Dictionary of Culprits and Criminals

by

GEORGE C. KOHN

THE SCARECROW PRESS, INC.

Metuchen, N.J., & London ● 1986

Library of Congress Cataloging-in-Publication Data

Kohn, George C.
   Dictionary of culprits and criminals.

   Includes index.
   1. Crime and criminals--Biography--Dictionaries.
I. Title.
HV6245.K64   1986   364.1'092'2 [B]   85-30426
ISBN 0-8108-1877-9

PREFACE

History is full of unsavory and criminal characters, male and female, young and old, rich and poor. Their deviousness and viciousness are disgusting and horrifying, and yet strangely fascinating. Newspapers, magazines, books, movies, and radio, television, and stage shows have all stimulated the public's seemingly inherent dark curiosity about their sinister brethren. But, out of the hundreds of thousands of despicable "little Somebodies and great Nobodies"--the culprits and criminals of society--very few of them actually deserve a niche of importance in history. But they cannot be forgotten; life certainly cannot be separated from the sinister in it. With this in mind, I have compiled and written this biographical dictionary of notorious and memorable persons whom history considers "outside the law."

The book contains known and proven assassins, murderers, spies, traitors, terrorists, kidnappers, poisoners, rapists, gangsters, racketeers, prostitutes, procurers, con artists, swindlers, impostors, forgers, counterfeiters, pirates, smugglers, thieves, burglars, robbers, gunfighters, Western outlaws, conspirators, highwaymen, megalomaniacs, war criminals, and others. For inclusion, an individual must have committed or been accused of committing an offense or crime that society at the time was prepared to punish by law. It was not the aim, and it is impossible, to include every famous criminal and antisocial character during the last five to six centuries, the time frame covered by the book. I have had to be highly selective in my choice of entries, generally picking those who have achieved, in one way or another, a notoriety or significance. In some cases, a kind of "criminal as hero" notoriety ruled for inclusion (for example, Rob Roy, Sam Bass, Roger Casement, and Charlotte Corday). However, if someone is generally regarded historically as a hero but punished or killed as a transgressor or criminal (for instance, Nathan Hale, John Brown, and Emiliano Zapata), then he or she is not included as an entry. Some culprits in the book are undoubtedly on the periphery of crime, or heroism. The reader will know. This "rogues gallery" ranges from such legendary and historic figures as Guy Fawkes, Moll Cutpurse, Blackbeard, Gilles de Rais, Jack Sheppard, and Johnny Ringo, to such contemporary villains as Lee Harvey Oswald, Mehmet Ali Agca, Meyer Lansky, Caryl Chessman, Peter Sutcliffe, Frances Schreuder, and Josef Mengele. American figures predominate, but Europeans and other Western-recognized wrongdoers are a major part of the book.

The concise biographical sketches are each about 100 to 200 words in length, with an occasional entry of 50 or 300 words. Each contains the full name of the culprit or criminal, including any well-known nickname, with brackets setting off those parts of the name not well known and, where appropriate, his or her real, legal, or birth name. Dates of birth and death, or when the person flourished, then follow, with a brief identifying phrase afterward. An outline or summary of his or her career generally concludes with how he or she died; interesting or peculiar quirks of personality may be part of the account. Names of persons in capital letters within entries indicate a cross-reference for the reader's benefit. In addition, "see also" cross-references at the end of entries direct the reader to other noteworthy people linked to a person. At the book's end, there is the usual index and another with the names of the notorious men and women listed under various types of culprits and criminals (assassin, spy, murderer, poisoner, racketeer, and so forth).

The inquisitive reader, whether a student, scholar, or general library user or book lover, will find the dictionary, I hope, an authoritative, quick, convenient, and easily comprehensible source of information about past and present evildoers of note in Western civilization. Maybe, he or she will also gain insight and understanding into man's inhumanity to man, not just more loathing; that would please me the most.

George C. Kohn
Madison, Conn.
February 1986

iv

DICTIONARY OF CULPRITS AND CRIMINALS

ABBANDANDO, [Frank] "Dasher" (1910-42). New York gangster and murderer. He was a top "hit" man for Murder, Inc., the enforcement squad of the national crime syndicate, and supposedly was involved in the killing of at least 50 persons in Brooklyn in the 1930s. Abbandando received the nickname "Dasher" after one of his early hits; when his gun failed to fire, he fled with his intended victim in pursuit and ran around a building so fast that he managed to come up behind the person. He then pumped several bullets into him to carry out his assignment successfully. Based on testimony from killer-turned-informer Abe RELES, Abbandando was arrested, convicted of murdering a loan shark operator, and sent to the electric chair on February 19, 1942.

ABBOTT, [Burton W.] "Bud" (1920-57). California kidnapper and murderer. In 1955 the dead body of 14-year-old Stephanie Bryan was found buried on Abbott's property in the Trinity Mountains of California. Abbott was arrested for kidnapping and murder. After a long trial, during which Abbott laughed at the prosecution's voluminous circumstantial evidence, he was found guilty of Stephanie's murder and sentenced to death. All his appeals were denied. On March 14, 1957, Abbott was executed in San Quentin's gas chamber, never having made a public admission of guilt.

ABBOTT, Jack Henry (b. 1943). American robber and alleged murderer. At the age of nine, Abbott was sent to a Utah reform school for "failure to adjust to foster homes." At 18, he went to prison for passing bad checks. By the age of 38, Abbott had spent over 25 years in U.S. prisons for forgery, robbery, murder, and escape. In 1967 he stabbed a fellow prisoner to death in "self-defense." About four years later Abbott escaped from a Utah prison but was caught six weeks later. He pleaded guilty to bank robbery in Denver, Colorado, in 1971 and received a 19-year prison sentence. Novelist Norman Mailer, with whom Abbott corresponded, helped him gain release to a halfway house in 1981 (Mailer had promoted Abbott's literary efforts, which had led to the publication of In the Belly of the Beast, Abbott's prison memoir). In early 1982 Abbott was convicted of first-degree manslaughter in the

1

stabbing death of Richard Adan, an East Village waiter and aspiring actor, on July 18, 1981. Abbott was sentenced to 15
years to life in prison.

ABDUL AZIZ, Faisal ibn Musad (1948-75). Arab assassin. On
March 25, 1975 Prince Faisal, a playboy with a reputed history
of mental instability, shot and killed his uncle King Faisal of
Saudi Arabia at a palace reception at Riyadh honoring the king
and marking the birthday of the Prophet Mohammad. Immediately afterward he yelled, "My brother is avenged!" (His
brother had been killed nine years earlier during a protest
against an Islamic ban on human images.) Judged sane, Prince
Faisal was tried and convicted under Islamic law on June 18,
1975; he was later beheaded in Riyadh's large public square.

ABDULLAH, Mohammed [born: Joseph Howk, Jr.] (b. 1939).
California murderer. Born of a black mother and white father,
he was labelled "schizoid" after trying to burn down his parents' house. He took an Islamic name when he was about 17.
Abdullah was a brilliant student and attended the University of
California-Berkeley, where he fell madly in love with Sonja Hoff.
Out of jealousy and rage, on July 13, 1960, he shot Hoff dead
and tried unsuccessfully to kill himself. In 1961 Abdullah's
death sentence was changed to life imprisonment without parole
on grounds of insanity.

ABEL, Rudolf [Ivanovich] (1902?-71). Soviet Russian spy. With
the name Andrew Kayotis on his passport, he entered the
United States in 1948 and later, under various identities, Emil
Robert Goldfus--Milton--Mark--Martin Collins, carried on clandestine espionage activities for about eight and one half years,
obtaining secret U.S. information and transmitting much of it
by shortwave radio to Moscow. Posing as a semiretired photo-
engraver, he lived on Manhattan's Upper West Side until late
1953, when he moved to Brooklyn Heights and played a similar
role as well as indulging in painting realistic portraits and
landscapes. In New York City on June 21, 1957, special FBI
agents arrested him. He evidently had the rank of colonel in
the Soviet KGB--intelligence agency. He shortly afterward
gave his real name, Abel, and admitted to being an illegal alien
and a Russian citizen but refused to say anything about spying.
The U.S. government brought Abel to trial in Brooklyn, New
York, on October 14-25, 1957, and relied largely on the testimony of Soviet defector Reino Hayhanen, who had worked with
Abel, for its case. A jury convicted the "master spy with six
faces" of conspiring to transmit military secrets to Soviet Russia. After receiving a 30-year sentence on November 15, 1957,
Abel was sent to the Atlanta federal prison. In February 1962,
the U.S. government exchanged Abel for U.S. pilot Francis
Gary Powers, who had been held captive by the Soviets since
his U-2 spy plane had been shot down near Sverdlovsk in May

1960. Afterward Abel reputedly worked for Soviet intelligence all over the world; in 1965 he was awarded the Order of Lenin for his long and distinguished career. He died in Moscow on November 15, 1971.

ABERSHAW, Jerry (1773-95). English highwayman. He began stealing from persons at the age of 17, and for nearly five years he evaded arrest. His favorite spots to prey on travelers were Putney Heath and Wimbledon Common in southeastern England. When Abershaw was stopped for questioning by two police officers in a local tavern, he fired on them and killed one. Caught soon afterward, he was tried, convicted, and sentenced to be hanged. Abershaw, with his shirt open at the neck and with a flower in his mouth, reportedly laughed and chatted all the way to the gallows at Kennington Common on August 3, 1795; he kicked off his boots at the last moment in order to squelch his mother's prediction that he would die with them on.

ABRAMS, [Michael] "Big Mike" (d. 1898). New York murderer. A bloodthirsty brute, Abrams worked as a slugger and killer for hire on the streets of New York City, mainly in the Chinatown area. He also was known to run opium-smoking dens on Pell Street and in Coney Island. Witnesses saw Abrams kill and decapitate members of the tongs (secret Chinese gangs in New York and other cities), including Ling Tchen, a chief of the Hip Sing Tong. Shortly after Ling's death, Abrams was found dead on his bed, a victim of asphyxiation. The room's door and windows were tightly sealed, and a thin hose extended from the gas line in the hallway to the keyhole.

ACCARDO, Tony or Anthony Joseph [born: Antonio Leonardo Accardo] (b. 1906). Chicago gangster. From about 1928 to 1931 he was a personal bodyguard to Al CAPONE in Chicago. Accardo worked his way through the ranks of the Mafia to become boss of the Chicago syndicate in 1943. He lost control to Sam GIANCANA in 1957 but regained it in 1966. Nicknamed "Big Tuna" because of his fondness for big-game fishing, Accardo has acquired considerable wealth from properties and businesses in Florida, California, Nevada, and South America.

ADAMS, Al[bert J.] (1844-1907). New York gambler and racketeer. He became a partner of Zachariah Simmons, who operated a large policy game racket in New York City in the 1870s. Adams took over the operation after Simmons's death and developed ways to rig the games and lessen the winners' payoffs. He also rigged the results in numbers games so that owners of independent policy (numbers) shops often suffered severe losses and were forced to sell out to him. An estimated 1,000 policy shops were run by Adams, who made enormous bribery payments to Tammany Hall and the police to remain in business. Finally, in 1901, New York authorities shut Adams's rackets down and sent him to Sing Sing Prison for more than a year. Afterward Adams turned to land speculation instead of returning to his numbers games and lived a lavish life at the Ansonia Hotel. He committed suicide in his apartment on October 1, 1907. See also TWEED, [William Marcy] "Boss."

ADAMS, John. See CHRISTIAN, Fletcher.

ADAMS, Mary (d. 1702). English thief and whore. As a poor working girl, she was severely disgraced publicly because she gave birth to two illegitimate children (the second was born dead) as a result of two separate seductions. Later, while living in London, she turned openly to whoring on Drury Lane, having a number of rich gentlemen as customers. Arrested when she tried to cash checks she had stolen from a customer, Adams was promptly tried, convicted, and sentenced to die. She appeared insouciant when she was hanged at Tyburn on June 16, 1702.

ADAMS, Millicent (b. 1942). Pennsylvania murderer. From an upper-class family in Philadelphia, Pa., she was jilted in a love affair with one Axel Schmidt, an emulous engineering student, who hoped to marry another girl with more money and prestige. Pregnant by Schmidt and now vengeful, as well as allegedly suicidal, she bought a .22 caliber gun. She also obtained a St. Bernard dog, which she, testing to see if the gun worked, shot dead in her home. Later Adams fatally shot Schmidt as they had their final sexual liaison in her Philadelphia townhouse (October 1962). Her lawyers' pleas of temporary insanity and manslaughter were accepted by the court, which gave her a ten-year probationary sentence in a mental institution, to which she voluntarily committed herself. She qualified for "rehabilitation" about three years later and was released.

ADLER, Polly [born: Pearl Adler] (1900-1962). Russian-born New York madam. In 1920 she rented an apartment on Riverside Drive in New York City and established the first of many successful brothels. Many of Polly's beautiful girls operated out of elegant, colorful apartments--some with dining rooms and bars--in Manhattan's East 50s and 60s, and they serviced notable politicians and celebrities, as well as gangsters like Dutch SCHULTZ and Charles "Lucky" LUCIANO. A celebrity in her own right, Polly attended the openings of many New York nightclubs, where she often showed off some of her most stunning girls. Hauled into court after police raids on her "houses," Polly generally appeared in dowdy dress, a far cry from her usual flamboyant style, and she often managed to be released "for lack of evidence" or through her powerful connections. In 1944 she reportedly retired from the bordello business, having amassed a small fortune, and later pursued a literary career of sorts. In 1950 her book, A House Is Not a Home, appeared and became a best-seller, allowing her to live very comfortably from the profits until her death on June 10, 1962.

ADONIS, Joe or Joseph [born: Joseph Doto] (1902-72). Italian-born American racketeer. He immigrated to the United States around 1918 and became a member of a New York City street gang. Adonis, or "Joey A," as he came to be known, was an important figure in the Mafia by 1932 and, for many years, controlled the rackets in parts of New York and New Jersey. He sat on the national syndicate board for 20 years. Found guilty of conspiracy to break gambling laws, Adonis was sentenced to a two- to three-year prison term in 1951. U.S. officials later discovered that Adonis' entry into the United States had been illegal and ordered him deported to Italy in 1956. He lived for the rest of his life in Milan, Italy.

ADORNO, George (b. 1959). New York robber and murderer. At the age of 15, Adorno, who previously had been arrested 16 times for theft, confessed to a charge of triple murder before a New York district attorney. About one year later a juvenile court judge nullified the confession on a technicality but found Adorno guilty of robbery and sentenced him to three years imprisonment. Released after 18 months, Adorno soon shot and killed a cab-driving black law student, Steven Robinson. He was arrested, tried, and sentenced to 15 years to life for the murder--the maximum penalty allowed by a plea of guilty in the juvenile court.

AGCA, Mehmet Ali (b. 1958). Turkish terrorist and murderer. Born and bred in Malatya, Turkey, he left and took up university studies in Ankara (1977) and then Istanbul (1978), but dropped out of both places and shortly became the leader of an extreme right-wing Turkish political party. In 1979 he shot and killed the editor of a liberal Istanbul newspaper, was caught and made a confession (which he later recanted), and was sent to a maximum security prison from which he soon managed to escape. As a fugitive sentenced to death in absentia for the murder, Agca used false identities and passports to travel to Iran, Bulgaria, and elsewhere, linking up with various underground figures. Bekir Celenk, a Turkish arms and drug trafficker who lived in Sofia, allegedly offered Agca $1,250,000 to kill the pope. On May 13, 1981, Pope John Paul II was severely wounded when Agca shot him as he rode through St. Peter's Square in Rome; Agca was arrested at the scene and later confessed to the shooting, during which two women tourists were also injured. In July 1981, Agca was found guilty by the Rome Assize Court and sentenced to life imprisonment. Italian authorities stated that Agca was part of an international conspiracy against the Pontiff, implicating three Bulgarians and five Turks in the crime.

AIELLO, Joey or Joseph (1891-1930). American bootlegger and racketeer. He was a leading bootlegger in Milwaukee. With his brothers, Andrew, Antonio, and Dominick, he tried to seize control of the Sicilian rackets in Chicago and sought help from other underworld characters, such as the GENNA brothers and George "Bugs" MORAN. A bloody bootleg war broke out between Aiello and Al CAPONE in 1927. Aiello tried unsuccessfully to poison Capone and then offered $50,000 to any thug who could kill him. Capone terrified Aiello and forced him into "retirement." Later, in 1930, Aiello was machine-gunned to death by Capone's henchmen.

AIKNEY, Thomas (d. 1776). English murderer. Involved in a secret love affair with Elizabeth Broadingham, the pretty wife of an English smuggler named John Broadingham, Aikney was induced by her to kill her husband in order that they could marry. At his home in York, John was mortally knifed in the stomach by Aikney, who foolishly left the murder weapon in his screaming victim when he fled. The knife was traced to Aikney, who promptly admitted his guilt and implicated Elizabeth as the ringleader. Aikney was hanged on March 20, 1776, five weeks after the killing; his corpse was dissected at Leeds hospital by medical students. Elizabeth confessed, was garroted, and then burned to ashes, which onlookers saved as mementos of her death.

AIUPPA, Joseph John (b. 1907). American gangster. He first served as a Chicago Mafia strongman under Al CAPONE. Since about 1935 Aiuppa has been arrested on various charges, including bribery, gambling, and assault with intent to kill. He was given the sobriquet "Mourning Doves" after he was arrested and imprisoned for illegal interstate shipment of mourning doves from Kansas to Chicago. Aiuppa has also served time in prison for illegally selling gambling equipment. Today he is the Mafia boss in Cicero, Illinois.

ALDERISIO, Felix Anthony (1922-71). American Midwest gangster. Known widely as "Milwaukee Phil," Alderisio was arrested numerous times for gambling, burglary, extortion, assault, and murder. In the 1950s and early 1960s, he was the Mafia's highest-ranking "hit" man in the United States. Alderisio designed the "hitmobile," a black, specially equipped car with switches that turned off the front and back lights during police chases, clamps to anchor rifles, shotguns, and pistols for steady shooting, and secret compartments. In 1962, Chicago police arrested Alderisio and Charles Nicoletti, another "hit" man, as both were apparently waiting to carry out a syndicate "contract" killing. Later Alderisio was arrested for extortion, found guilty, and sent to prison, where he died.

ALEXANDER VI [real name: Rodrigo Lanzol y Borja or, in Italian,

Rodrigo Borgia] (1431-1503). Spanish-born pope, intrigant, and profligate. Appointed a cardinal by his uncle, Pope Calixtus III, in 1456, he amassed a large fortune as vice chancellor of the Church and lived lavishly like a Renaissance prince. He had many mistresses and fathered a number of illegitimate children, including four by the Roman noblewoman Vanozza dei Catanei. Through simony, he was elected pope in 1492, began reforming papal finances, and supported the war against the Turks, with whom he later allied himself when King Charles VIII of France, claiming the kingdom of Naples, threatened to depose him in 1494. During his papacy (1492-1503), Alexander relentlessly pursued the aggrandizement of his family (the four offspring born by Catanei were legitimatized, awarded powerful religious or political positions, or married to monarchs), as well as indulged in political intrigues to increase his worldly power, neglecting the spiritual interests of the Church. In 1494 Alexander negotiated the Treaty of Tordesillas, which divided the New World into Spanish and Portuguese spheres of influence. He ordered the 1498 hanging of Italian religious reformer Girolamo Savonarola, who had attacked the vice and worldiness of the pope. Alexander frequently had private sex orgies, the most notorious of which was probably the so-called "chestnut supper" in 1501. Some fifty young naked whores from the slums of Rome evidently slithered like snakes on marble floors, picking up hot chestnuts when ordered to by Alexander and his then mistress, Giulia Farnese, a young whore. On August 18, 1503, Alexander died of a fever in Rome. His decadency helped undermine the papacy and bring on the Protestant Reformation.

ALLEN, Bill (d. 1882). Chicago murderer. After killing a black man and a policeman on November 30, 1882, Allen, a black himself, fled and hid in the basement of a building in Chicago. Again he ran from the law after shooting and wounding another policeman, who had discovered his hideout. A "posse" of some 200 police officers, assisted by several thousand citizens armed with rifles, pistols, and pitchforks, tracked Allen down and killed him in a gun battle. Afterward, however, an angry mob of people, believing Allen had not been killed, marched on the police station to seize Allen and lynch him. When Allen's dead body was displayed through a barred window, the mob and many others filed by for a look at the corpse, which remained in the window for 48 hours until the avengers and the curious were satisfied and drifted away.

ALLEN, Floyd (d. 1913). Virginia murderer. The Allen clan of Carroll County, Virginia, was furious when Floyd was arrested and charged with assaulting a police officer (Floyd apparently knocked the officer down and helped a clan member, arrested for moonshining, escape). Found guilty by an alleged "stacked" jury, Floyd was brought before the judge in the Hillsville, Va., courthouse on March 14, 1912. As the judge read the sentence, one year in jail, Floyd and about 17 of his kinsfolk who were watching the proceedings drew their guns and began shooting. Within a minute six persons lay dead: the judge, the sheriff, a lawyer, a juror, a female witness, and a spectator. Floyd and his son Claude, who had taken part in the shooting, were later convicted of murder and sent to the electric chair on March 28, 1913. Floyd's brother Sidna was given a 15-year prison sentence, and other Allen clan members received lesser ones. Released on a pardon from the Virginia governor in 1926, Sidna, along with other Allens, claimed the killings had been unpremeditated and nobody had tried to kill the unfortunate victims.

ALLEN, John (c. 1830-?). New York procurer. Allen, who came from a well-to-do New York family and whose three brothers were ministers, left theological school to pursue a different life. He and his wife operated a notorious dance hall-bordello on New York City's Water Street in the 1850s and 1860s. Allen, to whom journalists gave the sobriquet the "Wickedest Man in New York," placed Bibles and other religious material in the rooms in which his prostitutes serviced the customers. His "ladies," bouncers, and barmen often sang hymns and listened to scripture read by Allen. For a while he rented his establishment to the clergy for prayer meetings and provided "reformed sinners" for a price of 25 or 50 cents each. Allen's religious dealings made him suspect in the underworld. Finally he shut down his operation and disappeared. Some say he reformed and became a man of the cloth; others say he set up business in another city.

ALLEN, Lizzie (1840-96). Chicago prostitute and madam. At the age of 18, she arrived in Chicago from Milwaukee, her hometown, and began working as a prostitute. After stints in two city brothels, Allen, a stunning beauty, opened her own "house" and prospered until it was destroyed in the Great Chicago Fire of 1871. Quickly reestablishing herself on Congress Street, Allen again prospered and, in 1878, formed a partnership with her financial adviser and lover, Christopher Columbus Crabb. Ousted from a 24-room bordello that they had built on Lake View Avenue in 1888, the pair constructed an elegant "House of Mirrors" on Dearborn Street (later that bordello would be run by the infamous madam-sisters, Ada and Minna EVERLEIGH). In 1896 Allen, in bad health, retired and gave her property to Crabb. When she died on September 2 that year, her estate was estimated to be worth from $300,000 to $1 million.

ALLEN, Margaret (1906-49). English murderer. Born into a huge family of 21 children (of which she was the twentieth), she grew up preferring to be masculine rather than feminine, wearing men's clothing, doing physically hard man's work, and drinking in pubs with men (who called her "Bill Allen"). In 1935 she supposedly had a sex change operation in a hospital (a shocking thing at the time), and afterward she was increasingly looked upon as an oddity and was rejected publicly where she lived in the borough of Rawtenstall, Lancashire. She reputedly tried to have affairs with women. On August 28, 1948, the body of an old, reclusive woman named Chadwick, who had died from hammer-inflicted wounds to the head, was found on the road near Allen's house. While investigating the murder, Scotland Yard detectives were dogged by Allen as they discovered many clues that clearly implicated her. Strangely, she openly revealed incriminating evidence until suddenly, on September 1, 1948, she confessed to the crime. But no explicable motive was ever disclosed. Sentenced to death after a short trial, she cantankerously went to her hanging on January 12, 1949.

ALLISON, Clay (1840-87). American gunfighter. He owned a small cattle ranch on the Washita River in the New Mexico territory. An alcoholic with an ability as a fast gun, Clay became a "killer-for-hire." Wealthy ranchers hired him to settle boundary disputes in the 1870s. According to some accounts, Clay shot and killed about 15 men; he seldom if ever faced his opponent in an open gunfight. Clay's death was ironic: driving his heavily-laden ranch wagon while drunk, he fell onto the road and the wagon's wheels rolled over his neck, killing him. See also COLBERT, Chunk.

ALLMAN, "Bad John" (d. 1877). American murderer. Allman was a brash cavalryman in the U.S. Army in the Western territories in the 1870s. In the cavalry barracks in Prescott, Arizona, in 1877, he evidently shot and killed two army sergeants during a poker game and fled. He then killed two members of a posse in pursuit of him and went on a terrorizing murder spree in the Arizona territory, leaving about a half dozen men dead. A band of five Western bounty hunters, the Outlaw Exterminators, Inc., were sent to capture Allman, the so-called "Cavalry Killer," dead or alive. On October 11, 1877, they caught up with Allman, hiding in an Indian cliff dwelling, and reportedly killed him in a gunfight. Clay Calhoun, one of the Exterminators, claimed so, but the four bullet holes in Allman's body were in a nice straight line, indicating that he may have been shot while asleep.

ALTERIE, Louis "Two-Gun" [born: Leland Verain] (1892-1935). Colorado-born Chicago bootlegger. In the early 1920s Alterie, who got his nickname because he liked to carry two revolvers, worked as a bootlegger for his friend Charles Dion O'BANNION. He was an emotional man, quick to react. When mobster Samuel J. "Nails" MORTON was thrown and kicked to death by a horse, Alterie immediately went to the stable and shot the horse dead. After O'Bannion was assassinated, Alterie offered to pistol duel his killers at high noon in the middle of Chicago. Fellow mobsters said he would get them in trouble by his "mouthing-off" and suggested he leave. In 1924 Alterie moved to his ranch in Colorado. An unknown gunman shot Alterie dead during a visit to Chicago in 1935.

ALVORD, Burt (1866-1910?). American lawman, outlaw, and train robber. In 1886 he became deputy to Sheriff John Slaughter of Cochise County in the Arizona territory and earned a reputation for capturing rustlers and other crooks. About 1895 Alvord himself turned to cattle rustling in Mexico, and in 1899 he hooked up with Billie STILES, another lawman-turned-outlaw, and pulled off several train robberies. The Alvord-Stiles gang was caught twice but escaped both times and continued its operations. In 1904 the Arizona Rangers caught up with Alvord and Stiles (both of whom had tried unsuccessfully to cover their trail by faking their deaths) and captured Alvord after wounding him in a gun battle; Stiles got away. Alvord received a two-year prison sentence and afterward faded from sight completely; same say he became a canal worker in Panama and died there in 1910.

AMATUNA, Samuzzo "Samoots" (1898-1925). Chicago gangster. He worked as the personal bodyguard of the bootlegging GENNA brothers of Chicago, becoming an enemy of Charles Dion O'BANNION and Al CAPONE, two Chicago gangsters who were also enemies. In 1925 Amatuna seized control of the Unione Siciliane, a secret Sicilian crime cartel with ties to the Mafia, and attempted to muscle in on Capone's underworld operations. Two unknown gunmen shot and fatally wounded Amatuna in a Chicago barbershop on November 13, 1925. He died soon after in the hospital.

AMBERG, [Louis] "Pretty" (1898-1935). Russian-born Brooklyn gangster and racketeer. Amberg, nicknamed "Pretty" because of his extreme ugliness, operated lucrative loansharking and bootlegging businesses in Brownsville and other areas of Brooklyn in New York City. He also ran a number of speakeasies (saloons where liquor is sold illegally) and an extensive laundry service for businessmen. Other top mobsters, such as Owen MADDEN, Jack "Legs" DIAMOND, and Dutch SCHULTZ, were told not to encroach on Amberg's territory; Amberg often threatened to kill them if they did (many of his enemies were found stuffed in laundry bags, where they had died of strangulation). After Amberg's gunmen killed two of Schultz's top men in 1935, a large gang war broke out, during which Amberg was fatally shot in October 1935.

AMMON, Robert Adams "Colonel." See MILLER, Bill or William Franklin.

ANASTASIA, Albert (1903-57). New York racketeer, gangster, and

murderer. A feared Mafioso (Mafia leader), Anastasia made
huge profits from narcotics smuggling, gambling, and prostitution and by extortion. He was head of Murder, Inc., the crime
syndicate's enforcement squad, and was given the title "Lord
High Executioner" because of his leading role in carrying out
syndicate killings. Mayor William O'Dwyer of New York City
tried several times to obtain murder indictments against Anastasia but failed; key eyewitnesses were always killed at the
last moment. In 1950 and 1951, Anastasia testified before the
U.S. Senate Crime Investigating Committee, chaired by Senator
Estes Kefauver, that he was a legitimate partner in a dress
manufacturing business. Two gunmen of Vito GENOVESE, a
Mafia chief, shot Anastasia to death in the basement barbershop of Manhattan's Park Sheraton Hotel on October 25, 1957.
See also LUCIANO, Charles "Lucky"; TENUTO, Frederick J.

ANDERSON, Bella (fl. 1899). New York kidnapper. A nurse, she
abducted an infant, Marion Clarke, from her simple New York
City home in May 1899. The kidnapped child, for whom only a
$300 ransom was demanded, became a sensational cause célèbre
in the press, and the public was passionately stirred up until
the police found her in an upstate New York farmhouse in the
hands of Anderson and a married couple, George and Addie
Barrow. An outlandish scheme of mass kidnapping nationwide
was revealed by Anderson, who said that she and the Barrows
had hoped to take many children from families of modest means
and become rich by ransoming them for small sums (a volume
business). The three were tried and convicted; the Barrows
received long terms in prison, but 35-year-old Anderson was
sentenced to only four years because of her cooperation with
the prosecution.

ANDERSON, Bill or William (d. 1864). American Confederate
guerrilla and murderer. During the U.S. Civil War (1861-65),
he rode with William Clarke QUANTRILL's guerrilla band. Anderson always carried an arsenal of weapons with him--revolvers,
pistols, rifles, a saber, and a hatchet--and became known as a
ruthless killer with the nickname "Bloody Bill." On September
26, 1864, he led a raid against Centralia, Missouri, and destroyed the town. There, on Anderson's orders, his men shot
dead two dozen Union prisoners. The following month, his
guerrilla band was attacked by Union troops under Commander
S. P. Cox, who personally shot Anderson to death.

ANDRÉ, John (1750-80). British spy, During the American Revolution (1775-83), André, a charming British aide-de-camp with
literary talent, became adjutant general with the rank of major
in charge of intelligence for British General Sir Henry Clinton
in New York City. In September 1780, André secretly negotiated with American General Benedict ARNOLD, commander of
the West Point, New York, fort, for the surrender of West

Point to the British for ₤20,000. While returning to New York City after the negotiation, André, wearing civilian clothes, was seized by three American militiamen, who discovered papers about the deal in one of his boots. Tried and found guilty of spying, André was hanged at General George Washington's headquarters at Tappan, New York, on October 2, 1780.

ANGRIA, Kanhoji (d. 1729). Malabar pirate. In the 1690s he began to prey on private foreign shipping along the Malabar coast (southwestern coast of India). Kanhoji built a chain of 26 pirate fortresses on the coast, and his pirate fleet ruthlessly plundered the ships of the British, French, and Dutch East India companies in this part of the Indian Ocean for nearly 30 years. East India shippers were generally free from piracy for 14 years after Kanhoji's death, during which time his five sons fought over who would take control. See also ANGRIA, Tulaji.

AGRIA, Tulaji (d. 1756?). Malabar pirate. In 1743, after a 14-year internecine struggle with his four brothers, Tulaji took control of piracy along the Malabar coast (southwestern coast of India) as successor to his father Kanhoji ANGRIA. His pirate fleet attacked the shipping of European East India companies until 1755, when the British sent a small naval fleet under Commodore William James to crush Tulaji's pirates. For two days the Protector, a British 40-gun man-of-war captained by James, bombarded Tulaji's island fortress of Severndroog. The pirates abandoned the fortress when a powder magazine blew up. The British then forced Tulaji and his pirates from three nearby mainland fortresses. Another British fleet captured the pirate fort at Gheria in 1756 and took Tulaji prisoner. He was killed soon afterward.

ANSELL, Mary (1877-99). English poisoner. To claim a petty insurance policy of ₤22 that she had taken out on the life of her feeble-minded sister Caroline, who was confined in an asylum, Mary Ansell mailed her a poisoned cake which Caroline quickly and happily ate, resulting in her painful death. Mary, who worked as a London household servant, failed to prevent an autopsy of the body and to get the insurance claim. As soon as phosphorus poisoning was discovered, she was arrested and brought to trial (June 1899), during which she angrily proclaimed her innocence, but the jury convicted her. Reading her death sentence, the judge averred, "Never in my experience has so terrible a crime been committed for a motive so utterly inadequate." Many noisy spectators watched her die on the gallows in St. Albans Prison on July 19, 1899.

ANSELMI, Albert (d. 1929). Sicilian-born Chicago gangster and murderer. In the early 1920s he and his close friend John SCALISE went to work as hired killers (hit men) for the GENNA brothers in Chicago. They carried out dozens of "hits" and

gained a reputation as bloodthirsty murderers, feared by rival
gangsters and the police. Unbeknownst to the Gennas in 1925,
Anselmi and Scalise became hit men for Al CAPONE and were
involved in the killing of Tony Genna. Later, Capone, believing the two killers were conspiring to murder him, beat them to
death with a baseball bat during a party at his headquarters in
Cicero, Illinois, on May 27, 1929.

ANTONINI, Theresa [Marschall] (1785-1809). German thief and
    murderer. With her husband, a Sicilian, she engaged in thiev-
    ery throughout her native Germany and was imprisoned twice
    with him. On a trip by horse-drawn coach from Danzig (Gdansk)
    to Vienna in 1809, the Antoninis, along with Theresa's 15-year-
    old brother Carl, conspired to kill the fourth passenger--a rich,
    lovely, young woman named Dorothea Blankenfeld--and steal her
    valuables. Various murder plans were proposed, but none was
    effected until the coach stopped at a Bavarian town near Augs-
    burg. There Blankenfeld was drugged and fatally beaten on
    the head with a poker (Theresa had suggested they kill her by
    pouring hot lead into her eyes and ears). The threesome
    wrapped the corpse in a cloak and journeyed on with it, but
    foul play was quickly suspected by the innkeeper where they
    had stayed. The killers were caught and brought to Nurem-
    berg. First Carl and then Theresa confessed (her husband
    never did and committed suicide in his cell by starvation).
    Carl was sentenced to ten years' imprisonment, and Theresa
    was beheaded in public.

APACHE KID (1867-?). American Indian robber, rapist, and mur-
    derer. He served as a U.S. sergeant of scouts in the Arizona
    territory until he took Apache tribal revenge and killed his
    father's murderer. The Apache Kid was caught, after hiding
    for two years, and convicted of murder but was given a par-
    don by President Grover Cleveland. He turned to a life of
    lawlessness. In 1889, while being sent to prison in Yuma,
    Arizona, convicted of killing a whiskey salesman, the Apache
    Kid killed two guards and escaped. For several years he and
    some followers robbed and murdered white prospectors and
    settlers and raped their wives and daughters. A prospector,
    Edward A. Clark, claimed he fatally shot the Apache Kid in
    1894, near Tucson, Arizona. The Indian terror ceased. How-
    ever, the Apache Kid is believed to have taken this opportunity
    to cross into Mexico to live in peace, without fear of being shot
    by a bounty hunter.

APIS, Colonel. See DIMITRIJEVIĆ, Dragutin.

APTE, Narayan. See GODSE, Nathuran [Vinayak].

ARAM, Eugene (1704-59). English scholar and murderer. On
    February 7, 1745, a wealthy shoemaker named Daniel Clark

disappeared. Aram, a philologist and schoolmaster in Knaresborough was suddenly able to pay his many debts. He and
Robert Houseman, a linen weaver, were found with some of
Clark's property. Questioned by the police, Houseman confessed to killing Clark, implicated Aram in the crime, and disclosed the location of Clark's body. Aram, who denied he conspired in any plot to kill Clark, skillfully defended himself in
court but was found guilty and sentenced to death. He was
hanged after a futile attempt to commit suicide. For many years
Aram's body was hung in chains at Knaresborough. Aram's
crime was the basis of a novel, Eugene Aram, by Bulwer Lyt-
ton, and a long poem, The Dream of Eugene Aram, by Thomas
Hood.

ARBUCKLE, [Roscoe] "Fatty" (1887-1933). American comedian and
alleged murderer. Arbuckle, weighing nearly 300 pounds, was a
successful Hollywood-film comedian who lived a wild, lavish life
when he was accused of the rape-murder of 25-year-old actress
Virginia Rappe in 1921. At his St. Francis Hotel suite in San
Francisco, Arbuckle had allegedly seduced Rappe, whose bladder had ruptured during intercourse, causing her death. Arbuckle was indicted on manslaughter but was acquitted after
three sensational trials, during which details of his disreputable
private life were made public. The scandalous Arbuckle became
a scorned man; his films were boycotted in the United States,
England, and elsewhere. Later he acted in some vaudeville
shows and directed a few short films, but he never regained
his former prominence. Arbuckle died of a heart attack in a
New York hotel room on June 29, 1933.

ARCHER-GILLIGAN, "Sister Amy" (1869-1928). Connecticut mass
poisoner. After opening a nursing home for the elderly in
Windsor, Connecticut, in 1901, "Sister Amy" (as she was lov-
ingly called by her trusting boarders) systematically carried
out secret poisonings of old men and women in her home.
Through marriage to five men in her care who died, she obtained much money from insurance taken out on their lives;
she also profited from old women's wills naming her as beneficiary (relatives had agreed to these wills after Sister Amy
persuaded them her home care was costing more than she
charged). A suspicious relative notified the police about the
high death rate in the place, and a disguised female agent uncovered the poisonings while working there. Sister Amy was
tried (1914), convicted, and sentenced to life. After serving
time at the Wethersfield, Connecticut, prison, she was transferred to a mental institution, where she died in 1928.

ARDEN, Alice (1516-51). English murderer. Her husband Thomas
Arden, a nobleman twice her age, was unaware of her continu-
ous, longtime love affair with Richard Mosby, a tailor, with
whom she began to conspire to murder her elderly spouse in

Faversham, Kent, their place of residence. Alice, beautiful
and genteel, involved killers-for-hire, servants, and others in
the plot, which was eventually carried out on the night of
February 15, 1551. Helped by several conspirators, Mosby
and Alice strangled, clubbed, and stabbed Thomas to death
and moved the body from the house to the garden outside.
When the corpse was found shortly, suspicion immediately
focused on Alice because of bloodstains carelessly left on rugs.
Under interrogation she admitted her guilt, and Mosby and her
servants were apprehended and quickly tried along with her and
condemned to death. Some, like Mosby, were hanged; others
were burned at the stake, as was Alice before many cheering
spectators at Canterbury on March 14, 1551. Rounded up were
her killers-for-hire and anyone else who may have taken part,
however minor it was, and they were either executed or imprisoned. A popular tragic play, Arden of Faversham, published in 1592, is based on this crime and is thought to have
involved William Shakespeare in some literary way.

ARKANSAS TOM. See DAUGHERTY, Roy.

ARLINGTON, Josie [real name: Mary Deubler] (1864-1914). New
Orleans prostitute and madam. At the age of 17 she turned to
whoring and worked at various bordellos on Basin Street and
Customhouse Street until she became the madam of her own
place in 1888. Around 1890 Josie, who went by the name of
Josie Alton, changed her name to Lobrano d'Arlington (Philip
Lobrano was her lover), which she soon shortened to Arlington.
Josie established an opulent and gaudy sex palace, "The Arlington," in New Orleans's infamous red-light district, Storyville,
and amassed a fortune from the earnings of her "high-class"
girls supposedly from around the world. In about 1905 Josie
became funereal and religious, bought a plot in the Metairie
Cemetery, and built a tomb of red marble. She retired in 1909
and died five years later. For a while the tomb of New Orleans's
most notorious madam was bathed at night in the red glow of a
nearby traffic light. Finally city officials, embarrassed because
Josie's tomb had seemingly become a celebrated spot frequented
by tourists and others at night, removed the red traffic light.

ARMSTRONG, Karleton [Lewis] (b. 1946). American protestor.
Many political bombings of U.S. government property occurred
during the Vietnam War, which numerous students and others
actively protested. Armstrong and three other members of the
radical Students for a Democratic Society (SDS) were charged
with blowing up the U.S. Army Mathematics Research Center at
the University of Wisconsin in August 1970; the predawn blast
killed Robert Fassnacht, a physicist, and injured several others.
Wanted by the FBI, Armstrong was a fugitive until caught in
Toronto in 1972; his cohorts remained at large. He pleaded
guilty to second-degree murder, was sentenced to 23 years in

prison, and eventually gained release on parole from the Fox
Lake, Wisconsin, Correctional Institution in 1980.

ARNOLD, Benedict (1741-1801). American general and traitor. He
and Ethan Allen led an American force that captured British-
held Fort Ticonderoga, New York, at the beginning of the
American Revolution (1775-83). American armies under Arnold
and Richard Montgomery failed to capture the Canadian city of
Quebec in late 1775. Made a brigadier general by Congress in
1776, Arnold commanded a flotilla on Lake Champlain that halted
the southward advance of the British. He was greatly embittered by Congress's promotions in February 1777 (five brigadier
generals, his juniors, were promoted ahead of him) but, nonetheless, won an important victory against the British at Danbury, Connecticut, two months later, thus forcing Congress to
promote him to major general. In 1778 Arnold was made commander of Philadelphia, where he was criticized for mingling
with Loyalist sympathizers. In 1779 he was court-martialed
because of violations of civil and military regulations and was
reprimanded. From May 1779, Arnold corresponded with British
General Sir Henry Clinton and Major John ANDRÉ in New York,
offering his services to the British and informing them of a
proposed American invasion of Canada. After being appointed
commandant of the fort at West Point, New York, Arnold arranged to surrender West Point in exchange for a British commission and £20,000. The plot was discovered with the capture
of André on September 23, 1780, and two days later Arnold
went over to the British side. In 1781 he led two raids, one
against Virginia, the other against New London, Connecticut,
and at year's end he moved to England, where he was shunned
for the rest of his life. Arnold died in obscurity in London on
June 14, 1801.

ARNOLD, Philip (1829-73). American con man. In 1871 he and
John Slack pretended to be prospectors who had discovered a
fabulously rich diamond field in eastern Arizona. William C.
Ralston, president of the Bank of California, and other financiers in San Francisco shelled out $700,000 to buy Arnold's and
Slack's rights to the claim after mining experts verified its existence (they were led blindfolded--to keep the claim's location
secret in order to protect the discovers' rights--to a mesa in
Wyoming that Arnold and Slack had "salted" with industrial diamonds and other gems). In 1872 a mining company, financed
by American and European bankers and tycoons, was set up to
unearth the apparently incredible deposits. Slack disappeared
forever with his share of the money, and Arnold settled down
in Elizabethtown, Kentucky, near his birth place. U.S. government geologists investigated the claim and uncovered the
scam. The investors, embarrassed, suffered in silence except
for one who brought suit to recover $350,000 from Arnold, who
showed papers that the deal had been legal and backed up by

specialists in the field. However, he repaid $150,000 to settle the matter. In late 1873 Arnold, while recovering from a shotgun wound in his back inflicted by a business rival, developed pneumonia and died.

ARNOLD, Stephen (1775?-?). New York murderer. Arnold, a teacher in Cooperstown, New York, who often flew into a rage when his pupils made mistakes, clubbed his six-year-old niece to death for misspelling the word "gig." He was tried, convicted, and sentenced to be hanged. On the day of his execution in 1805, bands played music while thousands of spectators watched Arnold on the gallows. A minister delivered an hourlong sermon. Afterward the sheriff came forward, removed the rope from around Arnold's neck, and read a reprieve from the governor. Why had the sheriff waited until the end? To have Arnold experience the terror of death and not to disappoint the crowd. Later Arnold was pardoned on grounds of temporary insanity.

ASHBY, James (fl. 1830s). American gambler. Ashby and a young man, pretending to be a senile, whiskey-drinking, fiddle-playing father with his yokel of a son, worked the Mississippi riverboats, appearing to be the perfect victims to be ripped off by slick gamblers. Instead, they dubbed the best card sharks; while the "son" was gambling, Ashby played parts of tunes, which were signals known to the son, and consequently the seemingly stupid country boy won hand after hand. It was a long time before Ashby's musical signals were found out.

ASHLEY, John (1895-1924). Florida robber. From about 1915 to 1924 he led a gang of robbers who haphazardly held up banks and hijacked liquor shipments, especially those of rumrunners. After a holdup, Ashley and the others headed for the Florida Everglades, where they successfully evaded capture. To some backwoodsmen Ashley became a folk hero because he flouted the law. Several times he was caught but escaped. While he was in a Miami jail, his gang threatened to shoot up the town unless he was released. Soon afterward Ashley was convicted of bank robbery and sentenced to 17 years in prison, but he broke out in short order and resumed his robbery career. A 1924 "pirate" raid by the Ashley gang on a Bimini island netted only $8,000 from the liquor suppliers to rumrunners. Police, through a gang informer, tracked down Ashley and three other gang members and fatally shot them in a reported gunfight near Jacksonville.

AVERY, John or Long Ben. See EVERY, Henry.

AVINAIN, Charles (fl. 1830s-60s). French mass murderer. For about 30 years he apparently carried out many killings at his dilapidated farm near Clichy, just north of Paris. Telling unsuspecting farmers he would buy their hay for the lowest price on the market, Avinain, a butcher by trade, lured them to his farm, promptly smashed their skulls in, and then tossed the dead bodies in the Seine River. Afterward the farmers' hay, wagons, and horses were sold for a hefty profit. Apprehended after two of his victims, seen with him shortly before their deaths, were found on the riverbank, Avinain was found guilty but refused to confess his crimes to the very end, his execution by the guillotine.

AXIS SALLY [real name: Mildred Elizabeth Gillars] (b. 1900). American propagandist and traitor. At the outbreak of World War II (1939-45), Gillars, who had once hoped to be an actress, was teaching English in Berlin. According to what she later claimed, her love for a German named Max Otto Koischwitz, who was a member of the Foreign Ministry staff, propelled her into making English-language propaganda broadcasts on German radio during the war. American GIs and other Allied troops in southern Europe and elsewhere often listened to her entertaining radio shows of music and talk. Broadcasting such songs as "Lili Marlene," which became very popular with Allied soldiers, she served the Axis cause, earning the nickname "Axis Sally." Gillars tried to destroy Allied morale, speaking tartly about the soldiers' supposedly unfaithful wives and girlfriends on the homefront. After the war she was brought to trial (1949) and sent to prison on a conviction of treason. She was released in 1961.

- B -

BA CUT [real name: Le Quong Vinh] (1921-56). Vietnamese bandit, rebel, traitor, kidnapper, and murderer. First he was a cunning Vietminh Communist fighter against the French in Vietnam, indulging in killing and looting. Next, after deserting the Communists, he joined Hunyh Phu So, a Vietnamese religious teacher and prophet with a large following, to whom he pledged his allegiance by personally cutting off his left forefinger, thus becoming known as Ba Cut (Three Fingers). After Phu So was captured and executed by the Vietminh in 1947, Ba Cut and his formidable Hoa Hao guerrilla army fought intermittently on the side of the French, who were trying to contain the Vietminh and a strong Vietnamese nationalist movement. By 1954, when the French suffered defeat at Dien Bien Phu and Vietnam was partitioned, Ba Cut ruled the South Vietnamese provinces near Cambodia; his powerful army's terrorism ended when Ngo Dinh Diem's South Vietnamese government soldiers seized him in mid-April 1955. Tried and found guilty of armed revolt, treason, kidnapping, and murder, Ba Cut was guillotined near Can Tho on July 13, 1956.

BABINGTON, Anthony (1561-86). English conspirator. Son of a rich Roman Catholic family in Derbyshire, he served as a page at Sheffield Castle where the Roman Catholic Mary, Queen of Scots was held prisoner by Queen Elizabeth I. After 1580 Babington secretly helped Jesuits working covertly in England, and in 1586 he was induced by a priest, John Ballard, to organize a conspiracy to assassinate Elizabeth, to free Mary, and to make England a Catholic country. Babington's letters to Mary, detailing his plans, were intercepted by Elizabeth's spies. He then fled to Harrow but was caught in late August 1586. Babington, Ballard, and five others were found guilty of treason and were executed on September 20, 1586. Mary, implicated in Babington's plot, was condemned by an English court and, on February 8, 1587, was beheaded at Fotheringhay Castle.

BAILEY, Harvey (1889-1979). American bank robber. He pulled off several of the largest bank heists in U.S. history. In 1922 Bailey, Jim Ripley, and others stole more than $500,000 in untraceable bills from the U.S. Denver Mint. In 1931 Bailey, Eddie Bentz, and some others seized more than $1 million in cash and negotiable securities from the Lincoln National Bank and Trust Company, Lincoln, Neb. With Fred BARKER, Alvin KARPIS, and others in May 1932, Bailey robbed the bank in Fort Scott, Kansas, and was caught by the FBI soon afterward. Convicted of robbery, Bailey was sent to the Kansas State penitentiary, from which he led a successful breakout on May 31, 1933. Three months later he was captured by the FBI at the Shannon Ranch in Paradise, Texas, where "Machine Gun" KELLY was holding Charles Urschel for ransom. Bailey, or "Old Harve" as he was called, broke out of the Dallas County jail but was captured after a wild chase near Ardmore, Oklahoma. He was then mistakenly convicted of the Urschel kidnapping and sent to Leavenworth until 1965, when he was paroled. He retired as a cabinetmaker in Joplin, Missouri, and died at age 91.

BAKER, Cullen M. (1838-68). Texas outlaw and murderer. At different times during the U.S. Civil War, Baker, hunted for killing several men, joined and briefly served in both the Confederate and Union armies, using army service to hide from the law. He became the leader of a vicious band of Texas outlaws, who called themselves the Confederate Irregulars, after the war. The outlaws terrorized much of Texas, robbing and murdering farmers, lawmen, and "nigger police." Baker tried to hang Thomas Orr in a dispute over a girl, but failed. Orr, accompanied by a posse, tracked down Baker and shot him to death in late December 1868. See also LONGLEY, William P. "Wild Bill."

BAKER, Henry J. See McGINNIS, [Joseph Francis] "Big Joe."

BAKER, Joseph [real name: Joseph Boulanger] (d. 1800). Canadian pirate and murderer. In the late 1700s, sailing aboard U.S. vessels, Baker instigated mutinies and sold captured ships and their cargoes for profit. In 1800 the U.S. schooner Eliza, under Captain William Wheland, was seized by Baker, aided by two sailors named Berrouse and LaCroix. The pirates killed the ship's first mate and wounded Wheland, who was allowed to live after agreeing to sail the Eliza into pirate waters. Wheland later managed to lock Berrouse and LaCroix below deck and, brandishing an axe, forced Baker up into the ship's rigging, where he remained for 16 days until Wheland sailed the ship into port. In Philadelphia on May 9, 1800, Baker, Berrouse, and LaCroix were hanged for murder and piracy.

BAKER, Mary (1800-?). British impostor. As a wily, irresponsible youth, she pulled off an incredible imposture in Gloucestershire in 1817. Appearing in disguise and speaking in "a foreign language" that dumfounded British linguists, Baker was recognized by a sailor, with whom she was secretly in collusion, as a Javanese princess named Caraboo who had been taken from Sumatra by pirates and had landed in England when their ship foundered offshore. Treated as a celebrity for about a year, she was exposed by an old associate who knew about a verifying scar on her back. She admitted guilt and then sailed to the United States, where she vanished.

BALDRIDGE, Adam (fl. 1690s). English pirate and trader. In 1685 he reportedly killed a man in Jamaica and fled to the island of Madagascar in the Indian Ocean. There he erected a large fortress on a hilltop and established a trading business with the pirates. His warehouses on the bay at St. Mary's held guns, gunpowder, tools, clothing, and food, which Baldridge traded for pirates' plunder--ivory, gold, silks, coffee, spices, slaves, and so forth--from the Indian Mogul galleons and Arab Mocha fleets. Baldridge became the absolute ruler of St. Mary's, and the African natives called him "King of the Pirates." He kept a harem of native girls for use by the pirates and lived an easy, comfortable life until the local people forced him to flee from the island in 1697, when they learned he had been selling many of their friends into slavery. Baldridge went to New York and supposedly lived there until his death, many years later.

BALFOUR, Jabez Spencer (1843-1912). English swindler. At the age of 27, Balfour was made managing director of Lands Allotment Ltd., which built apartments, houses, and hotels in England. Under his management, the capital of Lands Allotment Ltd. increased fifty-fold between 1867 and 1888. Profits were created on paper by the sale of land and buildings at inflated prices from one company to another--companies directed or formed by Balfour. A public outcry occurred after a Balfour-directed company, the Liberator Building Society, collapsed in

1892 and Balfour fled to Argentina. Evidence of fraud was found in the Balfour Group, formerly Lands Allotment Ltd., and Balfour was brought back to England to stand trial in 1895. On November 28, 1895, he was convicted of fraud and sentenced to 14 years in prison.

BALL, Joe (1892-1938). Texas mass murderer. In the 1930s his tavern-inn in Texas was known for its attractive waitresses and its alligator pond (customers regularly watched the 'gators devour stray cats and dogs and "meat" thrown to them). Ball had affairs with his waitresses, a dozen or more of whom mysteriously disappeared, which resulted in an inquiry by the Texas Rangers. A former longtime inn employee, an old black cook, confessed that he reluctantly had helped Ball kill some of the waitresses. The corpses had been cut up and the pieces fed to the 'gators. When lawmen arrived at the inn on September 24, 1938, Ball took a gun from the cash register and fatally shot himself in the head.

BALLARD, John. See BABINGTON, Anthony.

BANFIELD, John S. See McGINNIS, [Joseph Francis] "Big Joe."

BANISZEWSKI, Gertrude Wright (b. 1929). Indiana sadist and murderer. In the summer of 1965 Baniszewski took temporary foster care of Jenny Likens, age 15, and her sister Sylvia, age 16, the daughters of traveling circus people. She began to beat and torture the two girls. Sylvia's fingers were burned with matches. Mrs. Baniszewski's own teenagers and neighborhood boys were encouraged to beat Sylvia, who was forced to dance naked before them. Using a hot needle, Mrs. Baniszewski branded Sylvia's stomach with the words, "I am a prostitute and proud of it." Sylvia then died when her head slammed against the cellar floor following a blow from Baniszewski. The Indianapolis police investigated and learned the details. Baniszewski was tried, convicted, and given life imprisonment.

BARBAROSSA I [born: Arouj, Aruj, Koruk, or Horush] (1473?-1518). Barbary pirate. He and his brother Khizr (BARBAROSSA II), sons of a Turk from the Greek island of Lesbos, engaged in piracy in the Mediterranean, especially along the Barbary Coast (North African coast west of Egypt), during the first decades of the sixteenth century. They seized European ships and raided Spanish and Italian coastal towns and villages. Hoping to establish an African stronghold, the brothers attacked the Spanish at Algiers in 1518 and gained partial control of the Barbary State of Algeria; Arouj, however, was killed by the Spaniards.

BARBAROSSA II [born: Khizr; adopted name: Khayr ad-Din] (1483?-1546). Barbary pirate. The European name Barbarossa ("redbeard") was applied to him and his brother Arouj (BAR-

BAROSSA I), who together harassed European shipping in the
Mediterranean, especially on the Barbary Coast, and plundered
Spanish and Italian coastal areas in the early part of the 1500s.
After Arouj's death in 1518, Khizr, who took the title Khayr
ad-Din, carried on the piratical raids, captured Algiers from
Spain in 1529, and later gained control of all the Barbary States
(present-day Algeria, Tunisia, Libya, and Morocco). Between
1533 and 1544, the main period of his conquests, Barbarossa II
was admiral of the Ottoman Empire fleet of Sultan Suleiman I
"the Magnificent"; he won a major victory against the Holy
Roman Empire at the naval Battle of Preveza in September 1538,
thus securing Turkish control of much of the Mediterranean.
He ravaged the coasts of Spain, Italy, and Greece as a Muslim
corsair (a privateer of the Barbary States) until the age of 60.
In 1546 he died at the court of Constantinople, a revered figure
to the Ottomans.

BARBIE, Klaus (b. 1913). Nazi war criminal. He served as Gestapo chief in Lyon, France, from 1942 to 1944 during the German Nazi occupation of France in World War II. At Lyon's Fort
de Montluc prison, Barbie, a skilled pianist and an admirer of
Friedrich Nietzsche, nineteenth-century German philosopher who
argued for the creation of a superior, dominant race, was supposedly responsible for the torture and murder of thousands of
French Jews and resistance fighters, including the resistance
leader Jean Moulin. Some 7,500 other Jews were deported, allegedly on Barbie's orders, to Nazi concentration camps, where
many of them died. In 1951 Barbie settled in Bolivia under the
name of Klaus Altmann and, in 1957, was granted Bolivian citizenship under that name. After French Nazi hunters made public his presence there in 1972, French and West German officials
sought his extradition. Apprehended and imprisoned in January
1983 on a charge of fraud in connection with a $10,000 debt to
a state mining company, Barbie was expelled from Bolivia and
flown under military guard to France on February 5, 1983. Indicted for "crimes against humanity" involving over 11,000 deaths,
he was incarcerated at Lyon's Fort de Montluc to await trial.

BARKER, [Arizona Donnie Clark] "Ma" or "Kate" (1872-1935).
American gang leader and outlaw. Although she was never arrested for or charged with any crime during her life, Ma Barker
became known as the "brains" behind the payroll, post office,
and bank robberies carried out by her sons, the Barker Brothers, and their colleagues in the early 1930s. According to most
accounts, she dominated as well as doted on her sons. At her
hideouts, Barker sheltered top criminals such as Alvin KARPIS,
Al SPENCER, and Frank "Jelly" NASH. She helped plan the
kidnappings of millionaires William A. Hamm, Jr. (1933) and Edward George Bremer (1934) and, reportedly, the murder of her
boy friend, Arthur V. Dunlop (1932). With her son Freddie,
Barker was chased to a hideout on Lake Weir, Florida, where

they were shot to death by FBI men on January 16, 1935. See also BARKER, [Arthur] "Doc" or "Dock"; BARKER, Fred or Freddie; BARKER, Herman; BARKER, Lloyd; ZIEGLER, "Shotgun" [George].

BARKER, Arthur "Doc" or "Dock" (1899-1939). American bank robber and kidnapper. The oldest son of Ma BARKER, he was considered the deadliest of the Barker Brothers. From 1910 to 1915 he was arrested several times on minor charges. Then, in Tulsa, Oklahoma, in 1920, Doc killed a night guard while attempting to rob a drug shipment at St. Johns Hospital and was sentenced to life imprisonment at Oklahoma State Penitentiary. Paroled in 1932, he joined with his brother Fred and others and robbed banks throughout the Midwest. He helped kidnap for ransom William A. Hamm, Jr. (1933) and Edward G. Bremer (1934). Led by Melvin Purvis, Chicago FBI men captured Doc in 1935. Convicted of the Bremer kidnapping, he was sentenced to life at Alcatraz, where he was killed during an attempted breakout on June 13, 1939. See also BARKER, Fred or Freddie; KARPIS, Alvin; ZIEGLER, "Shotgun" [George].

BARKER, Fred or Freddie (1902-35). American bank robber and murderer. In 1926 he was sentenced to a five-to-ten year term at the Kansas State Penitentiary for bank robbery. Paroled in 1931, Fred Barker joined his friend Alvin KARPIS to go on a bank-robbery spree in the Midwest. Law enforcement officers were killed during robberies. Barker also stole cars, clothing, jewelry, cigarettes, and whiskey before turning to a more profitable crime kidnapping. With his brother Doc BARKER and others, he kidnapped brewer-millionaire William A. Hamm, Jr. for a $100,000 ransom (1933) and banker-millionaire Edward G. Bremer for a $200,000 ransom (1934). He and his mother, Ma BARKER, were killed during a shootout with FBI agents at Lake Weir, Florida, on January 16, 1935. See also ZIEGLER, "Shotgun" [George].

BARKER, Herman (1894-1927). American bank robber and murderer. Several times he was arrested on minor robbery charges and was released into the custody of his doting mother, Ma BARKER. Herman organized a teenage gang in Tulsa, Oklahoma, that specialized in store burglary. In the early 1920s he became a member of a bank robbing gang, which included Ray TERRILL and Matt Kimes, that operated in Missouri, Oklahoma, and Texas. He killed a police officer and was seriously wounded during a store robbery in Newton, Kansas; he shot himself to death that day, September 19, 1927.

BARKER, Lloyd (1896-1949). American robber. One of the notorious Barker Brothers, he earned a reputation at an early age for robbery. His mother, Ma BARKER, managed to secure his release into her custody, and Lloyd continued his criminal ways.

With his brother Herman, Lloyd formed a teenage burglary gang in Tulsa, Okalhoma, in 1910. Twelve years later, in 1922, he was caught while robbing a post office in Oklahoma and was sent to Leavenworth Penitentiary. Lloyd was released in 1947. His wife killed him two years later.

BARNES, [Leroy] "Nicky" (b. 1933). New York narcotics racketeer. He allied himself with Brooklyn racketeer Joey GALLO, who taught him much about the narcotics underworld in organized crime. Barnes imported large quantities of heroin from overseas and set up his own "millworking" and distributing operations in Harlem and other areas of New York. He became fabulously wealthy, buying expensive cars and apartments, and carried around large amounts of cash. The "King of Harlem," as some called him, evaded long-term imprisonment for many years because he kept the authorities from obtaining any substantial evidence. Finally, in 1978, Barnes was tried for narcotics violations, convicted, and sentenced to life imprisonment plus a fine of $125,000.

BARRIE, [Peter Christian] "Paddy" (1888-1935). Scottish-born British and American horse race fixer. He was an expert "dyer" of racehorses, using special dyes, bleaches, and other materials to change the identities of fast, championship horses to those of lesser known and slower horses. The ringers usually won, and Barrie and others in the know would make a "killing" on their bets at the racetrack. Barrie disguised racehorses in Great Britain and the United States from about 1920 to 1934. He also often disguised himself and used aliases to avoid capture by the authorities. Pinkerton agents finally caught Barrie at Saratoga racetrack in New York, and because U.S. laws on horse race fixing were lenient at that time, Barrie was not imprisoned but deported to his native Scotland, where he died shortly after.

BARROW, Clyde (1909-34). American robber and murderer. In the late 1920s he and his brother Buck committed several robberies in the Dallas, Texas, area. Clyde met Bonnie PARKER, a cafe waitress, in January 1930, and they began living together. Sent to the Waco jail for burglary, Clyde escaped with help from Bonnie but was caught and then sent to the brutal Eastham prison farm in Texas. There he was tortured and became a confirmed homosexual. Clyde killed an inmate for informing on him in 1931. Released after serving 20 months, he swore he'd never go to prison again. In the fall of 1932, Bonnie and Clyde, with a renegade named Ray HAMILTON who served as a lover to both, took to the open road, robbing small banks and stores and killing lawmen and others. Hamilton soon left the pair, who were then joined by Buck and his wife, Blanche, and a gas-station-attendant-turned robber named William Daniel Jones. The five-member Barrow gang pulled off

many holdups, usually never getting more than a few hundred
dollars, and became widely known for its wild shootouts with
police, using shotguns, machine-guns, and revolvers. The
gang killed two lawmen while fighting its way out of a trap in
Joplin, Missouri, in April 1933. At Dexter, Iowa, in July 1933,
the police fatally wounded Buck and captured Blanche; the three
others escaped. Jones soon deserted, and Bonnie and Clyde
stayed on the run. On May 23, 1934, the pair were ambushed
and shot to death by a Texas posse, led by Frank Hamer, at a
roadblock near Gibland, Louisiana.

BARROW, George. See ANDERSON, Bella.

BARRY, Jeanne Bécu du. See GOURDAN, Madame.

BARTER, Richard "Rattlesnake Dick" (1834-59). English-born
California robber. He received his nickname because he pros-
pected briefly at the Rattlesnake Mine in northern California.
Barter organized a gang, led by George Skinner, to rob
$80,000 in gold from the Yreka Mine's mule train as it came
down out of the mountains. In 1856 Skinner and two others
stole the gold and waited for Barter and Skinner's brother Cy
to bring fresh mules to transport it away. However, Barter
and Cy were in jail, having been caught, drunk, stealing mules.
George Skinner and the others buried the gold nuggets and
went to Folsom to celebrate. They were soon hunted down and
killed by Wells Fargo agents during a shootout. When Barter
and Cy finally broke out of jail, they searched unsuccessfully
for the buried treasure. In July 1859, Barter was shot dead
by lawmen while robbing a stagecoach. See also SKINNER,
Cy[rus].

BASS, Sam (1851-78). American stage and train robber and outlaw. As a member of an outlaw gang, he held up and robbed
stagecoaches and trains in the Dakota and Nebraska territories
in 1876 and 1877. Bass fled south to Texas, where he formed
another outlaw gang that specialized in train robberies. Because he gave money he stole to the poor, he gained widespread
frontier fame as a "good badman," a kind of Robin Hood. Informed on by Jim MURPHY, one of his gang, Bass was shot in
the stomach by a lawman the day before he planned to rob the
Round Rock, Texas, bank. Bass died the next day (July 21,
1878), refusing to tell the Texas Rangers the names of his accomplices or where any of the loot of his robberies was buried.
See also DAVIS, Jack; JACKSON, Frank.

BASSITY, Jerome [presumed real name: Jere McGlane] (c. 1870-
1929). San Francisco brothel owner. During the early years
of the twentieth century, Bassity was considered the king of
San Francisco's red-light district, owning more brothels than
anyone else in the city. Despite numerous newspaper exposés

about Bassity, his sex rackets, and his own lascivious life style, he operated with little interference from the law (San Francisco's government was under the corrupt rule of political boss Abraham RUEF at the time). Except for two years, 1907-9, when the city was under a reform administration, Bassity's many brothels and other dives flourished and made much money for their owner. Finally, in 1916, feeling the weight of new reform efforts, Bassity retired and moved to Mexico, where he resided for years. When he died in 1929, his estate was less than $10,000; he had spent recklessly until the very end.

BATEMAN, Mary [Harker] (1768-1809). English thief and poisoner. After 1894 she lived with her husband, John Bateman, a simple wheelwright, in Leeds, Yorkshire, where she earned an ominous reputation as a fortuneteller with supernatural powers and became known as the "Yorkshire Witch." Increasingly feared by townspeople for her avowed witchcraft and black magic, she received much money from customers who sought to get rid of evil spirits or curses; her fraudulent operation took the savings of many gullible souls until she was arrested for the poisoning death of a Mrs. Perigo in 1808. Mr. Perigo, whom she had tried also to poison after stealing the couple's money, had notified the police when he fell ill eating Mary's poisoned pudding and learned from a doctor that it had been laced with mercuric chloride (which had killed his wife). Although she proclaimed innocence at her sensational trial, Mary was convicted of murder and, on March 20, 1809, was hanged before a large, silent crowd made up probably of many witch-fearing folk.

BÁTHORY, Elizabeth (1560-1614). Hungarian countess and mass murderer. After her husband, a wealthy Hungarian count, died in 1600, Countess Báthory, mentally unbalanced since childhood, conjured up the mad idea that her complexion and her body would stay smooth and youthful if she bathed in human blood. Helped by three loyal servants, all believers in black magic, she lured hundreds of servant girls over a period of years to her remote castle, where they were slaughtered and the blood from their bodies was drained into a large tub in which the countess took long baths. One of her intended victims managed to escape and warn the authorities, who found many human corpses in the castle. Brought to trial in January 1611, Countess Báthory was accused of killing 610 persons (a total she had allegedly written in a book recording the murders). Her three accomplices were found guilty and hanged, but the countess, although convicted of murder, was spared execution because of her connections in high places (the prime minister was her cousin) and entombed in her room at the castle (she was furnished food and water through a small hole in the wall). She died there more than three years later on August 21, 1614, wild-eyed and hysterical.

BATTAGLIA, Sam "Teets" (1908-73). Chicago gangster and racketeer. As a youth, he was a member of Chicago's wild juvenile
42 Gang. Battaglia, known more for his brawn than his brains,
became an important Mafia henchman and worked for Sam
GIANCANA. By 1950, he was the "juice king"--head of the
syndicate's loansharking business--and also operated several
gambling and prostitution rackets. Battaglia was arrested 25
times on charges from robbery to homicide. In 1967 he was
convicted of extortion and given a 15-year term in prison,
where he later died.

BEADLE, William (d. 1783). Connecticut murderer. According to
reports, he had planned for a year to kill his family. As
Beadle's wife and five children lay sleeping on December 11,
1783, Beadle struck each on the head with an axe and slit
their throats with a carving knife. Then, in the kitchen
downstairs, he committed suicide, shooting himself in the head.

BEAN, Sawney (fl. mid-1400s). Scottish highwayman, mass murderer, and cannibal. Illiterate and uncouth, he lived with his
wife and 14 children in a giant cave by the desolate seacoast
along the Galloway region in southwestern Scotland. For over
25 years the Bean family assaulted, robbed, and killed travelers
--men, women, and children--on their way to and from Edinburgh and Glasgow in the north. Their depredations included
cannibalism as well. Finally, an intended victim who had seen
his wife knocked from her horse, her throat immediately slit,
and her body cannibalized, managed to escape to warn the
Scottish king at Glasgow. Some 400 men and bloodhounds, led
by the king, tracked down and, after a fierce battle, captured
the Beans in their cave, in which were found numerous mutilated cadavers. Sawney and the rest were brought to Leith,
showed not the slightest repentance for their crimes, and were
promptly burned to death at the stake without a trial. It was
estimated that the Beans' murder victims totaled well over 1,000
persons.

BEAUCHAMP, Jereboam O. (1803-26). Kentucky murderer. In
1826 Beauchamp, a lawyer, married Ann Cooke, who charged
she had been seduced and made pregnant by Colonel Solomon P.
Sharp. Sharp refused to duel Beauchamp, who wished to
avenge Ann's honor. Wearing a red hood over his head,
Beauchamp went to Sharp's house and stabbed him to death.
But Beauchamp was recognized and thrown in jail, where Ann
and he, upon learning he was to be hanged, tried unsuccessfully to commit suicide by taking poison. On the day of the
hanging, July 7, 1826, the pair plunged knives into each
other's stomachs. Ann died. Severely wounded and with his
wife in his arms, Beauchamp was led to the gallows in a field
near Frankfort, Kentucky. Thousands of spectators witnessed
his death.

BECK, Dave or David D. (b. 1894). American labor leader convicted of income tax evasion. An aggressive labor negotiator
and founder of the Western Conference of Teamsters, Beck rose
to be elected president of the powerful International Brotherhood of Teamsters in 1952. Apparently, however, his ambition
and greed caused him to raid the union treasury for his personal use, taking funds to build a grand home in Seattle and to
live lavishly. When Senator John McClellan's committee investigated labor racketeering in 1957, Beck's underhanded dealings
presently came to light (Beck invoked the Fifth Amendment more
than 200 times in hearings before the Senate committee). The
AFL-CIO found him guilty of misuse of union funds and expelled
both him and the Teamsters union, then a part of the AFL-CIO.
Beck, indicted for income tax evasion (1957), was found guilty
(1959) and imprisoned; James R. Hoffa had earlier (1957) succeeded him as Teamsters' president. Still owing the government
$1.3 million in back taxes, Beck was permitted to suspend pay-
ments upon his release from prison in 1971.

BECK, Martha [Seabrook] (1920-51). American swindler and murderer. In 1947 Beck, an obese divorcee, teamed up with her
lover, Raymond Martinez FERNANDEZ, to make a business out
of mulcting members of Lonely Hearts clubs in New York and
elsewhere. Fernandez courted the women and arranged to marry them, while Beck posed as his sister. After the two had
obtained the women's money and other assets, they killed them.
As many as 17 women may have died by their hands. When the
murder of Mrs. Delphine Downing and her child were discovered
in Grand Rapids, Michigan, suspicion focused on Beck and Fernandez, who were both arrested. The pair confessed to the
murders, as well as to killing Mrs. Janet Fay in New York.
Extradited to New York because that state had the death penalty, the murderers were tried, convicted, and executed at
Sing Sing Prison on March 8, 1951, after appealing their case
in vain.

BECK, Sophie (1851-?). American swindler. With money gleaned
from her minor confidence rackets in New York City, she moved
(about 1900) to Philadelphia, where she soon set up the Storey
Cotton Company, a specious business promising investors a 50
percent return on their money within a month or two. Gullible
persons, impressed by Beck, unknowingly bought worthless
stock certificates for cash from her and were stalled by her in
receiving payments. In early 1903 Beck absconded with two
million dollars from the valueless firm, sailing to Europe where
she took up residence in grandeur in Paris.

BECKER, Charles (1869-1915). New York policeman, extortionist,
and murderer. In 1911 Becker was put in charge of the special
crime squad of the New York City Police Department. Becker
received kickbacks from gamblers, prostitutes, and other vice

racketeers and provided police "protection" to those who paid
and "penalties" (police raids) to those who refused. When
gambler Herman "Beansie" Rosenthal refused to pay any more
to Becker, Becker's squad raided and destroyed Rosenthal's
gambling casino. Rosenthal then exposed the whole police protection racket and Becker's connection and profits, and as a
result was shot and killed outside the Cafe Metropole in Manhattan on July 16, 1912. Later Becker was arrested after "Big
Jack" ZELIG, a gangster once hired by Becker, told a grand
jury that Becker had arranged the murder of Rosenthal. Becker
was tried, found guilty of first degree murder, and electrocuted
at Sing Sing Prison in Ossining, New York, on July 7, 1915.
See also GYP THE BLOOD.

BECKER, Marie [Alexander] (1877-c. 1938). Belgian mass poisoner.
Tired of her monotonous life and unromantic husband and seized
by a desire to recapture love and youth, the matronly Marie
first had a wild love affair with a middle-aged Lothario named
Lambert Beyer (1932), secretly poisoned to death her husband,
and then killed Beyer the same way when she grew bored with
him. In Liège, Belgium, where she lived, Becker now indulged
herself fully in carnal pleasures with paid gigolos in nightclubs
and in her bedroom. Because her dressmaking business did
not yield enough money to pay for her orgies, she stole from
female customers whom she secretly killed with digitalis poison.
A friend, to whom Becker had boldly asserted that she could
eliminate her unwanted husband without a trace, went to the
police and informed them. Becker was arrested, some of her
victim's corpses were exhumed, and poison was found in them.
She openly laughed about the poisonings at her trial, telling in
delight how her ten known victims died. She was convicted and
imprisoned for life.

BECKWOURTH, Jim [born: James Beckwith] (1800-1866?). Ameri-
can scout and horse thief. About 1824 Beckwourth, son of an
Irish aristocrat and a female mulatto slave, traveled west to the
Rocky Mountains with a U.S. Army expedition to fight in the
Indian wars. He soon became a guide for immigrants moving
through the mountains and supplied them with stolen horses.
Beckwourth set up a thriving horse-stealing operation with
Thomas L. "Pegleg" SMITH and William S. "Old Bill" WILLIAMS
in southern California in the 1840s. The gang engaged in nu-
merous gunfights with posses and vigilantes, who finally forced
Beckwourth to flee from California to Colorado territory in 1855.
As a scout for the U.S. Army, Beckwourth took part in the
Sand Creek Massacre, in which U.S. troops killed more than
400 Cheyenne and Arapaho Indians in 1864. It is believed that
he was poisoned to death in 1866 by some Crow Indians, with
whom he was trading.

BELAND, [Lucy] "Ma" (1871-1941). Texas drug trafficker. Her

increasing avarice drove her husband to desert her in 1912,
after which she sent her two teenage daughters, Cora and
Willie, into the Fort Worth, Texas, streets to earn money as
prostitutes and also began peddling narcotics, chiefly morphine
and heroin, with the help of her two sons, Charlie and Joe.
Within a few years, the Beland clan, led by Ma (as she was
called by friends and foes), became the most infamous wholesale traffickers in illegal drugs in Texas and the Southwest.
High Texas officials were bribed by her to close their eyes to
her lucrative operation, which was headquartered in an ostensi-
bly respectable clothing store in Fort Worth. The family members, all of whom became addicts, either died from overdoses
or were jailed on convictions of drug selling. Finally, Ma herself was fooled by an FBI undercover agent asking to buy
heroin in 1937. Arrested and convicted, she received only a
two-year prison sentence because of her advanced age.

BELCASTRO, James (fl. 1920s). Chicago gangster, extortionist,
and bomber. He was a leader in the Black Hand extortion
racket in Chicago, forcing prominent and well-to-do citizens to
pay much money in order not to be maimed, poisoned, or killed.
Belcastro became a trusted terrorist for Al CAPONE, a mob
boss and bootlegger, and specialized in blowing up saloons
(with customers) whose owners refused to take Capone's beer.
Rival breweries were also dynamited by Capone's chief "pineapple man," Belcastro, whom the Chicago underworld labeled
as "King of the Bombers." During the 1927 Chicago primary,
the so-called "Pineapple Primary" because of the many bombings, he planted explosives at voting places and outside homes
of political rivals opposing the election of William Hale "Big Bill"
Thompson, Capone's mayoral candidate. Belcastro lived to a
ripe age, dying in bed of natural causes.

BELL, Tom [real name: Thomas J. Hodges] (1825-56). American
doctor and stage robber. After serving as a physician in the
Mexican War (1846-48), he went to California in search of gold
but found the life of crime more lucrative. With a man named
Bill Gristy, Bell organized and led a hardened gang of stagecoach robbers in the mid-1850s. While attempting to rob a
$100,000 gold bullion shipment aboard the Marysville stage in
August 1856, the gang shot and killed a woman passenger,
wounded two men, but was driven off by the guards, who
fatally shot two gang members. Posses and vigilante groups
immediately took off after the gang and soon caught Gristy,
who turned informer and said Bell was the gang's leader. On
October 4, 1856, Bell was found dead, hanging from a tree near
Nevada City, California.

BELLAMY, [Samuel] "Black" (d. 1717). English pirate. He and his
pirate crew successfully plundered many Spanish and American
merchant ships in the Caribbean and Atlantic sea-lanes and were

greatly feared for several years because of their sudden raids
and ruthless slaughter of seamen. After robbing some vessels
in 1717, Bellamy, aboard his English-built ship Whidah, which
he had stolen, sailed north to New England. The ship, laden
with gold and silver coins, ivory, jewels, and other valuables,
encountered a severe storm, split apart, and apparently sank
off the coast of Cape Cod, Massachusetts. According to the
report of two pirate survivors of the Whidah, Bellamy, who
called himself a "free prince" with license to steal from the
rich, and about 150 of his crew drowned, taking to their sea
graves a fabulously rich booty. The two pirates were subsequently hanged in Boston.

BELLE, Earl (b. 1932). Pittsburgh financier and accused swindler.
Belle, a financial "whiz kid" and chief official of Cornucopia
Gold Mines, became successful and wealthy as a young man in
Pittsburgh. Through clever financial maneuvers, he and an
associate secured large bank loans for their company and raised
much money from stockholders. After being charged with defrauding banks and owners of stock in their company of more
than two million dollars, Belle fled to Rio de Janeiro in 1958
and took up "permanent exile" there.

BENDER, Kate (1832 ?). American mass murderer. A tall, pretty,
buxom, young woman, Kate, along with her father (William John
"Old Man" BENDER), mother, and brother, arrived in Cherryvale, Kansas, in the spring of 1872. She said she was a spiritualist who could heal the sick and talk with the dead. Bender
delivered spiritual lectures and held public séances in small
towns in southeastern Kansas, earning the title "Professor Miss
Kate Bender." All the while she helped murder and rob travelers who stopped overnight at the Benders' wayside inn. On
May 5, 1873, Kate disappeared with her family.

BENDER, Tony. See STROLLO, Anthony C.

BENDER, William John "Old Man" (1813?-84?). American mass murderer. He and his daughter, Kate BENDER, headed the notorious Bender family (which also included his wife and son, John).
The Benders built a one-room inn near Cherryvale, Kansas, in
1872. Travelers, seated with their backs against a canvas curtain that divided the room, used to touch their heads to the
canvas, and then the Old Man and his son, on the other side
of the curtain, would bash in their skulls with sledgehammers.
The dead guests' money and other valuables were taken, and
the dead bodies were dumped in the cellar until buried outside.
Dr. William H. York stopped and disappeared at the Benders'
place in March 1873. His brother, Colonel A. M. York, visited
the inn to question the Benders, who afterward, on May 5,
1873, disappeared. Colonel York and others then dug up 11
mutilated corpses (one of them his brother's) on the premises.

A posse reportedly failed to find any trace of the "Hell" or "Bloody" Benders, as they came to be known; later two members of the posse said they helped kill and bury the Benders. In 1884, a man looking very much like Old Man Bender was arrested in Montana territory for a murder similar to those in Kansas. The man tried to free himself from an ankle iron by cutting off his foot and bled to death.

BENI or BENE, Jules (d. 1861). French-Canadian robber and outlaw. In the 1850s he operated a trading post and stagecoach station in what is now Julesburg, Colorado. Wanted criminals were sheltered there. Beni reportedly stole horses and cash from the Overland Express Company, which sent Joseph A. "Jack" SLADE, a notorious gunslinger, to investigate. In 1859 Beni blasted Slade with a shotgun and left him for dead. Slade miraculously recovered and two years later seized Beni, who had been told to vacate the area but had returned. Slade lashed Beni to a fence post and used him for target practice, shooting him in the arms and legs and finally sticking his gun into Beni's mouth and blasting off his head. Slade then cut off Beni's ears, one of which he apparently used as a watch fob.

BENSON, Howard. See WELCH, Ed.

BERGDOLL, Grover Cleveland (1893-1966). American draft dodger. A wealthy Philadelphia playboy, Bergodoll did not report to his local draft board in 1917 during World War I and eluded federal authorities until early 1920. However, he soon escaped and was not recaptured for almost 20 years, during which time he hid in various spots in the United States, including his family's mansion in Philadelphia, and Europe. Returning from Germany aboard the steamship Bremen in May 1939, Bergdoll surrendered on his arrival in New York City, reportedly because he thought he would be drafted into the German army if he stayed abroad. Sentenced to seven years at hard labor, he was released from prison early in 1944. Bergdoll died at a psychiatric hospital in Richmond, Virginia, on January 27, 1966.

BERIA, Lavrenti [Pavlovich] (1899-1953). Soviet spy chief. Having helped the Bolsheviks (Communists) seize power in Russia in 1917, he became mastermind of Cheka (Soviet secret police) espionage and counterespionage activities in Georgia, his and Joseph STALIN's home state, and elsewhere in the Soviet Union in the 1920s. He helped Stalin secure dictatorial power by 1927; his investigations uncovered counterrevolutionaries and Stalin's enemies during the next decade. In 1938 Beria, who had ruthlessly deported countless enemies to the ice deserts of the Arctic and the plains of Siberia, became the Communist chief of all Soviet intelligence at home and abroad; he administered, in addition, all Soviet slave labor, correctional labor,

and concentration camps. His spy ring--the Rote Kapelle
("Red Orchestra")--successfully infiltrated numerous foreign
governments as part of the huge Soviet spying organization,
the OGPU (NKVD or MVD), which Beria headed. Beria, who
planted his agents everywhere, was made a Politburo member
in 1946. At Stalin's death (1953), his power was enormous and
menaced the balance of the Soviet power structure. Charged
with anti-party and anti-state crimes and convicted at his secret trial, Beria was executed in Moscow on December 23, 1953.

BERKMAN, Alexander (1870-1936). Lithuanian-born American
anarchist. Berkman, an avowed anarchist associated with Emma
GOLDMAN, was outraged by the strong-handed and murderous
tactics used by industrialist Henry Clay Frick to put down
striking workers at the Carnegie Steel Company's largest mills
in Homestead, Pennsylvania, during July 6-9, 1892. On July
23 Berkman stormed into Frick's office and fired two shots at
Frick, wounding him in the neck before being wrestled to the
floor by Frick's assistant, Mr. Leishman, and Frick himself
(Frick sustained seven additional wounds by Berkman, who
stabbed him with a knife during the struggle). The would-be
assassin was sentenced to 22 years in prison. Released early
in 1906, Berkman resumed his anarchist activities with Goldman
until both of them were arrested for agitating against the mili
tary draft and deported to Russia in 1919. Disillusioned by
Soviet authoritarianism, both later left Russia. Berkman, who
lived for periods in Sweden, Germany, and France, grew progressively despondent and finally killed himself in Nice, France,
on June 28, 1936.

BERKOWITZ, David Richard. See SON OF SAM.

BERMAN, Otto "Abbadabba" (1889-1935). New York numbers racketeer. He worked for Dutch SCHULTZ, who controlled much of
the numbers-game racket in New York City, and was considered
a mathematical genius because he developed a system for rigging
the results of numbers games. Berman's technique, enabling
bettors to figure out the amount of money to put in the mutual
machine to have a lesser-played number win, was extremely
profitable for Schultz and his friends. Berman was shot and
killed by two gunmen, whose principal target was Schultz, at
the Palace Chop House in Newark, New Jersey, on October 23,
1935.

BEVAN, Catherine (1680-1731). Delaware murderer. A clandestine
love affair between matronly Catherine and young Peter Murphy,
her husband Henry's servant, led to the lovers beating and
choking 60-year-old Henry to death in 1731. Publicly claiming
that he had perished from a stroke, the killers nailed shut the
lid of his coffin, preventing the customary viewing of the dead
before burial and consequently arousing suspicion. The lid was

removed; Henry's injured body effected the arrest of Catherine
and Peter, who promptly confessed. Both were executed; while
Catherine stood tied at the stake with a rope around her neck,
which was to strangle her beforehand, the rope burned up,
leaving her to be burned alive--the only woman to suffer such
an execution in America.

BIANCHI, Kenneth [Alessio] (b. 1951). American mass murderer.
In the fall of 1977 the Los Angeles area was terrorized by a
series of ten slayings of women 18 to 28 years old by a killer
or killers referred to as the "Hillside Strangler," so-called because the victims had all been choked to death and dumped,
partly nude, on hillsides along roads in the city's northeastern
Glendale area. A special 55-officer police task force questioned
suspects, including Bianchi, a former security guard under arrest in Bellingham, Washington, on charges of killing two Western Washington University coeds; at the time (April 1979),
Bianchi's cousin, Angelo Buono, was also suspected in the hillside murders. Before being extradited to Los Angeles for trial,
Bianchi pleaded guilty to killing the two coeds and received two
consecutive life prison terms (October 19, 1979). In a plea
bargaining deal with the Los Angeles District Attorney's office,
he admitted to five of the hillside murders and agreed to testify
against Buono, his accused accomplice, in return for being
spared a possible death sentence. On October 22, 1979, Bianchi
was sentenced to five concurrent life terms in prison, and later,
in 1983, he helped convict Buono as the chief prosecution witness. Bianchi's past, particularly his experience as an adopted
child who was kept ignorant of his origins, was brought out in
his defense during his 1979 trial.

BICHEL, Andreas (1770-1808). German mass murderer. In the
early 1800s he established himself as a fortuneteller in Regens-
dorf, Bavaria. Travelers, mostly young women, were always
his victims, never local villagers, whose disappearance would
undoubtedly bring about dangerous inquiries. Unsuspecting
women and others were told by Bichel that they had to be ab-
solutely still for him to read their futures and thus had to be
securely tied to a chair. He would then swiftly cut their spinal
cords from behind, thrust his sharp knife into their lungs, de-
nude their bodies, and bury them in a woodshed near his house.
Finally, a woman looking for her missing sister accidentally
spotted one of her sister's garments in a tailor's shop in Reg-
ensdorf. Told that the clothing had been sold to the tailor by
Bichel, she informed the police, who investigated and found
stacks of female clothes in Bichel's house and later uncovered
corpses in the woodshed. Bichel was convicted (he murdered
an estimated 50 persons) and, in 1808, was condemned to the
wheel, a torture device like a cartwheel designed to stretch,
disjoint, and mutilate a victim. Afterward his bones were
broken one by one by an executioner with a sledgehammer,
and his body was decapitated.

BIDDLE, Ed[ward] (1844-1902). Pennsylvania murderer and prison
   escapee. On January 30, 1902 he and his brother Jack broke
   out of the Allegheny County Jail near Pittsburgh, where they
   were awaiting execution for a double murder. The warden's
   wife, Katherine Scoffel, who had fallen in love with Ed, aided
   and accompanied them in the escape. Shortly afterward, near
   Butler, Pennsylvania, police stopped the trio, killed Jack in a
   wild gunfight, and fatally wounded Ed. Katherine begged Ed,
   as he lay dying, to shoot her so she "could be with him forever in death." He did so, but she survived, was tried, and
   sentenced to two years in the Allegheny prison. Released after
   18 months, Katherine lived as a shunned woman until her death
   in 1926.

BIGLEY, Elizabeth. See CHADWICK, Cassie L.

BILLEE, John (d. 1890). Oklahoma murderer and outlaw. In April
   1888, he killed a man and buried him in a gully in the Kiamichi
   Mountains in southeastern Oklahoma. Three U.S. deputy marshals captured Billee along with four other outlaws in Muskogee,
   Oklahoma, but were shot and wounded by Billee during an attempted escape before they were able to put a disabling bullet
   into Billee and subdue him. By bringing Billee and the others
   back alive to Fort Smith, the deputies were able to collect their
   fees for the outlaws (in those days, dead prisoners netted deputies nothing). Billee was hanged at Fort Smith on January 16,
   1890.

BILLINGTON, John (d. 1630). English-born American murderer.
   He became known as a foul-mouthed bully during the voyage
   aboard the Mayflower from England to America in 1620. His
   tongue got him in trouble with Captain Miles Standish, who
   once ordered his feet and neck tied together as punishment.
   At the Pilgrim colony at Plymouth, Massachusetts, Billington
   had a number of violent arguments and fights with neighbors,
   one of whom was John Newcomen. One day in 1630 Billington
   ambushed and shot Newcomen dead with a blunderbuss. The
   Pilgrims found Billington guilty of murder and hanged him.
   Billington is generally considered America's first murderer.

BILLY THE KID [real name: William H. Bonney] (1859-81).
   American gunfighter and outlaw. By the age of 16, he supposedly had become a master of the use of the .41 Colt revolver and the .44 Winchester rifle and had shot and killed
   several men in arguments. Billy headed a gang of gunslinging
   cattle rustlers and in 1878, during a cattle war in Lincoln County, New Mexico, killed Sheriff William Brady. He and his confederates led a wild life, drinking and gambling and killing
   several other lawmen in the Southwest. A posse under Sheriff
   Patrick Floyd Garrett, a former friend of Billy, trapped Billy
   and some of his gang and forced them to surrender in late 1880.
   Tried and sentenced to hang for the murder of Sheriff Brady,

Billy escaped from jail, killing two deputies. On July 14, 1881, Sheriff Garrett, after again hunting him down, shot Billy dead near Fort Sumner, New Mexico. See also BOWDRE, Charlie; O'FOLLIARD, Tom; RUDABAUGH, Dave.

BINAGGIO, Charley or Charles (1909–50). Kansas City political boss. He helped deliver votes for Thomas Joseph PENDERGAST in Kansas City, Missouri, in the 1930s and had control of all North Side wards by 1945. Binaggio was supposedly involved in many ballot frauds but was never indicted. A power struggle developed between him and Jim Pendergast, Tom's nephew and successor, that allegedly caused Binaggio to accept large sums from the underworld after promising to make both Kansas City and St. Louis "wide open" to gambling and other gangland interests. Binaggio apparently reneged on his promises and failed to repay the crime syndicate, which, from all indications, arranged the shooting death of Binaggio and his chief body-guard, Charley Gargotta, on April 6, 1950, at Kansas City's First District Democratic Club.

BIOFF, Willie [Morris] (1900–1955). Chicago procurer, union racketeer, and informer. At an early age Bioff became a pimp and acquired a bevy of prostitutes who worked Chicago's Levee area. His brutal treatment of the girls landed him in jail several times. Bioff was also a union slugger for Al CAPONE and extorted millions of dollars from movie studio executives through union infiltration and threats of closing down the film industry. Newspaper columnist Westbrook Pegler helped the authorities expose and convict Bioff in 1941 of breaking the anti-racketeering laws. Bioff then turned state's evidence, helping the government convict Frank NITTI, Charles Gioe, Paul RICCA, John ROSELLI, and other mobsters. Set free, Bioff settled in Arizona under the name of Nelson. On November 4, 1955, he climbed into his pickup truck, stepped on the starter, and was blasted to death by a bomb in the truck's motor.

BIRD MAN OF ALCATRAZ. See STROUD, Robert [Franklin].

BIRRELL, Lowell McAfee (b. 1907). American swindler. The smart, university-educated son of a poor Presbyterian minister, he became a successful lawyer in New York in the 1930s. In 1944, through the help of his dying friend Cecil B. Stewart, a rich broker, Birrell obtained directorships in many of Stewart's firms. He was then able to secure large loans to buy other companies, whose assets he used to pay back loans or switched from one firm to another, and created confusing interlocking directorates. He promoted collapsing companies on the stock exchange, floating stock, pushing for quick sales, and taking millions of dollars in profits. Birrell, who established an incredibly Byzantine financial empire, was a bold showman, gallivanting at nightclubs and giving lavish parties at his estate in Bucks County, Pennsylvania. Though some of his companies crashed and investors were burned, Birrell kept up his manipulations until a New York investigation into his dealings caused him to be subpoenaed in 1957. Later, in October of that year, he fled with reportedly $3 million to Rio de Janeiro. In 1964 Birrell suddenly arrived under Brazilian police escort in New York, where he was seized by authorities and charged with fraud, embezzlement, and tax evasion involving some $25 million. The U.S. government and the Security Exchange Commission took years to go through his voluminous records while Birrell used legal maneuvers to remain out of jail. On January 11, 1972, he was finally incarcerated, convicted of fraud in connection with unauthorized stock certificates.

BJORKLAND, [Rosemarie Diane] "Penny" (b. 1941). California murderer. On February 1, 1959, she took her .38 caliber pistol, which she used for target shooting, and went hunting for someone to kill in Daly City, California. Bjorkland picked at random landscape gardener August Norry and pumped six bullets into him. She then reloaded, shot another six bullets into the dead body, reloaded again, and put another six shots into the corpse. Later the police traced the 18 bullets taken from Norry's body to a gun shop, whose owner told them he sold the bullets to Bjorkland. Arrested, the 18-year-old blonde admitted the killing. After a long trial with much psychiatric examination, she was sentenced to life imprisonment.

BLACK BART [real name: Charles E. Bolton] (c. 1820-?). California stage robber. From about 1874 to 1883 he held up and robbed at least 27 stagecoaches in California. He often left behind bits of doggerel, signed "Black Bart," inside Wells Fargo strong boxes he looted. Wearing a long, white duster and a flour sack mask, Black Bart became a familiar figure along the California trails. In 1883 a lone rider forced him to drop his handkerchief and flee during a stage robbery. Pinkerton detectives traced the laundry mark on the handkerchief to a distinguished, elderly gentleman, Charles E. Bolton, in San Francisco. Bolton finally confessed to being Black Bart and was sentenced to ten years in San Quentin prison. Released on good behavior on January 21, 1888, after spending slightly more than four years in prison, Black Bart seemed to pass out of sight. One report said he died in Nevada; another said in New York City in 1917.

BLACKBEARD [real name: Edward Teach or Thatch] (d. 1718). English pirate. After serving as a privateer during Queen Anne's War (1702-13), he turned pirate and converted a captured French merchant ship into a 40-gun warship, Queen Anne's Revenge. He was given the nickname "Blackbeard" because he grew a long, black beard, which he wore in braids apparently to look more fierce. From 1716 to 1718 he attacked

shipping off the Spanish Main, the West Indies, and the coasts
of Carolina and Virginia. He committed many outrages and
shared his booty with Governor Charles Eden of Carolina, who
gave him protection. Finally, two British warships sent by
Governor Alexander Spotswood of Virginia at the urging of
southern planters who had lost valuable cargoes chased and
cornered the Queen Anne's Revenge off Ocracoke Island, North
Carolina. Blackbeard was killed on November 21, 1718, during
a furious battle, and his head was placed atop his ship's
bowsprit for all to see.

BLAKE, George [born: George Behar] (b. 1922). British secret
agent and Soviet spy. During World War II (1939-45) he was a
resistance fighter in the Netherlands, escaped to England in
early 1943, and soon entered the British Royal Navy, where his
espionage skills were subsequently recognized. (By the war's
end he had changed his name to Blake, perhaps because it
sounded more British than Behar.) In 1948 Blake, fluent in
five languages, entered the British Foreign Service as vice
consul and was assigned to Seoul, South Korea. Interned by
the North Koreans during the Korean War (1950-53), he secretly became a Communist. Later, while working as a double
agent for Britain in Berlin from 1955 to 1959, Blake was actually a triple agent: a spy trained to pretend to have become a
traitor who secretly is involved in betraying his country. He
turned over to the Soviets secret information selected by British
Intelligence as well as more valuable secret documents that the
British didn't know about; he gave the KGB (Soviet intelligence
agency) the names of more than 50 espionage agents working
for British, U.S., and German intelligence. Reports from de-
fectors to the West led to suspicion about Blake's activities.
Charged with offenses under the British Official Secrets Act,
Blake stood trial on May 3, 1961 (he had made a full confession before the trial and thus had nothing to say in his defense), and was sentenced to 42 years in prison. On October 22, 1966, Blake, helped by former fellow prisoner Sean
Bourke, and three others escaped from London's Wormwood
Scrubs Prison and disappeared behind the Iron Curtain. In
1970 the Soviets awarded Blake the Order of Lenin for his
intelligence work.

BLANDY, Mary (1719-52). English poisoner. Her father, the
highly regarded lawyer Francis Blandy of Henley on Thames,
opposed Mary's proposed marriage to Captain William Henry
Cranstoun when he discovered that Cranstoun was already
married (the captain, who was almost twice Mary's age, had
sought to forsake his wife and children in the hope of obtaining Mary's presumed £10,000 dowry after their marriage; later
the huge dowry was found to be nonexistent). In June 1751,
Mary put some poison, sent to her by Cranstoun, in her father's
tea and gruel. Gravely ill and bedridden, he eventually died on

August 14, 1751. The household servants accused Mary, who was arrested and later, on March 3, 1752, brought to trial (Mary's mother had died soon after the father's death). Found guilty, Mary, while mounting the gallows in an open field near Oxford, was disturbed when rowdies tried to look under her long skirts and told the hangmen, "Gentlemen, do not hang me high, for the sake of decency!" She covered her face with a handkerchief, and her execution took place. Cranstoun fled to a monastery in France after Mary's arrest and died there of illness on November 30, 1752.

BLISS, George M[iles] (fl. 1860-80). New York burglar. He headed probably the largest gang of bank burglars ever to work with the law in New York. The Bliss Bank Ring, which included at times the infamous safecracker Mark SHINBURN, bribed police and others in authority not to harass them (about ten percent of the loot from burglaries went to crooked authorities) and pulled off numerous heists, including the spectacular 1869 robbery of $2.75 million from New York's Ocean Bank at Fulton and Greenwich streets. Following a crackdown on the alliance between bank burglars and police in 1880, the Bliss Bank Ring fell apart and many members were arrested, including Bliss, who was sentenced to prison on a conviction of bank burglary. See also TWEED, [William Marcy] "Boss."

BLONGER, Lou (fl. 1880s-1920s). French-Canadian-born Denver con man. He operated a saloon in Denver, and became a master in the confidence racket, amassing millions of dollars. Through payoffs to the police, Blonger, a fat, red-faced swindler, remained untouched by the law and established the largest con ring in U.S. history. By 1920 some 500 flimflammers worked for Blonger and his partner KID DUFFY, both of whom were headquartered in Denver. Blonger's confederates pulled off scams in Colorado, Florida, Louisiana, Texas, and other states, bilking suckers of hundreds and thousands of dollars in various con games. In 1920 J. Frank Norfleet, a Texas cattleman in Fort Worth, was swindled out of $45,000 by one of Blonger's sub-gangs, led by Joe Furey. Norfleet, an ex-sheriff, doggedly tracked down Furey in Jacksonville, Florida, and had him arrested in 1924. Eventually Norfleet, who was determined to expose Blonger's flimflamming racket, succeeded in having Blonger, Kid Duffy, and hundreds of their associates sent to jail. Blonger died in prison at the age of 73.

BLOOD, Thomas (1618?-80). Irish rebel. Colonel Blood, who once fought for Oliver Cromwell, attempted several times to abduct or assassinate members of the English royal family and overturn the monarchy. On May 9, 1671, disguised as a minister and accompanied by two cohorts, he gained entrance to see the Crown Jewels in the Tower of London. After knocking unconscious the chief guardian of the jewels, Blood stuffed the

English crown into a leather pouch while his fellow thieves pocketed the royal orb's gold ball and the royal scepter. With a fourth man who had held the getaway horses at the tower's main gate, the thieves rode off but were immediately pursued and overtaken by militiamen who had been quickly alerted by an alarm sounded by a tower guard. Taken into custody, Blood contrived a personal interview with King Charles II, whom he greatly impressed and amused, so much so that Charles pardoned him and restored his Irish estates. Despite these magnanimous gestures, Blood continued to conspire against the throne until his death in August 1680.

BLUEBEARD. See LANDRU, Henri Désiré; RAIS [RAIZ or RETZ], Gilles de; WATSON, J. P.

BOGLE, Helen. See BOGLE, James H.

BOGLE, James H. (fl. 1909). American kidnapper. In March 1909, following the widely talked-about abduction of eight-year-old Willie Whitla from his school, his wealthy parents, Mr. and Mrs. James P. Whitla of Sharon, Pennsylvania, received a letter from the kidnappers demanding $10,000 ransom for the release of their son, who would be killed otherwise. The money was paid, and the boy was handed over while the press covered every move. Bogle and his wife, Helen McDermott, were soon picked up by police after they had gotten drunk in a Cleveland, Ohio, bar, where they had aroused the suspicions of the bartender because of their wasteful spending of new five-dollar bills with consecutive serial numbers. Most of the ransom money was found on 38-year-old Helen, who later bragged about master-minding the crime and made up far-fetched stories about her past. The Bogles were tried, convicted, and given life im-prisonment.

BOLBER, Morris (c. 1890-c. 1938). Philadelphia quack and mur-derer. Dr. Bolber and his two cousins, Paul and Herman Petrillo, ran a murder-for-profit ring in the Italian community of Philadelphia during the Depression in the 1930s. They se-duced lonely wives, who fell madly in love with them and agreed to plans to kill their husbands for insurance money on their lives. Carino Favato, a faith healer called "The Witch," teamed up with the Bolber-Petrillo ring and helped murder, usually by administering poison, some 30 to 50 men. Finally in 1937, an ex-convict, who had hoped to join the group and had suggested a murderless scheme to make money but had been turned down by Herman Petrillo, informed the police about the racket. Bol-ber, Favato, and the Petrillos were arrested and soon denounced each other in the hope of gaining lenient sentences. The testi-mony of some implicated wives, who turned state's evidence, helped convict the Petrillos, who were executed, and Bolber and Favato, both of whom received life in prison.

BOLTON, Charles E. See BLACK BART.

BOLTON, Mildred Mary (1886-1943). Illinois murderer. A fanciful and insanely jealous wife, she accused her peaceable, stay-at-home husband Charles, a Chicago businessman, of having love affairs with numerous women, including his secretaries. At their home in Chicago's Hyde Park area, she continually tormented and frequently assaulted him physically, drawing blood, alleging perfidy on his part. Finally, she went to his office in the Loop and fatally shot him at his desk (June 15, 1936). Convicted and sentenced to death, she was able to gain a commutation from the Illinois governor. While serving a 199-year term without parole, Mildred killed herself at the Dwight, Illinois, women's prison by cutting her wrists with stolen scissors (August 29, 1943).

BOMPARD, Gabrielle (1869-?). French murderer. A poor 20-year-old hussy kept by a married, middle-aged brute named Michel Eyraud, she apparently planned the murder (1889) of a prosperous Parisian bailiff named Gouffé, whom she sexually enticed to her small apartment and, with the help of Eyraud, hanged by a belt connected to an intricate pulley and rope contraption they had set up. The two killer-lovers absconded with only part of Gouffé's 14,000 francs, which they mistakenly thought would be on him, and dumped Gouffé's body near Lyons. The police soon found it and began a search for the killers, who by then had fled abroad to the United States and Canada. Leaving Eyraud to take up with an American lover, Bompard returned to Paris, confessed to the crime, but blamed it all on Eyraud, who was tracked down and caught in Cuba and brought back to stand trial with Bompard. Both were found guilty by a French jury (1890) which in typically French fashion gave a more lenient sentence to Bompard, the woman; she received 20 years of hard labor, and Eyraud went to the guillotine, fuming with resentment, in 1891.

BONANNO, Joseph C., Sr. (b. 1905). Sicilian-born American racketeer and gangster. He entered the United States illegally in 1924 and worked for the Mafia in Chicago and New York. Bonanno, better known as "Joe Bananas" to the Mafia bosses, built a lucrative crime empire from loanshark, gambling, and narcotics rackets throughout the country and in Canada. In 1964 he planned to kill the top Mafia (Cosa Nostra) chiefs, such as Tommy LUCCHESE and Carlo GAMBINO, and take complete control. His "hit" man, Joe COLOMBO, squealed, and Bonanno was forced out of the East coast rackets. A Mafia war erupted in 1967 in Brooklyn between mobsters loyal to Bonanno and those under Paul Sciacca, an East coast boss. Bonanno had a heart attack in 1968 and retired to his estate in Tucson, Arizona. In 1980 he was found guilty of interfering with a federal grand jury's investigation of his two sons' businesses.

BONNER, Antoinette (1892-1920). Rumanian-born American thief. Dubbed the "Queen of Diamonds" in New York City between 1910 and 1914, lovely young Antoinette, who had expertly learned the diamond business through her experienced father, sold to rich customers millions of dollars worth of gems entrusted to her by the best jewelers. In Paris in 1914, arrested for absconding with diamonds valued at over a million dollars, she was let go after protesting that she had only been trying to make a sale there. She regained her good reputation, but six years later was caught in her New York offices, attempting to close up and sail to Europe with stolen goods. Before the police would take her in, she swallowed strychnine poison and, saying "Go to hell!" died.

BONNET, Jeanne (1841-76). San Francisco thief. In about 1875 she gathered dozens of prostitutes from brothels and formed a strictly female gang of thieves in San Francisco. Bonnet, who wore men's clothing and went under the nickname "Little Frog Catcher" (because she reportedly caught and sold frogs as an honest livelihood), and her gang worked out of a shack on the city's waterfront for about a year, until Bonnet was found dead with a bullet through her heart. It is believed that a pimp or pimps, whose girls had sworn off prostitution to join Bonnet, had murdered her in revenge.

BONNET, Stede (c. 1670-1718). British pirate. After retiring from the British army as a major, Bonnet settled on his plantation in Barbados. In early 1718, he inexplicably turned pirate, outfitting his own ship, the Revenge, and plundering ships along the Carolina and Virginia coasts. His appearance-- portly, clean shaven, and with a gentleman's powdered wig-- brought laughter to BLACKBEARD, with whom Bonnet sailed for a few months. Bonnet is said to have originated forcing prisoners to walk the plank to their watery grave. After a battle in which all ships ran aground near Cape Fear, Bonnet was captured with 30 of his men and taken to Charleston, South Carolina. He escaped but was recaptured, tried, and hanged in November 1718.

BONNEY, William H. See BILLY THE KID.

BONNIE AND CLYDE. See BARROW, Clyde; PARKER, Bonnie.

BONNOT, Jules (d. 1912). French bank robber and murderer. He is credited with being the first person to use an automobile in a bank robbery in Europe. In 1912 he drove to the biggest bank in Chantilly, a town 26 miles north of Paris by road, left the car's motor running, and entered the bank. Bonnot gunned down three persons, seized about 80,000 francs, and fled in his car. Later he and another man died in a wild gun battle with some 200 French gendarmes. Bonnot rhetorically asked himself in his will if he was sorry for the crime and replied, "Yes, maybe, but I'm not guiltier than the sweatshop owners who exploit poor wretches."

BONNY or BONNEY, Anne (fl. 1720-21). Irish pirate. She ran away from her penniless, groveling husband when Captain Jack RACKHAM courted her lavishly on New Providence in the Bahama Islands. With him and other pirates, Bonny stole a fast merchant sloop in Nassau harbor, converted it to a pirate ship, and preyed on shipping in the Caribbean area. She helped Rackham press Mary READ, disguised as a man, into pirate service. In late October 1720, a British merchant sloop surprised the pirates' vessel as it lay anchored off the coast of Jamaica. Rackham and his male mates put up little resistance, apparently the worse for drink, but Bonny and Read fought valiantly. They were, however, all captured and brought to Jamaica for trial. Because Bonny and Read said they were pregnant, they were granted stays of execution. Bonny's death was never recorded; apparently she survived the birth of her child in prison (Read did not) and was released.

BOOTH, John Wilkes (1838-65). American actor and assassin. He was a noted Shakespearean actor and an ardent supporter of the Confederacy. In 1864 Booth began plotting to kidnap President Abraham Lincoln. However, after the South's surrender the next year, he decided to assassinate the president, vice president, and members of the cabinet and enlisted the help of George Atzerodt, David E. Herold, Lewis PAINE, Mary E. SURRATT, John H. SURRATT, and others. Booth, an egomaniac, chose to kill the president himself. On the evening of April 14, 1865, at Ford's Theatre in Washington, D.C., he fatally shot Lincoln through the head with a Derringer pistol. Shouting, "The South is avenged," Booth jumped to the stage and then escaped. Union troops found him hiding in a tobacco barn near Bowling Green, Virginia, on April 26, 1865. The barn was set ablaze, and Booth either shot himself or was shot to death by the Union soldier and zealot, Boston Corbett.

BORDEN, Lizzie [Andrew] (1860-1927). Massachusetts accused murderer. Lizzie's father and stepmother were found dead with their heads bashed in by blows from an axe on August 4, 1892, at their home in Fall River, Massachusetts. Circumstantial evidence led authorities to charge Lizzie with the murders and hold her in jail for almost a year. At a sensational 13-day trial in June 1893, the gruesome nature of the killings was dwelled upon by the prosecution and the defense, which pointed out the striking contrast between the bloody murders and Lizzie, a demure, gentle, kind, and charitable woman. The jury found Lizzie not guilty, but in the years afterward scandal-mongering reporters and gossipers tried to establish her guilt through animadversion. Lizzie lived with her sister Emma, who had been away at the time of the murders, in Fall River until 1905, when the sisters had a falling out and never spoke to each other again. When Lizzie died in 1927, she left about $30,000 (what remained of her approximate $250,000 inheritance from her parents) to an animal rescue organization.

BORGIA, Rodrigo. See ALEXANDER VI.

BORMANN, Martin [Ludwig] (1900-1945?). German Nazi leader and war criminal. After joining the German National Socialist (Nazi) party in 1925, he rose in the hierarchy to become a member of the party's highest governing body from 1933 to 1941, when he succeeded Rudolf HESS as third deputy Führer. After the suicide of Adolf HITLER, on April 30, 1945, Bormann vanished and was thought by many to have fled to Argentina. The International Military Tribunal at Nuremberg, West Germany, tried him in absentia and sentenced him to death as a war criminal in 1946. After a skeleton dug up in West Berlin was identified as that of Bormann, the West German government officially announced that he had committed suicide on May 2, 1945.

BORNE, Henry. See DUTCH HENRY.

BOSTON, Patience (1713-35). Puritan Maine murderer. After acquiring a nefarious record as a liar, curser, drunkard, and thief, she committed murder. In 1735 eight-year-old Benjamin Trot of Falmouth, Maine, walked on her toe. Patience flew into a rage, picked up the boy, and threw him down a well, where he drowned. For this, Patience was hanged in York, Maine, on July 24, 1735. She was the first woman to be hanged in what is now Maine.

BOSTON STRANGLER. See DeSALVO, Albert [Henry].

BOTKIN, Cordelia (1854-1910). California poisoner. In the early 1890s she left her husband and lived a Bohemian life in San Francisco. Cordelia lured journalist John Presley Dunning away from his wife, Elizabeth, and daughter. In 1896 Elizabeth moved to Dover, Delaware, with her daughter to wait for her husband. In 1898 John left Cordelia for news service in the Spanish-American War. Afraid Elizabeth would lure John back to her after the war, Cordelia bought arsenic, inserted it into chocolate candies, and mailed the "gift" (with a note from "Mrs. C.") to Elizabeth. Elizabeth and her sister, Mrs. Joshua Deane, died from eating the candy, which was traced back to Cordelia. After a sensational trial, Cordelia was found guilty and given life imprisonment. She was moved from the San Francisco county jail, ruined by the earthquake in 1906, to San Quentin, where she later died.

BOTTOMLEY, Horatio William (1860-1933). English proprietor and swindler. In 1889 he formed the Hansard Publishing Union and its affiliate, the Anglo-American Union, and enticed businessmen and others into investing in these printing and publishing ventures; most of the capital ended up in Bottomley's pocket. In 1893 Bottomley stood trial for conspiracy to defraud but brilliantly defended himself and was acquitted. He lived an extravagant life, spending money fast, drinking, gambling, and cavorting with numerous mistresses. In 1906 he established the weekly newspaper John Bull, by which he advertised his doubtful ventures. Brought to trial for fraud in connection with his Joint Stock Trust in 1908, Bottomley was released because of lack of substantial evidence against him. From 1906 to 1912 and from 1918 to 1922, Bottomley was a member of Parliament. Bankruptcy and a court judgment against him had forced him to resign in 1912. In 1922 he was convicted of fraudulent conversion of trust funds and was sent to prison for five years. After his release, Bottomley made some money in journalism but was again bankrupt in 1930. He died in poverty in 1933.

BOWDRE, Charlie (1853?-80). American outlaw. He teamed up with BILLY THE KID during the Lincoln County War in the New Mexico territory in 1778. A devoted "pal" of Billy's afterward, Bowdre engaged in cattle rustling, becoming one of the most feared "wanted" outlaws until December 21, 1880. That day possemen under Sheriff Patrick Floyd Garrett blasted him to death at Stinking Springs, where Billy and other gang members fought a wild gun battle but were forced to surrender.

BOYCE, Christopher (b. 1953). American spy. He worked as a security clerk at a TRW Inc. plant in Redondo, California, from mid-1974 to 1976. Boyce was arrested in mid-January 1977 and charged with selling highly classified material dealing with U.S. satellite surveillance systems to the Soviet Union. U.S. government officials claimed the information could have compromised the CIA's cryptographic communications systems. Boyce was given a 40-year prison sentence. On January 21, 1980, he escaped from California's Lompoc Correctional Institution and was on the loose for 19 months, until August 21, 1981, when he was caught by U.S. marshals in Port Angeles, Washington.

BOYD, Belle (1844-1900). American Confederate spy. Working out of Martinsburg, Virginia (now West Virginia) and Front Royal, Virginia, she informed the Confederate army about Union troop movements in the Shenandoah Valley during the U.S. Civil War (1861-65); she frequently carried messages through Union lines to hand them to General T. J. Stonewall Jackson in 1862. A charming Southern belle, she was betrayed by a lover, imprisoned, but released under a prisoner exchange and soon resumed her espionage work in Richmond, Virginia. In 1864 Belle, who had again been caught and released twice, went to England, allegedly to deliver secret letters from Confederate President

Jefferson Davis to agents there. Sam Wylde Hardinge, a Union officer who had once held Belle in custody, followed her and married her in England (she had sweet-talked him into becoming a Confederate spy). After Hardinge's death in 1866, Belle, who had now begun a stage career, returned to the United States and toured about giving dramatic lectures on her wartime experiences under the billing, "The Rebel Spy."

BOYD, Jabez (d. 1845). Pennsylvania robber and murderer. He was a "man of two beings." Thought to be a very religious man, Boyd used his church-going activities to find out when persons carried money on them. Later that same day he ambushed them and stole their money. One night in Westchester, Pennsylvania, Boyd accosted Wesley Patton to rob him. Wesley put up a fight and Boyd murdered him with a club. A witness to the killing identified Boyd, who was found sitting in a church pew with a hymnal in hand, singing. He was hanged soon afterward.

BOYLE, W. A. "Tony" (b. 1902). American labor leader and murderer. In late 1969, shortly after Boyle's reelection as president of the United Mine Workers (UMW), his bitter rival for the UMW union leadership Joseph A. Yablonski and Yablonski's wife and daughter were shot to death in their Clarksville, Pennsylvania, home. In 1972 Boyle became the first major U.S. labor leader to be convicted under the 1925 Corrupt Practices Act when he was found guilty of illegally spending union funds for political contributions; one month later, a federal judge overturned Boyle's 1969 election, saying UMW funds and facilities had been used illegally to defeat Yablonski. Based upon revelations by former UMW colleagues, Boyle was charged with instigating Yablonski's assassination. He was tried and convicted of ordering the Yablonskis' murders (1974) and was sentenced to three consecutive terms of life imprisonment (1975). Three others, including Albert Pass, pleaded guilty; Pass received the same sentence as Boyle. But Boyle, maintaining his innocence, brought the case to the Pennsylvania Supreme Court, which overturned his conviction on a legality. At a retrial in 1978, he was found guilty again on the three counts of first degree murder of the Yablonskis, and he was returned to prison to serve mandatory life terms.

BRADFORD, Priscilla [Ann Hadley] (b. 1944). Florida murderer. On the evening of March 28, 1980, police found the severely beaten dead body of John Young Bradford, a mild-mannered optometrist and owner of a lucrative optical laboratory, lying on the kitchen floor of his posh suburban home in Melbourne, Florida. His dumpy, unattractive wife, Priscilla, claimed that he had attacked her unmercifully, as he supposedly had done frequently before, and she had struck blows killing him in self-defense. The hasty cremation of the corpse, the general lack of emotion about the death by Priscilla and her 14-year-old daughter from a previous marriage, Eden Elaine, and other odd details resulted in an investigation that revealed the truth: it had been a premeditated murder carried out by Priscilla, Eden, and two female friends, 18-year-old Joyce Lisa Cummings and 34-year-old Janice Irene Gould. Priscilla, Cummings, and Gould had grown to be militant feminists with a loathing toward the optometrist and a longing to control and reap the profits from an "all-female" optical lab. They thought of shooting Bradford, attempted unsuccessfully to poison him, and then battered him to death that fateful night with a large cast-iron frying pan, apothecary jars, and a metal bottle capper, among other things. In agony, their victim drowned in his blood, swallowing his tongue. On orders from her mother, Eden had helped beat him at the end, but she later confessed and was granted immunity as a witness for the state. Priscilla, Cummings, and Gould were tried, convicted, and imprisoned for life.

BRADY, Al (d. 1937). American bank robber, murderer, and gangster. Brady, along with James Dalhover and Clarence Shaffer, pulled off a number of bank robberies in Indiana and other midwestern states in the mid-1930s. The gang shot and killed five people, including three lawmen, in the process and became "most-wanted criminals" by the FBI, which finally caught up with the trio in Bangor, Maine, on October 12, 1937, when they were trying to buy revolvers of a special make. Attempting to flee, Brady and Shaffer were shot to death in a barrage of bullets; Dalhover was wounded, seized, and later executed.

BRADY, Ian (b. 1936). British mass murderer. He initiated his girlfriend, Myra Hindley, who worked in the same company as he did in Manchester into his perverted life of sadism, pornographic photography, and eventually murder--all for thrills. To satisfy their maniacal, sensual cravings, the two lovers turned to abducting, sexually abusing, and killing youths, whose bodies they buried in the moors. In 1965, after nearly two years of this heinous activity, Myra's brother-in-law, whom the two killer-lovers tried to lure into their crime life by having him witness a grisly axe slaying, went to the police, who arrested them for murder. Tried and convicted in Chester, Brady and Hindley, called the "Moors Murderers," who committed three known murders (maybe five), were both sent to prison for life (1966). Their depravity and the case were the basis of Beyond Belief, a novel by Emlyn Williams.

BRANCH, Elizabeth (1673-1740). English murderer. Married to a prosperous farmer in Somersetshire, she abused their servants sadistically for years and grew even crueler after her husband died and left her the estate. Senseless beating and torturing gratified Elizabeth and her daughter, Mary (1716-40), who had developed the same warped mean streak in her, until they were

arrested for killing (1740) a poor orphaned girl, Jane Butters-
worth, who worked for them. Tried in Taunton in March 1740,
mother and daughter were convicted on testimony from witnesses. Furious citizens planned to dismember them bodily,
but were thwarted when the pair were transported to Ovel-
chester and hanged before a large, gaping throng.

BRAS-COUPÉ (d. 1837). Louisiana slave outlaw. Known first as
Squire, he was a strapping black slave who attempted three
times to escape from his master, succeeding on his third try
despite the handicap of an amputated right arm (he had lost it
after being wounded in the arm during the second escape).
He formed a gang of escaped blacks and vagrant whites that
terrorized the New Orleans area for nearly three years, robbing and killing with abandon. To black slaves, Bras-Coupé
("Arm Cut Off") became a kind of folk hero because of his
strength and supposed invulnerability. However, in April
1837 he was wounded by slave hunters but got away in the
swamps. On July 19, 1837, the dead body of Bras-Coupé was
brought into New Orleans by a Spaniard named Francisco Garcia, who claimed he had clubbed Bras-Coupé to death after
being attacked by him and who now demanded the posted $2,000
reward for his capture, dead or alive. It was thought, however, that Garcia let Bras-Coupé sleep in his hut and murdered him while asleep; Garcia received $250 and was told to
leave.

BRAUN, Tom or Thomas Eugene (b. 1945). American murderer.
He and his friend Leonard Maine went on a murdering spree in
August 1967. Carrying a .22 Luger and a .22 Colt pistol and
much ammunition, the two 18-year-olds stopped and seized Mrs.
Deanne Buse near Redmond, Washington. After Braun shot her
dead, they drove off in Mrs. Buse's car, crossing into Oregon.
There Braun fatally shot Samuel Ledgerwood, whose car the two
boys now took. In northern California, Braun and Maine picked
up two hitchhikers, Timothy Luce, whom Braun murdered, and
Luce's girl friend Susan Bartolomei, who was raped and severely wounded. On August 27, 1967, police seized the killers in
a small hotel in Jamestown, California. Later the boys confessed to all the killings. Braun received the death sentence;
Maine, life imprisonment.

BRÉCOURT, Jeanne [Amenaide] (1837-after 1892?). French courtesan and blackmailer. Although a lowborn, poor street girl of
Paris, she lived for several years with a rich baroness who
taught her the aristocratic ways of etiquette and imbued her
with a craving for money and status. Ravishingly beautiful,
Brécourt enraptured countless, highborn gentlemen-lovers as
a heartless, high-priced Parisienne courtesan, seducing them
to give her much money and jewels or blackmailing them with
false stories of being pregnant. At the age of 40 she saw her

beauty vanishing and wanted security. In early 1877 she persuaded Nathalis Gaudry, a lovesick brute desiring her, to throw acid into the eyes of a young, wealthy man named Georges de Saint Pierre, who was madly in love with her; by blinding Georges, she hoped to make him totally dependent on her and thus secure power and money for the rest of her life. After the crime was committed, a young French detective named Gustave Macé unraveled it and brought both Brécourt and Gaudry to trial in Paris in July 1877. France's ablest lawyer, Charles Lachaud, defended this notorious courtesan, who was widely written about in the press and who, using her great beauty and penetrating eyes, tried to intimidate the judge and jury. Brécourt and Gaudry were both convicted, the former receiving 15 years' imprisonment and the latter five.

BREMER, Arthur [Herman] (b. 1950). American would-be assassin. On May 15, 1972, in a shopping center at Laurel, Maryland, Bremer, a former janitor's assistant and busboy, shot at and seriously wounded Alabama Governor George C. Wallace, who was then campaigning for the Democratic presidential nomination. While being wrestled to the ground by Wallace's bodyguards, Bremer fired off several more shots, wounding three other people. Tried and convicted, he was sentenced to 63 years imprisonment and, to this day, has never said why he shot Wallace. The source of the considerable money he lived on while tracking Wallace before he shot him also remains a mystery. Wallace, who continued his political career, remained partially paralyzed from the waist down because of a bullet lodged near his spinal column.

BRIDGET FURY [real name: Delia Swift] (1837-72?). New Orleans prostitute, mugger, and murderer. Because of the fighting fury with which she plied her trade as a mugger and whore in the French Quarter of New Orleans in the 1850s and 1860s, Bridget received the nickname-surname "Fury" and lived up to it during her criminal career. In 1858 she killed a man and was sentenced to life imprisonment but, in 1862, was set free in a general amnesty of many prisoners during the U.S. Civil War (1861-65). In the late 1860s Bridget operated her own brothel on Dryades Street in New Orleans but later gave up the business after spending several months in jail on a robbery conviction in 1870. Bridget became a wretched drunk wandering the streets and, presumably, died of ill health in 1872.

BRIGGEN, Joseph (1850?-1903). California murderer. He raised magnificent Berkshire pigs on his ranch in central California and won blue ribbons exhibiting them at the state fair in Sacramento. In early 1902 a recently hired ranch hand of Briggen's informed authorities he had found human remains in his room at the ranch. An inquiry turned up human bones and a man's skull in the pigpen. In August 1902 Briggen was convicted of murder and received life imprisonment at San Quentin, where he died the next year.

BRIGGS, Hattie (fl, 1880s-1890s). American madam. A big, beefy woman, Briggs operated two brothels in Chicago in the 1880s and early 1890s. She was known to intimidate and often rob her clientele, few of whom testified against her in court for fear of reprisals. Hattie flourished and established her flamboyant lover-gambler William Smith in the saloon business, announcing she planned to get Smith elected mayor and get rid of the police department. A police force then raided Smith's saloon, arrested Smith, and took away his liquor license. Hattie was harassed, arrested frequently on blanket warrants, and finally moved her brothel operation to the suburbs and then to the South.

BRILEY, Linwood (1954-84). Virginia mass murderer and prison escapee. He was the mastermind behind the greatest death-row escape in U.S. history, which occurred on May 31, 1984, when he, his younger brother James, and four other convicted killers broke out of the Mecklenburg Correctional Center in Boydton, Virginia. While two escapees were caught within 24 hours and two others about a week later in Vermont, the notorious black Briley brothers remained at large for about 20 days until FBI agents captured them in Philadelphia. The Brileys, accompanied by another brother and an accomplice, had slain 11 persons in a crime spree in Richmond, Virginia, in 1979. Linwood died in Virginia's electric chair later that year (1984), and James died in the same chair six months after (1985); together they had been condemned for ten murders.

BRINVILLIERS, Marie de [born: Marie Madeleine Marguérite d'Aubray] (1630?-76). French mass poisoner. Born of a rich French noble family, beautiful Marie married the Marquis Antoine Gobelin de Brinvilliers in 1651 but soon took a lover, Godin de Sainte-Croix, whom her father later learned about and ordered sent to the Bastille in 1663. On his release, Sainte-Croix conspired with Marie to poison her father, and together they experimented with lethal poisons to discover the most undetectable one. At the Hôtel-Dieu, the public hospital in Paris, the Marquise, working as a nurse, secretly tested deadly drugs on patients, some 50 to 100 of whom evidently died because of her ministrations. In 1666 she poisoned her father and inherited his estate, which she soon dissipated. In 1670 the Marquise poisoned her two brothers to obtain their wealth; she failed to kill her husband because Sainte-Croix, not wanting so murderous a vixen for a wife, administered antidotes that counteracted the poisons given to the Marquis. Marie took to poisoning anyone who offended her. While testing new deadly drugs in his laboratory, Sainte-Croix accidentally inhaled some poisonous

fumes and died in 1673. An investigation led to the discovery
of Marie's sinister activities (a servant of hers confessed to
helping her and Sainte-Croix kill her brothers). The Marquise
fled abroad and was eventually arrested in Liège in March 1676.
Returned to Paris for trial, she was convicted and confessed
under torture on the rack. On July 16, 1676, before a large
crowd in front of Notre Dame Cathedral, Marie, almost naked,
wearing only a thin garment, made a public confession, asked
for God's and the King's pardon, but was taken to Place de la
Grève, where she was beheaded and her body burned.

BRISTOL BILL (fl. 1840s). British-born American bank robber and
counterfeiter. Supposedly fleeing from the British penal colony
at Sydney, Australia, Bristol Bill hooked up with English Jim,
another ex-Sidney prisoner, and held up many banks in New
York and New England in the 1840s. They also circulated
counterfeit money and swindled some businesses. In late 1849
lawmen in Vermont caught Bristol Bill (English Jim got away),
and he was sent to prison for 14 years. What became of Bristol Bill afterward remains a mystery. English Jim carried on
his criminal activities in California until vigilantes captured him
and lynched him.

BROADINGHAM, Elizabeth. See AIKNEY, Thomas.

BROCIUS or BROCIOUS, William "Curly Bill" (1857-82). American
gunfighter and outlaw. He is best remembered for the shooting
of Sheriff Fred White in Tombstone, Arizona, in October 1881.
Deputy Sheriff Virgil Earp (Wyatt Earp's brother) claimed
Brocius used a fancy gun spin to kill White. Some witnesses
to the killing said White caused his own death by grabbing
Brocius's cocked six-gun, setting it off. The jury ruled the
death accidental, and Brocius was released. Considered the
most important gunfighter in the McLowery-Clanton gang,
Brocius was absent from the gunfight between the Earps and
Clantons at Tombstone's O.K. Corral in 1881. Brocius and his
men rustled cattle and participated in numerous shootouts in
Arizona territory. Near the Whetstone Mountains outside Tombstone, a posse under Wyatt EARP met up with a band under
Brocius, who said he had a warrant for Wyatt Earp's arrest
issued by Sheriff Johnny Behan, Earp's rival. Brocius went
for his six-gun, but Earp was faster and shot him dead. See
also CLANTON, Billy or William; CLANTON, [Joseph Isaac]
"Ike"; CLANTON, [Newman H.] "Old Man."

BROOKS, Bill or William L. (1832?-74). American marshal and
horse thief. He was a skilled buffalo hunter, earning the
same nickname as the famous army scout William F. Cody,
"Buffalo Bill." In 1872 Brooks, who was also an expert with
the six-gun, was made marshal of Dodge City, Kansas, where
he successfully engaged in a dozen or more gunfights with

killers and "cleaned up" the town. However, he strangely turned bad and became involved in some illegal activities and left Dodge City. In July 1874 Brooks and two other men were arrested for stealing horses and mules from a stagecoach company (shortly before, Brooks had lost his stage driver's job at another company because its U.S. mail contract had been awarded to the company he later robbed). Vigilantes seized Brooks and his two confederates and hanged them on July 29, 1874.

BROOKS, Charles, Jr. (1942-82). Texas murderer. While stealing a car to obtain money to pay for narcotics, he and a friend, Woody Loudres, kidnapped and shot to death an auto mechanic in Fort Worth, Texas, in December 1976. Apprehended shortly after, neither of them admitted to pulling the trigger, and both were convicted of the murder and condemned to die. Loudres' conviction, however, was reversed on a legal technicality, and he received a 40-year prison sentence through plea bargaining. Brooks fought his execution through appeals as far as the U.S. Supreme Court, which refused to block it. At the state prison in Huntsville, Texas, on December 7, 1982, he became the first person ever to be executed by lethal injection (a combination of drugs and sedatives), as well as the first black and sixth prisoner to be put to death since the Supreme Court reinstated capital punishment in 1976. The execution stirred much controversy concerning its medical and ethical "humaneness," and objections to the death penalty itself were raised vociferously.

BROOKS, David. See CORLL, Dean [Allen]; HENLEY, Elmer [Wayne, Jr.].

BROTHERS, Leo Vincent (1899-1951). American gangster and murderer. He was a labor terrorist in St. Louis for many years. In 1930 Brothers, known as "Buster" to mobsters, came to Chicago to carry out Al Capone's murder contract on Jake Lingle, a corrupt newspaper reporter who was reportedly in debt to Capone for $100,000. (To pay off this gambling debt, Lingle had attempted to extort money from some of Al Capone's mobsters.) Disguised as a priest, Brothers shot and killed Lingle at the crowded Illinois Central railway station on June 30, 1930. Witnesses identified Brothers as the killer. After a long trial, the jury found him guilty of murder and sentenced him to 14 years in prison. Brothers was paroled eight years later.

BROWN, Hendry (1850?-84). American outlaw and lawman. He seemed unable to choose between a life of crime or not. In the 1870s Brown sold whiskey illegally in Texas, rode with BILLY THE KID in the 1878 Lincoln County War in the New Mexico territory, and then became a lawman in a Texas town. He turned outlaw again before long, traveled northward, and,

having a change in heart and using his Texas law badge, became marshal of Caldwell, Kansas. However, outlawry beckoned
him again, for in April 1884 he and three cohorts attempted to
rob the bank at Medicine Lodge, Kansas, and shot and killed
two persons. They fled but were caught by a posse. An angry
mob stormed the jail in which Brown and his fellow crooks were
held, dragged them outside, and lynched them.

BROWN, Sam[uel] (d. 1861). Virginia City slayer. Brown carried
a bowie knife and a revolver and enjoyed picking fights with
men who were armed less than he was. It is estimated he
killed more than a dozen men in Virginia City, Montana, before
he himself was slain. On July 16, 1861, Brown, drunk on
whiskey, went after a farmer named Vansickle, who left town
with Brown in pursuit, returned to his farm, and grabbed his
shotgun. When Brown saw the shotgun, he fled back to town
with Vansickle following him. Vansickle blasted Brown to death,
ridding Virginia City of one of its most cowardly slayers.

BROWN, Three-Finger. See LUCCHESE, Thomas [Gaetano].

BROWNE, Frederick Guy (1881-1928). English murderer. On
September 27, 1927, Constable Gutteridge was murdered in
Essex. Officers from Scotland Yard picked up Browne, who
had a record for burglary, for questioning and found in his
possession a gun believed linked to the Gutteridge killing. In
early 1928 William Henry Kennedy, who also had a criminal
record, was arrested for attempted car theft. Under interrogation, Kennedy was found to have been involved in the Gutteridge murder; Kennedy soon said Browne had shot the
constable to death. During the trial of Browne and Kennedy,
forensic witnesses and experts convincingly established that
Browne's gun had fired the spent cartridge case found at the
scene of the murder. Both Browne and Kennedy were found
guilty and hanged.

BROWNRIGG, Elizabeth (1720-67). English sadist and murderer.
Living in London in the mid-1760s, she was a skillful midwife
who was married to a prosperous plumber named James Brownrigg. Two workhouses and a foundling hospital bound over to
her three unwanted teenage girls whom she sadistically mistreated, half-starving and savagely beating them to the bone.
Fourteen-year-old Mary Clifford was tied naked to a hook in
the ceiling and whipped until she bled profusely (she died from
these horrific wounds). After mid-1767 the authorities learned
about Elizabeth's fiendishness, which her husband and son John
had found amusing, and finally managed to imprison the three
Brownriggs at Newgate (Elizabeth and John were picked up in
Wandsworth, where they had tried to escape in disguise).
Londoners clamored loudly for vengeance against them, especially Elizabeth, and had to be restrained from storming the

prison. At the trial, Elizabeth, on whom James and John
blamed everything, was found guilty and sentenced to death
by hanging, which was carried out supposedly before the
largest crowd ever to watch an execution at Tyburn (September 14, 1767). James and John were punished by fines of a
shilling each and six-month prison sentences.

BRÜHNE, Vera (b. 1910). German murderer. In 1960 Otto Praun,
a rich 65-year-old physician in Munich, tried to rid himself of
his attractive, blonde mistress Vera Brühne, to whom he had
promised but failed to give his large vacation villa on Spain's
Costa Brava. After Praun was found dead in his Munich mansion along with his female housekeeper-lover, police thought
that Praun had had a wild fit, killed the housekeeper, and
then himself, but they later discovered that he had been shot
twice in the head. Vera's outspoken teenage daughter Sylvia
revealed that her voyeuristic mother had numerous lovers, including a dumb stooge named Johann Ferbach. On Vera's orders, Ferbach had committed the murders. The two conspirators were convicted and imprisoned for life.

BRYANT, Charlotte (1904-36). British poisoner. An uneducated,
slatternly, and wanton wife, black-haired Charlotte continually
caroused and picked up men in the pubs of Dorsetshire in the
early 1930s. Her husband seemed indifferent and eventually
died of arsenic poisoning in December 1935, when she passionately wanted to marry an uncouth vagabond named Leonard
Parsons, with whom she had been whoring since 1933. Arsenic
was discovered in her husband's body and in her house near
Coombe. Tried and convicted of murdering her husband, Charlotte was sentenced to death, all the time showing no outward
worry, but when she was hanged about six weeks later, on
July 15, 1936, her hair had turned utterly white. Parsons was
apathetic about the execution.

BUCCIEREI, Fiore "Fifi" (1904-73). Chicago gangster. He was a
member of Chicago's juvenile 42 Gang and liked to wear wide-brimmed hats similar to those worn by gangsters in movies. In
1925 Buccierei began working for Al CAPONE as a thug. He
became an important enforcer in the Chicago syndicate and allegedly was the personal "hit" man of Chicago Mafia boss Sam
GIANCANA in the 1950s and 1960s. Arrested a number of times
for bribery, larceny, and murder, Buccierei was never convicted.
He died of cancer in 1973.

BUCHALTER, Louis "Lepke" (1897-1944). New York racketeer and
murderer. He and Jacob "Gurrah" SHAPIRO set up a strike-breaking service in the garment industry in New York City in
the early 1920s. Buchalter extended his operations into many
industrial and business rackets. With Charles "Lucky" LUCIANO, he funded wholesale liquor smuggling during Prohibition

and narcotics smuggling in the 1930s. As the Mafia controller of Murder, Inc., Buchalter carried out hundreds of murder contracts for the syndicate, of which he was a member of the board in the early 1930s. In 1939, after being tricked into surrendering to the FBI, Buchalter was convicted on charges of narcotics smuggling and sent to Leavenworth for 14 years. The New York district attorney's office, with testimony from Buchalter's former associates in Murder, Inc., succeeded in 1940 of convicting Buchalter of the 1936 murder of Joe Rosen, a Brooklyn candystore owner. All appeals for commutation of Buchalter's death sentence failed. Buchalter, along with his two loyal killers, Mendy Weiss and Louis Capone, was electrocuted at Sing Sing on March 4, 1944. Buchalter was the only national crime syndicate boss ever to be executed. See also RELES, Abe.

BUCHANAN, Robert (1855?-95). New York doctor and murderer. In 1892 Buchanan's second wife, Anna Sutherland, an ugly but rich brothel owner in Newark, New Jersey, died apparently of apoplexy. Some of Anna's friends suspected Buchanan, a vain, egotistical, and ambitious man, of killing her for her money. Newark newsman Ike White painstakingly investigated the curious case of a supposed respectable doctor who married a madam, uncovering evidence of morphine poisoning. Authorities examined Anna's body and found that atropine, or belladonna, had been used to reduce the contraction in the pupils of Anna's eyes (contraction occurs in morphine poisoning) and thus covered up the crime. Buchanan, who had collected Anna's money and remarried his first wife in Nova Scotia, was indicted, convicted, and electrocuted at Sing Sing (now Ossining Correctional Facility) on July 1, 1895.

BUCK, Rufus (1876?-96). American robber, rapist, and murderer. He led his gang on a senseless, two-week (July 28-August 10, 1895) rampage of robbery, rape, and murder in the old Indian territory of Arkansas-Oklahoma. His gang included Luckey Davis, Sam Sampson, Maomi July, and Lewis Davis. The five of them, all semiliterate, half-black and half-Creek Indian, first shot a deputy marshal to death and then held up a number of stores and ranches. Several women were raped by the Buck gang. A black boy working for a salesman was fatally shot in the back by the gang. A posse hunted the five down and captured them after a gun battle near Muskogee, Arkansas. At the trial, presided over by Hanging Judge Parker, none of the gang or their lawyers said much. Found guilty, the five were hanged on July 1, 1896.

BUCKMINSTER, Fred (1863-1943). American con man. Buckminster, a former plainclothes policeman, became a partner of Joseph "Yellow Kid" WEIL in 1908, and together they pulled off some of the most incredible scams. Buckminster and Weil once rented a vacant bank in Muncie, Indiana, and stocked it with fellow con artists pretending to be wealthy depositors. They tricked financiers into investing in the bogus bank, pocketing for themselves many thousands of dollars. The pair was involved in race horse swindles and phony boxing matches. Buckminster, along with con man Kid Dimes, worked the "fixed" fixed roulette wheel scam in several gambling houses in Chicago and elsewhere from about 1918 to 1928. Buckminster was convicted several times and spent many years in jail. When he was released from prison the last time in 1939, he announced he was going straight but reputedly pulled some old tricks till his death four years later.

BUFFALINO, Russell A. (b. 1903). American mob boss. The U.S. Senate's McClellan committee called Buffalino "one of the most ruthless and powerful leaders of the Mafia in the United States." Buffalino, who centers his activities in and around Pittstown, Pennsylvania, is suspected of involvement in labor racketeering, drugs, and dealing in stolen gems; he is considered the "Mafia boss" in much of Pennsylvania and in parts of New Jersey and upstate New York. Arrested repeatedly since 1927 for petty larceny, receiving stolen property, and conspiring to obstruct justice, Buffalino was finally sentenced to prison (four years) in 1977 after being convicted of an extortion charge. U.S. federal authorities have linked him to the disappearance of ex-Teamster Union president Jimmy Hoffa.

BUHRAM (d. 1840). Indian Thug mass murderer. He was a member of a 300-year-old secret murder cult, the Thuggee, which was made up of both Hindus and Muslims. The Thugs, as cult followers were called in India, worshipped Kali, the four-armed black Hindu goddess of generation and destruction. They killed people, usually travelers, with knives, pickaxes, and other weapons, robbing them and offering them as human sacrifices to Kali. In 1840 Buhram was tried for murder and found guilty of having strangled to death 931 victims in the Oudh region of north central India since 1790 (he had used his loincloth as a garroting weapon). He was promptly executed. By 1852 the British had managed to eliminate the Thuggee.

BUISSON, Émile (d. 1950). French robber and murderer. A wily, nondescript, little man, Buisson made crime his lifelong business, eventually becoming France's most-wanted fugitive by 1950. With his various gang confederates, he committed bank robberies, such as the spectacular nearly four-million-franc heist from the Crédit Industriel & Commercial in Paris (1941) and later the almost two-million-franc robbery of Crédit Lyonnais in Troyes, for which Buisson, caught and convicted, served time in Paris' Santé prison. But he obtained transfer as a madman to the asylum at Villejuif (his crazy pose was nonpareil) and soon after escaped to rejoin gang members (1947). For three years Buisson's swift, carefully planned raids (stealing a multimillion-franc fortune from Parisians and tourists) kept the Préfecture de Police (the Paris metropolitan police) and the Sûreté Nationale (France's FBI) busy hunting for the evasive thief, who disappeared as if by magic from crime scenes (at times, running across Parisian rooftops). Finally, on June 10, 1950, Buisson was caught hiding in a small inn outside Paris, following an intensive search headed by Monsieur Charles Chenevier, Sûreté criminal affairs director. Convicted of murder and robbery, Buisson was soon guillotined in a Parisian prison courtyard.

BULETTE, Julia (1832-67). Virginia City prostitute and madam. Beloved by the miners and railroad laborers and scorned by the "proper" ladies and gentlemen, Julia worked as a prostitute and ran a brothel for many years in Virginia City in present-day Montana. She wore jewels and furs and was noted for her acts of kindness and charity; when an epidemic or other disaster struck the community, Julia turned her "house" into a temporary hospital for the sick and disabled. On January 20, 1867, Julia was found beaten and strangled to death in her bed. Miners grieved and rounded up many suspects until John Millain, a "trail louse," was found with some of Julia's gems, was quickly tried and convicted, and hanged on April 24, 1868. Julia, who had received an elaborate funeral, was no longer a threat to the "right" side of Virginia City.

BULLION, Laura. See ROSE, Della.

BUNCH, Eugene (1850?-89). American train robber. Bunch, a former schoolteacher, started to rob trains in Louisiana, Mississippi, and Texas in 1888. A soft-spoken man, he always presented himself to train guards as "Captain Gerald" while ordering them to open safes or he would "blow their brains out." For about six months Bunch was an honest newspaper editor in Dallas, where he became known as "Captain Bunch" and was a charming society gentleman. But in 1889 he formed a gang and resumed robbing trains in Mississippi. Pinkerton detectives trailed the gang to its hideout on a little island in a Mississippi swamp. There Bunch and two cohorts were ambushed and killed during a gun battle.

BUNDY, Ted [full name: Theodore Robert Bundy] (b. 1946). American mass murderer. In late 1974 Bundy, a bright young man of seemingly outstanding character, moved from Seattle to Salt Lake City, Utah, where he entered law school and converted to Mormonism. However, in 1975 he was identified as the assaulter of a young woman, adjudged guilty, and sentenced from one to 15 years in prison. After escaping from jail in late 1977 (his second attempt that year), Bundy fled from Colorado (where he was in custody awaiting trial on a murder charge) to

Tallahassee, Florida, where he became a suspect in the strangulation murders of two sorority sisters at Florida State University on January 15, 1978 (Bundy had been picked up driving a stolen car in Pensacola). He went on trial for the killings, taking an active role in his own defense while cameras recorded, for the first time, the legal proceedings in a courtroom. Bundy was found guilty and sentenced to die (1979), and about six months later (1980) he was convicted of another 1978 killing--that of a 12-year-old Lake City, Florida, girl. Bundy then received his third death sentence; police have linked him to the murders of 18 to 36 other females in at least four states (Washington, Colorado, Utah, and Florida) over a span of about four years (1974-78).

BUNTLINE, Ned [real name: Edward Zane Carroll Judson] (1823-86). American writer and firebrand. In Nashville, Tennessee, where he established a sensational newspaper called Ned Buntline's Own in 1845, Buntline had an affair with a married woman and was arraigned for the murder of the cuckolded husband, who had threatened to shoot him. Put in jail (1846) to prevent an angry mob from lynching him for the murder, he later alleged that lynchers had grabbed him from his cell and hanged him, but before breathing his last, he had been cut down by some friends. Moving his business to New York City, Buntline was later a leader of the Astor Place Riot of 1849, violently opposing the British actor William Macready. Almost two dozen persons were killed in the riot, and Buntling was arrested and served a one-year prison term. After his release, he tended to "live" any criminality vicariously through his popular and profitable dime novels, some 400 of which he wrote, containing daredevil characters and wild plots.

BUONO, Angelo [A., Jr.] (b. 1933). California mass murderer. In 1979 Buono, an auto upholsterer and cousin of Kenneth BIANCHI, became a suspect in the "Hillside Strangler" case, in which ten young women had been sexually assaulted and stranged to death and left on hillsides along roads in Los Angeles's Glendale area in September-December 1977. Buono claimed he was innocent, but Bianchi pleaded guilty to five of the murders, agreeing to testify against his cousin in exchange for the prosecution not seeking the death penalty against him (1979). Buono's trial was the longest running criminal trial in U.S. history (nearly two years) and ended with Buono's conviction and sentencing to life in prison without parole (November 18, 1983) for the slayings of nine young women. The prosecution, whose chief witness was Bianchi, contended that Buono and Bianchi had abducted their victims, some of whom were hitchhikers and prostitutes, while they sometimes posed as police officers; they had committed most of the sexual assaults and murders in Buono's home in Glendale.

BURKE, Elmer "Trigger" (1917-58). American hired killer. Expert with a machine gun, Burke became a freelance killer for the underworld in the mid-1940s. After holding up a New York City liquor store in 1946, he was arrested and sent to Sing Sing for two years. Upon his release, Burke tracked down and shot dead George Goll, the hoodlum who reportedly killed his brother while he was in prison. He then became one of the most important "hit" men. His fee for murder was usually $1,000; occasionally he did a "job" free. In 1954 the mob hired Burke to kill Joseph "Specs" O'KEEFE, who took part in the 1950 Brink's robbery in Boston and reputedly was about to tell the police details of the crime. Burke succeeded only in severely wounding O'Keefe, who identified Burke as his attacker. Arrested, Burke managed to escape. FBI agents captured him a year later in Charleston, South Carolina. Extradited to New York, Burke was found guilty of killing Edward "Poochy" Walsh (Burke shot Walsh to death at a bar in 1952). On January 9, 1958, Burke was electrocuted.

BURKE, Martha Jane. See CALAMITY JANE.

BURKE, William (1792-1829). Irish-born Scottish body snatcher and mass murderer. He emigrated from Ireland to Scotland in 1817 and ten years later was living in an Edinburgh boardinghouse owned by William Hare, a fellow Irishman. Burke and Hare began robbing graves, exhuming corpses and selling them to unsuspecting anatomists, such as Dr. Robert Knox, who ran medical schools that needed cadavers for study (at the time, human dissection was illegal but was privately condoned for medical research). The two body snatchers, who received up to £14 for each body, soon turned to murder, waylaying old hags, derelicts, whores, and others, taking them to the boardinghouse, getting them drunk, and then smothering them to death. The murder victims were delivered for payment to Dr. Knox, with no questions asked. Finally two boardinghouse lodgers discovered Burke and Hare with one of their victims and notified the police, who caught the two with the corpse, a missing woman, and arrested them. Hare turned state's evidence at the ensuing trial, which began on Christmas Eve, 1828. (Hare was pardoned, left Scotland, and died years later as a disfigured, blind pauper in London after fellow workers discovered who he was--he had assumed another name--and avengingly tossed him into a limepit, which left him maimed and blinded.) Burke, who strangely and foolishly refused to give state's evidence, was convicted of 14 murders (he and Hare possibly killed as many as 32 persons) and was hanged in Edinburgh's Grassmarket on January 28, 1829, while a throng of 30,000 spectators stood in the rain to witness it. His body was then brought to the Edinburgh University Medical School, where it was dissected before many students. The verb "to

burke" came into the language to mean, "to murder by suffoca-
tion" and has today the figurative meaning, "to suppress quietly" as well.

BURNS, Robert Elliott (1890-1965). American convict, fugitive,
and writer. He was sentenced to six to ten years on a Georgia
chain gang for burglary (he and two others had stolen $5.80
from a grocery store). Burns escaped in 1922 and remained at
large until 1930, when Georgia authorities found him in Chicago.
He then voluntarily returned to Georgia, having a promise of a
pardon, but was again sent back to the chain gang. Miraculously, Burns escaped again. After finding him in New Jersey in
1932, Georgia authorities demanded his extradition but were refused after Burns's life on the chain gang was publicly exposed
(Clarence Darrow and other prominent people and New Jersey
officials defended Burns). In 1941 Georgia tried again to win
custody of Burns but failed. After the Georgia chain gang system was ended in 1945, Georgia's governor commuted Burns's
sentence to time served. Burns, a free man, who had earlier
written the bestseller I Am a Fugitive from a Georgia Chain
Gang and who had a movie made of his prison ordeal, was
much involved in penal reform for the rest of his life.

BURROUGHS, George (1650?-92). American minister convicted of
witchcraft. A massive persecution of persons suspected of practicing witchcraft, an evil of the Christian church, began in the
English colony of Salem, Massachusetts, in 1692. Burroughs, a
Puritan minister who had served in the Salem parish from 1680
to 1682, was removed from his clerical duties in Maine to stand
trial, having been accused of being a murderous witch by a
12-year-old "bewitched" girl, Ann Putnam. At his trial, he
was also accused of demonstrating psychic powers and conducting rituals flouting the communion service, and the jury easily
found him guilty. On August 19, 1692, Burroughs, declaring
his innocence, was hanged with other "witches" on Gallows Hill
near Salem; he was the only clergyman executed for witchcraft
in America.

BURROW, Rube or Reuben Houston (1856-90). American train robber and murderer. In 1887 he organized a gang of train robbers, which included his brother, Jim Burrow, and the Brock
brothers, Will and Leonard. The gang stopped express trains,
killed guards, looted safes, and stole wallets and jewelry from
passengers. Pinkerton detectives searched for months before
finding the Burrow gang in a mountain hideout near Nashville,
Tennessee. There Jim and the Brock brothers were caught in
February 1888. Rube escaped and for three months tried unsuccessfully to break his brother out of jail in Little Rock,
Arkansas (Jim died there of consumption in 1889). Rube,
wanted dead or alive, became the subject of a widespread manhunt in the South. In 1890 he singlehandedly robbed a train.

CARITATIVO, Bart (1906-58). Philippine-born California murderer. In 1946 he arrived in Stinson Beach, California, where he soon was hired as a cook and houseboy by the Lansburgh family. The Lansburghs' neighbors, Camille and Joseph Banks, were found murdered in their house in 1954. The police traced three documents, a handwritten note and letter and a typed will, to Caritativo, who was a close friend of Camille. Many misspellings and grammatical mistakes in the documents could not have been made by the Banks, both of whom were well educated. After a long trial, with testimony from handwriting experts, Caritativo was found guilty of murder. He died in San Quentin's gas chamber on October 24, 1958, never having made a public admission of guilt.

CARLTON, Harry (d. 1888). New York murderer. Carlton, a handsome, blue-eyed man, was convicted of murdering a policeman and, because the jury had not recommended mercy, seemed fated to die. However, his shrewd lawyers, William F. Howe and Abe Hummel, discovered that the New York state legislature had abolished hanging after June 4, 1888, and had stated that "electrocution shall apply to all convictions punishable by death on and after January 1" of the following year. When Carlton came up for sentencing in early December 1888 Howe pointed out the syntactical loophole in the law and demanded that his client be set free. The judge delayed sentencing while the case went to the state supreme court, which declared that hanging remained in force until the start of the new year. On December 23, 1888, Carlton was hanged at the Tombs in New York City. The law firm of Howe and Hummel, which almost succeeded in making murder legal for a while, was afterward approached by numerous felons and murderers for counsel.

CARPENTER, Richard (1929-56). Chicago robber and murderer. In 1951, while serving a one-year sentence in jail for robbery, Carpenter became known as a "Mama's boy" because of the many visits to the jail by his mother. A lone wolf, he never shared his mother's candies and cakes with his fellow inmates. For a while he was an honest taxi driver. Then, from late 1953 to 1955, Carpenter committed more than 70 robberies in the Chicago area. After shooting dead a policeman and severely wounding another in August 1955, he became the subject of a desperate manhunt. Carpenter held captive a truck driver and his family but fled when the police arrived. Caught soon after, he was found guilty of murder. His mother visited him before he died in the electric chair at Joliet State Prison on March 16, 1956.

CARR, Robert (c. 1590-1645). Scottish-born royal favorite and convicted poisoner. His good looks helped him become the court favorite of England's King James I, who granted him lands and honors between 1607 and 1614. While serving as James's personal secretary, Carr fell in love with beautiful Frances HOWARD, wife of the earl of Essex, with whom he sought to gain an annulment of her marriage so that they could marry. Carr's confidant and friend Sir Thomas Overbury, a gifted poet, opposed the plan, thus earning the wrath of both Carr and Frances and suffering imprisonment in the Tower of London on orders of King James (on a charge of plotting against the king, who actually thought that his homosexual relationship with Carr would best be served by supporting Carr and Frances). In 1613 Overbury died in the Tower, having been slowly and secretely poisoned by Frances, allegedly in collusion with Carr. Their marriage then took place, and Carr was made the earl of Somerset. In 1615 the plot against Overbury became publicly known, and the next year Carr was tried and convicted, despite his denial of guilt (earlier his wife had admitted guilt at her trial). Condemned to death, both were pardoned by the king but kept in the Tower until 1622. They retired to Oxfordshire, becoming estranged from one another for the rest of their lives.

CARR, Sam [born: Schmil Kogan] (b. 1906). Ukrainian-born Canadian political figure and Soviet spy. In the 1920s he immigrated to Canada, embraced the Communist cause, and became a leader in the Canadian Communist party. In about 1930 Carr, the name he took, and his Communist friend Fred ROSE began working for Soviet intelligence after traveling to Moscow and receiving espionage training there. Carr recruited Marxist-oriented Canadians for spy work and informed Moscow about party members who opposed Joseph STALIN. Though Carr professed to Canadian authorities that he was no longer a Communist agitator (1942), he carried on clandestine spying operations as part of an effective Soviet espionage network in Ottawa, Toronto, and Montreal. Top-secret military information was handed over to the Kremlin leaders during World War II. In 1945, when the Ottawa-based, Soviet cipher specialist Igor Gouzenko defected to the West and revealed the names of key spies in Canada, Carr went into hiding and managed to get out of Canada, going first to Cuba and then to New York. He was arrested (1948) by the FBI, returned to Ottawa, tried, and sentenced to six years' imprisonment. Freed in 1953, Carr emigrated from Canada to Poland. See also MAY, Alan Nunn.

CARSON, Ann (1790-1838). Pennsylvania counterfeiter. Her husband, U.S. Army Captain John Carson, was presumed dead in 1812 (he had disappeared while fighting the Indians two years earlier). Ann, a beautiful and vivacious woman who lived near Philadelphia, then married U.S. Army Lieutenant Richard SMITH. In 1816 her first husband returned home and was met by Smith, who refused him entry and shot him dead. During Smith's trial, Ann tried to kidnap Pennsylvania Governor Simon Snyder

and hold him hostage until Smith was released. She wasn't
successful, and Smith was convicted and sent to the gallows.
Ann was greatly embittered against the law. She organized a
counterfeiting ring, consisting of Sarah Willis, Sarah Maland,
William Butler, and others, and proceeded to successfully pass
phony bills for six years in Pennsylvania. She and her gang
were caught passing counterfeit notes on Girard's Bank in
Philadelphia in 1823. They were all given long prison sentences. Ann died in the Philadelphia prison while writing her
memoirs.

CARTER, John (fl. c. 1760-c. 1795). English smuggler. As a
young boy, Carter was nicknamed "The King of Prussia" because of his interest in playing soldiers, with himself as the
Prussian King Frederick the Great. Later, with his seven
brothers, Carter smuggled kegs of brandy and gin from Brittany across the English Channel to South Cornwall, where his
anchorage became well known as "Prussia Cove." Carter set
up cannons on the Cornish coast to drive off French privateers
and gave contraband to English custom officers to "make
peace." He carried on his smuggling for more than 30 years
and lived long enough to write his memoirs, The Autobiography
of a Cornish Smuggler.

CASEMENT, Sir Roger [David] (1864-1916). British consul and
Irish rebel. He worked for the British consular service in
Africa and exposed the cruel exploitation of native blacks by
white plantation owners and traders in the Congo. For this
and for exposing similar practices in Peru, Casement was
knighted in 1912. Although an Ulster Protestant, he joined
the Irish Catholic nationalists in their fight for independence
against British rule. After the start of World War I, Casement tried unsuccessfully to obtain aid from the United States
for the Irish struggle. He then sought assistance from Germany, securing some arms and supplies, but he failed to obtain a German expeditionary force to lead the planned Irish
rebellion on Easter, 1916. On April 20, 1916, when Casement
stepped ashore off a German submarine near Tralee Bay, Ireland, he was immediately arrested and taken to London, where
he and several other rebel leaders were tried and convicted of
treason. Casement's diaries, showing him to be a homosexual,
were made known at the trial in order to denigrate his character and to prevent any portrayal of him as a patriot and martyr.
Despite efforts by influential Englishmen to secure a reprieve,
Casement was hanged on August 3, 1916.

CASERIO, Sante Geronimo (d. 1894). Italian anarchist and assassin. Because President Sadi Carnot of France refused a reprieve for condemned anarchist Auguste Vaillant, who had
earlier made a vain attempt to blow up the French Chamber of
Deputies, Caserio, another political anarchist, began plotting

to assassinate Carnot and traveled to Lyons, France, to en-
counter the president, who was being honored there during an
exposition on June 24, 1894. After delivering a speech at a
banquet, Carnot was driven in his landau (four-wheeled carriage with a collapsible top) through the streets. The carriage stopped near Caserio, who immediately pushed the guards
aside, pounced upon Carnot, and thrust a large, sharp knife
into his midriff. The president died shortly afterward, and
Caserio, who had been seized by onlookers and nearly lynched
by them, was tried, convicted, and sentenced to die. Paralyzed by a paroxysm of fear, he had to be carried by guards
to the guillotine on August 16, 1894.

CASEY, James P. (d. 1856). California murderer. He was editor
of the Sunday Times in San Francisco and was publicly accused
by an archenemy, James King, editor of the Evening Bulletin,
of corrupt dealings with outlaws, thieves, and murderers in
the city. On May 14, 1856, Casey confronted King on the
street, ordered him to draw and defend himself, and then immediately shot him to death (King was unarmed and had no
chance to defend himself). Vigilantes stormed the jail where
Casey was being held, dragged him and three other prisoners
outside, pronounced them all guilty, and hanged them.

CASSIDY, Butch [born: Robert LeRoy Parker] (1866-1911?).
American train and bank robber and outlaw. In Colorado in
the 1880s, he rustled cattle with Mike Cassidy (whose name he
later adopted as his own) and robbed trains and banks with
the McCarty brothers and Matt Warner. In 1896, after serving
two years in jail for horse stealing and running a protection
racket, Cassidy organized the Wild Bunch, a gang of robbers
that included Elzy LAY, KID CURRY, the SUNDANCE KID, Ben
KILPATRICK, Bill Carver, and others. Led by Cassidy, the
Wild Bunch held up trains and banks and blasted open safes
with dynamite. Pinkerton detectives were unable to capture
Cassidy and his gang. The Union Pacific Railroad Company
finally sent its own band of gunmen after the Wild Bunch and
managed to kill some of the gang. In late 1901, Cassidy, along
with the Sundance Kid and his girl friend, Etta PLACE, fled to
New York and then to South America. The three held up several banks in Argentina. For a while Cassidy and the Sundance
Kid worked in a Bolivian tin mine. According to one report,
the two were killed by Bolivian soldiers in 1911 after robbing
the payroll of the tin mine. Another story by Cassidy's sister
says Cassidy returned to the United States and lived until
1937. See also McCARTY, Tom; WARNER, Matt.

CASTAING, Edmé (1796-1824). French physician and poisoner. In
1823 he poisoned one of his patients, a rich Frenchman named
Hippolyte Ballet, so that the victim's younger brother Auguste
would inherit a fortune. Castaing, who had suggested the

murder to Auguste and gained his approval, received much money from the latter but soon schemed to gain the entire inheritance. After forcing Auguste to name him as sole heir in a new will, Castaing used the recently discovered drug morphine to poison Auguste, but he was soon suspected because he had attended Auguste before he died and was the only legatee in the will. Arrested and tried for killing the two Ballet brothers, he was convicted of Auguste's murder, but not Hippolyte's (problems arose as to the kind of poison used since morphine was so new at the time; morphine was shown to have killed Auguste, but none was found in his brother). Castaing claimed he was innocent right up to his execution.

CASTRO, Thomas. See ORTON, Arthur.

CATESBY, Robert (1573-1605). English conspirator. Born into a steadfast Roman Catholic family, he developed a loathing of the English government when fellow Catholics, including his father, were persecuted for not joining the Protestant Church of England. Catesby was involved in the unsuccessful revolt by the second earl of Essex, Robert Devereux, against Queen Elizabeth I in 1601; he was supposedly in an abortive 1603 plot to capture King James I to force him to grant religious toleration to Catholics. In early 1604 Catesby began a conspiracy (later known as the Gunpowder Plot) whose object was to blow up Parliament and kill the king in revenge against harsh penal laws against the English Catholics. His accomplices included Thomas Percy, Thomas Winter, John Wright, Christopher Wright, Robert Winter, Robert Keyes, Francis Tresham, John Grant, Ambrose Rookwood, Sir Everard Digby, Thomas Bates, Guy FAWKES, and others. The plot was discovered, and Fawkes was arrested in the gunpowder-filled cellar under the Parliament buildings on the night before the intended explosion planned for November 5, 1605. After being tortured, Fawkes revealed the names of his co-conspirators. Catesby fled from London and hid in Holbeche House, Staffordshire, where he was killed on November 8, 1605, during his arrest. His cohorts were captured, murdered, imprisoned, or executed.

CATTLE KATE [real name: Ella Watson] (1866-89). American prostitute and presumed cattle thief. She set up a one-girl bordello in a cabin in the Sweetwater River valley of Wyoming in early 1888. She soon became known as "Cattle Kate" because her cowboy customers often paid for her services with stolen cattle. Cattle Kate and her friend Jim Averill, a homesteader who was fighting the big cattle barons, were seized by some cattlemen in July 1889. Intending only to scare the two, the cattlemen strung ropes from trees and attached them around their necks. The fooling, however, went too far when Cattle Kate and Averill were pushed off rocks into space and slowly strangled to death. No one bothered to cut them down.

Members of the group were arrested but never faced trial. Cattle Kate and Averill were made into vicious, big-time cattle rustlers in justification of the lynchings.

CERNY, Wenzel. See VELGO, Marie [Havlick].

CESARONI, Enrico (fl. 1958). Italian robber. An underworld kingpin in Milan, he was the mastermind of one of the biggest bank robberies in Italy's history when 590 million lire ($954,000) in cash and securities (mostly negotiable) were stolen from a Popular Bank of Milan delivery truck on the Via Osoppo in Milan on February 27, 1958. Cesaroni had been accompanied by six others--Luciano DeMaria, Arnaldo Gesmundo, Ferdinando Russo, Arnaldo Bolognini, Ugo Ciappina, and Eros Castiglioni-- all of whom were armed and wore masks and blue overalls when they successfully pulled off this swift, American-gangster-style robbery. Cesaroni was suspected, but Italian police had no proof until several pairs of blue overalls, found in a canal, were traced to DeMaria, who was rounded up with Russo, Ciappina, Gesmundo, and Bolognini about a month after the crime. One of them broke down and convessed; then they all confessed, giving details about using stolen vehicles during the robbery, abandoning them afterward, and meeting and dividing up the loot among them (most of it was recovered by police). Cesaroni managed to escape to Venezuela, where he was arrested and later brought back to Italy in 1959; Castiglioni eluded capture, and the others eventually received prison terms ranging from nine to twenty years; Cesaroni was sentenced to over 18 years' imprisonment. Numerous unsolved robberies of the preceding years were found to be the work of Cesaroni's gang members.

CHADWELL, Bill or William. See JAMES, Jesse [Woodson]; YOUNGER, Cole[man].

CHADWICK, Cassie L. [born: Elizabeth Bigley] (1857-1907). Canadian-born American swindler. Early in life, she learned how to con businessmen into giving her credit or money on the belief that she was a wealthy heiress. After marrying Dr. Leroy Chadwick of Cleveland, Ohio, she passed herself off as someone important in society. In 1894 Cassie pretended to visit steel tycoon Andrew Carnegie in New York City, duping a rich, prominent Cleveland lawyer into thinking she was Carnegie's illegitimate daughter. When Cleveland bankers heard about her fortune-to-be through Carnegie, they loaned her millions of dollars, which Cassie lavishly spent on diamonds, dresses, trips, dinner parties, and other things. After a dubious Boston creditor checked Cassie's background and discovered the hoax, she was arrested in 1904 and tried. Convicted of swindling millions of dollars, Cassie was sentenced to ten years in prison, where she died.

CHAMBERS, [Jay David] Whittaker (1901-61). American journalist and Communist spy. He joined the U.S. Communist Party in 1925 and was an editor for its newspaper, The Daily Worker. For about three years, between 1935 and 1938, Chambers was involved in espionage for the Soviets in the United States. In 1939 he left the Communist Party and worked for Time magazine. In August 1948, before the House Committee on Un-American Activities, he accused Alger HISS, president of the Carnegie Endowment for International Peace and a former State Department official, of being a Communist Party member in Washington, D.C., in the 1930s and of passing secret government documents to him. Hiss denied the allegations. Chambers then brought federal investigators to his farm in Maryland, where he produced microfilms of documents hidden in a pumpkin. These "pumpkin papers" had allegedly been given to him by Hiss. Later Hiss was indicted and found guilty of perjury in his testimony.

CHANG Hsüeh-liang (1898-?). Chinese warlord and kidnapper. After succeeding his father as military governor of Manchuria (Northeast Provinces) in 1928, Chang recognized the authority of Chiang Kai-shek's newly established Chinese Nationalist government at Nanking. The Japanese drove Chang's forces out of Manchuria in 1901. At Sian, China, in mid-December 1936, Chang and other army officers kidnapped Chiang to force him to form a united front against the Japanese (Chiang's Nationalists were then engaged in civil war against the Chinese Communists). Communist leader Chou En-lai brought about Chiang's release two weeks later (the Communists realized that Chiang alone could unite China against Japan; later Chiang led both the Nationalist and Communist forces against the Japanese). Chang was held under house arrest at Nanking and later at Taipei on Taiwan (in 1946 the Chinese Communists renewed the civil war with Chiang's Nationalists and forced them off the mainland to Taiwan). By 1961 Chang was no longer under guard, but he humbly remained under arrest until 1975, Chiang's death.

CHAPIN, Charles E. (1858-1930). New York editor and murderer. As a tough, autocratic city editor at the New York Evening World, Chapin earned the hatred of many of his staff. He lived lavishly, played and lost much money in the stock market, and fell deeply into debt. To stave off creditors, Chapin borrowed heavily from his employer, Joseph Pulitzer; he worried continually about leaving his wife penniless. One night in September 1918, Chapin shot his wife to death and went off to Central Park to kill himself, but somehow couldn't do it. He gave himself up to the police the next day and later was sentenced to 20 years to life at Sing Sing (now Ossining Correctional Facility). Chapin was made editor of the prison newspaper and filled it with juicy stories from fellow inmates.

Relieved of his job as editor, he turned to beautifying the prison grounds, planting roses, tulips, dahlias, and other plants all over the prison, becoming known as the "Rose Man of Sing Sing." Chapin died on December 13, 1930, shortly after a steam shovel had dug up and destroyed most of his gardens in order to install a new drainage system for the prison.

CHAPMAN, George [real name: Severin Klosowski] (1865-1903). Polish-born English mass poisoner. In 1888 he immigrated to England and settled in the Whitechapel district in London's East End. Assuming the name George Chapman, he became a tavernkeeper, although he had been trained as a barber surgeon in Poland. In 1902 Scotland Yard arrested Chapman for murdering his wife, Maud Marsh, after his mother-in-law suspected foul play and notified the police. The authorities delved into Chapman's background and discovered that he evidently had poisoned numerous women, including a drunkard-mistress named Mary Spinks and a former wife, Bessie Taylor, who had worked earlier as a barmaid for Chapman. For a while Scotland Yard thought it had finally caught JACK THE RIPPER, the notorious 1888 killer-mutilator of women in the Whitechapel area, but all of Chapman's known victims had been poisoned, not knifed in the Ripper's manner. Convicted of Maud's murder, Chapman was hanged in London's Wandsworth Prison on April 7, 1903.

CHAPMAN, Gerald [born: Gerald Chartres] (1892?-1926). American robber and murderer. He and George "Dutch" Anderson teamed up as con men and lived an expensive, stylish life in New York City. On October 24, 1921, the pair, accompanied by Charles Loeber, robbed a New York City mail truck of $1,424,127 in cash and securities (the largest mail theft in U.S. history to that date). Loeber, captured, informed on Chapman and Anderson, both of whom were caught. Chapman escaped twice from Atlanta Penitentiary. While attempting to hold up a department store in New Britain, Connecticut, on October 12, 1924, Chapman, along with Anderson (who had escaped from prison) and Walter Shean, shot and killed a police officer. Chapman was soon caught, tried, found guilty of murder, and sentenced to death. He was hanged in Connecticut on April 6, 1926.

CHAPMAN, John T. (1832-after 1892). Nevada train robber. Chapman, thought to be an upstanding, religious citizen, teamed up with Jack DAVIS to form a train robbery gang, which pulled off the first train robbery in the American Far West. The Davis-Chapman gang stole more than $40,000 from the express car of the Central Pacific's Train No. 1 near Verdi, Nevada, on November 4, 1870. Members of the gang, apprehended and interrogated by Wells Fargo agents, informed on

Chapman and Davis. Chapman, who denied any part in the crime, was convicted and sentenced to 20 years in prison (Davis confessed and received ten years). About nine months after his incarceration, in September 1871, Chapman and two fellow prisoners escaped but were soon caught. After serving his entire 20-year sentence (plus one year for the attempted breakout), Chapman was released and disappeared from sight.

CHAPMAN, Mark David (b. 1955). New York murderer. On the night of December 8, 1980, Chapman, who had worked as a security guard in Honolulu, Hawaii, shot and killed wealthy singer-composer John Lennon, a former member of the Beatles, outside the Dakota, the New York City apartment building in which Lennon lived with his wife, Yoko Ono. Millions throughout the world grieved the death of Lennon. Chapman, who had been apprehended without any trouble at the murder site, pleaded guilty to the killing and was sentenced to 20 years to life in prison. He said the novel Catcher in the Rye by J. D. Salinger must be read to understand the slaying of Lennon. According to psychiatrists, Chapman apparently had become obsessed by the famous rock star, identified very closely with him, and came to believe he (Chapman) was Lennon, who was now considered a "phony" by Chapman.

CHAPPLEAU, Joseph Ernst (1850-1911). New York murderer. He was convicted of killing a neighbor in a dispute either about some poisoned cows or a love affair with his (Chappleau's) wife, and became the first man sentenced to die in the newly devised electric chair. However, because "the chair" was not finished by the time of his scheduled execution in 1889, Chappleau's sentence was commuted to life imprisonment. Chappleau became one of the most popular prisoners in New York's Clinton Prison and was credited in 1905 with saving the life of a young prison guard, Lewis E. Lawes, who later became the reform-minded warden at Sing Sing. Chappleau died at Clinton Prison in 1911.

CHASE, John Paul. See NELSON, George "Baby Face."

CHERNOZAMSKY, Vlada (d. 1934). Macedonian terrorist and assassin. Continual political tensions among ethnic groups in the Kingdom of the Serbs, Croats, and Slovenes (which included Macedonians, Montenegrins, Bosnian Muslims, and others) culminated in the murders in the Belgrade Parliament in 1928 of several Croatian deputies, including peasant leader Stjepan Radić, who demanded autonomy for Croatia. Afterward, King Alexander I dissolved the Parliament, abolished the constitution, established a dictatorship, and renamed the kingdom Yugoslavia (1929). Croatian and Macedonian nationalists vowed to assassinate Alexander, a Serb. On October 9, 1934, Chernozamsky, a Macedonian agent of the Croatian separatists led by Ante PAVELIĆ, fired on the car in which Alexander and French

Foreign Minister Louis Barthou were riding through the streets of Marseilles, France, where Alexander was on a state visit to secure a treaty. The king was killed, and Barthou died of wounds hours later. Chernozamsky was grabbed at the scene by an angry mob, was shot in the head, and died later that day. His fellow conspirators (but not Pavelić) were then rounded up and received life imprisonment.

CHEROKEE BILL. See GOLDSBY, Crawford.

CHESIMARD, Joanne (b. 1948). American terrorist. A radical black leftist who had attended the City College of New York, Chesimard (later known as Assata Shakur) joined the Black Liberation Army, a small, seditious, terrorist group active in the New York-New Jersey area in the early 1970s, during the Vietnam War. Stopped on the New Jersey turnpike for a traffic infraction in 1973, she and companions James Costan and Clark Squire pulled guns during a violent affray with two state troopers; in the ensuing gun battle, Costan and a trooper were killed; the other trooper was injured, along with Chesimard and Squire, both of whom fled but later were caught. The crime brought a life term in prison for Chesimard in 1977, but she escaped in 1979 and has been a wanted fugitive ever since.

CHESSMAN, Caryl [Whittier] (1921-60). California robber, kidnapper, and sex offender. When he was arrested (January 23, 1948) and identified as the notorious "Red Light Bandit" of Los Angeles, Chessman had a record of car thefts, assaults, and robberies dating back to his teens and had spent about two-thirds of his life behind bars. The Red Light Bandit had approached victims in parked cars, flashing a red light to make them think he was a police officer, and had robbed the drivers and sometimes forced the women to perform unnatural sex acts with him. Chessman, who represented himself in court, was convicted of 17 counts, including two kidnapping charges which carried the death penalty, and was sentenced to die in the gas chamber. He made many appeals in the state and federal courts, winning eight official reprieves of execution while on San Quentin's Death Row for 12 years. And intense campaigning against capital punishment was waged by many on his behalf. His execution occurred on May 2, 1960--just seconds too late for an official ninth delay to reach San Quentin's warden. Chessman's 1954 autobiography, Cell 2455, Death Row, written in prison, is a moving account of his ordeal to save his life.

CHICAGO MAY. See CHURCHILL, May "Chicago May."

CHRISTIAN, Fletcher (d. 1790). English mutineer. The 220-ton British naval ship, H.M.S. Bounty, under Captain William Bligh, was commissioned to transport breadfruit trees from Tahiti in the South Pacific to West Indian plantation owners

seeking a cheap food supply for their slaves. On the return
voyage from Tahiti, Christian, the master's mate, led a successful mutiny near the Friendly Islands (now Tonga) on April
28, 1789. Bligh and 18 loyal followers were cast adrift in a
longboat with a scant supply of food and water; they miraculously reached Timor in the East Indies after sailing over 3,600
miles. Christian sailed the Bounty back to Tahiti, where 16 of
the mutineers chose to stay (some were later caught and in
1792 courtmartialed in England; three were hanged). With
eight other mutineers and 18 Tahitian men and women, he then
sailed the ship to Pitcairn Island, a remote island hideaway in
the South Pacific, and founded a colony there. In 1790 Christian was slain in a fight over a woman. The colony remained
in obscurity until discovered by U.S. whalers in 1808, at which
time mutineer Alexander Smith, who had assumed the name John
Adams, was the sole surviving male. In 1815 two British naval
ships accidentally discovered the island; Adams was not arrested
and was allowed to remain, dying there in 1829 at the age of 62.

CHRISTIE, John Reginald Halliday (1898-1953). English mass murderer. Soon after Christie vacated his apartment in London in
1952, the new tenant discovered the dead bodies of three women
hidden in the apartment's hollow walls. The police found Christie's wife's body under the floor and dug up two more women's
corpses in the garden outside. Quickly arrested, Christie soon
confessed to the six murders, which he committed at various
times between 1943 and 1953. During his trial in June 1953,
Christie admitted also to killing the wife and baby of Timothy
John Evans, who had lived in his apartment building in London
(Evans had been hanged in 1950 after being convicted of killing
his child). Evans had protested to the end that Christie had
been the murderer. Christie was found guilty of murder and
executed.

CHRISTIE, Ned (1867?-92). American Indian murderer and outlaw.
A full-blooded Cherokee Indian, he killed Deputy U.S. Marshall
Dan Maples in 1885 and was soon named the "Cherokee killer"
in the Oklahoma territory. For about seven years he roamed
the territory as a horse thief, rumrunner, and murderer until
U.S. marshals Heck Thomas and Paden Tolbert trapped him in
a nearly impregnable wooden fort near Tahlequah, Oklahoma,
in 1892. When army cannon balls and 2,000 bullets failed to
dislodge Christie, dynamite was used to breach the fort's walls.
The marshals and about 20 riflemen shot Christie dead when he
rode out, firing his rifle.

CHRISTOFI, Mrs. Styllou (1900-1954). Greek Cypriot murderer.
In mid-1953, on a visit to London to see her married son,
Stavros, whom she had not seen since he moved from Cyprus
to England about a dozen years before, poor frumpy Christofi
grew to loathe his attractive, German-born wife, Hella, whose

plans to go away for a while with the children (Christofi's grandchildren) provoked murder. While Stavros was away one evening (July 29, 1953) and the children were asleep, the mother-in-law knocked Hella unconscious, strangled her, and then tried to burn her body in the kitchen of their Hampstead apartment. The fire got out of control, and the mother-in-law fled to the street shouting, soon arousing a constable. In her broken English, Christofi unwittingly incriminated herself. At her trial, it was revealed that she had been charged with the burning death of her own mother-in-law in 1925. Mrs. Christofi was convicted and hanged.

CHRISTOPHER, Philip Bruce. See DINSIO, Amil [Alfred].

CHURCHILL, May "Chicago May" [born: May Lambert] (1876-1929). Irish-born American prostitute, blackmailer, and robber. In New York, Chicago, and other U.S. cities in the 1890s, she was the so-called "Queen of the Badger Game"--an extortion racket in which a gentleman is lured to a lady's room for sex and is later blackmailed on threats of exposing his activities. Her nickname "Chicago May" derived from her lucrative business in Chicago, where she swindled lovers by taking secret photographs of them in bed with her. This red-haired beauty once tried to bait the author Mark Twain, who was amused by her talk but saw right through her. Moving to England in 1900, she carried on her unsavory business, again making a fortune, and practiced it in France and other places, including South America. In 1901 she and criminal Eddie GUERIN, her lover, and "Dutch Gus" Miller and "Kid John" McManus burglarized the American Express Company in Paris; they were subsequently caught and jailed. Set free in 1904, she resumed her racket until imprisoned in 1907 in England on a conviction of attempted murder of Guerin, with whom she had had a hostile falling out. In 1918 British authorities deported her to America, where she solicited males, thieved, and talked about her "glorious" past until her death in a Philadelphia boardinghouse.

CINQUÉ (1813?-80). African mutineer. In the spring of 1839 he was seized by black slave traders in what is now Sierra Leone in west Africa and shipped with other black Africans to Havana to be sold into slavery. While being transported aboard the Spanish schooner Amistad to another Cuban port, Cinqué led a mutiny, killing the captain and the ship's cook. Cinqué and his 52 black followers, all of whom were ignorant of ship navigation, kept two crew members to sail them back to Africa and put the others over the side in boats. The two navigators, however, steered the Amistad north. Off Long Island, the ship was seized by a U.S. warship and taken to New London, Connecticut, where Cinqué and his men were arraigned on piracy and murder. Abolitionists defended them and appealed

their case to the U.S. Supreme Court in February 1841. Former President John Quincy Adams, acting as the slaves' attorney, eloquently argued their case, and the court ruled that
Cinqué and the others were freemen on the grounds that slave
trading was illegal. Cinqué returned to Sierra Leone in early
1842 and, ironically, later became a slave trader.

CINQUE, Field Marshall. See DeFREEZE, Donald [David].

CINQUEZ, Julian. See NOVENA, Colonel M.

CIUCCI, Vincent (1925-62). Chicago murderer. He fell in love
with a pretty 18-year-old girl and decided to kill his wife and
three children. On December 4, 1953, Ciucci chloroformed and
shot each family member in the head and then set fire to the
apartment. He was arrested, convicted, and sentenced to death.
Constant appeals for commutation kept Ciucci from the electric
chair for almost nine years.

CLAIBORNE, Billy (1860-82). American gunfighter. After the
death of BILLY THE KID in July 1881, Claiborne called himself "Billy the Kid," got into gunfights with men who refused
to call him that, and killed three men, including Jim Hickey,
for whose death Claiborne was imprisoned in San Pedro in the
Arizona territory. Claiborne was busted out of jail by "Ike"
CLANTON and the McLowery brothers and fired off a few shots
during the first seconds of the gunfight between the McLowery-
Clanton gang and the Earps at the O.K. Corral in Tombstone,
Arizona, on October 26, 1881. Claiborne then hid in a shop.
On November 14, 1882, Frank LESLIE shot and killed Claiborne
outside a Tombstone sallon in a dispute over Claiborne's sobri-
quet, "Billy the Kid."

CLANTON, Billy or William (1865?-81). American outlaw and gunfighter. A member of the wild Clanton gang, Billy bravely
confronted the three Earp brothers--Wyatt, Morgan, and Virgil
--and "Doc" HOLLIDAY in the shootout at the O.K. Corral in
Tombstone, Arizona, on October 26, 1881. Deserted early in
the gunfight by his friend Billy CLAIBORNE and his older
brother "Ike," Billy, along with the McLowery brothers, Tom
and Frank, traded shots with the Earps and Holliday. Billy,
wounded in his right hand and chest, switched his six-shooter
to the left hand and kept firing. Tom McLowery was blasted
to death by Holliday's shotgun; Frank McLowery, wounded in
the stomach by Wyatt Earp, was shot dead by Morgan Earp,
who received a bullet in the shoulder from Billy's .45. Billy
wounded Virgil Earp in the leg but was downed by shots from
Wyatt and Morgan. Trying desperately to cock and reload his
gun, begging for more bullets, Billy died with the final request
to pull off his boots because he had promised his mother he'd
not die with them on.

CLANTON, [Joseph Isaac] "Ike" (d. 1887). American cattle rustler and outlaw. A member of the notorious Clanton gang, Ike engaged in cattle rustling for most of his life, finally being killed in a gun battle with a posse under Perry Owens near the Blue River in the Arizona territory. Ike tried unsuccessfully to stop the shooting during the gunfight between the McLowery-Clanton gang and the three Earp brothers and "Doc" HOLLIDAY at the O.K. Corral at Tombstone, Arizona, on October 26, 1881. Ike fled from the bloody scene, leaving his younger brother Billy and the two McLowery brothers to be killed. Later Ike joined an unsuccessful plot to assassinate Virgil Earp and, allegedly, helped plan the murder of Morgan Earp in 1882. See also CLAIBORNE, Billy; CLANTON, Billy or William; CLANTON, [Newman H.] "Old Man."

CLANTON, [Newman H.] "Old Man" (d. 1881). American cattle rustler and outlaw. In the early 1870s he settled with his family on a ranch in Arizona territory and became head of an outlaw gang of rustlers and robbers. The Clanton gang, which included William "Curly Bill" BROCIUS, Johnny RINGO, and the McLowery brothers, robbed stagecoaches and mule trains loaded with silver bullion, becoming feared throughout the Southwest and across the border into Mexico. Days after the Guadalupe Canyon Massacre of July 1881, where the "Old Man" and his gang killed more than a dozen Mexicans guarding a mule train and stole about $75,000 in silver bullion, a large Mexican posse hunted down, ambushed, and killed the "Old Man" and four members of his gang. See also CLANTON, Billy or William; CLANTON, [Joseph Isaac] "Ike."

CLARK, Henry Lovell William. See FULLAM, Augusta [Fairfield].

CLARK, Lorraine (b. 1926). Massachusetts murderer. Secretly having extramarital affairs in Amesbury, Massachusetts, where spouse swapping was then in vogue, she attacked her uncorrupted husband, Melvin, on the night (April 10, 1954) he found her with another man. She killed Melvin and dumped the corpse wrapped in chicken wire and weighted down into the Merrimack River near the ocean. A week later, citing her husband's "cruelty," Lorraine filed for a divorce; about seven weeks later Melvin's unrecognizable body was discovered in a marsh and identified by fingerprints. His "loose" wife confessed and received a life term at the women's prison in Framingham, Massachusetts.

CLARKE, Mary Anne (1776-1852). British courtesan and swindler. She inveigled her way into British society by using her good looks and having love affairs with aristocrats and noblemen, who paid her handsomely for her charms. Through her long-time liaison with the influential duke of York, head of the British army, she secretly sold commissions in the army, often

undercutting the government's standard charge for a military
position in those days. Publicly exposed in 1807, she lost
society's favor, especially after she was imprisoned briefly for
libel (1814). In disgrace, Mary Anne Clarke moved from London to Paris, where she flourished as a wealthy exiled courtesan for several decades. Her death was at age 76 in her Bois
de Boulogne mansion.

CLÉMENT, Jacques (1567-89). French Dominican monk and assassin. In 1584 the Catholic Holy League under Henry of Guise
refused to recognize the Huguenot (French Protestant) leader,
Henry of Navarre, as heir presumptive to the French throne
and forced King Henry III to repeal concessions granted to the
Huguenots, thus bringing on the War of the Three Henrys or
the Eighth War of Religion (1585-89). Expelled from Paris by
the Catholics, Henry III allied himself with Henry of Navarre
after he had procured the murders of Catholic leaders Henry of
Guise and his brother Louis, cardinal of Lorraine. Before
Paris, at St. Cloud, on August 1, 1589, Henry III, planning to
besiege the city with an army, granted admission to Jacques
Clément, a fanatical Dominican monk, who claimed he had an
important message to deliver personally to the king. Clément
stabbed the king to death with a long dagger and immediately
afterward was killed by attending guards. France remained
torn by civil war.

CLEMENTS, Robert George (c. 1885-1947). British doctor and
presumed murderer. Married four times to wealthy women,
Clements evidently murdered each one to inherit her money.
His first wife, Edyth Anna Mercier, died in 1920 of apparent
encephalitis lethargica (sleeping sickness), which Clements
listed as the cause of death. His second wife, Mary McCleery,
unexpectedly died (1925) from endocarditis (acute inflammation
of the inner lining of the heart) after four years of marriage;
that's what the doctor reported. The death of his third
spouse, Katherine Burke, in 1939 was caused by cancer, according to Clements. Authorities became suspicious following
the demise of his fourth wife, Victoria Burnett, some 20 years
his junior, in 1947. An autopsy revealed she had perished
not from myeloid leukemia, as the death certificate stated, but
from morphine poisoning, which Clements himself then employed
to commit suicide before he could be taken into custody.

CLIFT, Martha. See COO, Eva.

CLIFTON, Dan (1865?-96?). American safecracker, robber, and
outlaw. He engaged in small-town robbery in Oklahoma's
Indian territory until he joined the Doolin gang in 1892.
Called "Dynamite Dick" because of his use of explosives in
heists, Clifton helped hold up stagecoaches, trains, and banks;
he lost three fingers, shot off during the famous gunfight

between the Doolin gang and the law at Ingalls, Oklahoma, in 1893. A man identified as Clifton because of the three missing fingers was shot to death near Blackwell, Oklahoma, in 1896. See also DOOLIN, Bill or William.

CLINE, Alfred L. (1888-1948). American forger and presumed murderer. For many years he went undetected, marrying women and apparently poisoning them to death after legally taking control of their estates. The corpses of Cline's wives were cremated, and so the authorities were unable to produce any concrete evidence of murder. Finally Cline was found guilty of having used forgery on documents and was sentenced to over 100 years in prison. He died in California's Folsom Prison.

COCHRANE, Henry S. (1826-1906). American government clerk and burglar. In 1893 some $130,000 in gold bars were discovered missing from the U.S. mint at Philadelphia. Because there were no signs of forced entry, the authorities were baffled at how the burglary had occurred until A. L. Drummond, head of the U.S. Secret Service, coaxed a confession to the crime from Cochrane, the mint's chief weighing clerk for the past 37 years. For a long while Cochrane had poked a rod through the wire cage surrounding a gold pile, knocked a bar to the floor, reached under the cage door, which was over six inches off the floor, and taken one or two bars on each occasion. At his home in Darby, Pennsylvania, Cochrane had melted down the bars into other forms, which he had sold under a pseudonym to the Philadelphia mint for an equal value in gold coin. Much of the stolen gold was found stashed in the walls of Cochrane's home. Cochrane was sentenced to seven years in the state prison, and after his release he lived to a ripe old age, dying in 1906.

COE, George [Washington] (1856-1941). American gunfighter. He was a fast draw with the gun, successfully battling other gunslingers in the 1870s. Coe rode with BILLY THE KID during the Lincoln County War between rival ranchers and merchants in the New Mexico territory in 1878. He was badly wounded in a gunfight in the bloody feud but survived. Coe went straight after accepting a pardon from the territory's new governor, Lew Wallace, and lived until a ripe old age.

COE, Phil (d. 1871). American gambler. Coe, a dapper man who wore a derby hat and carried a gold-knobbed cane, was an expert, but crooked, card player in Texas and other places in the 1860s and early 1870s. In 1871 he and gunfighter Ben THOMPSON opened the Bull's Head Tavern and Gambling Saloon in Abilene, Kansas. On the front of their saloon was a painting of an enormous bull whose genitalia were much larger than the rest of his body. The painting was dubbed the "Shame of Abilene" by the citizens, who asked Marshal James Butler "Wild

Bill" Hickok to remove it or have the painting redone. When Coe refused to do anything, Hickok himself repainted parts of the picture. On October 5, 1871, Coe and Hickok got into an argument, and Hickok, too hastily according to some accounts, whipped out his pistols and fatally shot Coe. Immediately afterward, Hickok, thinking he was being attacked from behind, turned and shot again, this time killing his own deputy, Mike Williams.

COHEN, [Meyer Harris] "Mickey" (1913-76). American gambler and gangster. He was a trusted friend of racketeer Benjamin "Bugsy" SIEGEL, whose West Coast gambling interests he acquired after Siegel's death by unknown gunmen in 1947. Cohen lived extravagantly and liked publicity. Several attempts were made to assassinate Cohen, who feuded with the national crime syndicate's bosses over profits from his lucrative bookmaking business in California. A number of gangland killings were attributed to Cohen's mobsters. Cohen was twice convicted of income tax violations, serving a total of 14 years in prison. Released from the Atlanta penitentiary in 1973, he pronounced himself law-abiding, worked for prison reform, and died of natural causes three years later.

COLBECK, Dinty (d. late 1920s). Missouri bootlegger, robber, and gangster. About 1920 he took control of "Egan's Rats," a feared St. Louis gang founded by "Jellyroll" EGAN. Colbeck redirected the gang's criminal activities into bootlegging, safecracking, and jewel thefts, operating mainly in the St. Louis-Kansas City area in the 1920s and 1930s. He paid huge bribes to corrupt policemen and politicians so that he could conduct his "business" without interference from the law. While engaging in a mail robbery, Colbeck and some "Rats" were surprised by the police and caught (some say Mafia members trying to destroy the independent gang informed the police). Unknown rival mobsters killed Colbeck, and his "Rats" were absorbed into other gangs in the late 1930s.

COLBERT, Chunk (d. 1874). American gunfighter. He evidently shot and killed at least seven men in gun duels before he went from the Colorado territory to the New Mexico territory to challenge Clay ALLISON, a notorious gunfighter, in 1874. Colbert and Allison sat down opposite each other at a table in an inn; they stirred their coffee and whiskey with the muzzles of their six-shooters, then put their guns back in their holsters, and began to eat. Colbert made a move beneath the table to draw, but Allison reacted swiftly before Colbert could raise his gun to fire and put a bullet above Colbert's right eye, killing him.

COLEMAN, Edward (d. 1839). New York thug and murderer. A New York City gang member in the 1830s, Coleman engaged in brawls, muggings, and other nefarious activities on the city streets. He wooed and eventually married the prettiest of the Hot Corn Girls, a famous group of strikingly attractive young women who sold ears of corn which they carried in cedar buckets hung from their shoulders. Dissatisfied with his wife's earnings, Coleman clubbed her so severely that she died. Arrested and found guilty of murder, he was executed at the newly built Tombs prison on January 12, 1839, becoming the first to be executed there.

COLL, Vincent "Mad Dog" (1909-32). New York gangster and murderer. He was hired by Mafia boss Salvatore MARANZANO to kill Lucky LUCIANO and Vito GENOVESE during a gangland war in New York City in 1930. When Maranzano was killed, Coll did not carry out the murder contracts. A bloody gangster war soon broke out between Coll and Dutch SCHULTZ over control of the bootleg business. In 1931 Coll murdered Schultz mobster Vincent Barelli and his girl friend Mary Smith. After he machine-gunned several of Schultz's hoods on a Manhattan street and hit five children (killing one), Coll was named "Mad Dog" and the "Mad Mick." Gunmen, on orders from Schultz, machine-gunned Coll to death in a drugstore phone booth in mid-Manhattan in late 1932.

COLLAZO, Oscar (b. 1914). Puerto Rican-born American would-be assassin. Collazo, a metal worker in New York, was an active leader in the Puerto Rican nationalist movement that agitated for the independence of Puerto Rico. Armed with pistols and much ammunition, he and 25-year-old Griselio Torresola, a fellow nationalist, attempted to assassinate U.S. President Harry S Truman in Washington, D.C. on November 1, 1950. Trying to shoot their way into Blair House, where Truman was residing while the White House was being remodeled across the street, they exchanged 27 shots with security guards in less than three minutes. Torresola was shot and killed by a fatally wounded guard, Leslie Coffelt, who died about four hours later. Collazo received a bullet in the chest, fell to the sidewalk, and was caught. He recovered to be indicted and convicted (March 7, 1951) on three charges: the killing of Coffelt, intent to assassinate Truman, and assault with intent to kill two guards. Collazo was sentenced to die in the electric chair on August 1, 1952, but a week before his execution Truman commuted the sentence to life imprisonment. He was placed in the federal penitentiary at Leavenworth, Kansas. On September 6, 1979, Collazo, along with three other Puerto Rican nationalists convicted of a shooting incident in the U.S. House of Representatives, were all released from prison under a grant of clemency from President Jimmy Carter.

COLLINS, Dapper Dan. See TOURBILLON, Robert Arthur.

COLLINS, John Norman (b. 1947). Michigan murderer. Seven

women students at Eastern Michigan University were shot, strangled, or clubbed to death in the Upsilanti, Michigan, area between August 1967, and July 1969. Police were baffled by the so-called "coed killer" until the death of the seventh victim, Karen Sue Beckemann. Evidence linking Collins to her resulted in Collins's arrest and trial in 1970. He was found guilty and sentenced to life imprisonment.

COLLINS, Michael. See DUNNE, Reginald.

COLOMBO, Joe or Joseph, Sr. (1914-78). New York gangster. In the 1960s he was involved in a plot to kill top New York syndicate leaders and take control of the whole Mafia operation. Colombo evidently told Carlo GAMBINO and Tommy LUCCHESE, both of whom were intended victims, about the murder plot and afterward became known as a "fink" to many rival mobsters. Colombo, made head of the Profaci Brooklyn crime family, engaged in a gangland struggle with Brooklyn racketeer Joey GALLO. In the early 1970s Colombo established the Italian-American Civil Rights League to better the image of Italians in America, especially to get rid of the stereotyped Italian-Mafia crime connection. On June 28, 1971, he was seriously wounded by a black gunman, Jerome A. Johnson, who was immediately shot to death by Colombo's bodyguards. Colombo, incapacitated by severe brain damage, lived as a kind of vegetable until his death seven years later.

COLONEL PLUG [real name: Fluger] (d. c. 1820). American river pirate. Colonel Plug, who claimed to have been a colonel in the American Revolution, organized and led a gang of river pirates along the Mississippi and Ohio rivers in the early 1800s. Hidden aboard a flatboat, he would bore holes in its bottom, causing it to sink while his colleagues came aboard, stole the cargo, and either killed the passengers or left them to drown. Colonel Plug, according to legend, failed to get out of the hold in time during one of his raids and drowned when the flatboat sank.

COLOSIMO, James "Big Jim" (1877-1920). Italian-born Chicago brothel keeper and gangster. At the age of 18, Colosimo worked for corrupt Chicago politicians, collecting kickbacks from brothel owners. In the early 1900s Colosimo began to operate a chain of whorehouses in Chicago and soon became known as the "King of Pimps." Money from the brothels and saloons attached to them made him a millionaire before he was 30. To protect his booze and brothel empire, Colosimo hired thugs and gangsters, such as Johnny TORRIO, to rub out extortionists who tried to take part of his wealth. Torrio, who soon began to run everything, wanted to branch out into other rackets, but Colosimo refused. On May 11, 1920, Al CAPONE, hired by Torrio, shot Colosimo dead at plush Colosimo's Cafe on South Wabash Avenue, Chicago.

COLT, John C. (1819-42?). New York murderer. John, the brother of Samuel Colt, the inventor of the Colt revolver, fancied himself a writer and claimed to cavort with authors such as Edgar Allan Poe and Washington Irving. He was convicted of killing a printer in a dispute about the printing of his book and was sentenced to hang. Prison authorities at the newly built Tombs in New York City granted John his wish to marry Caroline Henshaw on the morning of the day of his execution, November 18, 1842. After the wedding ceremony, the prison mysteriously caught fire, several prisoners were let out and escaped, and reportedly John was found dead with a knife in his heart. Though no official identification of the body was made, a coroner's jury declared that John had committed suicide. However, some believed John had escaped in the confusion, a dead man had been put in his place, and Caroline (who disappeared shortly afterward) and John later settled in California.

COLUMBO, Patty or Patricia (b. 1957). Illinois murderer. The sanguinary murders of her father, mother, and brother (May 4, 1976) at their home in Elk Grove Village, Illinois, was blamed on "young punks" by Patty, a tall, sexy brunette whom police soon arrested along with her married boyfriend Frank DeLUCA. The couple was charged with the slayings. During their lengthy trial in 1977, damning testimony was given by a number of witnesses who said Patty hated her family, especially her father, and had tried to hire two "hit men" to eliminate the family (she would also stand to gain a $250,000 life insurance policy on her father and his estate), but ultimately had been turned down by the two men, with whom she apparently fornicated often to gain their help. As Patty watched, DeLuca evidently did the killings for her and in revenge for an attack on him by her father, who had knocked out two of DeLuca's teeth. The jury's verdict was guilty, and Patty and her boyfriend were each sentenced to 200 to 300 years' imprisonment. At the women's prison in Dwight, Illinois, Patty was charged with arranging sex parties in 1979.

CONDENT, Christopher (fl. c. 1700-1720). French pirate. In the early 1700s Condent operated a pirate ship in the West Indies and seized numerous valuable cargoes from captured merchant vessels. When Woodes Rogers, the Bahamian governor, made war on the pirates in 1718, Condent sailed to the Indian Ocean and plundered a large Arab treasure ship near Bombay. Upon landing at Madagascar, his 40-man crew, with almost Ł1,200 per man, disbanded, and Condent gave up piracy. After receiving a pardon from the French governor of what is now the island of Réunion, Condent settled there for a while and then moved to Saint-Malo in France, where he became a prosperous shipowner.

CONEYS, Theodore. See SPIDER MAN OF MONCRIEFF PLACE.

CONNORS, Babe (1856-1918). St. Louis madam. In 1898 she opened her famous "Palace" of sexual pleasure in St. Louis and bedecked it with rich tapestries, lush expensive rugs, palatial crystal chandeliers, and many art objects. Babe, a hefty mulatto, employed the most beautiful prostitutes, most of whom were of mixed blood, part black and part white, and presented fabulous erotic stage shows filled with music, song, and dancing for her clientele. The well-known black singer Mama Lou, wearing her calico dress and bright bandana, entertained the Babe's customers with numerous bawdy songs. Until her death in 1918, Babe, who earned considerable money from her business, was a striking figure around town, resplendent in dress and regal in bearing.

COO, Eva (d. 1935). Canadian-born American prostitute, madam, and murderer. After immigrating to the United States in the early 1920s, she worked for several years as a whore in cities on the East coast and then established a roadhouse and brothel near Cooperstown, New York. Eva earned much money as a madam until the end of Prohibition, when her business dropped suddenly. In 1934 she and her best friend Martha Clift were charged with murdering Harry Wright, a janitor who worked for Eva and had been found dead near Eva's roadhouse, after Eva had put in a claim to collect Wright's life insurance. Martha turned state's evidence, testifying that Eva had planned the murder, had clubbed Wright on the head, and had induced Martha to drive over Wright's body as he lay unconscious in the road on the night of June 15, 1934. Convicted and condemned to die, Eva gave many interviews to the press, claiming her innocence. Strapped into Sing Sing Prison's electric chair on June 28, 1935, she waved to the matrons and merrily said, "Good-bye, darlings," just before her death. Martha Clift served a short prison sentence and afterward faded from sight.

COOK, Frederick A. See COX, Seymour Ernest J.

COOK, William (1929-52). American robber and mass murderer. As a youth, he spent several years in reform school and the state penitentiary in Missouri, serving time for robbery. In late 1950, Cook abducted Carl Mosser, his wife, and three children in their car and drove aimlessly through the Southwest until he shot them to death near Joplin, Missouri. Later Cook stopped another motorist, Robert H. Dewey, whom he killed in San Diego, California. Mexican police seized Cook in Santa Rosalia, about 400 miles below the U.S. border, and returned him to California, where he was convicted of the Dewey murder. On December 12, 1952, Cook was executed in San Quentin's gas chamber.

COOLEY, Scott (1845-after 1880). Texas Ranger, gunslinger, and murderer. After serving with the Texas Rangers, Cooley

worked for Tim Williamson, a wealthy cattleman, in Mason County, Texas, in the 1870s. When Williamson, arrested for cattle
rustling, was abducted and killed by an angry mob in 1875,
Cooley blamed his murder on Deputy Sheriff John Worley, whom
he said conspired with the mob. Cooley shot Worley dead and
cut off his ears, which he publicly displayed as a warning of
what awaited others involved in the Williamson killing. For about
a year the Mason County War raged between Cooley's group and
the anti-Williamson group, leaving about a dozen men slain. In
1876 the Texas Rangers stopped the bloodshed and looked for
Cooley, who disappeared and was never tried for his crimes.

COOLIDGE, Valorus P. (d. 1948). Maine doctor and murderer. The
principal doctor in Waterville, Maine, he attempted on September 30, 1847, to poison Edward Matthews, to whom he owed
much money and who visited the doctor's offices that day. The
poisoned brandy sipped by Matthews worked too slowly, so
Coolidge clubbed his victim to death. The autopsy was performed by Coolidge, who tried to cover up the crime, but a
curious accompanying physician discovered hydrocyanic (prussic) acid in the dead man's stomach. Coolidge was tried, convicted, and sentenced to be hanged but committed suicide in
his jail cell by taking the same poison, which had been smuggled
to him.

COONEY, Celia or Cecelia [Roth] (fl. 1924). Brooklyn robber.
New York newspapers romanticized her as the "Bobbed-Haired
Bandit," dwelling on her bold exploits, but actually 20-year-
old Celia, a laundry worker whose dark hair was bobbed, netted
only $1,600 in ten armed robberies in Brooklyn, New York, in
1924. She and her 24-year-old husband, Edward Cooney, an
out-of-work garage mechanic, sought a better life for their un-
born baby by stealing. Their vain attempt to rob the National
Biscuit Company in Brooklyn won them press headlines, which
helped result in their capture while in hiding in Florida. They
pleaded guilty, and Celia was sent to Auburn, Edward to Sing
Sing. Set free in 1931, they resumed married life on a farm in
upstate New York.

"COOPER, D. B." (?). Hijacker and extortionist. On Thanksgiv-
ing eve, November 24, 1971, a man wearing dark glasses and
calling himself "D. B. Cooper" hijacked a 727 Trijet en route
from Portland, Oregon, to Seattle, Washington. The plane
landed in Seattle, where the man's ransom demand of $200,000
in $20 bills was paid for the release of the 36 passengers.
"D. B. Cooper," holding three crew members hostage, ordered
the jet to be flown to Reno, Nevada, and apparently parachuted
out while in flight somewhere over southwestern Washington
State (the jet's rear exit door was found open). No trace of
the man has been found since, but it is thought he either died
on impact or of exposure to the freezing cold. In 1980 children

playing along the Columbia River near Vancouver, Washington, dug up marked bills of the ransom money worth several thousand dollars.

COPELAND, James (1815?-57). American Southern "land pirate" and hired killer. He headed a band of "land pirates" and hired killers in Mississippi in the 1840s. Copeland often worked for the powerful and corrupt Wages family, who owned much land around Augusta, Mississippi. In 1848 Gale H. Wages and Charles McGrath, two members of Copeland's band, were killed by James A. Harvey. After receiving $1,000 from "Old Man" Wages to avenge his son's death, Copeland eagerly shot and killed Harvey. Identified as Harvey's killer, Copeland was tried, convicted, and sentenced to death. Because he said nothing to implicate the Wages, Copeland remained alive for nine years, thanks to the power of the Wages clan. Finally he was hanged on October 30, 1857.

COPLON, Judith (b. 1920). American alleged spy. In New York City in 1949, she and her purported lover Valentin Gubitchev, a Russian engineer employed at the United Nations, were arrested and charged with securing secret U.S. documents for the Soviet Union. While awaiting trial in New York, Coplon, who had already been indicted in Washington, D.C., on charges of having stolen secret documents from the Justice Department where she had formerly worked as a political analyst, was found guilty and sentenced to prison; on appeal, she was freed on bail. Later (1950) she was convicted with Gubitchev, and each were sentenced to 15 years in prison. Gubitchev's sentence was suspended when he promised to leave the country; Coplon appealed and won a reversal of her New York conviction on grounds that the wiretapping evidence against her had been obtained illegally. Her Washington conviction was upheld, but she was entitled to a new trial to decide whether her phone had been tapped. Coplon was never retried, and in 1967 the Justice Department dropped all charges against her.

COPPINGER, Daniel (fl. c. mid-1700s). Danish-born English smuggler. His Danish ship was wrecked off the northern coast of Cornwall, England, in a violent storm and sank. Coppinger, a hulking giant of a man, swam to shore and made England his home. He organized a smuggling gang, using a cove at the foot of Steeple Brink, a high cliff, as his headquarters. Working out of "Coppinger's Cove," his gang led ships astray, wrecked them, looted their cargoes, and brought goods into the country illicitly. Coppinger was cursed for his cruelty by the English country people, who were glad when he was lost at sea during a storm.

COPPOLA, Frank (1944-82). Virginia burglar and murderer. Coppola, an auto mechanic and an ex-policeman, was convicted of burglarizing a Virginia farm equipment company in 1971. After serving over a year in prison of a four-year term, he was released and worked off and on for a used-car dealer. On April 22, 1978, Coppola, Joseph Miltier, and Donna Mills entered the Hatchell home in Newport News, Virginia, stole some jewelry and cash, fled, and were later apprehended. Muriel Hatchell was fatally beaten during the robbery. A Newport News jury found Coppola guilty of capital murder, sentencing him to the electric chair for the beating-death of Muriel Hatchell. Miltier received three life terms; Mills got life plus 117 years; and Karen Coppola, Frank's second wife, who had waited during the crime in a getaway car a few blocks away, got 55 years as an accessory. On August 10, 1982, Frank Coppola, who insisted he was innocent, became the first person executed in Virginia in 20 years.

COPPOLA, Michael "Trigger Mike" (1904-66). New York gangster. When Vito GENOVESE fled to Italy in 1937, Coppola took over the Mafia don's numbers racket in Harlem. Coppola's annual income from the racket was estimated to be $1 million. Because he often used automatic weapons to settle quarrels with his opponents, Coppola was given the nickname "Trigger Mike." In 1955 he married his second wife, Ann Drahmann, who grew to hate her husband's sadistic ways. Coppola divorced her in 1960 and sent thugs to beat her up after she testified against him during an IRS investigation. In 1962 he pleaded guilty to tax evasion. Released after serving nine months of a one-year sentence in the Atlanta Penitentiary, Coppola resumed his Mafia career and died in 1966 of undisclosed causes.

COPPOLINO, Carl (b. 1933). American doctor and murderer. At the age of 30, he retired as an anesthesiologist, citing a heart condition, and picked up annual benefits of $22,000 from his insurance company. With his wife, Carmela, he moved from New Jersey to Florida, where Carmela died of an apparent heart attack in 1965 (she had a $65,000 insurance policy on her life). Shortly afterward Marge Farber, who had known the Coppolinos in New Jersey, accused Carl of killing her husband and Carmela. Farber claimed she and Carl had had a love affair and Carl had murdered her husband out of jealousy in 1963; she said Carl had injected a drug into his victim before suffocating him with a pillow. Carl was indicted for murder in New Jersey and Florida and received an acquittal in the Farber case. Evidence was presented in Carmela's murder case in Florida that Carmela had not died of a heart attack and that she had had an injection in her left buttock just before death. "Store-bought" succinic acid, which used in excess could cause death, was discovered by a toxicologist in Carmela's body. Carl was convicted of second-degree murder and sentenced to life imprisonment.

CORDAY, Charlotte [full name: Marie Anne Charlotte Corday
d'Armont] (1768-93). French assassin. Beautiful, intelligent,
and from an impoverished noble family, she supported the
Girondists, moderate republicans, in their power struggle with
the radical Jacobins during the French Revolution (1789-92).
After the Girondists were crushed by the Jacobins in June 1793,
Corday sought to assassinate the powerful French journalist and
politician Jean-Paul Marat, who backed the Jacobins and the
bloody Reign of Terror against counterrevolutionaries. Walking
200 miles from Caen in her native Normandy to Paris, she gained
entrance to see Marat in his house on the pretext that she
wanted to inform him of conspirators. While Marat sat in his
bathtub, noting the names of Normandy dissidents who didn't
exist, Corday removed a long carving knife hidden in the bod-
ice of her dress and stabbed it into his chest through his
heart, killing Marat, whose cries before dying brought attendants who grabbed the assassin. Four days later, on July 17,
1793, Charlotte was brought to trial, during which her dress
was torn from her to show her breasts, was swiftly condemned
to die, and was guillotined that rainy evening in the Place de
la Révolution (Place de la Concorde) in Paris.

CORDER, William (d. 1828). English murderer. He had a love affair with pretty 25-year-old Maria Marton, who became pregnant.
On May 18, 1827, Corder, who had vowed to bring Maria from
her family's farm in Suffolk to Ipswich to marry her, lured her
to a red barn on his land and stabbed her to death with a pickaxe. Afterward he artfully wrote letters to Maria's parents,
saying he and Maria were living happily on the Isle of Wright,
but Maria's mother became upset by a nightmare in which she
saw her murdered daughter buried in the red barn. The mother
finally induced the police to dig up Corder's land, and Maria's
corpse was found in the red barn. At his trial, Corder pleaded
innocent but was convicted, mainly on the testimony of Maria's
younger brother who claimed he saw Corder walk from the barn
with a bloodstained pickaxe. Corder, who eventually confessed
in writing, was hanged on August 1, 1828.

CORLL, Dean [Allen] (1940-73). Texas mass murderer. Corll, an
electrician in Houston, was discovered to have killed at least 27
adolescent boys during a three-year period in the early 1970s.
Two teenage boys, Elmer Wayne HENLEY and David Brooks,
helped procure victims and were paid $5 to $10 by Corll for
each adolescent boy they brought to him. Corll took sadistic
sexual pleasure in raping, mutilating, and murdering the scared
youths, whose bodies were buried in a boat shed near Corll's
house or in the Gulf Coast region of east Texas. On August 7,
1973, 17-year-old Henley, fearing Corll would turn on him and
Brooks, killed Corll. Remains of Corll's victims were found,
and a police investigation implicated Henley and Brooks in the

murders. Henley, convicted on nine counts, received 594 years in prison; Brooks, convicted on one count, received a life sentence.

CORNELYS, Madame (d. 1779). Italian-born British madam. In the 1760s the lavishly furnished salon-bordello Carlisle House, operated by her in London's once fashionable Soho district, was frequented by the rich and powerful, nobility and royalty, and became the most notorious place of that kind in Europe. Madame Cornelys, who had once been Casanova's mistress, supplied the most gorgeous and seductive prostitutes, for whom her customers paid handsomely. As she grew wealthy, English clergy and others attacked her operation and eventually forced the closure of Carlisle House. To regain lost riches, Madame Cornelys opened another salon in the Knightsbridge area, but it soon collapsed when rich patrons stayed away because of her now odious repute. Thrown into debtor's prison in 1772, she remained there until her death.

CORNETT, Brack (1859-88). Texas bank and train robber. Most nineteenth-century robbers made little or no plans before they held up a bank or train. Cornett, however, became known for "casing"--looking over carefully--the bank or train he and his gang intended to rob and for practicing fast getaways from the planned site of the crime. After a train robbery near Pearsall, Texas, in 1888, lawmen recalled a recent report by a rancher who had seen a gang riding fast nearby a few days before (Cornett and his men practicing an escape), and soon cornered Cornett on a ranch and shot him dead in a gun battle when he refused to surrender.

CORONA, Juan (b. 1934). Mexican-born California mass murderer. In January 1973, in a courtroom in Yuba City, California, Corona, a labor contractor, was convicted of killing 25 transient farm workers in 1970-71 and was sentenced to 25 consecutive life terms. The bodies of the murder victims, found buried in peach orchards and along a river in Yuba County, had been mutilated with a machete-like weapon; some of the bodies were discovered after Corona's arrest in May 1971. In 1978 a state appeals court ruled that Corona's first defense had been inadequate and he was entitled to an insanity defense (in 1956 Corona had been admitted to a state hospital and diagnosed as "paranoid schizophrenic"). The court also said that the evidence proving Corona's guilt, "although circumstantial, was overwhelming" and ordered a new trial. Corona, who first served time in Soledad Prison, was then sent to a mental institution for observation. A seven-month-long retrial in 1982 ended with Corona being convicted again of the slaying of the 25 migrant workers.

CORTINA, Juan (1824-92). Mexican-Texan Outlaw. In the 1850s, when white Texans attempted to take some of his ranch land

(holders of shares in worthless oil companies were inveigled to
trade their shares plus money for other valueless shares by a
complex system of company mergers). Charges against Cox,
Cook, and eleven cohorts were brought in Fort Worth, Texas,
when their swindles were exposed in late 1923. They were
tried and found guilty of fraud in cheating buyers of oil leases
in Texas and sentenced to prison; Cox received eight years and
was fined $8,000; Cook was sentenced to 14 years and a fine of
$12,000.

COY, Bernie or Bernard Paul (1900-1946). Kentucky bank robber
and prison rebellion leader. He was convicted of bank robbery
in Kentucky and sentenced to 25 years in Alcatraz Prison in
San Francisco Bay. There, on May 2, 1946, Coy led the most
famous breakout attempt from "The Rock," during which five
men died and 15 more were wounded. While other convicts
instigated a prison riot, Coy and his accomplices, who included
Joseph Paul "Dutch" CRETZER, Sam Richard SHOCKLEY, Miran
Edgar "Buddy" THOMPSON, Clarence Carnes, and Marvin Hubbard, broke into the gun gallery to arm themselves, overpowered the tier guards, and took nine guards hostage. Because
of one locked door, the escape failed. Coy tried to negotiate
with the prison warden and subsequently lost control of his
men. Marines and prison guards stormed the prison, taking
the cell blocks with gunfire and heaving grenades. Coy was
killed by Cretzer, who had gone mad at the breakout's failure.
Cretzer was shot to death by guards, who put an end to the
affair after 48 hours.

CREAM, Thomas Neill (1850-92). Scottish-born doctor, arsonist,
and poisoner. As a youngster in 1863, he immigrated with his
family to Canada, where he later earned a medical degree at
Montreal's McGill University. In 1878 Cream committed arson
in London, Ontario, and collected insurance money on his own
torched property. By 1880 he was performing abortions in
Chicago, Illinois, where one of his patients died on the operating table and another died from prescribed medicine. Released
because of insufficient evidence, Cream, in 1881, was convicted
of poisoning an epileptic patient, Daniel Stott, whose medicine
he had laced with strychnine; at the trial, Stott's wife, with
whom Cream had been having an affair, turned state's evidence
against her lover. Sentenced to life imprisonment at the Illinois
State Prison in Joliet, Cream received a commutation when officials declared him "rehabilitated" and was set free in 1891.
Left much money by his father who had then recently died, he
moved to London, England, where he hung around prostitutes,
affectedly sporting a silk hat, evening dress, a velvet cloak, a
gold-crowned walking stick, and gold pince-nez (Cream was
cross-eyed since youth). After four prostitutes were murdered
by strychnine poisoning, Scotland Yard traced the crimes to
Cream, who was arrested in early June 1892. Tried and found

guilty of murder, he went to the gallows on November 15, 1892; as he fell through the gallows' trap, he shouted, "I am Jack --" before the rope cut short his words. Because he was in the Joliet prison at the time of the 1888 killings by JACK THE RIP-PER, theorists have generally discounted his apparent claim to have been the Ripper, but there possibly could have been two criminals who used the name Thomas Neill Cream, one of whom, a doppelganger, who committed the Whitechapel murders.

CRETZER, Joseph Paul "Dutch" (1911-46). American bank robber, prison rebel, and murderer. Convicted of bank robbery in 1939, Cretzer was sent to prison on McNeil Island, Washington, from which he tried to escape but was caught. At his trial for the attempted breakout, Cretzer beat a U.S. marshall with his handcuffed hands and killed him. He was then sent to Alcatraz for life. Cretzer joined Bernie COY, Sam Richard SHOCKLEY, Marvin Hubbard, Miran Edgar "Buddy" THOMPSON, and others in the bloody rebellion-breakout attempt on May 2, 1946. Armed with weapons from the prison gun gallery, Cretzer shot and killed a guard taken hostage when the convicts' escape was thwarted. While the Marines and prison guards made a final assault, Cretzer, maddened by Coy's "hick" leadership and failed plans, fatally shot Coy and was then killed by guards, who also shot Hubbard to death. The breakout attempt was over after a harrowing 48 hours.

CRIMMINS, Alice (b. 1939). New York murderer. On July 14, 1965, Crimmins, recently separated from her husband, reported the disappearance of her four-year-old daughter, Missy, and five-year-old son, Eddie, from her Queens, New York, apart-ment. Soon afterward the children were found murdered. In-vestigators surmised that Crimmins, wishing to be rid of the care of her children, had strangled Missy to death in a fit of rage and then killed Eddie because he had witnessed the crime. A 1968 manslaughter verdict against Crimmins, who was known to have had extramarital affairs, was overturned because of a technical illegality. Retried in 1971, she was convicted of man-slaughter in the case of her daughter and of first-degree mur-der in the case of her son, receiving five to 20 years' imprison-ment for the former crime and life for the latter. A higher court later overturned the murder conviction because of insuf-ficient evidence. Crimmins was imprisoned on May 16, 1975, and was released on parole on September 7, 1977.

CRIMMINS, Craig [Steven] (b. 1959). New York murderer. A boyish-looking stagehand at the Metropolitan Opera for four years, Crimmins of the Bronx, New York, was charged with the attempted rape and murder of blonde, 30-year-old Helen Hagnes Mintiks, an orchestral violinist, who was thrown--nude, bound, and gagged--down the ventilation shaft of New York's Lincoln Center building on the evening of July 23, 1980.

Crimmins, a high-school dropout with purported learning dis-
abilities and drinking problems, made a damaging confession to
the crime to the police just hours before he was charged on
August 30, 1980. At his sensational trial in 1981, the jury
convicted him of feloniously killing the violinist to cover up an
attempted rape (a charge that was dropped for lack of evidence). Crimmins received 20 years to life imprisonment.

CRIPPEN, Hawley Harvey (1862-1910). American-born British doctor and poisoner. Crippen's flamboyant and domineering wife,
Cora, who was a music-hall star known as Belle Elmore, disappeared after a party at their house in London on the evening of
January 31, 1910. Shortly afterward Crippen's ladylike secretary, Ethel Le Neve, moved in with Crippen, who, when asked
about Cora's whereabouts, said she had gone to California. He
later said she had died and been cremated. Suspicious friends
notified Scotland Yard, which began an inquiry but found nothing. Crippen, along with Le Neve, booked passage aboard a
steamship to Quebec. Meanwhile Chief Inspector Walter Dew of
Scotland Yard searched Crippen's house several times, finally
finding some human remains buried in the coal cellar. Sailing
aboard a faster ship, Inspector Dew landed in Quebec ahead of
Crippen and Le Neve, both of whom were arrested as they dis-
embarked and were brought back to England for trial. Crippen
was convicted of murdering Cora with the drug hyoscine and
was hanged on November 23, 1910. Le Neve, whose photo was
put in Crippen's coffin at his request, was acquitted (Crippen
had said that she had loved him "as few women love men" and
had insisted to the end that she was innocent).

CROSS, Phillip (1825-88). British doctor and poisoner. A retired
army surgeon, he settled down with his wife and four children
in County Cork, Ireland. Pretty 20-year-old Miss Skinner came
to work for the family as a governess and was amorously pursued by Cross, whose wife soon demanded that he dismiss the
young wench. Cross's wife suddenly and painfully died in 1887,
and very soon after he took off with Miss Skinner. Suspicious
authorities dug up the wife's body, which was found to contain
arsenic and strychnine poison. Tracked down and apprehended,
Cross was convicted of killing his wife and was promptly hanged.
Miss Skinner's presence was not to be seen at the proceedings.

CROWLEY, Francis "Two-Gun" (1911-31). New York robber and
murderer. In early 1931 Crowley and his partner, Rudolph
"Fats" Durringer, robbed a bank and then held up several
stores, shooting dead a storekeeper who resisted. In April of
that year, Crowley killed Virginia Banner, a dance hall hostess
who had spurned Durringer, and Frederick Hirsch, a policeman
who had asked for Crowley's license near North Merrick, New
York. Police found Crowley hiding in a Manhattan apartment
on May 7, 1931, and fought a fierce gun battle (later termed

the "Siege of West 90th Street") with him. Thousands of people watched as Crowley kept up a steady fusillade against 300 police officers. Wounded four times and overcome by tear gas, Crowley was finally seized. He was tried, convicted of murder, and executed in the electric chair at Sing Sing.

CUMMINGS, Joyce Lisa. See BRADFORD, Priscilla [Ann Hadley].

CUNNINGHAM, Charles (1787-1805). Pennsylvania murderer. A "bound" servant to an innkeeper in York, Pennsylvania, Cunningham was known to drink large amounts of whiskey and to enjoy gambling. On May 16, 1805, while shooting dice for money with Joseph Rothrock and another boy, he protested angrily that Rothrock had cheated him. In an alley later, Cunningham tried unsuccessfully to kill Rothrock with a knife and then strangled him to death with a thin rope. He also ground the dead boy's face into the cobblestones, obliterating the features. Quickly apprehended, Cunningham confessed and was hanged on September 19, 1805.

CURRY, George "Flat Nose" (1841-82). Wyoming robber and rustler. Curry, whose aliases were George Parrot and George Manuse, successfully engaged in stagecoach and train robbery and horse and cattle rustling in the Wyoming territory in the 1870s. He was convicted of an 1880 train robbery in which two deputy sheriffs were killed and was sentenced to hang on April 3, 1882, in Rawlins, Wyoming. Shortly before his scheduled execution, Curry escaped but was immediately caught by an angry mob, which tried to hang him on the spot. The rope broke during the hanging, and, as Curry lay on the ground, some of the mob shot him dead. Pieces of skin were peeled off Curry's corpse, tanned, and made into watch fobs and a pair of slippers by various Rawlins townspeople. Harvey Logan, who had ridden with Curry and greatly admired him, adopted his surname as his own, becoming known as KID CURRY.

CURRY, Kid. See KID CURRY.

CURRY, Peter. See WILCOXSON, Bobby Randell.

CURTIS, Winslow. See WHITE, John Duncan.

CUTPURSE, Moll [real name: Mary Frith] (c. 1584-1659). English highwaywoman and fence. She dressed, talked, and swore like a man and smoked a pipe. Cutpurse reputedly held up General Fairfax singlehandedly, but during her escape her horse faltered and she was caught. She managed to buy her way out of jail. Cutpurse operated a shop on Fleet Street in London, where she concentrated on buying and selling stolen property. Pickpockets, thieves, and others unloaded their goods at her shop, to which the rightful owners often came, after reading Cutpurse's

advertisements, to buy back their stolen items. Cutpurse died of dropsy in 1659.

CYCLONE LOUIE [real name: Vach Lewis] (1882-1908). New York gangster. Cyclone Louie, so named because of his violent and stormy nature, was a well-known hired mugger and killer in the Coney Island area in the early 1900s. His alibis managed to keep him out of jail. Cyclone Louie became a loyal friend of KID TWIST, for whom he reportedly performed a number of murder assignments free of charge. On May 14, 1908, outside a Coney Island dive, both Cyclone Louis and Kid Twist were shot and killed in a barrage of gunfire from enemies Louie the Lump (Louis Pioggi) and other Five Point gang members, who were settling a score with Kid Twist.

CZOLGOSZ, Leon F. (1873-1901). American anarchist and assassin. A semi-literate laborer, Czolgosz stood in line to shake hands with U.S. President William McKinley at the Pan-American Exposition in Buffalo, New York, on September 6, 1901. When the President was a few feet from him, Czolgosz revealed a .32-caliber pistol from under a phony white bandage wrapped around his right hand and fired two shots at McKinley. Seized by guards, Czolgosz said, "I done my duty." McKinley died eight days later of gangrene of the pancreas, partly caused by inept medical attention. Czolgosz was found guilty and sent to the electric chair at New York Auburn Prison on October 29, 1901. Affirming his anarchist beliefs, he said he killed the President for the good of the working people, and then he was executed.

- D -

DAGOE, Hannah (1730?-63). Irish-born British thief. For years she committed petty thievery in London's Covent Gardens area, finally being convicted of burglarizing the home of a needy widow; in those days theft brought a sentence of death. Fuming and cursing on the gallows at Tyburn on March 4, 1763, her execution day, this robust woman overpowered the hangman briefly, pulled off her clothes, and threw them at the shouting spectators (thus she robbed the hangman of his victim's garments --the usual recompense for the job). In a frenzy, with the rope at last around her neck, she killed herself by jumping to the ground.

DAGUE, Walter Glenn. See SCHROEDER, Irene.

DALTON, Bill or William [Marion] (1873-93). American train and bank robber and outlaw. In California on February 6, 1891, he and his brothers Bob and Grat attempted unsuccessfully to hold up a Southern Pacific express train. They were driven off by a guard with a shot gun. Bill and Grat were caught soon

afterward and tried. Bill was acquitted and did not ride the
outlaw trail until after his brothers Grat, Bob, and Emmett
failed to pull off the Coffeyville, Kansas, bank raid in 1892.
Bill then robbed some banks and trains with the Doolin gang
in Oklahoma. He was shot dead by a lawman on the front
porch of his farm. See also DALTON, Bob or Robert [Renick];
DALTON, Grat[ton]; DOOLIN, Bill or William.

DALTON, Bob or Robert [Renick] (1867-92). American train and
bank robber and outlaw. After serving as a U.S. marshal in
Fort Smith, Arkansas, and as a lawman on the Osage Indian
Reservation, Bob decided to follow the outlaw trail with his
brothers Grat, Emmett, and Bill. He was considered the
natural leader of the Dalton gang, which included his three
brothers and such outlaws as George "Bitter Creek" NEWCOMB,
Charlie "Black Face" Bryant, and Bill DOOLIN, who later led
his own notorious gang. Bob helped rob express trains in
California and Oklahoma. On October 5, 1892, Bob, Emmett,
and Grat, accompanied by Bill Powers and Dick Broadwell,
tried to rob two banks at the same time in Coffeyville, Kansas.
Forewarned, townspeople armed themselves and shot to death
four members of the gang (Emmett survived after he was shot
in the back while heroically trying to pull Bob into the saddle
to make an escape). See also DALTON, Bill or William [Marion];
DALTON, Emmett; DALTON, Grat[ton].

DALTON, Emmett (1871-1937). American train and bank robber and
outlaw. For a short time he was a U.S. marshal for Hanging
Judge Parker in Fort Smith, Arkansas. In the early 1890s
he took to the outlaw trail with his brothers Bob and Grat and
some others and robbed several express trains in Oklahoma.
Emmett, along with Bob and Grat, Bill Powers, and Dick Broadwell, attempted to rob the Condon and First National banks in
Coffeyville, Kansas, on October 5, 1892. They thought that
pulling off a double bank job at the same time would make them
famous. However, the town's citizens were alerted and armed
and confronted the Dalton gang as it emerged from the banks.
A fierce gunfight occurred during which four citizens were
killed and all the gang's members, except Emmett, who was
wounded many times, were shot to death. Emmett was sentenced to life imprisonment in the Kansas State Penitentiary in
Lansing and was later pardoned by the Kansas governor in
1907. He then led an exemplary life as a businessman in Los
Angeles until his death thirty years later. See also DALTON,
Bill or William [Marion]; DALTON, Bob or Robert [Renick];
DALTON, Grat[ton]; DOOLIN, Bill or William.

DALTON, Grat[ton] (1862-92). American train and bank robber
and outlaw. He wore a U.S. marshal badge in Fort Smith,
Arkansas, before turning outlaw with his brothers Bill, Bob,
and Emmett. As part of the Dalton gang, Grat participated in

several train robberies in California and Oklahoma in the early 1890s. He and his brothers Bob and Emmett, along with Bill Powers and Dick Broadwell, attempted to rob the First National and Condon banks at the same time in Coffeyville, Kansas, on October 5, 1892. Armed citizens shot Grat dead as he tried to mount his horse. See also DALTON, Bill or William [Marion]; DALTON, Bob or Robert [Renick]; DALTON, Emmett; DOOLIN, Bill or William.

DALY, John (1839-64). American gunfighter and outlaw. A cruel gunslinger from California, Daly led a gang of rustlers, robbers, and killers during the gold rush days in the Nevada territory in the early 1860s. He became a kind of vigilante outlaw who interpreted "justice" as he saw fit, intimidating, terrorizing, and slaying those who countered him. However, in February 1864, shortly after Daly and his gang had knifed and burned a man who had shot a gang member, the Citizens' Protective Association, a vigilante group, was formed, pursued Daly and his cohorts, captured, and lynched them.

DAMPIER, William (1652?-1715). English buccaneer, privateer, and explorer. He took part in English expeditions that plundered Spanish ships and settlements along the west coasts of Central and South America between 1679 and 1683. Dampier then sailed with Captain Swan in the Cygnet westward across the Pacific, and was left at his request on the Nicobar Islands in 1688. Before returning to England in 1691, Dampier and some others cruised about the East Indies, preying on foreign shipping. In 1697 he published a candid, best-selling book about his piracies, A New Voyage Round the World. Given command of the H.M.S. Roebuck, Dampier went on a voyage of exploration to Australia, New Guinea, and New Britain (1699-1701). He commanded a privateering expedition to the South Seas (1703-7). In 1704 Scottish sailor Alexander Selkirk, prototype of Robinson Crusoe, was marooned voluntarily by Dampier on the uninhabited South Pacific island of Mas-a-Tierra. Later, another privateering expedition (1708-11) under Sir Woodes Rogers and Dampier rescued Selkirk, who had remained on the island for four years and four months. Dampier netted nearly £200,000 from captured booty during his second privateering trip and retired.

DANIELS, Murl (1924-49). Ohio mass murderer. He and John Coulter West teamed up after they were paroled from the Mansfield Reformatory in Ohio and committed numerous robberies in the Midwest in 1948. The two returned to Mansfield to "take care of" some of the guards who allegedly had mistreated them in prison. A prison supervisor, his wife, and his daughter were seized and senselessly shot and killed in a field near the town. The killers then roamed through Ohio and murdered two other persons in order to get their vehicles, while a massive manhunt ensued. Refusing to halt at the police roadblock, they shot at the police, who returned fire, killing West. Daniels gave himself up, was convicted, and died in the electric chair on January 3, 1949.

D'AQUINO, Iva Ikuko Toguri. See TOKYO ROSE.

DAUGHERTY, Roy (1871-1924). American bank robber and outlaw. In 1892 Daugherty, nicknamed "Arkansas Tom," joined the robbery gang headed by Bill DOOLIN in Oklahoma territory. During the famous gun battle between the Doolin gang and lawmen in Ingalls, Oklahoma, on September 1, 1893, Daugherty shot dead Deputy Tom Houston and allegedly shot Deputy Ike Steel. His expert shooting enabled the Doolin gang members to escape, but Daugherty himself was cornered and forced to surrender. He was sentenced to 50 years in prison, received an early release in 1910, vowed to go straight, but engaged again in bank robbery. Caught and sent to prison for a bank job in Neosho, Missouri, in 1916, Daughtery was paroled in 1921 and before long was wanted again for robbery. On August 6, 1924, in Joplin, Missouri, a policeman recognized him and, before Daugherty could draw his gun from his hip holster like an old-time gunslinger of the West, shot him dead.

D'AUTREMONT, Hugh (d. 1959). Oregon lumberjack, train robber, and murderer. He led his twin brothers, Roy and Ray, in an attempted robbery of a Southern Pacific Railroad mail train near Siskiyou, Oregon, on October 11, 1923. A bomb set off by Hugh to blow away the locked door on the mail car caused the entire car to be set on fire and killed the mail clerk inside. The lumberjack brothers panicked, shot and killed the train's brakeman, fireman, and engineer, and then fled. The crime remained a mystery until criminologist Edward Oscar Heinrich deduced the identities of the murderers from bits of evidence. In 1927, after a three-and-a-half-year manhunt for the D'Autremonts, Hugh was arrested in the Philippines (he had enlisted as a U.S. soldier under the name Brice), and the twins were found under the name Goodwin working in an Ohio steel mill. They all confessed and were sentenced to life imprisonment. Hugh was paroled in 1958 and died the next year. Ray was paroled in 1961. Roy was later sent to a mental institution, where he died.

DAVIS, Angela [Yvonne] (b. 1944). American political activist and accused murderer. Davis, a self-avowed Communist with ties to a number of black militant groups, including the Black Panthers, taught courses in philosophy at the University of California at Los Angeles (UCLA) in 1969 and 1970. Black, beautiful, and bright, Davis gave speeches supporting the "Soledad Brothers," a group of black Marxist prisoners at the Soledad Prison. She purchased guns, which Jonathan Jackson, attempting to free his older brother George Jackson, a "Soledad Brother," passed to inmates at the Marin County Courthouse in San Raphael, California, on August 7, 1970. A shootout in the courthouse's parking lot that day left Judge Harold Haley, Jonathan Jackson, and two more inmates killed and District Attorney Gary Thomas critically wounded. Davis was indicted on charges of murder, fled, and became one of the FBI's ten most-wanted fugitives. She was caught in a New York City motel, extradited to California, and released on $102,000 bail. After a three-month trial (February 28 to June 4, 1972), Davis, who had gained worldwide notoriety, was acquitted by an all-white jury on charges of conspiracy, kidnapping, and murder.

DAVIS, Howell (d. 1719). Welsh pirate. For several years he raided ships in the West Indies. In 1718, when Bahama Governor Woodes Rogers began breaking up the pirates' havens, Davis ventured to West African waters to plunder European shipping and trading posts, from which ivory, gold, and slaves were shipped abroad. His pirate ship Royal Rover attacked many Portuguese settlements along the Gulf of Guinea. Among Davis's richest prizes was the British merchant galley Princess, which he seized in June 1719 at Anamaboe, an important slave trading station on the Guinea coast. One of the captured seamen taken aboard Davis's pirate ship was Bartholomew ROBERTS, who soon turned pirate. Shortly afterward, Davis was ambushed and killed by the Portuguese on Princes Island, a Portuguese colony in the Guinea Gulf.

DAVIS, Jack (1845?-79?). American train and stage robber and outlaw. The Davis-Chapman gang, led by Davis and John T. CHAPMAN, pulled off the first train robbery in the American Far West, stealing over $40,000 from the Central Pacific's Train No. 1 near Verdi, Nevada, on November 4, 1870. Caught soon afterward, Davis served less than six years in prison for the crime and then teamed up with Sam BASS, Joel Collins, and some others and engaged in stage and train robbery. The gang split apart and Davis later returned to Nevada, where he reportedly died while attempting to rob a stagecoach in 1879. Wells Fargo guard Eugene Blair claimed to have killed Davis with two close-range shotgun blasts to his face; recognition of the outlaw's face was impossible, however.

DAWSON, Charles (1864-1916). British lawyer and geological forger. Many scientists were impressed when Dawson, an attorney whose avocation was geology, discovered supposed 200,000-1 million-year-old fossilized human remains in a shallow gravel excavation at Piltdown Common near Lewes in 1912. Speculation about the authenticity of the find (fragments of cranium and jawbone) subsided after British Museum specialists accepted these remains of the so-called "Piltdown Man," who was considered the "missing link" between man and ape and was formally named Eoanthropus dawsoni in honor of the celebrated

Charles Dawson, who basked in fame until his death four years
later. However, by 1954 various scientific tests on the bones
had conclusively proven that Dawson had perpetrated a hoax,
that the jawbone belonged to an orangutan and the cranium was
that of a human being no more than 50,000 years old.

DEAN, Margie [born: Margie Celano] (1896-1918). French-born
American robber. Petite and flashy, she served some time in
Illinois' Joliet prison on a conviction of stealing diamonds in
Chicago, later on hooked up with a robbery gang led by Frank
"Jumbo" Lewis, and drove the gang's getaway car when they
robbed numerous banks in the Midwest. Married to a gang
member named Dale Jones, she deftly wielded a gun to escape
capture by lawmen until November 24, 1918, when she and
Jones were surprised by Pinkerton agents and police on a Los
Angeles street. A terrific barrage from the lawmen put an end
to Jones and Dean, who managed to kill a deputy sheriff with a
shotgun blast in the fierce battle before she died.

DeANGELIS, Anthony "Tino" (b. 1915). American swindler and
embezzler. In the 1950s DeAngelis, a pudgy little man and a
high-school dropout, established a complex of 12 closely held
companies centered around the "Allied Crude Vegetable Oil Re-
fining Corporation," which increasingly bought and sold huge
amounts of cottonseed, soybean, and other salad oils on the
American commodities exchanges. But DeAngelis bribed warehouse employees to falsify inventory records of oil stored in
huge tanks in Bayonne, New Jersey, and, using forged or
worthless warehouse receipts, acquired million-dollar cash loans
from many large U.S. banks and brokerages. Through overstated actual inventories and nonexistent inventories, this audacious con man, who liked the color grey to excess, cornered
the cottonseed and soybean markets and bought up futures contracts heavily in these two commodities with credit from brokers.
Huge losses by one brokerage firm that bought on margin led
to a U.S. government investigation (1963) that exposed the
scandalous "Great Salad Oil Swindle." In 1965 DeAngelis, convicted of fraud and conspiracy, was sentenced to 20 years' imprisonment; his swindling had netted $219 million. He was re-
leased in 1972, having promised to help bring other embezzlers
to justice.

DEEMING, Alfred or Frederick [Bailey] (1853-92). Australian con
man, swindler, and murderer. In Perth in early 1892, Deeming,
using an alias and pretending to be a baron, courted wealthy
Kate Rounsville, who became suspicious when he asked her to
draw up a will with him as beneficiary before their marriage.
He tried to flee from inquiring police but was caught. An investigation disclosed that Deeming apparently had killed at least
20 persons around the world and had carried out intricate
swindles while he posed as a British noble, a rich tycoon, and

a scientist in various places, including Johannesburg, Antwerp, and Montevideo. Authorities learned that he had killed his first wife and their children at Rainhill near Liverpool, England, and later had slain his second wife in Australia, burying all of his victims in cement (the murder of his first family in the late 1880s was for no reason other than to be rid of them; however, Deeming collected life insurance from his other wife's death). Convicted, "Mad Fred," as he was dubbed, went to the gallows at the Swanston Prison in Melbourne on May 23, 1892; before he was hanged, Deeming made an incredible confession to being JACK THE RIPPER.

DE FEO, Ronald, Jr. (b. 1951). New York mass murderer. He shot and killed his father, mother, two sisters, and two brothers while they were asleep in their home in Amityville, New York, in November 1974. The next owners of the De Feo house experienced alleged hauntings, which were later described in a book, The Amityville Horror. In 1975 Ronald made an unsuccessful plea of insanity and received a total of 150 years in prison.

DeFREEZE, Donald [David] (1944-74). American revolutionary and kidnapper. Calling himself "Field Marshal Cinque," DeFreeze, an escaped convict, was a leader of the Symbionese Liberation Army (SLA), a terrorist political group that kidnapped heiress Patricia C. Hearst from her Berkeley, California, apartment on February 4, 1974. At first asking $2 million as ransom for her release, DeFreeze later ordered her father, publisher Randolph Hearst, on threat of her death, to institute a $400 million food program for the poor in the San Francisco area. Messages from the SLA then announced that Patricia had joined it; later she was seen with SLA members robbing the Hibernia Bank of California on April 15, 1974. Pressing their search for her and the SLA, FBI agents cornered DeFreeze, Camilla Hall, Nancy Ling Perry, Patricia Soltysik, and two other SLA members in a hideout in a Los Angeles suburb and killed the six in the ensuing gun battle on May 17, 1974. See also HARRIS, William.

DE HORY, Elmyr [born: Josef Hoffman] (1906-76). Hungarianborn painter and forger. Unsuccessful at selling his expressionist paintings in Europe and elsewhere, this unrecognized artist turned to forgery for a livelihood, producing hundreds of works precisely in the styles of numerous famous painters and selling them as originals with the artists' signatures. Collectors and museums throughout the world purchased his fakes of Gauguin, Cézanne, Matisse, Picasso, Modigliani, Braque, and others. Living and working on the Mediterranean island of Ibiza, Spain, after 1962, de Hory was exposed in 1967 by two vainglorious agents of his phony paintings, and ultimately he was wanted on fraud charges in France in 1976. He then committed suicide with a barbiturate overdose on Ibiza.

DE KAPLANY, Geza (b. 1926). Hungarian-born California doctor
and murderer. When Dr. De Kaplany, an arrogant anesthesiologist living in San Jose, California, was unable to consummate
his marriage to his 25-year-old wife, Hajne, a former beauty
queen, he decided "to ruin her beauty" on August 28, 1962;
he tied Hajne to the bed in their honeymoon apartment, cut
wounds into her face and body, and poured nitric, sulfuric,
and hydrochloric acid into the cuts. Hajne was found and
brought to the hospital, where she suffered excruciatingly
from De Kaplany's acid torture and died about a month later.
At his trial, De Kaplany, dubbed the "acid doctor," said he
only wanted to spoil her looks, not kill her, and pleaded not
guilty and claimed insanity; defense psychiatrists stated he
was paranoid, a latent homosexual, and a transvestite. However, De Kaplany was judged sane, convicted of murder, and
given a life prison sentence. In 1975 he was released and
quietly flown out of the country to Taiwan; asked why he had
been let go six weeks before his official parole date (his parole
had been thought an impossibility), the state parole board ex-
plained that he was needed as a heart specialist in a Taiwan
missionary hospital, although De Kaplany was an anesthesiologist whose skills had waned in 13 years behind bars and whose
medical license had been revoked.

DE LACY, Patrick O'Brien. See PANCHENKO, Dimitri.

DeLUCA, Frank (b. 1937). Illinois murderer. Deserting his wife
and children to live with young sensual Patty COLUMBO in
Lombard, Illinois, he was accused of the heinous shooting and
stabbing deaths of Patty's father, mother, and 13-year-old
brother in Elk Grove Village, outside Chicago, in May 1976.
Implicated in the crime partly because of a bloody smear left
by a man without an index finger on one hand (as was DeLuca),
he and Patty were charged with the murders and brought to
trial in 1977. Employees in DeLuca's pharmacy gave incriminating testimony against their boss, who apparently sought revenge
for an assault on him by Patty's father and carried out her
long premeditated plan to kill the hated family members. A
jury convicted the two conspirators on three counts of murder
and gave them prison sentences they could not outlive.

DE LUSSAN, Raveneau (fl. late 1600s). French pirate and author.
A well-educated gentleman in good society in France, he fell
deeply in debt and eventually decided to take up piracy to pay
off his creditors. Monsieur de Lussan crossed the Atlantic in
his ship with a crew of mainly French and English rapacious
ruffians and proceeded to ransack and pillage Spanish settlements along the northern coast of South America. At times he
took women captive and secured handsome ransoms for their
release. A pious Catholic who attended church to give thanks
for his success, this gallant Frenchman captured Panama City

and led successful plundering expeditions down the western
coast of South America before sailing back to France with much
valuable booty. His debts were paid, and later he wrote a
vainglorious book about his buccaneering adventures in the
New World.

DEMARA, Ferdinand Waldo, Jr. (b. 1921). American impostor. His
resourcefulness and audacity as an impersonator of various pro-
fessionals became legendary, eventually earning him the moniker
the "Great Impostor" and more favor than reproach in the end.
Though a high-school dropout, in the 1940s Demara affected
distinguished roles: a Trappist monk in Kentucky, a cancer
specialist in Seattle, a psychology professor in Pennsylvania,
and a prison official in Texas. As a surgeon in the Canadian
Navy during the Korean War, he performed operations and am-
putations with the help of medical texts until he was finally
exposed and discharged. In time this "harmless" culprit, who
was arrested for posing as an accredited teacher in Maine (1956)
but not indicted, established himself as a genuine ordained minister.

DE MALKER, Daisy Louisa (c. 1885-1932). South African poisoner.
An avaricious nurse, she collected insurance money on the death
of her first husband, William Cowle, in 1923 and later inherited
the savings of her second husband, Robert Sproat, whom she
had induced to leave his money to her instead of his mother
shortly before he perished in 1927. Almost five years later,
while living with her third husband, Clarence de Melker, in
Johannesburg, South Africa, she was riled by Rhodes Cowle,
her 20-year-old son from her first marriage, who demanded his
legacy but who suddenly suffered an excruciating death. A
druggist from whom Daisy had bought arsenic told police, and
an examination of the young man's corpse revealed poisoning.
The corpses of Daisy's two former husbands were exhumed, revealing strychnine poisoning. Daisy was tried, convicted, and
hanged for the three murders in 1932.

DENKE, Karl (d. 1924). German mass murderer and cannibal.
From 1918 to 1924 he was the landlord of a boarding house in
the Silesian town of Münsterberg in eastern Germany (present-
day Ziebice, Poland). Denke axed to death an estimated 30
unsuspecting men and women who lodged with him between 1921
and 1924. After cutting the corpses into pieces, he would
meticulously pickle and preserve the human meat in large vats
of brine. Precise records of "preparation" were kept by Denke
so that he knew when the meat was ready to be eaten by him.
His murderous cannibalism was discovered when a would-be victim managed to escape and tell the police, who arrested Denke
on December 21, 1924. While awaiting trial, he committed suicide in his jail cell, hanging himself with his suspenders.

D'ÉON, Chevalier. See ÉON, Chevalier d'.

DeSALVO, Albert [Henry] (1933-73). Boston rapist and mass murderer. Between June 1962 and January 1964 an unknown man,
called the "Boston Strangler," sexually assaulted and strangled
to death 13 women in the Boston area, causing a wave of hysteria among many young and old women. In the fall of 1964 a
young woman identified the Boston Strangler as Albert DeSalvo
after he had molested but not killed her in her home. DeSalvo
had served time for indecent assault and been released in April
1962. He was apprehended, confessed to scores of rapes and
to the strangulation-murders, and was incarcerated. In February 1967 DeSalvo and two other inmates broke out of the Bridgewater State Mental Prison in Massachusetts, but they were soon
caught. In 1973 unknown convicts stabbed DeSalvo to death in
his cell at Massachusetts' Walpole State Prison, where he had
been sent earlier that year.

DESHAYES, Catherine "La Voisin" (d. 1680). French sorceress
and mass murderer. Of low birth, she was married young to a
Parisian shopkeeper named Deshayes, whose business failed,
causing her to take up the occult and fortunetelling to earn a
living in the late 1660s. Her crafty prophecies soon attracted
wealthy French aristocrats, men and women, who paid her handsome sums that allowed her to purchase a mansion on rue
Beauregard in the St. Denis section of Paris. There, for exorbitant prices, she began to dispense both aphrodisiacs and
poisons to her many patrons, to be used respectively either to
arouse reluctant lovers or to murder unwanted husbands, wives,
or children. At the secret chapel in her garden in the 1670s,
Catherine, known as "La Voisin" by the coven organized by her,
performed monstrous Black Masses, sexual and sadistic rites in
which infants were slaughtered before an altar on which naked
ladies lay to be fondled by priests. Along with numerous other
noble and royal personages, the stunningly beautiful Madame de
Montespan, a mistress of France's King Louis XIV, supported
La Voisin and her veritable witches' haven. Eventually the
courtesan hired La Voisin twice to kill the king, who had
threatened to abandon her for a new court lover. Failing the
first time, La Voisin's second plot to poison King Louis was
uncovered and she was arrested and tried, exposing those she
had involved in her atrocities and admitting to have killed over
2,500 children. She was tortured on the rack and, with her
tongue cut out, burned alive at the stake in public in Paris on
February 22, 1680. De Montespan and others were banished;
others were jailed or executed.

DE SOTO, Benito (d. 1832). Portuguese pirate. In the late 1820s
a sleek brigantine called the Black Joke, captained by de Soto,
menaced shipping throughout the Atlantic. De Soto was known
for his savagery, torturing and murdering captured sailors
capriciously. In February 1832 the unarmed British bark
Morning Star, homeward bound from Ceylon (now Sri Lanka),

was attacked by the Black Joke off Ascension Island in the
South Atlantic. The pirates blasted the British ship, cutting
the rigging into shreds. They raped the women passengers
and threw them and the men into the hold. Before leaving, de
Soto split the British captain's head apart with one blow of his
cutlass. De Soto was later recognized by survivors of the
Morning Star, arrested, and convicted of murder. At Cadiz,
Spain, he was executed.

DEVOL, George H. (1829-1902). American gambler. He was a
card shark, an expert at playing three-card monte, poker, and
faro. About 1850 Devol, who was a dapper dresser, teamed up
with "Canada Bill" JONES, another gambler, and the pair made
much money from suckers who traveled the Mississippi riverboats. Sometimes Devol was assaulted by his card-playing opponents and became known for using his massive skull as a
weapon, butting his foes into unconsciousness. In 1887 Devol's
autobiography, Forty Years a Gambler on the Mississippi, was
published. He said he had made over $2 million but had lost
most of it gambling in riverboats and throughout the West.
Devol, who married and settled down in Cincinnati, Ohio, reportedly won and lost more money than any other gambler in
U.S. history.

DIABOLITO ["Little Devil"] (fl. c. 1825-32). Cuban pirate. After
the mid-1820s Diabolito, aboard his fast-sailing two-masted
schooner, became a hunted outlaw pirate because of his vicious
attacks on merchant ships, especially American, in the West
Indies. U.S. warships were unable to capture Diabolito, whose
sleek schooner outraced them among the treacherous reefs of
the area. Finally, in April 1832 a large U.S. naval fleet, commanded by David Potter, tracked Diabolito down and in a sur-
prise attack killed about 70 of his pirate crew. Diabolito
dropped out of sight soon afterward.

DIAMOND, Jack "Legs" [born: John Thomas Noland] (1896-1931).
New York racketeer and murderer. Early in life he received
the nickname "Legs" because of his ability to elude police who
pursued him after robberies. During Prohibition Diamond
worked as a hijacker, bootlegger, and gem and narcotics smuggler for Jacob "Little Augie" ORGEN. He lived a wild, flashy
life, having affairs with showgirls and making many underworld
enemies because of his double-dealings and killings. At his
Hotsy Totsy Club in mid-Manhattan in 1929, Diamond and his
favorite henchman, Charles Entratta, shot and killed two hood-
lums, William "Red" Cassidy and Simon Walker, before many
witnesses. While hiding from the police, Diamond lost control
of some rackets to Dutch SCHULTZ. Later a full-scale mob war
broke out between Diamond and Schultz. After miraculously
surviving two assassination attempts by Schultz's gunmen,
Diamond (called "unkillable" by many mobsters) was fatally shot
as he lay asleep in his bed on December 18, 1931.

DILLINGER, John [Herbert] (1903-34). American bank robber and
murderer. He spent nine years (1924-33) serving time in an
Indiana reformatory and a prison on a charge of attempted robbery. Embittered by his prison experience, Dillinger robbed
banks to establish an escape fund for his friends still in prison.
Payoffs were made, and the Dillinger gang, which included Harry Pierpont, Charles Makley, John Hamilton, and others, was
formed in October 1933. The gang stole pistols, rifles, machine
guns, sawed-off shotguns, and ammunition from police arsenals
and robbed more than ten banks in the Midwest. Dillinger's
daring and casual style caught the public's eye, especially his
supposed "wooden gun" escape from the Crown Point, Indiana,
jail on March 3, 1934 (he had been caught in Arizona and extradited to Indiana to stand trial for robbery and murder). Other
hardened criminals, such as George "Baby Face" NELSON and
Homer Van Meter, became part of the Dillinger gang, which engaged in spectacular jail breaks, fought its way out of many
police traps, and murdered 16 persons. The FBI declared Dillinger "Public Enemy Number One" and pursued him relentlessly. Various gang members, such as Hamilton and Tommy Carroll, died in shootouts with police officers, and the gang
started to fall apart. Dillinger and Van Meter underwent plastic surgery to alter their faces and fingerprints. Using the
name Jimmy Lawrence, Dillinger took up with a Chicago waitress,
Polly Hamilton, whose friend Anna Sage betrayed Dillinger to
the FBI. Outside a Chicago movie theater on July 22, 1934,
FBI agents, headed by Melvin Purvis, shot him to death. See
also LAMM, Herman K. "Baron"; SINGLETON, Ed[gar];
YOUNGBLOOD, Herbert.

DIMITRIJEVIĆ, Dragutin (1876-1917). Serbian army officer and
conspirator. A member of the general staff, he began plotting
in 1901 with other military officers to assassinate Serbia's authoritarian king, Alexander Obrenović. On June 11, 1903 a
clique of officers invaded the royal palace and murdered Alexander, Queen Draga, and some 20 court attendants. Dimitrijević, who became a recognized master at planning regicides,
was made chief of Serbian intelligence in 1913 and was promoted to colonel in 1916. He headed the Serbian nationalist
secret society Union or Death (commonly called the Black
Hand), which he had helped establish in 1911 and in which he
was known as "Colonel Apis," and was involved in the plot to
assassinate Austrian Archduke Ferdinand at Sarajevo in 1914.
Convicted with six other officers of plotting to kill the regent
in 1916, Dimitrijević was shot to death in Thessalonica (Salon-
ica), Greece, on June 27, 1917. See also PRINCIP, Gavrilo.

DINSIO, Amil [Alfred] (b. 1936). American bank burglar. His
gang stole between five and seven million dollars in two bank
burglaries within 45 days in 1972. Dinsio, who was linked to
several bank jobs in his home territory of northeastern Ohio,

thoroughly cased United California Bank's Laguna Niguel branch
before defeating the vault alarm and blowing the vault open
with explosives on the weekend of March 24-27, 1972. Over
$5 million in negotiable instruments (cash, jewels, securities,
treasury notes, and so on) were taken by Dinsio, his brother
James, his brother-in-law Charles Albert Mulligan, Philip Bruce
Christopher, and the two brothers Ronald Lee and Harry James
Barber. When the Second National Bank of Warren, Ohio (Lords-
town branch) was burglarized on May 4-5, 1972, FBI investigators recognized a definite similarity to the Laguna Niguel heist
and zeroed in on Dinsio. Sufficient evidence was gathered finally to apprehend Dinsio, Christopher, and Mulligan, the three
of whom were tried in Los Angeles and found guilty on November 2, 1973; each received 20 years' imprisonment. James Dinsio and Ronald Barber, who were separately arrested in the
winter of 1973 and were separately tried and convicted in May
1973, both got consecutive five-year and ten year prison sentences. Harry Barber was a fugitive for eight years until arrested by the FBI in Pennsylvania in 1980. Total loot recovered
from the two heists was just under $4 million.

DIO, Johnny [real name: John DioGuardi] (1915-79). American
gangster and racketeer. He worked for Murder, Inc., the enforcement squad of the crime syndicate, and was involved in
labor union racketeering in New York and elsewhere. The 1956
acid-blinding of columnist Victor Reisel was attributed to Dio,
who allegedly carried out Teamster boss Jimmy Hoffa's wish to
"silence" Reisel and his reporting about the labor rackets. Dio
was convicted of securities fraud, sentenced to 15 years, and
imprisoned at Lewisburg, Pennsylvania. He died quietly in a
Pennsylvania hospital in 1979.

DIVER, Jenny [born: Mary Jones] (1700?-1740). Irish-born
British pickpocket and robber. Early in life, her dexterous
fingers enabled her to earn considerable money as a teenage
seamstress in Northern Ireland. Moving to London in hope of
greater prosperity, she fell in with a gang of pickpockets,
easily acquired their art, and became the best known pickpocket
in England's history; her cohorts named her Jenny Diver ("diver" is a British slang word for pickpocket). Swift and efficient,
Jenny stole purses, jewelry, pocketbooks, and silverware, duping ladies and gentlemen on London's streets and in their
wealthy mansions; she often posed as a fine, fashionable lady
to gain entrance to elegant homes, employing numerous aliases
throughout her career. Though arrested several times, she
escaped conviction until 1733, but her pickpocket gang soon
gained her release by bribing officials. In 1738, however, she
was convicted and sent to Virginia as banishment. The fortune
she brought with her helped bribe a ship's captain, who transported Jenny back to England about a year later. Again caught
in London (1740) for attempted thievery, she was found guilty
and hanged at Tyburn before a silent crowd in awe of her.

DIXON, Margaret (1670-1753). Scottish murderer. In Edinburgh in 1700, she was sent to the gallows on a conviction of murdering her child. After the hanging, her body was carried away by friends for burial, and at a tavern where the group had stopped for a drink Margaret miraculously came to life in her coffin and was helped out. She revived fully and returned to Musselburgh, her hometown. The laws disallowed her execution again, and Margaret became a celebrity of sorts. She bore several children thereafter.

DOANE or DOAN, Moses (d. 1788). American robber and outlaw. During the American Revolution (1776-81) and afterward, Doane led a gang of robbers, composed of five of his brothers and 10 to 15 others, that terrorized southern New Jersey and eastern Pennsylvania, especially Bucks County, Pennsylvania. Doane and his gang, aligned with the British in anticipation of their victory, pulled off a number of daring heists, including the $4,500 robbery (a king's ransom in those days) of Bucks County treasurer John Hart, a patriot, in Newtown, Pennsylvania, on October 16, 1781. With the British surrender at Yorktown three days later, Doane became a much-sought-after wanted outlaw, along with the others of his gang, such as James FITZPATRICK, "The Sandy Flash." The gang later split up, and members were apprehended. Shortly after Doane's brothers, Abraham and Levy, were caught and hanged in Philadelphia in 1788. Doane himself was seized and hanged, too.

DOBBERT, Ernest John, Jr. (1938-84). Florida murderer. Known as "the most hated man" on death row because of the nature of his crimes, Dobbert was a convicted child killer who was electrocuted on September 7, 1984, in the Starke, Florida, prison for the fatal beating and strangulation of his nine-year-old daughter on New Year's Eve in 1971. He was also found guilty of the second degree murder (by beating) of his seven-year-old son in 1972 and of abusing and torturing his two other children. While serving a life sentence for the son's death, Dobbert, a born-again Christian, avoided two death warrants signed by Florida's governor by filing appeals and winning stays of execution.

DOBBS, Johnny [real name: Michael Kerrigan] (d. 1892). American fence and bank robber. Dobbs, an expert safecracker, worked with other bank robbers, such as George Leonidas LESLIE, and took part in the famous $2.7-million robbery of New York's Manhattan Savings Institution in 1878. At a saloon he opened on Mott Street, he reportedly fenced more than $2 million in stolen cash and securities. Dobbs, an alcoholic, lived a lavish life and spent freely. Found lying drunk in a New York City gutter, Dobbs was brought to Bellevue Hospital, where he died on May 15, 1892.

DOENITZ or DÖNITZ, Karl (1891-1980). German Nazi naval com-

mander and war criminal. During World War I (1914-18), he
served as a German U-boat (submarine) officer in the Black Sea
and the Mediterranean. After Adolf HITLER came to power in
Germany in 1933, Doenitz worked secretly with other Nazis to
rebuild the navy, despite the 1919 Versailles Treaty's prohibition against a German naval force. He developed a new U-boat
fleet, over which Hitler gave him full command in 1936. During
World War II (1939-45), Germany's U-boats, trained in "wolf-
pack" tactics and in escaping Allied sonic detection, were successfully commanded by Doenitz, whom Hitler made grand admiral of the entire German Navy in January 1943 in place of
Admiral Erich RAEDER. Hitler also designated Doenitz his successor as the Nazi supreme commander, and after Hitler's death
Doenitz led the Third Reich (Nazi Germany) for several days
before ordering the unconditional surrender of Germany to the
Allies, effective May 7, 1945. He was brought to trial and convicted with other Nazi war criminals at Nuremburg, Germany.
In 1946 he received a ten-year sentence in Berlin's Spandau
Prison. Set free in 1956, Doenitz, an unreconstructed Nazi,
lived in the vicinity of Hamburg, West Germany, until his
death on December 24, 1980.

DOLAN, "Dandy Johnny" (1851?-76). New York gangster and murderer. Dolan, a member of the dreaded Whyos, a street gang
who ruled New York City's criminal underworld after the U.S.
Civil War, invented several implements to use in gangland
fights against rivals. He made an eye gouger of copper metal
that was worn on the thumb and special fighting boots with
pieces of an axe blade in the soles. In 1875 Dolan robbed the
factory of wealthy James H. Noe and beat Noe to death, crush-
ing his skull with an iron bar and gouging out his eyeballs,
which Dolan later proudly displayed as prizes. Police tracked
down Dolan, who was found with some of Noe's possessions (but
not his eyes) and arrested. Convicted of murder, Dolan was
hanged on April 21, 1876.

DOMINICI, Gaston (fl. 1952-60). French murderer. While on a
camping trip in Provence in early August 1952, British scientist Jack Drummond, his wife, and 12-year-old daughter were
found murdered near property belonging to Dominici, a 75-year-
old French farmer. French police began an exhaustive, but
unsuccessful, investigation for the murderer. Finally, Dominici's two sons accused their father of the crime, and soon afterward Dominici admitted his guilt, which he later retracted.
Before, during, and after the trial, the Dominici family members indulged in lies, retractions, accusations, counteraccusa-
tions, denials, and contradictions. Dominici was given the
death sentence, which was commuted to life imprisonment because of his old age. In 1960 Dominici was pardoned and set
free.

DONAHUE, [Cornelius] "Lame Johnny" (1850-78). American outlaw
and lawman. Donahue, nicknamed "Lame Johnny" because of a
lame leg from a deformity, was wanted for horse rustling in
Texas in the early 1870s. He moved to Deadwood in the Dakota
territory, where he served as a popular deputy sheriff until he
was recognized as an outlaw in early 1878. Donahue took to
horse stealing again but was caught. A masked man stopped the
stagecoach on which captive Donahue was being taken to Deadwood to be jailed and rode off with him. The next day Donahue
was found dead, hanging from a tree. Some say Donahue was
guilty of some dreadful crime that warranted his mysterious
lynching. Who did it and why remain a mystery.

DONNELLY, Edward (d. 1808). Pennsylvania murderer. He often
thrashed his wife, whose screams could be heard by the people
of Carlisle, Pennsylvania. One night in early February 1808,
Donnelly violently beat his wife to death. He then cut up the
dead body and burned the pieces in the fireplace. Suspicious
townspeople found the wife's jawbone and teeth in the ashes
and arrested him. Donnelly confessed and was hanged before
several thousand spectators on February 8, 1808.

DOOLIN, Bill or William (1863-96). American stage, train, and
bank robber and outlaw. He rode with the Dalton gang in the
early 1890s. Because his horse went lame, Doolin did not fol-
low the Daltons into Coffeyville, Kansas, where the gang was
annihilated in 1892. Doolin formed another band of robbers in
Oklahoma that held up many stagecoaches, trains, and banks.
The Doolin gang, which included Dan Clifton, George "Bitter
Creek" NEWCOMB, Roy DAUGHERTY, Charlie Pierce, Dick
WEST, and others, defeated a huge posse in a gun battle at
Ingalls, Oklahoma, in September 1893. The Doolin gang broke
apart in 1895. U.S. Marshal Bill Tilghman captured Doolin in
Eureka Springs, Arkansas, and brought him to Guthrie, Okla-
homa, to stand trial. Doolin soon escaped from the federal jail
and freed 37 other prisoners. U.S. Marshal Heck Thomas
hunted him down and shot him dead with a shotgun near Law-
ton, Oklahoma. See also DALTON, Bill or William [Marion];
DALTON, Bob or Robert [Renick]; DALTON, Emmett; DALTON,
Grat[ton].

DOSS, Nannie (1905-65). Oklahoma mass poisoner. Allegedly a
latent psychopathic personality, Mrs. Doss of Tulsa, Oklahoma,
poisoned to death 11 persons, among whom were her mother,
two sisters, two children, and four husbands, collecting life
insurance money on the victims during some 30 years of undetected criminality. Finally arrested, tried, and convicted,
she admitted to the murders (1964), fatuously claiming she
committed them because of her search for an ideal "romance"
in life. Imprisoned for life, she perished from leukemia the
following year.

DOTY, Sile (1800-1876). American burglar. Doty, who spent about
20 years of his life in jail on various burglary convictions, was
known as the "King of the Hotel Thieves" and used to brag
that he could get into any hotel room anywhere in the United
States. He studied and took apart all kinds of locks and made
skeleton keys to fit them. Doty, who said he "made crime
pay," was known to bribe crooked hotel clerks and managers,
who pointed out potential victims, and sheriffs and judges, who
kept him out of jail. Doty helped circulate counterfeit money,
too.

DREHER, Tom (c. 1882-1929). Louisiana doctor and murderer. His
torrid love affair with pretty Ada Le Boeuf, one of his medical
patients and the wife of his best friend, Jim Le Boeuf, was
common knowledge in the bayou country of southern Louisiana,
so that when Jim disappeared (1927) and was later found dead
in a Louisiana lake, suspicion immediately focused on Dreher,
who was arrested by police. He confessed straightaway to
shooting Jim Le Boeuf with the help of Ada and another, whom
he had hired; they had tried to sink the victim's body, weighted
and cut open in the stomach to release air, in the lake to eliminate evidence. All three were found guilty. After Ada failed
to gain clemency from Louisiana's Governor Huey LONG, both
she and Dreher were hanged together on February 1, 1929.

DRISCOLL, Danny (1860?-88). New York gangster and murderer.
He was a member of the Whyos, a feared street gang in New
York City, and administered beatings and killings for a fee.
Driscoll and Danny LYONS were co-leaders of the Whyos by
1887. Driscoll got into an argument with Five Points gang member John McCarthy over whom Breezy Garrity, a whore, was
working for. A stray bullet fired by Driscoll at McCarthy hit
and killed Garrity. Police picked up Driscoll, who was accused
of murder, found guilty, and hanged at the Tombs on January
23, 1888, leaving one less slugger and killer on the New York
streets.

DRUCCI, Vincent (1895-1927). Chicago bootlegger and gangster.
He earned the sobriquet "The Schemer" because of his fanciful
plans to rob banks and kidnap millionaires. Drucci worked as
a bootlegger and enforcer for Charles Dion O'BANNION. He
took charge after O'Bannion's death in 1924, fighting Al CA-
PONE for certain Chicago bootleg territory. Drucci engaged in
daredevil gunfights with Capone's mob and acquired another
sobriquet, "The Shootin' Fool." He was arrested on April 5,
1927, for planning Election-Day terrorism against opponents of
Chicago Mayor William Hale Thompson. In a squad car, Drucci
tried to take a gun away from a policeman and was shot dead.

DRUITT, Montague John (1857-89). English alleged murderer.
Brainy but unbalanced, Oxford-educated Druitt failed as a

young lawyer (not as a physician, as is repeatedly claimed) and undoubtedly became progressively sexually insane and suicidal (as his family believed). In 1888 Scotland Yard suspected him of being JACK THE RIPPER; at the time he taught in a run-down private school outside London and frequented areas in the city where prostitutes worked. After the murder of one of the Ripper's last victims, Druitt tried twice to drown himself in the Thames, succeeding in early 1889.

DU BARRY, Jeanne Bécu. See GOURDON, Madame.

DUBUISSON, Pauline (b. 1926). French murderer. Jealous and carnal, young and attractive, she fatally shot her paramour Felix Bailly in his apartment in Paris on March 17, 1951. His desire to marry someone else had provoked the shooting and her subsequent unsuccessful attempt to take her own life through asphyxiation by gas. Pauline's wanton lifestyle was divulged at her trial, and yet the jury discounted it to adjudicate the case as a woman's crime of passion. Found guilty, she was not executed but given life imprisonment--a common decision by a French court for a woman defendant.

DUCK, Mock. See MOCK DUCK.

DUELL, William (fl. 1740). English murderer. Tried and convicted of killing one Sarah Griffin, he was sent to the gallows in London on November 24, 1740. After the joint hanging of Duell and four other criminals, the bodies were removed to Surgeons Hall to be anatomized. Duell's body was laid bare upon a table for washing before its dissection and, moments before the cutting, was perceived to be breathing faintly. Several hours later Duell had indeed revived and soon became a marvel from the dead gawked at by Londoners. Later he was deported from the country.

DUFF, Adolph W. See KID DUFFY.

DUMOLARD, Martin (d. 1862). French mass murderer. A loutish farm owner near the French village of Montluel, he assaulted and killed at least ten (maybe as many as 25) peasant girls, whose bodies he sexually mutilated and whose clothing he brought home as gifts to his wife (she incited him to murder for almost a dozen years). In 1861 a would-be victim of Dumolard's escaped from his clutches on a deserted road and managed to tell the authorities, who arrested him. Dumolard denied any guilt, but his wife, under interrogation, exposed his many crimes. Both of them were tried at Bourg-en-Bresse and promptly convicted, while angry French citizens shouted for their immediate executions. About two months later, on March 8, 1862, Dumolard was beheaded; his wife gained a 20-year prison sentence.

DUNNE, Reginald (d. 1922). Irish terrorist and assassin. In London on June 22, 1922, he and fellow terrorist Joseph O'Sullivan, two members of the Sinn Fein (Irish nationalist movement), shot and killed Sir Henry Hughes Wilson, a recent member of Parliament from Northern Ireland and a long-time, outspoken advocate of drastic coercion against the Irish Catholics fighting for independence from British rule. While attempting to flee in a carriage from the site of the crime--the doorsteps of Wilson's home at Eaton Place--Dunne and O'Sullivan were run down by police, caught, and jailed. At their trial, the prosecution failed to have them implicate Michael Collins, the daring revolutionary leader of the Irish Republican Army (IRA) and hero of the Irish struggle for freedom. Dunne and O'Sullivan were hanged in London's Wandsworth Prison on August 10, 1922. Twelve days later Collins was assassinated by extremist republicans in Cork, Ireland.

DURRANT, [William Henry] Theo[dore] (1874-98). California murderer. He was a good student at San Francisco's Cooper Medical College and considered an upright member of the Emanuel Baptist Church. On April 3, 1895, Durrant led pretty 18-year-old Blanche Lamont to the church library and stripped naked before her. When she resisted him, Durrant strangled her to death and dragged the body to the belfry, where he had intercourse with the corpse. When asked by police about Lamont's disappearance, Durrant said she might have been seized by white slavers to be sold as a prostitute. Later that same month Durrant murdered 20-year-old Minnie Williams in the church library after having intercourse with her. When Williams' dead body was found in a church closet and Lamont's in the belfry, Durrant was arrested. At his trial he pleaded innocent but was found guilty. Appeals delayed his hanging for nearly three years until January 7, 1898.

DUTCH HENRY [real name: Henry Borne] (d. c. 1930). American mule and horse thief. At Fort Smith, Arkansas, in 1868, he was found guilty of stealing U.S. government mules and sentenced to a long term in prison, from which he soon escaped. He then organized and led a band of horse thieves (at one time Dutch Henry had some 300 men working for him) that operated in Texas, Kansas, and other areas--his gang stole whole herds at a time. Dutch Henry, who sold stolen horses to crooks and lawmen alike, became known as the "King of the Horse Thieves" and managed to beat charges of horse stealing for many years. Authorities finally discovered that Dutch Henry (whose name became a term used for a stolen horse and later a horse thief) was a prison escapee and sent him back to prison to serve out an extended term. About 20 years later, he was released and soon disappeared from sight.

DUVAL, Claude (1643-70). French-born English highwayman.

Duval, a young handsome Frenchman, went to England in attendance on the duke of Richmond after the restoration of the monarchy in 1660. Tempted by easy money through highway robbery, Duval became a highwayman noted for his daring robberies and his chivalry to ladies. His reputation for chivalry may be overstated, for he once snatched a silver feeding bottle from the mouth of a young lady's child during a robbery (Duval was forced by one of his companions to return the bottle). Duval was caught in London while in a drunken stupor. He was tried, convicted, and hanged at Tyburn on January 21, 1670. The epitaph on his grave's memorial in Covent Garden Church reads: "Here lies Du Vall: Reader, if male thou art, Look to thy purse; if female, to thy heart."

DYER, Amelia Elizabeth (1839-96). English mass murderer. The so-called "baby farmer," she was responsible for strangling to death seven young children placed in her custody in Reading, where she resided in 1895-96, posing as a charitable woman willing to take in young boarders for a fee. When the corpses of infants in her care were found in a waterway nearby, authorities became suspicious and eventually arrested and tried Dyer, who claimed to have worked for the Salvation Army at one time. She allegedly killed other children and babies in the same way during the preceding decade or more. Ruled not insane, convicted of the murders (which she admitted to doing), Dyer was hanged at Newgate Prison on June 10, 1896.

DYNAMITE DICK. See CLIFTON, Dan.

- E -

EARP, Wyatt [Berry Stapp] (1848-1929). American gunfighter, procurer, and law officer. Earp, a sharpshooter credited with "heroic" deeds, worked on both the right and wrong side of the law. In the 1860s he was a stagecoach driver, bartender, and card shark in California. In 1871 he was indicted for horse stealing and paid a bail to get off. Made a lawman in Wichita, Kansas, in 1874, Earp served a year until being dismissed on suspicion of taking funds. He then went to Dodge City, Kansas, was made deputy marshal, and gained a meritorious reputation for cleaning up the town, ridding it of many lawbreakers and gunslingers. Earp and his friend Bat Masterson, another lawman-gunfighter, were involved in gambling and procuring in Dodge City and became known as the "Fighting Pimps." In 1879 Earp went to Texas and was involved in a gold brick swindle before traveling on to the Arizona territory. In Tombstone, Arizona, he became a saloon keeper and deputy marshal under his brother Virgil, the town's temporary marshal. By early 1881 Wyatt was embroiled in a feud with the Clanton gang, and on October 26, 1881, he, Virgil, and Morgan (another Earp brother), and

"Doc" HOLLIDAY shot and killed the two McLowery brothers,
Tom and Frank, and Billy CLANTON in a famous gunfight at
the O.K. Corral. Townspeople, wary about Wyatt and his
brothers (Wyatt was thought to have provoked the gunfight),
forced the Earps to leave after Wyatt had been cleared of a
murder charge; Wyatt's shady dealings were still suspect.
When Clanton gang members seriously wounded Virgil and killed
Morgan in 1882, Wyatt sought revenge and gunned down Frank
Stilwell and other gang members. A warrant for his arrest for
murder compelled Wyatt to move to the Idaho territory, where
he was involved in claim jumping. Later he ran saloons in
California and Alaska. Fanciful tales about Wyatt and his fast
gun made him a legendary figure in his own time and after his
death in 1929. See also BROCIUS or BROCIOUS, William "Curly
Bill"; SHORT, Luke.

EASTERN JEWEL [adoptive name: Yoshiko Kawashima] (1906-48).
Manchu princess and Japanese spy. Raised as the adopted
daughter of a Japanese military official and educated in Tokyo,
she grew to loathe her Chinese heritage and turned against her
own countrymen, engaging in sabotage and espionage for the
Japanese militarists who sought to take control of Manchuria in
1931-32. Sexually promiscuous and aggressive all her life,
Eastern Jewel had a torrid love affair with Major Ryukichi
Tanaka, leader of the Japanese Intelligence Agency in Shanghai, who made her a ruthless spy (1931). Her terrorist tactics helped the Japanese secure Manchuria and forced the last
Manchu emperor of China, Henry Pu-Yi, to serve there as a
puppet of the Japanese militarists (1934-45). Eastern Jewel,
petite and pretty, often wore men's clothing, particularly riding breeches and high black boots, and seemed to enjoy over-
powering people. She became rich from her subversive work,
but at the same time became a sybarite and sexual deviant indulging in lesbianism and pederasty. When the Chinese Nationalists under Chiang Kai-shek gained control of China after
World War II, Eastern Jewel tried to hide but was exposed by a
former lover whom she had deceived. A court sentenced her to
death for treason, and she was beheaded in 1948.

EASTMAN, [Edward] Monk [born: Edward Osterman] (1873-1920).
New York gangster. In the early 1890s he was a bouncer in
the New Irving Hall, a New York City dance hall noted for its
robberies and rapes. Eastman gathered around him a vicious
group of thugs on the Lower East Side. The Eastman gang,
which was primarily Jewish, wiped out the Whyos, a tough Irish
street gang, and battled against the Italian Five Points gang
around the turn of the century. Eastman, who carried a huge
club with notches cut into it for every one of his victims, engaged in robbery, burglary, and murder for pay and was hired
sometimes by corrupt Tammany Hall politicians. In 1904 he was
arrested and found guilty of robbery and sent to Sing Sing for

ten years. On his release, Eastman found his power was gone and went to fight in World War I. He was shot dead on December 26, 1920, by a U.S. federal agent with whom he was running a small bootlegging business. See also KID TWIST; FITZ-PATRICK, Richie; ZELIG, Jack.

EGAN, "Jellyroll" (d. c. 1920). St. Louis gangster. He organized and led a vicious criminal gang in St. Louis after the turn of the century. Egan and his men, known as "Egan's Rats," were professional "legbreakers" hired by anti-union businessmen. After Egan's death, the "Rats" were taken over by Dinty COL-BECK, who revamped them and branched out into other criminal activities.

EICHMANN, [Karl] Adolf (1906-62). Austrian Nazi SS general and war criminal. As head of the Austrian office for Jewish emigration in 1938, Eichmann soon won recognition for his swift deportation of Jews and consequently, in 1939, was made the SS (Schutzstaffel) chief in charge of the Nazis' Jewish division. During World War II (1939-45) he was a major leader in the Nazi program for the extermination of European Jews, millions of whom were incarcerated in concentration camps to suffer maltreatment, torture, medical experimentation, or finally death--some six million Jews were murdered by firing squads or in special gas chambers, whose use Eichmann strongly advocated. In 1945 Eichmann was arrested by the Allies but escaped and secretly settled in Argentina, where he was located by Israeli agents in May 1960. He was then abducted to Israel, and after a four-month trial in Jerusalem, an Israeli court convicted him of crimes against humanity and the Jewish people and condemned him to death (December 15, 1961). Eichmann was hanged in Israel on May 31, 1962, after the country's supreme court affirmed the conviction and execution.

EISEMANN-SCHIER, Ruth (b. 1942). American kidnapper. In December 1968 she helped Gary Steven KRIST abduct 20-year-old Barbara Mackle and hold her for $500,000 ransom. Barbara, buried alive underground in a coffin-like box in a pine forest outside Atlanta, breathed through two specially supplied tubes and lived on some food and water left in the box. The kidnappers received the ransom, fled, and were tracked down by the FBI. Eisemann-Schier, who became the first woman ever to be put on the FBI's Most Wanted list, was arrested in 1969 when she applied for a nursing service job and her fingerprints were routinely checked by the FBI. She pleaded guilty, saying she and Krist did it for "kicks," and received a seven-year prison sentence.

ELLIS, Ruth (1927-55). Welsh-born British murderer. She was an attractive shill (one hired to keep customers buying) in several nightclubs in London in the 1950s. Her passionate love affair with a handsome racetrack driver, David Blakely, broke up when she simultaneously carried on another liaison with a friend of Blakely, Desmond Edward Cussen. She became jealous when Blakely was seen with other women, and in Hampstead on the evening of April 10, 1955, Ruth Ellis fatally shot him on a road at close range. Immediately she surrendered to police and confessed, saying at her trial (June 20-21, 1955) she murdered Blakely because she loved him and was "very upset." Convicted (the jury decided in less than half an hour) and sentenced to death, she failed to gain clemency despite much public uproar against her death and was hanged at London's Holloway Women's Prison on July 13, 1955. Hanging was abolished in England the next year, making Ruth Ellis the last woman hanged in the country.

ENGEL, George (1837-87). German-born American anarchist. After immigrating to the United States in 1873, he joined the labor union movement, working for better wages and working conditions. A self-proclaimed anarchist, Engel was brought to trail, along with August SPIES, Adolph FISCHER, and five others, on charges of conspiracy and murder during Chicago's Haymarket Square Riot in which seven policemen were killed and some 70 others were wounded (four civilians were also slain and many other citizens injured) on May 4, 1886. Of the eight defendants, all of whom were found guilty, Engel, Spies, Fischer, and Albert Richard PARSONS were hanged on November 11, 1887; 22-year-old Louis Lingg committed suicide in his jail cell; 34-year-old Michael Schwab and 40-year-old Samuel Fielden had their death sentences commuted to life; and 36-year-old Oscar Neebe received a 15-year prison sentence.

ENGEL, Sigmund Z. (fl. 1900-1949). European and American con man and thief. For nearly 50 years he successfully played a lucrative confidence game in Europe and the United States, charmingly courting and marrying young and old, lonely, unmarried women, particularly widows, and then absconding with their money and other valuables. Engel himself claimed to have married at least 200 women and mulcted them of about $6 million. He carried on his scams in Vienna, London, and Paris before fleeing from the law to America in 1917. Always posing as a wealthy gentleman--a lawyer, banker, millionaire businessman, oil tycoon, or movie mogul--and using numerous aliases, such as Carl Arthur Laemmle, Jr. and Eugene Walter Gordon, Engel persuaded his unsuspicious victims to entrust their money to him upon their marriage and thereafter departed with it, never to be seen again. Finally, in Chicago in June 1949 he was entrapped by police during one of his schemes and put in jail. At his trial, former victims of the then 73-year-old con man testified against him, helping secure his conviction on grand larceny and a prison sentence of from two to ten years.

ENGLAND, Edward (d. 1721). English pirate. In the early 1700s he menaced shipping along the West Indian and North American coasts. In about 1718 England decided to plunder in the Eastern seas. The pirate ships Fancy, captained by England, and Victory, captained by John TAYLOR, encountered the British East Indian ship Cassandra, under Captain James Macrae, off Johanna Island near Madagascar in August 1720. The pirates seized the Cassandra with its rich cargo and, at England's urging, permitted Macrae to go free in the damaged Fancy with a skeleton crew. Taylor and the other pirates soon banished England because of his clemency to Macrae. Left in an open boat, England managed to reach Madagascar, where he died a pauper.

ENGLISH JIM. See BRISTOL BILL.

ENRICHT, Louis (d. 1922). German-born American con man and thief. Immigrating to the United States in the latter 1800s, he indulged himself in duping investors in a number of phony business dealings. His promise to construct a railway from Cripple Creek to Canon City in Colorado netted him thousands of dollars. His fraudulent offers by mail of Tenessee land, which he claimed to have inherited through his family and distant relative Patrick Henry, earned him a conviction in 1903. A group of Europeans were "taken" for a large sum by buying his fake process for manufacturing artificial stone. In 1916, when he was an elderly "scientist" living in Farmingdale, New York, Enricht announced his development of a new low-cost automobile fuel that would replace gasoline. Benjamin F. Yoakum, a former railroad magnate, invested in Enricht's National Power Motor Company and in his secret formula to change water into a fuel for cars; Henry Ford was briefly interested in purchasing the fantastic formula. In 1918 Yoakum became suspicious, brought legal action against Enricht, and exposed the hoax--there was no formula. Later Enricht managed to cheat investors in the phony Enricht Peat Corporation out of some $50,000 but was found out and sent to Sing Sing (Ossinging Correctional Facility, New York) for ten years on a conviction for grand larceny. In 1922 he was pardoned by reason of his old age after only serving a year behind bars and died shortly afterward.

ÉON, Chevalier d' [full name: Charles Geneviève Louis Auguste André Timothée d'Éon de Beaumont] (1728-1810). French diplomat and spy. Made a chevalier (knight) at age 26, he was sent by King Louis XV on a secret mission to the Russian court in 1755; reputedly disguised as a female, he induced Czarina Elizabeth not to sign a military treaty between Russia and England against France. Later, after meritorious service as a French dragoon captain, Éon performed both diplomatic and espionage work in London, where as minister plenipotentiary (1762-63) he became embroiled in a dispute with the French

ambassador and remained there, rejecting his recall and claiming
he was under the king's orders to spy disguised as a woman.
In 1775, destitute and seeking a French pension, he returned
home under governmental orders that he dress as a female; he
got his pension but was forced by decree of the new king,
Louis XVI, to wear female clothing until his death. Debates
raged and bets were made about his "true" sex, which was
verified as male by an autopsy after his death in London on
May 21, 1810. From his name was derived the word "eonism,"
meaning the adoption by a male of female dress and mannerisms.

ESPINOSA, Felipe (d. 1863). Mexican murderer and outlaw. Seeking vengeance for the loss of family members during the Mexican
War (1846-48), Felipe, his two brothers Julian and Victorio, and
other Mexican kin invaded Colorado territory in 1861, declaring
they would kill 600 Americans as "justice." They managed to
slay 26 American miners, loggers, soldiers, and others by mid-
1863, when Felipe asked that the Espinosas be given 5,000
acres in exchange for an end to the killings. The territorial
governor rejected the offer and instead placed a $2,500 reward
on Felipe's head. Posses and vigilantes combed Colorado for
the Espinosas, especially Felipe. Victorio, though to be Felipe,
was caught near Fairplay and lynched. Tom Tobin, a scout commissioned by the U.S. Army, led a 15-man force that trapped
Felipe and Julian, but Tobin, not wanting to share the reward
money, slipped away, surprised, and shot the brothers dead.
He cut off their heads as proof he had killed them and returned
to Fort Garland, Colorado, to get the reward. Because of insufficient funds, Tobin only received $1,500 and some buckskins.
The "Espinosa heads," preserved in special fluid, were displayed for several years throughout the West.

ESPOSITO, Joseph "Diamond Joe" (1872-1928). Italian-born Chicago
bootlegger and racketeer. He organized union laborers and
financed businesses in Chicago in the early part of the 1900s.
In August 1908 Esposito shot and killed his barber Mack Gea-
quenta during an argument. The case was dismissed when witnesses disappeared or refused to testify. Esposito prospered
and earned the nickname "Diamond Joe" because of his habit of
wearing diamonds--cuff links, shirt studs, rings, diamond belt
buckles, and so on. During Prohibition he operated a vast
bootlegging business, with illegal stills in Melrose Park and
Chicago, and ingratiated himself with important Chicago politicians by delivering the "vote." Esposito was machine-gunned
to death during a mob war with Al CAPONE in 1928.

ESQUEMELING or EXQUEMELING or OEXMELIN, Alexander Olivier or
John (c. 1645-1707). Dutch or French pirate and author. In
1666 he sailed to the West Indies in the service of the French
West India Company and, for a while, served as a merchant
clerk on Tortuga Island off Haiti. Esquemeling became a servant

first owned by a cruel French official and then by a kind surgeon, who gave him his liberty. Joining with the buccaneers
on Tortuga, a notorious pirate rendezvous, he participated in
numerous piratical depredations, sea fights, and adventures,
which he recorded, along with stories told to him by other sea
rovers. In 1672 he returned to Europe, where he completed
a book entitled, De Americaenshe Zeerovers (The Buccaneers of
America, 1678), which became an important historical source
about piracy.

ESTES, Billie Sol (b. 1923). Texas farmer and con man. His
large, elaborate, and fraudulent farming scams were exposed
in 1962. Estes, a flamboyant Texas cotton farmer, was fined
by the U.S. Agriculture Department for cotton acreage allotment irregularities. Shortly afterward he was found guilty of
persuading farmers in Texas and other states to invest in nonexistent fertilizer tanks and was given a 15-year prison sentence. To cover the purchase of his fertilizer and equipment,
Estes evidently secured multimillion-dollar mortgages and loans
from many banks and financial institutions. In 1971 he was
paroled, with the stipulation he not engage in any promotional
schemes. In 1979 Estes was convicted of swindling investors,
securing loans on nonexistent oil-field cleaning equipment, and
received two five-year prison sentences.

EUSTACE THE MONK (d. 1217). Flemish pirate. Because of increased trade and shipping in European waters during the
Middle Ages, many persons turned pirate. Eustace, a Flemish
cleric with supposedly magical powers, was one; he sold his
services to King John of England and plundered French shipping in and around the English Channel. Because he began
to rob from English ships as well, Eustace was hunted down
and had to flee from England. He then became a pirate for the
French. In 1217, Eustace led an unsuccessful French invasion
of England across the Straits of Dover. He was captured by
the English and beheaded.

EUSTACHY, Lauren (fl. 1884). French doctor and would-be
poisoner. The sole, long-time physician in the village of
Pertius in southern France, Eustachy attempted unsuccessfully
to discredit young Dr. Tournatoire after he had established his
practice there and had taken away some of Eustachy's patients.
A libel suit ended with the old doctor paying a large sum. In
1884 Tournatoire received in the mail an anonymous gift (supposedly from an appreciative patient of his) of several cooked
thrushes, a delicacy. Tournatoire's wife and chef ate the birds
and afterward became gravely ill but recovered. Tournatoire
dissected the remains of the thrushes, discovering much atropine, a poisonous drug derived from belladonna. Suspicion
immediately centered on Eustachy, who was tried and confessed
to the attempted murder. He spent eight years in jail for the
crime.

EVANS, Chris[topher] (1847-1917). California train robber and
outlaw. With the Sontag brothers, Evans headed the notorious
California Outlaws, a band of train robbers who waged a bloody
campaign against the Southern Pacific Railroad in the 1880s and
early 1890s. Evans and the others were angry over the railroad's "seizure" of property from ranchers, farmers, and settlers in the San Joaquin Valley, California. The California
Outlaws robbed only the Southern Pacific's safes in its railroad
express cars, ignoring passengers' money and the U.S. mails.
Evans was wounded several times in gun battles with railroad
and Pinkerton men; one wound blinded his right eye. In June
1893 he and John SONTAG fought an eight-hour gunfight, the
battle of Simpson's Flats, against a huge posse at the outlaws'
hideout in central California. A deputy lawman was killed;
others were seriously wounded, including Evans and John.
Evans survived and was sent to prison in Fresno, California.
Later Ed MORRELL, a California Outlaw member who worked
as a spy, helped Evans escape from prison, but both were
captured weeks later and sentenced to life imprisonment. Evans
was paroled in 1911 and lived the rest of his life with his family in Portland, Oregon. See also SONTAG, George.

EVERLEIGH, Ada [real name: Ada Lester?] (1876-1960). American
madam. In 1898 she and her sister, Minna, both show girls,
bought a bordello in Omaha, Nebraska, as an "investment,"
stocked it with beautiful prostitutes who charged high prices,
and made money from steady customers during the Trans-
Mississippi Exposition in the city that year. Afterward Ada
and Minna moved to Chicago, where they purchased Madam
Effie Hankins's brothel, which had once belonged to Lizzie
ALLEN, and turned it into a magnificent high-class sex em-
porium filled with exquisite furnishings and 30 stunning, graceful, and intelligent courtesans. On February 1, 1900, the
Everleigh Club opened its doors and was soon patronized by
celebrities, millionaires, politicians, gangsters, and others who
paid the highest prices to indulge their sexual fantasies. "The
Scarlet Sisters," as Ada and Minna came to be called, remained
in business for slightly more than a decade, paying much money
to crooked politicians, policemen, and gangsters (such as "Big
Jim" COLOSIMO) for protection from the law. Ada, the "brains"
of the business, encouraged the girls to read and improve
their minds and to be proud to be in the Everleigh Club (more
than 400 girls worked in the club over the years, and many
of them retired with small fortunes). A reform movement to
clean up Chicago's red-light district forced the Everleigh sisters to close the club in 1911. After taking a long vacation
in Europe, Ada and Minna bought a mansion in Manhattan,
where they lived out their lives in grand, genteel fashion as
millionaires. See also EVERLEIGH, Minna.

EVERLEIGH, Minna [real name: Minna Lester?] (1878-1948).
American madam. After successfully running a whorehouse in

Omaha, Nebraska, Minna and her older sister, Ada, opened a grand sex palace in Chicago in 1900 and became world-renowned as madams who knew how to cater to male fantasies and chauvinism. The Everleigh Club on Dearborn Street was furnished with rich carpets and tapestries, expensive objects d'art and paintings, gilt-edged mirrors and spittoons, and large ornate brass beds inlaid with marble. Stylish and charming ladies of the evening serviced the clientele, who paid handsomely for the best "lovemaking" and who wined and dined at the club without fear of scandal. Minna and Ada wore silk gowns and glittering jewels and provided the same for their bevy of courtesans, who were coached in their dress, makeup, and manners (many of the young women who worked for the Everleigh sisters married millionaires, politicians, and gentlemen). Minna and Ada retired in 1911 when Chicago authorities began a reform drive against vice; they later settled in New York City and lived to ripe old age. Minna died on September 16, 1948, at the age of 71, and Ada died on January 3, 1960, at the age of 84. See also EVERLEIGH, Ada.

EVERY, Henry (c. 1653-c. 1710). English pirate. He drifted from honest seamanship to piracy, lured by the riches to be had by plundering Arab and Indian galleons. In 1694 Every, also known as John Avery or Long Ben Avery, led a successful mutiny aboard the Charles II, which was renamed the Fancy. For the next two years Every on the Fancy captured treasure ships in the Red Sea and the Indian Ocean. His seizure of the Gang-i-Sawai and the Fateh Mohamed in 1695 netted him and his crew some £600,000 in gold, silver, and jewels. Every became "The Arch Pirate," known for his depredations throughout the Eastern and Western seas. In the Bahamas he gave up piracy, dispersed his crew, and changed his name to Benjamin Bridgeman. About 1697 Every sailed to Ireland, landing near Londonderry and then dropping out of sight forever. Some say he lived the life of a squire; others say he died many years later as a pauper.

EYRAUD, Michel. See BOMPARD, Gabrielle.

- F -

FAHY, Bill or William J. (1886-1943). American postal inspector and robber. After the successful $2 million robbery of a U.S. mail train at Roundout, Illinois, on June 12, 1924, U.S. postal inspector Fahy was put in charge of solving the crime, but his investigation uncovered nothing. Other postal agents were assigned to the case and managed to capture some of the robbers, who said they had inside information that enabled them to pull off the perfectly timed heist. When it was discovered that Fahy was secretly trying to disrupt the case, he was suspected and was entrapped as the robbery gang's inside informant. Although he maintained he was innocent, Fahy was convicted with the other gang members and sentenced to 25 years' imprisonment. Released in 1937, he claimed he would prove his innocence but failed to do so in the next six years before his death.

FAISAL, Prince. See ABDUL AZIZ, Faisal ibn Musad.

FALL, Albert B[acon] (1861-1944). American politician convicted of graft. He served as U.S. senator from New Mexico from 1912 to 1921, when President Warren G. Harding made him Secretary of the Interior. Fall, who was in need of money (his properties were heavily mortgaged), secretly leased valuable naval oil reserves in Teapot Dome, Wyoming, and Elk Hills, California, to Harry F. Sinclair's Mammoth Oil Company and Edward L. Doheny's Pan-American Company. In return, Fall received $100,000 from Doheny and $260,000 from Sinclair. An investigation by the Senate resulted in the cancellation of oil leases and criminal prosecutions against Fall, Doheny, and Sinclair (the three were indicted for bribery and conspiracy to defraud the government). Doheny and Sinclair were acquitted, but Fall was convicted and served a year in prison (1931-32). After his release from the New Mexico State Penitentiary, Fall lived as a broken man and in poor health until he died in El Paso, Texas, in 1944.

FARNESE, Giulia. See ALEXANDER VI.

FARRINGTON, Hilary (d. 1870). American Confederate guerrilla and outlaw. He and his brother Levi fought with William Clarke QUANTRILL during the U.S. Civil War (1861-65). The Farringtons continued their depredations after the war. In 1870 Hilary and Levi, accompanied by William Barton and Bill Taylor, robbed a Southern Express train in Union City, Tennessee. William Pinkerton and railroad detectives caught Barton and Taylor at Lester's Landing, Mississippi, and Hilary at Verona, Missouri. While being extradited to Tennessee aboard the sternwheeler Illinois, Hilary tried to escape and fell overboard in a fight with Pinkerton. He was crushed to death by the ship's stern paddle. See also FARRINGTON, Levi.

FARRINGTON, Levi (d. 1871). American Confederate guerrilla and outlaw. During the U.S. Civil War (1861-65) he and his brother Hilary rode with William Clarke QUANTRILL, terrorizing towns in Missouri and Kansas. The Farringtons committed many robberies after the war, including the 1870 robbery of a Southern Express train at Union City, Tennessee. In 1871 Levi was caught by Pinkerton detectives in Farmington, Illinois. Brought back to Union City to stand trial, Levi was grabbed by angry citizens and hanged. See also FARRINGTON, Hilary.

FAWKES, Guy (1570-1606). English conspirator. A convert to

Roman Catholicism, he left Protestant England to enlist and fight in the Spanish army in Flanders. Eleven years later, in 1604, he returned to enter into a conspiracy (later called the Gunpowder Plot), led by Robert CATESBY, to blow up the English houses of Parliament at Westminster in reprisal for increasingly harsh penal laws against Catholics in England. The small band of conspirators rented a cellar area that extended under the Parliament buildings and secretly concealed there at least 20 barrels of gunpowder, ready to be exploded on November 5, 1605, when Parliament was to be opened by King James I. The plot was discovered through a letter sent by one of the conspirators, Francis Tresham, to his Catholic brother-in-law Lord Monteagle, urging him not to be present at Parliament's opening in order to avoid "a terrible blow." Fawkes was arrested when entering the cellar on the night of November 4, 1605. Under torture on the rack, he identified his co-conspirators, four of whom, including Catesby, were killed while resisting arrest. The rest were caught, tried, convicted, and executed (1606). Fawkes, who was hanged opposite the Parliament buildings on January 31, 1606, is remembered during England's annual celebration of Guy Fawkes Day (November 5), when there are fireworks, bonfires on which little effigies of the conspirator ("guys") are burned, and masked children begging for "a penny for the guy."

FAY, Larry (fl. 1920s). New York bootlegger and racketeer. A hedonist, he owned extensive bootlegging interests and several speakeasies (saloons) and clubs in New York City during Prohibition. For a while some of his establishments, which were partly financed by the gambler Arnold ROTHSTEIN, starred Texas Guinan, whose remark, "Hello, sucker" to a patron became famous as a literal come-on. Fay controlled, ironically, New York City's milk rackets at the time. Such leading racketeers as Jack "Legs" DIAMOND, Waxey GORDON, and Jacob "Little Augie" ORGEN fraternized with the wealthy, fun-loving Fay, whom the author F. Scott Fitzgerald, Fay's one-time neighbor in Great Neck, New York, in the early 1920s, used as the basis for his ill-fated main character in The Great Gatsby (1925).

FAZEKAS, Mrs. Julius (c. 1865-1929). Hungarian mass poisoner. The chief midwife in the neighboring Hungarian villages of Nagyrev and Tiszakurt, she successfully performed illegal abortions for fees from about 1911 to well into the 1920s. She began secretly selling arsenic poison to promiscuous village wives whose husbands and other family members were unwanted and thus suffered untimely deaths after consuming poisoned food. As scores of men perished in the district, police received anonymous tips implicating Mrs. Fazekas in 1929. But before she could be apprehended, she poisoned herself to death in her house, and afterward some of those involved with her, including the murderous prophetess Susanna, or Susi, OLAH, were rounded up and brought to trial for murder in Szolnok. Among the 26 tried, 18 received long prison sentences and eight were executed. Probably the vilest of those hanged was 66-year-old Juliane Lipka, who confessed to seven poisonings that included her husband, stepmother, brother, aunt, and sister-in-law--all committed in order to become a rich landowner by inheritance.

FEDORENKO, Fyodor (b. 1907). Ukrainian-born Nazi war criminal. Drafted into the Soviet army in 1941 during World War II, he was captured by the Germans and, while being held a prisoner, was chosen for training as a prison guard. As a Nazi guard in the Treblinka concentration camp in Poland in 1942 and 1943, Fedorenko took part in mercilessly persecuting Jews and other prisoners, some 900,000 of whom were exterminated at the camp during the war. In 1949 he entered the United States, concealing his Nazi service at Treblinka, and thus illegally obtained U.S. citizenship later in 1970. He worked in a factory in Waterbury, Connecticut, until his retirement to Miami, Florida, in 1976, and subsequently was exposed during a U.S. government investigation pursuing Nazi war criminals who fraudulently entered the country. In late 1984 Fedorenko, who had vainly appealed his case all the way to the Supreme Court, became the first war crimes deportee from the United States to the Soviet Union, which he had visited several times over the past decade and which had agreed to take him.

FELICIANI, Lorenza. See SERAFINA, Countess.

FENAYROU, Marin (d. 1882). French murderer. His much younger wife, Gabrielle, who had only married him--an apothecary-- because he could help her father's failing pharmacy in Paris, carried on a love affair with young Louis Aubert without Marin knowing it for years. Enraged because of Aubert's final decision to marry someone else, Gabrielle confessed her infidelity to Marin, inducing him to kill Aubert, whose corpse was found in the Seine River on May 28, 1882. Gabrielle acknowledged her part in the crime when questioned by gendarmes, and at the trial Marin told how he had stabbed her lover in the heart, where figuratively he had been speared by the affair. Marin was executed, and his wife received life imprisonment but was pardoned in 1903.

FERNANDEZ, Raymond [Martinez] (1914-51). American swindler and murderer. He and Martha BECK, two sexually maladjusted people, defrauded members of Lonely Hearts clubs in New York and elsewhere in the late 1940s. Fernandez wooed love-starved women, arranging to marry them and transferring their assets to him (Beck helped in the role of his sister). Afterward the pair murdered the women. Arrested in Grand Rapids, Michigan,

for the murder of a 41-year-old widow and her child, Fernandez
and Beck confessed, admitting also to murdering a 60-year-old
widow in New York. The sexual aberrations of the two murderers were exposed sensationally during their 44-day trial in New
York. Despite a defense of insanity, the pair was judged sane
and found guilty of murder. They died in the electric chair at
Sing Sing Prison on March 8, 1951.

FIELD, "Pinny" [Eugene, II] (1880-early 1940s). American forger.
Son of the celebrated American journalist and poet Eugene Field,
who is well known for his children's verse, "Pinny" (a nickname
given him in childhood when he wore a pinafore) apparently
shamelessly imitated his father's signature and handwriting, as
well as those of Mark Twain, Bret Harte, and other notables,
and adroitly wrote in their individual styles on flyleaves and
title pages of his father's books and other works, which he
then sold as authentic for tidy sums to unsuspecting customers.
Audaciously, he wrote inscriptions in books in his father's
hand, added false notarizations that stated books came from his
father's personal library, and forged sketches by his father
and Twain. After the 1920s, when Pinny disposed of much
bogus material, he faded from view and died sometime in the
early 1940s.

FIELDEN, Samuel. See ENGEL, George; SPIES, August.

FIESCHI, Giuseppe Maria or Joseph Marie (1790-1836). Corsican-
born thief, conspirator, and killer. After serving as a French
soldier during the Napoleonic Wars (1803-15), he returned to
his native Corsica, a French province since 1769, where he was
subsequently convicted of thievery and imprisoned for ten
years (1816-26). In the early 1830s Fieschi moved to Paris
and there secured government work under the alias Gérard.
Later he joined with Pierre Pépin and Pierre Morey, two republican rebels opposed to the repressive, conservative rule
of Louis Philippe, king of the French. Together they constructed an "infernal machine" of 25 guns that went off simultaneously and, on July 28, 1835, fired their contraption at the
king as he moved along the Boulevard du Temple in front of
their dwelling place. Louis Philippe was unscathed, but 18
persons were killed and many were wounded. Fieschi, Pépin,
and Morey were apprehended, convicted, and sent to the guillotine in Paris on February 19, 1836. The king instituted further repression after the attempt on his life, one of several
during his reign.

FINCH, [Raymond] Bernard (b. 1918). California murderer.
Finch, a doctor in Los Angeles, divorced his first wife to
marry Barbara Daugherty, the wife of his best friend. Their
marriage soon fell apart when Finch fell in love with Carole
Tregoff. On July 18, 1959, Barbara Finch was found shot to

death outside their home in West Covina, California. The
Finches' maid said she saw the doctor standing over his wife
with a pistol in his hand, while Tregoff huddled in the bushes.
Finch and Tregoff were charged with murder, but a hung jury
failed to convict at their first trial. At a subsequent trial on
March 27, 1961, both of them were found guilty of second-degree
murder and were given life imprisonment. Tregoff was released
in 1969, Finch in 1971.

FISCHER, Adolph (1859-87). German-born American anarchist. At
the age of 15 he immigrated to the United States and later became actively involved in the labor movement as an avowed socialist and anarchist. He participated in the Haymarket Square
Riot in Chicago on May 4, 1866, when seven police and four civilians were killed and some 100 other people were injured.
Fischer, August SPIES, George ENGEL, Albert PARSONS, Rudolph Schnaubelt, and four other indicted anarchists were to
stand trial for the Haymarket Square killings, but Schnaubelt
disappeared beforehand and was never located again. All were
found guilty, but only Fischer, Spies, Engel, and Parsons were
executed (November 11, 1887). One of the convicted killed
himself in his cell, and the three others received prison sentences.

FISH, Albert (1870-1936). American kidnapper, torturer, mass
murderer, and cannibal. He took a strange delight in inflicting
pain on himself and others. Fish encouraged children to beat
their buttocks until they bled, stuck countless needles into his
body, and burned himself with hot needles and pokers. Psychiatrists at New York's Bellevue Hospital examined Fish several
times and released him as disturbed but sane. From about 1910
to 1934 Fish worked as a house painter, moving from town to
town, state to state. During this time he abducted, tortured,
killed, cut up, and ate at least 15 children (he later admitted
to molesting more than 400 children over a 20-year span).
Fish's unsigned letter to the mother of one of his young victims, telling what he had done, was traced by the police. Soon
arrested, Fish confessed to butchering many children. At his
trial, he was judged guilty and sane and sentenced to death.
The prospect of dying in the electric chair excited Fish. Two
massive jolts of electricity were needed to kill him at Sing Sing
on January 16, 1936.

FISHER, John King (1854-84). Texas gunfighter and lawman.
Fisher, one of the fastest draws in Texas, was said to have
shot and killed seven men in gun duels in 1878. His cattle
ranch in southern Texas was the headquarters for numerous
cattle rustlers and gunslingers in the late 1870s. Fisher often
worked closely with Mexican cattle rustlers, buying and selling
their livestock, as well as brokering his own stolen cattle with
them. The Texas Rangers arrested Fisher many times but were

unable to prove him guilty of rustling or murder. Suddenly in 1880 Fisher reformed himself into a respected rancher and was made deputy sheriff of Uvalde County the next year. By chance he ran into an old friend from his gunfighting days, Ben THOMPSON, in 1884, and together they rode to San Antonio, where they were both killed in a gunfight with Billy Simms, Joe Foster, and Jacob Coy while attending a show in a vaudeville theater.

FITZGERALD, Elizabeth McMullin. See ZINGARA, Madame.

FITZPATRICK, James (1760?-87). American robber and outlaw. He rode with the loyalist Doane gang during the American Revolution (1776-81), robbing wealthy patriotic landowners and others in eastern Pennsylvania and parts of New Jersey. Fitzpatrick, a handsome, dashing, and daring Irishman, became the model for "The Sandy Flash" in American author Bayard Taylor's best-seller, Story of Kennett. By 1783 Fitzpatrick had formed his own gang, and he brazenly committed robberies until a posse trapped and caught him near Chester, Pennsylvania, where he was hanged in January 1787. See also DOANE or DOAN, Moses.

FITZPATRICK, Richie (1880-1905). New York gangster. He was one of the few non-Jews in Monk EASTMAN's gang that operated in New York City around the turn of the century. Eastman particularly delighted in Fitzpatrick's murderous trickery when doing away with enemies. In 1904, when Eastman was sent to prison on a conviction of robbery, a rivalry developed between Fitzpatrick and KID TWIST for leadership of the Eastman gang, which broke into warring factions. In 1905 Kid Twist arranged a conference to settle the internecine gang war. As supposed peace talks began between Fitzpatrick and Kid Twist in a Chrystie Street bar, the lights suddenly went out and gunshots were heard. When the police arrived, Fitzpatrick lay dead on the floor with his arms neatly folded across his chest.

FLAHERTY, James I. See McGINNIS, [Joseph Francis] "Big Joe."

FLANNELFOOT. See VICARS, Henry Edward.

FLORES, Juan (1835-57). Mexican-born California robber, murderer, and outlaw. Flores, convicted and imprisoned for horse rustling, and several fellow prisoners broke out of San Quentin in 1856, seizing a ship tied up at the prison's wharf and sailing off to "take over" Australia. But strong winds and tides drove the ship ashore south of Los Angeles, and the fugitives hid in the hills near San Juan Capistrano and went on a blood-thirsty rampage of robbery, holding up stagecoaches, supply wagons, and stores. The gang seized settlers and travelers, held them for ransom, and killed them if the ransoms were not paid. Flores was pursued by large posses, whose members were often

gunned down, and remained at large until February 1, 1857,
when possemen under Doc Gentry captured him. Flores quickly
escaped but was recaptured two days later. He was sentenced
to death by a "popular vote" and was hanged in Los Angeles on
February 14, 1857.

FLOYD, [Charles Arthur] "Pretty Boy" (1901-34). American bank
robber and murderer. Unable to find legitimate work in eastern
Oklahoma in the mid-1920s, Floyd turned to crime, committing a
payroll robbery for which he was arrested and sent to prison.
Released after three years, Floyd hooked up with other robbers
and gangsters in Kansas City, Missouri, and learned how to use
a machine gun, his main weapon. In 1930 he was arrested for
robbing a bank in Sylvania, Ohio, and while being taken to
prison made a daring escape through an open window of a moving train. Floyd teamed up with Bill "The Killer" MILLER and
went on bank robbing sprees in Michigan, Kentucky, and Ohio.
Part of the time they traveled with two girls from Mother Ash's
brothel in Kansas City, where Floyd supposedly picked up his
nickname "Pretty Boy" from the whores (he always loathed the
name). After a shootout with lawmen in Bowling Green, Ohio,
in June 1931 (Floyd killed the chief of police), Floyd ran for
cover to Oklahoma, where he joined forces with preacher George
Birdwell to rob more banks. To the poor Okie sharecroppers
Floyd became "The Robin Hood of the Cookson Hills," where
"sometimes a fella got to sift the law." To his dying day, Floyd
denied the FBI claim that he was the machine-gunner who murdered five lawmen in the Kansas City Massacre of June 17, 1933.
FBI agents, led by Melvin Purvis, cornered him in an open field
near East Liverpool, Ohio, and shot him dead on October 22,
1934.

FORD, Bob or Robert [Newton] (1860-92). American robber, outlaw,
and assassin. A cousin of Frank and Jesse JAMES, he was a
member of the Jameses' second gang, which included his brother
Charles Ford, Dick LITTLE, Wood HITE, Ed Miller, and Bill
Ryan. The gang robbed banks, trains, and stagecoaches in
Missouri, Iowa, and Alabama between 1879 and 1881. Missouri
Governor Thomas T. Crittenden secretly met with the Ford
brothers, evidently offering them pardons and $10,000 in re-
ward money to kill Jesse James. On April 3, 1882, Charles and
Bob Ford visited Jesse at his home in St. Joseph, Missouri,
and Bob fatally shot him in the back while he was hanging a
picture. Bob surrendered to authorities, was tried, and convicted of murder; however, he and Charles were granted pardons by the governor and handed the reward money. Billed
as "The Outlaws of Missouri," the Fords made stage appear-
ances throughout the country, telling how they killed Jesse,
but they often received boos and catcalls from audiences that
considered them "cowards." Charles committed suicide in a
Richmond, Missouri, hotel room on May 6, 1884. Bob, who

turned to drinking heavily, moved west and operated a gambling
saloon in Walsenburg, Colorado, for a short time and then a tent
saloon-brothel in Creede, Colorado. On June 8, 1892, Edward
O'KELLY, a relative of the outlaws John, Jim, Bob, and Cole
YOUNGER, blasted Bob to death in his saloon.

FORD, Charley or Charles. See FORD, Bob or Robert [Newton].

FORD, Emma (1870?-1903?). American robber and mugger. She
was a large, powerful black woman, over six feet tall and
weighing more than 200 pounds, who terrorized Denver, Chicago, and New York in the 1890s and early 1900s. Ford was
particularly notorious in Chicago's South Side, where she alone
or with her sister Pearl Smith used brass knuckles, razors,
knives, bats, and guns to attack and rob men. She worked in
"panel houses"--brothels that specialized in robbing the customer while he was occupied in bed with a prostitute. Ford disappeared in 1903 and was thought to have been killed by a gang
of male hoods.

FRANCIS, Willy (1930-47). Louisiana murderer. Sentenced to die
for a murder he committed at the age of 15, Francis was sent
to Louisiana's electric chair in 1946 but, because of a current
malfunction, received a low jolt and survived. His lawyers then
argued that sending Francis a second time to the chair was
"cruel and unusual punishment." The case was appealed to the
U.S. Supreme Court, which said that the first attempt to execute Francis was only cruel because of an accident and thus
"did not make the subsequent execution any more cruel in the
constitutional sense than any other execution." Francis was
successfully electrocuted in May 1947.

FRANK, Hans (d. 1946). German Nazi lawyer, leader, and war
criminal. In 1927, soon after his graduation from law school,
Frank joined the German National Socialist (Nazi) party and
rose to become head of the party's legal department by the
early 1930s. After the establishment of the Third Reich (Nazi
Germany) under Adolf HITLER in 1933, he was made a Reichsminister and helped formulate and institute laws against the
Jews and opponents of National Socialism, the Nazis' ideology.
In addition, he carried out Hitler's will to regiment the country's institutions and culture. With the Nazi conquest of Poland in 1939, Hitler appointed Frank governor general of Poland, a position in which he soon ruthlessly and summarily
sentenced and executed over 3,500 Polish intellectuals, many
of them Jews. By orders of Frank, the property of hundreds
of thousands of Poles and Jews was confiscated without compensation, and many of Poland's inhabitants were seized and
placed in camps as slave workers during World War II (1939-
45). At the Nuremberg war-crimes trial (1945-46), Frank
showed penitence for his enormities. He was convicted and

later was hanged as a war criminal at West Germany's Nuremberg
Prison on October 16, 1946.

FRANKLIN, Ed. See MUSGROVE, Lee H.

FRANKLIN, [Rufus] "Whitey" (1912-?). American bank robber and
murderer. Before the age of 18, Franklin received a life sentence in prison for murder in Alabama, but authorities there
released him after six years because of his youth. Shortly afterward he was arrested for bank robbery and sent to Alcatraz
for 30 years. In 1938 Franklin, Jimmy LUCAS, and Tom Limerick made an unsuccessful attempt to escape, during which a
prison guard and Limerick were killed. Franklin and Lucas
were tried and received life sentences for the guard's murder
(many Alcatraz guards felt they deserved the death penalty
instead). Franklin was placed in solitary confinement and reportedly was beaten by guards. He remained in isolation, never
seeing another prisoner and not being talked to by the guards
for more than seven years, probably until his death. There
are no public reports that Franklin was released from solitary
confinement, paroled, or died in prison.

FRICK, Wilhelm (1877-1946). German Nazi minister of the interior
and war criminal. Although he took part in the abortive 1923
Munich "beer-hall putsch" (coup) staged by Adolf HITLER,
Frick was not imprisoned because of his strong connections in
Munich's police department, where he was an official. In 1924
he was elected to the Reichstag (Germany's legislature), where
he became the leader of the Nazi politicians there in 1928. Appointed minister of the interior of the Third Reich (Nazi Germany) in 1933, Frick was instrumental in the promulgation of the
1935 Nuremberg Laws depriving Jews of civil rights, including
marriage with non-Jews, and persons of partly Jewish descent
of certain rights; he also helped institute strict Nazi party control of all local governments in Germany. During World War II
(1939-45), Frick lost his ministerial post to Heinrich HIMMLER
and was made Reich "protector" of Bohemia and Moravia, German-
occupied territories (1943). In 1946 the International Military
Tribunal convicted him of war crimes, crimes against humanity,
and crimes against peace, and he was hanged in Nuremberg,
West Germany, on October 16 of that year.

FRISCO SUE (1853-?). American prostitute and stagecoach robber.
In 1876, after a stint as a whore in San Francisco, Frisco Sue,
a stunning beauty, moved to Nevada to make it rich as a gold
robber. She and Sims Talbot held up a stagecoach, netted only
$500, and made plans to hold up the same stage again, thinking
the stage line would now put a valuable shipment aboard because robbers wouldn't immediately be expected to hold up the
same stage twice in a row. During the second holdup, Talbot
was shot dead by a stage guard and Frisco Sue was captured.

She served three years in prison and afterward disappeared. Some accounts say she married a millionaire in San Francisco and thus "struck it rich."

FRITH, Mary. See CUTPURSE, Moll.

FROMME, [Lynette Alice] "Squeaky" (b. 1950). American would-be assassin. A devoted disciple of Charles MANSON, Fromme, wearing a long bright red robe, stood in a large crowd that greeted U.S. President Gerald R. Ford as he arrived at California's state capitol in Sacramento on September 5, 1975. Somehow not listed by the Secret Service as one who might pose a threat to the President, Fromme managed to move very close to Ford, point a .45-caliber revolver at him, and pull the trigger. The gun didn't go off, and immediately Secret Service agent Larry M. Buendorf grabbed it. Fromme became the first person charged with and convicted of attempted assassination of a President under a 1965 law that carries a possible life sentence. She was incarcerated for life on December 17, 1975.

FUCHS, Klaus [Emil Julius] (b. 1911). German-born British physicist and Communist spy. In 1933 Fuchs, a German Communist opposed to the Nazis, fled from Germany to England, where he continued his studies in physics, receiving two doctorates. He became a British citizen in 1942 and was by that time actively involved in secret research on the atomic bomb. In 1943 Fuchs went to the United States to help develop the bomb. After World War II, he became head of the physics division of the Harwell Atomic Energy Research Establishment in England. Information acquired by the U.S. FBI from confessed Communist spies led to Fuchs' arrest in 1950. Charged with espionage, he pleaded guilty to supplying information to Soviet agents since 1943. Fuchs was convicted and sentenced to 14 years in prison. Released in 1959, he went to live in East Germany and reportedly later moved to the Soviet Union. See also GOLD, Harry.

FUGMANN, Michael (1884-1937). Pennsylvania murderer. Independent unionists fought the encroachment of the United Mine Workers of America in the coal-mining town of Wilkes-Barre, Pennsylvania, in 1936. Booby-trap dynamite bombs hidden in wooden cigar-box gifts were mailed to several members of the United Mine Workers, causing the death of Tom Maloney, his four-year-old son, and 70-year-old Mike Gallagher. Suspects were rounded up but no evidence was discovered to incriminate them. Finally, noted wood expert Arthur Koehler traced wood scraps from the bomb packages to Fugmann, a unionist opposed to the UMW. Fugmann was found guilty of the triple murder and died in the electric chair in June 1937.

FULLAM, Augusta [Fairfield] (1876-1914). British Indian poisoner. In 1911 in Agra, India, Augusta, wife of Lieutenant Edward

Fullam, began a torrid love affair with Henry Lovell William
Clark, a 42-year-old married Eurasian physician whose medical
duties sent him to various spots in India. A lengthy corres-
pondence developed between the lovers until finally Augusta
decided to poison her husband (later found was her note to
herself, "So the only thing is to poison the soup"). After Edward miraculously survived an attempted arsenic poisoning,
Clark "medically" injected him with gelsemine (a poisonous
drug), which killed him on October 19, 1911, and then listed
his death as "heatstroke." Thirteen months later Clark's wife
was stabbed to death by four Indian natives, assassins hired
by Clark. The authorities questioned Clark and then Augusta,
whose lodgings were searched. The lovers' letters were found
and implicated them in the killings. Augusta and Clark were
tried twice in Allahabad, India, and eventually convicted of
murder after Augusta had turned state's evidence in testimony
against Clark. Later Clark confessed fully and was executed
on March 26, 1913. Sentenced to life imprisonment, Augusta
died in her cell, ironically, of heatstroke on May 29, 1914.

FUNK, Walther (1890-1960). German Nazi journalist, economist,
and war criminal. He edited a leading German financial newspaper, the Berliner Boersenzeitung, until 1931, when he left
and joined the German National Socialist (Nazi) party later that
year. An ingratiating but weak man, Funk raised much money
for the party under Adolf HITLER, wheedling out of rich,
prominent German bankers, businessmen, and industrialists
(especially coal, steel, and munitions barons) large contributions that helped the Nazis assume power in 1933. Funk was
made head of the Nazi press bureau in 1933 and succeeded Dr.
Hjalmar H. G. Schacht in 1938 as German minister of economics
and in 1939 as president of the Reichsbank (national bank).
Schacht had been dismissed from the latter post because he opposed the huge Nazi armament program; later, in 1944, he was
put in a concentration camp for allegedly taking part in a plot
to assassinate Hitler and, in 1946, was acquitted of war crimes.
Funk was involved in the Nazi slave-labor programs in the concentration camps during World War II (1939-45). Secretly deposited in his Reichsbank vaults were gold fillings, gold jewelry,
and many other valuables taken from condemned and dead Jews
in extermination camps. After the collapse of the Third Reich
(Nazi Germany) in 1945, the International Military Tribunal at
Nuremberg convicted Funk of war crimes and sentenced him to
life imprisonment. He died in 1960. See also KRUPP, Alfried,
[von Bohlen und Halbach].

FUREY, Joe. See BLONGER, Lou.

FURY, Bridget. See BRIDGET FURY.

- G -

GABRIEL [full name: Gabriel Prosser] (c. 1776-1800). Virginia slave and insurrectionist. In the spring of 1800 Gabriel, a devotedly religious black slave owned by Thomas H. Prosser of Henrico County, Virginia (he assumed his master's surname), began plotting a large slave insurrection, intending to set up an independent black state in Virginia and eventually become the "king" of Virginia. On the night of August 30, 1800, Gabriel's "army" of some 1,000 blacks armed with guns, cutlasses, and clubs started marching on Richmond, Virginia, from a meeting point about six miles outside the city. The rebels, however, were forced to disperse when a heavy rainstorm washed out bridges and roads along the march. Before they could regroup, Governor James Monroe, informed of the plot, called out militiamen. Gabriel and 34 of his followers were caught, found guilty, and hanged in Richmond in September 1800.

GACY, John Wayne, Jr. (b. 1942). Illinois mass murderer. Between 1972 and 1978, Gacy, a building contractor, roamed "Bughouse Square," a haven for male prostitutes on Chicago's North Side, picking up boys and young men and luring them to his Chicago suburban home in Knollwood Park Township with promises of a job. Gacy apparently paid them for sexual favors, drugged and killed them, and buried most of them in the crawl space beneath his house (28 corpses were later found there). Police, investigating a missing boy, discovered the mass murders after tracing the boy to Gacy, who had once spent 18 months in an Iowa prison for sodomy with a teenage boy. Charged with a total of 33 deaths (dead bodies were found in Gacy's garage, as well as under the house and in the Des Plaines River), Gacy was tried, convicted, and sentenced to the electric chair in March 1980. Today he is a death row inmate at the Menard Correctional Center in Chester, Illinois.

GALANTE, Carmine (1910-79). American gangster, racketeer, and murderer. In the 1930s and 1940s he was a top enforcer for Mafia boss Vito GENOVESE and carried out murder contracts including the killing of anti-fascist newspaper editor Carlo Tresca in 1943. Galante, known as "Lillo" and "The Cigar," became an underboss of Joseph C. BONANNO and set up a powerful network of narcotics smuggling in the United States, Canada, and Europe. In 1960 he was convicted of dope smuggling and imprisoned. After his release in 1974, Galante became New York's Mafia boss and controlled the East Coast rackets. Rival mob leaders issued a contract on him. On July 12, 1979, an unknown gunman shot and killed Galante with a shotgun in a Brooklyn Italian restaurant.

GALLO, Joey or Joseph (1929-72). Brooklyn gangster and racketeer. He worked for Mafia boss Carlo GAMBINO and was a top

gunman. Rival Mafia figures nicknamed Gallo "Crazy Joe" because of his unpredictable, ruthless nature. In the late 1940s
and early 1950s Gallo and his brothers, Larry and Albert "Kid
Blast," engaged in a mob war against the Joseph PROFACI
family to gain control of the Brooklyn drug racket. Gallo later
continued the war against Joseph COLOMBO, Sr. Realizing the
gradual shift in power from Italians to blacks, Gallo made
friends with black gang leaders, who helped run his rackets.
An unknown gunman shot and killed him at a New York City
restaurant on April 7, 1972. See also BARNES, [Leroy]
"Nicky."

GALLUS MAG (fl. late 1850s and 1860s). English-born New York
mugger and bouncer. Gallus Mag, so-called because she wore
galluses (suspenders) to hold up her skirt, was a belligerent,
six-foot-tall brute of a woman who engaged in muggings and
other crimes along New York City's waterfront for more than a
decade. She also worked as a bouncer for One-Armed Charley
Monell in his Hole-In-The-Wall saloon on Water Street. Gallus
Mag, who carried a pistol in her shirt and a club attached to
her wrist, beat up troublesome saloon customers and often bit
off their ears before dragging them out the door. The severed
ears were kept as trophies in a large jar of alcohol behind the
bar. Once Gallus Mag bashed in Sadie the Goat's skull (Sadie,
her chief female rival, was another mugger who received the
name "the Goat" because she used her hard head to butt victims unconscious), chewed off her ear, but later fished it out
of the jar and returned it to her when Sadie made peace with
her. When the Hole-In-The-Wall was closed by the police in
1871 after several murders were committed there, Gallus Mag
soon faded from sight but was talked about for many years.

GAMBI, Vincent (d. 1819). Italian-born pirate. One of the most
bloodthirsty of pirates, Gambi roamed the Gulf of Mexico in his
pirate ship, plundering all shipping and killing captive seamen
indiscriminately in the first two decades of the nineteenth century. He had a volatile relation with the famous pirate captain
Jean LAFFITE, with whom he joined in piracy raids at times and
whose leadership he once challenged (Laffite shot and killed
Gambi's top lieutenant for questioning his orders, and Gambi
withdrew). Gambi, who helped the Americans defeat the British
at the Battle of New Orleans in early 1815, was granted a full
pardon with rights as a U.S. citizen but soon resumed his career as a pirate and looted shipping for about three more years.
While asleep on a sack of stolen gold, Gambi was slain by his
own men with his favorite weapon, a broadaxe, in 1819.

GAMBINO, Carlo (1902-76). New York gangster and racketeer. He
rose through New York's Mafia ranks with Charles "Lucky"
LUCIANO and Meyer LANSKY. In the 1940s and 1950s Gambino
was underboss to Mafia chief Albert ANASTASIA and controlled

rackets, such as narcotics smuggling, in Brooklyn. After the death of Vito GENOVESE in 1969, Gambino was considered by many to be the most powerful figure in organized crime or the national syndicate in the United States; he became the model for Mario Puzo's Godfather. His henchmen carried out gangland killings to protect the Gambino family interests. Gambino died of a heart attack in Massapequa, New York, on October 15, 1976.

GARCIA, Manuel Philip (d. 1821). Virginia highwayman and murderer. He robbed travelers in the Norfolk, Virginia, area. On March 20, 1820, Garcia, accompanied by his friend Jose Castillano, killed Peter Lagoardette, a rival highwayman, in a dispute over a local girl. Lagoardette was lured to a deserted house and butchered. Later his half-burned head, hands, and feet were found in the fireplace, along with bloodstained clothing, which was traced to Garcia and Castillano. The two killers confessed and were hanged in Norfolk on June 1, 1821. This was the first time U.S. police had used laundry marks on clothes to solve a murder.

GARDNER, Roy (1888-1940). American teacher, robber, and escape artist. He graduated from college with honors, took a job at an American midwestern university as an English teacher, and published a scholarly book on seventeenth-century literature. A restless and adventurous type, Gardner dropped out of the academic life and went to Mexico to fight with the rebels in 1908. Later he moved to California, where he did some prizefighting and turned to a life of crime. Twice caught and convicted of robbery, Gardner escaped from custody both times as he was being transported to the federal penitentiary at McNeil Island, Washington. The "Escaping Professor," as the press dubbed him, was finally caught and brought to the prison under heavy guard. On Labor Day 1921 Gardner made a sensational escape, fooling the authorities by retracing his escape route, hiding in the prison barn, and waiting until the coast was clear before swimming to the mainland). Gardner, who evidently wanted to begin "life anew" according to a letter he sent to President Warren Harding, fell back into crime and was caught attempting to rob a train in Arizona in late 1921. Sentenced to Leavenworth, he was later transferred to Alcatraz for security reasons in 1934; two years later Gardner was returned to Leavenworth because of his good behavior and in 1938 was released in poor health. He lived alone in a shabby hotel in San Francisco, where he committed suicide in January 1940.

GAYLES, Joseph. See SACCO THE BRACER.

GEAGAN, Michael V. See McGINNIS, [Joseph Francis] "Big Joe."

GEE, Dorothy or Dolly [born: Chang Hor-gee] (1897-1978).

Chinese-born California embezzler. Her father, who had emigrated from China to California with his family in 1901, prospered first as a shoe store owner and then as a bank officer in San Francisco. After 1914 Gee helped her father solicit business for the French-American Bank in Oakland, which thrived with their new Chinese accounts and deposits. In 1929 she took over her father's ledgers written in Chinese figures and further enhanced the bank (then part of Bank of America) by obtaining more savings and accounts for the next 30 years; operating the bank's Oriental branch on San Francisco's Grant Avenue, she was honored frequently as the "first woman banker in America." Unexpectedly, in late 1963 she confessed to the embezzlement (begun 50 years ago by her father to cover losses from gambling and bank speculative ventures) of more than $300,000 from the bank; she said she had to "save face" before retiring that year and could not be lauded for a banking career of fraud. Sentenced to five years in prison, Gee was freed in 16 months and faded into obscurity in San Francisco's Chinatown.

GEIN, Ed[ward] (b. 1906). Wisconsin murderer and necrophile. He lived alone on his farm in Plainfield, Wisconsin, after his mother and brother died. Gein developed a strong interest in female anatomy and apparently desired to change his sex. Around 1947 he began digging up female corpses from remote graves and bringing them to his farm for "experiments." Gein later turned to killing women to obtain his cadavers. The town's sheriff, on a hunch after Bernice Worden was discovered missing in 1957, went to Gein's farmhouse and found human skins, heads, hearts, livers, sex organs, and so on--the remains of at least 15 dead women, human "trophies" to Gein. Gein confessed to looting graves and to two murders (those of Mary Hogan in 1954 and Bernice Worden; others he couldn't remember). He was sent to an institution for the criminally insane, where he remains.

GENNA, Angelo (d. 1925). Sicilian-born Chicago bootlegger and murderer. In 1919 he and his five brothers (Tony, Mike, Pete, Sam, and Jim) established an extensive bootlegging business in Chicago. Angelo, known as "Bloody Angelo," engineered numerous killings against the Gennas' enemies. He and three gunmen killed Paul A. Labriola, a political rival, before a dozen witnesses (none testified against Angelo and the others). A three-way bootlegging competition developed among the Gennas, Charles Dion O'BANNION, and Al CAPONE. On May 25, 1925, Capone's gunmen shot Angelo dead with three shotgun blasts after an automobile chase through the Chicago streets. See also GENNA, Mike; GENNA, Tony or Antonio.

GENNA, Mike (d. 1925). Sicilian-born Chicago bootlegger and murderer. In the 1920s he and his brothers supplied cheap

(and sometimes unsafe) liquor to Johny Torrio and Al Capone.
Mike, called "The Devil," was a treacherous killer who led
Genna gunmen during rub-outs of rivals. A bootlegging war
developed among the Genna family, Charles Dion O'BANNION,
and Al CAPONE, who sought to wipe out the Genna influence
and take complete control. On June 13, 1925, Mike, while
searching for his brother Angelo's murderers with John SCA-
LISE and Albert ANSELMI (his supposed friends but really Capone's gunmen hired to kill him), was badly wounded by police
in a gunfight and bled to death. See also GENNA, Angelo;
GENNA, Tony or Antonio.

GENNA, Tony or Antonio (d. 1925). Sicilian-born Chicago bootlegger. He helped run the rich Genna family bootlegging business in Chicago in the early 1920s. Tony, considered the
"brains" behind the family, lived elegantly and often attended
the opera, earning the sobriquet, "Tony the Gentleman." He
never took part in a killing himself. After the deaths of his
brothers Angelo and Mike, Tony decided to leave Chicago. On
July 8, 1925, he was slain by Giuseppe Nerone, John SCALISE,
and Albert ANSELMI, all of whom had worked for the Gennas
but deserted to Al CAPONE. The remaining Genna brothers,
Pete, Sam, and Jim, fled from the city, their influence ended.
See also GENNA, Angelo; GENNA, Mike.

GENOVESE, Vito (1897-1969). Italian-born New York racketeer,
gangster, and murderer. As underboss to Charles "Lucky"
LUCIANO in the 1920s, he ran lucrative narcotics and brothel
rackets in Manhattan. Genovese worked his way through the
Mafia ranks, killing off his rivals and establishing himself as a
director of the national crime syndicate. In 1937 he fled to
Italy to escape prosecution for the 1934 murder of mobster
Ferdinand "The Shadow" Boccia. A close friend of Benito
Mussolini, Genovese took control of the Italian black market
and directed narcotics smuggling into the United States. After World War II, he returned to the U.S. to face the murder
charge (it was dismissed) and set about making himself king of
the American underworld. Genovese ordered the killing of
Mafia chief Willie MORETTI in 1951, Steven Franse in 1953, and
Albert ANASTASIA in 1957. At the famed Appalachian meeting of
the Mafia in upstate New York in 1957, Genovese, or "Don
Vitone," was recognized as the "boss of bosses." Two years
later he was convicted of smuggling and selling narcotics and
sentenced to prison in Atlanta. While behind bars, Genovese
directed rackets and ordered dozens of killings. Transferred
to Leavenworth, he died there in his cell of a heart attack.
See also COSTELLO, Frank; GALANTE, Carmine; GAMBINO,
Carlo; GIGANTE, Vincent.

GENTLE ANNIE [real name: Annie Stafford] (1838-after 1880).
Chicago prostitute and madam. A stunning, sensuous whore

in the Sands district of Chicago, Gentle Annie, who was totally
misnamed, was a brutal fighter in the city's so-called "Whore
War" of 1857, when the "lowly" Sands whores and pimps overpowered the more "mannerly" ones of State Street in a dispute
over services and ownership of "goods." By early 1860 Annie
had opened her own brothel, which boarded about three dozen
prostitutes. In 1866 she married her paramour Cap Hyman, a
top Chicago gambler, and received as a wedding gift from him
an inn called Sunnyside outside the city limits. Annie and Cap
tried unsuccessfully to turn the place into a classy bordello
(customers were reluctant to travel that far out of the city)
and resumed their operation in Chicago again. In 1876 Hyman
died after suffering a total mental and physical breakdown the
year before. Annie operated a brothel until about 1880, when
she disappeared and was thought to have died soon afterward.

GÉRARD, Balthasar (1558-84). French assassin. In 1581 the seven
northern provinces of the Netherlands formally deposed King
Philip II of Spain as their ruler and set up a republic with
William I "the Silent," prince of Orange, as hereditary stadt-
holder (chief magistrate). Philip promptly denounced William
as a traitor and offered a huge reward to anyone who assassinated him. Several unsuccessful attempts were made on William's life. On July 10, 1584, Gérard, a French Catholic fanatic,
gained entrance to William's palace at Delft, Holland, and shot
and killed William there. Caught while trying to flee, Gérard
was put in prison, where his body was disjointed on the rack
and burned with fire. Afterward, atop a scaffold before a
crowd of Dutch spectators, Gerard was further tortured; first
his right hand--the one that had committed the act of regicide--
was burned off; then his body was pierced with hot irons; his
stomach slit open; his arms and legs cut off; and, while still
breathing, he had his heart cut out. The corpse was decapitated, thus ending Gérard's inquisitional death sentence.

GIANCANA, Sam "Momo" [born: Salvatore Giancana] (1908-75).
Chicago gangster and racketeer. He started his criminal career
as a gun runner for Al CAPONE in 1925. Giancana was arrested countless times on charges such as bookmaking, gambling, assault to kill, burglary, larceny, bombing, and suspicion of murder. He was imprisoned for auto theft (30 days),
operation of an illegal still (four years), burglary (five years),
and contempt of a federal grand jury (one year). In the early
1960s Giancana was considered head of the Chicago Mafia. He
was thought to be involved in alleged CIA plots to assassinate
Cuban Premier Fidel Castro. An unknown gunman shot and
killed Giancana in his Chicago home.

GIBBS, Charles (c. 1800-1831). Rhode Island pirate and murderer.
At an early age he became a seaman. Gibbs instigated many
mutinies and gained a reputation for savagery and murder. He

once cut off a captured seaman's arms and legs and another
time ordered an entire merchant crew burned to death (he
boasted later he had murdered more than 400 persons during
his life). Four pirate schooners commanded by Gibbs were
seized by the U.S. brigantine Enterprise, under Lieutenant
Commander Lawrence Kearney, off the Cuban coast in 1821.
Forty pirates were captured, and the rest, including Gibbs,
fled into the jungles. Sailing aboard the Vineyard in 1830,
Gibbs and a black cook, Thomas G. Wansley, led a mutiny and
killed the captain and first mate. Shipmates later informed on
them. Gibbs and Wansley were found guilty and hanged on
Ellis Island, New York, on April 22, 1831.

GIGANTE, Vincent (b. 1926). New York gangster. Gigante, six
feet, four inches tall and weighing about 300 pounds, was reportedly the gunman sent by crime boss Vito GENOVESE to
assassinate rival Frank COSTELLO in 1957. Costello was shot
and wounded as he entered the lobby of his New York City
apartment building on May 2 of that year. Gigante, brought to
trial for attempted murder, was set free when Costello refused
to identify him. In 1959 Gigante, nicknamed "The Chin" because of that prominent facial feature, and other Genovese
aides were implicated in a dope-smuggling plot and sentenced
to long stints in prison.

GILBERT, Pedro (d. 1834). American pirate. In the early 1830s
the schooner Panda, captained by Gilbert, plundered many
European and American vessels in the Atlantic. In September
1832 Gilbert captured and looted the American brigantine Mexican, laden with silver and bound from Salem, Massachusetts,
to Rio de Janeiro. The pirates locked the crew of the Mexican
in the fo'c'sle, tore the rigging and sails to shreds, set fire to
the ship, and left. The crew miraculously got loose, put out
the fire, and sailed the ship back to Salem. The British caught
Gilbert in Africa in 1834 and extradited him to Boston, where he
was tried and hanged.

GILLARS, Mildred Elizabeth. See AXIS SALLY.

GILLETTE, Chester (1884-1908). New York murderer. Gillette,
deserted by his parents at the age of 14, began to work at his
uncle's shirt factory in Cortland, New York, in 1906. He had
ambitions to make it into high society. When Grace Brown, a
company secretary, became pregnant by him and threatened his
plans of success and prominence, Gillette brought Grace to the
Adirondacks on vacation. On July 11, 1906, Grace's battered
body washed ashore on Big Moose Lake, New York. Gillette
was arrested and tried for the murder. He told many conflicting stories during a long, sensational trial and sold photos of
himself to admiring women, using the money for catered meals
to his cell. Found guilty, Gillette was electrocuted at Auburn

Prison on March 30, 1908, never having confessed to the murder. The character Clyde Griffiths in Theodore Dreiser's novel An American Tragedy is based on Gillette.

GILLIS, Helen [Wawzynak]. See NELSON, George "Baby Face."

GILLIS, Lester J. See NELSON, George "Baby Face."

GILMORE, Gary Mark (1940–77). Utah murderer. He was convicted of killing a motel clerk during a petty robbery in Utah in July 1976. Gilmore, who also admitted to slaying a Utah gas station attendant in a similar holdup, was condemned to die, refused to appeal his death sentence, and asked to be executed. His impending execution drew worldwide attention because it marked the return of capital punishment in the United States after a ten-year moratorium (in 1976 the U.S. Supreme Court reinstated the death penalty under certain constitutional limitations). Groups opposed to capital punishment attempted unsuccessfully to block Gilmore's death, which took place before a five-man firing squad on January 17, 1977, at the Utah State Prison at Point of the Mountain. American author Norman Mailer's Pulitzer Prize-winning book Executioner's Song, which was made into a television movie, was based on Gilmore's life and controversial execution.

GLANTON, John J. (1815?–50). American murderer and scalp hunter. In 1845 he escaped from prison in Nashville, Tennessee, where he was serving time for murder, and took refuge in the U.S. Army during the Mexican War (1846-48). Afterward Glanton led a bloodthirsty and greedy band of scalp hunters, who killed over 1,000 Apaches and other Indians and sold their scalps to Mexican and U.S. government agencies (payment for scalps was a way of getting rid of hostile and unwanted Indians; a male Indian scalp procured $100, a female $50, and a child $25). Discovered illegally scalping Mexicans and dark-skinned American settlers, Glanton and his men fled from the law and later attempted to take over the business run by the Yuma Indians of ferrying settlers and covered wagons across the Colorado River on the Arizona-California border. The Indians massacred Glanton and most of his gang on April 23, 1850.

GLATMAN, Harvey Murray (1928-59). California rapist and murderer. In 1957 Glatman, posing as a magazine photographer, abducted Judy Ann Dull, raped her repeatedly, took lewd pictures of her, and then drove her to the desert west of Los Angeles, where he strangled her to death with a five-foot-long piece of rope. In 1958 Glatman abducted and killed two more young women (Shirley Ann Bridgeford and Ruth Rita Mercado), sexually abusing them and leaving them in the desert. The police had no idea who the sadistic killer was until a highway patrolman, cruising on the Santa Ana Freeway, found Glatman being held at gun point by Lorraine Vigil, who had successfully resisted Glatman's efforts to tie her up in his car and had seized Glatman's gun. Convicted of murder (Glatman proudly recounted his murderous acts), he was sent to San Quentin's gas chamber on August 18, 1959.

GLENCAIRN, Lord. See GORDON-GORDON, Lord.

GODSE, Nathuram [Vinayak] (1911-49). Indian Hindu assassin. He was the editor of a Hindu nationalist newspaper and a member of the Hindu Mahasabha, a rabidly anti-Muslim organization that loathed Mahatma Gandhi, India's preeminent spiritual and political leader and a Hindu himself, for attempting to bring about unity between Hindus and Muslims in India. A conspiracy to assassinate Gandhi, begun and led by Godse, failed to kill the 78-year-old advocate of nonviolence on January 20, 1948 at Birla House, Gandhi's holy place near Delhi; one of the conspirators, Mandanlal Pahwa, was caught; the others escaped. Ten days later, on January 30, Godse fatally shot Gandhi as he was leaving Birla House to hold an evening prayer meeting in Delhi. Grabbed immediately by onlookers, Godse was beaten and taken to prison. Later he and seven accused fellow conspirators--Pahwa, Narayan Apte (Godse's newspaper production manager), Vishnu Karkare, Shankar Kistayya, Digambar Badge, Vinayak Savarkar, and Gopal Godse (Nathuram's younger brother)--underwent a nine-month-long trial in Delhi, during which Godse took sole and full responsibility for the assassination. On February 10, 1949, Godse and Apte were condemned to death, Savarkar was acquitted, and the other five were sentenced to life imprisonment. Apte's hanging death on November 15, 1949, was very swift because of a broken neck, but Godse's that day was not: he slowly and excruciatingly strangled to death.

GOEBBELS, [Paul] Joseph (1897-1945). German Nazi propagandist and leader. Exempted from military service in World War I (1914-18) because of his clubfoot, Goebbels graduated from the University of Heidelberg in 1921 with a Ph.D. in German philology and began a journalistic career. He supported the National Socialist (Nazi) party, whose leader, Adolf HITLER, appointed him the party's district leader in Berlin in 1926 and the propaganda minister for all of Germany in 1928. With brilliant insight into mass psychology, Goebbels staged enormous party celebrations, demonstrations, and parades to help convert the German masses to Nazism and the leadership of Hitler. After Hitler came to power in 1933, he made Goebbels head of the newly formed National Ministry for Public Enlightenment and Propaganda for the Third Reich (the Nazi state). Goebbels, who also became director of Germany's new Chamber of Culture, controlled all propaganda, all publications, cinema, visual arts, radio, music, and theater. Through skillful manipulation of the media, he led and misled the German public and seemingly justified Hitler's excessive use of power, especially against the Jews during World War II (1939-45). Although Germany faced impending defeat in early 1945, Goebbels publicly insisted that victory could be had. Loyal to Hitler to the end, he killed his family (wife and six children) and himself in Berlin on May 1, 1945, one day after Hitler named Goebbels in his will as the new chancellor of the Reich.

GOERING or GÖRING, Hermann Wilhelm (1893-1946). German politician and war criminal. An early member of the National Socialist Party (the Nazis), Goering took part in the Munich "beerhall putsch," an abortive attempt to overthrow the republican government of Germany in 1923. Five years later he became one of the first 12 Nazis elected to the Reichstag (legislative assembly), of which he became president in 1932. When Adolf HIT-LER was made German chancellor in 1933, Goering, one of Hitler's most trusted friends, became air minister of Germany and president and interior minister of Prussia. Goering was probably involved in the 1933 Reichstag Fire, blamed on Marinus VAN DER LUBBE. Founder of the Geheime Staatspolizei, or Gestapo, Goering participated in the Blood Purge of 1934 and directed much of the Nazis' drive toward war-preparedness. Goering, who liked important-sounding titles and resplendent uniforms and decorations, collected large quantities of costly artifacts from all over Europe before and during World War II. As Germany collapsed, he tried to take control from Hitler, who dismissed him as a traitor. In May 1945 Goering surrendered to U.S. troops and became the chief defendant at the Nuremberg Trial for war crimes. He was convicted and condemned to die. On the night of October 16, 1946, about two hours before his scheduled hanging, Goering committed suicide by taking a poison capsule that he apparently had concealed under a false navel.

GOETZ, Fred. See ZIEGLER, "Shotgun" [George].

GOHL, Billy (1860?-1928). Washington mass murderer. In 1913 Gohl, an official of the Sailors' Union of the Pacific in Aberdeen, Washington, was convicted of killing two seamen and was held responsible for the murders of at least 40 others. He apparently shot and killed new merchant sailors in his office, took their cash and other valuables (which they had entrusted to him), and cast their bodies into the nearby fast-flowing Wishkah River, which flowed into Gray's Harbor. Between 1909 and 1912 authorities found 41 corpses in the harbor. Because the state of Washington had outlawed capital punishment in 1912, Gohl escaped the death penalty and received life imprisonment (the state reinstated capital punishment in 1914; Gohl's murders were a strong impetus in doing so). He died in prison in 1928.

GOLD, Harry [born: Heinrich Godolnitsky] (b. 1911). Swiss-born
American Communist spy. Born in Berne, Switzerland, to Russian emigrant parents who brought him to the United States at
the age of three and anglicized his name, Harry Gold became an
expert university-educated chemist who secretly espoused Communism and handed over to Soviet agents industrial processes
of American companies he worked for. Unmarried, he lived
with his parents and worked in Philadelphia, where he was an
important Soviet courier of information given to him by other
spies, particularly Klaus FUCHS and Julius and Ethel ROSEN-
BERG, during and after World War II; Gold passed on to Moscow highly secret research about the atomic bomb. In 1950
the FBI tracked down and arrested Gold, then working in the
Philadelphia General Hospital. Pleading guilty to spying, he
was convicted and sentenced (December 9, 1950) to 30 years'
imprisonment.

GOLD DUST TEDDY. See JONES, Edward.

GOLDMAN, Emma (1869-1940). Lithuanian-born American anarchist.
In 1886 she emigrated from Russia to the United States, where
she became actively involved in the anarchist movement. Goldman was a close friend of Alexander BERKMAN, another anarchist, and made many fiery speeches throughout the United
States. In 1893 she was imprisoned for inciting a riot in New
York City. After 1906 Goldman and Berkman edited and published a libertarian-anarchist periodical called Mother Earth and
campaigned tirelessly for the rights of convicted political prisoners and unemployed workers. Goldman was briefly imprisoned in 1916 for publicly advocating birth control, and she and
Berkman were sentenced in 1917 to two-year prison terms for
obstructing the military draft. Upon their release in 1919, the
two were deported to Russia but became disillusioned with the
despotic Soviet government and left in 1921. Goldman married
a Welshman named James Colton in 1926 and lived for periods
in England, Spain, and Canada, where she died at the age of
70.

GOLDSBOROUGH, Fitzhugh Coyle (1880-1911). American murderer.
He doted on his socialite sister, who he mistakenly thought had
been maligned by novelist David Graham Phillips in his book
The Fashionable Adventures of Joshua Craig. In New York
City's elegant Gramercy Park on January 23, 1911, Goldsborough
accosted Phillips and shot and killed him. He then fatally shot
himself in the temple before several horrified spectators.

GOLDSBY, Crawford (1876-96). American outlaw and murderer.
In 1894 he joined an outlaw band led by Bill and Jim Cook in
the Oklahoma territory. Goldsby, who was part Cherokee Indian, became known as "Cherokee Bill" and earned a widespread
reputation for his quick gun. Before his twentieth birthday he

had shot and killed thirteen men, including several lawmen, and had robbed numerous stores and trains. Hanging Judge Isaac Parker offered a $1,300 reward for Goldsby dead or alive. In early 1895 Goldsby was caught and taken to Fort Smith, from which he attempted unsuccessfully to escape a number of times. Legal appeals stalled his hanging until March 17, 1896.

GONDORF, Charley or Charles (fl. c. 1895-1914). American con man. He and his brother Fred successfully practiced "the big store" confidence racket, bilking wealthy suckers of an estimated $15 million before being arrested and imprisoned. They would set up a phony posh betting parlor, "the big store," supposedly wired to receive horserace results before they were sent to the bookmakers. A rich, gullible customer, convinced he would make a "killing," would bet heavily, eventually lose, but be reconciled when other bettors also lost badly (he didn't know that the parlor's patrons, like its employees, were all fakes). In 1906 Charley opened the biggest permanent big store in New York City and operated it until he was arrested during a police raid in 1914. After Charley was tried, convicted of swindling, and sent to Sing Sing (Ossining Correctional Facility, New York), Fred took over the operation but about a year later, in 1915, was arrested after a businessman, who had lost over $17,000 to Fred in the big store scam, led police to the con man in Manhattan. Convicted, Fred joined his brother in Sing Sing. A successful movie, The Sting, was based on the careers of the Gondorf brothers, who were played by actors Paul Newman and Robert Redford.

GOOCH, Arthur (1909-36). American kidnapper. On November 26, 1934, he and a fellow criminal became involved in a gun battle with two police officers in Texas, wounded one of the officers, and then forced the lawmen to drive them to Oklahoma. There federal agents stopped them and, in another gun battle, killed Gooch's cohort and captured Gooch. The Federal Kidnapping Statute or the so-called Lindbergh Law of 1932 made kidnapping a person across a state line "for ransom, reward, or otherwise" a capital crime. Gooch was convicted and condemned to die. Despite his lawyers' appeals to overturn the court verdict, stating that Gooch had not committed a kidnapping for ransom, Gooch was executed on June 19, 1936, becoming the first person to die under the Lindbergh Law. (The U.S. Supreme Court had ruled that abducting a police officer was included as a capital offense in the wording of the law.)

GOOLDE, Marie [born: Marie Girodin] (1877-1908). French-born adventuress and murderer. Her origins and early life are vague, but she did have three marriages, the first two ending in the mysterious deaths of her husbands. While operating a dress shop in London, she met and married an Irishman, Vere GOOLDE, with whom she journeyed to France's Monte Carlo

casino in the hope of taking home a gambling fortune in 1907.
There the Gooldes stabbed to death and robbed a wealthy Swedish widow, cut her body into pieces, and tried to ship it to
England via Marseilles, where the odor and blood of the dissected cadaver leaked out of the trunk to alert authorities.
The two were arrested (inside Marie's purse was found the dead
woman's jewelry), convicted of murder, and sent to French
Guiana to serve life prison sentences. Marie died there of
typhoid fever in July 1908.

GOOLDE, Vere (d. 1909). Irish-born British murderer. He and
his attractive wife, Marie GOOLDE, were arrested in Marseilles,
France, while trying to flee the country with the dismembered
corpse of a woman stuffed in a trunk and handbag (August
1907). A suspicious railway clerk had notified gendarmes after
noticing a peculiar smell and a red liquid coming from the trunk,
which was to be shipped to England. The Gooldes had gone to
Monte Carlo to win at the gambling tables and instead had murdered and robbed there a rich Swedish widow, who had loaned
them some money. Tried and convicted at Monte Carlo, the
Gooldes were imprisoned for life in French Guiana. Vere killed
himself in captivity in September 1909.

GORDON, Nathaniel (d. 1862). American slave trader and pirate.
In the mid-nineteenth century Captain Gordon and his crew
aboard the 500-ton ship Erie engaged in old-time piracy, con-
centrating chiefly on the smuggling of slaves into the United
States. The Erie regularly transported about 1,000 black
African captives, many of whom never survived the ocean voyage because of wretched living conditions aboard ship. Gordon
took great risks to reap huge profits from the slave trade.
About 50 miles off the African coast, the U.S. Mohican captured the Erie carrying some 890 blacks, 600 of whom were boys
and girls, to a slave market. The captives were released in
Liberia. Charged with piracy, Gordon was tried in New York,
convicted, and sentenced to die. Protesters claimed that it was
unfair to kill a person for a crime that was virtually nonexistent
for some 40 years. They sent a petition to President Abraham
Lincoln, who, however, upheld the law of May 15, 1820, which
declared slave trading as piracy, a crime warranting the death
penalty. On February 21, 1862, Gordon was hanged in the
Tombs in New York City, becoming the first person to be fed-
erally executed for slave trading in the United States.

GORDON, Waxey [real name: Irving Wexler] (1888-1952). American
pickpocket, bootlegger, and racketeer. At an early age he became an expert pickpocket who could lift a person's wallet from
a pocket as if it were coated with wax (hence his nickname
"Waxey"). During Prohibition Gordon, a short, dumpy man
with little hair, was a junior partner of racketeer Arnold
ROTHSTEIN and operated a number of rackets including

prostitution, dope dealing, and bootlegging. Gordon owned
large distilleries and breweries in Philadelphia and New York,
cities in which he also held much real estate, including speakeasies (saloons), nightclubs, and gambling casinos. Living in
grand style on an estimated income of $1 million to $2 million a
year, Gordon stayed in business through payoffs to crooked
politicians and others. In December 1930 he was found guilty
of income tax evasion (allegedly, information about Gordon's
false tax payments was leaked to federal agents by gangsters
working for Charles "Lucky" LUCIANO and Meyer LANKSY,
both of whom wanted to take over Gordon's operations). After
serving a ten-year term in prison, Gordon was released in
1940, declared he was Irving Wexler, a legitimate salesman, but
in 1951 was arrested for delivering a $6,300 package of heroin
to a federal agent disguised as a buyer. He was given 25
years to life and sent to Alcatraz, where he died of a heart
attack on June 24, 1952.

GORDON-BAILLIE, Mrs. See SUTHERLAND, Mary Ann [Bruce].

GORDON-GORDON, Lord (d. 1873). Scottish and American swindler. In 1868-69 under the name of Lord Glencairn, he successfully bilked a leading jeweler in Edinburgh out of Ŀ25,000
worth of fine gems. In 1871, now using the name Lord Gordon-
Gordon and claiming an aristocratic and wealthy background,
he surfaced in Minneapolis, Minnesota, and announced he intended to purchase vast tracts of railroad land on which to re-
locate his poor Scottish tenants. After being lavishly wined
and dined by the Northern Pacific Railroad, which hoped to
get enormous funds from him, Gordon-Gordon departed for New
York City to arrange transfer of money from Scotland. Carrying on as a fabulously rich, important, and fashionable lord,
he managed to mulct wily financier Jay Gould out of $150,000,
pretending to have powerful connections and influence that
would help Gould gain control of the Erie Railroad. Gordon-
Gordon, who appeared in court to answer Gould's suit against
him, fled to Canada when authorities discovered he was an imposter. He took refuge in Fort Garry, Manitoba, where he
fought off extradition to the United States. Minnesotans allegedly financed by Gould attempted several times to kidnap
Gordon-Gordon and return him to the states, but failed. His
case became internationally known, resulting in Scottish officials swearing out a warrant for Gordon-Gordon's arrest after
learning that he was "Lord Glencairn," a much wanted criminal.
Soon afterward Gordon-Gordon committed suicide, shooting himself in the temple.

GOSSMANN, Klaus (b. 1941). German mass murderer. Between
1960 and 1966 he indiscriminately shot and killed seven persons
in and around Nuremberg, West Germany. Gossmann was
dubbed the "Midday Murderer" because his killings occurred at

noon when loud church bells tolled, thus deadening his shots
and any victim's yells. Two shootings in 1962 took place in
banks which he then robbed. Finally captured, Gossmann, who
was a resident of Hersbruck near Nuremberg, claimed he had
planned to abduct or kill the actress Elke Sommer during her
next trip to Nuremberg to visit her family there; cut into his
gun's handle was "Elke." Showing not the least remorse for
his crimes and referring to human beings as "things," Gossmann was sentenced to life imprisonment in July 1967. An intelligent student, he had come to believe he was an Übermensch
(superman), possibly attempting to emulate his father who had
often told him about how, as a German soldier in World War II,
he had gunned down many enemy troops.

GOTTFRIED, Gesina [Margaretha] (d. 1828). German mass poisoner. A vain, iron-willed, beautiful, blue-eyed blonde, she poisoned to death with white arsenic at least 20 persons in German
households in which she lived or served as a housekeeper and
cook. Undetected for a dozen years until her arrest in 1828,
Gesina, catering to her own strange self-indulgent ends, murdered her two husbands (men named Miltenberg and Gottfried),
her parents and brother, a wealthy suitor, a friend to whom
she owed money, and members of the Rumf family, among
others. In late March 1828 Mr. Rumf, a wheelwright in Bremen, became suspicious of his housekeeper Gesina after discovering an unusual white powder on his food, which he
brought to the police. The powder was found to be arsenic,
and Gesina was put in jail on a charge of murder. At her
trial, she was hideous looking, like a wizened old hag (middle-
aged Gesina's earlier youthful, fresh appearance was all pretense and self-gratification), and haughtily admitted to having
killed her victims, evidently having received a kind of sexual
ecstasy while committing the poisonings. Convicted and sentenced to die, Gesina was beheaded in Bremen in 1828.

GOULD, Janice Irene. See BRADFORD, Priscilla [Ann Hadley].

GOURDAN, Madame (fl. latter 1700s). French madam. She operated one of Europe's most infamous bordellos, located on the
Rue des Deux Portes in Paris, which was frequented by numerous wealthy aristocrats, nobles, and royal personages. At
her lavish establishment, which was as splendid and comfortable
as a palace, Madame Gourdan instructed young, beautiful, sensual females, many of them from the countryside, in the lascivious art of prostitution. Flourishing harlots and courtesans
sometimes obtained advice from Gourdan, who allegedly personally trained Comtesse Jeanne Bécu du Barry, the beauteous and
last mistress of King Louis XV of France. Comtesse du Barry,
a courtesan of illegitimate birth, was banished to a nunnery in
1774 after the king's death. Later she was arrested as a counterrevolutionary during the French Revolution, tried, convicted,
and guillotined on December 8, 1793.

GRABEZ, Trifko. See PRINCIP, Gavrillo.

GRADY, [John D.] "Travelling Mike" (fl. c. 1860-80). New York sneak thief and fence. His gang of sneak thieves, consisting of Eddie Pettengill, Hod Ennis, "Billy the Kid" Burke, "Boston Pete" Anderson, and others, pulled off the largest reported sneak theft on March 7, 1866, when they took $1.9 million in cash and negotiable securities from the Manhattan office of penurious Wall Street financier Rufus L. Lord. Except Grady, all of the gang retired afterward. Grady later undermined his archrival Fredericka "Marm" MANDELBAUM by buying loot from criminals working for her at very low prices.

GRAHAM, Barbara [born: Barbara Elaine Wood] (1923-55). California murderer. In the late 1930s she spent time in a girls' reformatory and later was drawn into organized crime. In 1947 Graham was a star call girl for Sally Stanford, San Francisco's most notorious madam. She married four times, the last to a man named Henry Graham, who introduced her to drugs. As a member of a murderous robbery gang which included Emmett Perkins and Jack Santos, Graham apparently murdered an elderly Burbank, California, widow during a jewelry robbery in 1953. Arrested, Graham was convicted and sent to San Quentin's gas chamber along with Perkins and Santos on June 3, 1955. She asked for a blindfold, saying, "I don't want to have to look at people."

GRAHAM, John or Jack Gilbert (1932-57). Colorado mass murderer. On November 1, 1955, United Airlines Flight 629 blew up over a Colorado beet farm, killing 44 passengers and crew members. Suspicion centered on Graham, whose mother died on the plane. He had taken out insurance worth $37,500 on his mother's life just before takeoff and stood to inherit her $150,000 estate. The FBI interrogated Graham, who finally confessed to planting a bomb in his mother's suitcase. Graham also admitted to having blown up his service station to collect insurance money and to having parked his pickup truck at a railroad crossing where it was demolished by a passing train, also for insurance. Convicted of murder, Graham died in the gas chamber at the Colorado Penitentiary on January 11, 1957.

GRAIVER, David (1941-76?). Argentine financier and alleged swindler. Graiver, a former Peronist government official, was reputedly the chief money handler for the outlawed Montonero guerrillas in Argentina. He was suspected of using guerrilla funds to purchase a New York bank in 1975. Graiver established a huge banking empire in the United States, Europe, Latin America, and Israel, commuting weekly from New York City to his residence in Mexico. On August 7, 1976, he was allegedly killed in a jet plane crash on a mountain side in Acapulco, Mexico. A Manhattan grand jury, apparently unsatisfied that Graiver was dead (a charred, headless, limbless

torso was identified as his), indicted Graiver on 83 counts of
felony, including misappropriation of funds and alteration of accounts of American Bank & Trust Company in New York (the
bank collapsed five weeks after the plane crash).

GRANNAN, Riley (1868-1908). American gunfighter and gambler.
He earned a reputation as a fast draw in Kentucky, where he
was born, and other states, winning several gun duels. However, Grannan was better known for his shrewd, successful
gambling on horse races; he supposedly bet over $250,000 on a
horse and won. In 1907 Grannan bought $40,000 worth of des-
ert land in Rawhide, Nevada, with the intention of building an
enormous, "honest" gambling center, but he suddenly died in
April 1908 without any money. To some people, his dream became a reality when Benjamin "Bugsy" SIEGEL built the Flamingo
Hotel, a gambling paradise, in Las Vegas in 1945.

GRANS, Hans. See HAARMANN, Fritz.

GRAVES, Thomas Thatcher (1843-93). American murderer. Graves,
a scheming physician, endeared himself to Josephine Barnaby, a
wealthy Rhode Island heiress, and was given power of attorney
over her finances. He secretly began to seize her estate.
Barnaby grew suspicious. In April 1891 she visited a friend,
Mrs. Worrell, in Denver, where she received an anonymous gift
of a bottle of whiskey. The two women drank the whiskey and
died six days later. When poison was found in the bodies,
suspicion focused on Graves, who was tried and found guilty of
murder (a prosecution witness testified that Graves, claiming
he could not write, had asked him to write a note that was sent
with the poisonous whiskey). While awaiting a new trial, Graves
committed suicide in his jail cell by taking poison.

GRAY, George (fl. c. 1895-1902). American con man. Gray, who
came from a well-to-do Brooklyn family, perpetrated a confidence
game in which he pretended to have either an epileptic fit or a
heart attack in front of a wealthy stranger, who then readily
gave him money for fare to a hospital and for medical treatment.
Known as "the professional fit-thrower," Gray operated in New
York City, Newark, Buffalo, Boston, New Haven, and other
eastern cities in the United States, bilking suckers of about
$10,000 a year (his estimate). While feigning a convincing
heart attack in Manhattan in March 1902, he was arrested by
an alert policeman who recognized him. Gray served a nine-
month term in jail and then faded into obscurity.

GRAY, [Henry] Judd (1893-1928). American murderer. In June
1925 Gray, a meek-mannered corset salesman from New Jersey,
began a love affair with Ruth SNYDER, a sexy Long Island
housewife. They met regularly in Manhattan hotel rooms for
about two years. Judd reluctantly agreed to help Ruth murder

her husband, Albert, and on March 20, 1927, they used a sash weight to bash in Albert's skull, killing him as he lay asleep. The murderer-lovers were soon arrested on the basis of circumstantial evidence and charged with murder. Judd confessed under separate interrogation and blamed Ruth for the killing. Both were convicted and later sent to die in the electric chair at Sing Sing Prison on January 22, 1928.

GRAY, James Atwood. See SEADLUND, John Henry.

GREEN, Eddie (d. 1934). American "jug marker." He was hired by various bank robbing gangs as a "jug marker," one who checks out and studies the particular details of a bank to ensure a successful robbery. Green "cased" (looked over carefully) banks for John DILLINGER in 1933-34, selling him information about security systems, locks, vaults, bank employees, bank deposits, and other things. FBI agents gunned Green down in St. Paul, Minnesota, in April 1934.

GREEN, Edward W. (1833-66). Massachusetts bank robber and murderer. Green, postmaster of Malden, Massachusetts, was deep in debt and began to drink. On December 15, 1863, he entered the town's bank to find only the president's 17-year-old son there. Green impulsively went home, got his pistol, returned to the bank, fatally shot the teenager, and stole $5,000 in cash. Green's lavish spending caused police to question him. He confessed to the robbery and murder and was hanged on February 27, 1866. Many people consider Green America's first bank robber.

GREENGLASS, David. See ROSENBERG, Ethel [Greenglass]; ROSENBERG, Julius.

GREENHOW, Rose [O'Neal] (1817-64). American Confederate spy. At the outbreak of the U.S. Civil War (1861-65), Greenhow, a middle-aged socially prominent Southerner living in Washington, D.C., secretly obtained military information about Union activities from top government officials with whom she had earlier ingratiated herself. Greenhow apparently passed on intelligence that aided the Confederates at the First Battle of Bull Run (or Manassas) on July 21, 1861, when Union forces were routed. On August 23, 1861 she was arrested by Allan Pinkerton, head of the federal intelligence service, charged with espionage, and subsequently expelled from the North. Venturing to reenter the North in 1864, Greenhow perished at sea off North Carolina's coast while failing to run a Union blockade.

GRESE, Irma (1923-45). German Nazi war criminal. A fanatical member of Nazi youth organizations in the 1930s (against her father's wishes), she became (1942) a concentration camp supervisor at Ravensbrück and afterwards at Auschwitz, where she earned a reputation as a brutal, sadistic torturer and killer. Usually wearing a man's SS uniform and hobnailed boots, carrying a pistol and whip, she took pleasure in tormenting many thousands of female prisoners in her charge, particularly Jewish women and girls. Inmates who displeased her were often killed or severely whipped or kicked by her in a wild frenzy; she had lampshades made out of skin from murdered inmates. In 1945 Grese spent a short time at the Bergen-Belsen concentration camp before being captured by Allied soldiers. Tried by a British court which heard damning testimony against her by survivors of the camps, she showed no remorse for her war crimes, was convicted, and hanged in Hameln, West Germany, on December 13, 1945.

GRINDER, Martha (1815-66). Pennsylvania poisoner. While supposedly taking care of Mrs. Carothers, her neighbor in Pittsburgh, she poisoned her to death by mixing arsenic into her food. Grinder, plainly sadistically demented, confessed to the murder, stating her love "to see death in all its forms and phases" and a desire she "should have done more" [killing]. Tried and convicted, she died on the gallows on January 19, 1866.

GRINEVITSKY, Ignaty (d. 1881). Russian assassin. He was a member of a Russian militant revolutionary group called "The People's Will," led by Andrei Zhelyabov and his lover Sophia PEROVSKAYA, which had been plotting since 1879 to assassinate Czar Alexander II in order to end his totalitarian monarchy and begin a general uprising that would bring liberal reforms for the populace. Unsuccessful attempts were made to blow up the Czar in his train and in the Winter Palace and to shoot him. In St. Petersburg (Leningrad) on March 13 (March 1, O.S.) 1881, Grinevitsky ran from a crowd watching Alexander's entourage pass by and set off a bomb in the Czar's carriage, mortally wounding Alexander and himself. (Just before the assassination, Zhelyabov and a student named Rysakov had thrown an explosive at the Czar as he went by; both were arrested.) Later six conspirators, including Zhelyabov and Perovskaya, were convicted and executed, and repression of the Russian citizenry increased.

GUAJARDO, Jesús (d. 1920). Mexican army officer and assassin. A Yaqui Indian half-breed and a cavalry officer in the Mexican army of General Pablo González, Colonel Guajardo was ordered to pretend to desert and join Emiliano Zapata, Mexican revolutionary hero and leader of agrarian reform in his native Morelos. Zapata's forces were battling those of González and President Venustiano Carranza, Zapata's arch rival. Zapata agreed to meet with Guajardo, who had offered to bring some 800 troops with him and had supposedly proved his sincerity by taking the government-held town of Jonacatepec and executing there 59

Carrancista prisoners. On April 10, 1919, Zapata and ten of his men entered the San Juan Chinameca hacienda near Cuautla, Morelos, to meet Guajardo, whose troops, assembled in ranks like an honor guard, suddenly opened fire at Guajardo's command. Zapata and some of his comrades were killed. Afterward Guajardo was promoted to brigadier general and received 50,000 pesos. When Carranza was ousted from the presidency by Álvaro Obregón in 1920, González was arrested as a possible subversive. Soon Guajardo was also arrested and found guilty of plotting to free González; a Mexican government firing squad shot him to death in July 1920.

GUAY, Albert (d. 1950). Quebec murderer. After a Canadian Pacific Airlines plane exploded and crashed while on a flight from Quebec to Baie Comeau on September 9, 1949, investigators found evidence of a dynamite bomb at the crash site and then traced a suspicious package listed on the plane's manifest to a Marguerite Pitre, who was arrested along with her brother Genéreaux Ruest and Albert Guay. Evidently Guay had enlisted the help of Pitre, a petty crook, and Ruest, a watchmaker, to devise a bomb and put it aboard the plane in which Guay's plump wife was taking a trip at Guay's request. Guay detested his wife and wished to kill her in order to marry his sweetheart, a 19-year-old waitress. Twenty-three persons, including Guay's wife, were killed aboard the plane. Guay, Pitre, and Ruest were convicted of murder and hanged.

GUBITCHEV, Valentin. See COPLON, Judith.

GUERIN, Eddie (1860-c. 1920). American and French robber. He acquired an international reputation as a jewel thief and expert safe cracker. After serving a long prison term for an 1888 bank robbery in Lyons, France, Guerin teamed up with "Chicago May" CHURCHILL, an expert at playing the badger game (enticing a gentleman to a "lady's room" for sex and then taking his money through robbery or blackmail). The two became lovers and succeeded in stealing some $250,000 from the Paris office of the American Express Company (April 26, 1901); both were caught and sent to prison, Churchill to Montpellier Prison in France and Guerin to the infamous Devil's Island in French Guiana. In 1905 he made a miraculous escape from this prison and eventually made his way to Chicago, where he cracked a few safes and then returned to Europe. Guerin and Churchill had an angry falling out, which resulted in the latter's attempt (with help from Cubine Jackson, alias Charlie Smith, her new criminal-lover) to kill Guerin in London in 1907. Wounded, Guerin testified against the two assailants, who received long prison sentences.

GUERRE, Martin. See TILH, Arnaud du.

GUIMARES, Alberto Santos (1890-1953). American swindler and con
man. In 1922 he used showgirl Dot King to bilk large sums of
money from a Boston banker. When King was found murdered
on March 15, 1923, Guimares was arrested on suspicion of murder. On the night of the murder Guimares said he was with
socialite Aurelia Drefus, who supported his story. In 1924
Drefus fell to her death from her Washington, D.C., hotel's
balcony. An affidavit signed by her and found by the police
stated she had perjured herself by providing Guimares with an
alibi on the night of King's murder. Guimares was released on
lack of evidence and continued his swindling career unpunished
until his death.

GUITEAU, Charles Julius (1844-82). American assassin. Guiteau,
a self-styled lawyer, sent Republican presidential nominee
James A. Garfield a disjointed campaign speech. Garfield never
used the speech, but Guiteau believed his words had swayed
the public to elect Garfield and sought an ambassador's appoint-
ment to Paris. Denied the post, Guiteau resolved to gain vengeance by killing Garfield. In a railroad station in Washington,
D.C., on July 2, 1881, Guiteau fatally shot the president with
a .44 caliber pistol (Garfield died more than two months later).
Arrested immediately, Guiteau acted as his own lawyer at his
trial, during which he mocked the judge, jury, and witnesses
and said that God had told him to kill Garfield. He was found
guilty and sent to the gallows on June 30, 1882. Guiteau began to recite on the scaffold a poem he had written and memo-
rized: "I am going to the Lordy...."

GUNNESS, Belle (1859-1908?). Indiana mass murderer. In 1901
she began to run a hog farm near La Porte, Indiana, and to
place advertisements in magazines announcing she was looking
for a wealthy husband who was "kind and willing to help pay
off the mortgage." More than 14 suitors came to Belle's farm,
where they were poisoned and their money taken. It is estimated that Belle collected more than $100,000 before her disap-
pearance on April 28, 1908, when her farmhouse burned down
and inside were found the bodies of Belle's three children and
a headless woman (believed by many not to be Belle). Belle's
farm helper Ray Lamphere was arrested and confessed that he
had helped Belle in some of her murderous activities, cutting
up and burying corpses on the farm. Lamphere was sent to
prison, where he died in 1911, and Belle was never heard from
nor seen again.

GUSCIORA, Stanley H. See McGINNIS, [Joseph Francis] "Big Joe."

GUZIK, Jake (1886-1956). Russian-born Chicago mobster. In about
1922 he began to work for Al CAPONE and soon became Capone's
most trusted financial adviser. Guzik, who supposedly never
carried a gun, later managed the Chicago mob's finances and

paid large sums of protection money to crooked police and politicians, earning the nickname "Greasy Thumb Jake" because he counted out huge payoffs (he was the mob's top bagman--collector of money from racketeers). Paul RICCA, Sam "Momo" GIANCANA, Tony ACCARDO, and other Chicago gangsters entrusted Guzik with the financial arrangements of the syndicate until his death on February 2, 1956, when Guzik died of a heart attack in a Chicago restaurant.

GYP THE BLOOD [real name: Harry Horrowitz] (1889-1914). New York bouncer, gangster, and murderer. He was a bloodthirsty bouncer in New York City's East Side dance halls, where he became well-known as "Gyp the Blood" because he often drew blood cracking skulls and breaking the backs of men. He led the Lenox Avenue Gang, a violent group of muggers, sluggers, bombers, and killers that terrorized the area around 125th Street. Gyp the Blood and three of his gang--Lefty Louie, Whitey Lewis, and Dago Frank--helped Jack ZELIG carry out the murder of gambler Hermann Rosenthal, who had publicly disclosed payoffs by gangsters to the police in New York. Gyp was arrested, convicted of murder, and electrocuted on April 13, 1914. See also BECKER, Charles.

- H -

HAARMANN, Fritz (1879-1925). German sex pervert, burglar, and mass murderer. He had a disturbed youth, suffering beatings by his father, seeing his three sisters become whores, indulging in dressing in his sisters' clothing, and being sent to a mental hospital after he had assaulted several children. Later Haarmann, a homosexual, committed burglaries and sex crimes unrestrainedly. In Hanover, Germany, between 1918 and 1924, he was an informer for the police, carrying a badge and secretly using it to question and pick up poor, homeless, loitering youngsters in the city's railway station. Many young boys were taken by Haarmann to his third-floor apartment which overlooked the Leine River. There, accompanied sometimes by his homosexual lover Hans Grans, he sexually attacked the boys, strangled them to death, and then carried the bodies to the attic, where he had a room for a black-market butcher business. After cutting up and deboning the bodies in the room, whose walls became crusted with blood, Haarmann took the human flesh to Hanover's outdoor market, where he sold it as horsemeat to impoverished Germans. Into the Leine River he dumped his victims' bones and skulls, some of which were found in May 1924. A dragging of the river turned up hundreds of human bones, and soon afterward Haarmann was apprehended while accosting a boy in the train station. Police discovered many clothes from his victims in his quarters and the bloody attic room. Haarmann finally confessed and

implicated Grans, who was arrested, and together they stood
trial. Convicted of 24 murders, Haarmann, who had contemptuously estimated the number of his victims to be 30 to 40 during
the trial, was sentenced to death and later beheaded in January
1925. Grans received life imprisonment, a sentence later reduced to 12 years; he served his time and disappeared after
his release.

HAHN, Anna Marie (1906-38). German-born American mass poisoner. In 1929 she settled with her husband and son in Cincinnati, Ohio, where she met rich old gentlemen in poor health
and volunteered to provide them "tender, loving care" in their
final years. One by one the old men died and left their houses,
estates, or bank accounts to Hahn. Similarities in the deaths of
two elderly gentlemen under Hahn's care (they experienced severe stomach pains and vomiting) led to an investigation by the
Cincinnati police, who ordered an autopsy of one corpse and
discovered lethal amounts of arsenic in it. Other patients of
Hahn were then exhumed, and poison was found in them, too.
Brought to trial for the murders of five men, Hahn, named
"the beautiful, blonde killer" by the press, was convicted by an
11-woman, one-man jury, which recommended no mercy and sentenced her to death. She broke down hysterically while being
strapped into the electric chair on June 20, 1938, regained her
composure with the help of a chaplain, and died without the
authorities knowing exactly how many she actually murdered in
all (it is estimated she may have poisoned 15 men).

HAIGH, John George (1909-49). English murderer. After the disappearance of Mrs. Durand-Deacon in 1949, inquiries were made
and the police soon learned that she had last been seen with
Haigh, who was then apprehended. Haigh shockingly announced
he had "destroyed her with acid," in an acid bath. The police,
who found some bone fragments but no body, heard Haigh state
he had destroyed other people and had drunk their blood.
Haigh confessed to murdering five persons between 1944 and
1949. Tried and convicted of Mrs. Durand-Deacon's murder,
Haigh was executed at Wandsworth Prison on August 6, 1949.
The jury had rejected the defense's plea of mental instability
or insanity and had reached its verdict in 15 minutes.

HALL, Carl Austin (d. 1953). Missouri kidnapper and murderer.
An alcoholic with a long criminal record, Hall joined up with
Bonnie Brown HEADY after his release from the Missouri State
Prison in the spring of 1953. Needing money, the two lovers
put into operation a plan that Hall had dreamed up while in
prison. On September 28, 1953, Bonnie Heady abducted six-
year-old Bobbie C. Greenlease, Jr., son of a wealthy car dealer in Kansas City, Missouri, taking the child from his private
school on the pretense she was his aunt. Together Hall and
Heady drove with the boy across the Kansas state line, and in

a desolate field Hall choked and shot Bobbie to death. After
burying the boy's body in the garden of Heady's home in St.
Joseph, Missouri, the lovers sent a $600,000 ransom demand
(the largest in U.S. history up to that time) to the Greenlease
family for the boy's safe return. The ransom was paid. In
St. Louis, Hall went on a drunken binge and was turned in to
the police by a cabbie who heard him boast about the kidnapping. Hall and Heady, who was picked up, admitted to the
crime, were tried and convicted of murder, and were sent to
the gas chamber at the same time on December 16, 1953.

HAMILTON, Mary (1705-?). English impostor and bigamist. Posing
as a man, she managed to marry 14 women over a period of a
decade without being publicly revealed. Finally brought before
a court in Taunton and accused of bigamy by her wife Mary
Price in 1746, Mary Hamilton refuted none of the revelations
and charges but spurned the court by saying there was no law
against what she did. Although temporarily bewildered, the
court ruled that she had committed bigamy and sentenced her
to six months in prison, during which time she would be
whipped in public in Taunton, Glastonbury, Wells, and Shipton-
Mallet--the towns where she had her "uncommon" marriages.

HAMILTON, Ray[mond] (1912-35). American robber and murderer.
He served time for robbery in the Eastham prison farm in
Texas, where he met Clyde BARROW and later traveled with
him and Bonnie PARKER as a member of the Bonnie and Clyde
gang. Alone or with accomplices, Hamilton held up banks, oil
refineries, plants, and other establishments for about three
years. He once broke into the National Guard Armory in Fort
Worth, Texas, and stole machine guns, rifles, shotguns, and
ammunition. Hamilton was caught several times but escaped
soon afterward; miraculously he broke through two police road
traps "no human could escape." Finally caught and imprisoned
in Eastham, Hamilton, along with Joe Palmer and Henry Meth-
vin, escaped, using guns smuggled into them by Bonnie and
Clyde. Hamilton remained at large for many months, evidently
indulging himself in robbing and killing until his recapture.
On May 10, 1935, he was executed on a conviction of murder.

HANKS, O. C. "Camilla" (1863-1902). American train and bank
robber and outlaw. He rode with BUTCH CASSIDY, the SUN-
DANCE KID, and other outlaws, becoming a slick robber of
banks and trains in the West. Hanks, also called "Deaf Charley" because he was deaf in the right ear, was captured by a
posse in Teton, Montana, in 1892 after robbing a Northern Pacific train at Big Timber, Montana. Sentenced to ten years at
Deer Lodge Penitentiary, he was released in 1901 and quickly
rejoined Cassidy and his Wild Bunch. Hanks pulled off train
robberies in Wyoming and Montana with the Wild Bunch and
then headed for Texas to live it up. He was shot and killed

by lawman Pink Taylor during an argument in a Texas saloon
on October 22, 1902.

HARDIN, [John] Wes[ley] (1853-95). American gunfighter. He
developed a fast gun as a teenager in Texas and fatally shot
his first man in 1868 (later he claimed he had killed 44 men--
all in self-defense--during his lifetime). For a while Hardin
worked as a trail cowboy driving cattle between Texas and
Kansas. He gained a widespread reputation as one of the
quickest "draws" in the West. In Abilene, Kansas, in 1871,
Hardin reportedly backed down Marshal Wild Bill Hickok with a
quick gun-spin. A reward of $4,000 was placed on Hardin's
head after he killed Sheriff Charlie Webb of Brown County,
Texas, in 1874. Hardin fled east to Florida, where he was
trapped and captured by Texas Rangers at the Pensacola railroad station in 1877. Tried and found guilty of the Webb murder, Hardin was sentenced to 25 years in prison at Huntsville,
Texas. He studied law in prison, reformed himself, and was
released in 1894 with a full pardon. Hardin then became a
lawyer in El Paso, Texas, where he gained the hatred of
gunfighter-turned-lawman John SELMAN. On August 19, 1895,
Hardin, standing at an El Paso bar, was fatally shot in the
back of the head by Selman, who later claimed self-defense and
was acquitted. See also HELM, Jack.

HARE, Joseph T[hompson] (d. 1818). American highwayman. He
became famous as the leader of a band of cutthroats who stopped
and robbed stagecoaches traveling the Natchez Trace (the trail
from Natchez, Mississippi, to Nashville, Tennessee). He evaded
the law for many years, for no description of him was obtain-
able. Finally, in 1813 Hare was caught and sent to prison for
five years. Upon his release, he returned to robbery, stopping
the night stagecoach from Baltimore near Havre de Grace, Maryland, and taking about $16,000, a huge haul for those days.
Captured soon afterward, Hare was tried and hanged in Baltimore on September 10, 1818.

HARE, William. See BURKE, William.

HARGRAVES, Dick (1824-82). American gambler. A smart dresser
who wore clothes imported from Europe, Hargraves was probably the most famous "honest" gambler in New Orleans and on
the Mississippi riverboats in the 1840s and 1850s. Though he
prided himself on his professional skill, he was unsympathetic
to those he beat, some of whom sought revenge but were supposedly shot down by Hargraves. Also involved in numerous
love affairs, Hargraves once killed a banker, whose wife he
was seeing, in a gun duel and then killed the banker's avenging
brother in another duel. Weary of the gambling life and seeking adventure, Hargraves joined an unlawful military expedition
to Cuba in the late 1850s and afterward served as an officer in

the Union Army during the U.S. Civil War (1861-65). He
moved to Denver, where he died of tuberculosis in 1882.

HARPE, [Wiley] "Little" (1770-1804). American highwayman. In
the 1790s he and his brother William Micajah "Big" HARPE robbed
and murdered dozens of men, women, and children in the Appalachian frontier region. One of the so-called "Terrible Harpes,"
Little Harpe escaped capture by Ohio possemen in 1799 and
later joined a gang led by Kentucky outlaw Samuel MASON. He
and another gang member, Sam Mays, killed Mason in late 1803,
cut off Mason's head, and brought it to Natchez, Mississippi,
to claim a reward. Little Harpe, who went under the name of
Setton, was recognized and arrested along with Mays. Both
men were hanged at Greenville, Mississippi, on February 8,
1804. Their heads were cut off and displayed on poles as
warnings to others who thought of taking up the highwayman's
life.

HARPE, [William Micajah] "Big" (1768-99). American highwayman.
He and his brother Wiley "Little" HARPE robbed and killed
scores of westward-moving settlers along the Wilderness Road
(trail from Virginia to Kentucky) and the Natchez Trace (trail
from Mississippi to Tennessee) in the 1790s. Known as the
"Terrible Harpes," they moved to the Ohio territory and continued to prey on pioneers. In 1799 a large posse of frontiers-
men hunted them down; Big Harpe was shot from his horse and,
while still alive, had his head cut off; Little Harpe escaped.

HARRIS, Emily. See HARRIS, William.

HARRIS, Jean [Struven] (b. 1924). American headmistress and
murderer. Police found Dr. Herman Tarnower, prominent, 69-
year-old cardiologist and originator of the popular Scarsdale
Diet, fatally shot in the bedroom of his home in Purchase, New
York, on March 10, 1980, and the next day they charged Harris, his lover for 14 years and the head of an exclusive girls'
school in Virginia, with the murder. She later confessed to the
shooting but claimed that she had wanted Tarnower to kill her
and that he, attempting to save her during their violent con-
frontation, had received three bullet wounds and died instead.
During her sensational three-month jury trial in White Plains,
New York, the prosecution suggested that she had been moti-
vated to kill through jealousy over Tarnower's affair with his
female assistant. Despite Harris's plea of innocence, on February 24, 1981, the jury found her guilty of murder in the second
degree. She received 15 years' imprisonment, the minimum sentence allowed under New York law. Her case was detailed in
Shana Alexander's bestseller Very Much a Lady.

HARRIS, Leopold (fl. 1930-33). English arsonist and swindler. An
extensive investigation of 29 large fires of suspicious origin

resulted in the arrest of Harris, a fire assessor, in February
1933. Conclusive evidence showed that Harris had run an elaborate organization that profited handsomely from arson. Insurance officials, assessors, firefighters, accountants, and others
were involved in defrauding insurance companies of hundreds of
thousands of dollars annually, receiving kickbacks. Harris and
15 others were found guilty in July 1933. Harris was released
from prison in 1940.

HARRIS, Phoebe (1755-88). English counterfeiter. For many years
she made counterfeit coins (one known as a coiner in Britain),
but was eventually caught in the act and sentenced to death in
1788. Before an insensitive, boisterous throng outside of Old
Bailey (the central criminal court of London), she prayed
tremblingly as she was tied to a stake, hanged, and then
burned to death. This barbaric form of capital punishment was
outlawed in England in 1793, thus earning Harris notoriety as
the last criminal to suffer such an execution in the country.

HARRIS, William (b. 1945). American kidnapper. On a street in
San Francisco on September 18, 1975, FBI agents apprehended
William Harris and 26-year-old Emily Harris, the alleged last
members of the radical-terrorist Symbionese Liberation Army
(SLA). An hour later heiress Patricia C. HEARST, abducted
by the SLA on February 4, 1974, was found in an apartment in
San Francisco's Mission district. Written evidence by William
Harris implicated the Harrises in the Hearst kidnapping. In
August 1978 William and Emily pleaded guilty to "simple kidnap-
ping" and on October 3, 1978, were sentenced to ten years to
life in prison. See also DeFREEZE, Donald [David].

HARRISON, Carter (1825-93). Chicago politician and mayor. In
the 1850s and 1860s he made much money in real estate in Chicago, securing considerable financial and political clout in the
city. In 1877, after being elected mayor, Harrison was exposed
as owning properties rented to vice operators such as saloon,
gambling house, and brothel managers. Despite stories in the
press about his alleged close ties to the underworld and top
criminal figures such as gambler Mike McDONALD, Harrison was
a popular mayor, serving five separate terms in the office.
On October 28, 1893, during his fifth term, he was shot and
killed by a malcontent named Prendergast.

HART, Pearl (1878-1925?). Canadian-born American stage robber.
At the age of 20, she moved to Arizona, determined to become
America's most famous woman outlaw. She had read many tales
about the Western outlaws and had been greatly impressed. On
May 30, 1899, Hart and a miner named Joe Boot held up the
stagecoach near Globe, Arizona, taking about $450 from three
passengers. The pair got lost during their getaway and were
caught. Hart was sentenced to five years in the Yuma prison,

where she posed for pictures and became a celebrity. After
her release she toured as the "Arizona Bandit," later claiming
the distinction of having taken part in the last stagecoach robbery in the United States. She supposedly died a year after
making a nostalgic visit to Arizona's Pima County Courthouse
in 1924.

HART, Steve. See KELLY, Ned.

HARTZELL, Oscar Merrill (d. 1943). American swindler. In the
early 1920s he joined up with two con artists, Mrs. Sudie
Whiteaker and Milo F. Lewis, to operate a lucrative scam: selling worthless shares in the imaginary fortune of Sir Francis
Drake. In Iowa, Missouri, Illinois, and other midwestern states,
Hartzell and his agents contacted persons named Drake and
others, persuading them they would inherit large sums of money
when the Drake estate was finally legally settled in England.
Letters soliciting prospective investors, who received phony
receipts for investing in the supposed legal settlement of the
ancient Drake treasure (pegged at times from $22 billion to
$400 billion), were sent through the U.S. mails. Leaving a
loose organization of "Drake agents" under his brother Canfield,
Oscar traveled to London in 1924 and carried on the fraud there
for nearly nine years; Scotland Yard investigated him. Eventually, in early 1933, Oscar was extradited from England as an
undesirable alien. Federal authorities picked him up in New
York and brought him to Sioux City, Iowa, to stand trial for
postal fraud. Twice convicted (freed on bond after his first
conviction), Hartzell was sentenced to ten years imprisonment at
Leavenworth, which he entered in November 1933. His confederates were rounded up in 1935; some were convicted of fraud
in Chicago, others were freed. Some 70,000 suckers had handed over almost $2 million to Hartzell and his cohorts over the
course of the swindle; Hartzell became demented in prison and
died there in 1943.

HARVEY, Julian (1916-61). American mass murderer. Rescued
from a dinghy in November 1961, Captain Harvey told authorities his ketch Bluebelle had caught fire and sunk about 50
miles from Nassau in the Bahamas. He said he had been unable
to save his wife and the five-member Dupperrault family, all
passengers on board. Almost four days later, 11-year-old Terry
Jo Dupperrault was found alive floating on a cork raft, and she
detailed how Harvey had slain his wife and members of her family. Left by Harvey on a sinking boat (Harvey had opened the
sea cocks), Terry Jo had managed to escape and attach herself
to the cork piece. When Harvey learned that Terry Jo was
alive, he committed suicide by slashing his wrists with a razor
in a Miami motel. An inquiry revealed that Harvey had been
married before and that his first wife and her mother had
drowned in a car that Harvey had crashed through a bridge

barrier into a Florida bay in 1949. Harvey had claimed he had been thrown free during the "accident."

HAUPTMANN, Bruno Richard (1899-1936). German-born American kidnapper and murderer. On March 1, 1932, the infant son of Charles and Anne Morrow Lindbergh was taken from his crib in the Lindbergh home in Hopewell, New Jersey. A ransom of $50,000 for his release was paid by a go-between, Dr. John F. Condon, to a man (later known as Cemetery John) in the Woodlawn Cemetery in the Bronx, New York. After the body of the baby was found not far from the Lindbergh home on May 12, 1932, a nationwide manhunt began. In 1934 more than $11,000 of the ransom was found in the garage of Hauptmann, an unemployed carpenter who had entered the United States illegally in 1923 and had an arrest record in his native Germany. In a sensational trial in Flemington, New Jersey, from January 2 to February 13, 1935, Hauptmann was found guilty and was sent to the electric chair in the New Jersey State Prison on April 3, 1936, never having confessed to the crime.

HAYER, Talmadge (b. 1943). American convicted assassin. In the winter of 1966, Talmadge Hayer (also known as Thomas Hayer or Hagan) and two members of the Black Muslims, Norman 3X Butler and Thomas 15X Johnson, were tried before a jury and convicted of the assassination of Malcolm X, militant black founder and leader of the Muslim Mosque and the Organization of Afro-American Unity (OAAU). However, conflicting testimony and lack of a full investigation cast uncertainty on the identities of the actual murderers who gunned down Malcolm X on February 21, 1965, in a public auditorium in Harlem, New York. Shot and wounded by one of Malcolm X's bodyguards, Hayer was caught and later stood trial with Butler and Johnson. Hayer denied being a Black Muslim but confessed to the murder of Malcolm X, who had broken away from the Black Muslims to form the Muslim Mosque, Inc. (a bitter rivalry had subsequently ensued between these organizations). Some accomplices are thought to have helped in the assassination by igniting a smoke bomb in the back of the auditorium and creating a noisy disturbance at the time.

HAYES, Catherine [born: Catherine Hall] (1690-1726). British whore and murderer. She grew into womanhood as an attractive, buxom, and seductive whore operating in Worcestershire and Warwickshire in central England, where army officers and others were serviced by her. Although she married John Hayes (1713) and later (1719) moved with him to London, where he prospered as a coal merchant, Catherine indulged herself with different lovers and came to hate her husband. In March 1725 in conspiracy with Thomas Billings and Thomas Wood (both of whom were lovers of hers and lodged in Hayes' London house), she killed her husband and cut up the body; his head was

found thrown in the mud near the Thames River and was impaled
on a pole for public display for identification. In time, the
authorities traced the crime to Catherine, Billings, and Wood,
who admitted guilt. All three were tried, convicted, sentenced
to die; Wood died of fever in his cell, but Billings was hanged
and Catherine was burned alive at the stake when the executioner failed to strangle her beforehand at Tyburn before a
gleeful, ghoulish crowd.

HAYWOOD, William Dudley [original name: William Richard Haywood]
(1869-1928). American radical labor leader. In 1896 he joined
the newly formed Western Federation of Miners and by 1900 was
a top official of the labor organization. Haywood, called "Big
Bill," was accused of advocating violence by workers in industrial disputes. When former Idaho Governor Frank Steunenberg
was assassinated in late 1905, labor activist Harry ORCHARD,
the confessed assassin, claimed he was carrying out Haywood's
orders (Steunenberg's anti-labor actions during a strike at the
Coeur d'Alene mines had embittered Haywood, who allegedly
sought vengeance). Defended by Clarence Darrow during a
78-day trial, Haywood was acquitted and continued his labor
militancy. In 1905 he helped found the Industrial Workers of
the World (IWW), the so-called Wobblies, who hoped to overthrow capitalism and rebuild American society on a socialistic
basis. Haywood, who led large textile workers' strikes in 1912
and 1913, was arrested on a charge of sedition in 1917; he was
tried, convicted, and sentenced to 20 years' imprisonment. Released on $30,000 bail pending a new trial, Haywood fled to
Soviet Russia in 1921 and resided there until his death on May
18, 1928.

HEADY, Bonnie Brown (1912-53). Missouri kidnapper. Running
around with gangsters and craving excitement, paunchy Heady,
whose imprisoned husband (one-time bank robber) was killed
during an escape attempt, became the lover of Carl Austin HALL,
who hoped to make a quick fortune by kidnapping the son of a
wealthy auto dealer in Kansas City, Missouri. On September 28,
1953, Heady took six-year-old Bobbie C. Greenlease, Jr. from
his private school by pretending to be the boy's aunt and by
fraudulently convincing the school officials that she was taking
him to see his ill mother in the hospital. In a field Hall killed
the youngster while Heady remained placidly at a short distance.
The lovers then buried the boy's corpse in the flower garden at
Heady's home in St. Joseph, Missouri. Their $600,000 ransom
demand for the safe return of the boy was met by the Greenlease family after much confusion about the delivery of the
money. Drinking and bragging about the crime, Hall was
turned in to authorities by a St. Louis cabdriver; Heady was
soon apprehended and confessed. The two were tried and
found guilty of murder; they died simultaneously in the Missouri gas chamber on December 16, 1953. (Heady was the
first female ever executed for kidnapping in U.S. history.)

HEARST, Patty or Patricia [Campbell] (b. 1954). California bank robber. Daughter of publishing magnate Randolph Hearst, she was abducted (February 5, 1974) from her Berkeley, California, apartment by the Symbionese Liberation Army (SLA), a radical terrorist group, which demanded a $2 million ransom for her release and the distribution of $230 million of free food to the poor in California. But on April 15, 1974, she participated with SLA members in the armed holdup of a San Francisco bank, whose automatic cameras took pictures showing her with a carbine; in taped messages, Patty soon declared she had joined the SLA to fight for "the freedom of the oppressed people." The FBI seized her in San Francisco on September 18, 1975, and a protracted legal dispute about her criminal status followed until she was convicted of bank robbery and sentenced to seven years in a California prison. The powerful Hearst family later obtained a presidential commutation of her sentence, and Patty, who once described herself as an "urban guerrilla" before a court, was released on February 1, 1979, having served 22 and one half months. See also DeFREEZE, Donald; HARRIS, William.

HEATH, John (d. 1884). Arizona outlaw. While robbing a store in Bisbee, Arizona, in 1883, five masked men shot and killed four innocent townspeople before fleeing. A posse from nearby Tombstone apprehended Heath, a suspected outlaw leader, who named five men as the robbers. Heath was believed to have been involved in the Bisbee Massacre and was sentenced to life imprisonment. However, an angry mob from Bisbee stormed the Tombstone jail, seized Heath, and lynched him from a telegraph pole on February 22, 1884. See also KELLEY, Daniel.

HEATH, Neville [George Clevely] (1917-46). English murderer. On June 21, 1946, the naked, mutilated corpse of 32-year-old Margery Aimee Gardner was discovered in a London hotel room registered under the name of Lieutenant Colonel Heath. Several days later police received a letter from Heath, who disclaimed any involvement in the murder. Heath was arrested posing as Group-Captain Brooke, a false identity he had used to give police information about the missing young woman, Doreen Marshall. Incriminating evidence was found linking Heath to Marshall, whose severely mutilated dead body was discovered near the shore at Bournemouth. Heath, who had a past criminal record (theft and fraud) and who liked to pretend he was a war hero, pleaded insanity at his trial, but the jury convicted him of murder and sentenced him to death. On the way to his hanging on October 26, 1946, Heath reportedly asked for a double whiskey.

HEDGEPETH, Marion (d. 1910). American gunfighter and robber. He usually dressed in a well-cut black suit and wore a derby hat--a dapper appearance that fooled many of his gunfighting opponents. Hedgepeth's draw was said to be so quick that he once killed a man whose gun was already out of his holster. He led a band of outlaws, the "Hedgepeth Four," that robbed trains in the Midwest in the early 1890s. Caught in 1893, Hedgepeth was convicted of robbery and served time in prison in Jefferson City, Missouri. He helped H. H. HOLMES, arrested for fraud, get a lawyer to gain release (Holmes never paid his promised $500 to Hedgepeth for the help; consequently, Hedgepeth later exposed the murderous activities of Holmes, who had revealed them to Hedgepeth while in jail). Released in 1906, Hedgepeth turned to robbing banks in the Midwest. A policeman shot him dead while he tried to rob a bar in Chicago on January 1, 1910.

HEIRENS, William (b. 1929). Chicago murderer. As a youth he committed several burglaries in 1945, murdering two Chicago women in the process. Police found a note written on the bathroom mirror of one of his victim's apartments: "For heaven's sake, catch me before I kill more. I cannot control myself." In early 1946 Heirens took six-year-old Suzanne Degnan from her home, killed her, cut up the body, and shoved the pieces down several sewers. Later caught while trying to enter an apartment, Heirens insisted that "George Murman" (discovered to be his alter ego by psychiatrists) was the murderer. He finally confessed and was given life imprisonment, never to be paroled.

HELD, Leo (1928-67). Pennsylvania mass murderer. On October 23, 1967, he unexpectedly went berserk in Lock Haven, Pennsylvania, as he was walking into the Hammermill Paper Company, where he worked as a laboratory technician, and opening fire with two guns on his coworkers, four of whom were killed. Then returning home, Held fired on his neighbors and others until the police shot and seized him in his backyard. Unconscious from his wounds, he died about a day later; his hour-and-a-half rampage had taken the lives of six persons and left six others wounded.

HELLIER, Thomas (d. 1678). Virginia thief and murderer. After committing several thefts in the Virginia colony, Hellier was sentenced to bondage on a plantation. A rebellious bonded servant, Hellier passed from one plantation owner to another until he was sold to a gentleman farmer named Cutbeard Williamson. Late one night in 1678 Hellier entered the Williamson mansion and slew Williamson, his wife, and the maid. He was caught and hanged on August 5, 1678, at Westover, Virginia. Hellier's body was chained to a tall tree near the James River, an ominous warning to other bonded servants coming up the river who thought of rebellion.

HELM, Boone (1824-64). American outlaw and murderer. In 1851 he stabbed a man to death in Missouri, fled from the law to Oklahoma Indian territory, but was captured and returned to

Missouri for trial. Helm was acquitted when witnesses, apparently afraid of being killed by Helm, denied having seen anything. Later Helm was hired by Elijah Burton to guide him and others through the snow-covered mountains from Oregon to Utah; everybody in the party dropped out except Burton and Helm, but only the latter arrived in Salt Lake City. Helm later admitted to murdering Burton and eating his flesh in order to survive. He also knifed a man to death in a San Francisco brothel. In about 1863 Helm joined Henry PLUMMER and his outlaw band, the Innocents, in Montana and soon became wanted for the slayings of several men. Vigilantes caught Helm and four colleagues on January 14, 1864, and immediately hanged them.

HELM, Jack (1838?-73). Texas sheriff and murderer. In the early 1870s he became a captain in the Texas state police and was named sheriff of DeWitt County, where he was involved in the bloody Sutton-Taylor feud on the side of the Suttons. Accused of cold-bloodedly killing Sutton supporters, Helm was removed from the state force but remained sheriff; a number of murders were credited to him. In 1873 Helm became embroiled in a feud with the gunfighter John Wesley HARDIN, a distant relative of the Taylor clan. While meeting with Hardin to make peace, Helm was blasted with a shotgun by Hardin and died from shots fired by Jim Taylor, an attendant at the meeting.

HENDRICKSON, John, Jr. (1833-53). New York murderer. After marrying his 19-year-old fiancée, Maria, Hendrickson took her to live with seven members of his family in Bethlehem, New York. Maria, a bossy, imperious young woman, came to be loathed by the family, which suggested that Hendrickson get rid of her. He thus murdered Maria, using aconite poison (the first recorded instance of such poisoning in America). The family tried to cover up the crime but the police found out. Hendrickson was hanged on March 6, 1853.

HENLEY, Elmer [Wayne, Jr.] (b. 1956). Texas mass murderer. He and another teenage boy, David Brooks, were accomplices of Dean Allen CORLL, who raped, tortured, and killed at least 27 adolescent boys in and around Houston, Texas, in the early 1970s. Henley and Brooks were paid $5 to $10 for luring a boy to Corll's house, where the youth became a victim after becoming "high" on marijuana or acrylics. On August 7, 1973, Henley, believing Corll intended Brooks and him as victims, killed Corll in self-defense at an acrylic-sniffing party and then notified the police. Dead bodies in plastic bags and covered with lime were found in various places, including a boat shed near Corll's house. Henley and Brooks were implicated, tried, and convicted of nine counts and one count of murder, respectively. Henley received 594 years; Brooks was sentenced to life imprisonment.

HENSZLEIN, Klein (d. c. 1573). German pirate. A treasure-hungry pirate, Henszlein and his pirate crew plundered shipping in the North Sea after the mid-1500s, gaining a reputation as merciless killers and robbers. Finally a fleet sent from Hamburg cornered Henszlein and captured him and 33 of his companions. Henszlein and the 33 others were beheaded before the citizens of Hamburg, and their heads were fixed on the ends of sharp stakes as an ominous warning to would-be pirates.

HERRIN, Richard [James] (b. 1954). American manslayer. Described as an "All-American boy" and an outstanding Yale University graduate student on scholarship, Herrin apparently was distraught over attempts by his 20-year-old girlfriend Bonnie Garland to break off their two-year relationship; on the night of July 7, 1977, he used a claw hammer to bludgeon to death Bonnie while she slept in her bedroom at her parents' house in Scarsdale, New York. Shortly after, Herrin surrendered to a priest and confessed to the slaying, and at Yale a "crusade of compassion" was launched to help understand the case; Herrin had had a traumatic childhood, mental problems aggravated by pressures at Yale, and a so-called symbiotic relationship with Bonnie, a Yale undergraduate student. At his trial he was convicted of first-degree manslaughter (June 18, 1978) and afterward received the maximum sentence, eight to twenty-five years in prison.

HERRING, Bob or Robert (1870-1930). American robber and outlaw. As a Texas teenager engaged in horse stealing across the border in Mexico, Herring earned a reputation for betraying his cohorts in crime by stealthily riding off alone with the money from the sale of the stolen horses. In the mid-1890s he pulled several gold robberies with three other Texas outlaws and then fled with the loot. The search for Herring, the so-called "Herring Hunt," ensued throughout much of the West until 1899, when Herring was apprehended by lawmen in Dallas. He had killed two innocent townspeople there while he was fighting a gun battle with one of the outlaws he had betrayed. Sentenced to 35 years imprisonment, Herring died in prison in 1930, carrying to the grave the location, supposedly in Oklahoma's Wichita Mountains, of his buried treasure.

HESS, [Walther Richard] Rudolf (b. 1894). German Nazi leader and war criminal. He joined Adolf HITLER's German National Socialist (Nazi) party in 1920, took part in the abortive 1923 Munich putsch (coup), and wrote down Mein Kampf from Hitler's dictation while in the Landsberg prison. After Hitler gained complete power in Germany in 1933, he appointed Hess deputy Nazi party leader and a cabinet member. In 1939 Hess became third deputy Führer, second in line of succession after Hermann GOERING, but his influence on Hitler declined steadily, perhaps

undermined by Martin BORMANN, another top Nazi leader. On
May 10, 1941, Hess stole an airplane at Augsburg and secretly
flew alone to Scotland, hoping evidently to negotiate peace between Germany and Britain. Authorities arrested Hess, whose
peace proposals were discredited, and held him as a prisoner of
war during the rest of World War II (1939-45). With his sanity
in doubt, Hess was tried by the international tribunal at Nuremberg, convicted of war crimes, and sentenced in 1946 to life imprisonment at the Spandau Prison, Berlin.

HEYDRICH, Reinhard [Tristan Eugen] (1904-42). German Nazi
police official. Forced to resign from the German navy because
of misconduct in 1931, Heydrich joined the Nazi party under
Adolf HITLER and became head of the party's security branch,
the Sicherheitsdienst (SD). Heinrich HIMMLER made Heydrich
deputy chief of the Gestapo (secret police that became part of
Himmler's elite Black Shirts, the SS or Schutzstaffel) and involved him in the Nazis' plans to exterminate the Jews in Europe.
A brutal, ruthless man, Heydrich was appointed Reich "protector" of Bohemia and Moravia in September 1941 and initiated
there a reign of terror, arresting, executing, and imprisoning
in concentration camps Jews and others the Nazis wanted eliminated. Heydrich's numerous executions earned him the moniker,
"The Hangman of Europe" or "der Henker" (the hangman). In
May 1942 Czech resistance fighters shot and killed Heydrich.
In retaliation, the Nazis demolished the Czech village of Lidice
on June 10, 1945, killing the entire male population and deport-
ing the women and children. See also KALTENBRUNNER,
Ernst; NEURATH, Konstantin von.

HICKMAN, [William] Edward (1907-28). California kidnapper and
murderer. On December 15, 1927, he abducted 12-year-old
Marion Parker, one of twin daughters of Los Angeles businessman Perry Parker. Hickman then sent Parker a ransom note
demanding $7,500 (later he claimed $1,500 of it to be for college
tuition) and several other notes, one of which was written by
Marion. At an appointed spot outside Los Angeles, Parker gave
the money to Hickman, who dropped the blanket-wrapped youngster on the road and drove off. The girl was dead, strangled
with her legs cut off. Soon apprehended, Hickman was tried,
convicted, and hanged on February 4, 1928, in San Quentin
Prison.

HICKOCK, Richard E. (1932-65). Kansas murderer. While serving
time in a Kansas prison, he was informed that Herbert W. Clutter, a well-to-do wheat farmer, kept much money in a safe at
his home in Holcomb, Kansas. Paroled, Hickock, along with
Perry E. SMITH, another ex-convict, went to the Clutter home
on November 15, 1959, and terrorized the family, finally killing
Clutter, his wife, daughter, and son with shotgun blasts at
close range. Tracked down and arrested by police in Las Vegas,

Hickock and Smith confessed to the murders, were tried, convicted, and hanged in April 1965. The senseless Clutter murders were the basis of Truman Capote's bestselling book In Cold
Blood.

HICKS, Albert E. (d. 1860). American thug and murderer. He belonged to no gang but worked alone as a vicious thug and killer
for hire along New York City's waterfront in the 1850s. While
in a drunken stupor, Hicks, called "Hicksie" by many fellow
criminals and the police, was shanghaied (drugged and kidnapped
for service aboard a ship) and put aboard a fishing sloop bound
for Virginia. Hicks murdered the ship's three crewmen, decapitated them and threw them overboard, set the ship adrift, and
returned to New York with much booty. Later he came under
suspicion when the sloop was discovered, bloodstained and looted,
and was arrested when some of the captain's personal belongings
were found in his possession. He was tried and convicted of
piracy and murder and sentenced to die. Hicks, who confessed
to the crimes while awaiting his execution in the Tombs, was
sent to the gallows on Bedloe's Island on July 13, 1860; an estimated 10,000 spectators witnessed the hanging of this infamous
villain.

HIGGINS, [John Calhoun Pinckney] "Pink" (1848-1914). Texas
rancher and gunfighter. In the 1870s Higgins, who was an expert shot with a Winchester rifle, engaged in a bloody feud with
another ranching family, the Horrells, in Lampasas County in
central Texas. An officer in the Ku Klux Klan, Higgins frequently fought gun battles with the Horrells and others over
cattle rustling charges. He was known to stuff the corpse of
a dead foe inside the dead body of a disemboweled cow and
parade the sight as a "cow giving birth to a man." A ferocious
shoot-out took place between the Higgins and Horrell clans in
the town of Lampasas in July 1877; several persons were killed.
Shortly afterward the Texas Rangers arranged a truce after
they seized some members of each clan, persuading the bitter
rivals to sign an agreement that miraculously ended the feud.
A heart attack took the life of Higgins in 1914.

HILL, Mildred (fl. 1942-45). American con artist. In 1942 Hill,
at the age of about 61, initiated a matrimonial confidence game
out of Washington, D.C., writing love letters to gullible, lonely
men with the supposed intention of marrying them in the future.
A photograph of her attractive 21-year-old daughter (she had
ten children, some of whom helped her in the scam) was sent
to entice the prospective husbands, who mailed cash and checks
to Hill in response to her phony plea for funds to meet the medical expenses of her sick mother. Hill made sure her would-be
suitors were at least 500 miles distant from Washington, D.C.
If a suitor showed up, she impersonated the ailing mother, saying her daughter was out of town or had eloped with a used-car

salesman. A mimeograph machine was used for a time to copy
the many letters sent to the suckers in the West. In Chicago
in 1945, she was exposed by a suspicious suitor, was arrested
and promptly tried, and received a five-year prison sentence
for mail fraud.

HILL, Virginia (1918-66). American syndicate bag lady and narcotics peddler. While working as a waitress in Chicago in 1934,
she met and eventually married bookie Joseph Epstein, who was
head of the Chicago mob's wire service. Virginia, a beautiful
woman with a voluptuous figure, became a trusted playmate and
lover of many of the national crime syndicate's top gangsters,
including Joe ADONIS, Tony ACCARDO, Charles "Lucky"
LUCIANO, Frank COSTELLO, and Benjamin "Bugsy" SIEGEL.
She lived a rich and flamboyant lifestyle, wearing expensive
dresses, furs, and jewelry, giving wild and lavish parties in
syndicate-owned nightclubs in New York, Chicago, and other
places, and traveling extensively in the United States and
abroad. Virginia was the syndicate's main connection with
Mexican narcotics smugglers. As the mob's bag lady, she
transported large sums of money to various syndicate leaders
and evidently delivered funds to unnumbered Swiss bank accounts and elsewhere. In 1946 Siegel, Virginia's "true love,"
named his newly built gambling casino and hotel in Las Vegas,
The Flamingo, in honor of her nickname. During the Kefauver
Committee hearings into national crime activities in 1951, Virginia was asked why top mobsters gave her enormous sums of
money. She replied, "It's because I'm the best goddam lay in
the country!" For nearly the last 15 years of her life, she
traveled and lived in Europe (she faced charges of fraudulent
tax returns in the United States) and attempted to commit suicide several times. On March 25, 1966, in Salzburg, Austria,
Virginia swallowed an overdose of sleeping pills, lay down in a
snowbank, and died.

HILLSIDE STRANGLER. See BIANCHI, Kenneth [Alessio]; BUONO,
Angelo [A., Jr.].

HIMMLER, Heinrich (1900-1945). German Nazi leader. He took part
in the 1923 abortive Munich "beer-hall putsch" staged by Adolf
HITLER to overthrow Germany's republican government. Himmler, a fanatic racist, joined the National Socialist (Nazi) party
in 1925 and became head of the Schutzstaffel (SS), the party's
black-shirted elite corps, in 1929. After the Nazi purge of
1934 (Ernest Roehm, Hitler's rival and head of the Sturmabteilung,
the Nazi militia or brown-shirted storm troopers, was killed),
Himmler's SS developed into the strongest armed body in Germany next to the armed forces. Appointed chief of the Gestapo
(secret police that was absorbed into the SS) in 1936, Himmler
gained vast powers in the Third Reich (Germany's Nazi state),
whose enemies he ordered arrested, imprisoned, or executed.

After the outbreak of World War II (1939-45), his SS squads rounded up Jews and others in Germany and occupied countries and sent them to concentration camps in Eastern Europe, where they were tortured and killed en masse (Himmler established the Reich's first such camp in Dachau in 1933). He was named interior minister in 1943 and head of the Wehrmacht (armed forces) inside Germany in 1944. When Hitler found out that Himmler was secretly attempting to negotiate the surrender of Germany to the Western Allies in April 1945, he ordered his arrest, but Himmler, disguised as a common soldier, escaped to be seized by British troops and promptly committed suicide by taking poison on May 23, 1945. See also HEYDRICH, Reinhard [Tristan Eugen].

HINCKLEY, John W[arnock, Jr.] (b. 1955). American assailant. On March 30, 1981, Hinckley, an on-and-off college student and the son of a wealthy Colorado oil executive, shot and wounded U.S. President Ronald Reagan in front of the Hilton Hotel in Washington, D.C. Hinckley, using a .22-caliber revolver, fired four to six shots and also wounded three other men: presidential press secretary James S. Brady, Secret Service agent Timothy J. McCarthy, and policeman Thomas K. Delahanty. Hinckley was immediately grabbed at the scene. Based on the contents of an unmailed letter found in his Washington, D.C., hotel room, the FBI concluded that Hinckley's "motive" for the shooting was to show his love for actress Jodie Foster, whom he had never met and to whom he had written several letters. At his arraignment on August 28, 1981, Hinckley pleaded not guilty to charges of attempting to kill Reagan and the three others. On June 21, 1982, after a highly publicized eight-week trial, a U.S. District Court jury in Washington, D.C., found Hinckley not guilty by reason of insanity, and he was hospitalized for psychiatric treatment. The verdict caused a wave of protest and legislative attempts to tighten or abolish the insanity defense.

HINDLEY, Myra. See BRADY, Ian.

HIRASAWA, Sadimacha (fl. 1948). Japanese artist, bank robber, and mass murderer. One of Japan's most horrific crimes occurred at Tokyo's Teikoku (Imperial) Bank on January 26, 1948, when Hirasawa, pretending to be a Dr. Jiro Yamaguchi, entered the bank at closing time and, claiming an immediate danger of a dysentery epidemic, induced the 15 bank employees to swallow a medicine that supposedly prevented dysentery. The "doctor" then fled with 181,400 yen ($600) while the victims collapsed in pain; only three of them survived poisoning by potassium cyanide. A nationwide manhunt for the killer immediately ensued, and a painstaking police investigation led after 200 days to the arrest of Hirasawa, an artist whose paintings had gained some favor in the art world. He had allegedly attempted two similar robbery-murders earlier, posing first as a Dr. Matsui and second as Dr. Yamaguchi. At a sensational trial, two of the survivors positively

identified Hirasawa, who proclaimed innocence but was found
guilty and sentenced to death. Inexplicably, the warrant for
his execution was never signed by the justice minister, and
Hirasawa carried on his painting in his jail cell.

HISS, Alger (b. 1904). American public official and perjurer. In
1936 Hiss, a lawyer, entered the U.S. State Department and
later served as an advisor at international conferences, including
the Yalta Conference in 1945. Before the House Committee on
Un-American Activities in August 1948, U.S. journalist Whittaker
CHAMBERS identified Hiss as a fellow Communist Party member
in Washington, D.C., in the 1930s. Hiss, who was then president of the Carnegie Endowment for International Peace, was
also accused by Chambers of having helped transmit confidential
government information to the Russians. Hiss denied these
charges and sued for libel. Documents supplied by Chambers
to federal officials resulted in Hiss being indicted by a grand
jury in December 1948 on two counts of perjury. No decision
was reached by a jury at a trial in New York City in 1949. At
a second trial, Hiss was convicted of perjury (1950) and sentenced to five years' imprisonment. Many people believed Hiss'
conviction had come from tampered evidence, and controversy
remains today about the case. Released in November 1954, Hiss
later wrote a book, In the Court of Public Opinion, in which he
denied all charges against him.

HITE, Wood (1848-81). American robber and outlaw. For over a
decade, from 1870 to 1881, Hite rode with his cousins Frank and
Jesse JAMES and took part in numerous bank and train robberies in Missouri and other states. When the James gang began to
dissolve in 1881, Hite apparently learned of a plot by members
of the gang to kill Jesse in order to collect the large reward
posted for him, dead or alive. In any case, Hite was unable to
inform Jesse about it and was shot and killed by either Robert
FORD, Jesse's eventual assassin, or Dick LITTLE, both members
of the gang.

HITLER, Adolf (1889-1945). Austrian-born German Nazi dictator.
During World War I (1914-18) Hitler served in the German army
and became a corporal. Hitler blamed Germany's defeat on the
perfidy of the Communists and the Jews. In 1921 he was made
president of the German National Socialist (Nazi) party, which
was ardently nationalistic, anti-alien, and anti-Semitic and which
Hitler molded into a paramilitary organization. On November 8,
1923, attempting to start a revolution against the republican
government, he led the unsuccessful Munich "beer-hall putsch."
Arrested afterward, Hitler was sent to Landsberg prison, where
he composed a book called Mein Kampf (My Struggle), which
contained his ideas for world domination. By the late 1920s the
Nazi party, led by Hitler, Gregor Strasser, Paul Joseph GOEB-
BELS, Heinrich HIMMLER, Hermann GOERING, and others, had

many German supporters who believed in the party's promise to bring back prosperity to Germany. In 1932 the party gained control of the Reichstag (legislature), and in 1933 Hitler became chancellor with dictatorial powers. The Führer, as Hitler was titled, set in motion his plan to achieve supremacy of the so-called Aryan race by harassing, arresting, or assassinating Jews, Communists, and political opponents. In addition, he built up the armed forces of the Third Reich (Germany's Nazi state) and instituted a policy of territorial expansion. After seizing Austria and part of Czechoslovakia, Hitler's troops invaded Poland in 1939, starting World War II (1939-45). During the war he called for the mass extermination of the Jews, overseen by Adolf EICH-MANN and others, a policy which he fanatically pursued to its disastrous end. On April 30, 1945, Hitler and his wife, Eva Braun, committed suicide in the chancellery in Berlin. See also ROSENBERG, Alfred.

HOBBS, James (1819-79). American scalp hunter. In the 1830s, 1840s, and 1850s he practiced scalp hunting in the American Southwest and in northern Mexico. Hobbs, who sometimes lived with the Comanches, Navahos, Shawnees, and other Indians, received bounties from the U.S. and Mexican governments to bring in Indian scalps (scalping was a way of disposing of unwanted Indians at that time). For a period he and James KIRKER worked together as scalp hunters, and they reputedly cashed in on some scalps of dark-haired, dark-skinned Mexicans and North Americans, as well as Indians. Hobbs was a U.S. officer in the Mexican War (1846-48). He clandestinely helped the Yuma Indians kill rival scalp hunter John GLANTON in 1850. He lived to the age of 60, dying in Grass Valley, California, in 1879.

HOBECK, Ole. See WELCH, Ed.

HOCH, Johann [Otto] (1855-1906). German and American mass poisoner. Before he emigrated from Germany to the United States in the late 1870s, Hoch evidently married a number of European women, poisoned them to death, and then absconded with their money. He practiced the same thing in the United States, marrying women in Chicago, Ohio, West Virginia, and on the West Coast. Hoch located his victims by placing ads in newspapers, seeking congenial females who desired marriage to a responsible, well-off widower. Police estimated that Hoch may have married as many as 55 women, some of whom he just robbed of all their savings and disappeared, and others (perhaps 25) whom he poisoned to death with arsenic. Police tracked down Hoch in New York City, where he was attempting to marry his landlady. Returned to Chicago on charges of murder, Hoch was identified by several women as their missing husband and later was given the nickname "Stockyard Bluebeard" because he had once worked in Chicago's packing plants and was the accused murderer of many females. He was convicted of one murder (that of Marie Walcker) and hanged in the Cook County jail on February 23, 1906. See also LANDRU, Henri Désiré.

HODGES, Thomas J. See BELL, Tom.

HOESS, Rudolf (1900-1947). German Nazi war criminal. Born into a German Catholic family which hoped he would become a priest, Hoess instead left home to join the army and then the Nazi party in 1922. Involved in a killing in 1923, he received a ten-year prison sentence but was released after five years. In 1933 he joined the Schutzstaffel (SS) and became first (1934) an officer at the Dachau concentration camp, next (1938) a top official at the Sachsenhausen camp, and later (1940-43) commandant at the Auschwitz extermination camp, where he used Zyklon B gas for mass execution of Jews and other prisoners. Insensitive and imperturbable, Hoess carried out orders dutifully, a major reason why Heinrich HIMMLER considered him one of his most trustworthy officers. After World War II, Hoess was arrested, imprisoned (while behind bars he wrote his memoirs, which show no sense of guilt for any atrocities), testified piously at the Nuremberg trials, and finally was condemned to death by a Polish people's court. In April 1947 he was hanged at Auschwitz, the scene of his war crimes.

HOFFMAN, Harold [Giles] (1896-1954). New Jersey governor and embezzler. A banker from South Amboy, New Jersey, he became a popular elected public official in the 1930s, serving as a U.S. congressman and then as governor of New Jersey. Touted by the Republicans as a possible candidate for the U.S. presidency, Hoffman stayed the execution of convicted killer Bruno Richard HAUPTMANN, thus incurring a storm of criticism and losing much popularity. In 1954 an investigation by the New Jersey attorney general uncovered gross financial irregularities in the state agency which Hoffman directed at the time. Hoffman's long-time embezzlement of hundreds of thousands of dollars of public (state) and private (bank) funds was revealed after his death from a heart attack later that year.

HOFFMAN, Harry. See LENNON, [Patrick Henry] "Packy."

HOHENAU, Walter [real name: Frederick Jonas] (fl. 1927-32). German and American swindler. In 1927 Hohenau, who had been imprisoned twice in Germany for fraud, arrived in Houston, Texas, where he pretended to be a humble but brilliant scientist who had just invented an electrical machine ("the hydro-atomizer") that could provide energy strictly from water for practically no cost. After selling some $100,000 worth of stock to investors in his nonexistent Hydro Production Company, he fled to Mexico when the sham was discovered. Mexican President Plutarco Elías Calles, convinced by Hohenau that the invention was of great value, helped the perpetrator of the

fraud to secure large sums of money from the government.
Afterward Hohenau sailed to Germany and carried on his con
game there with another fuel machine. Scientists were deceived;
businessmen in London, Paris, and Rome gave him much money
to develop his device when he traveled to these and other places
to explain and sell it; Benito Mussolini was a sucker-investor.
Finally uncovered as Frederick Jonas and a swindler by German
President Paul von Hindenburg, Hohenau (who had taken the
title "count") was imprisoned, killed a guard in a vain breakout
attempt (his way of preventing his extradition to Britain, France,
Italy, or the United States to face charges), and was sent to
prison in Germany. During World War II he reportedly escaped
when the prison was bombed; Hohenau had vanished forever.

HOLLIDAY, [John Henry] "Doc" (1852-87). American dentist,
gambler, and gunfighter. In 1873 he moved west from Atlanta,
giving up a career in dentistry for a life of gambling, drinking,
and gunfighting (occasionally he performed as a dentist when
coaxed to). In about 1879 Holliday opened a gambling saloon-
brothel in New Mexico territory and once shot dead an ex-U.S.
Army scout who tried to lure away one of his prostitutes. With
a bowie knife, Holliday killed a man in an argument over cards
in Griffin, Texas, was arrested and locked in a hotel room (the
town had no jail). While an angry mob assembled to lynch him,
he escaped by the help of prostitute-friend "Big Nose" Kate
Elder, whom he later reputedly married. In Tombstone, Arizona, on October 26, 1881, Holliday helped Wyatt EARP and his
brothers, Virgil and Morgan, win the infamous gunfight at O.K.
Corral, in which the two McLowery brothers, Tom and Frank,
and Billy CLANTON were killed. (Holliday, who blasted Tom
McLowery to death with his shotgun, was wounded in the hip
by Frank McLowery, who was then shot dead by Morgan Earp.)
Afterward Holliday rode with Wyatt Earp, gunning down Clanton-
McLowery supporters. Holliday's health deteriorated because of
heavy drinking, but he continued to roam the West as a gambler
and gunfighter until he was forced to enter a sanatorium at
Glenwood Springs, Colorado, in 1887. He died there about six
months later on November 8, 1887.

HOLMES, Alexander William (1812-?). Finnish-born American seaman
accused of murder. On a voyage from Liverpool, England, to
Philadelphia in April 1841, Holmes's ship, the William Brown,
struck an iceberg and sank, but not before two lifeboats with
some survivors had been launched. Captain George L. Harris
and eight sailors in a jolly boat set out to reach Newfoundland,
while nine seamen, including First Mate Francis Rhodes, Holmes,
and 32 passengers foundered in heavy seas in a longboat designed
for 20 persons. When high winds and gigantic waves began to
batter the longboat, loaded to the very gunwales, the boat was
in danger of sinking unless it was quickly lightened. Holmes,
Rhodes (who bemoaned the decision), and other seamen seized

14 passengers and jettisoned them overboard; 16 persons went
to a watery grave (two sisters allegedly jumped overboard after
their brother was thrown out). The next day the longboat was
picked up by a schooner bound for France, and Holmes and
the others were later returned to New York, where they learned
that the jolly boat had reached Newfoundland safely. The murderous events were made public, causing ferocious debates about
the ordeal and the justification for murder. Holmes and Rhodes
were indicted for murder in Philadelphia; Rhodes disappeared
and Holmes faced trial. David Paul Brown defended Holmes during an eight-day trial, at the end of which the jury convicted
Holmes with a recommendation for mercy. Public opinion was on
the side of Holmes, who served a six-month prison term and
then vanished back at sea.

HOLMES, H[arry] H[oward] [real name: Herman Webster Mudgett]
(1858-96). American swindler, arsonist, and mass murderer.
He was expelled from medical college for stealing cadavers in an
insurance swindle. Later Holmes bought several cheap buildings
in Chicago, heavily insured them, and set fire to them to collect
the insurance money. In 1892 he built a huge mansion (later
termed "Murder Castle") in Chicago, to which he lured many
young women with offers of finding them jobs or husbands.
His mansion had rooms without doors in which women were imprisoned, tortured, and murdered. Holmes became involved in
an insurance swindle with a crook named Benjamin F. Pitzel and
was put in jail in St. Louis, where he met Marion HEDGEPETH,
a robber, and revealed to him his murderous activities. After
his release, Holmes killed Pitzel in Philadelphia during a dispute.
Hedgepeth, who had helped Holmes get out of jail on a promise
of money and who had received nothing, told the police what he
knew about Holmes. Holmes was arrested, convicted of the Pitzel murder, and hanged at Moyamensing Prison in Philadelphia
on May 7, 1896. Chicago police found the remains of at least
200 female corpses in Holmes's "Murder Castle."

HOLMES, John Maurice. See THURMOND, Thomas Harold.

HOLZWEBER, Franz. See PLANETTA, Otto.

HOOLEY, Ernest Terah (1859-1947). English financier and swindler.
He was a stockbroker who acquired control of established companies, manipulated their books, and issued company prospectuses
with greatly inflated values. Between 1887 and 1897 he became
well known for his many spectacular, money-making business
deals. Hooley's company promotions attracted numerous investors, who poured money into the schemes and Hooley's own
pocket. In 1904 and 1912 Hooley was charged with obtaining
money under false pretenses; he served one year in prison after his conviction in 1912. In 1922 Hooley was found guilty of
conspiracy in connection with one of his property businesses and

sentenced to three years in prison. He was in and out of court on various charges after his release, but managed to remain out of jail until his death.

HOPE, Jimmy (1840-c. 1900). New York policeman and burglar. A member of the New York Police Department, Hope helped bank robbers, such as George Leonidas LESLIE, in their crimes. As a police "fixer," he bribed bank watchmen, guards, and policemen to stay away during robberies and also to hinder any police pursuit that might occur. He was instrumental in the success of Leslie's $2.7 million robbery of the Manhattan Savings Institution in 1878. The following year, Hope was uncovered, tried, convicted of burglary, and given a long prison sentence. After his release in the late 1890s, Hope disappeared and was thought to have died within a couple of years.

HORN, Tom or Thomas (1860-1903). American lawman and murderer. He served as a U.S. Army scout in the war against the Apaches under Geronimo, whose final surrender he negotiated. Horn then worked as a cowboy, deputy sheriff, and Pinkerton agent, finally quitting the law-abiding life to become a callous hired killer who would shoot down anyone for the right price. During the 1890s Horn was hired by big Wyoming cattlemen to settle scores for them and to eliminate small ranchers. Horn considered his killings works of art, often waiting for days to get the one sure shot at his victim. Deputy U.S. Marshal Joe Lefors won Horn's confidence one night; Horn, drunk, admitted to many killings, including that of 14-year-old Willie Nickell (Horn, lying in ambush for the boy's father, had killed the boy in error). Horn was tried, found guilty, and hanged on November 20, 1903 in Cheyenne, Wyoming.

HORNER, Joe or Joseph. See CANTON, Frank M.

HORROWITZ, Harry. See GYP THE BLOOD.

HORSLEY, Albert E. See ORCHARD, Harry.

HOTSUMI, Ozaki. See SORGE, Richard.

HOUSDEN, Nina (b. 1916). Michigan murderer. Her henpecked husband, whom she continually and wrongly accused of infidelity, finally filed for divorce, but Nina's irrational jealousy drove her to strangle him to death with a clothesline while he was in a drunken stupor in their Highland Park, Michigan, apartment (December 18, 1947). Using a meat cleaver and carving knife, she cut up the body, wrapped the pieces in pretty Christmas paper, threw them in her car, and then drove toward her native Kentucky, where she planned to deposit the parcels in the wilds. When the car broke down in Toledo, Ohio, Nina lived and slept in the front seat while a mechanic worked to fix it for two days. A dreadful odor coming from the Christmas packages caused the mechanic to open one in secret and discover a human leg; he told the police, who arrested Nina. Returned to Michigan, she was tried, convicted, and sent to prison for life.

HOWARD, Frances (1593-1632). English noblewoman and poisoner. The wife of the third earl of Essex, she fell passionately in love with Robert CARR, court favorite of England's King James I, who helped the lovers arrange an annulment of Howard's marriage in order that they could wed. However, Sir Thomas Overbury, friend and adviser to Carr, violently opposed the annulment plan and consequently was imprisoned in the Tower of London (1613) on charges of plotting against King James. Frances Howard, seeking to get rid of Overbury (who was a talented writer), sent poisoned food and drink to him in the Tower, where he perished on September 15, 1613. Afterward she married Carr, whom the king made the earl of Somerset. As Lady Somerset, she had much power and wealth until the circumstances of Overbury's death were revealed publicly (1615) and she and her husband were brought to trial (1616). Prosecuted by the famous Sir Francis Bacon, she confessed in tears to the poisoning and was sentenced to death, as was her husband (though his guilt was never positively established during his separate trial later). The king pardoned them both, however, and they remained in the Tower until 1622. Living together in Oxfordshire afterward, they grew to hate one another, resulting in Frances not speaking to Robert during the last five years of her life.

HUBERTY, James [Oliver] (1943-84). American mass murderer. The worst mass killing by a single person in a single day in U.S. history occurred in a McDonald's fast-food restaurant in San Ysidro, California, on July 18, 1984, when Huberty, dressed in combat fatigues and armed with a 12-gauge shotgun and two other firearms, walked in and began shooting indiscriminately. He fired about 140 shots, killing 21 persons and wounding 19, before a police marksman shot him dead 90 minutes later. At the time Huberty was an unemployed security guard who had moved to the area with his family in late 1983 after losing a job in Ohio; he told his wife he was "going hunting humans" on the afternoon of the massacre. No known motive for his behavior was revealed, although his despondency over the recent loss of another job may have ignited Huberty, an unemotional man who owned an arsenal of weapons and was known to have sometimes beaten his young daughter.

HUMBERT, Theresa [born: Theresa Daurignac] (fl. 1877-1902). French swindler. Homely, uneducated, ambitious, shrewd, and dissimulating, she went from being a poor peasant girl in southern France to being a supposed Parisian heiress to a $20 million fortune in securities. Pretending she was rich, she married

Frederic Humbert, a lawyer, to whom she later confessed her deception. They settled in Paris and beginning in 1877 carried on a colossal fraud by pretending that Madame Humbert was the daughter of Robert Henry Crawford, an American multimillionaire industrialist, and had inherited his money ($20 million). However, Madame Humbert said she was disbarred from touching the securities, which must remain in a huge steel safe in her Parisian apartment until lawsuits by two Crawford nephews who claimed rights to the fortune were settled in the courts. Parisian society was deceived, and financiers loaned her much money on credit (eventually a total of $14 million). Madame Humbert, her husband, her unmarried sister, and two brothers (who posed as the Crawford nephews) were privy to the fraud and stalled its disclosure for 25 years by instituting false claims and counterclaims in the courts. The law finally forced the opening of the safe on May 8, 1902; found inside were some negotiable bonds (about $1,000 worth), an empty jewel box, and one trouser button. Madame Humbert and her four cohorts had fled the night before, but they were found masquerading as Armenian refugees in Madrid and brought back to Paris to stand trial on charges of fraud. All were found guilty; Madame Humbert received a five-year sentence of solitary confinement, as did her husband; the others got lesser sentences.

HUME, Alexander Douglas. See WILBY, Ralph Marshall.

HUMPHREYS, Murray (d. 1965). Chicago gangster. As a young man, he was a torpedo (hired gunman or assassin) for Chicago underworld boss Al CAPONE and later worked his way up to become a board member of the Chicago syndicate. Nicknamed "The Hump" and "The Camel," Humphreys frequently wore camel's-hair coats and drove high-priced automobiles while engaging in mob activities. According to popular belief, he shotgunned to death old Roger TOUCHY, a bootlegger and Capone's enemy, before being sent to jail, on a Chicago street on December 17, 1959, just 23 days after Touchy's release from prison. A heart attack ended the life of Humphreys in his Marina City apartment about six years later.

HUNT, Sam[uel McPherson] "Golf Bag" (d. 1956). Chicago gangster and murderer. Credited with the murders of at least 15 men, Hunt worked for Al CAPONE as a top "hit man" in Chicago; he was involved in Capone's gang war with gangster George "Bugs" MORAN. In 1927, while investigating a shooting along Chicago's Lake Michigan shore, police came upon Jack "Machine Gun" McGURN and Hunt, who was toting a golf bag that contained golf clubs and a semiautomatic shotgun. Police were unable to link McGurn and Hunt with any crime, but Hunt quickly received the nickname "Golf Bag." Hunt served as a pallbearer at Capone's funeral in 1947. In 1956 Hunt died in bed of natural causes.

HYDE, Bennett Clarke (fl. 1909-13). Missouri doctor and poisoner.
His wealthy wife was a member of the distinguished Swope family of Kansas City, Missouri, where he resided and practiced
medicine. Avariciously hoping to make her the sole inheritor of
her uncle Thomas Swope's fortune (over $2 million to be left to
relatives through a will), Hyde used cyanide and strychnine
(one offset the other to hide symptoms of poisoning) to murder
the uncle and his executor, James Hunton, in 1909. Using typhoid germs, the doctor tried to kill other Swopes, doing away
with one before suspicious officials disinterred the corpses of
Thomas Swope and Hunton and found poison in them. In April
1910 Hyde stood trial for multiple murder and was found guilty
and sentenced to life imprisonment; appeals were made, costly
lawyers were hired by Hyde's wife (who thoroughly rejected the
verdict), and three more trials followed without reaching a conviction. At the start of a fourth trial, the court dropped the
charges against Hyde at the request of his lawyers; the doctor
was let go, to the chagrin of some.

- I -

INGENITO, Ernest (b. 1924). American burglar and mass murderer.
As a youth, he spent time in the Pennsylvania State Reformatory
for attempted burglary. While serving in the U.S. Army in
1943, Ingenito provoked a fight with a sergeant, was sent to
prison for two years, and was dishonorably discharged. Unable
to get along with his wife, who refused to let him see his two
young sons, Ingenito went into a rage on November 17, 1950,
shooting eight of his relatives (seven died) in Vineland, New
Jersey. Apprehended by police, who stopped him from committing suicide, Ingenito was judged insane and was imprisoned
for life in the New Jersey State Hospital.

INSULL, Sam[uel] (1860-1938). English-born American securities
manipulator. In 1881 he became Thomas A. Edison's secretary,
was soon directing the operations of several Edison electric companies, and was heading Chicago Edison by 1902. After forming
Commonwealth Edison in Chicago in 1907, Insull struck out on
his own, helping other utilities companies grow and prosper, as
did Insull himself, who was a multimillionaire in the 1920s. Buying stock in Insull's Middle West Utilities group was considered
a safe and profitable investment. In June 1932 Insull's financial
manipulations (underhanded buying and selling of properties
and funds between companies) were discovered, and most of his
companies collapsed, with investors losing some $750 million.
Nearly broke, Insull fled to Europe and refused to return to
the United States to face charges of embezzlement and mail
fraud. Finally arrested by the Turkish authorities and sent
home, Insull was set free when the U.S. government failed to
prove its charges due to the complexity of Insull's financial

dealings and the ambiguity of the law. He then moved to Paris, where he died on a street corner in 1938, having only $1,000 cash and about $14 million in debts.

IRELAND, William Henry (1777-1835). English forger and author. For two years (1794-96) the literary world was excited by the Shakespearean "discoveries" which he, the precocious teenage son of a London engraver and antique dealer, claimed to have been given by a wealthy English gentleman who wished to remain anonymous. Many scholars and notables including James Boswell, Edmund Burke, William Pitt, and the Prince of Wales were impressed by the mass of material in William Shakespeare's handwriting: legal documents, a new version of King Lear, a portion of the original Hamlet, and two unknown ("lost") plays called Vortigern and Rowena and Henry II. However, after the derisible, first performance of Vortigern and Rowena at London's Drury Lane Theater on April 2, 1796, much of the public doubted the authenticity of Ireland's discoveries, and later the Shakespearean scholar Edmond Malone exposed Ireland as a fraud. In late 1796 the latter openly confessed that he had forged all the "new" Shakespeareana and exonerated his father, whom many had blamed for the hoax. Ireland later wrote some original romances and verse.

IRVING, Clifford (b. 1930). American writer and forger. In 1971 he duped the McGraw-Hill Book Co. into paying him $750,000 for a phony autobiography of reclusive billionaire Howard R. Hughes. Irving also swindled Life magazine, which intended to publish excerpts of the book. In a telephone press conference from his hideaway in the Bahamas, Hughes told reporters he had never met Irving and denied any knowledge of the biography. A Swiss bank disclosed that a $650,000 check, cashed by one "H. R. Hughes," had been deposited to the account of "Helga R. Hughes," soon revealed as Irving's wife. In New York on March 13, 1972, Irving and his wife admitted that the purported book of Hughes was a hoax and pleaded guilty to federal charges of conspiracy to defraud McGraw-Hill; they returned what remained of the publisher's money. Sentenced to two and one half years' imprisonment, Irving was released after 17 months and resumed a writing career.

IRVING, Johnny or John (d. 1883). New York pickpocket. He organized and led the famous "Dutch Mob," a gang of more than 200 pickpockets that operated in the Bowery (lower Manhattan) in the 1870s. In 1877, when the police managed to break up the gang, Irving turned to working single-handedly. In late 1883 in a New York bar owned by bank robber Shang Drapper, Irving was shot and killed by Johnny "The Mick" WALSH. Billy Porter, who had accompanied his friend Irving to the bar, then killed Walsh with a blast from his gun.

IRWIN, Robert [born: Fenelon Arroyo Seco Irwin] (fl. 1930s). New York murderer. In the early 1930s he visited doctors in New York hospitals to receive treatment for a mental disorder. In October 1932 Irwin severely injured himself in an attempted self-castration. Five years later, jobless and depressed, he went to the home of his girl friend, Ethel Gedeon, in New York and strangled Ethel's mother and sister to death and, using an ice pick, killed a visitor in the house. Afterward Irwin roamed about the country, finally resting in Chicago, where he revealed his crime to the press. Taken into custody, Irwin was judged insane; he pleaded guilty to second degree murder in November 1938 and was sentenced to 139 years' imprisonment.

IRWIN, Stella Mae (b. 1923). South Dakota bank robber. At age 15, she ran away from home and married an ex-convict named Bennie Dickson, who taught her to be a sharpshooter. Together they held up two banks in South Dakota, escaping with a total of almost $50,000 in 1938. Police and FBI agents pursued the couple throughout the Midwest without capturing them. Bennie was finally killed in a gun fight with agents in St. Louis; Stella Mae was caught the next day (April 7, 1939) traipsing about in Kansas City, Missouri. At age 17, this one-time "Little Sure Shot" emulator of Annie Oakley received ten years' imprisonment after being tried and convicted of bank robbery in South Dakota.

IVANOV, Igor A. (b. 1930). Soviet spy. In October 1963 the FBI apprehended four Soviet agents and a U.S. engineer, John Butenko, for attempting to gain possession of secrets concerning the U.S. Strategic Air Command electronic communications system. Three of the Soviet agents, who worked in the United Nations, were deported as unwelcome persons, but the fourth, Igor Ivanov, a chauffeur without diplomatic immunity, along with Butenko, faced trial. Each was convicted of espionage and sentenced to 30 years' imprisonment (1964). The Soviet embassy posted bond ($100,000) which freed Ivanov, who became the first spy ever convicted and held who stayed out of prison. In 1965 the U.S. government rejected a Soviet attempt to exchange Ivanov, a detainee in the U.S. while appealing his case all the way to the Supreme Court, for Newcomb Mott, an American held in the Soviet Union for illegal trespass. In 1971 Ivanov was permitted to visit Russia, on the condition that he would return when his trial was rescheduled; he never came back.

IVERS, Alice. See POKER ALICE.

- J -

JACK THE RIPPER (fl. 1888). Whitechapel murderer. An unknown person killed seven (maybe 14) women, all prostitutes, in or

near the Whitechapel district in the East End of London between
August 6 and November 9, 1888. The victims all had their
throats cut by a long-bladed knife after being ferociously stabbed,
and all of the victims' bodies (except the first) were savagely
mutilated. The killings occurred sometime between 11 p.m. and
4 a.m. The last murder was the most horrific, with the killer
cutting off the woman's breasts, removing her heart and kid-
neys, and laying these things out to be seen. From the way
the body was cut up, the killer seemed to have a good knowledge of human anatomy and surgical talents. The police once
received half a human kidney in the mail, supposedly from
Jack the Ripper who had extracted it from a victim. They also
received notes of ridicule from someone called Jack the Ripper.
Despite a strong public outcry and many efforts to find the killer,
various authorities, including Scotland Yard, failed to catch
the Ripper, who vanished as abruptly as he or she had appeared.
A number of theories as to the identity of the killer have been
put forth, and there have been numerous suspects, including
poisoner George CHAPMAN, deranged M. J. DRUITT, Dr.
Mikhail Ostrog, and Dr. Thomas Neill CREAM.

JACKSON, Eddie (1873-1932). Chicago pickpocket. Jackson, often
called America's most dexterous and expert pickpocket, worked
the Loop area of Chicago from the 1890s until the early 1930s.
The "kiss-the-sucker" technique was his specialty: bumping a
victim directly in front and, at the same time, nimbly lifting his
or her money with one quick movement. Arrested almost two
thousand times during his life, Jackson was regularly bailed out
by lawyer-politician Black Horton, whom he kept on retainer.
Although he sometimes made $1,000 a week, Jackson was a home-
less pauper when he died in 1932.

JACKSON, Frank (1856-?). Texas train robber and outlaw. He
rode with the famous outlaw Sam BASS and his gang, robbing
three express trains in Texas in 1878. While planning to rob
the bank at Round Rock, Texas, in July 1878, Bass, Jackson,
and other gang members were surprised by lawmen who had been
informed of the impending robbery by a traitorous gang member,
Jim MURPHY. Jackson helped Bass, gravely wounded, to escape, but Bass soon died and Jackson was never seen again.
Some Texans believe Bass told Jackson where the loot from his
robberies was buried, and Jackson retired as a wealthy man
somewhere in the far West.

JACKSON, Humpty (d. 1914). New York gangster and murderer.
Jackson, a well-educated man who liked to read books by Vol-
taire, Huxley, Darwin, and Spencer, led a cutthroat gang of
robbers and killers in New York City in the 1890s. He always
carried three revolvers--one in a pocket, another in a holster
tied to his hunchback (from which he got his name "Humpty"),
and a third in a special compartment in his derby. Jackson was

arrested and convicted more than twenty times for various crimes, including burglary and murder. In 1909 he was convicted of ordering the murder of someone he'd never met and given a 20-year term in prison, where he later died. See also SPANISH LOUIE.

JACKSON, [Mary Jane] "Bricktop" (1836-after 1862). New Orleans prostitute, mugger, and murderer. At the age of 13, she became a whore in New Orleans. Because of her violent, murderous temperament, Jackson (nicknamed "Bricktop" because of her flaming red hair) was kicked out of brothels and dance halls along New Orleans' toughest street, Gallatin Street. The "scourge of Gallatin Street," as she was also dubbed, then operated mainly alone, selling her services as a whore and a street mugger. In the late 1850s police had credited her with the murders of four men and the maimings of at least a dozen others. After Jackson stabbed her lover, mugger John MILLER, to death in 1861, she was sentenced to ten years in prison, but nine months later she was released under a blanket pardon given by the military governor of Louisiana to most prisoners during the U.S. Civl War. Jackson soon vanished entirely.

JAMES, [Alexander] Frank[lin] (1843-1915). American bank and train robber and outlaw. During the U.S. Civil War (1861-65), he rode with Confederate guerrilla leader William Clarke QUANTRILL and took part in the bloody raid on Lawrence, Kansas, in 1863. Frank and his brother Jesse, hunted as guerrilla-murderers by Union soldiers after the war, formed an outlaw gang that committed numerous bank and train robberies and killings in Missouri, Kansas, Iowa, and other states. In 1881 the state of Missouri posted a $10,000 reward for the capture of the James brothers, dead or alive. On October 5, 1882, six months after Jesse's assassination, Frank surrendered to Governor Thomas T. Crittenden in his office in Jefferson City, Missouri, saying he was tired of the outlaw's life. After a series of trials, Frank, now part of the romantic James legend, was set free and retired to his farm in Clay County, Missouri, where he died many years later. See also JAMES, Jesse [Woodson].

JAMES, Jesse [Woodson] (1847-82). American bank and train robber and outlaw. He gained legendary fame for reportedly stealing from the rich and giving to the poor, like Robin Hood, but in truth he was a murderous robber who kept what he stole. At the age of 17, Jesse rode with Confederate guerrilla leader Bill ANDERSON and participated in the massacre at Centralia, Missouri. In 1866 Jesse and his brother Frank formed a gang of outlaws, which included brothers Cole, Jim, John, and Bob Younger, Charlie Pitts, Clell Miller, and Bill Chadwell, and began robbing banks in Missouri and other midwestern states. The gang, which took up train robbery in 1873, became known for its daring raids and many incredible escapes from law officials, including Pinkerton detectives. While attempting to rob the First National Bank in Northfield, Minnesota, on September 7, 1876, the outlaws were trapped by the town's citizens. Only Jesse and Frank managed to escape; the other gang members were either killed or captured later. The James brothers stayed quiet until 1879, when Jesse formed a new gang, which included Robert and Charles FORD. The James gang again robbed banks and trains. In 1881 the Missouri governor secretly offered the Fords a $10,000 reward to kill Jesse. At his home in St. Joseph, Missouri, where he was living under the name of Thomas Howard, Jesse was shot in the back and killed by Robert Ford on April 3, 1882. See also HITE, Wood; JAMES, [Alexander] Frank[lin]; LITTLE, Dick.

JEANNERET, Marie (d. 1884). Swiss nurse and mass poisoner. Until finally being arrested and found guilty of fatally poisoning seven persons during her nursing career, Jeanneret apparently derived libidinal gratification and a thrill from pain and murder, managing for a considerable time to cover any evidence against her. A physician named Rapin, extremely wary of her, had her taken into custody. Examination of the corpses of patients once under her care brought to light her penchant for belladonna, along with other poisons such as antimony and morphine. Pretty and appealing, Jeanneret received only 20 years' incarceration from the jury that convicted her.

JEGADO, Hélène (d. 1851). French mass poisoner. Employed as a cook and maid in households in France for over 20 years, she secretly and sadistically used poison to kill family members and servants who annoyed her, lacing their food with arsenic and watching gleefully as the victims grew violently sick and died in pain. In one place, her own sister and six others fell victim to Jegado in this way. In the early 1850s she was hired by Professor Théophile Bidard in Rennes in Brittany. After two of Bidard's servants suffered painful deaths, the suspicious professor called in the authorities to investigate; poison was discovered in one body. The illiterate and now panic-stricken Jegado was apprehended when her background revealed a series of strange poisonings. In December 1851 she was tried, convicted, and guillotined in Rennes for the murders of at least 26 persons (she may have killed as many as 60, according to some accounts).

JENNINGS, Al (1864-1961). American robber. Al and his brother Frank, two Oklahoma cowboys, robbed a Rock Island express train on October 1, 1897, netting $60 apiece. Lawman Bud Ledbetter caught the pair a day later, and the court sentenced the two to life imprisonment for the trivial robbery (the pardon business flourished in those days). Released after five years, Al later traveled to California, where he became well known for his fanciful tales about his robberies (we have only his word

that there was more than one) and his expert marksmanship
(friends said he was a poor shot). In 1948 Al backed up 101-
year-old J. Frank Dalton's false claim to be Jesse JAMES, who
many believed had not been killed in 1882. When Al died in
1961, the press called him "the last of the Western outlaws" with
tongue in cheek.

JIM THE PENMAN [real name: Alonzo James Whitman] (1854-after
1910). American con man. During his life he squandered a
large inheritance, served as a state senator in Minnesota, was
awarded an honorary degree from New York's Hamilton College
(where he almost was elected as a member of the board of
trustees), and made a fortune through illegal activities. He is
probably best remembered for his confidence wizardry--his
skillful forgery and slick passing of thousands of worthless
checks (hence his sobriquet "Jim the Penman"). In 1899 he
was apprehended as the head of a lucrative confidence gang in
New York City and later was found guilty of obtaining bank
loans through the use of spurious credit and subsequent cashing of bad checks. In his scams, Jim the Penman managed to
swindle some fashionable hotels, such as Boston's Parker House,
Chicago's Grand Pacific, New York's Bartholdi, and Atlantic
City's Isleworth Hotel. He was caught over 40 times for passing
bad checks and served stints in prison on various convictions
involving fraud.

JIM THE PENMAN. See SAWARD, James [Townshead].

JODL, Alfred (1890-1946). German Nazi general and war criminal.
In 1935 he became head of the Home Defense Department in the
war ministry of the Third Reich (Nazi Germany). Adolf HITLER,
to whom Jodl was fanatically loyal, named him chief of staff of
operations in the armed forces supreme command, the Oberkom-
mando der Wehrmacht (OKW), on August 23, 1939, about a week
before Hitler launched Germany's invasion of Poland that pre-
cipitated World War II (1939-45). Jodl and Wilhelm KEITEL,
Hitler's two key figures in the supreme command, worked out
and directed almost all of the German military campaigns in the
war. Captured Allied troops were summarily shot to death on
orders by Jodl. At Reims, France, on May 7, 1945, Jodl signed
the unconditional surrender of Germany to the Allies. The International Military Tribunal convicted him of war crimes, including particularly a wide variety of crimes against persons
and property. He was hanged at West Germany's Nuremberg
Prison on October 16, 1946.

JOHNNY BEHIND THE DEUCE [real name: John or Michael
O'Rourke] (1862-82). American gambler and gunfighter. In
early 1878 he came to Tucson, Arizona, where he soon became
known for his slick card playing and shooting prowess. Labeled
a cheater by many, Johnny managed to stay clear of the law

until early 1881, when he was arrested for shooting dead a miner who had accused him of thievery. Wyatt EARP, for whom Johnny had dealt cards in the Oriental Saloon (partly owned by Earp) in Tombstone, Arizona, took Johnny from an angry mob planning to lynch him in Tombstone and imprisoned him in Tucson, where Johnny soon broke free. In a card game in 1882, gunfighter Pony Deal, whose close friend Johnny RINGO was allegedly fatally shot in the head while asleep by Johnny Behind the Deuce, called the gambler a cheat and, before "The Deuce" could raise his gun, shot him to death.

JOHNSON, John (d. 1824). New York murderer. He killed his roommate James Murray in his sleep to steal his money in 1824. Johnson then carried Murray's body, wrapped in a blanket, to the New York harbor to dispose of it. When he was accosted by a policeman, Johnson dropped the corpse and fled. The unknown corpse was displayed at City Hall Park for someone to identify it. At least 50,000 people viewed it before it was identified. Johnson was arrested, tried, and sentenced to be hanged for murder. Many thousands watched his execution on Second Avenue and Thirteenth Street on April 2, 1824.

JOHNSON, [John V.] "Mushmouth" (d. 1907). Chicago gambler and racketeer. Johnson, a flamboyant black man seen habitually with a cigar in his mouth, controlled successful policy rackets and gambling saloons in parts of Chicago from about 1885 until his death in 1907. His gambling operation on South Clark Street allowed bets as low as five cents. Despite attempts by civic reformers to shut down his gambling joints, Johnson managed to stay in business, paying enormous sums to crooked police for protection. Just before he died, Johnson claimed he had only $15,000 to show for having pocketed some $250,000 from his operations.

JOHNSON, Richard (d. 1829). New York murderer. With a pistol loaded with buckshot, Johnson shot and killed his mistress, Ursula Newman, on November 20, 1828. He had grown enraged when Newman, who had given birth to his child, had refused to admit it was his and to give it his name. Soon arrested, Johnson confessed, was tried, and sent to the gallows on Blackwell's Island on May 7, 1829.

JONAS, Frederick. See HOHENAU, Walter.

JONES, Charles T. See PATRICK, Albert.

JONES, Edward (fl. latter 1800s). American swindler. Unsuccessful as a chemist and mining assayer in San Francisco, Jones turned his scientific skill to a life of crime as a modern "alchemist" capable purportedly of manufacturing gold. The underworld called him "Gold Dust Teddy" because of the elaborate

swindles he organized to sell bags of gold which contained
brass filings covered by gold dust. Jones also originated the
famous gold brick swindle: selling to prospective victims gold-
covered lead bricks that corresponded perfectly in weight with
solid gold bricks. Hounded by the law, Jones moved across
country and then to Europe, where he continued his nefarious
operations until a suspicious jeweler in London informed the
police when Jones tried to sell him a mysterious powder (actually just red marble) supposedly capable of turning silver
into gold. Arrested, Jones pleaded guilty to an attempt to obtain money by false pretenses and got off with a light sentence.
Later, he disappeared from public view.

JONES, Jim or James Warren (1932-78). American minister and accused mass murderer. Born in Lynn, Indiana, he became a
reverend of the Disciples of Christ and subsequently leader of
the People's Temple, a socialist-religious cult, in San Francisco
and Los Angeles. In the 1970s he built up the Temple's mem-
bership, gained some public recognition for his social work, and
was appointed to the San Francisco Housing Authority in 1976.
But press reports of flagrant mistreatment of members within
the Temple caused Jones in 1977 to decide to move to northwest
Guyana, where he and many of his followers set up a commune
called Jonestown. Temple members complained about gross sexual abuses committed or ordered by Jones, some of whose followers shot and killed U.S. Representative Leo J. Ryan of
California and four others at Guyana's Port Kaituma airport as
they were leaving after a visit to investigate nearby Jonestown.
After the shootings that same day, November 18, 1978, Jones
reportedly forced his followers at the commune to drink cyanide-
laced Kool-Aid to commit mass suicide. The next day Guyanese
soldiers discovered 911 men, women, and children lying dead
at Jonestown, and Jones himself, dead with a bullet in his head.
A Guyanese coroner's jury blamed the deaths on Jones and one
or several unknown accomplices.

JONES, William (d. 1877). English-born Canadian and American
gambler and con man. An expert card player, Jones fleeced
gullible Canadians for many years, playing three-card monte.
About 1850 he moved to Mississippi, where he met and formed
a partnership with gambler George H. DEVOL, who gave Jones
the sobriquet "Canada Bill." The pair worked the Mississippi
riverboats, cheating greenhorn card players for nearly a decade.
When river traffic dwindled, Jones turned to the railroads and
cheated greenhorns at three-card monte for about 15 years. In
1874 Jones and gamblers Jimmy Porter and Charlie Starr opened
up several crooked gambling dens in Chicago. After a while
Jones, who had amassed about $150,000 in six months and then
lost it playing faro (to Jones, gambling itself was more important
than the money), moved to Cleveland, plying his "trade," and
then to Pennsylvania, where he later died in the Charity Hospital
in Reading, Pennsylvania.

JOYCE, William (1906-46). American-born British Nazi propagandist and traitor. As a youngster, he was taken to England, where he became involved in the fascist movement. At different times between 1913 and 1938, Joyce was a member of the British Fascist Party, Sir Oswald Mosley's Union of Fascists, and his self-established National Socialist League. In August 1939 Joyce, who held a British passport because of his claim to have been born in Ireland, disappeared on a trip abroad. After the outbreak of World War II, he was heard broadcasting on the radio in English from Berlin, Germany, trying to induce the British and other allies to capitulate. Joyce was given the nickname "Lord Haw-Haw" because of the derisive manner of his speech, whose timbre was unusual. His English-language Nazi propaganda lasted throughout the war. In May 1945 Joyce was captured by British soldiers, who recognized his voice, in a forest on the German-Danish border. He was tried under British law because of his British passport (Joyce had been granted German nationality in 1940), found guilty of high treason, and hanged at Wandsworth Prison on January 3, 1946.

JUANITA (1828-51). Mexican prostitute. A young, dazzling Spanish-speaking woman, she serviced the Mexican and American miners of Downieville, California, until settling down with one she loved in mid-1851. A popular ruffian-miner, attempting to force himself upon Juanita (known only by that name) in her cabin, was knifed to death by her on July 4, 1851. A quick jury "trial" in a saloon ended in her conviction despite a strong case of self-defense, and she was hanged by a blood-thirsty mob soon afterward. Later many people inveighed against the barbaric frontier justice inflicted upon her, the first woman to be "tried" and hanged in California.

JUDD, Winnie Ruth (b. 1909). Arizona murderer. In 1932 she became known as the "trunk murderer" after being found guilty of killing two friends, Agnes LeRoi and Hedvig Samuelson, in Phoenix, Arizona, cutting up the bodies, and shipping the pieces to Los Angeles. Sentenced to be hanged, Judd was granted a special sanity hearing shortly before her execution. At the hearing, the "Tiger Woman," as the press dubbed her, clapped her hands, laughed and yelled, and pulled at her hair and clothes. Her father traced insanity in the family back 125 years. Judged insane, Judd was sent to the Arizona State Mental Hospital for life. She made seven successful escapes, once staying out more than six years. Finally psychiatrists judged her sane and she was sent to prison. In 1971 Judd was paroled and went to live in California.

JUDSON, Edward Zane Carroll. See BUNTLINE, Ned.

- K -

KALOUMENOS, Nicholas. See VAVOUDIS, Nicholas.

KALTENBRUNNER, Ernst (d. 1946). German Nazi police official and war criminal. A loyal member of the German National Socialist (Nazi) party, he succeeded Reinhard HEYDRICH as head of the Sicherheitsdienst (SD), the clandestine security and intelligence branch of the Schutzstaffel (SS), during the Third Reich (Nazi Germany). Many Nazi atrocities and killings in concentration and extermination camps in Germany and German-occupied territories during World War II (1939-45) were committed on Kaltenbrunner's orders. After several assassination attempts (1943-44) on the life of Adolf HITLER, Kaltenbrunner and Heinrich HIMMLER carried out a vicious purge of fellow Germans suspected of disloyalty and conspiracy. Many were arrested, tortured, hanged, or interred in camps. After the war the International Military Tribunal tried and convicted Kaltenbrunner, who denied all charges against him, of war crimes, especially crimes connected with concentration camps, and on October 16, 1946, he was sent to the gallows in West Germany's Nuremberg Prison.

KAPLAN, Nathan. See KID DROPPER.

KARPIS, Alvin [born: Francis Albin Karpoviecz] (1907-79). Canadian-born American burglar, bank robber, and kidnapper. In 1926, while serving time in a Kansas reformatory for attempted burglary, Karpis befriended Larry DeVol, a gangster who taught him how to crack open safes. Later the pair went on a burglary spree in Kansas, Missouri, and Oklahoma. Arrested in 1930, Karpis met fellow-prison-inmate Fred BARKER, who later nicknamed Karpis "Old Creepy" because of his dour expression after undergoing plastic surgery on his face in 1934. Karpis participated in the ransom-kidnappings of brewer William A. Hamm, Jr. (1933) and of banker Edward G. Bremer (1934). After the deaths of Fred and Ma Barker in 1935, Karpis, accompanied by Harry Campbell and others, pulled a number of bank and payroll robberies and became the FBI's Public Enemy Number One. Caught by FBI agents in New Orleans on May 1, 1936, Karpis was sentenced to life imprisonment, spending almost 33 years at Alcatraz before being transferred to Washington's McNeil Island Penitentiary. Paroled in early 1969, Karpis was deported to his native Canada. He retired to Spain in the late 1970s.

KEARNEY, Patrick (b. 1939). California mass murderer. Between late 1972 and 1977 dead bodies and parts of bodies of 28 persons were discovered in plastic trash bags, garbage bins, junk piles, and highway ditches along California's coastline. Police were baffled by the so-called "Trash Bag Murderer" until Kearney, a former aerospace worker, turned himself in and later pleaded guilty in court to 21 killings (he gave no reason for his murder rampage). He was sentenced to two concurrent life prison terms.

KEELY, John E. W. (1827-98). Philadelphia swindler. In 1872 Keely, a former carnival pitchman, presented his new, miraculous energy-producing machine, which he claimed could convert a quart of water into enough fuel to propel a 30-car train from Philadelphia to New York City. Keely's elaborately connected metal contraption demonstrated amazing power by shredding iron and shooting bullets through foot-thick boards. In 1874, after four leading financiers visited Keely in his Philadelphia workshop and became convinced of the value of his "invention," the Keely Motor Company was formed for the development of the machine, and thousands of dollars of stock in the company were sold to gullible investors. Large sums of money advanced to Keely for research were pocketed by him during the next 25 years. Though The Scientific American called Keely's machine foolish, investors were conned by Keely's scientific-sounding verbiage. After his death, the mysterious source of power that ran his machine was discovered to be a compressed air assembly hidden in Keely's cellar.

KEENE, John (d. 1865). American murderer and robber. After the outbreak of the U.S. Civil War in 1861, Keene enlisted in the Confederate navy and, soon after, knifed to death his ship's captain. A fugitive from Southern authorities, Keene joined the Union forces at Memphis, Tennessee, but again killed a man and fled. Using the name Bob Black, he then formed and led a gang of highway robbers that terrorized Tennessee until Keene was seized by Union authorities. However, he escaped and went west, where he rode with some outlaws in Utah and Montana. Arrested on a charge of murder in Montana, Keene was promptly convicted and hanged in 1865.

KEITEL, Wilhelm (1882-1946). German Nazi general and war criminal. Advancing steadily through the German military ranks, Keitel had become a major general by 1934, when Adolf HITLER had established himself as Führer (leader) of the Third Reich (Nazi Germany). One of Hitler's closest and most loyal military advisers, he was appointed chief administrative officer in the ministry of war in 1935 and was promoted, in 1938, to head of the armed forces supreme command, a new post created by Hitler, who remained the absolute supreme commander of Germany's forces. During World War II (1939-45) Keitel presented the terms of the French surrender in June 1940 and directed troops on the Eastern Front in 1941. After the war at the Nuremberg trials he was convicted of war crimes, especially crimes in occupied territories and against prisoners of war, and was hanged at Nuremberg, West Germany, on October 16, 1946. See also JODL, Alfred.

KELLEY, Daniel (d. 1884). Arizona outlaw. He and four other
men robbed a store in the mining town of Bisbee, Arizona, on
December 8, 1883, and in the process shot to death four innocent bystanders. The robber-killers fled, and a massive manhunt for them ensued. At Deming, New Mexico, a barber recognized Kelley while shaving off his beard (Kelley's identity
had been made known by a suspect named John HEATH) and
held a razor to his throat while lawmen were summoned. Kelley, arrested, was quickly tried for the Bisbee Massacre, convicted, and hanged on March 8, 1884.

KELLY, Dan or Daniel. See KELLY, Ned.

KELLY, Edward O. See O'KELLY, Edward.

KELLY, [George R.] "Machine Gun" (1895-1954). American bootlegger, gangster, and kidnapper. He was a bootlegger in Texas
in 1927 when he met and later married Kathryn Shannon, who
taught him how to use a machine gun and pumped up his reputation as a fearless gangster. Kathryn, who also gave him the
sobriquet "Machine Gun," urged Kelly to take up bank robbery
and join a gang. Between 1931 and 1933 Kelly took part in
several minor bank holdups in Texas and Mississippi. At
Kathryn's insistence, Kelly turned to kidnapping to get more
money, and on July 22, 1933, accompanied by Albert Bates, he
abducted millionaire oilman Charles F. Urschel from his home in
Oklahoma City, Oklahoma, and held him for $200,000 in ransom.
Urschel, released when the ransom was paid, put the FBI on
Kelly's trail. On September 26, 1933, Kelly and his wife were
captured at their hideout in Memphis, Tennessee (Bates was
earlier arrested in Denver). The trio received life imprisonment. Kelly was transferred from Alcatraz to Leavenworth,
where he died of a heart attack. See also KELLY, Kathryn
[Shannon].

KELLY, [Joseph] "Bunco" (1838-1934). English-born Oregon shanghaier. Kelly, unrelated to SHANGHAI KELLY of San Francisco
notoriety, practiced, however, the same trade--shanghaiing
(kidnapping seamen and others to fill orders by crew-short sea
captains)--in Portland, Oregon, for about 35 years. Arriving
in Portland from Liverpool, England, in 1861, Kelly quickly became known as a ruthless, money-hungry shanghaier, seizing
drunken men from waterfront saloons and brothels and handing
them over to captains for $30 to $50 a head. He received the
nickname "Bunco" because of his double dealings: collecting
payments for dummies and corpses (supposedly alive drunken
sailors wrapped in blankets). In 1894 Kelly, despite his claim
of innocence, was convicted of killing an ex-saloon keeper,
George Sayres, for $2,000 and sentenced to the Oregon State
Penitentiary. Released in 1907, Kelly soon moved to South
America, where he lived to the age of 96.

KELLY, Kathryn [Shannon] (b. 1904). American kidnapper. In the late 1920s she promoted her husband, George, as tough, bold "Machine Gun" KELLY and encouraged him to rob banks in Texas and other states. When "Machine Gun" carried out her scheme to kidnap Oklahoma oilman Charles F. Urschel for a ransom of $200,000 in July, 1933, Kathryn wanted to kill Urschel after the ransom was collected but was persuaded not to by her husband (the only time "Machine Gun" stood up to his wife). Apprehended with her husband in Memphis, Tennessee, on September 26, 1933, Kathryn was sentenced to life in prison. She was released from the Cincinnati Workhouse in 1958 and faded quickly from the public's view. See also SHANNON, Robert K. G.

KELLY, Ned [born: Edward Kelly] (1855-80). Australian bushranger. In 1878 he and his brother Dan, both of whom were wanted by the law for horse and cattle thievery, formed an outlaw gang with Joe Byrne and Steve Hart, two other bushrangers (outlaws living in the bush of Australia). The gang successfully held up banks (1878-80) in the Victoria-New South Wales border area, where the poor and lawless country folk frequently sympathized with the attempt to fight the in-coming, mighty landowners and their wealth. The Government of Victoria, after learning that the four gang members had shot and killed three out of the four lawmen sent into the treacherous bushland to track down the gang (October 1878), offered a reward of Ł1,000 (later increased to Ł8,000) for information leading to the gang's capture. The Kellys escaped several shootouts with police and other pursuers until June 1880, when they were boxed in at Glenrowan, a town on the main railway line from Melbourne. The two Kellys, Byrne, and Hart, failing to loot the town before being confronted by the police, took a stand in the Glenrowan Hotel and fought a wild, day-long gun battle during which Byrne was killed and Ned Kelly, who had crawled outside the hotel, was wounded in the leg. Police set fire to the building to force out Hart and Dan Kelly, who both continued to shot at police and perished in the flames. Ned Kelly recovered from his wound in custody and later, in the Melbourne jail, was hanged on November 11, 1880.

KELLY, Shanghai. See SHANGHAI KELLY.

KEMMLER, William (1861-90). New York murderer. Kemmler, alias John Hart, was convicted of axing to death his mistress, Matilda Ziegler, a crime he committed in Buffalo, New York, on March 29, 1889, and was sentenced to death. While awaiting execution on death row, Kemmler became the focus of much attention because he was to be the first to die in the newly developed electric chair. On August 6, 1890, while doctors and news reporters watched, Kemmler was strapped into the chair at the Auburn Prison, New York; calm and collected, he seemed to enjoy the occasion as electrodes were attached to his head and back and a mask placed over his head. After 1,000 volts went through him for 17 seconds, Kemmler was still alive. The current was then sent fitfully through him until he was finally pronounced dead. The nearly botched execution was severely criticized by some of the press, which saw electrocution as perverse and inhuman.

KEMPER, Ed[mund Emil, III] (b. 1948). California mass murderer. At the age of 16 he shot and killed his grandmother and grandfather while living with them. Judged insane, Kemper was held in California's Atascadero State Hospital until 1969, when he was pronounced "fully recovered" and released. In 1972 and 1973 he offered rides to female students and other women in Santa Cruz, California, killing six of them, decapitating them, and indulging in depraved sexual activities with them. On April 20, 1973, Kemper clubbed his mother to death while she was asleep, cut off her head and hands, and threw the hands in a garbage disposal. He then strangled his mother's best friend, a neighbor, to death. Three days later, in Pueblo, Colorado, Kemper called the Santa Cruz police, told them about the killings (the police knew nothing about them), and surrendered, saying he might kill again if not confined. Kemper, who was found guilty of eight counts of first-degree murder, was sentenced to life imprisonment. When asked earlier what his punishment should be, he had answered, "Death by torture."

KENNEDY, [James W.] "Spike" (1855-c. 1900). American murderer. One night in 1878 he was kicked out of a saloon in Dodge City on orders from Mayor James H. Kelley. Kennedy, son of a wealthy rancher, had been too attentive to beautiful showgirl Fannie Keenan, whom Kelley loved. Kennedy later fired a shot into Kelley's bedroom and unknowingly killed Fannie, who was asleep on the sofa. He then fled from town and was chased by Wyatt Earp, Bat Masterson, Charlie Bassett, and Bill Tilghman across more than 100 miles of open range. Finally wounded and caught, Kennedy said he wished he had been killed when told of Fannie's death. He was tried and acquitted and later became a cowboy drifter, never returning to Dodge City.

KENT, Constance [Emilie] (1844-?). English murderer. In late June 1860, in the village of Road (now Rode) near Trowbridge, Somersetshire, her three-year-old half-brother was found dead, his throat slit, lying near the Kents' mansion-like home. Local police and Scotland Yard investigated after a board of inquiry determined that the boy had been murdered. No real evidence was discovered, but it was surmised that someone in the family was responsible, possibly Constance, a pretty, demure, and strong-willed 16-year-old. Afterward Constance entered a convent in Brittany, France, and in 1863 entered a convent in Brighton, England. Unexpectedly, on April 25, 1864, she calmly confessed to the murder, implying that hatred for her stepmother was the motive. At an emotional trial before a justice in 1865, she was convicted and sentenced to death. Because of her age at the time of the crime, the sentence was later commuted to life imprisonment. Released from England's Millbank Prison 20 years later, in 1885, she went to live in Canada and died in obscurity on an unknown date. Speculation has persisted that Constance took the blame under pressure from others who were really involved.

KENT, Frank (fl. latter 1800s). English counterfeiter. An electrician by trade in London, he secretly turned his skills to "coining" (counterfeiting money), first making coins by means of a galvanic battery and acid bath, then by casting them in molds, and finally by striking them from a die by means of a stamping machine. His nearly perfect specimens, ranging from sixpences to sovereigns, which were usually amalgams of gold and silver, aluminum, or zinc, earned him the sobriquet "King of the Coiners." Kent, who passed out his spurious coins while traveling about England, was eventually uncovered by Scotland Yard after the noise of his stamping machine in his workshop at Peckham caused suspicious neighbors to alert the police. Found guilty of coining, Kent received five years imprisonment and, after his release, supposedly went straight. In time, however, he disappeared; his fake coins turned up again; and Scotland Yard caught and charged him again. Kent was given a 16-year sentence this time.

KERRIGAN, Michael. See DOBBS, Johnny.

KETCHUM, Sam[uel] (1884-99). American train robber and murderer. He followed his brother Tom into crime, robbing trains and killing innocent people in the late 1890s. After Tom's capture in July 1899, Sam, now head of the Ketchum gang, stupidly attempted to rob the same train his brother had held up near Twin Mountains, New Mexico, on four different occasions. Sam was shot in the arm by train conductor Frank Harrington and fled to a nearby ranch, where a cowboy badly amputated his arm. He died of blood poisoning shortly afterward. See also KETCHUM, Tom or Thomas "Black Jack."

KETCHUM, Tom or Thomas "Black Jack" (1862-1901). American train robber and murderer. He and his brother Sam were cowboys who took up robbery when times were tough. In 1898 Tom formed an outlaw band that held up the same train at the same place near Twin Mountains, New Mexico, four times. On the last time, July 11, 1899, possemen were waiting for the Ketchum gang, which included Elzy LAY (Sam did not take part). Tom and Elzy were pursued and caught, but not before they shot and killed two lawmen. Tried and convicted of train robbery, Tom was hanged at Clayton, New Mexico, on April 26, 1901. See also KETCHUM, Sam[uel].

KHAYR AD-DIN. See BARBAROSSA II.

KID CURRY [real name: Harvey Logan] (1865-1904). American
robber, gunfighter, and murderer. In the mid-1880s he was
taught the art of cattle rustling and train robbery by Wyoming
outlaw George "Flat Nose" CURRY, whom he so admired that he
adopted the outlaw's surname as his own in 1882. Kid Curry,
a ruthless, quick tempered gunslinger, killed eight men in gun
duels, becoming one of the West's most feared gunfighters (he
was a deadly marksman with his famous pearl-handled Peacemaker
with a 14-inch-long barrel). In 1896 Kid Curry joined the Wild
Bunch, a loose gang of outlaws formed by Butch CASSIDY, and
took part in every major robbery the gang pulled off. After
Cassidy left for South America in 1901, Kid Curry continued
robbing banks and trains and became the most-wanted outlaw in
America. In the fall of 1902 he was caught near Knoxville, Tennessee, imprisoned in an "escape-proof" jail, but broke out in
June 1903. Hunted continuously by posses and Pinkertons, Kid
Curry was wounded during a gun battle with lawmen in Colorado
in 1904; not to be taken, he committed suicide by shooting a
bullet through his temple.

KID DROPPER [born: Nathan Kaplan] (1891-1923). New York
gangster and racketeer. As a youth he earned the name "Kid
Dropper" because he used to drop a wallet filled with counterfeit bills on the sidewalk, then pretend to accidentally find it,
and persuade a gullible passerby to take it from him for a price
and return it to the supposed rightful owner. After World War
I, Kid Dropper organized a gang of vicious labor sluggers and
extortionists in New York City. He vied with Johnny SPANISH,
a gang member, for leadership, which he assumed when the
latter was murdered in July 1919. In 1923 Jacob "Little Augie"
ORGEN and his gang waged war against Kid Dropper's mobsters
for control of the bootlegging and labor rackets. Arrested for
carrying a concealed weapon in August 1923, Kid Dropper, while
being moved by police from one court to another, was shot and
killed by a hoodlum named Louis Kushner, who wished to impress
the "Little Augies," Orgen's gang, with a heroic deed. Kushner
was caught and received a 20-year prison sentence.

KID DUFFY [real name: Adolph W. Duff] (fl. 1904-24). Denver
con man. In 1904 he became a partner of Lou BLONGER, who
operated a large confidence ring headquartered in Denver,
Colorado. Kid Duffy, his well-known underworld name, controlled Blonger's con empire, which eventually included some 500
colleagues, and collected Blonger's cut from the various scams,
which supposedly netted Blonger about $10 million each year
during the first two decades of the century. Through the per-
sistent efforts of Texas rancher J. Frank Norfleet, who had
been bilked by members of Blonger's con ring, Kid Duffy, along
with Blonger, were exposed and imprisoned in the mid-1920s.

KID TWIST [real name: Max Zwerbach or Zweibach] (1882-1908). New York gangster. Kid Twist, so named because of his uncanny ability to evade the arm of the law, was the righthand man of Monk Eastman and took command of Eastman's gang after Eastman was convicted of robbery and sent to prison in 1904. Kid Twist, who had a sadistic streak, was credited with killing at least 15 men during his life, including rival gang leader Richie FITZPATRICK in 1905. On May 14, 1908 Kid Twist ridiculed Louie the Lump (Louis Pioggi), a member of the Five Points gang, about having made love to his girl, Carroll Terry, a dancehall star. That same day Louie the Lump, accompanied by other Five Pointers, gunned down Kid Twist and CYCLONE LOUIE (Vach Lewis) outside a Coney Island bar, killing them both. Louie was arrested, pleaded guilty to two counts of manslaughter, and served 11 months in the Elmira Reformatory. See also ZELIG, Jack.

KID TWIST. See RELES, Abe.

KIDD, Captain [William] (c. 1645-1701). British privateer and pirate. After sailing as a privateer in the British king's service against the French in the West Indies in 1689, Kidd became an established shipowner and sea captain in New York. While in England in 1695, he received a special royal commission as a privateer to attack French and pirate ships preying on British shipping in the Indian Ocean. In 1697, however, on board the Adventure Galley Kidd turned pirate after failing to take a prize and began plundering Arab and Indian Mogul ships. In 1698 he seized his biggest prize, the rich Armenian treasure ship Quedah Merchant, and scuttled the Adventure Galley. Piracy charges were made against Kidd, who claimed his captured ships were lawful prizes. In 1699 he surrendered on promise of a pardon. At his trial in London, Kidd was found guilty of piracy and murder and was hanged on May 23, 1701.

KILPATRICK, Ben[jamin] (1865?-1912). American train and bank robber and outlaw. Kilpatrick, a slick, handsome gunslinger sometimes referred to as the "Tall Texan," successfully rode the outlaw trail during the 1890s, hiding out at the Hole in the Wall, an almost impregnable natural fortress on the Wyoming-Utah border. He worked with two gangs: one headed by Tom "Black Jack" KETCHUM and the other, the Wild Bunch, led by Butch CASSIDY. After the Wild Bunch fell apart in 1901, Kilpatrick and his girlfriend, Della ROSE, called the "Rose of the Bunch," went to St. Louis, Missouri, and wildly spent money from a recent train robbery in Wagner, Montana. Suspicious lawmen apprehended them, found currency from the robbery in their hotel room, and forced Kilpatrick to confess. On December 12, 1901, Kilpatrick was sentenced to 15 years at the federal prison in Atlanta; Della, convicted as an accomplice, received five years in a Tennessee women's prison. Released in June 1911, Kilpatrick hoped to rob trains like in the old days but had a short career. On March 14, 1912, at Dryden, Texas, he and an ex-convict named Ed WELCH attempted to hold up and rob a Southern Pacific train, but express guard David A. Truesdale surprised them when they weren't looking, struck Kilpatrick on the head with an ice mallet, killing him with one blow, grabbed Kilpatrick's gun, and shot Welch dead.

KING, Kate [real name: Kate Clarke?] (1842-after 1870). St. Louis madam. Abducted by Confederate raiders in Missouri in 1862, Kate became the mistress of the raiders' leader, William Clarke QUANTRILL, who wantonly slaughtered helpless citizens during raids on Missouri and Kansas towns. Quantrill left half of his estate to Kate, who established a stylish bordello in St. Louis, Missouri, in late 1865 and prospered for a number of years. After marrying a man named Woods, she retired as a madam and disappeared.

KINTPUASH. See CAPTAIN JACK.

KIRKER, James (1810-52). American scalp hunter and gunrunner. As a teenager he saw his parents killed by Apaches in the Arizona territory and soon after began lifting Indian scalps, which he sold to Mexican and American authorities (scalping was a lawful practice to get rid of hostile Indians). In 1842 Kirker teamed up with another scalp hunter, James HOBBS, and together they slaughtered hundreds of Indians. To earn more money, Kirker ironically began gunrunning for an Apache chief but ended the operation after the Mexicans posted a large reward for his capture. Resuming scalping with Hobbs and aided by friendly Shawnees, the pair scalped some three hundred Apaches and Navahos in one village, rode to Mexico to collect the bounty, but, because the Mexican treasury was short, received only 2,000 of the 23,000 gold pesos due them. Kirker deserted Hobbs, stealing the 2,000 pesos, and fled to California, where he drank himself to death in 1852. (Mexican authorities eventually gave Hobbs the 21,000 pesos due the scalp hunters, and Hobbs retired a rich man.)

KISS, Béla (1878-after 1930?). Hungarian robber and mass murderer. Although he disappeared during World War I (1914-18) and was never caught, Kiss was held responsible for the murders of at least two dozen persons over a 15-year span, beginning in 1912 when he killed his wife, about 15 years his junior, and her lover. Afterward Kiss, a reserved and respected Hungarian tinsmith from Czinkota (his native village), turned vengeful and rapacious, seemingly possessed by an uncontrollable sexual and murderous desire. He lived in Budapest under an alias, indulging himself constantly at brothels and luring women through matrimonial advertisements to his apartment, where he robbed and strangled them. The dead bodies were brought by him to his Czinkota house, where they were kept in alcohol in tin casks in the cellar for long periods until he could safely bury them on his grounds outside. Public outrage about the crimes after their discovery did not deter Kiss, who went underground forever.

KLAUSEN, Max. See SORGE, Richard.

KLIMEK, Tillie (1865-1936). Illinois mass poisoner. Married five times while living in Chicago's Polish laboring community, big and brawny Tillie secretly killed her first four husbands by serving them arsenic-laced stew, afterward collecting considerable money from life insurance taken out on them; Tillie also poisoned a nosy neighbor who questioned her self-proclaimed clairvoyance predicting the deaths of her husbands before they occurred in 1914, 1915, 1916, and 1920. The fifth husband, Anton Klimek, whose demise she foretold to a clerk while buying a funeral dress in 1927, was found dying in bed when police entered on the clerk's report. Klimek was saved, but his weighty, bumptious wife was found guilty and sentenced to life; she died later in Dwight, Illinois, women's prison.

KNAPP, Joseph (c. 1770-1830). Massachusetts murderer. On the night of April 6, 1830, Joseph, his brother John, and Richard Crowinshield clubbed and stabbed retired sea captain Joseph White to death. They had conspired to rob the captain of his hoarded money. Crowinshield, already having a bad reputation, was questioned and put in jail. A fellow prisoner, after learning of the crime from Crowinshield, wrote a letter to extort money from the Knapp brothers. The police seized the letter and arrested the Knapps. Joseph confessed and was promised immunity if he testified against the others. Crowinshield hanged himself in his cell, and John was found guilty and hanged without his brother's testimony. Daniel Webster, the prosecutor, said Joseph had consequently lost his immunity because he failed to testify against his brother. Joseph was tried, convicted, and hanged, despite a public outcry against his conviction, termed "vindictive" by many.

KOCH, Ilse (1917-71). German Nazi war criminal. A bosomy, blue-eyed blond, she became an ardent supporter of Nazism and Adolf HITLER's storm troopers, or Schutzstaffel (SS), in the mid-1930s. Heinrich HIMMLER, leader of the SS, arranged her marriage to his chief aide, Karl Koch, with whom she lived in a villa near the Buchenwald concentration camp during World War II (her husband was commander there). Oversexed and sadistic, she frequently indulged in orgies with SS junior officers and enjoyed ordering the deaths of prisoners, especially Jews, who displeased her. From human skins, she had lampshades and pairs of gloves made; her villa's dining room was adorned with cut-off, shrunken heads of prisoners. Arrested when Germany was defeated, Ilse was convicted of war crimes by a U.S. military tribunal at Nuremberg (1948) but was released, despite worldwide protests, by a U.S. review board two years later. A German court then put her on trial in Augsburg (1950-51), found her guilty of multiple murder, and imprisoned her for the rest of her life.

KORETZ, Leo (1881-1925). Chicago swindler. In 1917 Koretz, a bon vivant stockbroker, began selling shares in the Bayano Timber Syndicate of Panama, a company supposedly prospering from its extensive and valuable land holdings of mahogany. When oil was reportedly discovered on company lands in Central America, top tycoons in Chicago invested heavily and were sometimes rewarded with dividends (Koretz paid investors dividends out of their original investments and often persuaded them to take additional oil stock instead of their dividends). Once, at a gala banquet in Chicago's Congress Hotel, Koretz was honored as a financial genius; during the festivities newsboys broke in and raced about, shouting, "Extra, extra, read all about it! Leo Koretz's Oil Swindle!" The partygoers were momentarily stunned until they were informed that the newspapers were a joke--just part of the entertainment; it caused a great laugh. However, Koretz's scam was soon exposed when some stockholders visited the company's holding in November 1923 and found undeveloped swampland owned by the Panamanian government. Koretz fled with $5 million to Canada, but authorities, knowing Koretz was a diabetic, managed to trace him to Halifax because of his need for insulin (a rare and costly hormone medication then). Arrested and imprisoned to await trial, Koretz ate an entire five-pound box of chocolates which he had persuaded an admiring lady friend to bring to him in his cell and keeled over dead on January 9, 1925.

KREUGER, Ivar (1880-1932). Swedish financier and swindler. The Swedish Match Company, a holding firm organized by Kreuger in 1917, solely controlled the making of matches in Sweden when, in 1919, Kreuger decided to expand his operations overseas with the intention of eventually securing an international match monopoly. A secretive and silent megalomaniac with a craving for unlimited power and money, Kreuger began a vast speculative financial operation throughout Europe and the United States after receiving enormous loans from Swedish banks (he used as security $100 million in forged phony Italian bonds, which were kept hidden in a Stockholm bank vault). Kreuger bought up match companies everywhere, controlling probably over half the match production in the world by 1928. U.S. bankers and businessmen and others invested millions of dollars in his company, and Kreuger made huge loans to countries and, in return, received monopoly rights for the manufacture and sale of matches, thus eliminating much competition worldwide. His fraudulent industrial and financial empire began to fall apart after the stock market crash of 1929. "The Match King," as Kreuger was called, failed to make good repayment of the phony Italian bonds (which he had resold over and over in the past decade) when they came due in November 1931. Investigations into his dealings ensued, and on March 12, 1932, Kreuger shot and killed himself in his lavish apartment in Paris. With public disclosure of his fraudulent practices, his enterprises collapsed generally. An estimated $750 million had been conned by Kreuger from his numerous investors--individuals and governments.

KRIST, Gary Steven (b. 1945). American kidnapper. On December 17, 1968, Krist and Ruth EISEMANN-SCHIER abducted Barbara Mackle, 20-year-old daughter of a wealthy Florida real estate developer, and held her for a $500,000 ransom. They buried Barbara alive in a coffin-like box nine feet below the surface, near Atlanta. Two tubes extending to the surface allowed Barbara to breathe; she also was given some food and water. After the ransom was paid, the kidnappers released Barbara and fled. FBI agents tracked Krist down and arrested him in a crocodile-infested swamp near Hog Island, Florida (Eisemann-Schier was caught later). Krist was convicted and sentenced to life imprisonment. He was released on parole in 1979 with the stipulation he had to live in Alaska, where his family operated a fishing business.

KRUPP, Alfried, [von Bohlen und Halbach] (1907-67). German industrial magnate and war criminal. The great Krupp Works of munitions factories, shipyards, and other industries secretly aided in the rearmament of Germany after World War I (1914-18). Alfried's father, Baron Gustav, supported the National Socialist (Nazi) party under Adolf HITLER in 1933 at the start of the Third Reich (Nazi Germany) and helped expel Jewish industrialists from the country. Alfried, Gustav's eldest son, who had backed the Nazi Schutzstaffel (SS) since 1931, assumed control of the Krupp empire soon after World War II erupted in 1939; he seized property in all German-occupied territories during the war and exploited slave labor at many concentration camps to construct Krupp factories. At the Nuremberg war-crimes trial (1945-46) Gustav was indicted as a major war criminal but, because of senility and deteriorating ill health, was not tried (he died on January 16, 1950). Later Alfried was tried before an American military tribunal at Nuremberg, West Germany, and sentenced as a war criminal to 12 years' imprisonment in 1948. Released on a general amnesty in 1951, Alfried regained the Krupp's confiscated personal and corporate property and managed the firm until his death on July 31, 1967 in Essen. In early 1968 the firm became a public corporation. See also FUNK, Walther.

KUEHN or KÜHN, Bernard [Julius Otto] (1895-?). German doctor and spy. He served as a midshipman in the German navy during World War I, became a physician after his discharge, and espoused the Nazi cause after his practice failed, becoming a minor Gestapo official and a personal friend of Heinrich Himmler. In 1935 he was sent with his wife, Friedel, six-year-old son, Hans Joachim, and beautiful, 18-year-old stepdaughter, Susie Ruth, to live in Hawaii to work as espionage agents for both Japan and Germany. With his family, Kuehn, posing as retired and well-to-do and studying history and language, collected and transmitted to the Japanese much secret military information about U.S. naval operations in Hawaii and the Pacific. The amicable Kuehns aroused no suspicions as they relayed exact data about the American fleet at Pearl Harbor; the infamous Japanese attack there (December 7, 1941) was largely success-ful because of information from the Kuehns, who were caught outright that same day by U.S. intelligence agents while flash-ing signals from their Oahu house to the Japanese. Tried and sentenced to be shot, Kuehn gained (1942) a commuted sentence (50 years at hard labor in Alcatraz) by revealing all he knew about Axis espionage in the Pacific. He was released after serv-ing four years; his family members were interned for several years and then returned to Germany.

KÜRTEN, Peter (1883-1931). Germany pyromaniac, sexual pervert, and mass murderer. Kürten, who spent 21 years of his life in jail, gained sadistic, sexual satisfaction from the murder of more than two dozen persons in Germany between 1913 and 1930. He first set fire to buildings in Cologne, Germany, in 1904, delight-ing in seeing the destruction of other people's property, but soon "graduated" to assaulting and killing others to get his thrills. Kürten's first victim was an eight-year-old girl, whose throat he cut and body he ravished in 1913. Between 1923 and 1930 Kürten, who lived quietly with his wife and worked as a molder, roamed at night through the streets of Düsseldorf, lur-ing his victims, mostly women, by his "youthful appearance" (he used cosmetics). He strangled them, cut their throats, stabbed them with scissors, or clubbed them to death, rejoicing in com-mitting murder with bestiality and in cold blood. Sometimes Kürten raped them when they were dead and sucked their blood. Later he masturbated at his victims' graves and con-versed with them. In May 1930 a victim of his escaped being murdered and told the police, who began a widespread manhunt. Kürten then told his wife all about his crimes, and she turned him over to the police. In 1931 "The Düsseldorf Vampire," as Kürten came to be known, was convicted of murder in nine cases, of attempted murder in seven others, and was sentenced to death. He looked forward to his death by the guillotine, which took place at Klingelpütz Prison in Cologne on July 2, 1931.

- L -

LABBÉ, Denise (b. 1926). French murderer. A secretary at the
National Institute of Statistics and an aspiring university student in Rennes, she became enthralled by her over-weening
lover, 24-year-old Jacques Algarron, an illegitimate son of a
military man who treated all women as slaves. In 1954 she
drowned her two-and-one-half-year-old daughter, Catherine,
whom she had borne out of wedlock by another man, in order
to prove her love to Algarron (he had demanded that she make
the "sacrifice" and at the time had her under his sinister spell).
Spurned by Algarron afterward, Labbé confessed to the crime
and implicated Algarron. At Blois in 1955, both of them stood
trial; the distinguished lawyer Bâtonnier Simon defended Labbé,
suggesting she was temporarily insane at the time of the murder and managing to obtain life imprisonment (instead of the
guillotine) for his client. Algarron was also found guilty by
the jury and received a 20-year sentence.

LACENAIRE (Pierre-François, called Gaillard) (1800-1836). French
assassin, thief, and forger. Around 1830 Lacenaire turned to
a life of crime, being opposed to Louis-Philippe (who was chosen
"king of the French") and his support of the wealthy bourgeois.
He indulged in assassination, theft, and forgery at the expense
of the French government. Lacenaire wrote articles and poems
about crime, showing great insight into the criminal mind and
saying prison was the university of crime (he spent about three
years in prison). Although he collaborated with numerous hard
criminals, Lacenaire tended to hold them in contempt as illiterate
and uncultured (he came from a middle-class family and was well
read). Finally sentenced to death, he wrote his memoirs while
awaiting execution in prison, tracing his criminality to his family's lack of love and his own lack of status. Lacenaire, with
aristocratic composure, died on the scaffold in Paris in 1836.

LAFARGE, Marie [born: Marie Fortunée Cappelle] (1816-52).
French noblewoman and poisoner. Highborn, well-educated,
and cultured, she married (1839) Charles Joseph Pouch Lafarge
without realizing she was not bettering her social status (her
lifelong craving was to be accepted as royalty) until immediately
afterward. Her coarse-mannered, unrefined husband, who hoped
to restore his iron works in Corrèze with help from Marie's
100,000-franc dowry, nauseated her. At the dilapidated Lafarge
château, Le Glandier, in Corrèze, she supposedly schemed to
get rid of him. When Charles died on January 14, 1840, family
members accused Marie of murder; she had openly bought arsenic to kill rats at Le Glandier. An autopsy by doctors revealed arsenic in Charles's stomach, and Marie was taken into
custody at Brive and later sent to Montpellier Prison, where
she awaited trail and became a celebrated case in France as the

citizenry disagreed over her guilt. Marie's brilliant young
lawyer Charles Lachaud fell in love with her but failed to gain
her freedom at her 17-day sensational trial (1840), during which
testimony from the esteemed toxicologist Dr. Mathieu Orfila condemned her. Pleading innocent, she nonetheless was sentenced
to hard labor for life and public exposure in the pillory at Tulle.
King Louis Philippe quickly commuted the sentence to life imprisonment. Released from Montpellier Prison in 1852 after successfully appealing to Emperor Napoleon III because of her wor-
sening tuberculosis, Marie sought to renew her health at a spa
in the Pyrenees, where she died within several months.

LAFFITE or LAFITTE, Jean (1780?-1826?). French-born pirate,
privateer, and smuggler. In 1806 he and his brother, Pierre,
arrived in New Orleans and soon set up a mercantile operation
that evidently profited greatly from the sale of smuggled goods
and slaves. Holding a privateering commission from Cartagena
(in modern Colombia), Laffite went to sea to plunder Spanish
shipping, becoming the leader of an illicit pirate colony on the
islands of Barataria Bay off the Louisiana coast. Many valuable
stolen cargoes passed from the Baratarian pirates such as Rene
Beluche, Captain Dominique, Vincent GAMBI, and others who
worked with Laffite through the bayous to New Orleans. In
1814 (during the War of 1812) the British offered Laffite much
money and a naval captaincy if he would help them capture New
Orleans, but he offered his services to General Andrew Jackson
and helped the U.S. win the Battle of New Orleans on January
8, 1815. President James Madison then granted Laffite and his
men full pardons with rights of U.S. citizenship, but they took
to piracy in late 1816. Laffite and 1,000 followers moved down
the coast and founded a new pirate colony called Campeche at
what is now Galveston, Texas, in 1817 and preyed on Spanish
trade in the Gulf of Mexico and the Caribbean. In 1820 the
pirates attacked U.S. vessels, which caused the U.S. government to send a naval force against Laffite. In 1821 Laffite
burned Campeche to the ground and set sail aboard The Pride,
his special ship, with his closest followers and supposedly established another pirate haven farther down the coast. He continued his piracy along the Spanish Main (the northern coast of
South America) until his death, which, according to strong evidence, occurred in a Yucatán village in Mexico in 1826. Just
how he died remains unknown.

LAFFITE, John [born: John Andrechyne Laflin] (1893-1970). American forger and swindler. An engineer on the Missouri Pacific
Railroad until his retirement in the early 1940s, he then traveled
about the United States offering for sale documents written,
signed, or owned purportedly by the notorious pirate Jean
LAFFITE, whose great grandson he claimed to be. In Kansas
City, New Orleans, and other cities, rare book dealers and
historians and collectors, especially spinsters who fell for him,

shot to death in her bedroom in Jackson, Michigan. Jackson Police Chief John Boyle found evidence linking Latimer to the crime. Arrested and tried, Latimer was found guilty (the jury said he committed murder to collect life insurance and to inherit the family fortune) and was sentenced to life in prison. Latimer became a model prisoner and gained access to lethal drugs. In 1893 he poisoned the food of two guards, one of whom died and the other fell unconscious, permitting him to escape. Soon apprehended, Latimer again became a model prisoner and remained incarcerated until 1935. He died a vagrant in a Michigan home for the aged.

LA TOFFANIA. See TOFFANIA, La.

LA VOISIN. See DESHAYES, Catherine.

LAW, John (1671-1729). Scottish financier, gambler, and con man. Forced to leave England in 1694 after killing a man in a duel over the affections of a woman, Law went to Amsterdam, where he studied banking, and later reappeared in Scotland to propose, unsuccessfully, revenue and trade reforms. After winning much money by gambling, he moved to Paris and founded the Banque Générale in 1716. To solve France's financial difficulties caused by extravagant wars and exorbitant spending by the king, Law proposed to float government-backed paper currency and to develop the supposedly enormous riches of French Louisiana and other French colonies. The French government was persuaded to support Law's "Mississippi Scheme" of commercial exploitation and colonization, and Law was made director-general of France's finances and merged his Compagnie d'Occident, or Mississippi Company, with the royal bank and assumed the national debt. Public confidence soared, causing wild speculation in the company, whose stock became greatly inflated in value. Some French citizens made huge profits by buying and selling stock before the "bubble" burst in October 1720, when the company's almost complete lack of any real assets was publicly revealed. Thousands of investors were ruined, and Law, called a fraud and threatened with being lynched, fled disguised as a beggar in December 1720, leaving behind a fortune he had accumulated in gold and jewels. France then abolished Law's financial system. In 1729 Law died in Venice, where he had earned a living as a gambler during the last years of his life.

LAY, Elzy or Elsa (1868-1934). American train and bank robber and outlaw. A hardcore member of the Wild Bunch, an outlaw gang organized by Butch CASSIDY in 1896, Lay helped plan the gang's robberies in Wyoming, Colorado, and elsewhere. Lay was Cassidy's closest friend, much closer than the SUNDANCE KID, despite the popular tradition. When not working with the Wild Bunch, Lay pulled off jobs with outlaw Tom "Black Jack" KETCHUM and his gang. In 1899, after robbing

a train at Twin Mountains, New Mexico, the Ketchum gang with
Lay were pursued by possemen and caught after a sheriff was
killed in a gun battle with the outlaws. Lay managed to escape,
but a month later was trapped by a posse in Clayton, New Mexico. He tried to shoot his way out and killed a lawman. Sentenced to life imprisonment, Lay completely reformed himself in
the Santa Fe prison and was released on the governor's pardon
in 1906. He then married, settled down as a rancher, and, for
a while, speculated about oil drilling (land he had claimed but
was taken over by Standard Oil of California was later found to
contain oil). There are reports that Lay and Cassidy were
seen together in Baggs, Wyoming, in 1929-30. Lay died on November 10, 1934.

LAYFAYETTE, Justine (d. 1888). French witch and murderer. In
the 1880s, while running a meager boardinghouse in Lyons, this
hulking woman secretly practiced black witchcraft and influenced
her good-looking husband, at least 15 years her junior, to carry
out submissively her evil desires to celebrate the rites of death.
Over a five year period, her husband lured young women to
spots where he cut their throats, sucked their blood, and sliced
off hunks of their flesh which he brought home for his wife to
eat. He was finally caught attacking a victim, and Justine was
then arrested. On trial in 1888, the two were found guilty;
Justine was judged sane and died on the guillotine; her husband,
declared insane, was sentenced to life in an asylum, where he
died in 1927.

LeBLANC, Antoine (d. 1833). French-born murderer. LeBlanc, a
tall, handsome fellow, arrived in the United States on April 26,
1833, and went to work for the Sayre family in rural New Jersey. He apparently resented his position as a common laborer
and the fact that he had to sleep in the woodshed. On May 2,
1833, he beat Mr. and Mrs. Sayre to death with a shovel and
buried their bodies in a pile of manure. LeBlanc, upon discovering the Sayre's black maid in the attic of the house, murdered her, too. The corpses were soon found, and LeBlanc
was arrested, quickly tried, and convicted. A crowd of about
12,000 persons, the majority of them women, watched LeBlanc
go to the gallows on the Morristown green on September 6, 1833.
LeBlanc reportedly had had affairs with several local women.

LEBRON, Lolita (b. 1920). Puerto Rican nationalist and terrorist.
Leading three Puerto Rican men on March 1, 1954, she entered
the gallery of the U.S. House of Representatives in Washington,
D.C., where she unfurled and waved a Puerto Rican flag before
she and her companions sprayed gunfire at the congressmen on
the main floor below, wounding five of them. Lebron and the
others were seized, arrested, and received 75-year prison sentences each. A commutation of their sentences by President
Jimmy Carter on September 6, 1979, resulted in their release,

and Lebron, then avowing herself "a revolutionary," journeyed with the others to Puerto Rico.

LECHLER, John (d. 1822). Pennsylvania murderer. He found his wife in bed with his neighbor John Haag and threatened to kill them both. Haag bought him off with a promissory note. However, when Lechler failed to collect his money from Haag, he became enraged, strangled his wife to death, and hung her in the attic. He then went to Haag's house and called for him to come out. When Haag refused, Lechler, armed with two pistols, fired through the door and killed Haag's wife. Lechler was convicted and hanged. The newspapers in the area (Lancaster, Pennsylvania) conducted probably the first poll ever taken concerning a verdict and found that the majority of people favored Lechler's execution.

LEE, John D. (d. 1877). Utah murderer. On September 7, 1857, Indians supported by some Mormons attacked a wagon train of 140 immigrants at Mountain Meadows in Utah territory. The immigrants held off the attack until the arrival of more men under Mormon Bishop Lee, who was also an Indian agent. Lee promised to lead the wagon train safely to Cedar City if the immigrants would put down their arms. However, as soon as they laid them down, Lee and his men shot them dead (only 17 very young children were spared). Later Brigham Young, the Mormon leader, excommunicated Lee because of the massacre. U.S. officials finally tried Lee in 1875, found him guilty, and executed him by firing squad near the site of the massacre on March 23, 1877.

LEHMANN, Christa (b. 1922). German poisoner. From an unstable family in Worms, West Germany, she married (1944) a drunkard, Karl Franz Lehmann, a tile setter by trade, and had several love affairs which only left her increasingly hostile and depressed. Her husband died in convulsions in 1952, her father-in-law did likewise in 1953, and her close friend, Annie Hamann, died in 1954. Though Christa shed many tears while attending the Hamann funeral, detectives suspected her and took her in for questioning; suddenly, in jail, she confessed to using poisonous E-605 (a new insecticide) on the victims, the last of whom (Hamann) she had not intended to kill, but had hoped to poison instead Hamann's elderly mother who disliked Christa. The murderer received life imprisonment following her trial and conviction (1954).

LeMARCA, Angelo John (1925-58). American bootlegger and kidnapper. In financial straits, he rashly abducted 32-day-old Peter Weinberger on July 4, 1956, taking the infant from his carriage on the veranda of his home in Westbury, New York, and leaving a note demanding $2,000 ransom for his release (the money was never paid). The dead body of Peter was later found. The FBI uncovered LeMarca's identity through hand-writing analysis (his writing on an illegal liquor case fit that on the ransom note), and LeMarca was arrested on August 22, 1956. Found guilty and sentenced to die, he was sent to the electric chair in Sing Sing (Ossining Correctional Facility) on August 8, 1958.

LEMAY, Georges (b. 1926). Canadian burglar. An elusive underworld figure, he masterminded the largest bank burglary in Canadian history on July 1, 1961, a national holiday in Canada (Dominion Day). His gang members drilled through the concrete walls and ceiling of the Bank of Nova Scotia in Montreal and broke into hundreds of safe-deposit boxes to steal $633,605 in cash, jewels, negotiable securities, and other valuables. Gang members were in time caught, but Lemay, who absconded with most of the loot, evaded arrest until May 1965, when he became the first criminal to be captured through the international communications of the Early Bird satellite; seeing his photo on a TV screen, a boat repairman in Fort Lauderdale, Florida, informed police that Lemay, using the alias Rene Roy, was on a yacht in Bahia Mar basin. In custody in Miami, Lemay hurriedly married his girl friend (June 1, 1965) so that she couldn't be forced to testify against him. He escaped from the Miami jail and was a notorious fugitive for almost a year until his recapture in August 1966. At his trial in Montreal for the 1961 burglary, Lemay was convicted (December 1968) and sentenced to eight years' imprisonment. Set free in· 1975, he has never disclosed what happened to the vanished loot.

LEMOINE (fl. 1906-8). French swindler. Posing as a scientist who had solved the secret of manufacturing marketable diamonds, Lemoine demonstrated to diamond merchants and rich mining magnates, all of whom were sworn to secrecy by him not to divulge the formula, his process at his laboratory in London in 1906. (The samples of uncut diamonds he produced actually came from a South African mine.) Sir Julius Wernher, one of the heads of the De Beers Company, and others were conned into advancing Lemoine capital (at least Ł75,000) to build and equip his proposed diamond factory at Argeles near Pau, France. No diamonds were produced, leading Wernher to visit Argeles and find a mere shed. The authorities were notified and arrested Lemoine in Paris in January 1907. Lemoine pleaded innocent, saying he had made diamonds (as proof, he made several exceedingly minute ones, but they were not of the large size shown in his laboratory). In July 1908 in Paris, Lemoine was tried and convicted of fraud and swindling and sentenced to six years' imprisonment with hard labor.

LENNON, [Patrick Henry] "Packy" (fl. 1926-56). New York swindler. He and his stock market ring manipulated big businessmen, mainly wealthy industrialist Augustine Joseph Cunningham of Rochester, New York, selling them shares in a worthless firm, Inter-City, for nearly three years (1926-29) before being uncovered and given prison sentences for fraud. Later, in 1951, Lennon (under the alias Harry Hoffman) headed a con group that again preyed on gullible A. J. Cunningham, who failed to recognize his former bilker. Cunningham was taken in by a ridiculous story that he had been left valuable patents but had to help pay off Hollywood moguls and investors (who supposedly had claims against the inheritance or wanted the patents but would settle out of court) in order to secure the legacy valued at some $60 million. For four years millionaire Cunningham was mulcted out of over $425,000 by the Hoffman-Lennon con gang, who also took over $300,000 from seven other trusting business-men during this period. By early 1956 Cunningham had finally become somewhat suspicious. His bankers and postal officials investigated the matter. Hoffman-Lennon was apprehended, along with some of his cohorts, and they were tried and con-victed and sent to jail. Lennon received a five-year sentence, the others less.

LEOPOLD, Nathan F., Jr. (1906-71). Chicago kidnapper and mur-derer. He and his friend Richard A. LOEB, spoiled sons of wealthy Chicago families and brilliant university students, de-cided to commit the "perfect murder," one that would be an in-tellectual challenge. On May 22, 1924, the pair abducted 14-year-old Bobbie Franks, a Chicago millionaire's son, and stabbed and killed him with a chisel. They then stuffed the body in a drain pipe. Leopold sent a typewritten note to the Franks de-manding $10,000 in ransom for the release of their son. A work-man soon found Bobbie's body, and police found eyeglasses near the body and traced them to Leopold. The ransom note was also traced to Leopold's typewriter. Leopold and Loeb were both questioned and broke down and confessed to the killing. During a sensational trial Clarence Darrow, hired by the par-ents of Leopold and Loeb, pleaded his clients guilty and asked the court for mercy. Each killer was sentenced to life imprison-ment and sent to the Illinois penitentiary near Joliet. Leopold became a reformed man and was paroled in 1958, seeking re-demption for himself. He worked as a $10-a-month laboratory technician in Puerto Rico, where he died of heart failure on August 30, 1971.

LEPKE, Louis. See BUCHALTER, Louis "Lepke."

LE ROY, Kitty (1850-78). American gambler. Kitty, a vivacious and stunning beauty by the age of 16, had a brief career on the stage in Dallas before she turned to card playing and gambling, becoming one of the West's best faro dealers. She carried several bowie knives and guns, masterfully using these weapons to settle arguments arising at the gambling tables. Wooed by many male admirers, Kitty was married four times and in 1878 was killed by her fourth husband, presumably out of jealousy (he committed suicide afterward). During the last two years of her life, Kitty and her husband had operated the Mint Gambling Saloon in Deadwood, South Dakota, a dive frequented by outlaw Sam BASS and lawman Wild Bill Hickok.

LESLIE, Frank "Buckskin" (1842-after 1922). American gunfighter. In 1880, after a stint as a U.S. Army scout in the Indian wars, Leslie settled in Tombstone, Arizona, where he quickly earned a reputation as a pitiless gunslinger, always armed and ready for a gun duel. Some 10 to 15 killings, including that of gunfighter Billy CLAIBORNE in 1882, were credited to Leslie, who practiced his fast draw and shooting continually wherever he went in the West. In 1889 he shot and killed Mollie Williams, a whore with whom he had had an affair, and was incarcerated until 1896. For several years Leslie mined gold in the Klondike, then worked as a bartender in saloons in California, and afterward ran a pool hall in Oakland, California, until 1922, when he disappeared.

LESLIE, George Leonidas (1838-84). American bank robber. He led a double life, by day a respectable, educated gentleman, by night the mastermind of bank robberies. From 1865 to 1884 Leslie and his gang of thieves stole an estimated $12 million from banks in Philadelphia, Baltimore, New York City, and other cities. His biggest heist was the $2.7 million robbery of the Manhattan Savings Institution on October 27, 1878. Leslie, who posed as a man of inherited wealth and belonged to prestigious clubs, advised other bank robbers for many years, sometimes charging a fee of $20,000 for his artful knowledge. Known as the "King of the Bank Robbers," Leslie never spent a day in jail and lived a lavish life, spending much time and money on women. He was murdered by members of his own gang during a dispute over a woman. See also HOPE, Jimmy.

LEWIS, Vach. See CYCLONE LOUIE.

LEY, Robert (1890-1945). German Nazi leader and war criminal. While serving in the German army in World War I (1914-18), he was captured and imprisoned in France. Released in 1920, Ley joined the German National Socialist (Nazi) party in 1924 and became a top party leader in the Rhineland (1924), Munich (1931), and in all Germany (1932). Intensely anti-Semitic, he was named by Adolf HITLER to head Germany's Labor Front in 1933, promptly abolished the free trade unions, and brutally procured Nazi domination of all workers. Many atrocities in Germany and its occupied lands during World War II (1939-45) were committed under Ley's order. After Germany's defeat by the Allies, Ley was arrested and indicted on war crimes, including especially crimes connected with forced labor, but committed suicide in prison on October 25, 1945, before his trial in Nuremberg, West Germany.

LIEBSCHER, William, Jr. (b. 1918). California bank robber. Living in the fashionable section of Fairfax, California, this well-mannered used car salesman, who acted in the community's amateur theater group, successfully committed 18 bank robberies in the San Francisco area during a 17-month period (1956-57), each time taking small amounts ranging from $700 to $2,555 and afterward using the money to pay off personal and business debts or to keep a good credit rating. He would disguise himself using make-up and wearing dark sunglasses, give bank tellers his demands on handwritten notes, then quickly flee in a car. The FBI received important clues from witnesses which helped locate Liebscher, who readily confessed when confronted; he was sentenced to 15 years' imprisonment on September 11, 1957.

LIGHTFOOT, Captain [real name: Michael Martin] (1775-1822). Irish and American highwayman. He and another highwayman, known only as "Captain Thunderbolt," held up and robbed coaches and lone travelers in Ireland and Scotland from about 1792 to 1818. Fellow bandits gave him the sobriquet "Captain Lightfoot" because of his ability to escape capture. In 1818 Lightfoot fled from Ireland and landed at Salem, Massachusetts, determined to lead an honest life. Failing as a farmer and then a brewer, he turned to highway robbery again, preying on travelers throughout New England from 1819 to 1821. Lightfoot, a romantic Robin Hood figure to many because he once refused to rob a lady passenger on a coach, was hunted down and caught in a barn near Springfield, Massachusetts. Convicted, Lightfoot went to his hanging "calm and serene," putting the rope around his own neck and dropping a handkerchief as a signal for the hangman.

LINCOLN, Warren (1870-1941). Illinois lawyer and murderer. In about 1921 Lincoln, a Chicago defense lawyer, settled into retirement with his wife in Aurora, Illinois. His wife's puritanical ways began to infuriate him, and his brother-in-law, who had moved in as a permanent house guest, bored him to distraction. One day the latter two disappeared, and a while afterward authorities became suspicious of foul play when Lincoln was caught in a number of lies about his wife and brother-in-law. A search ensued that uncovered the severed heads of the missing two buried in flower boxes filled with slaked lime, which had mistakenly been put in the boxes instead of quicklime, a disintegrating substance, and thus had preserved the heads. Lincoln received life imprisonment at Joliet prison and died there in 1941.

LINGG, Louis. See SPIES, August.

LINGLEY, William "Big Bill" (d. 1915). New York gangster and murderer. He and Freddie Muehfedt organized the Car Barn Gang, a vicious group of thugs, thieves, and murderers that operated mainly from East 90th to 100th Street in New York City.

Lingley, the principal leader of the gang, always carried two revolvers and a blackjack. In the fall of 1911 the Car Barn Gang publicly declared war on the police, who then were constantly attacked for almost four years. In 1915 Lingley and Muehfedt killed a liquor dealer in the Bronx, were caught, and sent to the electric chair in Sing Sing. Soon afterward the Car Barners disbanded.

LIPKA, Juliane. See FAZEKAS, Mrs. Julius.

LITTLE, Dick [real name: Dick Liddell or Liddil] (1852-after 1890). American robber and outlaw. When Frank and Jesse JAMES formed their second gang in the fall of 1879, Little joined it and participated in bank, express train, and stagecoach robberies in Missouri, Alabama, and elsewhere. Little felt no loyalty to Jesse, who had a large reward posted for him, and evidently conspired with Charles and Robert FORD, two other gang members, to murder Jesse. Gang member Wood HITE, who reportedly uncovered the traitors, was shot and killed by Little or Robert Ford in 1881. After Jesse's assassination by Ford in 1882, Little surrendered to lawmen and spent eight months in prison in Alabama. Later he operated a saloon in Las Vegas, New Mexico, with Robert Ford but completely disappeared after 1890.

LITTLE PETE [real name: Fung Jing Toy] (1864-97). Chinese-born San Francisco tong leader. By the late 1880s Little Pete, as the English-language newspapers called him, controlled the Sum Yops, a powerful tong (secret Chinese bandit organization that engaged in illegal activities) in San Francisco's Chinatown. He accumulated a fortune from rackets such as peddling opium, gambling, prostitution, smuggling aliens (especially female slaves), and carrying out murder contracts. Rival tongs grew to fear the Sum Yops under Little Pete, a seemingly indestructible hatchet man (the hatchet was the tongs' favorite fighting weapon) who survived numerous bloody gang wars. Little Pete, who wore a coat of chain mail and a hat lined with steel for protection, was credited with the killings of at least 50 rival hatchet men, many of whom belonged to the Sue Yop Tong. On January 23, 1897, two hired tong warriors, Lem Jung and Chew Tin Gop, murdered Little Pete in a San Francisco barber shop; a revolver was shoved down inside the back of Little Pete's coat of chain mail and five bullets were pumped into his spine. The killers escaped capture and later fled to China.

LOEB, Richard A. (1907-36). Chicago kidnapper and murderer. He and Nathan F. LEOPOLD, Jr., two outstanding university students and egotistical sons of rich Chicago families, decided to commit the perfect crime. On May 22, 1924, they kidnapped 14-year-old Bobbie Franks, a millionaire's son and a distant cousin of Loeb, near his school in Chicago. They stabbed the

boy to death, poured hydrochloric acid over his face to conceal
his identity, and shoved the body in a drain pipe. A railroad
workman soon found the body, near which were found eyeglasses
that were traced by police to Leopold. Also, a typewritten ransom note sent to the Franks demanding $10,000 for their son's
release was traced to Leopold's typewriter. The "fun killers"
were arrested. Loeb confessed first, then Leopold; each
blamed the other for the killing. At their trial, defense lawyer Clarence Darrow, hired by the parents of the killers, eloquently defended Leopold and Loeb against execution. Both
were given life imprisonment in the penitentiary near Joliet, Ill.
Loeb became an aggressive homosexual in prison and preyed
upon fellow inmates. In January 1936 he was slashed to death
in a shower by another prisoner.

LOGAN, Harvey. See KID CURRY.

LOHMAN, Ann Trow. See RESTELL, Madame.

L'OLONNOIS, Francis (1630?-71). French pirate. Known also as
Jacques Jean David Nau, he was perhaps the most bloody and
cruel buccaneer of his day, capturing and plundering Spanish
galleons and towns in the West Indies, gleefully torturing and
killing captured prisoners and town inhabitants. His abominable
piracy began in 1653, when he first captained a ship and crew
out of Tortuga, an island pirate haven off northern Haiti. He
fiendishly enjoyed mutilating his prisoners before slaying them;
once he personally cut off the heads of 90 captured Spanish seamen. In a land battle with Spaniards near Campeche, Mexico,
his crew was destroyed, and he pretended to be a corpse on
the battlefield, was overlooked, then stealthily slipped away; in
disguise, he watched the Spanish in Campeche celebrate his
death. Soon afterward L'Olonnois gathered a new crew, seized
a Spanish man-of-war off Cuba, and continued his enormities.
With a fleet of eight ships, he captured the prosperous town of
Maracaibo in present-day Venezuela in 1667; Spaniards here and
in nearby villages were taken and butchered and spoils (money,
jewels, and slaves) were apportioned among his men. Later
landing on the coast near Cartagena (northern Colombia),
L'Olonnois and his men were furiously attacked by wild Indians
who hated whites, and they were killed.

LOMBARDO, Antonio or Tony (1892-1928). Sicilian-born Chicago
gangster. In the 1920s Lombardo, a smart, courteous Sicilian,
worked for Chicago crime boss Al CAPONE, to whom he gave
much counsel and remained always loyal. Through peaceful
negotiations arranged by Lombardo, Capone was able at times
to settle gangland disputes without resorting to violence against
his enemies. Lombardo always feared being poisoned to death
and often had his assistants taste his food before he ate it.
For his loyalty, Capone appointed Lombardo president of the

Chicago branch of the Unione Siciliane, a Sicilian fraternal underworld organization, in 1925. Two unknown gunmen shot and killed Lombardo and one of his bodyguards on the corner of State and Madison streets in Chicago on September 7, 1928.

LONERGAN, Wayne (b. 1916). Canadian-born New York murderer. On October 24, 1943, Patricia Burton Lonergan, 22-year-old heiress to a multimillion-dollar brewery fortune, was found murdered in her apartment bedroom in New York City; she had been strangled and beaten with antique, heavy candlesticks. Her husband, Wayne, who had two months earlier gone to Canada to enlist in the Royal Canadian Air Force, was discovered to have been in New York at the time of the murder. Apprehended in Toronto, Wayne was brought back to New York and supposedly confessed to the crime after a long, grueling police interrogation (he never did sign a confession). Wayne, who disclosed he had taken part in sex orgies as a bisexual, was convicted of second-degree murder despite the absence of conclusive evidence that he had gone to his wife's apartment or touched the candlesticks on the day of the murder. After serving 21 years of a 35-years-to-life sentence, Wayne was released from Sing Sing (Ossining Correctional Facility) in 1965 and deported to Canada.

LONG, Huey [Pierce] (1893-1935). Louisiana politician and demagogue. An ambitious and flamboyant attorney, Long was overwhelmingly elected governor of Louisiana in 1928, afterwards establishing a powerful political machine that had almost absolute control over the state. A champion of the "little folk" (mainly poor whites) and a foe of the privileged rich (especially oilmen), the "Kingfish," as he was nicknamed, succeeded in pushing through welfare legislation, large taxations, and public works programs. He was accused of bribing state legislators and of gross misconduct but was never convicted. Through supposed use of intimidation and tactics of the underworld, Long expanded his powers and crushed his opposition. In 1932 he began serving as Louisiana's newly elected U.S. Senator, commuting regularly between Washington, D.C. and Louisiana. He gained absolute authority over the state militia and election process. His federal program to "share-the-wealth" (or "every man a king," mercilessly taxing the rich and guaranteeing every American family an annual income of $5,000) brought him national attention during this Depression period. Long was shot and fatally wounded in a hallway of the Louisiana capitol on September 8, 1935; about 30 hours later he died. His assassin, Carl Austin Weiss, a mild-mannered 29-year-old physician, was immediately gunned down by Long's bodyguards, who pumped 61 bullets into him. Long's ruthless character and career have been the basis of films and novels, notably All the King's Men by author Robert Penn Warren.

LONGBAUGH, Harry. See SUNDANCE KID.

LONGLEY, William P. "Wild Bill" (1851-77). American gunfighter
and murderer. At the age of 15 he shot a black lawman to
death because he didn't like his "arrogant manner." Longley.,
a firm believer in the South, hated blacks, carpetbaggers, and
Northerners. For about a year (1867-68) he rode with a Texas
band of outlaws, the Confederate Irregulars, led by Cullen M.
BAKER. He then roamed as a lone wolf from the Rio Grande to
the Black Hills, shooting and killing people almost everywhere
he went (he is credited with killing at least 32 men during his
life). In Evergreen, Texas (Longley's birthplace) in April 1875,
he ambushed and killed Wilson Anderson, whom he suspected of
killing his cousin, and became a much sought-after fugitive for
almost two years. Finally caught, Longley was convicted and
hanged in Giddings, Texas.

LOOMIS, Cornelia (d. 1897). New York robber and murderer. She
was a member of the powerful Loomis gang that stole from and
killed many farmers in upper New York state in the latter half
of the nineteenth century. Cornelia, an expert rider and sharpshooter, escaped capture many times, hiding with other gang
members in the Nine-Mile Swamp near Brookfield, New York. In
the early 1880s, after her brothers Denio, Wash, Grove, and
Plumb had died, Cornelia became leader of the Loomis gang and
continued to run a lucrative horse-, cattle-, and sheep-stealing
business until her death in 1897. See also LOOMIS, Grove[r];
LOOMIS, [George] Wash[ington, Jr.].

LOOMIS, [George] Wash[ington, Jr.] (1813-65). New York robber
and murderer. His mother encouraged him and his brothers
and sisters at an early age to steal "little things" as long as
they didn't get caught. In the 1840s Wash became leader of
the Loomis gang, which robbed and killed farmers and others
in New York's Mohawk and Chenango valleys. In 1857 vigilantes
raided the Loomis farmhouse, found huge quantities of stolen
goods, and arrested the gang's members. The case against the
gang was dropped when court records were burned and witnesses
disappeared. During the U.S. Civil War (1861-65) the Loomis
gang ran a massive horse-, cattle-, and sheep-stealing operation,
earning much money from livestock sold through fences, such as
Frederick "Marm" MANDELBAUM, to the Union Army. In 1865
a posse led by Constable James L. Filkins broke into the Loomis
farmhouse and attacked gang's members with pipes and guns.
Wash was literally beaten to death. See also LOOMIS, Cornelia;
LOOMIS, Grove[r].

LOOMIS, Grove[r] (d. 1870). New York robber, counterfeiter, and
murderer. He and his brothers--Wash, Bill, Wheller, Plumb,
and Denio--and his sister, Cornelia, formed a gang in the 1840s
that terrorized farm communities in upper New York state.
Grove ran the gang's counterfeiting operation. He was arrested several times but was always released after evidence

against him disappeared and local lawmen were beaten up. In 1857 and 1865 vigilante committees tried unsuccessfully to break up the Loomis gang, which was reselling hundreds of stolen items--livestock, furs, and equipment--to markets in Albany, New York City, and elsewhere. During a vigilante raid on the Loomis farmhouse in 1867, Grove and his brother Plumb were hung by their hands over a fire until they confessed their crimes. When Grove died in 1870, the gang continued to operate for a time under Denio, then under Cornelia. See also LOOMIS, Cornelia; LOOMIS, [George] Wash[ington, Jr.].

LORD HAW-HAW. See JOYCE, William.

LOVING, "Cockeyed" Frank (1854-82). American gambler and gunfighter. Loving, a cool-headed gambler, had a long-running feud with feisty gunfighter Levi RICHARDSON over a dance-hall girl whom they both loved. On April 5, 1879, at the Long Branch Saloon in Dodge City, Kansas, Richardson fired five shots at Loving at point blank range but missed him; Loving then fired and killed Richardson with three hits. Arrested, Loving was soon acquitted on grounds of self-defense and, for the next three years, related his art of gunfighting at the poker tables in Colorado. In April 1882, in Trinidad, Colorado, Loving and ex-lawman Jack Allen fought a celebrated gun duel in which the pair exchanged 16 shots without drawing blood. The next day Allen surprised Loving, shot quickly and killed one of the West's "coolest" gunfighters and gamblers.

LOW, Edward or Ned (fl. 1720s). English pirate. Low grew from a boy pilferer on the streets of London into a rapacious and cruel pirate who sailed in North American waters. For a short time he sailed with pirate captain George Lowther, preying on shipping in the West Indies. As owner of his own brigantine, Low attacked many trading vessels along the coast of New England, seizing much booty and many ships. Later he commanded one of the biggest piratical forces in American waters and became known as a "ferocious brute of unequalled cruelty." He was reputedly responsible for killing 53 defenseless Spanish captives. Low was also known to rob shipwrecked crews and then leave them to starve to death. Once the English man-of-war Greyhound surprised Low and nearly disabled his ship by heavy fire. Another pirate ship had accompanied Low's ship and had become disabled. Seeing his imminent capture, Low set full sail and sped away, leaving his companion pirates to fight alone and eventually to be captured, tried, convicted, and hung near Newport, Rhode Island. Low continued his piratical escapades for several more years. How and when he died are not recorded.

LOWE, Joseph "Rowdy Joe" (1846?-99). American brothel-saloon owner, gambler, and gunfighter. He and his sexy wife, "Rowdy

because German law prohibited a murder indictment against a mental defective, as he was legally designated. The Nazis sent him to a hospital in Vienna to be used as a subject in medical experimentations. He died from a lethal injection on April 8, 1944.

LUETGERT, Adolph Louis (1848-1911). German-born Chicago murderer. Luetgert, the owner of a large Chicago sausage factory, installed a massive bed in his factory for his many trysts with his mistresses. Louisa, his wife, became outraged at his affairs. On May 1, 1897, Louisa was found missing. Adolph told her relatives he had hired private detectives to find her but to no avail. The police, informed of Louisa's disappearance, searched Adolph's sausage plant and found pieces of human bone, some teeth (Louisa's), and two gold rings (also Louisa's) in one of the steam vats. Luetgert was arrested, tried, and found guilty of having killed his wife and boiled her to a gluey substance in a vat. Luetgert received a life sentence at Joliet Prison, where he later died, never having admitted to the crime.

LUPO, Ignazio [real name: Ignazio Saietta] (1870?-1944). Sicilian-born New York extortionist, murderer, and counterfeiter. From the 1890s until 1918 he directed the fearsome Black Hand Society in New York City, becoming well-known as "Lupo the Wolf" because of his cruel and rapacious nature. The Black Handers practiced extortion against Sicilian and Italian families, sending letters demanding payoffs on threats of maiming or murdering family members if they refused. In 1901 the U.S. Secret Service uncovered the so-called Murder Stable, a property in the Italian section of Harlem owned by Lupo, where the remains of some 60 victims were found buried (some of whom had balked at demands by the Black Hand). Lupo, who demanded absolute obedience from his gang, was often contracted as a killer-for-pay by other gangs and was credited with numerous slayings. Before World War I (1914-18) he became head of the Unione Siciliane, an amiable Sicilian brotherhood, and soon turned it into a national crime cartel involved in extortion, white slavery, kidnapping, and robbery. Arrested for counterfeiting, Lupo was convicted and sent to Sing Sing (now Ossining Correctional Facility) in 1918 for 30 years. Paroled in the late 1930s, he went into retirement and died in 1944. See also MASSERIA, Joe or Giuseppe.

LUSTIG, "Count" [Victor] (1890-1947). Czechoslovakian-born international swindler. He served short stints in jail (1908-1912) in several European cities on convictions of fraud and embezzlement. Around 1920 Lustig turned up in Paris, posed as an important French ministry official, and twice managed to sell the famous Eiffel Tower to leading scrap metal dealers on phony claims the tower was too costly to repair and was to be torn down and sold for scrap (one dealer paid Lustig about $50,000 for the tower's iron; the other gave him $75,000). Sought by the law, Lustig moved to the United States, where he sold a new "money-making machine," which supposedly duplicated precisely currency fed into it. Lustig was said to have made more than $1 million from gullible bankers, businessmen, madams, and gangsters who bought the money boxes, which produced only those real bills previously concealed in them. Lustig was involved in many money scams such as selling bogus money and worthless securities and, as the urbane "Count," suckered rich and poor by various impressive schemes. In 1925 he managed to fleece crime boss Al CAPONE out of $5,000 in a simple investment scam. In 1935 Lustig was arrested for counterfeiting and, while awaiting trial, escaped from the FBI's detention center in New York City by climbing out a window and, posing as a window cleaner, descended the building, scrubbing windows. About six months later he was caught near Pittsburgh and sent to Alcatraz on a 20-year sentence for counterfeiting and breaking out of jail. Later he was transferred to Leavenworth, where he died in 1947.

LUTZ, Rudolf (fl. 1920-50). Austrian burglar and murderer. Descended from a well-off Austrian family in Vorarlberg, Lutz lived by fraud and burglary for many years and was arrested and convicted several times, notably in 1930 for burglarizing a post-office delivery truck. In 1949 police in Vienna linked him to the mysterious murder of Blanche Mandler, a textile factory owner whose killer they thought (based on strong circumstantial evidence) was her factory manager Richard Kraus, with whom she had had violent arguments over his proper work authority. Lutz, who had recently admitted to a burglary of office typewriters, confessed finally to the killing, saying he and Mandler had made some foreign currency deals together and that he had strangled her to steal money she was to invest in a deal. Lutz then stabbed her and placed her corpse naked in a bathtub full of water in her Vienna apartment, where police, accompanied by Kraus, had found her on the night of November 8, 1949. Lutz was sentenced to life imprisonment on December 5, 1950.

LYLES, Anjette [Donovan] (b. 1917). Georgia poisoner. In 1958, while investigating several mysterious deaths in Cochran, Georgia, police focused on Anjette Lyles, an attractive, widowed restaurant owner whose young daughter Marcia had recently died and whose two husbands and a mother-in-law had earlier perished without clear explanation. Examinations of the four bodies revealed arsenic in all, and Lyles, who had collected life insurance on the victims' deaths, was brought to trial and convicted, despite pleas of innocence from this white mother who practiced voodoo witchcraft as an avocation. She escaped the death sentence by being pronounced insane, receiving life incarceration at the Milledgeville, Georgia, state hospital.

LYONS, Danny (1860?-88). New York gangster and murderer. He and Danny DRISCOLL headed the Whyos, a terrifying New York City street gang that engaged in beatings and killings for payment (the Whyos would punch a victim for $2, break a nose or jaw for $10, break an arm or leg for $19, and do the "big job" [murder] for $100 and up). Lyons had three whores working for him. When he tried to recruit a fourth, he got into a fight with her pimp, Joseph Quinn, who was shot and killed by Lyons on July 5, 1887. Lyons hid but was caught by the police, who wanted to get rid of one more criminal in New York. Convicted of murder, Lyons was hanged in the Tombs on August 21, 1888.

LYONS, Sophie (1848-1924). American thief, swindler, and columnist. Attractive, audacious, and artful, she operated on both sides of the law to amass a fortune (some $1 million at the time of her death). In about 1862 she began her criminal career in New York City, her birthplace and home, shoplifting, picking pockets, and other thievery, graduating ultimately to confidence games and bank burglary after marrying English-born master thief Edward "Ned" Lyons. The two of them served time in Sing Sing (Ossining Correctional Facility) in the 1870s, Ned for bank burglary and Sophie for grand larceny. On her release, she went into robbery in a big way, becoming an international thief and swindler and pulling off jobs in America and Europe. Frequently pretending to be a wealthy grand dame, Sophie hobnobbed with the social elite, members of whom she robbed of diamonds and jewelry; she maintained an elegant lifestyle, with several residences at home and abroad, and often used aliases when pulling off her jobs, which sometimes involved harlotry. Arrested numerous times and having spent terms in jail, she decided to reform herself "to gain the respect of good people." In 1897 Sophie, who had by then learned several languages and become a cultured woman of means, joined the staff of the New York World, where she soon became America's first society columnist, writing about the doings of the upper crust with whom she was in close contact. Later at her home in Detroit, Sophie was fatally beaten by thieves, whom she had hoped to reform, and died of a brain hemorrhage.

- M -

McCALL, "Black Jack" (1851-77). American gunrunner and assassin. In the 1870s McCall, a cross-eyed lush and saddlebum, engaged in gunrunning to the Indians in the Western territories (he had gotten his cross eyes when a lawman, whom he had assaulted, hit him on the head with a board, knocking him unconscious and forever messing up his eyes). On August 2, 1876, McCall slipped up behind lawman James Butler "Wild Bill" Hickok, who was mulling over his poker hand in a Deadwood, South Dakota,

saloon, and shot him dead through the head. Hickok's hand—
two aces and two eights—thereafter became known as the "dead
man's hand." McCall claimed he was avenging the murder of his
brother, whom he said Hickok had fatally shot, pleaded self-
defense to a miners' jury, and was found not guilty. A U.S.
marshal later arrested McCall for the Hickok assassination and
brought him to trial in a law court in Yankton, South Dakota.
McCall's story about his brother was found to be a fabrication:
he had had no brother. Asked why he hadn't come face-to-face
with Hickok, he replied, "I didn't want to commit suicide."
McCall was convicted of murder and hanged on March 1, 1877.

McCARTY, Tom (fl. c. 1885-95). Colorado bank and train robber.
The two McCarty brothers, Tom and Bill, accompanied by young
Butch CASSIDY, held up and robbed an express train near
Grand Junction, Colorado, on November 3, 1887. The McCarty
gang then switched to bank robbery, taking $20,000 from the
First National Bank in Denver on March 30, 1889, and over
$10,000 from the bank in Telluride, Colorado, on June 24, 1889;
both bank heists were pulled off without any shooting. With
large posses on their trail, the gang went into hiding, mainly
at the Hole in the Wall, a rocky natural fortress on the Wyoming-
Utah-Colorado border. In 1893 Tom and Bill, along with Bill's
son Fred, attempted to rob the bank at Delta, Colorado, but were
overwhelmed by angry townspeople, who fatally shot Bill and
Fred. Tom escaped and claimed he would avenge the deaths of
his brother and nephew, but never returned to Delta, where a
good reward was posted for him, dead or alive.

McCOLLUM, Ruby (b. 1915). Florida murderer. In the town of
Live Oak, Florida, in 1952, this black woman killed a white local
political leader, Dr. LeRoy C. Adams, with whom she had had a
love affair and by whom she was alleged to have had a child.
Tried and convicted, she spent about two years in prison before
being officially declared insane and sent to a mental institution;
her white lawyer Frank Cannon, who worked without compensation, saved her from death in the electric chair. Eventually
Ruby McCollum was released into the custody of her daughter.

McCONAGHY, Robert (1810-40). Pennsylvania mass murderer. On
May 30, 1840, McConaghy, distraught over family problems,
killed six of his relatives (his wife and mother-in-law and four
of her other children). Immediately arrested, McConaghy refused to admit his guilt but was convicted and sentenced to the
gallows. He was hanged twice on November 6, 1840, in Huntingdon, Pennsylvania. The first time the rope broke. Standing on
the scaffold a second time, McConaghy confessed to the murders.
The rope held this time. Afterward a pamphlet about his case
became a bestseller for about ten years.

MacDONALD, Jeffrey [Robert] (b. 1944). American army captain,

doctor, and convicted murderer. His 26-year-old wife and two
young daughters were brutally stabbed to death in the early
morning hours of February 17, 1970, at their home in Fort
Bragg, North Carolina, where MacDonald was stationed as a
physician with the Green Berets. Army investigators learned
from clean-cut, Princeton-educated MacDonald, who had survived stab wounds that night to telephone the military police,
that supposedly four drug-crazed hippie intruders had committed
the three murders, which were similar to those committed by the
Charles MANSON family in 1969. Although MacDonald himself
was accused of the killings, the army exonerated him because of
insufficient evidence, but later his father-in-law, Alfred Kassab,
who had defended MacDonald's innocence, came to believe he was
guilty and launched a crusade to reopen the case. Finally, on
July 16, 1979, MacDonald, who had become a respected surgeon
in California, was placed on trial in federal court in Raleigh,
North Carolina, and was convicted (August 29, 1979) by a 12-
member jury of having committed the crimes and staging them
to look like cult slayings. He was set free about one year later
because of a legal technicality--a ruling that the U.S. Supreme
Court overturned (1982)--and subsequently his appeal was denied.
He is now serving three consecutive life sentences in the federal
prison at Bastrop, Texas, and will be eligible for parole in 1991.
MacDonald's controversial case was chronicled in author Joe
McGinniss' bestseller, Fatal Vision (1983).

McDONALD, Mike or Michael [Cassius] (1832-1907). Chicago con
man, gambler, and political fixer. During the U.S. Civil War
(1861-65) he directed a highly organized and profitable bounty
jumping racket, collecting commissions from enlistments in the
Union Army, then having the new soldiers immediately desert to
reenlist in another place and collecting commissions again. In
the 1870s McDonald built up a large confidence game operation
in Chicago, ruling a colony of gamblers and swindlers and making large payoffs to politicians and police to remain in business.
By 1880 he had accumulated a fortune as controller of almost
all the gambling rackets in the city (he coined the phrase,
"Never give a sucker an even break") and had become Chicago's
most influential political boss, which he remained for over 25
years. Through his political clout, McDonald was able to "fix"
juries so that he was untouched by the law for any underworld
operations. Marital problems (he was married twice) greatly upset him and, some say, led to his death on August 9, 1907.
Shortly before, his second wife, showgirl Dora Feldman, 35
years his junior, had shot and killed her secret lover, artist
Webster Guerin, and had disclosed she did not love McDonald,
who was apparently heartbroken. See also HARRISON, Carter.

McERLANE, Frankie or Frank (fl. 1920-30). Chicago gangster and
bootlegger. He joined bootlegger Joseph "Polock Joe" SALTIS
to become his right-hand gunman in Chicago in the 1920s.

McErlane introduced the use of the Thompson submachine gun in gangland wars and reportedly killed at least ten gang rivals, mobsters working for Al CAPONE, Edward "Spike" O'DONNELL, Ralph SHELDON, and others. In late 1929 McErlane quit working for Saltis because he felt he was being cheated out of his share of Saltis's bootleg profits. McErlane, wounded by an unknown assailant in 1930, then worked for himself and other gangsters, disappearing from sight in the 1930s.

McGINNIS, [Joseph Francis] "Big Joe" (fl. 1940s-56). Massachusetts bank robber. A Boston liquor dealer with a criminal record, McGinnis and his friend Anthony "the Pig" (or "Fats") Pino spent about 18 months planning the so-called "robbery of the century": their 11-member gang's heist of $2,775,395 in bills, coins, checks, and money orders from Brink's Inc., a Boston armored car service, on the night of January 17, 1950. McGinnis and Pino, who had a long-time criminal record, recruited nine accomplices: Vincent J. Costa, James I. Flaherty, Henry J. Baker, Stanley H. Gusciora, Joseph James "Specs" O'KEEFE, Adolf "Jazz" Maffie, John S. Banfield, Thomas F. Richardson, and Michael V. Geagan, all of whom were professionals in the underworld. Although a Brink's cashier who had been tied up along with guards and others during the robbery managed to get loose and push an emergency button, the seven armed and masked members of the gang who entered the Brink's office successfully executed the heist in about 17 minutes, fleeing afterward to a house in Roxbury, Massachusetts. The gang divided up about $1.1 million after destroying all traceable monetary items. The FBI and local police were unable to solve the crime until 1955, when O'Keefe (who had been tricked out of most of his share of the money, having given it to Maffie for safekeeping, and who had been shot at by gunman Elmer "Trigger" BURKE, hired by gang members to kill O'Keefe to prevent him from becoming a police-informer as he threatened to do) talked openly and thus secured the arrest of his ten accomplices. They were all tried, convicted, and imprisoned (Banfield and Gusciora had meanwhile died of natural causes); the case was closed in 1956.

MacGREGOR, Robert. See ROB ROY.

McGURN, "Machine Gun" Jack [real name: James Vincenzo De Mora] (1904-36). Chicago gangster and murderer. In the 1920s and 1930s he worked for Al CAPONE as a hit man. An expert with the Thompson submachine gun (hence his nickname "Machine Gun"), McGurn was credited by police with at least 28 killings, including six members of the GENNA gang and seven members of the MORAN gang (St. Valentine's Day Massacre of 1929). McGurn was arrested on suspicion of murder several times, but he was never brought to trial. On the eve of St. Valentine's Day in 1936, he was shot to death by three unknown gunmen in a Chicago bowling alley. See also HUNT, Sam[uel McPherson] "Golf Bag."

McKINNEY, James (1861-1902). American gunslinger and murderer. in the 1890s the so-called "McKinney Touch"--shooting a person in the buttocks for sport, thereby maiming or killing him or her --made him a much-sought-after fugitive from the law. McKinney was known to have left his "touch" on at least half a dozen victims from Colorado to California, including a cancan dancer, miners, and lawmen. On April 18, 1902, in Bakersfield, California, McKinney died in a gun battle in an opium den with six arresting law officers, two of whom were fatally wounded.

MacLEOD, Banda (1900-1950). Indonesian-born spy. A petite, well-educated, cosmopolitan, Eurasian beauty who was the daughter of the infamous spy MATA HARI (some historians doubt this), Banda lived and worked as a schoolteacher in Batavia (Djakarta, Java), where she frequently gave social parties attended by diplomats, military officers, and journalists. A Dutch uncle of hers who was in the Japanese army forced her to become an espionage agent for the Japanese by threatening to expose the secret of her parentage (1942). However, because her sympathies at the time (World War II) lay with the Dutch, she collaborated secretly with her lover Abdul, an underground resistance fighter for Indonesian independence, against the Japanese and passed along valuable information to the Allies. She found out about the Japanese plans for the Battle of Guadalcanal beforehand and about various Japanese troop concentrations and ship movements. After the war Banda fought against Dutch occupation of Indonesia and helped secure support and funds in America for her cause. Hired by the U.S. intelligence service after Indonesia became independent, she gathered information in Communist China about Soviet supplies and in North Korea about the intended invasion of South Korea (1950) that led to the Korean War. Caught accidentally by the Communists, she received no trial and was shot by a firing squad at the same time her mother had been executed: 5:45 a.m.

McLOWERY or McLAURY, Frank and Tom. See CLANTON, Billy or William; EARP, Wyatt [Berry Stapp].

MADDEN, Owen or Owney (1892-1964). English-born New York bootlegger, gangster, and murderer. Madden, a leader of the murderous Gopher Gang on New York City's West Side, was involved in hundreds of gang fights from 1903 to 1914. He was an expert user of the blackjack, brass knuckles, and his favorite weapon, a lead pipe wrapped in a newspaper. By the time he was 21, he had been arrested more than 40 times, charged with robbery, assault, and murder. In 1914 he was convicted of killing "Little Patsy" Doyle, a rival gang leader, and sentenced to 10 to 20 years in prison. Released on parole in 1923, Madden became an important bootlegger and speakeasy owner in New York and worked with such top criminals as Dutch SCHULTZ, Charles "Lucky" LUCIANO, Meyer LANSKY, and Abner "Longy" ZWILLMAN. In the mid-1930s he retired from the New York world of crime and moved to Hot Springs, Arkansas, where he died in 1964.

MAFFIE, Adolf "Jazz." See McGINNIS, [Joseph Francis] "Big Joe."

MAHANEY, Jack (1844-?). New York pickpocket, mugger, burglar, and prison breaker. The son of a wealthy New York family, Mahaney ran away from boarding school and hooked up with Italian Dave and his gang of some 40 boys who roamed New York City's streets as pickpockets and muggers in the 1850s and 1860s. He and Italian Dave, who taught him the art of crime, often worked together on important jobs. A dispute over the sharing of loot caused the pair to break up, and Mahaney formed his own gang and committed numerous burglaries and robberies. Taken into custody several times by police, Mahaney became known as the American version of English, prison breaker Jack SHEPPARD because he twice escaped from New York City's Tombs Prison and twice broke out of Sing Sing (now Ossining Correctional Facility). Mahaney also escaped custody several times by jumping from speeding trains without incurring any injury. He later assumed a number of aliases, supposedly taking up the confidence racket, and was not seen again.

MAINWARING, Sir Henry (1587-1653). English privateer and pirate. Mainwaring, well educated with a degree from Oxford, served in the army before he was commissioned to plunder Spanish shipping in the West Indies. Instead he plundered Spanish ships off the African coast and became a much-feared pirate. At the age of 24, Mainwaring commanded a fleet of 30 ships that terrorized foreign shipping for nearly four years (he never plundered an English vessel). Offers by the Spanish king of a pardon and command of a Spanish fleet, or a commission as a privateer by the duke of Florence, and of a partnership by the bey (governor) of Algiers were all rejected by Mainwaring, who accepted the English Crown's offer to drive Barbary corsairs (pirates) out of English waters. In 1618 Mainwaring was knighted, and in 1621 he was elected to Parliament. He wrote a textbook on pirates and a naval manual, the latter published by Parliament. Mainwaring died, however, in poverty.

MAJOR, Ethel Lillie (1890-1934). English poisoner. In 1934 her husband Arthur Major, to whom she had been married for 16 years, died in Kirby-on-Bain, a village in Lincolnshire; he had informed others that his wife was trying to poison him. Their marriage had collapsed that year when he discovered (and she admitted) that her "sister" Auriel was actually her own child,

but Ethel refused to tell him who Auriel's father was. When
strychnine was found in Arthur's body, Scotland Yard questioned Ethel, who unintentionally mentioned strychnine poisoning although she wasn't supposed to know the cause of death.
She was convicted and hanged at Hull.

MALCOLM, Sarah (1711-33). Irish-born British murderer. A
strongly built laundress, she unexplainably and maniacally
strangled her sleeping employer, 80-year-old Lydia Dunscomb,
who lived in the Inner Temple area of London, on the night of
February 5, 1733. She then killed two possible witnesses and
fled with some items but was soon caught and placed on trial
for the so-called "Temple Murder." Despite her denial of guilt,
Sarah was convicted and condemned to death; while in jail she
had her "wicked" portrait drawn by William Hogarth, the noted
English painter. A noisy throng watched Sarah stoically go to
her hanging in London on March 7, 1733.

MALEDON, George (1834-1911). American hangman. After the U.S.
Civil War, in which he served in the Union Army, Maledon became a lawman in western Arkansas, which included Indian territory, and volunteered to be the hangman whenever an execution took place at Fort Smith, Arkansas, seat of the district
federal court. After 1875 he worked faithfully and meticulously
for a notorious jurist, Isaac C. "Hanging Judge" Parker (1838-96),
who ruled the Fort Smith court for 21 years during which time
he condemned 172 persons to death on the gallows. Nearly all
of the 88 who were hanged were done so by the hand of Maledon, a cold-blooded craftsman proud of his specially made, well-
oiled hanging ropes which he used again and again; he once
remarked, "I never hanged a man who came back to have the
job done over." Maledon, who earned about $100 per hanged
man, was criticized by some for staging multiple hangings, sending simultaneously three, four, five, or even six to their so-
called "dance of death" through the gallows' traps. When Parker died of illness, Maledon carried on for awhile and then retired, touring around showing off his ropes, traps, and other
paraphernalia. He tried his hand at farming with little success
and died on May 6, 1911.

MALLON, "Typhoid" Mary (1870-1938). New York cook and typhoid
carrier. The New York City Health Department, investigating
a minor epidemic of typhoid fever in Oyster Bay, New York, in
1906, traced the cases of this highly contagious disease to hired
cook Mary Mallon, who in 1907 was detained, tested, and proven
to be a public menace as a carrier of typhoid. But she felt fine
and refused any treatment by health officials, who held her responsible for outbreaks during the past several years when she
cooked in numerous restaurants, hotels, clubs, and private
homes. She was finally released in 1910 after much litigation,
promising to cease cooking. "Typhoid Mary," as the press

dubbed her, dropped out of sight, using a new identity and knowingly spreading the disease by working as before. A serious typhoid outbreak in a hospital in 1915 was traced to Mary, who had been employed there. Again she was taken into custody, refused treatment, and spent the rest of her life confined in New York's Riverside Hospital, where she died of a stroke on November 11, 1938. She caused at least 53 cases of typhoid and three deaths between about 1904 and 1915.

MANDELBAUM, Fredericka "Marm" (1818-94). Prussian-born New York fence. She was the most notorious fence (receiver of stolen goods) during the 1800s. Her elegantly furnished brownstone house on Clinton Street in New York City was often frequented by top criminals, such as George Leonidas LESLIE, Mark SHINBURN, Johnny DOBBS, and the LOOMIS gang, who all fenced their stolen goods through her. Mandelbaum gave lavish parties at which judges, politicians, burglars, and thieves mixed and talked. In her house she established a crime school where men and women, young and old, were taught professional methods of stealing, burglary, safecracking, and swindling. In 1884 Mandelbaum was indicted for grand larceny and receiving stolen wares. Informed by her lawyers (Howe & Hummel) that her career as a fence was over, Mandelbaum fled with her family and about $1 million in cash to Canada. Several times she returned to New York in disguise to visit her relatives and old friends in the underworld. She died in Canada, and her body was brought back to New York for burial.

MANNING, Maria (1825-49). Swiss-born murderer. A pretty maid who worked for British aristocrats, she married Frederick George Manning in the hope of becoming wealthy but was deceived. Her weak-willed husband, however, helped her kill a well-to-do customshouse officer named Patrick O'Connor (August 9, 1849) with whom Marie had had extramarital sex and whose body they buried in lime under the kitchen floor of their house in London. O'Connor's disappearance led to a Scotland Yard investigation that implicated the Mannings; Maria fled to Edinburgh, where she was picked up carrying O'Connor's railway stock certificates and money, and Frederick was found hiding on the island of Jersey. Each blamed the other for O'Connor's murder. Tried together at London's Old Bailey, the Mannings were found guilty and sentenced to death. Maria made vain appeals to Queen Victoria and other royal personages before her hanging on November 13, 1849, outside of Horsemonger Lane jail. She and Frederick were hung together before the largest crowd ever to witness a public execution in England; novelist Charles Dickens, a witness, expressed outrage at such a gruesome public spectacle relished by some 40,000 gleeful people of all ages and classes.

MANSON, Charles [Milles] (b. 1934). American mass murderer. In the 1950s he did time in several reform schools and prisons for stealing, procuring, and forgery. In the late 1960s Manson established a commune for a cult of hippies at the Spahn Ranch near Los Angeles. There his followers practiced free love, used drugs, and conducted pseudoreligious ceremonies centered around Manson as a satanic Christ-like figure. On Manson's orders, several members of his "family" (Charles "Tex" Watson, Susan Atkins, Patricia Krenwinkel, and Leslie Van Houton) broke into the Beverly Hills residence of film director Roman Polanski, who was away at the time (August 9, 1969), and shot, stabbed, and clubbed to death five persons (Polanski's pregnant wife, actress Sharon Tate, coffee heiress Abigail Folger, Polish writer Voyteck Frykowksi, hair stylist Jay Sebring, and 18-year-old Steven Earl Parent). The killers wrote slogans ("War" and "Pig") on the walls of the house with the blood of their victims. Two days later, on August 11, 1969, they entered the home of Leno and Rosemary La Bianca, slaughtered them, and again scrawled slogans in blood on the walls. Soon identified as the leader of the killers, Manson was arrested and tried along with the three female killers; Watson was tried separately. All were found guilty in early 1971. Manson and the four others were sentenced to death but were given life imprisonment when the Supreme Court abolished capital punishment in 1972.

MANSVELT [Mansveld or Mansfield], Edward (d. 1667). West Indian buccaneer. In 1665 in Jamaica (an English possession since 1655), Governor Modyford commissioned Mansvelt, who may have been born in Curaçao of Dutch descent, to assemble an expedition to sail against the Dutch, with whom the English were then at war. The expedition (15 ships with 600 fighting pirates), led by Mansvelt and his vice-admiral Henry MORGAN, moved instead against Spanish settlements and fortifications in Cuba, Nicaragua, Costa Rica, and Panama, successfully seizing and looting a number of places. On an island near Costa Rica captured by the pirates, Mansvelt planned to establish a permanent pirate principality, but the Spaniards were able to recapture the island, thwarting the plan. Mansvelt returned to Jamaica, where he was upbraided by the governor for his actions with impunity; the old buccaneer died before long, and Morgan succeeded him as the pirates' leader.

MARANZANO, Salvàtore (1868-1931). Sicilian-born American bootlegger and gangster. He was an old-guard Mafia leader, a so-called "Mustache Pete," who wanted to organize crime throughout the United States with himself as super boss. During Prohibition Maranzano ran a lucrative bootlegging operation in New York City. In 1930 an internecine war (the so-called "Castellammarese War") broke out between him and Giuseppe "Joe the Boss" MASSERIA. After Masseria's death in April 1931, Maranzano set up a new Mafia organization, calling it La Cosa Nostra ("Our Thing"), which included dividing the New York Mafia into five family groups. He schemed to eliminate his enemies, such as Vito GENOVESE, Al CAPONE, Dutch SCHULTZ, Frank COS-TELLO, and Charles "Lucky" LUCIANO. On September 10, 1931, four gunmen hired by Luciano stabbed and shot Maranzano to death in his Manhattan office.

MARCELLO, Carlos [born: Calogero Minacore] (b. 1910). Tunisian-born American crime boss. For over 60 years his private life and business dealings have been shrouded in secrecy in New Orleans, his place of residence with his wife and family, and throughout the Southwest. In 1930 he was convicted of assault and robbery but received a full pardon from Louisiana Governor O. K. Allen; in 1938 he was convicted of drug peddling but got released in less than a year. For years Marcello, called "The Little Man" because of his short height, passed himself off as a tomato salesman earning $1,600 a month but later said he was an investor and land developer. The FBI, one of whose agents he was convicted (1968) of slugging in 1966, claims that Marcello has bribed public officials at every governmental level and that he oversees a huge criminal empire (gambling, prostitution, narcotics, and labor racketeering, among other operations) that takes in an estimated $2 billion a year. At congressional crime hearings, Marcello has refused to answer questions; he has been cited for contempt of Congress twice but escaped imprisonment through legal technicalities. Several times he has thwarted federal attempts to deport him. In 1980 an FBI undercover operation resulted in his indictment in New Orleans for racketeering, conspiracy, and fraud; in 1981 a federal court there convicted him of conspiracy in a bribery case.

MAREK, Martha [Lowenstein] (1904-38). Austrian swindler and mass poisoner. A foundling in Vienna, she became the ward of a rich, elderly man named Moritz Fritsch, who on his death (1923) left her his fortune and mansion at Mödling. In 1924 lovely Martha married a handsome young engineer named Emil Marek, with whom she soon wasted her inheritance through extravagances and then managed, despite much suspicion by authorities, to collect insurance money from an "accident" to Emil (he and Martha used an axe to amputate Emil's leg below the knee, a ghastly ordeal that netted them in the end only 3,000 pounds). Later they again became impoverished, and in 1932 Martha collected life insurance on the deaths of Emil and their seven-year-old daughter. Several months later she claimed insurance on the death of an aunt and subsequently on the death of a boarder in her home in Vienna. A vain attempt to collect insurance on "stolen" expensive paintings which she had hidden in a warehouse focused the authorities' attention on Martha's past, resulting in the discovery of thallium poisoning in the exhumed bodies of the four deceased above. Tried for murder in Vienna in 1938, she pleaded innocent but was convicted and, on December 6, was beheaded.

MARTIN, Michael. See LIGHTFOOT, Captain.

MASON, Sam[uel] (1755?-1803). Kentucky highwayman. In the
early 1800s he led a large band of cutthroats who robbed and
killed travelers in Kentucky and along the Natchez Trail (trail
from Mississippi to Tennessee). At the scene of each crime,
Mason usually carved the words, "Done by Mason of the Woods,"
which became his trademark. The governors of Mississippi and
Louisiana offered rewards for Mason's capture, dead or alive.
Sam Mays and Wiley "Little" HARPE, who then went under the
name of Setton, joined Mason's gang, killed Mason in late 1803,
and brought his severed head to Natchez, Mississippi, to collect their reward. Both were recognized as highwaymen and
hanged in 1804.

MASSERIA, Joe or Giuseppe (1880?-1931). Sicilian-born New York
extortionist, bootlegger, and gangster. In the early 1900s he
worked for Ignazio LUPO, leader of the Black Handers (extortionists), in the Italian section of Harlem in New York City.
Masseria later took control of Lupo's operation and branched
out into bootlegging in the 1920s. He managed to survive unscathed assassination attempts by Mafia rivals such as Umberto
Valenti, who was apparently gunned down on Masseria's orders.
"Joe the Boss," as Masseria was called, was one of the "Mustache Petes" (Mafia leaders filled with Old World traditions) and
was loathed by many of the newer and younger gangsters, such
as Joe ADONIS, Vito GENOVESE, Albert ANASTASIA, and Benjamin "Bugsy" SIEGEL (the four of whom reputedly assassinated
Masseria, though the police record listed the assassins as "persons unknown"). In 1930-31 Masseria battled against Mafia boss
Salvatore MARANZANO in the so-called "Castellammarese War,"
which ended with the murder of Masseria at Scarpato's Restaurant in Coney Island, Brooklyn, on April 15, 1931. Charles
"Lucky" LUCIANO, Masseria's "trusted" aide, had accompanied
his boss there but had been taking a "long leak" in the bathroom when the killing occurred.

MASSIE, Thomas H. (1900-1944). American murderer. Massie was
a lieutenant in the U.S. Navy stationed in Hawaii. One night
in September 1931, his attractive socialite wife, Thalia, was allegedly raped by five Hawaiian beach boys, who were soon arrested. The case against the boys was weak, and they were
released on bond. Massie, helped by Albert O. Jones, Edward
J. Lord, and his wife's mother, Mrs. Granville Fortescue, tried
to force a confession out of one of the boys, Joseph Kahahawai,
whom they had abducted, and shot him to death. Massie and
the others were caught while trying to dispose of Kahahawai's
body. With Clarence Darrow as their attorney, the four were
tried and found guilty of murder in the second degree. Riots
erupted in the United States over the verdict and the sentences
of ten-year prison terms. Hawaii's governor commuted each

sentence to one hour "held" in court and released them. The
Massies were divorced two years later in Reno, Nevada.

MATA HARI [born: Margaretha Geertruida Zelle] (1876-1917).
Dancer, courtesan, and spy. Her seven-year disastrous marriage to Captain Rudolf MacLeod, a Dutch officer who exploited
and beat her while they lived in wedlock in the Dutch East Indies during those years, ended in divorce in her native Holland
in 1902. She then trained herself to be an exotic and erotic
Oriental dancer and moved to Paris, where at first striptease
work, streetwalking, and whoring were her means of earning a
living. In 1905 she began calling herself Mata Hari, a Malay
phrase meaning "eye of the dawn". The Parisian nightclub audiences before whom she danced as a newly found love-goddess
began raving ardently about her rich erotic style and charms;
she titillated men's greatest sexual desires with her undulating
motions, throwing off her red veils to reveal her naked flesh as
if in orgasm. She was soon paid fortunes for her performances,
and captivated men of power and wealth made her their secret
courtesan, giving her costly gifts. By 1913 Mata Hari had been
recruited by the Germans to work as an espionage agent (she
had numerous affairs with German military officers) and, during
World War I, turned over to them important plans about Allied
supplies and offensives which she obtained from her French and
other lovers. Her activities became suspicious to the Allies,
resulting in her arrest in Paris on February 13, 1917. Although
her exact role as a spy was not clarified with facts at her military trial (July 24-25, 1917), Mata Hari was found guilty and
later executed by a 12-man firing squad at Vincennes, near
Paris, on October 15, 1917. Many grieved because she met her
death so proudly.

MATHER or MATHERS, David (1845-?). American lawman and outlaw. He operated on both sides of the law and managed to get
away with it, receiving the nickname "Mysterious Dave." Mather,
who kept a tight lip, was a cattle rustler in Kansas in 1873, a
con man selling "gold bricks" to cowboys in Texas in 1878, and
a lawman in Nevada and Texas in the early 1880s. Named assistant marshal in Dodge City, Kansas, in 1883, Mather lost the
post in an election the next year and was succeeded by Tom
Nixon. He and Nixon, both of whom owned saloons, got into a
price war over beer which led to Mather shooting Nixon in the
back, killing him. Mather was arrested, tried, and acquitted
on grounds of self-defense. Soon afterward he disappeared;
some say he served as a marshal in small towns in Nebraska
and then became an outlaw in Canada in the early 1900s.

MAY, Alan Nunn (b. 1912). British scientist and Soviet spy.
Early in 1943 May, a nuclear physicist, went to Canada to help
develop the atomic bomb (the Manhattan Project) and later (1944)
was appointed chief of the Montreal laboratories. He knew the

details of the progress of the atomic research in the various
installations in Canada and the United States. Long a secret
Communist party member, May became involved in Soviet espionage, handing over reports on atomic development and samples of
uranium-233 and -235 (vital components of the bomb) to Soviet
agents. The spying network of which he was a part was exposed when cipher clerk Igor Gouzenko at the Soviet embassy
in Ottawa defected to the West with incriminating documentary
proof (1945). May, who had gone back to Britain after World
War II, was arrested, tried, and sentenced (1946) to ten years'
imprisonment. He was released on December 30, 1951. See
also CARR, Sam; ROSE, Fred.

MEAD, [William] Elmer (fl. 1895-1935). American swindler. He had
a long and lucrative career as a master of confidence games,
pocketing some $2 million over 40 years of successfully duping
well-to-do farmers, ranchers, building contractors, and others.
Nicknamed "The Christian Kid" because of his affected piety
and regular Sunday church attendance, Mead used many aliases
during his life and originated the magic-wallet con game, his
cleverest scam. He would plant a money-filled wallet with phony
identification papers in it, which an "honest" sucker would purposely find and return to the owner (Mead); impressed then by
Mead's seeming wealth and influence, the person would be conned
into handing over his or her money for a sure money-making
deal, and Mead would abscond with the funds. In 1922 Mead
was caught in Denver and imprisoned; three years later he was
released. Carrying on his flimflamming operations as before, he
was again caught in late 1935, and three years later Mead, now
at age 63 and in jail, faced tax evasion charges that ended his
fraudulence for good.

MEANS, Gaston Bullock (1880-1938). American investigator, hoaxer,
and con man. From 1910 to 1915 he worked for a private detective agency, secretly bilking clients, but quit to run the financial affairs of eccentric millionaire-heiress Maude King, whom
he managed to mulct out of $150,000 through fraudulent invest-
ments by mid-1917. When King became suspicious, he took her
on a hunting trip during which she "accidentally" shot and killed
herself, according to the decision of the coroner's jury. During
World War I Means hired himself out as a spy to the British,
Germans, and Americans, impersonating intelligence agents and
inventing elaborate espionage activities to stay in business. In
1921 he was made special investigator in the Bureau of Investigation (later the FBI), where he continued his flimflamming and
made large sums of money. Hired by Mrs. Warren G. Harding,
Means uncovered an extramarital affair between President Harding and Nan Britton, an Ohio poet. He attempted to blackmail
the Hardings for an alleged $50,000 with the accusation that the
President had fathered a child by Britton. Harding died before
Means could collect. Later Means tried to capitalize by writing

The President's Daughter about the alleged illegitimate child
and The Strange Death of President Harding, a scandalous
bestseller in which he implied that Mrs. Harding had poisoned
her husband in revenge for his affair with Britton. Means
continued his con games into the mid-1930s, when he fleeced
wealthy heiress Evalyn Walsh McLean out of $100,000 on his
promise that he could get back the kidnapped Lindbergh baby
through his underworld contacts. The money, supposedly to
be paid as ransom, was never recovered, and Means was convicted of fraud and sentenced to 15 years at Leavenworth, where
he died of a heart attack in 1938.

MEEGEREN, Hans Van. See VAN MEEGEREN, Hans.

MEINHOF, Ulrike (1934-76). German terrorist. A noted radical
journalist and an organizer of the leftist Red Army Faction,
which sought to change the politics of West Germany, she and
Andreas Baader (whom she helped free from German police
custody in 1970) established a rabid terrorist group (the so-
called Baader-Meinhof gang) which engaged in numerous revolutionary and criminal activities, such as kidnappings, killings,
and bloody bank robberies. This paramilitary gang was eventually squashed by German police, who caught Ulrike Meinhof
in possession of an arsenal of various weapons in mid-July 1972.
She committed suicide using ripped-up towels to make a rope to
hang herself in Stammheim Prison in May 1976, having become
depressed about her predicament.

MELDRUM, Robert (1865-after 1929). American gunslinger. Western mine operators and cattle ranchers often hired Meldrum to
get rid of squatters and troublemakers, some of whom were
found shot to death. In 1900 Meldrum became marshal in Dixon,
Wyoming, where he won fame for killing Noah Wilkinson, a notorious Texas outlaw with a price on his head. The killings of
some strikers at the Smuggler Union Mine in Telluride, Colorado,
in 1901 were attributed to Meldrum, who managed to evade the
law and continue working as a hired gunman until 1916. Convicted of manslaughter (mine operators and ranchers helped reduce the murder charge against him), Meldrum received five to
seven years but was paroled after serving only three months.
After Meldrum's saddler's business in Walcott, Wyoming, burned
down in 1929, he disappeared and was thought to have moved
east.

MENGELE, Josef (b. 1911-79?). German Nazi doctor, war criminal,
and fugitive. Born to an affluent family in Germany, Mengele
earned university degrees in medicine and anthropology before
going in 1943 to work as the chief Nazi SS doctor at Auschwitz
concentration camp in Poland. He was in charge of choosing
which new arriving prisoners should be sent immediately to the
gas death chambers (judged as "unfit") and which should be

put to work. Mengele became known for conducting hideous
medical experiments on inmates, especially on dwarfs and twins,
hoping to unlock the "secret" of multiple births (so that Germany could produce more children) and to breed a blue-eyed
"master race." Called "The Angel of Death" and "The Butcher
of Auschwitz," he deformed, tortured, and murdered many
through chemical injections, drugs, starvation, disease, suffo-
cation, and other means in his so-called genetic research. The
killing of more than 400,000 Jews, Gypsies, and others--more
than 200,000 of them children--was attributed to Mengele, directly and indirectly. After World War II he lived openly in
Germany until 1951, then moved to Buenos Aires in Argentina
and later to Paraguay, where he gained citizenship in 1959.
West Germany's requests for his extradition to stand trial on
war crimes charges were stalled first by Argentina (1959) and
then by Paraguay (1960), which later insisted that he had left
the country when other extradition requests were made. He
supposedly lived reclusively in Brazil between 1961 and 1979,
when he apparently drowned at a beach resort. Human skele-
tal remains, exhumed from a grave in Embu, Brazil, in June 1985
were verified "with reasonable scientific certainty" to be Mengele's.

MENTEN, Pieter (b. 1899). Dutch art collector and Nazi war
criminal. For 30 years Menten's close association with Dutch
royalty shielded him from prosecution for crimes committed during World War II. As a Nazi SS officer during the war, he led
troops through the Polish village of Podhorodse in 1941, slaugh-
tering its Jewish inhabitants. During this period he was able
to filch many valuable art works from places in Europe and bring
them home to Holland, where he became enormously wealthy, estimated to be worth $100 million. By 1976 Dutch authorities had
gleaned enough evidence against Menten to arrest him, and in
1977 an Amsterdam court found him guilty of murdering 20 to
30 Jews at Podhorodse. His conviction, however, was overturned (1978) on his claim to have been promised immunity by
the Dutch justice minister in the 1950s. The Supreme Court
soon ordered a second trial, which was delayed until 1980 when
Menten was pronounced mentally and physically fit to defend
himself. Again convicted of the war crime by a Dutch court
(1980), he was sentenced to ten years' imprisonment and fined
$51,700. Menten was released from prison in March 1985 and
now lives in Holland. The long struggle to bring Menten to
justice is chronicled in Malcolm C. MacPherson's book The Blood
of His Servants.

MERCADER [del Rio Hernandez], [Jaime] Ramón (b. 1914).
Spanish-born assassin. A political activist on the side of the
Communist totalitarianism advocated by Soviet dictator Joseph
Stalin, Mercader, who had been born in Barcelona, was hired
by Stalinist agents to do espionage work in Mexico in the late

1930s. There he successfully infiltrated the Trotskyite ranks, becoming ultimately a trusted friend of exiled Russian Communist revolutionist Leon Trotsky, an outspoken critic of the Stalinist regime and a proponent of a worldwide revolution to establish pure Communism. Stalin's secret police, using machine guns and incendiary bombs, failed to assassinate Trotsky at his villa outside Mexico City on May 23, 1940. Afterward Mercader was directed to do the job alone, and on August 20, 1940, under the name Jacques Mornard (he also used the alias Frank Jackson) gained entrance to Trotsky's villa's study, where he suddenly took a piolet (mountaineering ice axe) from beneath his raincoat and bashed in the skull of Trotsky, who sat reading at his desk; Stalin's enemy died about 25 hours later. Mercader was taken into custody after being severely beaten, was found guilty in a court trial, and was imprisoned for 20 years (the maximum sentence for murder under Mexican law). In 1960 he was set free and promptly fled to Czechoslovakia.

MERCIER, Euphrasie (1823-?). French poisoner. After losing a large inheritance through mismanagement, she worked for many years in menial jobs until finally, at the age of 60, she opened a boot shop in Paris. A rich lady friend, Elodie Ménétret, allowed Euphrasie to move into her villa at Villemomble, outside of Paris, in 1883. There Euphrasie indulged herself in maniacal religious rites which frightened Elodie, who suddenly disappeared in April 1883. Euphrasie's brother and three sisters (all of whom were thought mad) came to live with her in the Ménétret house, and she told the police and others that Elodie had gone to a convent in France. In 1885 Euphrasie's young nephew, Alphonse Chateauneuf, deduced that his aunt had poisoned the missing woman and obtained her arrest. Human bones were found buried in the Ménétret garden. At her sensational trial (April 6-10, 1886), she pleaded innocent but was found guilty and received a 20-year prison sentence.

MERRICK, Suds (d. 1884). New York river pirate and burglar. In the 1860s and 1870s he was a river pirate in New York City. Merrick was a leader of the Hook Gang, which looted docks on the East River and cargo ships there. In 1874 the police surprised Merrick and three colleagues (Jimmy Gallagher, Tommy Bonner, and Sam McCracken) while they were looting the canal boat Thomas H. Brick. Merrick escaped but the others were caught and later sent to Auburn Prison for long terms. Merrick then fell out of favor with the Hook Gang and operated as a lone-wolf burglar until 1884, when he was mysteriously murdered on New York's Bowery.

MERRIFIELD, Louisa [Highway] (1907-53). British poisoner. In 1953 she married her third husband, and they were hired as housekeepers by one Mrs. Ricketts in Blackpool. After the aged Mrs. Ricketts died soon after (April 14, 1953), authorities grew suspicious of Louisa when she hastened to have the body cremated. Traces of phosphorous poison were found in the corpse and supposedly on a spoon in Louisa's purse. Damning testimony against Louisa was given by neighbors and others at her trial in Manchester, showing that she had schemed openly to kill the old woman to inherit her property. Louisa was convicted and hanged; her husband had known nothing of her plans.

MESSINA, Attilo (fl. 1940s-50s). Egyptian-born Italian white slaver and procurer. One of the four Messina brothers, Attilo was involved in white slavery in London after World War II. He helped import girls from Belgium, France, Italy, and other European countries, arranged for their phony marriages to gain British citizenship, and established them in nice apartments in London's West End to ply their service as fancy whores. In 1951 Attilo spent six months in prison on a conviction of procuring. Afterward he continued his vice operation until April 1959, when several of his white slaves and others were induced to testify against him (the Messina brothers often threatened girls who tried to escape or inform the police with beatings or razor slashings). Attilo was convicted and sentenced to four years' imprisonment. Long-time confusion over the nationality of the Messina brothers, whom British authorities sought to deport but whom other countries refused to take, ended when it was established that by Italian law the Messinas were Italian citizens (their father had been an Italian). Attilo was deported to Italy after his release from prison. See also MESSINA, Carmelo; MESSINA, Eugenio.

MESSINA, Carmelo (d. 1959). Egyptian-born Italian white slaver and procurer. In 1934 the Messina brothers—Carmelo, Eugenio, Attilo, and Alfredo—immigrated to England, where they engaged in white slavery. They imported hundreds of girls from Belgium, France, Italy, Spain, and Greece for prostitution in London, securing British citizenship for them through phony marriages. The prostitutes, given fancy clothing and set up in fashionable apartments in London's West End, were controlled totally by the Messinas, who received 80 per cent of their earnings. In 1955 Carmelo and Eugenio were arrested by authorities in Belgium on charges that included procuring. Carmelo was set free, but Eugenio was extradited to England for trial. Carmelo, refused admission to England, later entered illegally, was arrested, imprisoned for ten months, and then deported to Italy, where he later died. See also MESSINA, Attilo; MESSINA, Eugenio.

MESSINA, Eugenio (fl. 1940s-50s). Egyptian-born Italian white slaver and procurer. He and his three brothers—Carmelo, Attilo, and Alfredo—operated a large and lucrative prostitution business in London. Hundreds of girls brought in from other European countries and set up in smart apartments in the West

End worked as white slaves for the Messinas, handing over enormous earnings (one girl said she had serviced 49 customers in one night, which was slightly above average for a Messina prostitute). Eugenio and Carmelo were arrested in Belgium in 1955 on charges of procuring Belgian girls. Brought back to England, Eugenio was tried, convicted of running a prostitution ring, and sentenced to six and one half years in prison. He was released in 1959 and was immediately deported to Italy. See also MESSINA, Attilo; MESSINA, Carmelo.

METESKY, George [Peter] (b. 1903). New York City's "Mad Bomber." From about 1950 to 1957 he terrorized New York City, setting off homemade bombs in Grand Central Station, Penn Station, Radio City Music Hall, and many other places. The bombs, which injured 15 persons (eight seriously), were followed by notes that raged against Consolidated Edison, the utility company. One note was traced to Metesky, a former employee of the company, who claimed it was responsible for his contracting tuberculosis. Police discovered that Metesky had also planted bombs, all duds, in the city in 1940 and 1941. Charged with attempted murder, Metesky was judged criminally insane and sent to a New York state mental hospital. In 1973 he was released, considered cured.

MILLER, Bill "the Killer" (1905-31). American bank robber, prison breaker, and murderer. In 1930 in Toledo, Ohio, Charles "Pretty Boy" FLOYD teamed up with Miller, who was wanted for five murders and prison breaking. Miller had miraculously escaped while handcuffed with other prisoners in Detroit in 1929 and had become a fugitive at large. After pulling some small robberies in Michigan, Miller and Floyd, accompanied by two whores whom they had fallen in love with in Kansas City, robbed some banks in Kentucky and Ohio in May and June 1931. Police officers, attracted by the robbers' foolishly lavish spending and show of large bills, attempted to apprehend them in Bowling Green, Kentucky, in early June 1931. Miller and a police chief were killed and the two whores were wounded in the ensuing gun battle; Floyd managed to escape.

MILLER, Bill or William Franklin (1874-after 1920). American swindler. In January 1899 Miller, a bookkeeper in a brokerage office in New York City, talked of "inside tips" from top Wall Street financiers through which fortunes could be made, offering to pay 10 percent interest a week on money invested with him (a fabulous 520 percent each year!). Gullible investors paid thousands of dollars into Miller's Franklin Syndicate, which was simply a "robbing-Peter-to-pay-Paul" scheme, taking in money more rapidly than paying it out. Miller went into partnership with "Colonel" Robert Adams Ammon, a shady lawyer involved in other scams, who persuaded Miller to hand over $180,000 and to flee to Canada to escape impending arrest in November

1899. Soon afterward the Franklin Syndicate collapsed, with investors filing over $2 million in claims. Miller was soon caught, tried, convicted, and sentenced to ten years' imprisonment. Ammon, indicted in 1901 for receiving stolen money, was convicted in 1903 on testimony against him by Miller, who was later pardoned for helping to convict Ammon and released in 1905. Miller then worked briefly as a bookkeeper again, disappeared for about a decade, and was last seen operating a grocery store in Long Island, New York, in 1920.

MILLER, Clell. See JAMES, Jesse [Woodson]; YOUNGER, Cole[man].

MILLER, Jim (d. 1909). American lawman and gunfighter. In 1890 Sheriff Bud Frazer of Reeves County, Texas, made gunslinger Miller, nicknamed "Killin' Jim" because of his reputed killing of several men in gunfights, his deputy sheriff. A feud began between them over Miller's unlawful activities, and Frazer fired Miller, who soon afterward became marshal of Pecos, Texas. There were three wild shootouts between Miller and Frazer, who won the first two, leaving Miller both times severely wounded and certain to die. However, Miller survived to confront Frazer in a saloon in Toyah, Texas, on September 14, 1896, and to blast him to death with a shotgun. Miller was tried twice but went free and became a dreaded gunfighter-for-hire (he boasted he had "downed" 51 men in duels). He was lynched in Ada, Oklahoma, for killing a former lawman.

MILLER, John (1829–61). New Orleans mugger and murderer. In the 1850s he stalked the French Quarter of New Orleans, mugging people as a way of living. Miller, who briefly managed a prize-fighter named Charley Keys, lost his left arm in a fight over money from an upcoming boxing match. To the remaining stump of his left arm, he attached a chain and iron ball which he effectively used as a weapon thereafter. Imprisoned for killing a man in 1857, Miller supposedly reformed himself in prison but later met, fell in love with, and teamed up with a red-haired whore named "Bricktop" JACKSON. The two of them were probably the cruelest muggers New Orleans ever had. In a brutal fight in their living quarters on December 5, 1861, Miller, attempting to "tame" his wife, lashed her with a bullwhip and clubbed her, but in turn was beaten and stabbed to death by Jackson, who was sent to jail but later released.

MILLER, Lucille (b. 1930). California murderer. A liaison between her, an attractive housewife in San Bernardino, California, and Arthwell C. Hayton, a successful lawyer, resulted in the murders of Hayton's wife (by asphyxiation) and Lucille's 39-year-old husband--Dr. Gordon E. "Cork" Miller--a prosperous dentist whom Lucille drugged unconscious (as she had done earlier before killing Hayton's wife) and then burned to death inside the family Volkswagen (October 8, 1964). Evidence at the latter murder site implicated Lucille, who was apprehended, tried, and found guilty of killing her husband (Arthwell Hayton had nothing to do with Lucille's schemes, which were designed so that she could eventually marry Hayton). Sentenced to life imprisonment, she was later released on parole in 1972.

MINA, Lino Amalia Espos y (1809-32). American impostor, poisoner, and thief. Mina, who said he was the son of the Spanish governor of California, stayed in Dr. William Chapman's mansion in Philadelphia in 1831. Servants discovered Mina embracing Mrs. Chapman. Two weeks after Mina bought arsenic for the "stuffing of birds," Dr. Chapman suddenly died. Mrs. Chapman and Mina were soon married. Authorities grew suspicious when valuables in the mansion began to disappear and when they learned that Mina had posed as Dr. Chapman to do business. The doctor's body was then exhumed and large amounts of arsenic were found in it. Mina and Mrs. Chapman were arrested and tried; he was convicted of being a false, thieving murderer and hanged. She was acquitted, having convinced the jury she had been hoodwinked by Mina.

MINER, [William] "Old Bill" (1847-1913). American stage, train, and bank robber. From the 1860s to 1911 he robbed stagecoaches, express trains, and banks in California, Colorado, Oregon, Washington, and Georgia. Twice Miner was caught after robbing California's Sonora stage, in 1869 and 1881, and afterward served 10- and 20-year terms repsectively in San Quentin. For a brief time in 1880 he was a slave trader in Turkey and then a gun runner in South America. Miner, a free-wheeling, roaming robber, is reputed to have invented the phrase, "Hands up!" In the early 1900s he moved to Canada to continue his robbery career. The Northwest Mounties caught him in 1906 and sent him to New Westminster Penitentiary at Victoria, British Columbia, from which he escaped the next year by tunneling under the walls. Miner was tracked down and caught by Pinkerton detectives in a Georgia swamp in February 1911; he had led a gang of bandits who had held up a train near White Sulphur, Georgia. While serving a life sentence at the state prison in Milledgeville, Georgia, Miner escaped three times but was soon recaptured after each. He died in his cell in 1913.

MIRANDA, Ernesto (1941-75). American rapist. In 1963 Miranda was arrested for stealing $8 from a bank in Phoenix, Arizona. While in a police lineup, he was identified as a kidnapper and rapist. Under police interrogation, Miranda made a written confession to the kidnapping-rape charge, which was used at his trial to convict him. The U.S. Supreme Court later overturned his conviction, saying the police had not properly advised Miranda of his constitutional rights against self-incrimination. Miranda was later found guilty of the rape charge and sent to prison. Released on parole, Miranda was slain in a fight in a Phoenix bar in 1975.

MITCHELL, William.   See RUSSELL, Baldy.

MOCK DUCK (1878-1942).   New York tong leader.   At the beginning
of the 1900s, Mock Duck, leader of the Hip Sing Tong, challenged the power of Tom Lee, head of the On Leong Tong, which
controlled and greatly profited from extensive illegal enterprises
in New York City's Chinatown (the tongs, secret Chinese organizations, engaged in such rackets as peddling opium, prostitution, gambling, and smuggling aliens, especially female slaves).
A prolonged, fierce, and bloody struggle ensued between the
Hip Sings and the On Leongs, who tried unsuccessfully to kill
the upstart leader Mock Duck on orders from Tom Lee.   Mock
Duck, who wore a bulletproof vest of chain mail, miraculously
survived knifings and shootings and through cunning and
force took control of Chinatown after the tong war of 1909-10
in which some 300 tong casualties occurred.   In 1912 Mock Duck
was convicted on a numbers racket charge and served two years
in Sing Sing Prison (now Ossining Correctional Facility).   Afterward the On Leongs tried to depose him as the supreme power
in Chinatown but failed.   Accused of the murders of a dozen
men, Mock Duck remained free because of lack of evidence.
Finally, in 1932 a truce was arranged between the Hip Sings
and On Leongs, and soon after Mock Duck left Chinatown to
live in Brooklyn but regularly visited his former domain until
his death in 1942.

MODERS, Mary (1643-73).   English harlot, actress, swindler, and
thief.   Lowly born, intelligent, and beautiful, she pretended
fancifully to be a highborn lady of quality and was married several times but deserted her husbands, stealing their riches.
Several times she was arrested and tried for bigamy, always
gaining release because of lack of evidence against her.   For a
period Mary Moders was a highly paid prostitute in Cologne,
Germany, and after her return to England in 1663 she posed
haughtily as an abandoned German princess and deceived many
rich young aristocrats who lavished much money and gifts upon
her for sexual favors.   She cheated numerous married men,
bilking them of fortunes by threatening to expose their scandalous liaisons with her.   Her notoriety led to a theatrical career for a time, during which the "German Princess" was seen
in that role on the stage by many, commoners and nobles both.
But her beauty began to fade and she was shunned by admirers, causing her to turn to thievery to make ends meet.   Finally caught and convicted of robbery, Mary was banished to Jamaica but managed to return about two years later, which was
a violation punishable by death.   Found out, she was tried and
condemned and, on January 2, 1673, hanged at Tyburn, London.

MOLINEUX, Roland B. (1868-1917).   New York accused poisoner.
A wealthy, aristocratic New Yorker, Molineux belonged to the
Knickerbocker Athletic Club in the 1890s.   He was known to
loathe certain club members, including Henry C. Barnet, who

died mysteriously in November 1898, and Harry Cornish, who
was nearly poisoned to death in December of that year (Cornish's
landlady Katharine Adams was poisoned by accidentally drinking
a bottle of Bromo Seltzer intended for Cornish and found loaded
with cyanide of mercury). The bottle was traced to Molineux,
who was charged with murder and tried. After a sensational
three-month trial that cost the prosecution more than $200,000
Molineux was found guilty and sentenced to die in Sing Sing's
electric chair. He spent 18 months on death row and finally
was granted a retrial on a technicality. Molineux had become a
celebrity in prison, writing a small book, The Room with the
Little Door, which was considered the work of a sensitive, talented writer. A jury acquitted him in four minutes in 1902.
Eleven years later Molineux, who had become a newspaper writer
about other murder trials, was committed to an insane asylum
where he died in 1917.

MOLL CUTPURSE. See CUTPURSE, Moll.

MONGE, Luis José (1918-67). Puerto Rican-born Colorado mass
murderer. A driver-salesman working and living in Denver,
Monge loved his wife and ten children but became mentally
troubled by his strong sexual attraction to one of his young
daughters. In fear of public discovery of his sexual mania, he
impulsively killed his wife and three of his children before thinking about committing suicide on the night of June 28-29, 1963.
He then called the police, telling them to come before he killed
somebody else. Prison psychiatrists declared him legally sane
at the time of the murders. Monge pleaded guilty, was convicted at his trial, and was sentenced to die in the gas chamber. His appeal automatically delayed his execution but was
denied by the Colorado Supreme Court in 1965. His execution,
rescheduled for February 1966, received a reprieve from the
Colorado governor and, after voters decided to retain capital
punishment in a referendum later that year, was again rescheduled for June 2, 1967. Tormented by what he had done
nearly four years before, he readily died for his family that
day.

MONK, Maria (1817-49). Canadian-born American hoaxer. The
Rev. Mr. W. K. Hoyt turned up with Maria in New York in
1836, claiming to have saved her from a sinful life at the Hotel
Dieu nunnery in Montreal. Soon Maria's alleged life as a novice
and nun was published in The Awful Disclosures of Maria Monk,
in which she charged that the sisters at the nunnery were
visited nightly by lusty priests from a nearby monastery and
that the remains of sisters who had resisted the priests' carnal
desires could be found in the nunnery's cellar. A clergyman
had supposedly fathered Maria's child, whom she displayed (later
it was discovered that a Montreal policeman was the father).
Maria's mother declared that her vagabond daughter had never

entered a nunnery, and Maria's scandalous story was discovered to be a hoax. However, she wrote another anti-Catholic book, Further Disclosures of Maria Monk, in which she said she had been held hostage in a convent after being abducted by some priests and had escaped by promising to marry one of them. Later Maria drank excessively, frequenting Bowery bars in New York City, and evidently died of ill health in 1849.

MOORE, Flossie (1866-after c. 1900). Chicago mugger. A strong-willed black woman, Moore engaged in mugging in the vice districts of Chicago between 1889 and 1893 and earned a reputation for profiting greatly from her trade. She liked to flaunt her newly acquired wealth, displaying a roll of bills in the bosom of her dress and another in her stocking, and wore expensive gowns at dances put on by brothel owners. Flossie also had a lawyer on retainer at $125 a month and used him constantly to keep her out of jail (she was arrested hundreds of times during her career). In 1893 she was sent to Joliet Prison on a conviction of mugging and served much of a five-year sentence in solitary because she twice nearly killed a prison matron there. After being released, Flossie left Chicago for New York in about 1900, hoping to get away from the law's ever watchful eye, and vanished forever.

MOORE, Sara Jane (b. 1930). American would-be assassin. A twice-divorced political activist, she shot a .38-caliber revolver at U.S. President Gerald R. Ford in front of the St. Francis Hotel in San Francisco on September 22, 1975. Ford was not hit because an alert bystander, a former marine named Oliver Sipple, saw the gun and spoiled her aim when it was fired. Seized and held on $500,000 bail, Moore maintained that she was an FBI undercover informer (in fact, the FBI strangely had earlier accepted her services as an informant on underground radicals and terrorists). The night before the assassination attempt, the Secret Service had questioned her about activities, confiscated a gun, but failed to detain her; she was not considered a threat since she had indeed operated as an informer for the San Francisco police as well as the FBI. Moore, who had attempted for years to obscure her identity, was given a life sentence and sent to the Alderson, West Virginia, federal prison.

MORAN, George "Bugs" (1893-1957). Chicago robber, bootlegger, and gangster. Before he was 21, he had taken part in 26 known robberies and had served three prison sentences. In about 1914 he joined Earl "Hymie" WEISS, Charles Dion O'BANNION, and Vincent DRUCCI to form the North Side Gang in Chicago. After O'Bannion's death in 1924, Moran swore an eternal vendetta against Al CAPONE, the North Siders' chief rival. He shot up Capone's headquarters in broad daylight in 1926 and reportedly killed at least eight of Capone's henchmen between 1926 and

1932. Moran was absent when Capone's mobsters machine-gunned to death members of Moran's gang on February 14, 1929, the St. Valentine's Day Massacre. After that the North Siders fell, and Moran's power rapidly declined. In 1946 Moran was arrested and imprisoned for bank robbery in Ohio. Released briefly in 1956, Moran was rearrested for an earlier bank robbery and sent to Leavenworth, where he died of lung cancer the next year.

MORAN, Thomas B. "Butterfingers" (1892-1971). American pickpocket. In San Francisco on the day of the earthquake in 1906, Moran began picking pockets and went on to pick more than 50,000 during the next 65 years, earning the title the "King of the Pickpockets." He roamed as a lone wolf throughout the United States and Canada, plying his "trade" at race tracks and bus stations, in subways, and on busy city streets. Moran, nicknamed "Butterfingers" because his fingers could move in and out of pockets like butter, was arrested 64 times, in every state of the United States and in Canada. He died in a charity mission in Miami on September 14, 1971.

MORANO, Pelligrino. See MORELLO, Nick or Nicholas.

MORELLO, Nick or Nicholas (1866-1916). Sicilian-born New York racketeer and gangster. By 1900 the Morello family, a clan of brothers, half-brothers, and other relatives from Corleone, Sicily, had firmly established a Mafia power base in New York City and was deeply involved in food rackets, extortion, contract killings, and counterfeiting. Nick Morello, a Mafia leader, dreamed of a national crime organization controlling all the rackets in the United States. However, the Camorristas (members of the secret Camorra society of Naples, Italy), led by Pelligrino Morano who controlled the docks and rackets in Brooklyn, waged a bloody gangland war against the Mafia under Nick Morello, who was shot to death with his lieutenant Charles Umbriaco outside a cafe in Brooklyn in 1916. In 1918 Morano was convicted of murdering Morello on damning testimony from Tony Notaro, a killer-turned-informer, and sentenced to life imprisonment. Soon the Camorristas and Mafiosi made peace, with the latter eventually leading the national crime syndicate in the country.

MORETTI, Willie (1894-1951). New York and New Jersey gangster and racketeer. He rose through the Mafia ranks to become a syndicate chief in charge of gambling rackets in New Jersey and parts of New York City. In the late 1940s Moretti, suffering mental illness from an advanced case of syphilis, talked openly about mob activities, endangering syndicate leaders. Frank COSTELLO sought to protect his friend Moretti, who was considered unfit by many mobsters, especially after his testimony in 1950 before the U.S. Senate Crime Investigating Committee

headed by Senator Estes Kefauver (actually Moretti revealed
very little about the mob). On October 4, 1951, Moretti was
shot and killed in a New Jersey restaurant; the "mercy killing"
was evidently ordered by rival gangster Vito GENOVESE.

MORGAN, Henry (1635-88). Welsh buccaneer. As an adventurous
youth, he traveled to the West Indies where he quickly took to
buccaneering. In 1668 Morgan was chosen as the buccaneers'
commander, secured the backing of Governor Modyford of Jamaica (which the English had seized from the Spanish in 1655),
and began to daringly and successfully raid and plunder Spain's
Caribbean colonies. He seized Puerto Principe (Camagüey),
Cuba (1668), sacked Portobello, Panama (1668), ravaged Spanish colonies around Lake Maracaibo, Venezuela (1669), raided
the coasts of Cuba and North America (1670), and captured
Panama City (1671); this last feat he accomplished with almost
2,000 fellow buccaneers sailing in 36 ships. However, England
and Spain had agreed to peace by the Treaty of Madrid in 1670,
and so Morgan, who had absconded with most of the loot from
the Panama City raid, was arrested and taken to England to
stand trial for his piratical crimes (1672). But his exploits
gained favor with King Charles II, who knighted Morgan in
1673 and sent him to Jamaica to serve as lieutenant governor.
For the rest of his life, Morgan lived on that Caribbean island,
eventually dying in Port Royal (near Kingston, Jamaica) on
August 25, 1688. See also MANSVELT, Edward.

MORNAND, Jacques. See MERCADER [del Rio Hernandez], [Jaime]
Ramón.

MORRELL, Ed (1871-1946). California outlaw, convict, and prison
reformer. Morrell, the youngest member of the California Outlaws, worked as a spy for them among railroad detectives in
the San Joaquin Valley, California. He helped Chris EVANS, a
member of the outlaws, escape from prison, thwarting an apparent plot by railroad detective Big Bill Smith to have Evans
killed during an attempted breakout. Morrell and Evans were
hunted down and caught. Morrell received a life sentence at
hard labor at Folsom Prison, where he endured brutal, inhu-
mane torture for years. Finally he was transferred to San
Quentin, where he once again suffered punishment after punishment for minor infractions. Morrell, framed on a charge of
having a gun smuggled in, was ordered to spend the rest of
his life in solitary confinement in the prison's dungeon. Publicity about the "Dungeon Man of San Quentin" and about Morrell's hellish ordeal in prison finally resulted in his release in
1907. Morrell became a national hero, talking before audiences
throughout the country on prison reform. In 1918 he advised
Congress on prison labor problems. Morrell and his experiences
in prison were the basis of Jack London's The Star Rover. See
also SONTAG, George; SONTAG, John.

MORRIS, Earl (b. 1920). American bank robber. In 1951 Morris, a native of Oklahoma, committed bank robbery in Texas and was caught, convicted, and given a ten-year sentence at the Huntsville, Texas, state prison, where he soon became friends with Paul and Donald Scott, two brothers from Kentucky captured and convicted of robbery in Texas that same year. Morris was paroled two years later, and the Scotts were released after serving three years. By 1956 the three of them organized a scheme to rob the Farmers and Traders Bank in Campton, Kentucky. When they attempted the robbery on the night of January 5, 1957, they were surprised by a bank guard and took flight after a wild machine-gun battle with local police. Within three days, the three were found hiding in the Kentucky foothills by FBI agents, police, and members of a citizens' posse. Morris and the Scotts each received a 30-year prison term.

MORTON, Samuel J. "Nails" (d. 1924). Chicago gangster. Morton, who had won France's Croix de Guerre for leading successful attacks against the Germans in World War I, joined Charles Dion O'BANNION and his gang in Chicago and participated in robberies and killings from about 1920 until his untimely death in 1924. While on one of his daily horseback rides in Chicago's Lincoln Park, Morton was thrown and kicked to death by a horse. Louis "Two-Gun" ALTERIE, Morton's good friend and an O'Bannion gang member, then went to the park's stables, grabbed the same horse, led it to the place where Morton had been killed, and shot the animal dead with several bullets through the head. This strange, comical scene was later repeated in the films Public Enemy and The Godfather.

MUDGETT, Herman Webster. See HOLMES, H[arry] H[oward].

MULLER, Franz (1839-64). German-born British murderer. In 1862 Muller arrived from Germany in England, where he became a tailor after seeking vainly to find work as a gunsmith, his former trade. About two years later, the dead body of Thomas Briggs, an elderly bank clerk and frequent train traveler, was discovered on the tracks of the North London Railway. Near the body were a bag and cane belonging to Briggs and a hat belonging to Muller, who had been engaged to one of Briggs's daughters. Muller, who had sailed to the United States, was tracked down and extradited to England for trial. Convicted of murder (the first one on a railroad in England), Muller was publicly executed in front of Newgate Prison on November 14, 1864.

MULLIGAN, Charles Albert. See DINSIO, Amil [Alfred].

MULLIN, Herbert (b. 1947). California mass murderer. Voted "most likely to succeed" by his 1965 high school class, Mullin dropped out of college and became a member of the hippie-drug cult in San Francisco's Haight-Ashbury district, where he

experimented with LSD. During four months prior to mid-
February 1973, he went on a murder rampage killing ten (maybe 13) men, women, and boys in the Santa Cruz Mountains of
northern California. Mullin confessed, stating he had been
preternaturally commanded to slay them as a human sacrifice to
prevent a popularly, but not scientifically, predicted major
earthquake in the region in early 1973. Declared legally sane,
he was found guilty of ten counts of murder (through he confessed to 13 killings, he was tried for only ten) and sentenced
to life imprisonment in 1973.

MULLINEN, Joe (d. 1781). American robber. During the American
Revolution, Mullinen, who indulged in the good life of wine,
women, and song, led a band of robbers in what is now southern
New Jersey, working out of a marshy, wooded region called Pine
Barrens. Much of the loot, which was generally stolen from the
rich, was hidden in Pine Barrens, but Mullinen also gave some
of it to the poor and thus gained their favor and became a Robin
Hood figure. Finally caught at a barn dance, he went to the
gallows in August 1781 without revealing where he had buried
any of his treasure.

MURIETA or MURRIETA, Joaquin (c. 1830-53?). Mexican-born
California outlaw. In the early 1850s he led a murderous group
of outlaws who held up stagecoaches to loot passengers and who
stole gold from prospectors in California. Murieta, of whom little is actually known, terrorized California until 1853, when the
state governor offered a $1,000 reward for his capture, dead or
alive. The California Rangers under Captain Harry Love claimed
they killed Murieta that year and displayed his decapitated head
in a jar of preserving liquid in San Francisco and other places
as proof. Many people insisted the head was not that or Murieta, whom they said fled to his native Mexico to live out his
life as a farmer in Sonora.

MURPHY, Jack (b. 1937). American burglar and murderer. A
beach boy who became a champion surfer with the nickname
"Murph the Surf," handsome Jack Murphy and two friends broke
into the American Museum of Natural History in New York City
and stole the famous 535-carat Star of India sapphire, worth
some $400,000 then (1964). The three, who left the jewel in a
locker in a bus terminal in Miami were caught and spent less
than two years behind bars in New York. Later Murphy was
sentenced to life imprisonment for killing a young woman in
Florida. In late 1984 he was released from a Florida prison
to live in a halfway house until granted complete freedom; he
asserted he was fully reformed after the last 17 years of incarceration.

MURPHY, Jim (1861-79). Texas outlaw and informer. His family
often gave the notorious outlaw Sam BASS refuge from the law

on their ranch in Denton County, Texas. Because of this, Jim, his father, and brothers were arrested and put in jail. After secretly making a deal with the Texas Rangers to turn in Bass, Jim hooked up with the outlaw and told the Rangers about a planned robbery of the bank at Round Rock, Texas, in July 1878. Bass was ambushed and mortally wounded. Many Texans considered Jim a rotten coward and traitor (Bass had earned a gallant reputation for giving money to impoverished souls), which eventually drove him to commit suicide by drinking some poisonous eye solution in June 1879.

MURRAY, George C. (1919-49). American gunrunner. Having worked as a U.S. Army officer in the Philippines at the end of World War II, Murray became a successful businessman operating an import-export company trading in surplus goods in Manila during the period 1945-49. However, after his mysterious murder (August 13, 1949), Philippine authorities discovered that Murray's large yacht had been smuggling arms, ammunition, war vehicles, and other matériel to various rebel groups in Southeast Asian countries; using his connections in high places in the Philippines and elsewhere, he had bought much U.S. Army-surplus materials which he profitably passed off in his black-market operations. The authorities also unraveled his murder supposedly by obtaining strong circumstantial evidence that his pretty Filipino wife, Esther del Rosario Murray, shot him because of jealousy over his womanizing. Esther pleaded innocent but was convicted; when her appeal was denied by the Philippine supreme court, she was incarcerated for life in 1959.

MURREL, John A. (1794-?). Tennessee robber, mass murderer, and conspirator. Murrel, a Tennessee plantation owner, led a band of cutthroats who robbed and murdered travelers and settlers along the Natchez Trace (trail between Tennessee and Mississippi). He may have killed more than 500 people. In 1834 Murrel told a young man, Virgil Stewart, about his plan to lead an armed black slave revolt to take over various cities, including New Orleans, Memphis, Nashville, and Natchez. Stewart informed the authorities of Murrel's incredible plot. Murrel was seized, tried, and sent to the Nashville prison for 10 years. His slave revolt began without him in 1835 but soon fell apart. Murrel was released from prison in about 1842 and soon disappeared.

MUSGROVE, Lee H. (d. 1868). American gunslinger and outlaw. In the 1850s he settled in Napa Valley, California, and quickly became known as a mean gunslinger, quick to resolve a dispute with his fast draw. In 1863 Musgrove, who had been born in Mississippi, killed a man who had offended his Confederate honor and fled from the law to Nevada, where he was involved in two killings and had to flee again. Later he organized and led a cruel gang that stole cattle and horses from Kansas to Texas.

Numerous murders were attributed to Musgrove and his men, who were finally tracked down almost single-handedly by a Colorado lawman named David J. Cook. Caught in Wyoming territory, Musgrove was jailed in Denver to lure Musgrove's top sidekick, Ed Franklin, into a rescue attempt. Franklin came to Denver for that purpose but was surprised by Cook in his hotel room and shot dead. Afraid others might try to free Musgrove, a mob of townspeople stormed the jail and lynched him on November 23, 1868.

MUSICA, Philip (1877-1938). Italian-born American swindler. In 1909 Musica, a food importer in New York City, was found guilty of bribing customs officials and sent to Elmira Reformatory for one year. He won a presidential pardon in five months. Musica then attempted to swindle banks out of $1 million by taking loans on nonexistent hair shipments, based on false invoices, to his wig-making business. Caught and imprisoned for three years, Musica turned to pharmaceutical swindling upon his release in 1918. He received a federal permit to buy large amounts of raw alcohol to manufacture into a hair tonic called Dandrofuge, but instead he converted the alcohol into bootleg liquor and sold it to gangsters. His bogus hair-tonic firm, Girard & Co., made Musica a very wealthy man, who now went under the name of F. Donald Coster. In 1926 he bought the respected drug firm of McKesson & Robbins, which unknowingly "bought" drugs from phony companies set up by Coster (Musica). No questions were asked, and Coster became known as a financial wizard on Wall Street, especially after McKesson & Robbins weathered the Great Depression of 1929 (Coster issued thousands of fake inventory notices to cover his swindling of his own company). In December 1938 Julian F. Thompson, treasurer of McKesson & Robbins, discovered and disclosed that an alleged $21 million worth of inventory didn't exist. Coster was publicly exposed and on December 16, 1938, shot himself to death in the bathroom of his mansion.

MUSSOLINI, Benito (1883-1945). Italian Fascist dictator. An active socialist as a young journalist, Mussolini turned nationalist soon after the start of World War I (1914-18), founded his own newspaper, Il Popolo d'Italia, in which he urged Italy to enter the war on the side of the Allies, and then enlisted in the Italian army to fight in the war. After recovering from a combat wound (1917), he returned to his newspaper, became violently anti-leftist and nationalistic, and established the Fascist party between 1919 and 1921. Overseeing the spread of Fascism throughout Italy, Mussolini ordered the Fascists to march on Rome in October 1922, threatened to overturn the government, and was appointed the new Italian premier by King Victor Emmanuel III. Italy was transformed into a dictatorship under Mussolini, who suppressed all opposition parties and regimented the press. "Il Duce" (the leader), as Mussolini was called by his followers, had imperialistic designs to create a great Italian empire; he initiated the Italo-Ethiopian War of 1935-36, which ended with Italy's conquest and annexation of Ethiopia, and the Italian occupation of Albania in 1939. Mussolini's ties with Adolf HITLER (the Rome-Berlin Axis) led to Italy's entry into World War II (1939-45) on Germany's side after the fall of France in 1940. Italian military failures in Greece and Africa and the successful Allied invasion of Italy resulted in his deposition and imprisonment in July 1943. Rescued by German commandos, Mussolini was installed as head of a puppet government in northern Italy. On Germany's defeat, he was caught fleeing, quickly tried, and shot to death with his mistress, Claretta Petacci, by Italian partisans near Azzano on April 28, 1945.

MYRTEL, Héra [born: Marie-Louise Victorine Grônes] (1868-?). French novelist and murderer. While married to a prosperous silk merchant named Paul Jacques, she wrote romantic popular novels under the pseudonym of Héra Myrtel, gained some success, became the center of a washed-out group of artists in Paris (her residence), and indulged her vanity in many short-lived love affairs. Her husband's death in the bedroom of their Paris apartment (March 5, 1914) was ruled a suicide, but allegedly Myrtel had shot him. With their daughter Paule, she then moved to Mexico City, where she set up a dilettante literary salon and married an opportunist named Charles Bessarabo. After returning to Paris to live in 1916, Myrtel set up another literary group, reveled in a life of drugs (especially hashish) and debauchery, and grew to loathe her cuckolded husband. When Bessarabo's mangled corpse was found by police in a trunk in the railroad station in Nancy, Myrtel and Paule were put on trial (February 15, 1921), during which the latter said she had been forced by her mother to help ship her stepfather's body from Paris to "anywhere" where "it won't be found for a long time." The jury found Myrtel guilty of murder and acquitted Paule; Myrtel received 20 years in prison, where she later died on an unknown date.

- N -

NASH, Frank "Jelly" (1884-1933). American bank robber, murderer, and escapee. After being tried and acquitted for a 1913 murder in Oklahoma, Nash, known for his violent and uncontrollable temper, killed a witness who had testified against him at his trial. Apprehended and given life imprisonment, he was granted a full pardon in July 1918 but soon afterward was caught robbing a bank and sentenced to 25 years at McAlester Penitentiary, Oklahoma. But, with his sentence remarkably commuted to five years by the governor, Nash was set free at the end of 1922 and then participated in bank robberies and killings in 1923-24. Caught again, he was sent in March 1924 to Leavenworth Penitentiary, where he supposedly reformed himself to become a trustee prisoner and escaped while outside the prison on an assignment in October 1930. Nash reputedly hooked up with Al CAPONE and his gang in Chicago and got involved in the rackets in Kansas City. For a while he worked with Arthur "Doc" BARKER, Al KARPIS, and others pulling off bank robberies. While in hiding in Hot Springs, Arkansas, Nash was seized by FBI agents and brought to Kansas City, where unknown gangsters machine-gunned him and four lawmen to death on June 17, 1933, in busy Union Station (the so-called Kansas City Massacre). Whether the gunmen were attempting to free Nash from federal custody or to kill him to prevent him from talking to the authorities remains unresolved.

NATION, Carry [born: Carry Amelia Moore] (1846-1911). American temperance firebrand. She soon left her first husband, a doctor and an alcoholic, and about ten years later, in 1877, married David Nation, an itinerant minister and lawyer who later divorced her on grounds of desertion in 1901. A resident of Kansas, a dry state, since 1889, Carry denounced liquor and became convinced that she should personally stop the illegal sale and drinking of alcoholic beverages in Kansas saloons. Alone or with supporters, this militant woman (about six feet tall and weighing some 175 pounds), usually dressed in religious-style black and white clothing, entered saloon after saloon, smashing bottles, furniture, and fixtures with a hatchet. From Kansas, she traveled to other states to carry on her saloon-destroying campaign and soon became a notorious national figure for temperance (although her tactics gained her little support from national temperance movements). Frequently she was assaulted and beaten severely; at least 30 times she was arrested and jailed, but paid her fines with money from selling souvenir hatchets or from lecture tour fees. She also strongly advocated woman's suffrage. Her ambitious and constant crusading took its toll; finally she collapsed during a speech in Eureka Springs, Arkansas, and died in a Leavenworth, Kansas, hospital on June 9, 1911.

NAU, Jacques Jean David. See L'OLONNOIS, Francis.

NAUMOFF, Nicholas. See TARNOWSKA, Maria.

NEEBE, Oscar. See SPIES, August.

NELSON, Earle Leonard (1892-1928). American mass murderer, rapist, and necrophile. Nelson, a Bible-reading fanatic who had suffered a head injury in a childhood accident, was put in a mental hospital after raping a young Philadelphia girl in 1918. He promptly broke out but was soon caught and sent to a prison farm, from which he quickly escaped. Recaptured again, Nelson was sent to a state penitentiary but escaped from there in late

1918. Later, in 1926 and 1927, Nelson, who went under the name of Roger Wilson, murdered 20 landladies throughout the United States and in Canada. He strangled them with his powerful hands and raped them after death. Finally Nelson was caught in Manitoba, where he was tried, convicted of murder, and hanged on January 12, 1929. On the gallows before his execution, Nelson said, "I stand innocent before God and man.... God have mercy!"

NELSON, George "Baby Face" [real name: Lester J. Gillis] (1908-34). American bank robber, murderer, and gangster. He wanted recognition his whole life, dropping his real name because it sounded "sissy" and asking to be called "Big George" Nelson (instead he was called "Baby Face" behind his back). In 1929 Nelson worked for Al CAPONE in Chicago but was let go when he proved to be unreliable, killing persons whom he was supposed to only beat up. Nelson was arrested in 1931 for a jewelry store robbery and sentenced to the Joliet, Illinois, penitentiary for one year. Afterward he hooked up with John DILLINGER, who was not too fond of Nelson and his quick trigger finger, and robbed banks in the Midwest. During a shootout with FBI agents near Little Bohemia Lodge in northern Wisconsin on April 22, 1934, Nelson killed Special Agent H. Carter Baum and escaped in an FBI car at high speed. After Dillinger's death in July 1934, Nelson was declared "Public Enemy Number One" by the FBI. Nelson, along with his wife, Helen Gillis, and his best friend, John Paul Chase, fought a wild machine-gun battle with FBI agents Sam Cowley and Herman Hollis in a field near Barrington, Illinois, on November 27, 1934. Cowley and Hollis were killed but not before they pumped 17 slugs into Nelson, who managed to drive off with his wife and Chase. The next day Nelson's bullet-riddled corpse was found 20 miles away on a country road in Illinois. About a month later, Chase was seized in California and was sentenced to life imprisonment. Also caught was Helen Gillis, who served a year in a Madison, Wisconsin, women's prison and then disappeared.

NEURATH, Konstantin von (1873-1956). German diplomat and Nazi official and war criminal. Neurath, a baron, served as Germany's ambassador to Denmark (1919), to Italy (1922), and to Great Britain (1930-32) before becoming foreign minister at the start of the Third Reich (the Nazi state under Adolf HITLER). After Joachim von RIBBENTROP took his post in 1938, Neurath was made Nazi "protector" of Bohemia and Moravia, two Czech territories occupied by German troops after the beginning of World War II (1939-45). His harsh treatment of the inhabitants was thought not effectively brutal enough by Hitler, who replaced him with Reinhard HEYDRICH in 1941. Later the International Military Tribunal at Nuremberg convicted Neurath of war crimes, including particularly crimes in the occupied territories, and sentenced him in 1946 to 15 years' imprisonment. He was released in 1954 because of poor health and died two years later.

NEVISON, William (1640?-84). English highwayman. He was given the nickname "Swift Nicks" by King Charles II of England because of his nimble-footedness in evading capture after committing highway robbery. Nevison, who was noted for his gentlemanly manner, earned a reputation as a latter-day Robin Hood, robbing from the rich and giving to the poor. For many years he led a large band of robbers in Yorkshire country, where he also ran a protection racket. Caught in 1676, Nevison was tried, convicted, and condemned to die. After falsely promising to turn king's (state's) evidence, he had his death sentence commuted to one of military service. Nevison deserted and returned to the highway to continue preying on travelers. He was caught while asleep in a tavern and hanged at York on March 15, 1684.

NEW ORLEANS AXEMAN (fl. 1911-19). New Orleans mass murderer. An unknown person committed at least eleven murders in New Orleans from 1911 to 1919. Most of the victims were Italian grocers and members of their families. The killer would cut out a door panel to gain entrance to a victim's home and use an axe as a murder weapon, which was then left behind to be found by authorities. Several citizens survived attacks by the Axeman and afterward identified neighbors and others as their assailant. But the killings continued, terrorizing the city and confirming the innocence of suspects in custody. In Los Angeles a man named Joseph Mumfre was shot and killed by an Italian woman whose husband had fallen victim to the Axeman but who had herself survived the attack (she claimed to have recognized the killer as he fled from the scene). The murders ceased, but the Los Angeles authorities held the woman, charged her with murder despite her story, and handed her a ten-year prison sentence (she was set free after three years).

NEWCOMB, George "Bitter Creek" (1866?-95). American robber and outlaw. He worked as a cowboy in Texas and then moved to the Oklahoma territory, where he joined Bob Dalton and Bill Doolin, two famous outlaw leaders, and engaged in robbery for a livelihood in the 1890s. Newcomb was a handsome ladies' man who called himself the "wild wolf from Bitter Creek." According to several accounts, his young love, Rosa Dunn (supposedly the legendary "Rose of Cimarron" but most likely not), shielded him with her body at the Battle of Ingalls, Oklahoma, in September 1893 and helped him, wounded, escape from the possemen. A $5,000 reward was posted for Newcomb, dead or alive. Returning to the Cimarron River country to visit Rosa, Newcomb and his friend Charlie Pierce were gunned down by Rosa's two brothers in May 1895. The brothers then carted the dead outlaws to Guthrie, Oklahoma, to collect the reward money.

NEWELL, Susan (1893-1923). Scottish murderer. Ill-disposed toward her husband, whom she attacked in their one-room apartment in Glasgow, Scotland, she was discovered trying to dispose of the dead body of a 13-year-old newsboy named John Johnstone (June 1923). The police had been notified when Susan and her eight-year-old daughter, Janet, had been seen pushing a cart with a large sack on it through the streets, alarming a woman when she spied a human foot and head protruding from the bundle. At the trial Janet innocently told that her mother, evidently refusing to pay the newsboy a few pennies for his papers, had gone into a rage and strangled him. Ruled sane and guilty of murder, Susan Newell spitefully went to her execution on October 10, 1923, becoming the first woman to be hanged in Scotland in 50 years.

NEWMAN, Julia St. Clair (1818-?). West Indian-born thief and swindler. As a youth of Creole parentage, she was educated in France before settling in London, where, although being cultured and talented as a singer and musician, she turned to dulicity and thievery for a living. In 1837 Julia was incarcerated in England's Millbank Prison for swindling. As a prisoner, she became extremely violent and uncontrollable, assaulting guards, destroying things, fomenting upheavals by other inmates, and trying to kill herself several times. Deemed mad, she was put in a straitjacket but chewed her way out of it. English authorities finally deported her aboard a convict ship to Australia, where she vanished.

NICHOLSON, Margaret (1750?-1828). English would-be assassin. On August 2, 1786, Nicholson, a housemaid, approached Britain's King George III to present a grievance petition; the king, who had just stepped from his coach at the gates of St. James's Palace in London, was suddenly lunged at by Nicholson, who attempted to kill the king with a dessert knife but only managed to rip his coat's sleeve before being seized by guardsmen. Before a court, she was judged raving mad as she screamed incoherently about her legal rights to the crown. She was then confined in Bethlem Royal Hospital, popularly known as Bedlam (England's oldest and most famous institution for the mentally ill), where she died 42 years later still believing the crown was rightfully hers.

NITTI, Frank (1884-1943). Chicago gangster. Nitti, a barber by trade, joined Al CAPONE at the start of Prohibition and became head of Scarface's special machine-gun squad. Numerous killings were attributed to Nitti, nicknamed "The Enforcer," during Chicago's bootleg liquor wars. Nitti rose in the Mafia ranks and later took control of the Chicago syndicate after Capone's imprisonment in 1931 (his leadership, however, was often questioned by other top gangsters, such as Paul RICCA, Tony ACCARDO, and Jake GUZIK). Nitti, who had served 18 months

in prison for income tax violations in the early 1930s, was faced
with another prison sentence for tax evasion but chose to commit suicide instead, shooting himself while walking along some
Chicago railroad tracks on March 19, 1943. See also BIOFF,
Willie.

NORTH, John (d. 1835). Mississippi gambler and alleged insurrectionist. He ran a corrupt saloon-brothel-gambling house in
the criminal-infested Landing area of Vicksburg, Mississippi.
In 1835 a rumor spread that North, caught up in the proposed
black slave revolt of John A. MURREL of Tennessee, was about
to unleash an army of criminals to loot Vicksburg. Vigilantes
quickly invaded the Landing area, rounded up dozens of "undesirables," and hanged them. North escaped but was caught
the next day and hanged on a high hill above the city. His
corrupt saloon's roulette wheel was tied to his body, which was
left dangling as an ominous warning to other lawless types.

NOVENA, Colonel M. [real name: Julian Cinquez] (fl. 1859).
Cuban-born American con man. He successfully pulled off the
first large real-estate swindle in U.S. history. Using several
important-sounding aliases, of which Colonel M. Novena was his
favorite (others included Sir Richard Murray, General Alverosa,
and Count Antonelli), he gained access to the homes of many
famous, rich, and socially prominent persons in Washington,
D.C., Richmond, Baltimore, Philadelphia, and New York City,
exploiting his natural charm, good looks, and sophistication.
Often asked to dine and to attend lavish parties, Novena, a
perfect ladies' man, persuaded wealthy speculators whose wives
doted on him to lend him large sums of money for business ventures. Proposing to build a supposed architectural masterpiece,
the Novena Building in New York City, he sold off optioned
properties surrounding it (he had not paid for them) and even
the land on which the Novena Building was to stand. With
thousands of dollars bilked from the gullible, Novena left New
York and soon faded into obscurity.

NOZIÈRE, Violette (b. 1915). French poisoner. An only child on
whom her parents doted, she was full of pretensions by the
time she was 19; a student who indulged herself in whoring in
the Latin Quarter of Paris, Nozière fell in love with fellow student
Jean Dabin and told him that they soon would be rich. Twice
she secretly tried to poison both her mother and father in order
to inherit the family's entire savings (180,000 francs). When
Nozière finally did fatally poison her father but not her mother
(August 23, 1934), the gendarmes were suspicious and managed
to charge her with murder. Admitting that she killed her father
and calling him a "satyr," Nozière was promptly tried, convicted,
and sentenced to be guillotined. A higher court commuted the
sentence to life imprisonment.

NUNN MAY, Alan. See MAY, Alan Nunn.

NUSSBAUM, Albert Frederick. See WILCOXSON, Bobby Randell.

- O -

OATES, Titus (1649-1705). English priest, conspirator, and perjurer. Ordained as an Anglican priest, he became close friends
with a rabid anti-Jesuit English divine named Israel Tonge, with
whom he fabricated the story of the Popish Plot of 1678: a
widespread conspiracy by Roman Catholics to massacre Protes-
tants, seize power, assassinate England's King Charles II, place
his Catholic brother James on the throne, and reestablish the
Catholic Church in England. Oates swore to the plot's truth
before a prominent judge, Sir Edmund Berry Godfrey, whose
unexplained murder shortly afterward (October 1678) lent cre-
dence to the Catholic plot and caused a wave of terror in London. Blamed for the murder were three Catholics, who were
convicted in a kangaroo court and then executed (later Oates
and others were found to have instigated the crime, but the
actual killer was never uncovered). Catholics were apprehended
or persecuted; 35 were judicially murdered on account of testimony from Oates. Finally his false accusation of a plot by Queen
Catherine to poison her husband Charles on behalf of the Pope
brought Oates' downfall in 1684; in addition, he lost a libel suit
to James, whom he had called a traitor, and paid about £100,000
in damages. After James ascended the throne in 1685, Oates
was convicted of perjury, pilloried, flogged, and sent to prison
for life. When James was deposed and William III took the
throne in 1689, Oates was set free on a pardon and given a
pension; he then gradually faded into obscurity and died in
London on July 12, 1705.

O'BANNION or O'BANION, [Charles] Dion (1892-1924). Chicago
bootlegger, gangster, and murderer. O'Bannion, nicknamed
"Deanie," worked for the Hearst newspapers as an enforcer,
beating up Chicago newstand owners who refused to sell Hearst
papers. At the same time, in the 1910s, he organized a gang
of safecrackers, burglars, and killers, including Earl "Hymie"
WEISS, George "Bugs" MORAN, and Vincent DRUCCI, that became known as the North Side Gang. O'Bannion, a devoted
churchgoer, bought breweries and distilleries in the early 1920s
and controlled bootlegging operations in Chicago's 42nd and 43rd
wards. He tried to undermine Italian and Sicilian gangsters and
bootleggers, such as Johnny TORRIO, Al CAPONE, and Angelo
GENNA, and take over Prohibition rackets throughout the city.
O'Bannion, whom police credited with 25 murders, was labeled
"Chicago's arch-criminal" until 1924, when three unknown gunmen, supposedly hired by Capone, entered O'Bannion's headquarters, a floral shop on North State Street, and shot O'Ban-

nion to death. More than 15,000 persons attended his funeral, one of the most elaborate in Chicago's history.

O'CONNOR, [Thomas] "Terrible Tommy" (1886-?). Irish-born Chicago murderer. In 1921 O'Connor was convicted of first degree murder and sentenced to be hanged. Earlier that year at his sister's home in Chicago, he had shot and killed police officer Patrick J. O'Neill in a gunfight with officers who had come to arrest him for an Illinois Central train station robbery in which a night watchman had been killed. Four days before O'Connor was scheduled to hang, he escaped from the Cook County Jail and disappeared completely. Under a court order, the scaffold on which O'Connor was to hang is stored in the basement of the Chicago Criminal Courts Building and will be kept until O'Connor's fate is decided.

OCUISH, Hannah (1774-86). American Indian murderer. In New London, Connecticut, on December 20, 1786, Ocuish, a 12-year-old part Pequot Indian girl deserted by her parents, was hanged after being convicted of murdering six-year-old Eunice Bolles. According to reports, Ocuish had killed Bolles after being accused by the younger girl of stealing her strawberries. Ocuish is usually considered to be the youngest person ever executed in America.

O'DONNELL, [Edward] "Spike" (fl. 1923-25). Chicago bootlegger. He and his three brothers, Tom, Steve, and Walter, ran a bootleg operation in southwestern Chicago in an Irish neighborhood known as Kerry Patch. The O'Donnell gang, led by Spike, used strong arm tactics to persuade bartenders to take their liquor, causing the outbreak of a gangland war between the O'Donnells and Al CAPONE, who felt his "territory" was being encroached upon. Several members of the O'Donnell gang were reportedly shotgunned to death by Frankie McERLANE and Joseph "Polock Joe" SALTIS, mobsters at that time working for Capone. Spike was wounded and unnerved in a machine-gun attack by McErlane in September 1925; he gave up bootlegging and dropped out of sight.

O'DONNELL, [William] "Klondike" (fl. 1921-26). Chicago gangster and bootlegger. No relation to Edward "Spike" O'DONNELL and his brothers, Klondike and his two brothers, Bernard and Myles, operated their own speakeasies (saloons) on Chicago's West Side. Klondike worked briefly for Al CAPONE, forcing saloon keepers to sell Capone's needle beer. He tired of taking orders from Capone and, in 1926, sided with George "Bugs" MORAN in his gangland war against Capone. Klondike's gang ceased to exist following the killing of five members in 1926.

OERTEL, Albert. See WEHRING, Alfred.

O'FOLLIARD, Tom (1859-80). American gunfighter and outlaw. In 1878 he became an accomplice of BILLY THE KID, and together they fought numerous gun battles with lawmen in the Southwest. O'Folliard's bullet could have been the one that killed Sheriff William Brady during the 1878 cattle war in Lincoln County, New Mexico; although Billy the Kid was charged with the crime, O'Folliard had accompanied him and fired off many rounds at the sheriff. A posse under Sheriff Patrick Floyd Garrett stalked Billy the Kid's gang and, in one ambush at night in December 1880, killed O'Folliard, whom they mistook for Billy. See also BOWDRE, Charlie.

OGILVIE, Patrick (1745?-68). Scottish murderer. In 1765 he fell passionately in love with his older brother Thomas's recent bride, beautiful, rich, 19-year-old Catherine Nairn Ogilvie, whose reciprocal passion led them to openly become lovers. The cuckolded Thomas seemed to understand and forgive them, strangely, and went so far as to offer Patrick control over part of his large estate at East Miln, Scotland. After Patrick returned to his military duty, he sent arsenic to Catherine, who killed Thomas by serving him poisoned tea. Love letters between Catherine and Patrick and samples of arsenic were found in Catherine's rooms, causing the lovers to be tried and convicted of murder. Patrick was hanged in Edinburgh on November 13, 1768. Catherine, whose execution was delayed until she gave birth to Patrick's child, was secretly helped to escape to France, where she disappeared.

O'KEEFE, [Joseph James] "Specs" (b. 1907). Massachusetts bank robber and informer. He was a member of the gang organized by Joseph Francis "Big Joe" McGINNIS and Anthony "the Pig" (or "Fats") Pino that successfully carried out the spectacular Brink's robbery in Boston on January 17, 1950. About $1.1 million was split up among the 11 members of the gang, who then went their individual ways to spend their shares as they pleased. O'Keefe arranged to have Adolf "Jazz" Maffie, an accomplice in the robbery, hold $93,000 of his share but later had misgivings. In 1954, set free on parole from a sentence he was serving for possession of stolen firearms, O'Keefe demanded his money, threatening to turn informer if the gang members kept his share any longer. Gunman Elmer "Trigger" BURKE was hired by the gang to rub out O'Keefe, who was wounded as Burke wildly fired his submachine gun while pursuing his victim through Boston's Dorchester streets in June 1954. Because of O'Keefe's testimony, all gang members were arrested (1955), tried, found guilty, and sent to prison. O'Keefe was released in 1960 and later escaped several murder attempts. His nickname, "Specs," which he loathed, originated in his youth when his face was dotted with freckles.

O'KELLY or O. KELLY, Edward (d. 1904). American murderer. He

was related by marriage to the four outlaw YOUNGER brothers--
Bob, Jim, John, and Cole--close friends of Frank and Jesse
JAMES. At Creede, Colorado, on June 8, 1892, O'Kelly, using
a double-barreled shotgun, shot and killed Bob FORD, "the
dirty rotten coward who shot Mr. Howard" (i.e. Jesse James).
O'Kelly was convicted and sentenced to 20 years in the Colorado
State Penitentiary. However, because his act of avenging Jesse's
murder was more or less acceptable, O'Kelly's sentence was
quickly reduced, and he was released in 1894 with a full pardon.
Ten years later, while engaged in a robbery in Oklahoma City,
Oklahoma, he was fatally shot by a law officer.

OLAH, Susanna or Susi (1869-1929). Hungarian prophetess and mass
poisoner. After settling in the Hungarian village of Nagyrev in
1909, she engaged in nursing and midwifery while convincing the
villagers she could foretell the deaths of undesirables--diseased
and handicapped persons, young and old, and others (like vagrants or faithless husbands). For some 20 years Olah, who was
well paid for her predictions and was secretly helped by numerous female "spiritual assistants," put to death at least 100 persons by arsenic poisoning. She was finally exposed in 1929
when an anonymous assistant denounced her. She promptly
killed herself before she could be tried, but three of her assistants were found guilty and hanged. See also FAZEKAS,
Mrs. Julius.

O'LEARY, "Big Jim" (1860?-1926). Chicago gambler. He established a lucrative and lavish gambling house on South Halsted
Street in Chicago and owned bookie joints and pool halls
throughout the city. Called "Big Jim" because of his big
ideas and gambling ventures, O'Leary converted the steamboat
City of Traverse into a floating gambling resort, the first such
in U.S. history, which sailed on Lake Michigan until the police
shut down the resort. O'Leary's operators took bets on horse
races and other sporting events, elections, and even the
weather. When O'Leary died in 1926, he was a multimillionaire
and one of Chicago's most prominent citizens.

OLIVE, [Isom Prentice] "Print" (1840-86). American cattle baron
and murderer. He and his brother Bob owned a vast cattle
ranch along the Platte River in Nebraska. They waged a vicious war against homesteaders, who they felt were taking over
the area. In November 1878 Bob was killed in a gun battle with
two homesteaders, Ami Ketchum and Luther Mitchell, who were
arrested and handed over to Print. Print then meted out his
own justice, shooting them dead, then hanging them, and finally burning the corpses. Brought to trial for this outrage,
Print was found guilty and sentenced to life imprisonment. In
1880 he was freed on a technicality. A new trial was ordered
but never took place, and Print later moved to Colorado. In a
saloon in Trail City, Colorado, in 1886, Print was shot to death

by a former cowboy employee, Joe Sparrow, in an argument
over a $10 debt.

ORCHARD, Harry [real name: Albert E. Horsley] (1866-1954).
American assassin. In late 1905 former Governor Frank Steunenberg of Idaho was killed by a bomb that had been placed in
his home. Orchard later confessed to the assassination, claiming he had done so on orders from labor leader William D. HAY-
WOOD, a foe of Steunenberg. Orchard, who admitted he was a
hired union bomber, said he had committed many terrorist acts
on orders from Haywood and others. In a long, well-publicized
trial in 1906-7, the prosecution led by future senator William E.
Borah failed to substantiate Orchard's charges against Haywood
and alleged fellow conspirators Charles H. Moyers and George A.
Pettibone. Defense attorney Clarence Darrow compared the evils
of capitalism with the justice of the labor movement. Haywood
and his fellow defendants were acquitted. Orchard was convicted, sentenced to hang, but secured a commuted sentence of
life imprisonment. He died in prison on April 13, 1954.

ORGEN, Jacob "Little Augie" (1894-1927). New York gangster and
racketeer. He headed a gang of labor sluggers, hijackers,
smugglers (dealing chiefly in narcotics and stolen gems), and
extortionists in New York in the 1920s. The "Little Augies,"
as the gang was called because of their leader's sobriquet, engaged in vicious gun battles with their principal rival gang led
by Kid DROPPER. Orgen finally succeeded in wresting control
of New York City's bootlegging and labor rackets from Kid Dropper, who was fatally shot in August 1923. Orgen was king of
a lucrative bootleg-and-narcotics empire that extended from Manhattan to Albany, New York, until October 15, 1927, when he
was machine-gunned to death while walking with his bodyguard
Jack "Legs" DIAMOND along a New York City street near his
Lower East Side headquarters.

ORTON, Arthur (1834-98). English impostor. A butcher's son
from Wapping, a district of London, Orton emigrated (1852) to
Australia where he drifted about and eventually worked as a
butcher under the alias of Thomas Castro in Wagga Wagga, New
South Wales (he changed his name after being caught stealing
horses). After seeing a newspaper advertisement for information about Sir Roger Tichborne, the eldest son of a wealthy
landed family in Britain, who had been lost at sea off Brazil in
1854, Orton-Castro got in touch with the gullible Lady Tichborne, the son's dowager mother, and identified himself as her
missing son whom she had refused to believe was dead. After
his arrival in England (1866), Lady Tichborne incredibly believed Orton to be Roger, though both men looked and acted
quite differently: when last seen, Roger was thin, had straight
hair and a tattoo, and spoke French fluently, whereas Orton
was obese, had wavy hair and no tattoo, and spoke only coarse

English. Numerous persons disbelieved Orton, but not until after Lady Tichborne's death (1867) was he exposed while involved in litigation to his supposed rightful claim to the large Tichborne estate in Hampshire, which had passed to Roger's nephew. Orton lost a long, sensational court case (1871-72) to the Tichborne family, which paid out £90,000 to win. Declared an impostor, Orton again stood trial (1873-74) and was convicted of perjury and sentenced to 14 years in prison. Released after ten years (1884), he made a vain attempt to test his claim again, became destitute, sold his "confession" to a newspaper, and later died in poverty in London on April Fools' Day, 1898.

OSMAN, Sülün (1912-?). Turkish thief and swindler. An amiable raconteur living in Istanbul after 1930, he had a long criminal record mainly for thievery and swindling and served time in jail for several convictions during his 30-year career. Osman, who used a score of aliases and usually operated alone, was one of the greatest confidence men, convincing gullible Turkish strangers to buy public property, such as railway cars of the Orient Express, city trolley cars, clock towers of Istanbul University, and other things he pretended to own, have a right to, or find. He made about 150,000 Turkish lira ($200,000) before promising to the police to quit his con games.

O'SULLIVAN, Joseph. See DUNNE, Reginald.

OSWALD, Lee Harvey (1939-63). American presumed assassin. Oswald, a former U.S. Marine, lived and worked in the Soviet Union from 1959 to 1962. He then returned to the United States and became involved in leftist and right-wing political organizations. In October 1963 Oswald took a job at the Texas School Book Depository in Dallas. Rifle bullets apparently fired by him from the sixth floor of the depository building killed President John F. Kennedy and severely wounded Texas Governor John B. Connally on November 22, 1963. Stopped for questioning shortly after the assassination, Oswald shot and killed patrolman J. D. Tippit and fled into a Dallas movie theater, where he was soon apprehended by police officers. Oswald consistently denied having killed Kennedy and Tippit. On November 24, 1963, while being transferred to the Dallas county jail, Oswald was shot to death by Dallas nightclub owner Jack RUBY. Subsequently, the Warren Commission investigated the Kennedy assassination and concluded that Oswald acted alone as assassin. However, many persons disagree, advocating that Oswald was part of a vast conspiracy. The fact that 18 key material witnesses to the assassination died in the three years that followed has disturbed experts looking into the event.

- P -

PACKER, Alfred or Alferd G. (1847-1907). American murderer,

thief, and cannibal. In late 1873 Packer guided five gold prospectors into the San Juan Mountains of southwestern Colorado.
Exhausted and starving, the party camped in a mountain shack,
where Packer killed the prospectors and took their money.
Packer then cut up the corpses and lived on strips of human
flesh until he reached the Los Pinos Agency, where authorities
grew suspicious after seeing Packer with much cash and in good
health. In 1874 the bodies of the five missing prospectors were
found. Packer had vanished. Finally, in 1883, he was arrested
in Salt Lake City, tried, found guilty of murder, and sentenced
to 40 years in prison. A model prisoner, Packer was released
early, in 1901, and then worked as a ranch hand in Colorado,
where he died six years later.

PAINE, Lewis [born: Lewis Thornton Powell] (1844-65). American
conspirator. He hated blacks and the Union and fought for the
Confederacy during the U.S. Civil War (1861-65). As a Confederate soldier at Gettysburg in 1863, Paine was severely
wounded and captured by Union troops. Later he escaped.
While John Wilkes BOOTH was assassinating President Lincoln
on April 14, 1865, Paine attempted to kill Secretary of State
William Henry Seward at Seward's home in Washington, D.C.
Though he stabbed Seward several times, Paine failed to kill
him and was seized by federal authorities. Along with three
other co-conspirators--David E. Herold, George Atzerodt, and
Mary E. SURRATT--Paine was hanged at Washington's Old Penitentiary on July 7, 1865.

PALMER, Annie [May] (1802-31). Jamaican mass murderer. While
she reigned as mistress of Rose Hall, a magnificent house and
6,600-acre sugar cane plantation located along the north coast
of Jamaica in the West Indies, all three of her husbands met
death at her hands: she poisoned the first, stabbed the second,
and strangled the third. Many of her some 2,000 slaves, who
cursed her as a white witch, were tortured (oftentimes in Rose
Hall's lower dungeon) or hanged on her orders for minor offenses (she murdered the young girl with whom her own favorite slave master had fallen in love). Annie Palmer's atrocities
ended when she was fatally strangled by a witch doctor in 1831,
and according to legend, Rose Hall is considered to be haunted
by her ghost.

PALMER, William (1825-56). English doctor and mass poisoner. He
was known to have poisoned six persons to death--his wife, his
brother, his mother-in-law, one of his children, a bookmaker,
and a close friend (he may have killed another six, but there
is no proof). Palmer, who was well educated and came from a
wealthy family, became a doctor in London in 1842; he had previously squandered his inheritance on gambling on horses. In
the late 1840s Palmer used funds from life insurance policies on
his relatives to pay off his gambling debts. He killed a book-

maker to eliminate having to pay him his considerable betting losses, and he murdered his friend and fellow gambler John Parsons Cook using strychnine poison because he needed Cook's winnings to cover his large debts. Suspicion centered on Palmer after Cook's death. Brought to trial, Palmer was convicted mainly on testimony from the druggist who had sold Palmer the strychnine and from a doctor who was an authority on strychnine. (Palmer had used it because it left no traces in a victim's stomach.) Palmer, showing no remorse, was hanged on June 14, 1856.

PANCHENKO, Dimitri (fl. c. 1900-1911). Russian doctor and poisoner. Soon after the turn of the century, he gained notoriety as a reputed murderer-for-hire in St. Petersburg (Leningrad). Disposing of one's undesirable relatives seemed to be his specialty. An impoverished noble, Patrick O'Brien De Lacy, of Grodno hired Panchenko for over 600,000 rubles to poison his in-laws in order for his wife to inherit the family fortune. In 1911 De Lacy's brother-in-law suddenly died, and an autopsy revealed poisoning by diphtheria and cholera. An inquiry soon led to the arrest of De Lacy and Panchenko, who had been heard telling his mistress Madame Muraviora how he intended to put the aforementioned poisonous bacteria in the brother-in-law's caviar. De Lacy and Panchenko were both found guilty, with the former being sentenced to life imprisonment and the latter to 15 years.

PANZRAM, Carl (1891-1930). American arsonist, burglar, robber, and mass murderer. He led a life of crime throughout the United States and in several foreign countries. In 1903 Panzram was sent as an incorrigible to the Minnesota State Training School. Two years later he set fire to the school's warehouse and, in his words, "The whole place burned down.... Nice, eh?" While serving in the U.S. Army, Panzram was courtmartialed and served three years in the old Fort Leavenworth military prison for attempted robbery of government property. Traveling about the country, Panzram was arrested for burglary and robbery in various states, including Montana, Oregon, Connecticut, New York, and Maryland, and did time in various correctional institutions and penitentiaries, from which he frequently escaped. Panzram, who served time under a number of aliases, said he was brutally beaten and tortured while behind bars. At times he traveled abroad and claimed he burned down an oil rig in Panama and murdered at least a half a dozen young blacks in what is now Angola. Panzram admitted, without any remorse, to having killed 21 persons and sodomized at least 1,000 during his lifetime. While imprisoned at Leavenworth in 1929, he bashed in the skull of a prison laundry foreman with an iron bar and killed him. Panzram was tried, convicted, and hanged in the prison yard at Leavenworth on September 5, 1930.

PARDUE, John [Russell], Jr. (1942-71). American bank robber, bomber, and murderer. Between 1968 and 1970 he and his younger brother, James Peter Pardue, committed six bank robberies (two each in New York, Connecticut, and Missouri), four murders (their own father and grandmother and two black accomplices), and two bombings (both in Danbury, Connecticut, during a bank robbery there in 1970). An FBI investigation finally ended their violence and destruction when the Pardue brothers were taken into custody in March 1970; John, the blond, blue-eyed "All-American" boy, was picked up in Connecticut, James in Maryland (James had traveled back and forth from his residence there to help his brother mastermind bank heists, and together they had gone back and forth from Connecticut to Missouri). John was mortally wounded trying to escape custody before his trial in Bridgeport, Connecticut; before he died about two weeks later (April 28, 1971), he fully confessed to the robberies, bombings, and killings. James was imprisoned by Connecticut and Missouri authorities until released from a state hospital in Fulton, Missouri, in the spring of 1976. Arrested for a 1976 attempted bank robbery in Colorado, James was tried and convicted and given a 25-year prison sentence in 1977.

PARISH, Frank (d. 1864). Montana rustler and robber. In the 1860s vigilantes in Montana territory sought to wipe out the criminal element that had disrupted life there. Though they had no evidence against Parish, who had a bad reputation in the territory, they decided to hang him as an example of what would happen to other "criminals." The vigilantes' "preventive hanging," however, was spoiled when Parish, moments before his death, admitted to livestock rustling and stagecoach robbery; he was just another guilty man!

PARKER, Bonnie (1911-34). American robber and murderer. She was a cafe waitress in Dallas when she first met Clyde BARROW in early 1930. In her words, she was "bored crapless" and saw a life of excitement with Barrow, even if it was outside the law. Bonnie helped Clyde escape from the Waco, Texas, jail by passing a .38 Colt through the jail bars to him. Lovers Bonnie and Clyde then began a wild lawless rampage, robbing small banks and stores and killing policemen and others. She liked reading about her exploits in the newspapers and sent editors poems she wrote. Pictures of Bonnie smoking a cigar and brandishing a machine-gun were printed in many papers. A five-man Texas posse under Frank Hamer shot Bonnie and Clyde dead near Gibland, Louisiana, on May 23, 1934.

PARKER, Isaac C. "Hanging Judge." See MALEDON, George.

PARKER, Robert LeRoy. See CASSIDY, Butch.

PARSONS, Albert Richard (d. 1887). American anarchist. Born in Alabama, he served in the Confederate army in the U.S. Civil War (1861-65). Afterward Parsons, who was well-educated and an excellent speaker, became involved in radical causes, giving numerous fiery speeches in public decrying the wretched state of the poor and the common worker. He declared himself a steadfast anarchist while joining the labor movement's fight to organize and receive better pay. August SPIES, Adolph FISCHER, George ENGEL, and Parsons were sent to the gallows in Illinois on November 11, 1887, after having been convicted of conspiring to commit violence and murder at the Haymarket Square Riot in Chicago. The riot on May 4, 1866, caused when a dynamite bomb was thrown at police trying to disperse a mob of labor protestors in the square, resulted in the killing of seven police and four civilians and the wounding of about 100 other persons.

PATRIARCA, Raymond L. S. (b. 1908). New England gangster and racketeer. Around 1933 he took control of Frank Iacone's Mafia gang in New England. Patriarca, called the "Padrone," was convicted of armed robbery in 1938 and served nearly two years in the Old Charleston jail in Massachusetts. In the 1940s and 1950s he established large gambling and loansharking operations, which he ran from his office in Providence, Rhode Island, and managed to keep out of the public's eye. In 1966 Patriarca was convicted of conspiracy to commit murder. After several appeals, he went to prison in 1970 to serve five years and continued to run the New England Mafia while there.

PATRICK, Albert (d. 1940). American forger and murder conspirator. Patrick, a lawyer in New York, was involved in litigation for Texas multimillionaire William Marsh Rice, who lived with his valet-secretary Charles T. Jones. On September 23, 1900, Rice died. Shortly afterward suspicion focused on Patrick when he attempted to cash a $250,000 check on Rice's account (he had previously forged a will leaving half of Rice's fortune to himself). Patrick and Jones were arrested and imprisoned. While in prison, Jones attempted suicide and said he had been paid by Patrick to murder Rice (which he had done, using chloroform). Patrick, sentenced to death in 1902, delayed his execution by appeals and finally had his sentence commuted to life imprisonment in 1906. Patrick was released from prison in 1912; he died many years later in Tulsa, Oklahoma.

PATTEN, C[arl] Thomas (d. 1959). American evangelist and con man. His evangelist wife, Bebe Harrison, taught him the scriptures, helping him become ordained by the Fundamental Ministerial Association and then traveling with him on the revivalist circuit for about ten years until they settled in Oakland, California, in 1944. Soon many trusting souls came under

the spell of C. Thomas Patten (he joked the "C" stood for
"cash"), who led and sermonized to large congregations at re-
vival meetings as well as at his temple in Oakland. Usually
wearing cowboy boots, a Stetson, and flashy clothes, he swayed
the gullible and faithful under his threats of eternal damnation
to donate huge sums of money to support his work and his proj-
ects, which never materialized. The Pattens, however, lived in
great luxury but in 1948 came under investigation by Oakland's
district attorney because of their monetary dealings. Indicted
for grand theft, Patten stood trial (1950) and was convicted
and sentenced to five to fifty years in prison. In 1953 he was
paroled on the condition he would never collect from a congre-
gation again (the evangelistic activity under Bebe, who had remained free, dwindled and brought in small sums). At his death
in California in 1959, Patten was a little-remembered religious
personage.

PATTERSON, Nan (1882–after 1910). New York accused murderer.
Nan, a stunning Floradora Girl on Broadway at the turn of the
century, had a love affair with a married horse race gambler
named "Caesar" Young, whose wife refused to divorce him and
attempted to break up the affair by persuading Caesar to sail
with her to Europe in June 1904. During a ride with his paramour in a hansom cab down Broadway, Young was fatally wounded
in the chest by a gunshot. Nan was arrested and stood trial
three times, accused of murdering Caesar, but she pleaded innocent, saying he had shot himself out of grief over having to
leave her (his suicide seemed improbable because of the location
of the wound and the fact that the gun had been replaced in
Young's pocket). The public sympathized with Nan, who was
discharged and left jail to the cheers of over 2,000 of her supporters. Now a celebrity and offered leading roles in musicals,
Nan, the so-called "Girl in the Hansom Cab," was discovered to
have no acting ability and soon dropped out of the limelight and
later disappeared.

PAVELIĆ, Ante (1889–1959). Croatian revolutionist and leader. A
lawyer and city official at Zagreb, Pavelić became a Croatian
representative in the Yugoslav national parliament at Belgrade.
He spurned the unification of the country and helped establish
a separate parliament at Zagreb in 1928. When King Alexander I
of Yugoslavia set up a royal dictatorship in 1929, Pavelić fled to
Italy, where he formed a Croatian terrorist group called the
Ustashe (Revolutionists). The 1934 assassination of King Alexander, carried out by terrorist Vlada CHERNOZAMSKY, was apparently planned by Pavelić and the Ustashe (Pavelić was tried
and sentenced to death in absentia for the murder). When the
Axis powers seized the Balkans in 1941 during World War II
(1939–45), Pavelić, who had adopted a zealous pro-Axis stance,
was appointed by Adolf HITLER to head the Independent State
of Croatia, which was under German-Italian protection. Pavelić's

fascist regime, attempting to "purify" the Croatian land and faith, persecuted and murdered thousands of Jews, Muslims, and Orthodox Serbs. Upon the defeat of Germany in 1945, Pavelić fled from Croatia to hide in Austria and Italy, from which he escaped to Buenos Aires, Argentina, in 1948. The Argentine government refused Yugoslavia's request for his extradition in 1957, and soon afterward Pavelić secretly moved to Spain, where he later died in Madrid on December 28, 1959.

PEACE, Charles (1832-79). English burglar and murderer. He spent time in prison for a series of burglaries in the 1850s. Peace was a "cat burglar" or "portico thief" who had amazing ability to break into the most secure houses, often through upstairs windows. Skilled also in the use of disguise, he often posed as a proper citizen for the purpose of surveying the premises he intended to burgle. Peace, who used various aliases, was caught in Manchester in 1866 and sent to prison for six years. In the mid-1870s he burglarized homes in Peckham, and was later caught by the police in 1878. At his trial, Peace was convicted of burglary as well as murder (killing a railway engineer in 1876). Before his death sentence--hanging--was carried out on February 25, 1879, Peace admitted to the killing.

PEACH, Arthur (d. 1638). American murderer. Peach, accompanied by three runaway servants, waylaid and killed a Narragansett Indian man who was returning home from the Massachusetts Bay Colony after receiving cloth and beads in trade. Peach and two of the runaways were caught, tried for the crime, and convicted. A debate then ensued about whether three whites should be punished by death for the killing of one Indian; some colonists wondered whether "any English should be put to death for the Indians." Peach and the two others were eventually hanged (probably to avert war with the Indians), becoming the first whites executed in America for murdering an Indian--a rare act of justice for the Indians during the next 250 years.

PEARL, Cora [born: Elizabeth Crouch] (d. 1886). English-born courtesan. Living as a notorious high-class prostitute in Paris in the 1860s, she gave risqué dinner parties during which man-servants used to carry her, naked on a large platter, into the room to be served to the guests as dessert--a special delight to noble Frenchmen. A wealthy Bonaparte prince and a young aristocratic heir to a French fortune both became enamored by Pearl, keeping her as their mistress and lavishing great gifts upon her; the latter tried to kill himself because of her. French authorities were urged to deport Pearl to her native England but failed, and she took to gallivanting around Europe as a high-priced courtesan in the 1870s. Later, back in Paris, she died in obscurity of cancer.

PECK, Ellen [born: Nellie Crosby] (1829-1915). New York swindler.

For almost 35 years she carried on her flimflamming schemes,
becoming known as the "Queen of Confidence Women," a title
given her by New York City Police Inspector Thomas A.
Byrnes, who apprehended her on numerous occasions. At age
51 she began her criminality, leaving her family, moving to New
York City, and soon absconding with negotiable bonds from an
old millionaire soap tycoon B. T. Babbit. Hunted down and
convicted of swindling (1884), Peck served time in prison, then
resumed her con games (robber-baron Jay Gould was defrauded
by her, along with others), and was repeatedly put behind bars
(from 1887 to 1911) on convictions of fraud (her seemingly un-
quenchable sexual appetite physically ruined one of her dupes,
an elderly doctor in Brooklyn). Serving a 20-year sentence in
New York's Auburn Prison beginning in 1908, she gained a full
pardon in 1911 (at the age of 82), but again bilked another
businessman, using sex and threatening to inform the man's
wife, in 1913 (at age 84!). Sick in bed at her family's New
York homestead when the authorities caught up with her, Peck
was not arrested and shortly thereafter died.

PEEL, Fanny (1828-58). American prostitute. At the age of 15,
Fanny, the beautiful and educated daughter of a Troy, New
York, clergyman, was seduced and subsequently turned to a
life of prostitution. After working in several bordellos, she became the mistress of a number of wealthy businessmen in New
York City, Chicago, and elsewhere and accumulated a sizable
fortune. In 1857 Fanny arrived in New Orleans, where she
quickly became known as the city's loveliest courtesan. Believing herself superior to the dandies she serviced, Fanny grew
disillusioned after several months and was soon dismissed from
the chic Dauphine Street bordello where she worked. She moved
to Mobile, Alabama, where she died in the summer of 1858.

PEETE, Louise [born: Lofie Louise Preslar] (1883-1947). California
murderer. Married several times, she ran away from her husbands (the last being Richard C. Peete of Denver) and engaged
in prostitution and blackmail in numerous U.S. states in the
first part of the century. In 1920 she became housemaid-lover
of Los Angeles millionaire Jacob Charles Denton, whom she killed
when he refused to marry her. When police dug up his corpse
in the Denton mansion's cellar, Louise was arrested and convicted
of murder and imprisoned for life. After serving 18 years, she
was paroled in the custody of Mr. and Mrs. Arthur Logan of
Pacific Palisades, California. Mrs. Logan's disappearance in 1944,
as well as Mr. Logan's commitment by Louise to an asylum,
aroused police suspicion and led to the discovery of Mrs. Logan's
buried body in the Logan garden. Again charged with murder
and convicted, Louise was imprisoned at Tehachapi until her execution at San Quentin in 1947; she became the second woman to
die in the gas chamber in California.

PEGLOW, Karl (d. 1955). German counterfeiter. A luckless artist who had become an expert photographer and engraver while working for a time in the German government printing office, Peglow was convicted twice of counterfeiting rationing cards in the Hannover area. After two years' imprisonment (1948-50), he settled in Hameln with his wife, worked as a truck driver, and secretly produced a steady stream of almost-perfect bank notes. His expert imitations of ten and twenty-mark bills, which he passed one by one to merchants and businesses in widely separated towns, nearly went undetected except for some minute flaws noticed by the banks. A painstaking investigation by police uncovered Peglow, who possessed incriminating evidence: engraving plates for fifty-mark notes of perfect quality. Convicted and imprisoned (1954), he proudly demonstrated his counterfeiting skill as part of a police documentary film about bogus currency which he helped make before dying in July 1955.

PELTZER, Armand (1844?-85). Belgian engineer and murderer. In Antwerp, Belgium, he fell madly in love with the young wife of attorney Guillaume Bernays, whom Peltzer decided to murder in order to marry Madame Bernays. Concocting the "perfect crime," Armand met with his brother Leon PELTZER in Paris in November 1881, and together they put into action Armand's scheme: the crime would be committed by a nonexistent person named Henry Vaughan, a fictitious shipping tycoon who would actually be Leon in disguise. In early 1882 Vaughan (Leon) contacted Bernays in Antwerp and persuaded him to come to Brussels to discuss possible legal work with Vaughan's new steamship line. In a Brussels apartment, Leon shot and killed Bernays, then discarded his disguise and disappeared. Not seeing mention of the killing in the newspapers, Leon vainly thought to help to get his press glory. A letter written by Leon from Switzerland, signed "Henry Vaughan" and sent to the Belgian police, was traced through handwriting analysis to Leon, who had failed to change his writing style. Soon both Peltzer brothers were arrested, tried (November 27-December 22, 1882), and convicted of murder. Condemned to die, they instead received life imprisonment since executions had been done away with in Belgium. Armand died of illness in Louvain prison in 1885.

PELTZER, Leon (1847-1922). Belgian murderer. Working abroad in New York under an alias (he had earlier committed some financial wrongdoing in Argentina), Leon was summoned by his older brother Armand PELTZER to meet him in Paris, where Leon was informed he would be able to pay off his sizeable debts to his brother. At their Paris meeting (November 1881), Leon agreed to kill a Belgian attorney named Guillaume Bernays, whose young wife Armand loved desperately and wanted to marry. The blond-haired Leon changed his appearance completely, posing as one Henry Vaughan, a nonexistent wealthy shipper (part of Armand's "foolproof" murder plot). In time, Bernays received a letter from Vaughan (Leon), who asked him to come to Brussels to talk about legal work for Vaughan's steamship line. The attorney came and was shot dead in secret by Leon, who then dispensed with his disguise and fled to Switzerland. Stupidly, he wrote a letter to the Belgian police because he had seen no notice in the press about the murder (he desired press coverage to appease his vanity), and subsequently the police were able to trace the letter to Leon because of his handwriting, which he had failed to alter. Leon and Armand both stood trial (November 27-December 22, 1882) and were found guilty of murder. They were sent to Louvain prison for life. Armand died there in 1885, and Leon worked on his language skills, eventually becoming an informal translator for the Justice Ministry. At age 65 he was released on the condition he leave the country. Living abroad for many years, Leon was permitted finally to return to Belgium but soon grew despondent and ultimately killed himself by drowning in the sea off Oostende.

PENDERGAST, Tom or Thomas Joseph (1872-1945). Kansas City political boss. After 1910 he was the Democratic leader in Kansas City, Missouri, and by 1920 his powerful political machine ruled the city, which became "wide open" to gangland interests, such as liquor, gambling, and vice. "Boss Tom," as he was called, participated in discussions with reputed underworld chiefs in the early 1930s, when the national crime syndicate was being formed; the Pendergast machine was known to use fraud and violence to achieve its goals and to maintain absolute control. In the late 1930s, the FBI discovered evidence of ballot fraud (stuffed ballot boxes and vote theft), and over 250 Pendergast associates were found guilty in the fraud case. In 1939 Pendergast himself was convicted of tax evasion and sent to Leavenworth, from which he was paroled in 1940 with the stipulation that he would refrain from politics for five years. His political machine was broken. See also BINAGGIO, Charley or Charles.

PERKINS, Josephine Ameilia (1818-after 1841). English-born American horse thief. She arrived in America about the mid-1830s and soon fell into a life of crime, chiefly horse thievery. She was arrested several times for stealing horses, released because of her sex or supposed insanity, but served a two-year term in Kentucky's Madison County jail in the late 1830s. There is no further record of Josephine, known as America's first female horse thief, after 1841, when evidently she decided to reform to avoid possible longer incarceration in the future.

PEROVSKAYA, Sophia (1855-81). Russian assassin. She and her lover Andrei Zhelyabov led a violent nihilist organization (which called itself "The People's Will") against the totalitarian regime of Czar Alexander II of Russia. Undeterred by several attempts

to kill him, the czar continued to show himself publicly until he
was assassinated by terrorists directed by blonde-haired Perovskaya in St. Petersburg (Leningrad) on March 13 (March 1, O.S.),
1881. Two bombs were thrown, the first exploding behind Alexander's sleigh-carriage which was traveling along the Nevsky
Prospekt, the second blowing up right beside the czar and mortally wounding him and the bomb thrower, Ignaty GRINEVITSKY.
A member of the People's Will, Nikolai Rysakov, later informed
on Perovskaya and others involved in the assassination plot;
Rysakov had been arrested with Zhelyabov at the scene of the
crime. Six conspirators, including Perovskaya, Zhelyabov, and
Rysakov, were found guilty and sentenced to death. On April
15 (April 3, O.S.), 1881, they were hanged before more than
100,000 hushed spectators in Semenovsky Square in St. Petersburg.

PERRY, Oliver Curtis (1864-1930). American train robber. In 1891
Perry, a former Wyoming cowboy who admired the exploits of the
Western outlaws, single-handedly robbed the New York Central
No. 31 train near Albany. The following year he robbed, again
alone, two more New York Central trains, the first near Syra-
cuse, the second near Lyons, New York. A posse chased him
after the second robbery and caught him. Perry was tried, convicted, and sent to Auburn Prison for 49 years. Newspaper
stories about his daring, ingenious methods of breaking into
trains' express cars made Perry a celebrity. After creating
several disturbances at Auburn, Perry was moved to the State
Hospital for the Criminally Insane at Matteawan, New York, in
1893. He escaped in 1895 but was soon caught and sent to the
maximum-security prison at Dannemora, from which he tried unsuccessfully to escape several times. Perry was put in solitary
confinement, where he lived for the next 25 years. Driven half
mad, he blinded himself in 1920 and tried to starve himself to
death during the last six years of his life (during that time he
spoke not a word to the guards, who had to force-feed him).
Perry died in his cell on September 10, 1930.

PERUGGIA, Vincenzo (fl. 1911-13). Italian thief. On the evening
of August 21, 1911, while employed as a janitor in France's
Louvre Museum in Paris, he stealthily and carefully cut the
portrait painting of "Mona Lisa" from its frame and carried it
hidden under his overcoat to his apartment, where he stashed
the 400-year-old masterpiece in the false bottom of a trunk.
After two years, during which time he came under suspicion,
Peruggia smuggled the stolen painting to his native Italy, trying to sell it to Italian officials for $95,000 without luck. He
was quickly apprehended, and the "Mona Lisa" was recovered
and sent back to the Louvre. At his trial in Florence, Peruggia claimed his thievery was done out of patriotism (his desire
to bring the painting home to the country of its creator, Leonardo da Vinci); the court mildly reproved him and sentenced
him to about a year in jail.

PETERS, Frederick Emerson (1885-1959). American con man and
imposter. In 1902 he began writing worthless checks, posing
as someone else, and was so successful that authorities did not
catch him until 1915. Peters' modus operandi was generally the
same: he would purchase an item in an expensive store, impress
the clerk by pretending to be someone important or the son or
relative of a well-known figure, write out a check much larger
than the cost of the purchase, and then pocket the extra money
(the item itself was usually sent to Peters' supposed club or
university, but occasionally he walked out of the store with it).
Released after serving five years in the Atlanta federal penitentiary, where Peters broadened his knowledge about the world
and people through much reading, he resumed his con operation
with greater finesse. In his check cashing scams he now impersonated such figures as Franklin Delano Roosevelt, Theodore
Roosevelt, Jr., Booth Tarkington, Philip Wylie, and other notable men. In 1924 Peters was apprehended and sent to the
McNeil Island, Washington, federal prison, where he helped establish a large prison library (there he read voraciously to develop his con art). After his release, he again worked many
remarkable scams, at times actually believing that he was indeed
the person he was impersonating. Peters, who spent many years
behind bars during his life, was apprehended for the last time
in Washington, D.C., in 1952. Later set free, he continued his
bad check passing until the age of 74, when he suffered a fatal
stroke in New Haven, Connecticut, and was given a pauper's
funeral there.

PETIOT, Marcel (1897-1946). French doctor and mass murderer.
He was a French army surgeon during World War I, after which
he spent several months in an asylum suffering from "war psy-
chosis." Petiot continued his career as a doctor but often robbed
his patients and burglarized their homes. During the Nazi occupation of Paris in World War II, he promised to smuggle Jews
and others out of the country for cash or jewelry, but these
"emigrants" never left Petiot's Paris house. Petiot killed them,
either by poison or toxic gas, and disposed of their bodies in a
quicklime pit or his furnace. Neighbors grew suspicious of
Petiot, resulting in the discovery by police of smoldering human
remains in his furnace. At his trial, Petiot claimed he had
killed only German soldiers and French collaborators (later he
boasted of having killed 63 persons, disclaiming the prosecution's figure of 27 persons). Found guilty, Petiot was beheaded
on the guillotine at the Santé Prison in Paris on May 25, 1946.

PETRILLO, Herman and Paul. See BOLBER, Morris.

PHILBY, [Harold Adrian Russell] "Kim" (b. 1912). British intelligence officer and Soviet spy. He became a Communist when he
was a student at Cambridge University in England. Philby, who
started spying for the Soviet Union in 1933, entered the British

Secret Intelligence Service in 1940 after being recruited by Guy Burgess, a British agent who was also a Soviet spy. Philby worked for many years as one of the Soviet's most important "moles," or double agents, in British intelligence. He was in charge of liaison between British intelligence and the Central Intelligence Agency (CIA) from 1949 to 1951, when he worked at the British embassy in Washington, D.C. According to reports, Philby tipped off Soviet double agents Burgess and Donald Maclean when they were about to be arrested in 1951 (the two spies then escaped to Russia). Philby, after mysteriously disappearing in Beirut, Lebanon, turned up in Moscow in 1963. His espionage activities were then fully exposed, causing an infamous scandal. Philby, now a Soviet resident, became a colonel in the KGB and in 1980 was awarded by the Kremlin the Order of Friendship of the People for his "more than 40 years of difficult but honorable work."

PHILIPSE, Frederick (c. 1630-1702). Dutch-born New York pirate-broker. In about 1647 he immigrated from Holland to Nieuw Amsterdam (now New York City), where he established a shipping business. He acquired much property through his two marriages and became deeply involved in pirate trading in the 1690s. Philipse's ships supplied the Madagascar pirates with rum, guns, ammunition, food, and clothing and brought back cargoes of slaves and booty. Corrupt colonial officials often let his cargoes pass inspection. After 1698, however, Philipse and his son and partner, Adolph, came under much suspicion because of their "ventures" and wealth. Philipse was never prosecuted and died one of the richest men in New York.

PHILLIPE, Joseph (d. 1866). French mass murderer. Phillipe's origins and early career are obscure, as are the reasons he began attacking and cutting the throats of French prostitutes in Paris in the early 1860s. Seven persons (six streetwalkers and a youngster) were slain by him in 1864. His night attacks ended in 1866 after one of his intended victims, saved by a gendarme, told the authorities her attacker had a tattoo on his arm with the words "Born under an evil star." This guided them to Phillipe, who was arrested, found guilty of killing at least eight (indubitably more than a dozen) prostitutes, and put to death in July 1866.

PHILLIPS, Clara (1899-?). California murderer. After finding out that her wealthy husband, Armour Phillips, who sold oil-securities in Los Angeles, was having a love affair with a lovely, 22-year-old widow named Alberta Meadows, Clara pursued the latter for days until finally confronting her on July 6, 1922. Clara, accompanied by her friend Peggy Caffee had picked up Alberta and driven to a deserted spot where she assaulted and killed her rival with a hammer. Soon afterward Armour Phillips, to whom Clara admitted the crime, informed the authorities and had his wife apprehended. Peggy's testimony against Clara, whom newsmen nicknamed the "Tiger Woman" because she had stalked her victim like a tiger, helped sentence her to ten years to life imprisonment. Released from California's Tehachapi prison in 1935, she soon faded from public view.

PINO, Anthony "the Pig" (or "Fats"). See McGINNIS, [Joseph Francis] "Big Joe."

PIPER, Thomas W. (1849-76). Boston rapist and mass murderer. Between 1873 and 1875, Boston was terrorized by a series of rapes and the murders of three women and a girl. After five-year-old Mabel Hood Young was found murdered in the tower of the Old Warren Avenue Baptist Church, suspicion fell on Piper, the church sexton, who had been seen with the child shortly before her death. Piper was arrested and soon confessed to the killings. Some people said that drugged whiskey (apparently mixed with laudanum) drunk by Piper had turned him temporarily into an uncontrollable creature who lurked in the night after females. Piper was tried, found guilty, and hanged.

PITTS, Charlie. See JAMES, Jesse [Woodson]; YOUNGER, Jim or James.

PITTSBURGH PHIL. See STRAUSS, Harry.

PLACE, Etta (1880?-after 1907). American outlaws' accomplice. In 1897 Etta, a tall, raven-haired beauty who craved excitement, joined Butch CASSIDY, the SUNDANCE KID, and the Wild Bunch and rode with them on their robbery forays in Wyoming, Utah, and elsewhere. Some people claimed she had been a schoolteacher, and others said she had been a prostitute whom the Sundance Kid had picked up at Fannie Porter's posh brothel in Fort Worth, Texas. Nevertheless, she loved the Sundance Kid, even caring for him when he "caught cold" (contracted venereal disease, in whorehouse slang) after one of his jaunts to a fleshpot. Etta went with Cassidy and the Sundance Kid to South America in 1902 and later acted as a scout on their robbery raids there. In 1907 the Sundance Kid took Etta to New York for an appendicitis operation and then to Denver to recuperate. The Sundance Kid left her in 1908 to return to Cassidy in Bolivia, and Etta faded away. There is some slight evidence that the lovers eventually rejoined and settled down in Mexico City, where they had a reunion with Cassidy years later.

PLACE, Martha M. (1848-99). New York murderer. At her home in Brooklyn, New York, on February 7, 1898, she used an axe to kill her disagreeable stepdaughter Ida and later that day, after her husband William had returned from work, attacked and wounded him with the axe. He fled to safety, and the police seized and imprisoned Martha, who was convicted of murder and condemned to die. New York's Governor Theodore Roosevelt denied her request to commute her sentence, and at New York's Sing Sing Prison (Ossining Correctional Facility) on March 20, 1899, she became the first woman ever to die in the electric chair.

PLANETTA, Otto (d. 1934). Austrian Nazi assassin. Austria's Chancellor Engelbert Dollfuss established an authoritarian government in an effort to crush the Nazi movement in his country in 1933-34. Reputedly with the backing of Adolf HITLER, Germany's Führer, some 150 members of the Austrian Nazi party, led by Planetta, Franz Holzweber, and others, attempted to seize power on July 25, 1934; they took over government buildings in Vienna, Austria's capital, and burst into the chancellery to confront Dollfuss in his office. Planetta impetuously fired two shots at Dollfuss, who had tried to dissuade the Nazi rebels from their intentions. The chancellor was fatally wounded in the throat and spine and died shortly after in the hands of his captors, who were assaulted and captured by Austrian government troops. The coup d'état failed; Hitler denied any knowledge of it, and Planetta, Holzweber, and most of their cohorts were executed, crying, "Heil Hitler!" just before their deaths in 1934.

PLANTAIN, John (fl. 1720s). English-born Jamaican pirate. He went to sea at the age of 13 and became a pirate at 20. After several years of successful piracy in and around the Red Sea, Plantain settled down at Ranter Bay in Madagascar, where his pirate booty allowed him to live a life of leisure. He kept a harem of native girls for his pleasure. With pirate friends, Plantain fought and defeated the tribal chieftains and proclaimed himself "King of Madagascar." However, the natives rose up against Plantain, who often tortured and killed them at whim, and forced him to flee from the island. It is believed he sailed to India's Malabar coast and later died there.

PLUMMER, Henry (1837-64). American lawman, robber, and murderer. About 1860 he formed a gang of outlaws in Lewiston, Idaho, and pretended to be an upstanding citizen while his gang plundered the area. In 1862 Plummer and some of his gang moved to Bannack, Montana, organized another outlaw band (absurdly called the "Innocents"), and robbed stagecoaches carrying gold. Plummer, who grew rich and portrayed himself as a lawful vigilante, managed to get himself elected sheriff of Bannack on May 24, 1863. He soon expanded his operations to Virginia City, Montana, where he was made marshal. In late 1863 Plummer, who reportedly killed at least 15 men, was openly identified as the leader of the Innocents. In Bannack on January 10, 1864, vigilantes hanged him and two of his cohorts on the very gallows Plummer himself had erected to hang criminals. See also SKINNER, Cy[rus]; YAGER, [Erastus] "Red."

PODOLA, Guenther (1930-59). English murderer. In London in 1959 he was brought to trial for shooting a policeman dead while resisting arrest. For the first time in English legal history, a defendant pleaded amnesia or loss of memory about his alleged crime. Podola said he remembered nothing about his life before a date a few days after the shooting. A jury judged Podola sane and said he was not suffering from genuine loss of memory. Another jury found him guilty of murder and ordered the death sentence to be carried out.

POILLON, Charlotte (1872?-1935?). New York swindler. She and her sister Katherine, buxom women each weighing more than 200 pounds, bilked lonely, wealthy men out of their savings on promises of marriage. They entrapped men with their sexual "favors" and threatened to expose them. Between 1903 and 1923 they worked many shady deals and were brought to court by several wealthy businessmen on charges of blackmail. Charlotte, a semi-professional boxer, was well known for beating up hotel owners and restaurant waiters in New York City. See also POILLON, Katherine.

POILLON, Katherine (1870?-1933?). New York swindler. She and her sister Charlotte, two towering women of great girth, used sex to trap rich, lonely men into promises of marriage. In 1903 Katherine sued wealthy William G. Brokaw of New York for $250,000 for breach of promise. To avoid any public scandal, Brokaw settled out of court for $170,000. The Poillon sisters were ejected numerous times from New York hotels for failure to pay their bills and were thrown out of city restaurants for disorderly conduct. See also POILLON, Charlotte.

POKER ALICE [real name: Alice Ivers] (1851-1930). English-born American gambler, gunfighter, and madam. While earning a living as a schoolteacher in Colorado territory in the 1870s, she took up poker and became an expert gambler and card dealer, earning the nickname "Poker Alice." Smoking black cigars and toting a gun, she later traveled the railroad gambling circuit and won much money in card games. About 1891 Poker Alice landed in Creede, Colorado, where she briefly worked as a card dealer in a saloon owned by Bob FORD, the killer of Jesse JAMES. She moved on to Deadwood, South Dakota, became known for settling arguments with her quick gun, and married a card shark named William Tubbs, with whom she settled down as a chicken farmer. After Tubbs died in 1910, Poker Alice set up a gambling saloon-brothel near Fort Meade, South Dakota, servicing the soldiers and others for a number of years and voicing her two favorite remarks: "I'll shoot you in your puss, you cheating bastard!" and "I never gamble on Sundays" (nor did she let her girls service clientele on Sundays). When some drunken soldiers tried to crash down her door in 1920, Poker Alice shot dead one of the men. Tried and found guilty, she was set free by the judge who refused to sentence a white-haired old lady to jail. Poker Alice soon retired and lived the rest of her life on a ranch.

POMEROY, Jesse H. (1860-1932). Boston mass murderer. In the early 1870s youngsters began to disappear mysteriously in Boston. In 1874 a boy, William Barton, informed the police he had almost been killed by Pomeroy, who was then arrested, tried, convicted of murder (police found 27 bodies of youngsters buried behind Pomeroy's father's shop), and sentenced to be hanged. Though the public demanded the death penalty, Pomeroy's sentence was commuted to life imprisonment in solitary confinement in the Old Charleston jail. Pomeroy spent 41 years in solitary before being allowed to mingle with other prisoners in 1916. He was denied parole many times and died in the Bridgewater State Farm for the Criminally Insane on September 29, 1932.

PONZI, Charles (1878-1949). Italian-born American swindler. In 1919 he developed a get-rich-quick money trading scheme, buying international postal-union reply coupons at depressed rates in foreign countries and selling them in the United States at a large profit. Investors, lured by Ponzi's offer to pay them up to 50 percent profit in three months, poured their money into Ponzi's Financial Exchange Company in Boston. As investors put in new funds, Ponzi kept paying out interest on old funds. The "Great Ponzi Plan" made him a millionaire until investigations by newspapers exposed him. Ponzi was convicted of using the U.S. mails to defraud and sent to prison for four years in 1921. Later he tried to defraud real-estate investors in Florida, was again caught, and was sent to jail in 1925. Ponzi, who was also convicted under Massachusetts law for the mail-fraud swindle and sentenced to seven-to-nine years, finally emerged from prison in 1934 and was immediately deported to Italy, where he supposedly worked as a "financier" for Benito Mussolini. Eventually Ponzi immigrated to Rio de Janeiro and died there in a charity hospital in January 1949.

POOLE, William (d. 1855). New York gangster and murderer. He worked for the Know-Nothing Party and, for a fee, administered beatings to members of rival political groups. Poole, who headed a gang on New York City's West Side, received the nickname "Bill the Butcher" after he killed several enemies with a carving knife. In 1855 Lew Baker, a Tammany Hall hood, shot and fatally wounded Poole during a brawl in Manhattan's Stanwix Hall bar. Poole's last words to his gang before dying 14 days later were, "Good-bye, boys. I die a true American!"

PORTEOUS, John (d. 1736). Scottish police officer lynched for

murder. A riot broke out after the execution of a well-liked
smuggler in Edinburgh. City Guard soldiers, on orders from
Captain Porteous, fired into a mob, killing and wounding a number of people who had viewed the unpopular hanging. Porteous
was brought to trial, found guilty of murder, and condemned to
die. When he was granted a reprieve, an angry mob marched
on the prison where he was held on September 7, 1736, forced
the gates, seized Porteous, and lynched him. This open defi-
ance of law brought a long governmental inquiry into the affair.
Little was discovered, and the city of Edinburgh was finally
fined Ł2,000 for its mishandling of the law.

PORTUGUEZ, Bartholemy (fl. mid-1600s). Portuguese pirate. Calling himself a "flibustier" (freebooter) and seeking riches, he
sailed his small ship from Portugal to the West Indies, where he
and his hand-picked crew attacked Spanish commercial vessels
with considerable success. Frequently preying on well-armed
and larger Spanish ships laden with treasure and bound for
home from South America, Cuba, or Hispaniola, Portuguez liked
to run his vessel alongside the bigger ships, board them, and
capture them in hand-to-hand fights on their decks. Although
captured once himself by some Spaniards and taken to Campeche,
Mexico, where he was to be hanged in the public square, he
managed to escape and make an incredible, obstacle-impeded
journey on foot down the coast to safety. He then continued
his exploits until finally settling in Jamaica, where he disappeared.

POWELL, Lewis Thornton. See PAINE, Lewis.

POYAS, Peter. See VESEY, Denmark.

POYNTZ, Juliet [Stuart] (1896-?). American-born Soviet spy.
Born and raised in Omaha, Nebraska, she moved to New York
City, becoming a staunch member of the American Communist
Party in the 1920s. Poyntz made several trips to the Soviet
Union where she was well instructed in espionage work; as a
Soviet agent based in New York, she indoctrinated other Ameri-
cans eager to undermine the U.S. government by passing along
top military and other secrets. The bloody terrorism and mur-
derous political purges instituted by Joseph Stalin to make his
dictatorship absolute in Russia in the 1930s supposedly caused
Poyntz to disavow the Communist Party and denounce Stalinism.
Poyntz disappeared from her New York City residence in early
June 1937 and may have been abducted and killed by Stalinists
sent to eliminate disloyal party members.

PRESCOTT, Abraham (1816-36). New Hampshire murderer. On
June 23, 1833, he beat Mrs. Sally Cochran to death after she
rejected his amorous advances. Prescott was arrested and tried.
His lawyer argued that Prescott was a sleepwalker (the first time

sleepwalking was used as a defense) and whatever he had done had been done while he slept. The public was outraged at such a defense. Prescott was convicted and sentenced to be hanged, but appeals delayed his execution until early 1836. At Pembroke, New Hampshire, a crowd gathered to witness Prescott's hanging and rioted when it learned that Prescott had received a stay of execution. Quickly Prescott was moved to Hopkinton, New Hampshire, and hanged there.

PRILUKOFF, Donat. See TARNOWSKA, Maria.

PRIME, Geoffrey A. (b. 1938). British intelligence officer and spy. He was a linguist and Russian language expert at an intelligence headquarters in London from 1968 to 1981. During the period from 1976 to 1977, Prime worked at the Government Communications Headquarters, Britain's main electronic spying and computer center, in Cheltenham in west central England. In 1982 he was charged with supplying the Soviets with secret information "of an exceptionally grave nature." At his trial in London in November 1982, Prime pleaded guilty to seven separate espionage charges and was sentenced to 38 years in prison.

PRINCIP, Gavrilo (1894-1918). Bosnian-born Serbian conspirator and assassin. He was a member of a secret Serbian terrorist organization, the Black Hand, led by Dragutin DIMITRIJEVIĆ or "Colonel Apis," which wanted to recover lost Serbian territory and destroy Austro-Hungarian rule in the Balkans. Princip, with fellow Serbian students Nedjelko Cabrinović and Trifko Grabez, received revolvers, grenades, and some cyanide (with which to commit suicide if their plot to kill an important Austrian failed) from Dimitrijević and secretly crossed the Serbian border to Sarajevo, Bosnia-Hercegovina (now part of Yugoslavia). There, on June 28, 1914, Cabrinović tossed a grenade at the car in which Archduke Francis Ferdinand and his consort, Countess Sophie, were riding; the grenade bounced off the car, rolled under another, exploded, and injured an army officer. Cabrinović swallowed the cyanide but it did not work, then jumped into a river but was seized by pursuing police. Shortly afterward, the royal couple's car stopped in front of Princip, who drew his revolver and fired twice, killing Ferdinand and Sophie (later he claimed the bullet killing Sophie had been intended for General Oskar Potiorek, a rider in the car). Seized immediately, Princip, who had taken the cyanide but with no result, was put in jail and soon informed on 25 fellow conspirators who were arrested and received long prison sentences. Princip was tried and sentenced to 20 years' imprisonment (the maximum punishment for a criminal under age 20). On April 28, 1918, he died of tuberculosis in an Austrian hospital at Theresienstadt (now Terezin, Czechoslovakia) near his prison. The assassination had caused Austria-Hungary to declare war on Serbia, thus precipitating World War I (1914-18).

PRIO, Ross (1900-1972). Chicago gangster and racketeer. From the mid-1930s until his death of a heart attack in 1972, Prio was a quiet but important member of the national crime syndicate in the United States. His "territory" was Chicago's North Side, where he helped run hotels, motels, restaurants, nightclubs, and currency exchanges. Prio allegedly had major interests in gambling rackets in Las Vegas. During the 1963 Senate investigation into organized crime, Prio was named one of the top Mafia, or Cosa Nostra, leaders in Chicago.

PRITCHARD, Edward William (1825-65). British doctor and poisoner. An egotistical, flamboyant physician known for his extramarital seductions of young women, Pritchard seemed to grieve too ostentatiously when his wife died unexpectedly in 1865; he kissed her somber lips as she lay in the coffin, whose lid had been removed on his order. Shortly thereafter, his wife's mother, who supposedly suspected him of murder, perished, too. The crimes were traced to Pritchard, who eventually admitted to poisoning (with aconite, mainly) the two women; some claimed that he had also killed a young girl several years before. On the day after he confessed, Pritchard was hanged before a reported crowd of 100,000 persons; he was the last person to be executed publicly in Scotland. No motive was ever revealed by him for the killings, but many think he had delusions of committing them with impunity.

PROBST, Antoine (d. 1866). Pennsylvania mass murderer. Probst, a farm worker, was fired by his employer Christopher Deering because of his continual drunkenness. Maddened by Deering's refusal to rehire him, Probst invaded the Deering farm house near Philadelphia one night in 1866 and killed eight persons, including the six Deering family members, a boy servant, and a woman visitor. Arrested soon afterward, Probst confessed, was convicted, and died on the gallows. Doctors removed his eyes as an experiment to see if the retinas retained the final image seen before his death; nothing was discovered.

PROFACI, Joe or Joseph (1896-1962). Brooklyn gangster and racketeer. He was boss of one of the five original top Mafia "families" established in New York in the 1930s (the other four were headed by Charles "Lucky" LUCIANO, Joseph C. BONANNO, Sr., Tom Gagliano, and Vince Mangano). The Profaci crime family owned and operated numerous businesses throughout Brooklyn (Profaci was the leading American importer of olive oil and tomato paste in the late 1940s). Joey GALLO, a top Brooklyn mobster, attempted to destroy the power of Profaci's Mafia family and take control of the gambling and narcotics rackets in Brooklyn. From the late 1940s to the early 1960s an intermittent Gallo-Profaci gangland war resulted in many killings. In 1962 Profaci died of cancer, and leadership of his family was taken over eventually by Joe COLOMBO, Sr., not Gallo.

PROSSER, Gabriel. See GABRIEL.

PSALMANAZAR, George [real name: unknown] (c. 1679-1763).
French-born English literary impostor. As a poor but educated
young man with a gift for languages, he roamed through western
Europe, passing himself off convincingly as "a Japanese converted
to Christianity." In Holland a Scottish Protestant chaplain,
William Innes, who saw through the fraud but encouraged it on
a larger scale to gain personal credit for the conversion, brought
Psalmanazar in late 1703 to London, where the latter hoodwinked
British clergy and other learned gentlemen by pretending to be
a Christianized pagan from Formosa (Taiwan) who had embraced
the Church of England. Psalmanazar, the center of public
adulation, endeared himself to London's Anglican bishop, for
whom he translated the catechism of the church into "Formosan"
(a language Psalmanazar invented and convinced British authorities to hire him to teach at Oxford University). In addition, he
wrote in Latin a best-selling history of his supposed homeland,
The Historical and Geographical Description of Formosa (1704),
which was translated into English. His imposture collapsed in
1707 when doubters showed that his claims were fraudulent, and
afterward he fell into despair for the hoax, living the rest of
his life as a guilt-ridden and repentant hack writer. Only in
his memoirs, published posthumously (1764), did he admit the
imposture.

PURDY, Sam (d. 1805). American white slaver. In the early 1800s
he headed a notorious gang of procurers who engaged in white
slavery (the practice of forced prostitution). Girls living along
the Ohio and Mississippi rivers were kidnapped or bought from
their impoverished parents and "sold down the river" (Purdy
was thought to have originated the phrase), especially at Natchez, Mississippi, to brothel keepers and "floating hog pen"
operators, who in turn sold them to whoremasters in New Orleans and elsewhere. Purdy, who specialized in procuring good-
looking girls, received much more than the average $125 price
per girl. A reformer named Carlos White finally destroyed the
operation, tracking down the Purdy gang and rescuing several
girls, including the famous Beckett sisters of St. Louis, from
brothels in New Orleans. Purdy was found dead in his bed in
1805, knifed, and his gang members were eliminated one after
another. All were shot to death except one, who was brought to
trial by White and sent to jail for ten years.

- Q -

QUANTRILL, William Clarke (1837-65). American Confederate guerrilla leader and murderer. At the start of the U.S. Civil War
(1861-65), Quantrill organized a pro-Confederate guerrilla band,
which later numbered about 450 men. Though he engaged in

fights with Union troops in Missouri and Kansas, Quantrill busied himself with robbery, arson, and murder. On September 6, 1862, his band raided Olath, Kansas, looting and burning the town and killing a dozen men. On August 21, 1863, Quantrill's raiders attacked Lawrence, Kansas, where Quantrill ordered 150 men and boys to be rounded up and shot to death with their hands tied behind their backs and with their wives and daughters watching. Later, in Texas, Quantrill attacked defenseless wagon trains and killed travelers, stealing their possessions. During a raid into Kentucky in early June 1865, Quantrill was fatally wounded by Union soldiers under Captain Edward Terrill. See also ANDERSON, Bill or William; JAMES, [Alexander] Frank[lin].

QUERIPEL, Michael (b. 1937). English murderer. Pretty, 46-year-old Elizabeth Currell was attacked and battered to death while she took a walk on the golf course of Potter's Bar, a small town north of London, on the evening of April 30, 1955. The killer had accidentally left a clear palm print on his murder weapon, a blood-smeared iron tee marker, and so Scotland Yard painstakingly took, by request, palm prints from thousands of males over age 16 known to have been in the region that fatal night. Queripel, a loner and town clerk in Potter's Bar, was identified by his print (which he had reluctantly given at his younger brother's request) and taken into custody, readily confessing to the crime. At his trial on October 12, 1955, he pleaded guilty and was sentenced to life imprisonment.

QUISLING, Vidkun (1887-1945). Norwegian official and traitor. He was a Norwegian army officer who served as a military attaché in Russia (1918-19) and Finland (1919-21). Later he became Norway's minister of defense (1931-33) as a member of the ruling Agrarian Party, but resigned to form the fascist National Unity Party, which never attracted many followers in Norway. Quisling and his party opposed unionism and Communism and backed Adolf Hitler's National Socialism in Germany. At a meeting with Hitler in Berlin in early April 1940, Quisling gave strategic information that helped the German Nazi invasion of Norway succeed later that same month. After the Norwegian king and government fled to England, Quisling made himself premier, but public opposition forced his retraction within a week. The Nazis allowed him to remain as head of Norway's sole political party, eventually naming him premier in 1942. A brutal and incompetent administrator who even embarrassed the Nazis at times, Quisling lived in extreme luxury on an island near Oslo, becoming more and more megalomaniacal as he issued self-serving and cruel orders. In May 1945, after the Germans in Norway surrendered, he was arrested and charged with treason, theft, and murder, particularly the deaths of some 1,000 Norwegian Jews whom he had deported to concentration camps. Convicted of these crimes, he was executed by a firing

squad on October 24, 1945, in Oslo. The word "quisling" has
since become a synonym for traitor.

- R -

RACKHAM or RACKAM, Jack or John (d. 1720). English pirate.
In the early part of the 1700s, Rackham, captain of a pirate
ship, plundered coastal trading vessels, becoming the scourge
of the West Indies. Known as "Calico Jack" because of the
bright cotton clothing he wore, Rackham sometimes pressed
sailors from captured vessels into service as pirates. His lavish, romantic courtship of Anne BONNY endeared him to other
pirates on the island of New Providence in the Bahamas. With
Bonny and others, Rackham seized a fast-sailing sloop and went
on a wild, short-lived piratical escapade in the Caribbean in
1720. Anchored off the coast of Jamaica in October 1720, Rackham's sloop was unexpectedly attacked by a British merchant
sloop under Captain Barnet, who had been commissioned by the
governor of Jamaica to catch Rackham. Bonny and Mary READ,
both dressed as male pirates, put up a fierce fight, but Rackham and the other males were too drunk. The pirates were all
captured. Rackham was convicted of piracy and hanged in
Jamaica on about November 21, 1720.

RAEDER, Erich (1876-1960). German Nazi naval commander and
war criminal. In World War I (1914-18) he served as chief of
staff under German Admiral Franz von Hipper and participated
in the battles of Dogger Bank and Jutland. Appointed head of
Germany's naval department in 1928, Raeder clandestinely re-
constructed the country's navy, emphasizing U-boats (subma-
rines) and fast cruisers, in violation of the 1919 Versailles
Treaty. Adolf HITLER, Germany's Führer (leader), named him
grand admiral in 1939, but during World War II (1939-45)
Raeder's aggressive naval strategy conflicted with Hitler's
plans, which usually downplayed the importance of sea power.
Consequently, Raeder was replaced as grand admiral by Karl
DOENITZ in early 1943. At Nuremberg, West Germany, in 1945,
the International Military Tribunal sentenced Raeder to life imprisonment as a war criminal, but he was released because of
ill health in 1955. He died in Kiel on November 6, 1960.

RAIS [Raiz or Retz], Gilles de (1404-40). French baron, satanist,
and mass murderer. The eldest son of a rich French landown-
ing noble family in Brittany, he added to the wealth he inherited
by marrying a rich heiress, becoming the greatest landowner in
France and financing the armies led by Joan of Arc against the
English in 1429-30. Trained in the arts of war, Rais distinguished himself in battle, fought side by side with Joan of Arc
at Orléans, and was made marshal of France by King Charles VII.
However, after the "Maid of Orléans" was burned alive as a

witch-heretic in 1431, Rais changed drastically in character, shut himself up in his castle in Brittany, and developed an obsessive interest in alchemy and satanism. With help from servants, he abducted children (mainly boys) and sadistically tortured and killed them at his court. Offering his victims to the devil, he was said to have ejaculated into them at the moment they died. His killings became known to the bishop of Nantes, who tried Rais in an ecclesiastical court and gained his confession, under threat of torture, to having mutilated and murdered more than 100 children (some claim his victims numbered as many as 800). Rais was then handed over to a civil court which sentenced him to death, along with his two closest associates Poitou and Henriet, who had confessed under torture to the crimes. On October 26, 1440, the three were hanged outside the city of Nantes; Rais died having asked for forgiveness (which the bishop gave) and having resigned himself to his fate as a penitent Christian.

RALSTON, James W. See WILBY, Ralph Marshall.

RANN, Jack or John (d. 1774). English highwayman. Nicknamed "Sixteen-String Jack" because of the 16 silk strings attached to his buckskin breeches around his knees, Rann was an elegantly dressed highway robber who loved good clothes, bad women, and a royal life style. Rann, who teamed up and lived with a stylish whore named Eleanor Roche, was arrested several times but released for lack of evidence. Arrested for the seventh time in 1774, he was found guilty and condemned to die. Rann held a lavish dinner party in his Newgate Prison cell three days before his hanging, which took place before a huge crowd at Tyburn.

RASPUTIN [Novykh], Grigory Yefimovich (1872?-1916). Siberian-born Russian mystic and profligate. As a youth he joined and later became the leader of a sex cult, the Khlysty (Flagellants), that engaged in weird, frantic orgies. He was given the surname Rasputin, meaning "The Debauched One," because of his depraved life and enormous sexual appetite, which caused him to believe he had divine powers that could work miracles. Branded a heretic by the Church, Rasputin wandered about as a "holy man," preaching a doctrine of religious salvation through sexual indulgence. He seduced many aristocratic Russian women, who endured the stench of Rasputin's body (he sometimes went without a bath for months) all for "purification" or "healing" (mysticism and the occult were in fashion at the time). In 1905 in St. Petersburg, Rasputin miraculously improved the condition of Empress Alexandra's son Alexis, a hemophiliac, gaining a hypnotic hold over the empress and, through her, Emperor Nicholas II, and assuming a powerful position in the Russian court. "The Mad Monk," as Rasputin came to be called, continued his debauchery, with seductions, lavish parties, and mystic faith healings. During World War I, while Nicholas II

was fighting with the Russian army, Alexandra made Rasputin
her chief advisor. He removed many officials who opposed him,
often replacing them with unscrupulous incompetents. In December 1916 right-wing conspirators, including Prince Felix
Yusupov, Grand Duke Dimitry Pavlovich, and Dr. Lazovert,
attempted to assassinate Rasputin. Failing to kill him with
cyanide-laced cakes and wine, they stabbed and shot Rasputin,
tied his wrists and ankles, and dumped him in the frozen Neva
River, where he finally drowned.

RATTLESNAKE DICK. See BARTER, Richard.

RAVAILLAC, François (d. 1610). French assassin. Huguenot
(Protestant) leader Henry of Navarre was crowned King Henry
IV of France in 1594, having abjured Calvinism and converted
apparently to Roman Catholicism the year before (the latter religion was predominant in the kingdom). Although he brought
prosperity to France, many militant Catholics remained uncon-
vinced of Henry's religious sincerity (he signed the Edict of
Nantes [1598] which granted qualified freedom of worship to the
Huguenots). In the early afternoon of May 14, 1610, while riding in his carriage through the streets of Paris, Henry was assaulted by a religious fanatic named François Ravaillac, who
jumped aboard the carriage when it slowed down in the narrow
Rue de la Ferronnerie and twice plunged a long knife into the
king. Henry perished as his coach hastened to the Louvre
palace. The assassin was nearly slain by the king's guards
but they were stopped by the duke of Épernon (Henry's companion in the coach), who inflicted murderous torture on Ravaillac afterward. Tied to a cross, Ravaillac's right hand was slowly burned off; large open wounds made by hot irons on his body
were filled with hot oil and lead. At the end he was decapitated.

RAY, James Earl (b. 1928). American assassin. In the 1950s and
1960s he served time in prison for armed robbery. Ray escaped
from the Missouri State prison in April 1967 and was a fugitive
when he shot and killed civil rights leader Dr. Martin Luther
King in Memphis, Tennessee, on April 4, 1968. Immediately
after the assassination, Ray fled to Canada and then a month
later to London. He took a mysterious trip to Lisbon, Portugal, for five days and then returned to England. On June 8,
1968, London police, informed by the FBI that Ray was King's
assassin, arrested Ray at the Heathrow Airport just before he
was to fly to Brussels. After being extradited to the United
States, Ray pleaded guilty to murdering King and was sentenced
to 99 years in prison. He soon reversed his plea, dropped his
original lawyer, and retained a new one. In 1977 Ray and six
other prisoners broke out of the Bushy Mountain State Prison in
Tennessee but were shortly recaptured. In 1978 a House committee suggested that Ray, who had no apparent reason for killing King and had been obviously well-financed during his escape
afterward, was in "likelihood" involved in a conspiracy.

RAYNOR, William P. (d. 1884). Texas gunfighter. Raynor, a dandy with a fast draw, had killed eight men in gun duels when he strode into the Gem Saloon in El Paso, Texas, on April 14, 1884. A gunfight broke out between him and Bob Rennick, who was playing faro in the saloon's gambling room with Bob Cahill. Rennick was not hit, but Raynor, with two bullets in him, staggered into the street and collapsed beside Wyatt Earp, a visitor in town, asking him to tell his mother that he "died game." Raynor's friend Buck Linn thought Cahill had fatally wounded Raynor and immediately vowed revenge. Cahill, who had never fired a shot in his life, received a quick lesson in gunfighting from Earp and managed miraculously to kill Linn in a gunfight without getting shot himself. Raynor died an hour later in an El Paso doctor's office.

READ, Mary (d. 1721). English pirate. Disguised as a cabin boy, Read joined the British Navy and sailed aboard a man-of-war. Later, after serving as a soldier, again pretending to be a male, during the War of the Spanish Succession (1701-14), Read married a young Flemish innkeeper and settled in Holland. When her husband suddenly died, she ran away to sea, disguised as a male sailor. The Dutch ship she was on was later captured by the pirate Captain Jack RACKHAM. Pressed into pirate service, Read and Anne BONNY, who both dressed in men's clothing, helped Rackham plunder ships in the West Indies. In late October 1720, Read was caught, along with the rest of Rackham's pirate crew, by the British off the coast of Jamaica. She and Bonny had fought bravely while Rackham and the other male pirates lay in a drunken stupor below decks. Taken to San Jago de la Vega, Jamaica, Read and Bonny were tried on November 28, 1720, one week after Rackham and the other pirates were hanged. Their pleas of pregnancy kept them from the gallows. Mary died in prison during childbirth.

REAVIS, James Addison (d. 1908). American forger and swindler. In the late 1860s he skillfully forged real-estate documents in St. Louis to earn large commissions. To escape arrest, Reavis moved to Santa Fe, New Mexico, where he began to forge ancient Mexican and Spanish land claims alleging that vast tracts of land in Arizona territory were deeded to Miguel Silva de Peralta, a fictional Spanish nobleman Reavis invented. In the 1870s Reavis, who worked as a legal records clerk, made fraudulent documents to prove the existence of Peralta and his descendants and traveled to Madrid, Seville, Mexico City, and other places where he planted his false papers about the Peralta family in state libraries, archives, and monasteries. In 1881 Reavis publicly declared himself to be Baron de Arizonaca and Caballero de los Colorados, husband of the last of the fictional Peraltas, a young Mexican woman whom he had sent to finishing school and married (she came to believe she really was a Peralta descendant). Reavis laid claim to 10.8 million acres of

Arizona territory, including the city of Phoenix, and filed his claim with the Surveyor General of the United States. Legal experts said his documents were valid. For years hundreds of businesses and thousands of families on his supposed land paid rent to Reavis, who collected more than $10 million. In 1894 Reavis was exposed as a fraud after the documents were shown to have been doctored. He was tried, convicted of forgery and fraud, and sent to prison for six years. Released in 1901, Reavis was penniless and lived as a vagrant in Phoenix until his death seven years later.

REED, Ed[ward] (1871-95). American horse thief, lawman, and murderer. He was born out of wedlock, the son of Belle STARR and Jim REED. Ed, like both of his parents, engaged in horse stealing in Texas and Oklahoma. Although he was never con-victed, he was suspected of killing his mother, who had often whipped her son with a bull whip and with whom he allegedly had an incestuous relationship. Ironically, in about 1894 Ed became a deputy sheriff at Fort Smith, Arkansas, and soon af-ter killed two former lawmen for being drunk. He himself was shot dead during a brawl in a saloon.

REED, Jim (c. 1845-74). American horse thief, stage robber, and outlaw. He began to live with Belle STARR in Texas in 1869. The pair trekked to California to engage in stagecoach robbery. After attacking and robbing a prospector of $30,000 in gold, they returned to Texas, where Belle bought a ranch and began to play "Bandit Queen." Reed struck out on his own and soon joined Tom STARR and his band of horse thieves in Oklahoma. In August, 1874, Reed was shot and killed by Deputy Sheriff John T. Morris, who once rode with Reed as a stage robber. See also REED, Ed[ward].

REED, [Nathaniel] "Texas Jack" (1862-1950). American bank, stage, and train robber. Between about 1885 and 1895 he and several accomplices successfully held up banks, stagecoaches, and ex-press trains in Texas, California, Colorado, and the Arizona territory. While attempting to rob a train in the Oklahoma ter-ritory, they were ambushed by a posse led by Deputy U.S. Marshal Bud Ledbetter. Reed, who was severely wounded in the ensuing gun battle, managed to escape but was later cap-tured. Sentenced to prison, he was paroled about two years later, reformed himself, and established a road-show called "Texas Jack, Train Robber" that toured the country (at the start of his robbery career, he had taken the sobriquet "Texas Jack" because it sounded tough, the right name for an outlaw). The road-show was highly profitable, and later Reed wrote an autobiography, The Life of Texas Jack, of which some 70,000 copies were sold. He lived to a ripe old age, dying in Okla-homa City, Oklahoma, in 1950.

REES, Melvin David (1933-61). American rapist and mass murderer.
In Maryland and Virginia in the late 1950s, Rees murdered nine
persons, mainly women whom he brutally raped before strangling
or shooting them. A massive FBI dragnet produced information
that led to Rees's arrest in 1959. In a police line-up, a U.S.
Army sergeant identified Rees as the killer of his girlfriend,
Margaret Harold, near Annapolis, Maryland, in June 1957. Notes
written by Rees were found in his home describing his sadistic
sex crimes against women, especially the rape and slaying of
Carroll Jackson in January 1959. Rees, labelled the "Sex Beast"
by the press, was tried by the state of Virginia, found guilty,
and executed in 1961.

REIS, Arturo Alves (1896-1955). Portuguese con man and forger.
Aided by others, he audaciously forged letters and documents
which induced the esteemed London firm of Waterlow & Sons,
Ltd., the official printers of Portuguese currency, to print
much new money for the Bank of Portugal, which he pretended
to represent (February 1925). Reis said the money (eventually
more than $10 million worth of 500-escudo bank notes) was des-
ignated exclusively for the Portuguese African colony of Angola,
but he deftly manipulated it into his accounts and even started
his own private bank in London. The scam was uncovered because of serial-number duplication, and finally Reis was placed
on trial for fraud and forgery in May 1930. Found guilty, he
was imprisoned for eight years and later died in poverty.

REISER, Charles (1878-1921). American safecracker and burglar.
Nicknamed "The Ox" because of his large size and enormous
strength, Reiser was the best safecracker (an expert in the
use of nitroglycerine) in the United States in the first decades
of the century. A number of times he was charged with burglary in Chicago and Seattle but managed to beat the rap when
witnesses were killed or disappeared. During World War I,
Reiser, who lived a double life under the name of Shopes as a
respectable family and community man, hooked up with Chicago
gangster Charles Dion O'BANNION and successfully cracked
safes, netting large sums of money. During an attempted robbery of a Chicago storage firm on October 10, 1921, Reiser
killed the watchman but received two bullet wounds, one through
the lungs, and was caught. Hospitalized, he supposedly committed suicide (according to his wife, who had visited him in the
hospital just moments before he was found with ten bullets in
him). Because both his right hand and left arm had been
broken in the robbery attempt, the wife's story was suspicious.
However, a coroner's jury concurred with her. She inherited
Reiser's estate of over $100,000 which, according to some odd
press reports, would have been confiscated and handed over to
his past burglary victims if Reiser had been convicted.

RELES, Abe (1907-41). American gangster, murderer, and police informer. In the 1930s he was a member of Murder, Inc., the national crime syndicate's enforcement squad. During that time, Reles, nicknamed "Kid Twist," was arrested on various charges, including murder, robbery, burglary, and possession of narcotics. Taken into police custody in the spring of 1940 on a homicide charge, he became one of the most famous police informants in underworld history, hoping to save his own skin on a promise of immunity from prosecution made by New York City's district attorney. In his courtroom testimony, Reles admitted to killing dozens of people; gave explicit details about the coast-to-coast, murder-for-profit business of Murder, Inc., introducing the words "contracts" (assignments to kill), "hits" (actual killings), and "bums" (victims); and named his accomplices, such as Mafia boss Louis "Lepke" BUCHALTER, Harry STRAUSS, Frank "Dasher" ABBANDANDO, Buggsy Goldstein, and Happy Maione, and important syndicate leaders, such as Charles "Lucky" LUCIANO and Albert ANASTASIA. A much hated stool pigeon, Reles was kept under heavy police protection at the Half Moon Hotel in Brooklyn's Coney Island section while he testified in 1941. On November 12, 1941, he jumped, fell, or was thrown out of the sixth-floor window of the hotel to his death. The underworld sighed in relief, but Reles's testimony doomed many mobsters.

REMUS, George B. (1874-1952). Ohio bootlegger and lawyer acquitted of murder. Although he served years in the Atlanta federal penitentiary on a conviction of bootlegging, Remus is best remembered for a bizarre murder trial in Ohio in 1927. After his release from prison, he was soon brought to trial for the shooting death of his wife, whom he claimed had been unfaithful during his time behind bars. Remus, a disbarred lawyer, defended himself, pleading not guilty on grounds of insanity. The foolish testimony of his witnesses, who said he was unbalanced and dangerous, finally convinced the jury to acquit Remus by reason of insanity; the prosecution, however, persuaded the judge to commit the defendant to a state mental institution because of his supposed threat to the public. About four months later, Remus appealed his case, proved he was sane, and was let go.

RENDALL, Martha (d. 1909). Australian poisoner. Between 1906 and 1909 she was married to one Thomas Morris, a railroad worker in Western Australia. During that period three of the Morris children by Thomas's first wife, whom he had thrown out because of her chaotic ways, died in agony, all complaining beforehand of sore throats. In April 1909 the youngster George Morris told authorities that his stepmother would kill him if allowed to swab his throat with muriatic (hydrochloric) acid, as she had often done with the other Morris youngsters. Found guilty of poisoning the children, apparently because of jealousy over her husband's love for them, Martha Rendall became the first and only woman hanged in Western Australia when she was executed in Fremantle in 1909.

RENO, Frank (1837-68). American robber and outlaw. He and his brothers John, Simeon, and William, accompanied by several other men, committed the first train robbery in America on October 6, 1866, when they held up the Ohio and Mississippi railroad near Seymour, Indiana, and stole $10,000 in cash and gold from the Adams Express car. Frank, the eldest Reno brother, led the gang across the Midwest, robbing trains, banks, post offices, and county treasury offices from 1866 to 1868. To escape vigilantes and Pinkerton detectives, Frank and four of his men fled to Canada but were soon arrested there and brought back to Indiana to stand trial. On December 11, 1868, vigilantes broke into the New Albany, Indiana, jail, seized Frank, Simeon, William, and Carl Anderson (one of the Reno gang), and hanged them mercilessly from the ceiling beam in the jail. See also RENO, John; RENO, Simeon or Simon; RENO, William.

RENO, John (1839-?). American robber and outlaw. In 1866 and 1867 he was second in command of the vicious Reno gang, which brazenly robbed trains and county treasury offices in Indiana, Iowa, Missouri, and other states. In the spring of 1867 the Renos robbed the Daviess, Missouri, county treasury of $22,000 and rode home to Seymour, Indiana, with the Pinkerton detectives hot on their trail. Shortly afterward, the Pinkertons grabbed John at the Seymour train station, hustled him aboard a train pulling out of town, and delivered him to authorities. John was sent to jail for two years, during which time the Reno gang was caught and some members lynched. See also RENO, Frank; RENO, Simeon or Simon; RENO, William.

RENO, Simeon or Simon (1843-68). American robber and outlaw. An important member of the notorious Reno gang, Simeon took part in numerous train and bank robberies in the Midwest from 1866 to 1868. With his brother Frank and other gang members, Simeon fled to Windsor, Canada, to escape being lynched by a vigilante committee from Indiana. However, they were soon caught and returned to Indiana for trial. On December 11, 1868, Simeon was dragged from his cell in the New Albany, Indiana, jail and hanged by vigilantes. After the vigilantes left, Simeon suddenly revived and fought to free himself from the rope that was choking him. He slowly strangled to death. See also RENO, Frank; RENO, John; RENO, William.

RENO, William (1848-68). American robber and outlaw. He was the youngest member of brutal Reno gang of Seymour, Indiana, and helped rob the Ohio and Mississippi train outside Seymour in 1866 (the first train robbery in the history of the United States), the county treasury in Daviess, Missouri, in 1867, the Harrison

Bank in Magnolia, Iowa, in 1868, and the Jefferson, Missouri, and Indianapolis train near Marshfield, Indiana, in 1868. Possemen caught William soon after the latter robbery and threw him in the New Albany, Indiana, jail. On December 11, 1868, vigilantes stormed the jail and hanged him, along with his brothers Frank and Simeon and Reno-gang member Carl Anderson, all of whom were being held there for trial. See also RENO, Frank; RENO, John; RENO, Simeon or Simon.

RESTELL, Madame [real name: Ann Trow Lohman] (1812-78). English-born New York abortionist and purveyor of contraceptives. In the nineteenth century, when abortion and contraception were considered illicit and immoral, Madame Restell operated a business on New York City's Greenwich Street that sold contraceptives, performed abortions, and served as a maternity hospital for pregnant women. She was called "the wickedest woman in the city" and served short stints in jail for various offenses. For nearly 40 years, through large payoffs to police, Madame Restell stayed in business and accumulated a fortune while living in a mansion on Fifth Avenue with her husband, Charles R. Lohman, a quack doctor who dispensed sundry medicines that supposedly prevented pregnancy and aborted fetuses. In 1878, facing charges of possession and selling of contraceptives, Madame Restell became gravely despondent over the adverse effect the trial would have on her adored grandchildren and committed suicide in her bathtub by cutting her throat with a knife. Her legacy totaled $1 million.

RIBBENTROP, Joachim von (1893-1946). German Nazi foreign minister and war criminal. In 1932 Ribbentrop, a wealthy champagne merchant, joined the German National Socialist (Nazi) party led by Adolf HITLER, who made him his chief foreign policy adviser after the Nazis came to power in 1933. As German ambassador-at-large (1935-36), he negotiated the Anglo-German agreement of 1935 that permitted Germany's naval rearmament; he then served as ambassador to Great Britain (1936-38) and developed into a rabid Anglophobe. Ribbentrop was instrumental in forging the Rome-Berlin Axis (1936) that strengthened the tie between Hitler and Italian fascist Benito MUSSOLINI. In 1938 he succeeded Konstantin von NEURATH as foreign minister; later Ribbentrop successfully forged a nonaggression pact with Joseph STALIN of the Soviet Union (August 1939), paving the way for Germany's invasion of Poland and the start of World War II (1939-45). The Italo-German-Japanese alliance of 1940 (Tripartite Pact) was signed by Ribbentrop, who faithfully carried out Hitler's orders until Germany's collapse and defeat in 1945. Arrested by the Allies in Hamburg on June 14, 1945, he was tried and convicted by the Nuremberg war-crimes tribunal, which found him guilty on all counts. Ribbentrop was hanged at Nuremberg, West Germany, on October 16, 1946.

RICCA, Paul [born: Felice DeLucia] (1897-1972). Italian murderer
and Chicago gangster. In 1919 Ricca fled from Italy to the
United States to avoid prosecution for murder in Naples (he was
convicted in absentia and given a 21-year sentence). He worked
as a Mafia henchman for Al CAPONE in Chicago in the 1920s
and became an underboss to Capone's successor Frank "The Enforcer" NITTI in the early 1930s. In about 1940 Ricca took control of the Chicago mob. In 1943 he and other gangsters, including Louis "Little New York" Campagna and Phil D'Andrea,
were convicted of attempting to extort about $1 million from the
motion-picture industry; they were given ten-year prison terms.
Ricca, known to have influence with many politicians, managed
to be paroled in 1947 (arrested more than 12 times during his
life for conspiracy, income-tax evasion, mail fraud, falsification
of papers for U.S. citizenship, and other charges, Ricca went
to prison several times but always managed to serve short sentences). In 1950 the U.S. Senate Crime Investigating Committee
under Estes Kefauver named Ricca the "national head of the
crime syndicate." Ricca, nicknamed "The Waiter" because he
once waited on tables and cited that as his occupation at immi-
gration hearings, was stripped of his U.S. citizenship in 1957
and ordered deported in 1959. Through many appeals, Ricca
remained in the country and discouraged Italy and other foreign
countries from taking him in by sending foreign government
officials news clippings about his criminal activities in the United
States. He died of natural causes in Chicago on October 11,
1972.

RICHARDSON, Levi (1851-79). American gunfighter. He killed
several men in gun duels, earning a reputation as a fast draw
with a .44-caliber Remington pistol. In Dodge City, Kansas, in
1879 Richardson and "Cockeyed" Frank LOVING argued over a
dance-hall girl whom they both loved. On April 5, 1879, they
goaded each other into a gunfight at Dodge City's Long Branch
Saloon. Richardson, after fanning his gun in amateur fashion,
fired off five shots and missed Loving at close range; Loving
then emptied his gun into Richardson, killing him instantly.
Loving was arrested but soon released on grounds of self-
defense.

RICHARDSON, Thomas F. See McGINNIS, [Joseph Francis] "Big
Joe."

RINGO, Johnny [born: John Ringgold?] (1844?-82). American gunfighter and outlaw. In the 1870s he rode with Scott Cooley, an
ex-Texas Ranger turned outlaw, and participated in the 1875
Mason County War in Texas (a feud between cattlemen) that resulted in the killing of at least a dozen men and the wounding
of many more. Ringo, a brooding, silent type of gunslinger
who was college educated and reputedly came from a genteel
Southern family, became a member of the Clanton gang and a

bitter enemy of Wyatt EARP and his brothers in Tombstone,
Arizona (he was not present during the famous gunfight at the
O.K. Corral, but he did ride with "Old Man" CLANTON during
the 1881 Guadalupe Canyon Massacre, helping kill a number of
Mexicans and rob $75,000 in silver bullion from a Mexican mule
train). Ringo indulged himself in senseless killings and earned
the wrath of numerous people on both sides of the law. In 1882
he began drinking heavily and, that summar, was found dead
in Arizona's Turkey Creek Canyon with a bullet through his
head. Suspected of being Ringo's killer were Frank "Buckskin"
LESLIE, a fellow gunfighter who had turned against Ringo;
JOHNNY BEHIND THE DEUCE, a gambler who supposedly shot
him in retribution; and Wyatt Earp, who believed Ringo helped
murder his brother Morgan Earp in February 1882. Who killed
Ringo remains a mystery today.

RINTELEN, Franz von (d. 1949). German saboteur, spy, and labor
agitator. Under the pretense of setting up a supposedly legitimate American import-export company in New York City in 1915,
Captain von Rintelen, disguised as a businessman when he entered the U.S. earlier that year, proceeded to carry out important sabotage of war supplies being shipped abroad to the Allies
in Europe during World War I (the United States was a neutral
nation at the time). His incendiary devices secretly placed in
the holds of cargo ships caused "accidental" fires at sea, forcing the sailors to jettison ammunition needed by the Allies.
Rintelen, whose company profited from Allied contracts, also
organized a militant labor union that fomented strikes in the
U.S. While returning to Germany he was held under arrest in
England, having been exposed by another German agent, and in
1917 was sent back to the U.S., where he was imprisoned. Set
free in 1920, he returned to Germany but later settled in England, where he died in 1949.

ROB ROY [real name: Robert MacGregor] (1671-1734). Scottish
Highland outlaw. When the Scottish parliament renewed pro-
scription against the MacGregor clan in 1693, he assumed his
mother's name, Campbell, and continued his career as a freebooter, rustling cattle and exacting tribute for protection
against thieves. The name Rob Roy ("Red Rob") was given
him because of his dark red hair and ruddy complexion. On
his inherited Highland territory, Balquhidder, he raised cattle
for the English market until 1712, when he fell deeply in debt
to the duke of Montrose, from whom he had borrowed large
sums for unsuccessful speculative ventures. Deprived of his
land by the duke, Rob Roy, noted for his skill with the sword
and his strength, took to brigandage with vengeance, especially
against Montrose. During the Jacobite Rebellion of 1715, he
and his armed men plundered both English and Scottish nobles.
In 1717 Rob Roy was captured but escaped and carried on his
exploits against Montrose until 1722, when he was arrested and

imprisoned in Newgate Prison, London. Sentenced in 1727 to be transported to Barbados, he was given a pardon and returned to Balquhidder, where he lived until his death on December 28, 1734. His outlawry is described in Sir Walter Scott's novel Rob Roy (1818).

ROBERTS, Bartholomew (c. 1682-1722). Welsh pirate. After about 20 years of honest seamanship, Roberts turned to piracy aboard Howell DAVIS's ship in 1719. He was made captain when Davis was slain. Roberts, or "Black Bart" as he came to be known, plundered ships throughout the Atlantic Ocean and the Caribbean. Around the 28-gun flagship Royal Fortune he built a daring pirate fleet that reportedly captured and looted more than 400 ships in less than four years. His pirates revered him for his brains and courage. The British warship H.M.S. Swallow under Captain Chaloner Ogle pursued Roberts's pirate fleet for many months and finally cornered it near Cape Lopez on the Gulf of Guinea in West Africa (February 1722). During a ferocious battle, Roberts was killed. Later 52 members of his crew were hanged at Cape Coast Castle on the Guinea Gulf.

ROBIN HOOD (1200s?). English outlaw. According to various accounts, he lived with loyal followers in either Sherwood Forest in Nottinghamshire or in the woodlands of Barnsdale in neighboring Yorkshire-West Riding. Robin Hood evidently led his band in rebellion against the central government's laws restricting forest hunting rights. English officials, notably the sheriff of Nottingham, and wealthy ecclesiastical landowners were robbed and sometimes killed by the rebels, who also earned money levying tolls on travelers and freely hunted the deer of the forests. (The sheriff of Nottingham was shot dead by the rebels' arrows and decapitated.) Women and the poor were never preyed upon and were often helped by Robin Hood, who reputedly robbed the rich to help the poor and came to be portrayed in legend as chivalrous and good-natured, despite his streak of cruelty toward lawmen and rich clergymen. His band's chief members, according to some 30 medieval English ballads which are the only evidence of Robin Hood's existence, were Little John (his chief archer), Friar Tuck, George-a-Greene, William Scathlock, and Maid Marion (his lady love). A treacherous cousin, a prioress pretending to help Robin Hood when he had a fever, caused him to bleed to death through bloodletting. Today he is conjecturally identified as an early Saxon leader, an early earl of Huntingdon, an outlaw follower of Simon de Montfort, or a thirteenth-century agrarian rebel.

ROBINSON, Henrietta (1816-1905). New York poisoner. An enigmatic beauty whose origins and early career were obscure (perhaps a patrician emigrant from Ireland, England, or France who became the abandoned mistress or wife of a New York City politician or millionaire), Henrietta Robinson settled in the early

1850s in Troy, New York, where her odd and secretive behavior was the gossip of the citizenry. In May 1853 she was charged with fatally poisoning Timothy Lanagan, who had publicly upbraided her for some highhandedness. Arsenic was found both in Lanagan's body and hidden in Henrietta's cottage. At her sensational trial, she wore an elegant black silk dress and several heavy blue lace veils over her face, thus becoming known as "the Veiled Murderess." She lifted the veils only for seconds to allow witnesses to identify her, maintained an aura of mystery, and was found guilty of the murder. After the New York governor's commutation of her death sentence to life imprisonment, Henrietta was taken to Sing Sing (Ossining Correctional Facility), where she became a model prisoner. Transferred to Auburn prison in 1873, she attempted to kill herself in 1890 and consequently was sent to an institution for the criminally insane, where she died of old age 15 years later. No woman in U.S. history has remained incarcerated longer than Henrietta's 52 years.

ROBINSON, Sarah Jane [Tennent] (d. 1905). Irish-born Massachusetts mass poisoner. A strong-headed woman living in Cambridge, Massachusetts, she used arsenic poison to kill seven persons (six relatives and a landlord) and received money from life insurance on family members. In the 1880s her husband and two children, as well as her sister, brother-in-law, and their son, perished from eating poisoned food (Sarah Jane, hoping to marry her wealthy brother-in-law, killed her sister and later the brother-in-law after he rejected her marriage proposal). Later an insurance investigator, suspicious of Sarah Jane, had the graves dug up and discovered poison in the bodies. Tried and convicted of murder, Sarah Jane spent the rest of her life in prison.

ROC THE BRAZILIAN (fl. 1660s-70s). Brazilian-born pirate. As a young man, Roc, whose actual name is unknown, turned to piracy first as a crew member aboard a pirate ship and then as captain of his own vessel. His vicious plundering of Spanish settlements and merchant ships and torturing of prisoners made him notoriously feared throughout the Caribbean. Much of the rich loot he seized was brought to Jamaica, where he frequently cavorted drunkenly with his companion buccaneers. While attempting to pillage the Mexican town of Mérida in Yucatán, Roc and a French buccaneer named Tributor, accompanied by their crews, were overwhelmed by Spanish cavalry and a cannonade from the garrison there. Tributor and many other pirates were slain; Roc fled safely from the region. His activities afterward are obscure, with reports that he lived on Jamaica and other islands.

ROGERS, George W. (1898-1958). New Jersey hero and murderer. On September 8, 1934, the U.S. steamship Morro Castle, en

route from Havana, Cuba, to New York, caught fire off Asbury
Park, New Jersey. Rogers, the ship's radioman, sent SOS signals that brought help and saved many lives (134 passengers,
however, died in the fire). Four years later Rogers, an ac-
claimed hero, severely wounded his supervisor at the Bayonne,
New Jersey, police radio bureau in a bomb attack (he wanted to
take over his supervisor's job) and was sentenced to 12 to 20
years in the New Jersey State Prison at Trenton. Paroled in
1942, Rogers later fell deeply in debt to William Hummel, whom
he clubbed to death along with Hummel's unmarried daughter, in
Bayonne in 1953. Again sent to the Trenton prison, Rogers
died there of a heart attack on January 10, 1958. Evidence
later showed that he may actually have started the fire on the
Morro Castle and that his apparent heroism was a cover-up.

ROMAINE, Henry G. (?). New York grave robber. In 1876 Alexander T. Stewart, a New York department-store owner, died, leaving an estimated $30-million estate. His body, buried on the
church grounds of St. Mark's-in-the-Bouwerie, was dug up and
stolen in mid-November 1876. The grave robbing was widely
publicized, and the Stewart family offered $25,000 reward for
the recovery of the body and the capture of the robber. In
January 1877 a ransom note signed by a "Henry G. Romaine"
was delivered to the Stewarts demanding $200,000 for the return
of Alexander's body. After negotiations, Romaine was given
$20,000 for the remains of Alexander. Romaine was never
caught. Some people believe he was actually bank robber
George Leonidas LESLIE or master thief "Travelling Mike"
GRADY, but it remains a mystery today.

ROSE, Della [real name: Laura Bullion] (1873-after 1906). American outlaws' accomplice. A pretty dance-hall girl, she hooked
up with the outlaws at the Hole in the Wall, an outlaw hideout
on the Wyoming-Utah border, and rode with them on numerous
raids. After 1896 she hung around with the Wild Bunch, joining them during their robberies and becoming known as the "Rose
of the Bunch." In November 1901 she and Ben KILPATRICK,
one of the Wild Bunch, were captured in St. Louis; they were
found with part of the money stolen from a train at Wagner,
Montana, in July of that year. Kilpatrick received 15 years in
prison; Rose, convicted as an accomplice, was sentenced to five
years in a Tennessee women's prison. Rose disappeared after
her release in 1906. See also CASSIDY, Butch.

ROSE, Fred [born: Fred Rosenberg] (b. 1906). Polish-born Canadian politician and Soviet spy. After coming to Canada in the
mid-1920s, he became prominent in the country's Communist party
and, around 1920, secretly entered into spy work for the Soviets.
Rose, his assumed name, was active in Canadian politics while
helping to mount an effective intelligence operation in Ottawa,
Montreal, and Toronto. In 1942, however, he repudiated verbally

all Communist party agitation, which may possibly have helped him win election to the Canadian Parliament in 1943 and reelection in 1945 as a member of the Labor Progressive party (organized in 1942 as a cover for the Communist party). During this time Rose and Sam CARR were the two key Canadians in a large Soviet-controlled spy apparatus obtaining confidential technical, economic, and political information for the Kremlin. After the Ottawa-based Soviet spy and defector Igor Gouzenko exposed the espionage ring in the fall of 1945, Rose was apprehended, tried, and sentenced to six years in prison. See also MAY, Alan Nunn.

ROSE MAN OF SING SING. See CHAPIN, Charles.

ROSE OF CIMARRON. See NEWCOMB, George "Bitter Creek."

ROSELLI, John [born: Fellippo Sacco] (1905-76). Italian-born American gangster, extortionist, and racketeer. In the 1930s he was a Mafia mobster in California and later became the national syndicate boss of the West Coast. In 1944 Roselli was found guilty of extorting $1 million from Hollywood motion-picture studios (he threatened to have Mafia-controlled stage workers slow down movie production). Roselli, head of various gambling rackets, ran the Sans Souci gambling casino in Havana, Cuba, in the 1950s (later, in 1975, he testified before a special U.S. Senate committee that he and Sam "Momo" GIANCANA had been recruited by the CIA to assassinate Fidel Castro). In 1968 Roselli and four others were convicted of swindling some $400,000 from members of the Friars Club, to which he belonged. In 1976 Roselli's dead, decomposed body was found sealed in an empty 55-gallon oil drum floating in the ocean off the Florida coast.

ROSEN, Joseph or "Doc." See STACHER, Joseph "Doc."

ROSENBERG, Alfred (1893-1946). Estonian-born German Nazi leader, writer, and war criminal. In 1919 he fled to Munich, Germany, to avoid arrest for counterrevolutionary speeches in his native Reval (Tallinn, Estonia), then a part of Russia. Soon joining the nascent German National Socialist (Nazi) party, Rosenberg became editor of the party newspaper, Völkischer Beobachter, in which he fanatically expounded Nazi doctrines of racial inequality (the Nordic, Germanic, or Aryan "master race" must dominate the Blacks, Jews, and other inferior races) and nationalist expansion (necessary conquest by Germany of adjoining lands). Rosenberg wrote a number of books, including Der Mythus des 20. Jahrhunderts (The Myth of the Twentieth Century), whose pseudoscientific ideas greatly influenced Adolf HITLER and helped establish Hitler's rabid anti-Semitism and other prejudices as well as fueled his desire for world domination. During World War II (1939-45) Rosenberg directed the

removal of captured art from France to Germany. In 1941 he
was appointed Reichsminister for the occupied territories in
eastern Europe. After the war the International Military Tribunal convicted Rosenberg on all four of its counts of war
crimes, including a wide variety of crimes against persons and
property. He was hanged in Nuremberg, West Germany, on
October 16, 1946.

ROSENBERG, Ethel [Greenglass] (1915-53). Convicted American
spy. She and her husband, Julius ROSENBERG, were accused
of helping turn over U.S. atomic secrets to the Soviet Union
and were brought to trial in March 1951. The federal government claimed that the Rosenbergs gained possession of military
data through Ethel's brother, David Greenglass, who worked at
the Los Alamos, New Mexico, atomic bomb project in 1944-45.
It was also stated that the data were passed to the Soviet vice
consul in New York City through espionage courier Harry GOLD,
who had earlier been arrested in connection with British-
Communist spy Klaus FUCHS and had been sentenced to 30
years' imprisonment on December 9, 1950. The jury found the
Rosenbergs guilty (March 29, 1951) under the Espionage Act of
1917, and U.S. District Court Judge Irving Robert Kaufman
sentenced them to death (April 5, 1951). Subsequently appealing the verdict and pleading for executive clemency without
success, the convicted couple (both were native-born Americans)
bravely said goodbye to their two young sons and went to their
electrocution at Sing Sing (Ossining Correctional Facility), New
York, on June 19, 1953. They proclaimed their innocence to
the end.

ROSENBERG, Julius (1918-53). Convicted American spy. An active
Communist Party member in the late 1930s and an electrical engineer who served in the U.S. Army Signal Corps from 1940 to
1945, Julius and his wife, Ethel ROSENBERG, stood trial (March
6-29, 1951) on charges of conspiracy for handing over top-
secret military information to the Soviet Union. The U.S. government claimed that the Rosenbergs had received highly classified data on nuclear weapons from Ethel's brother, Sergeant
David Greenglass, who had worked as an army machinist at the
atomic bomb project in Los Alamos, New Mexico, in 1944-45.
The data had been passed to Harry GOLD, a Swiss-born espionage agent in the United States, who had in turn passed it on to
the Soviet consulate in New York (Gold, apprehended in 1950,
was sentenced to 30 years' imprisonment later that year). Fellow espionage agent Morton SOBELL, who had escaped to Mexico
City but had been extradited to the United States, was tried
along with the Rosenbergs, who were found guilty mainly on the
testimony of Greenglass and his wife (Greenglass was later sentenced to 15 years in prison); Sobell was also convicted and received a 30-year prison term. Condemned to death, the Rosenbergs made several appeals (gaining worldwide attention from

liberals and others who claimed that the strong anti-Communist
political climate had hurt the defense's case), but secured no
clemency from President Harry S. Truman or his successor,
Dwight D. Eisenhower. On June 19, 1953, Julius and Ethel
died in the electric chair at Sing Sing (Ossining Correctional
Facility), New York, becoming the first U.S. citizens executed
for treason during peacetime.

ROTHSTEIN, Arnold (1882-1928). New York gambler, racketeer,
and fixer. Rothstein, an expert poker player and crapshooter,
gambled his way to a fortune as a teenager in New York City,
sometimes taking in $10,000 a week. Money soon made him
powerful, allowing him to buy gambling casinos, nightclubs, and
whorehouses, as well as racehorses. Rothstein, called "Mr.
Big" or "A. R.," became known also as "The Man Uptown" who
could fix anything--a bet, a night in bed with a beautiful showgirl, or a murder. He had many political and police contacts,
as well as gangland friends, such as Jack "Legs" DIAMOND,
Charles "Lucky" LUCIANO, and Waxey GORDON, and always
managed to stay out of trouble with the law. Rothstein was allegedly involved in the Black Sox Scandal of 1919, when eight
Chicago White Sox baseball players were bribed to throw the
World Series to the Cincinnati Reds. In the 1920s Rothstein
operated a liquor importing racket and financed illegal speakeasies (saloons) in New York City. Suddenly and strangely he
fell apart in 1928; he began to look sickly and to lose heavily
on the horses and at the poker tables. From September 8 to 10,
1028, Rothstein lost $320,000 in a poker game with two California
gamblers, "Nigger Nate" Raymond and "Titanic" Thompson. Afterward Rothstein refused to pay up, saying the game had been
fixed. On the night of November 4, 1928, he was found shot to
death at New York's Park Central Hotel. Earlier that day Rothstein had bet more than $500,000 that Herbert Hoover would beat
Al Smith in the U.S. presidential election on November 6, 1928.

RUBY, Jack [real name: Jacob Rubenstein] (1911-67). Dallas murderer. Ruby, owner of a nightclub in Dallas, was reportedly
distraught over the assassination of President John F. Kennedy
in that city on November 22, 1963. Two days later, while Kennedy's presumed assassin Lee Harvey OSWALD was being escorted
by police officers through the basement of the Dallas municipal
building to a waiting car that would take him to the county jail,
Ruby stepped in front of Oswald and, using a .38-caliber revolver, fatally shot him in the abdomen. The murder was seen
live on television. Ruby, who claimed he acted out of patriotism, was convicted of murder and sentenced to death. While
awaiting a retrial on appeal, Ruby, who was then suffering
from cancer, died of a blood clot on his lung on January 3, 1967.

RUDABAUGH, Dave (1841-86). American robber and outlaw. As a
teenager, he began rustling cattle and robbing travelers in

Missouri and Kansas; later he turned to holding up express
trains and seizing payrolls. In the late 1870s he formed the
Dodge City gang and committed a number of crimes in Texas
and the New Mexico territory. Rudabaugh hooked up with
BILLY THE KID in 1880, and late that year both were captured
at Stinking Springs in New Mexico territory. Rudabaugh managed to escape, was caught again, and was sentenced to 40
years' imprisonment. In early December 1881 he escaped from
the San Miguel jail by tunneling under the wall and crossed into
Mexico's Chihuahua province, where he organized an outlaw gang
that plundered the area for the next five years. During a raid
on the town of Parral, the townspeople opened fire on the outlaws, and Rudabaugh was killed. His head was cut off and
mounted on top of a pole during the town's celebration.

RUDENSKY, Morris "Red" [born: Max Motel Friedman] (b. 1908).
American reformed safecracker and robber. He spent time as a
youth in a New York state reformatory, where he was brutalized
and learned how to pick locks and blow up safes. In the 1920s
Rudensky, along with others, went on a robbery spree in the
Midwest, stealing jewelry, bonded whiskey, and money. Finally
caught, Rudensky was sent to Leavenworth, from which he escaped several times (once upside-down, squeezed into a magazine crate shipped from the prison's print shop) but was always
recaptured. In 1929 he stopped a riot in Leavenworth's mess
hall and saved the life of warden Tom White. Rudensky then
totally reformed himself. Transferred to Atlanta, he was made
editor of the prison magazine and won widespread praise for his
work helping convicts rehabilitate themselves. Rudensky was
set free, a responsible citizen; he later became chief locksmith
for the 3M Company in Minneapolis, Minnesota.

RUEF, Abraham (1864-1936). San Francisco political boss. In 1901
Ruef, a lawyer and political bigwig, became head of the newly
formed Union Labor Party, secured the election of Eugene E.
Schmitz, a musicians' union leader, as mayor, and gained political control of the city. San Francisco became a "wide open
city" under the ruling Ruef machine, which accepted bribes by
vice operators, such as brothel owner Jerome BASSITY, who
wanted no interference from the law and other officials. The
newspapers printed many stories about corruption in the city
administration, but to little avail. Finally, in 1908, when San
Francisco was under a reform administration, Ruef was convicted of bribery after a sensational trial and given a 14-year
prison sentence. He served time in San Quentin from 1911 to
1915, when he was paroled as a reformed man and entered the
real estate business.

RULOFF, Edward H. (d. 1871). New York murderer and robber.
In 1846 he apparently killed his wife and child and dropped
their bodies into Lake Cayuga, New York. Convicted of

kidnapping (not murdering) his wife, Ruloff served ten years
in prison, was retried, and this time found guilty of murdering
his child. He escaped from prison before his scheduled hanging
(later an appeals court reversed his death sentence). For a
while Ruloff pretended to be a professor (he had learned several languages while in prison) and gave lectures at colleges
for large fees. He and others turned to robbery, breaking
into stores and offices in New York. In 1870 Ruloff shot and
killed a store clerk during a robbery in Binghamton, New York.
Caught soon afterward, he was convicted of murder and hanged.
(Ruloff's brain was dissected by Cornell University medical
school doctors and compared with that of Daniel Webster!)

RUSSELL, Baldy [real name: William Mitchell] (1853-1928). American murderer, robber, and outlaw. In 1874 his father's ranch
in Texas was raided by the Truitts. He retaliated by invading
the Truitt ranch and shooting down two members of the Truitt
family. Russell's father was blamed for the murders and hanged
by vigilantes, causing Russell to shoot the last Truitt family
member, James Truitt, to death and then become an outlaw and
stagecoach robber in the Southwest. Captured in 1912 and sentenced to life for the Truitt killings, Russell escaped from jail
after a few months and remained a fuigitive for the rest of his
life.

RUSSIAN BILL [real name: William Tattenbaum] (1855-81). Russian-
born American outlaw. He was the son of a rich Russian noblewoman named Countess Telfrin, and while serving as a lieutenant
in the Czar's White Hussars (cavalry regiment), he struck a
superior officer and deserted in order not to face a court-
martial. In 1880 he showed up in Tombstone, Arizona, where
the townspeople dubbed him "Russian Bill" because of his background (doubted by most), fine clothes, and elegant manner.
For about a year Russian Bill rode with "Curly Bill" BROCIUS,
Billy CLANTON, and other outlaws and supposedly participated
in a minor way in several illegal escapades. He broke away to
rustle horses on his own in the New Mexico territory but was
soon caught, promptly tried, convicted, and hanged.

- S -

SACCO, Nicola (1891-1927). Italian-born anarchist. On May 5,
1920 Sacco and Bartolomeo VANZETTI, two Italian immigrants to
the United States and acknowledged anarchists, were arrested
for the murders of a paymaster and a guard during a $15,776
robbery (April 15, 1920) of a shoe factory in South Braintree,
Massachusetts. The pistol found on Sacco was later linked by
ballistics experts to the bullet that killed the guard. On July
14, 1921, Sacco and Vanzetti were found guilty of murder after
a trial in Dedham, Massachusetts. Immediately there were

widespread protests accusing Judge Webster Thayer and the jury
of bias against the politically radical, alien defendants and damning the supposed scientific evidence of experts. In 1925 a condemned gangster said the murders had been committed by the
Morelli gang, not Sacco and Vanzetti. Appeals were made for a
new trial but were denied by the Massachusetts Supreme Court.
Governor Alvan Tufts Fuller appointed a special commission to
study the case (June-August 1927), accepted the commission's
findings that the trial had been fair, and refused clemency for
the two immigrants who had been sentenced to death on April 9,
1927. Despite national and international demonstrations against
the sentence, Sacco and Vanzetti were electrocuted on August 23,
1927. Controversy still swirls about the case, whether justice
was administered or not.

SACH, Amelia (1873-1903). English mass murderer. A seemingly
kind lady, she operated a "nursing home" in London where
desperate, unmarried mothers could deliver their babies and
could supposedly arrange for foster parents to take them, if
they chose, all for special fees. Sach, however, frequently
handed the babies to her simple-minded associate Annie Walters,
who was paid to kill the infants, usually through poisonous
sedation, and dispose of them either by throwing them in the
Thames River or burying them in garbage dumps. Their gruesome practice was uncovered by police in 1902, and Sach and
Walters were convicted of murder and later hanged together,
becoming the first females put to death in Holloway Prison.

SADE, Marquis de [Count Donatien Alphonse François de Sade]
(1740-1814). French aristocrat, debauchee, sadist, and writer.
He gave up a military career at the end of the Seven Years'
War (1756-63), in which he fought, and turned to a life of
debauchery after his marriage to a well-to-do bourgeois girl
(1763). He began having affairs and consorting with prostitutes, many of whom he sexually abused, subjecting them to
brutality and unnatural acts. Public knowledge of his gross
sexual perversion led to his confinement by the authorities in
several institutions: the fort of Pierre-Encise, near Lyons
(1768-69), the dungeon of Vincennes (1777-84), the Bastille in
Paris (1784-89), and the asylum at Charenton (1789-90, 1801-
14). While incarcerated or free, Sade wrote erotic essays,
novels, short stories, and plays (his obscene romances, Justine
and Juliette, are probably his best-known works); the term
"sadism"--receiving sexual gratification by inflicting pain on
others--derived from him. During his last years at the Charenton asylum, Sade had his fellow inmates perform as the actors
in his plays, which he staged in this place of refuge. He died
there on December 2, 1814.

SADIE THE GOAT. See GALLUS MAG.

SAIETTA, Ignazio. See LUPO, Ignazio.

SAINTE-CROIX, Godin de. See BRINVILLIERS, Marie de.

SALOMEN, Edith (1849-after 1908). American con artist and swindler. Around 1870, while publicly posing in Baltimore, Maryland, as the illegitimate daughter of Bavaria's "mad" King
Louis I and his adventuress-mistress Lola Montez, she managed
to dupe a young suitor from one of Maryland's high-society families out of over $200,000 before she was proved a fraud. Later
she began a confidence racket called "hypnotic mysticism,"
married a wealthy gentleman named General Diss Debar, and
operated a notorious séance salon in New York City. Many gullible, affluent persons paid Ann O'Delia Diss Debar (the name
she used) large sums of money for her conjurings of spirits of
the dead until she was exposed as a fraud and imprisoned for
six months. She then divorced her husband, assumed a new
identity as Madame Vera P. Ava, and gave lewd "shows" in
Chicago and other cities, talking about sex and singing and
dancing on stage. Afterward she entered into a number of
bigamous marriages, abandoning husbands after wasting their
money while pretending to be a spiritualist in contact with the
dead. On the run from the law, she moved to Cape Town,
South Africa, briefly selling degrees from a bogus theosophical
university there before moving on to England to carry on her
religious scams. Calling herself "The Swami," she was exposed
by Scotland Yard in 1901 and sent to prison for fraud. Seven
years later she was freed and returned to the United States,
where she soon faded into obscurity.

SALTIS, Joseph "Polock Joe" (fl. 1920-30). Chicago gangster and
bootlegger. During Prohibition Saltis was an important bootlegger and saloon operator on Chicago's southwest side. Although he paid tribute to Al CAPONE and apparently did "rub-
outs" (hired killings) for him, Saltis secretly worked with other
gangsters to put Capone out of business. Saltis employed
Frankie McERLANE, Frank Koncil, and other mobsters to keep
rival bootleggers and gangsters out of his territory. In 1926
and 1927 the Saltis-McErlane gang waged war against Ralph
SHELDON's gang, which was really controlled by Capone.
Saltis, who had become very wealthy from his bootleg operations, retired in 1930 to his country house in Wisconsin (the
nearby town of Saltisville was named for him). See also
O'DONNELL, [Edward] "Spike."

"SANDY FLASH, THE." See FITZPATRICK, James.

SANGERMAN, Joseph (fl. 1921-25). Chicago bomber. Sangerman,
a top manufacturer of barbershop supplies and boss of Chicago's barbers' union, headed a vicious gang called "Sangerman's

Bombers" that carried out numerous terrorist labor bombings
for organized crime and some politicians. Through bombings
he coerced barber shop owners opposed to union rules to fall
into line; his bombers-for-hire participated in bootleg and union
wars between rival mobsters, and one of them, George Matrisciano, who always carried two sticks of dynamite in his pockets,
gained a reputation as Chicago's best bomber. Sangerman was
arrested in 1925 and sent to prison after telling the authorities
all about his bombing-for-profit operation, similar to the Black
Hand extortion racket practiced by Italian and Sicilian gangsters
from about 1890 to 1920. Afraid Matrisciano might be arrested
and testify like Sangerman, union gangsters killed the bloodthirsty bomber in 1925, marking the decline of spectacular bombings as a tactic in the gangland wars. See also SWEENEY, Jim.

SAUCKEL, Fritz (1894-1946). German Nazi leader and war criminal.
    After joining the National Socialist (Nazi) party, Sauckel, a
    German newspaper publisher, was appointed in 1925 as gauleiter
    (Nazi district leader) of the state of Thuringia in central eastern
    Germany. At the onset of the Third Reich (Nazi German state
    under Adolf HITLER) he became governor of Thuringia in 1933,
    and after the outbreak of World War II (1939-45) he was put in
    charge of the entire slave labor program in the German-occupied
    territories. Millions of foreign workers, Slavs, Poles, Czechs,
    and others, were exploited and received atrocious treatment un-
    der Sauckel's orders. After the war, the International Military
    Tribunal convicted Sauckel of war crimes, particularly those
    connected with forced labor. He was hanged in the Nuremberg,
    West Germany, prison on October 16, 1946. See also SPEER,
    Albert.

SAWARD, James [Townshead] (d. c. 1915). British lawyer and
    forger. For years before 1900, Scotland Yard suspected Saward,
    a wellborn barrister, of being a redoubtable expert in the for-
    gery of checks, letters of credit, and other similar documents,
    but police visits to his lodgings in London's Temple area had
    uncovered no incriminating evidence. "Jim the Penman," as
    Saward was nicknamed, baffled bankers and financiers by his
    masterful and clever alterations ("cleaning" or "doctoring") of
    papers that enabled him to gain payments worldwide. He used
    numerous aliases to pass off his handiwork, such as changing
    Ł2,000 to Ł20,000 on a note. Saward tried in vain to go straight
    in London, but was eventually arrested, tried, convicted of
    many counts of forgery, and sentenced to life imprisonment.

SAXE, Susan [Edith] (b. 1947). American terrorist. A Brandeis
    University honor student, she became a radical anti-Vietnam
    War militant and feminist in the late 1960s. Sought in connec-
    tion with a 1970 bank robbery in Boston in which a policeman
    was killed, Saxe was an underground fugitive hunted by the
    FBI, which put her on its Most Wanted List, until 1975, when

she was arrested in Philadelphia. On June 9, 1975, while being tried in federal court in Philadelphia, she unexpectedly pleaded guilty to armed robbery and manslaughter, having been charged with a Philadelphia bank robbery and a federal arsenal break-in at Newburyport, Massachusetts, both committed in 1970. She served about eight years of a 12- to 14-year sentence, gaining release from the State Correctional Facility at Framingham, Massachusetts, in 1982.

SCALISE, Frank (1894-1957). New York gangster. He rose through the Mafia ranks to become underboss to Albert ANASTASIA, Mafia chief in New York. Scalise, nicknamed "Don Chreech," directed operations to recruit new members into the Mafia in the 1950s. Anastasia learned that his number two man, Scalise, was apparently receiving kickbacks of up to $50,000 for successful recruits and issued a "contract" on him. Two unknown gunmen in an automobile fatally shot Scalise in the neck as he stood on a sidewalk in the Bronx in 1957.

SCALISE, John (d. 1929). Sicilian-born Chicago gangster and murderer. He and Albert ANSELMI worked as hired killers for Angelo, Mike, and Tony GENNA, Chicago bootleggers, and received tens of thousands of dollars for numerous "hits" (killings) on rival gangsters and police officers. Scalise and Anselmi were thought to be two of the three gunmen who killed bootlegger Charles Dion O'BANNION in 1924. The murderous pair double-crossed the Gennas and became hit men for Al CAPONE and supposedly took part in the St. Valentine's Day Massacre of 1929. Capone heard that Scalise and Anselmi were plotting against him, had them tied up at a party in honor of the pair, and clubbed them to death with a bat on May 27, 1929.

SCHACHT, Hjalmar H. G. See FUNK, Walther.

SCHIRACH, Baldur von (1907-74). German Nazi leader and war criminal. Schirach, whose mother was an American, claimed he had turned anti-Semite in 1924 after reading a book entitled Eternal Jew by Henry Ford. In 1925 he joined the German National Socialist (Nazi) party led by Adolf HITLER, whom he idolized. Also a follower of Alfred ROSENBERG and Julius STREICHER, Schirach, youthful-looking and handsome, helped organize the Hitler Youth movement and became Youth Leader of the Nazi party (1931) and of the Third Reich, Nazi Germany (1933). Under his leadership the Nazification of German boys and girls took place with all youth organizations incorporated within the Hitler Youth movement, which was organized on para-military lines. Schirach was gauleiter (Nazi district leader) of Vienna from 1940 to 1945 during World War II. In 1946 the Nuremberg International Military Tribunal convicted him of war crimes against humanity, especially crimes against the Jews, and sentenced him to 20 years' imprisonment. Schirach died in 1974.

SCHMID, Charles Howard, Jr. (b. 1942). Arizona murderer. In the early 1960s he hung out in the Speedway Boulevard area of Tucson, Arizona, becoming known for his wild tales and bizarre appearance. In 1964 Schmid raped and killed 15-year-old Alleen Rowe; in 1965 he murdered two sisters, 17-year-old Gretchen and 13-year-old Wendy Fritz. Richard Bruns, to whom Schmid had boasted about the Fritz killings, informed the police, who arrested Schmid. The jury convicted Schmid and sentenced him to death for the Fritz murders (later Schmid pleaded guilty in the Rowe case and was convicted of second-degree murder). Appeals delayed his execution, which was finally nullified by the U.S. Supreme Court's decision to abolish capital punishment. Schmid was resentenced to two life terms in prison. In 1972 Schmid and another inmate broke out of the Arizona State Prison but were soon recaptured.

SCHNAUBELT, Rudolph. See FISCHER, Adolph.

SCHOENFELD, James L. (b. 1951). California kidnapper. On July 15, 1976, three masked armed men stopped a school bus with 26 children aboard near Chowchilla, California, then transported them and their bus driver as prisoners in two vans to a rock quarry near Livermore, California, and entombed the 27 victims in a large moving van buried in the quarry, leaving them with meager food supplies. The kidnappers demanded a $5-million ransom for the release of the hostages, who managed to free themselves after about 30 hours and notified the authorities. The identities of the three kidnappers were discovered, and on July 29, 1976, James Schoenfeld was arrested six days after his 22-year-old younger brother Richard Allen Schoenfeld had given himself up to the police; 24-year-old Frederick N. Woods was caught by Canadian lawmen in Vancouver, British Columbia. The trio pleaded guilty and were convicted of kidnapping in 1977; in 1978 the three were sentenced to mandatory life terms. The life sentences of the elder Schoenfeld, James, and Woods barred parole under a criminal age law.

SCHRANK, John N.(1876-1943). German American would-be assassin. To Schrank, a New York City bartender, ex-president Theodore Roosevelt was "power mad" and "treasonous" for seeking a presidential third term in office as the candidate of the "Bull Moose" party in 1912. Schrank's hostility dated back to the mid-1890s when Roosevelt, then New York City's police commissioner, shut down Schrank's saloon for some weeks because of a city-ordinance violation. With a .38-caliber revolver, Schrank dogged Roosevelt's campaign trail, finally shooting his intended victim in an open car outside the Gilpatrick Hotel in Milwaukee, Wisconsin, on October 14, 1912. Schrank was immediately seized by Roosevelt's secretary and companion, E. E. Martin; Roosevelt survived a minor bullet wound in the chest. Readily admitting the shooting, Schrank was judged insane by psychiatrists and spent the rest of his life in mental institutions.

SCHREUDER, Frances [Bernice] (b. 1938). American socialite and
murderer. A divorcee living in New York City, she was finan-
cially dependent upon her penurious Mormon multimillionaire
father, Franklin Bradshaw, founder of a chain of auto-parts
stores, who lived and worked in Salt Lake City, Utah. Afraid
of eventually being disinherited, which her father had talked
about, Frances instructed and then sent her 17-year-old son,
Marc Francis Schreuder, to kill his 76-year-old grandfather in
Utah. On July 23, 1978, Marc fatally shot Bradshaw in his
Salt Lake City warehouse. For the next three years, he was
not suspected as the killer until the murder weapon, a .357
magnum, was found and traced to him. Marc was found guilty
of second-degree murder in a Salt Lake City court on July 6,
1982. His mother, who fought extradition from New York, was
brought to jury trial in Salt Lake City in September 1983.
Damning testimony against her by her son, who was then serving a prison term of five years to life, helped convict her of
first-degree murder and gain her life imprisonment. This
gruesome case is the subject of Jonathan Coleman's book At
Mother's Request and Shana Alexander's Nutcracker.

SCHROEDER, Irene (1909-31). Pennsylvania robber and murderer.
In late 1929 she and 34-year-old Walter Glenn Dague, both of
whom had deserted their spouses, teamed up together as lovers
and began robbing stores and small banks in western Pennsylvania. While fleeing from a robbery in Butler, Pennsylvania,
the pair was chased by two highway patrolmen, one of whom
Irene shot and killed, the other of whom Dague wounded. The
lovers escaped but were later pursued through many states to
Arizona, where they were forced to surrender to lawmen after
running out of ammunition in a wild gun battle. Although Irene
assumed all the blame for the crimes they had commited, she
and Dague both were found guilty and condemned to death.
"Iron Irene" or "Tiger Girl," monikers given her by the press,
went calmly to her execution in the Rockview Penitentiary in
Pennsylvania on February 23, 1931. Strapped into the electric
chair, she was asked if she had a final request and replied,
"Yes, ... tell them in the [prison] kitchen to fry Glenn's eggs
on both sides. He likes them that way." Irene became the
first woman to be electrocuted in Pennsylvania. Dague was
executed several days later.

SCHULMEISTER, Carl (d. 1853). French spy. As a young man
during the Napoleonic Wars (1803-15), he worked as a double
agent in the service of France; the Austrians believed his fictitious story of having been expelled by the French for spying,
of having noble Hungarian ancestry, and of desiring to help
Austria triumph, and they made him head of intelligence in the
Austrian army. While sending critical Austrian military information to Napoleon, Schulmeister gave the Austrians misleading
French strategies which led to battlefield defeats for Austria.
After faking his seizure by the French and subsequent "escape,"

he secretly obstructed Austria to help Napoleon gain victory at Austerlitz (December 2, 1805). Schulmeister, whom the French paid very handsomely for his espionage in several countries, was taken captive after Waterloo (1815) and a large ransom was paid for his release. He died in the French city of Strasbourg.

SCHULTZ, Dutch [real name: Arthur Flegenheimer] (1902-35). New York bootlegger, racketeer, and gangster. In about 1920 he took the name of Dutch Schultz, the name of a once-feared boxer at the turn of the century. In the mid-1920s he organized a gang that gained control of the beer trade in the Bronx and the numbers racket in Harlem. Schultz operated speakeasies and restaurants throughout New York City by the end of the 1920s. When gangster rivals such as Jack "Legs" DIAMOND and Vincent "Mad Dog" COLL attempted to take over some of his rackets, Schultz ordered his gunmen to get rid of them. In 1933 Schultz was tried for income-tax evasion and was acquitted. The "Dutchman," as Schultz was widely called, wanted to "rub out" (kill) Special Prosecutor Thomas E. Dewey, who was investigating racketeering and vice in New York, but board members of the newly-established national crime syndicate, notably Louis "Lepke" BUCHALTER, Charles "Lucky" LUCIANO, and Meyer LANSKY, rejected the idea. The syndicate put out a contract on Schultz when it learned he intended to carry out the Dewey killing. On October 23, 1935, in the Palace Chop House and Tavern in Newark, New Jersey, two gunmen (one was later identified as Charles "the Bug" WORKMAN) shot and killed three of Schultz's gang members—Otto "Abbadabba" BERMAN, Abe Landau, and Lulu Rosenkrantz—and fatally wounded the Dutchman, who died two days later in the hospital, mumbling about friends, family, and money.

SCHWAB, Michael. See ENGEL, George; SPIES, August.

SCHWARTZ, Charles Henry (1895-1925). California swindler and murderer. At his experimental laboratory in Walnut Creek, California, in the early 1920s, Schwartz, a chemist, pretended he possessed a secret formula for the manufacture of artificial silk in order to attract investors willing to give him money for a share of the formula. When he produced no silk, some investors talked of fraud. In 1925 Schwartz murdered travelling evangelist Warren Gilbert Barbe, blew up his laboratory with Barbe's corpse in it, and fled. Schwartz had altered the dead evangelist to look like himself, hoping to collect a $200,000 life insurance policy he had recently taken out on himself. However, Barbe's body was identified. Insurance investigators and police traced Schwartz to a rooming house in Oakland, California, where he shot himself to death just before being arrested.

SCIERI, Antoinette (fl. 1914-26). Italian-born French thief and mass poisoner. At the start of World War I, this young woman nursed sick and wounded British and other soldiers at Doullens in northern France. She was discovered stealing money and valuables from her patients and imprisoned for a time (1915-16). An Italian soldier named Salmon then married her but several years later left because of her promiscuity. In 1920, with her second husband Joseph Rossignol, a drunkard who beat her, "Nurse Scieri" settled down in Saint-Gilles in southern France. By 1926 her husband and five elderly patients under her care had died, and a suspicious doctor helped police discover massive amounts of a lethal weed poison in the bodies of Rossignol and the others, whose bodies had been exhumed. Arrested, Scieri freely confessed, never gave a motive for the poisonings, and later received life imprisonment upon commutation of her death sentence.

SCOFFEL, Katherine. See BIDDLE, Ed[ward].

SEADLUND, John Henry (1910-38). American robber, kidnapper, and murderer. In the late 1920s and 1930s he drifted about the United States, robbing stores, restaurants, gas stations, and homes. On September 25, 1937, Seadlund and fellow robber James Atwood Gray kidnapped 72-year-old greeting-card manufacturer Charles S. Ross in Franklin Park, Illinois, and held him for $50,000 ransom (they had changed their plans from robbery to kidnapping after hearing Ross say whimsically, "I've often thought of being kidnapped."). Seadlund received the ransom but did not release Ross. The marked money turned up everywhere, leading the FBI eventually to the Santa Anita racetrack in Los Angeles. There Seadlund was arrested while placing a ten-dollar bet. He later confessed to killing Ross and Gray, whose bodies were found in graves near Spooner, Wisconsin. Seadlund was convicted and executed in the electric chair at the Cook County jail in Illinois on July 14, 1938.

SELMAN, John (1839-96). American gunfighter, cattle rustler, and lawman. He became deputy to Texas Sheriff John LARN, successfully gunning down bad characters and earning a reputation as a cruel gunslinger in the 1870s (many of Selman's victims-- he was credited with 20 killings during his life--were found unarmed, but the shootings were listed as "justifiable homicide"). Together Selman and Larn started a ranch and engaged in cattle rustling until Larn was arrested and killed by a lynch mob. Selman fled and soon formed a gang, "Selman's Scouts," that pretended to help ranchers fight rustlers but actually stole livestock. In 1880 Selman was arrested for rustling but bribed the guards on the way to jail and escaped to Mexico. After 1888 he worked honestly as a cowboy in El Paso, Texas, where the townspeople elected him constable in 1892. While indulging himself at a brothel in 1894, Selman shot and killed a fellow drunken lawman who had gone wild, shot up the place, and killed a client, a Texas Ranger; this became Selman's most popular killing. In 1895 he walked up behind gunfighter Wes HARDIN, who was standing at a bar in El Paso, and fatally shot him in the head. Selman claimed self-defense and was let go; he was not so lucky the next year, when a lawman named George Scarborough got into an argument with him and gunned him dead in the street on April 1, 1896.

SELZ, Ralph Jerome von Braun (b. 1909). California murderer. In 1936 Selz, a handsome vagabond, was arrested and charged with murdering 58-year-old Ada French Rice, with whom he had been living in San Francisco. He said the murder was an accident and led police, news reporters, and photographers to the remote spot in the Santa Cruz Mountains where he had buried her body. While Rice's stinking corpse was being lifted from a shallow grave, Selz laughed and joked with newsmen, who later termed him "The Laughing Killer." Selz pleaded guilty, was convicted, and sentenced to life imprisonment. In 1945 he escaped from prison and was recaptured about a year later in Calgary, Alberta. In 1962 Selz broke out again but was caught three days later. He was paroled in 1966 but arrested one year later for welfare fraud and returned to prison.

SERAFINA, Countess [real name: Lorenza Feliciani] (1754-?). Italian whore and con artist. As a poor, pretty 14-year-old girl in Rome, she was seduced by Giuseppe Balsamo, later well known as Count Alessandro CAGLIOSTRO. Together they traveled to many European cities, living on forged letters of credit and money from confidence tricks. Countess Serafina (she titled herself that about 1777) whored with customers chosen by Cagliostro, who eventually settled with her as his wife in Paris. There she assisted him in his many dupes. In 1790 in Rome, she denounced Cagliostro to the Inquisition as a sorcerer. The Inquisition later ordered her to be confined in a convent in Trastevere for the rest of her life. There is no record of when she died.

SEYSS-INQUART, Arthur (1892-1946). Austrian Nazi leader and war criminal. Pressure from the Third Reich (Nazi Germany under Adolf HITLER) forced Chancellor Kurt von Schuschnigg of Austria to appoint Seyss-Inquart minister of the interior, with authority over the police and security. Less than a month later, on March 11, 1938, Schuschnigg resigned and Seyss-Inquart became chancellor. The next day German troops invaded Austria and the new chancellor proclaimed the Anschluss (union) of Austria and Germany. Seyss-Inquart served briefly as governor of Nazi-controlled Austria, then became deputy governor of occupied Poland under Governor General Hans FRANK, and subsequently in 1940 during World War II (1939-45) was made Reichs commissioner of the occupied Netherlands. In this latter post which he held until the war's end, Seyss-Inquart ruthlessly deported many thousands of Dutch Jews to extermination and slave-labor camps. The International Military Tribunal at Nuremberg found him guilty of war crimes, particularly those in occupied territories, and sent him to the gallows with other convicted Nazis on October 16, 1946.

SHANGHAI CHICKEN [real name: John Devine] (1839-71). San Francisco thief and shanghaier's runner. A noted figure on the San Francisco waterfront in the 1860s, he was involved in different kinds of thievery, from picking pockets to burglary, and hired himself out as a slugger and killer. Shanghai Chicken (how he got the name is unknown) became a runner for SHANG-HAI KELLY, supplying sailors and others for his shanghaiing operation (kidnapping men and forcibly impressing them into a ship's crew). In 1869 his left hand was cut off in a fight, and he attached a big iron hook in its place and used it as a weapon. He killed a sailor during a robbery, was caught trying to escape as a stowaway on a steamer, and was hanged in 1871.

SHANGHAI KELLY (c. 1835-c. 1900). San Francisco shanghaier. He ran a notorious shanghai operation in San Francisco during the last half of the nineteenth century. Kelly, a stout, red-bearded American Irishman, lured sailors and other men into his boarding house by supplying them with prostitutes and liquor. There the men were drugged, clubbed unconscious, or tied up and sold to shipmasters who needed to complete their ships' crews. Shanghai Kelly provided hundreds of shanghaied (forcibly impressed) men and collected much money until the federal law against shanghaiing began to seriously impair his operation near the end of the 1890s; Kelly then disappeared from sight and presumably died a short time later. See also CALICO JIM.

SHANNON, Robert K. G. (1877-1956). Texas rancher and criminals' confederate. The so-called "Boss" of Wise County, Texas, he was a political wheeler-dealer with connections in the underworld. Shannon, stepfather of Kathryn KELLY, wife of George "Machine Gun" KELLY, provided criminals on the run with a safe haven at his ranch in Paradise, Texas, and sometimes charged them for using it as a hideout. In 1933 the Shannon ranch was used by the Kellys and Albert Bates to hide their kidnap-victim Charles F. Urschel, Oklahoma oil millionaire, while they negotiated his release for a $200,000 ransom. Afterward the FBI took Shannon and his wife, Ora, into custody; the Shannons were sentenced to life imprisonment for their part in the Urschel crime. The Boss's sentence was later reduced to 30 years, and in 1944 he was pardoned by President Franklin Delano Roosevelt because of poor health and advanced age. He died in the Bridgeport, Texas, hospital on Christmas Day, 1956.

SHAPIRO, Jacob "Gurrah" (1899-1947). New York gangster and racketeer. He and his close friend Louis "Lepke" BUCHALTER

were involved in labor racketeering in New York's clothing
industry in the 1920s and 1930s. They terrorized union locals
to gain control of them, took kickbacks from fearful union members, and extorted large payoffs from clothing manufacturers
who wished to prevent strikes. They also supplied strikebreak-
ing services to the manufacturers. Shapiro (nicknamed "Gurrah"
because he used to yell "Get out of here," which came out gut-
turally as "Gurrah here") frequently used blackjacks, knives,
guns, and bottles of acid to crush rivals opposed to the crime
syndicate's operations. In 1936 he was convicted of labor racketeering and sent to the Atlanta penitentiary for life, where he
died in 1947.

SHARPE, Mary Churchill. See CHICAGO MAY.

SHELDON, Ralph (fl. 1920-33). Chicago bootlegger. During Prohibition he organized a bootlegging gang that worked much of
the time for Al CAPONE. Sheldon's liquor and beer was mostly
supplied to speakeasies and restaurants on Chicago's South Side.
In 1926 Sheldon waged war against bootleggers Joseph "Polock
Joe" SALTIS and Frankie McERLANE after his best beer runner,
John Tucillo, was murdered by the Saltis-McErlane gang. Sheldon's gang disbanded in around 1934 with the formation of the
national crime syndicate.

SHEPPARD, Jack (1702-24). English robber and prison breaker.
He started as a pickpocket and progressed to robbery under
"Prince of Robbers" Jonathan WILD. Caught a number of times,
Sheppard managed to break out of prison, filing through bars
and knotting sheets and blankets together into rope to make his
escape. Twice he escaped from Newgate Prison in London, a
feat nobody else had ever done before. One time, Sheppard,
heavily ironed and chained to the floor of Newgate's famous
Stone Room, used a crooked nail to pry loose the irons,
squirmed out of his handcuffs, and escaped through the chim-
ney. While celebrating his breakout, he got drunk in a tavern
and was seized. This time in prison, Sheppard was shackled
with specially forged irons and was guarded every minute until
his pronounced execution. On the day of his hanging, a small
knife was found in Sheppard's pocket; he had evidently hoped
to cut the noose from his neck and escape into the large crowd
of spectators. He died at age 22.

SHEPPARD, Sam[uel H.[(1924-70). Ohio doctor accused of murder.
On July 4, 1954, his 31-year-old wife, Marilyn, was found
clubbed to death in the bedroom of their suburban home in
Cleveland, Ohio. Dr. Sheppard, an osteopath, stood trial for
his wife's murder, which he vehemently denied having committed; he claimed to have been awakened by her screams, to have
rushed to her aid, and to have been knocked unconscious by "a
bushy-haired man." Marilyn had died from more than 25 blows

came to mean fraud at a gambling table. In 1847 Skaggs, a
millionaire by then, retired and became a gentleman plantation
owner in Louisiana. During the Civil War (1861-65) he put his
money into Confederate bonds and lost it all. He died a poor
drunkard in Texas in 1870.

SKINNER, Cy[rus] (d. 1864). American robber and outlaw. He
was an important member of the so-called "Innocents," a gang
of robbers led by Henry PLUMMER that terrorized what is now
southwestern Montana. In 1862 and 1863 Skinner ran a saloon
in Bannack, Montana, that was a favorite meeting place for the
Innocents. At the saloon he used to overhear miners talk about
gold shipments and would give the information to Plummer and
the others. Skinner himself took part in only a few stagecoach
holdups. About two weeks after Plummer's lynching by vigilantes, Skinner was seized and, despite his pleas to be shot
rather than hanged (often a lingering death), was hanged on
January 26, 1864. See also BARTER, Richard "Rattlesnake
Dick."

SKULL, Sally [born: Sarah Jane Newman] (1813-67?). Texas
alleged murderer. Though she was married six times, she
came to be known by the surname of her third husband. Sally
claimed that her first husband (name unknown), whom she married at the age of 14, wandered off to fight the Indians about
1828; her second husband, Jesse Robinson, mysteriously died
in 1843 after about five years of marriage; George Skull, with
whom Sally ran a horse ranch in Goliad, Texas, suddenly disappeared in the late 1840s; John Doyle, her fourth marriage
partner, apparently tumbled, drunk on whiskey, into the
Nueces River and drowned; her fifth spouse, a man named Mr.
Watkins, was fatally shot by Sally, who said she had mistaken
him for an intruder while the pair were in Corpus Christi, Texas,
on a trip (the authorities accepted her story and released her).
In 1867 she married William Harsdoff and the pair immediately
departed for Mexico. A woman's rotting cadaver, thought to be
Sally, was later discovered beside the road to Mexico, but ru-
mors persisted that Sally was still alive and carrying on her
deadly skulduggery somewhere else.

SLACK, John. See ARNOLD, Philip.

SLADE, [Joseph A.] "Jack" (1824-64). American gunfighter and
murderer. He became a feared gunslinger in Colorado, Montana,
and other western states in the 1850s and 1860s. Slade committed numerous murders against those who offended him, engaging
at times in horrible acts of cruelty such as the slow, sadistic
shooting of French-Canadian robber Jules BENI in 1861. Liquor
made Slade a defiant killer, willing to take on anyone at any
time anywhere. In Virginia City, Montana, on March 3, 1864,
Slade went on a drunken rampage, shooting up much of the town

and threatening people. Vigilantes dragged him out of a saloon
and hanged him from a beam in front of the building. Slade's
wife packed his body in a tin coffin filled with alcohol and set
out to bury him in his birthplace in Illinois. By the time she
reached Salt Lake City, the body was decomposing and odiferous.
She buried it there in the Mormon Cemetery on July 20, 1864.

SLATER, Oscar [real name: Oscar Leschziner] (1873-1948). German-
born British convicted murderer. Settling in Great Britain after
fleeing from Germany to avoid conscription, he lived an evasive,
underworld existence, gambling, trafficking illegally in jewelry,
traveling about with a prostitute, and using numerous aliases.
Identified as the attacker of an elderly spinster, Marion Gilchrist,
who had been murdered in her Glasgow, Scotland, apartment on
December 21, 1908, Slater was tracked down and arrested in New
York City in early 1909; claiming complete innocence, he willingly
returned to Scotland to face trial in Edinburgh for the crime.
False statements from the prosecution and its witnesses convinced
the 15-member jury to convict Slater of murder. Sentenced to
hang (1909), he was instead given a life sentence at Peterhead
Prison because of vehement public support for him. Many persons tried to reopen his case, which finally received a special
review thanks to the help of Sir Arthur Conan Doyle, the author
of the Sherlock Holmes stories. Released (1928) on a technicality, Slater soon gained Doyle's furious disgust for his contemptu-
ousness for not being declared innocent. Slater did obtain some
compensation (£6,0   out gave nothing to Doyle and others who
had helped him.   suspicious figure, he was later temporarily
interned in Scot' 1 during World War II.

SLOVIK, Eddie o   ward [D.] (1920-45). American deserter. At
the time when   was drafted into the U.S. Army during World
War II, Slovik   as happily married and had a satisfactory work
record, havin   apparently learned to control the frustrations
that had helr d land him in early life first in reform school and
then in prisr i.   In August 1944 while advancing with his unit
from Francr j Omaha Beach toward Elbeuf, he became frightened
under hea'   enemy fire, fled from the battle front, and then
hooked uɪ with some Canadian forces. Six weeks later, when
Private ℉ ʌvik showed up for duty at the U.S. 28th Division, he
confessɾ to desertion and stated that he would run away again
if thrʋ into bloody combat. At a short court-martial (November 1   1944), he was convicted of desertion to avoid dangerous
dutv   he 58th Article of War) and was sentenced to be executed,
tho' . the army evidently had no intention of enforcing the sen-
ter but wanted to make an example out of Slovik's case to dis-
co ɩge desertion. However, because of numerous blunders, the
sɾ ence was ultimately confirmed by General Dwight D. Eisen-
ɪ ʲer and carried out by a firing squad in France's Vosges
untains on January 31, 1945. Slovik was the last person exe-
ɪted that way in U.S. military history.

SMITH, Alexander. See CHRISTIAN, Fletcher.

SMITH, Edgar [Herbert] (b. 1933). New Jersey murderer. He
spent a record 14 years on death row at New Jersey's Trenton
State Prison on a conviction of murdering 15-year-old Victoria
Zielinski in 1957. In his cell, Smith, continually affirming his
innocence, corresponded at length with journalist William F.
Buckley, Jr., who encouraged him to write a book, Brief
Against Death, about his ordeal. Smith later wrote another
book, A Reasonable Doubt, that purported his innocence. At
a new trial in 1971, he pleaded guilty to second-degree murder
and received 25 to 30 years. Soon afterward he was set free
on probation, having had time credited for good behavior. Smith
then wrote a third book, Getting Out, in which he questioned
whether justice had won in his case. In October 1976 FBI men
arrested Smith for abducting and stabbing a young woman in San
Diego, California. He confessed to the crime and, to nearly
everyone's amazement, to killing Victoria Zielinski about 19 years
earlier. Smith was imprisoned for life.

SMITH, George Joseph (1872-1915). English murderer. He wooed
lonely young women and supposedly proposed marriage to them.
After the women or "wives" died or disappeared, Smith collected
money from their wills and life insurance policies made out to
him. Finally apprehended because of a victim's father inquiries,
Smith was discovered to have drowned his victims (three known
women) in baths. He was found guilty of murder and hanged
at Maidstone on August 13, 1915.

SMITH, [Jefferson Randolph] "Soapy" (1860-98). American gambler
and con man. At an early age he learned the tricks of successful dishonest card sharps and gamblers, becoming a master at
the pea-in-the-shell game and three card monte. In the 1880s
Smith teamed up with V. Bullock-Taylor, another con man, and
sold soap in towns throughout the West. Smith would tell them
some bars of soap he was selling contained $20 bills inside the
wrappers. When his shill, Bullock-Taylor, would buy a bar and
find a $20 bill, suckers would rush to buy. Thus Smith acquired
the nickname "Soapy." He opened up a gambling dive in Denver
where he engaged in gold brick and phony mining stock swindles.
In 1892 Smith moved to Creede, Colorado, to fleece the silver
miners with his con rackets. He then went to Skagway, Alaska,
to fleece the miners going to and coming from the goldfields.
"Soapy's men" operated rigged card games, the pea-in-the shell
tricks, and tilted roulette wheels; they also robbed prospectors
who tried to hoard their money. Skagway was virtually controlled
by Smith, who named the marshal and the judges. In July 1898
Soapy's men mugged and robbed a gold miner in broad daylight.
A vigilante group, the Committee of 101, rose up in protest,
stormed into Smith's saloon, and shot Soapy to death despite
his attempt at the very end to con his way out.

SMITH, Madeleine (1836-1928). Scottish alleged murderer. At age 19 Smith, beautiful and vivacious, became the paramour of Émile L'Angelier, a 29-year-old clerk and ladies' man living in Glasgow, to whom she wrote many passionate love letters. Her father, a wealthy Glasgow architect, demanded that she end the relationship, which L'Angelier hoped would result in marriage and his rise to a higher station in life through inheritance. By early 1857 Madeleine's ardor for her lover had cooled, but Émile threatened to show her father her sensual love letters if she broke off with him; Madeleine's trysts with him resumed while she made plans to marry an affluent Scottish businessman who was a good friend of her father. In March 1857 L'Angelier suffered three violent attacks of vomiting after supposed visits to Madeleine and died during the third attack in his seedy Glasgow quarters on March 23, 1857. An autopsy revealed much arsenic inside his stomach, and Madeleine, who had openly bought arsenic (commonly used then cosmetically), was arrested and tried for murder (early July 1857). She was graceful and poised at the nine-day trial in Edinburgh, at the end of which the verdict was "Not Proven," which implies the jury thought her culpable but had no proof (there was no tangible evidence that the lovers had met just before the death of L'Angelier, who was known to eat arsenic, a fad of the time). Afterward, shunned by her family (except for her brother), Madeleine moved to London where she became involved with artists and socialists; her marriage (1861) to artist George Wardle resulted in two children and was long and happy. In 1909 she, now a widow, moved to the United States where she remarried. Again widowed in 1926, she later died in poverty in Hastings-on-Hudson, New York.

SMITH, Mary [Eleanor] (1866-after 1938). American shoplifter, swindler, and murderer. As "Shoebox Annie" she was well known by police in many U.S. cities in the 1910s and 1920s; the name derived from her successful use of a shoebox wrapped like a store purchase as a device for shoplifting (things were slipped into it through a slit in the top). With her son Earl, who was a habitual criminal, she stole automobiles and swindled wealthy businessmen, a number of whom disappeared. Apparently, after killing them the Smiths dissolved their bodies in a tank of hydrochloric acid beneath their house in Anaconda, Montana. Finally the two were convicted of grand larceny, Earl receiving a life term because of previous arrests and jail stints, Mary earning an eight-year sentence because of a "cleaner" record. About to be paroled in 1938, she was retried on an earlier murder charge, convicted, and imprisoned for life.

SMITH, Perry E. (1928-65). Kansas murderer. On November 15, 1959, he and Richard E. HICKOCK, two ex-convicts and vagrants, invaded the Clutter family home in Holcomb, Kansas, expecting to seize more than $10,000 believed to be kept there. Instead, they netted less than $50 after terrorizing the four family members and leaving them dead. Perry and Hickock were caught in Las Vegas by police; each confessed and tried to blame the other for the crime. A jury found them guilty, and they were hanged in April 1965. Truman Capote's book In Cold Blood is based on the Clutter murders.

SMITH, Richard (d. 1816). American murderer. In 1812 Smith, a U.S. Army lieutenant stationed near Philadelphia, met and fell in love with and married Ann CARSON, whose husband, Captain John Carson, had been away in the Indian wars for two years and was listed as presumed dead. They lived happily married until January 20, 1816, when Captain Carson returned home. Smith denied him entry, drew his revolver, and fatally shot him in the head. During Smith's trial, Ann Carson tried to kidnap Pennsylvania Governor Simon Snyder and hold him hostage until Smith was set free. She failed, and Smith was convicted of murder and hanged in Philadelphia on February 4, 1816.

SMITH, Robert [Benjamin] (b. 1948). Arizona mass murderer. Considered an upright high school student, he calmly walked into a beauty salon in Mesa, Arizona, on November 12, 1966, and, brandishing a gun, made seven persons (five women and two children) lie down on the floor in a configuration resembling wheel spokes. Smith then shot and killed them all and gave himself up to the police, to whom he announced that he "wanted to be known." He was convicted (October 24, 1967) and given life imprisonment.

SMITH, [Thomas L.] "Pegleg" (1801-66). American mountaineer, kidnapper, horse thief, and con man. As a young man he moved from his native Kentucky to the Santa Fe area, where he became a fur trapper and traded pelts with the Indians. Shot in the right knee by an Indian during a dispute, Smith acquired a wooden leg, hence the nickname "Pegleg," but continued to engage in nefarious dealings with the Indians. He kidnapped Indian children and sold them to rich Mexicans who were looking for slaves. Pursued by the law, Smith moved to California, where he teamed up with Jim BECKWOURTH and William S. "Old Bill" WILLIAMS to form a notorious horse-stealing gang. Later, when gold was discovered in California, Smith turned con artist, selling phony stakes in alleged gold mines, such as the now famous "Lost Pegleg Mine," or maps showing the supposed locations of rich gold veins. Smith died in a San Francisco hospital in 1866.

SMOLIANOFF, Solomon (1897-?). Russian-born counterfeiter. When Joseph STALIN began his pogrom against the Jews in Russia, this talented Jewish artist fled and wandered for years in Germany and other lands, earning a livelihood mainly by forging passports and counterfeiting English and American currency in the 1920s and 1930s. He was in and out of German jails for counterfeiting and, during World War II, was imprisoned first at Mauthausen and then Sachsenhausen concentration camps. In 1942 Smolianoff was brought to the slave camp at Friedenthal near Berlin to make engraving plates to print bogus British money on specially produced paper (Adolf HITLER, Heinrich HIMMLER, Bernhard Kruger, and other Nazis hoped to flood the world with counterfeit Bank of England notes and thus to destroy the value of Britain's currency). With other Jews, Smolianoff was forced to manufacture currency which only the Bank of England itself, with difficulty, was able to detect; Smolianoff's plates produced notes almost identical to genuine British ones. The secret counterfeiting operation was moved to Redl-Zipf in Austria just months before Germany's defeat, having put into circulation several hundred million dollars worth of English money in 1943-45. Most of the evidence of this operation was destroyed by the Nazis. Smolianoff managed to escape, fled to Italy, and later to South America supposedly. See also ZOTOW, Eugene.

SNYDER, Ruth [Brown] (1895-1928). New York murderer. Bored with her loveless marriage to Albert Snyder, Ruth began a torrid love affair with corset salesman Henry Judd GRAY in 1925. For nearly two years they met in Manhattan hotels. Ruth talked of doing away with Albert and took out a $48,000 life insurance policy on him with double indemnity. Several times she tried unsuccessfully to poison her husband. Finally, in the early morning of March 20, 1927, she and Judd killed Albert, smashing in his skull as he lay asleep. Circumstantial evidence led to the arrest of Ruth and Judd, both of whom confessed after undergoing separate interrogations. During a sensational trial each blamed the other for the murder. Both were convicted and later were electrocuted at Sing Sing Prison on January 22, 1928.

SOBELL, Morton (b. 1917). American conspirator and convicted spy. From information gained from testimony from confessed Communist spy Klaus FUCHS, the FBI was able to round up other conspirators, including Julius and Ethel ROSENBERG and their close friend Morton Sobell, a New York electrical engineer who had worked for the U.S. Navy on top-secret radar equipment from 1942 to 1947. To escape prosecution, Sobell had earlier fled to Mexico but had been picked up by Mexican undercover agents and handed over to FBI men at the border. In New York City, 1951, Sobell and the Rosenbergs faced trial together on espionage charges of having sold classified U.S. military information to Soviet agents; the former was found guilty and sentenced to 30 years' imprisonment; the latter two, convicted also, were executed for their crime in 1953. Sobell served time in the Atlanta and Lewisburg, Pennsylvania, federal penitentiaries, and was freed from the latter prison in early 1969, after almost 18 years behind bars.

SOCCO THE BRACER [real name: Joseph Gayles] (1844-73). New

York gangster and river pirate. He led the Patsy Conroy gang In New York City in the 1860s and 1870s. Socco The Bracer, who always carried two guns and several knives, was credited with killing at least 20 men in fights. His gang preyed on cargo ships docked along the East River, stealing whatever it could. While attempting to loot the brig Margaret at Pier 27 on the night of May 29, 1873, Socco The Bracer, accompanied by Bum Mahoney and Billy Woods, awakened the ship's crew, who shot at them and forced them over the side into their rowboat. Two harbor policemen in boats spotted them and traded shots with Socco, who was seriously wounded. Thinking their leader was dead, Mahoney and Woods dumped Socco overboard in the middle of the river. Socco immediately revived and begged the two to pull him back in, which they reluctantly did. Socco then died and the two once again threw his body overboard. Four days later the body floated ashore at the foot of Stanton Street.

SON OF SAM [real name: David Richard Berkowitz] (b. 1953). New York mass murderer. For about a year, from 1976 to 1977, New York City was terrorized by an unknown killer called first the ".44-Caliber Killer" (because of the revolver he used) until given the nickname "Son of Sam" (the name used by him in letters sent to newspapers). In eight separate attacks, Son of Sam fired bullets at 13 young women and men (they were usually lovers parked in cars at night), killing six and seriously wounding seven of them. A large manhunt ensued while many parents waited fearfully, restricting the nightly activities of their teenagers. Finally, on August 10, 1977, police, using some seemingly unrelated clues, apprehended David R. Berkowitz, believed to be Son of Sam, near his home in Yonkers, New York, and held him for psychiatric tests. Berkowitz pleaded guilty and was sentenced to 25 years to life three different times by three separate state supreme court judges in the three counties (Bronx, Queens, and Kings or Brooklyn) in which the killings occurred; these were the maximum sentences allowed by law.

SONTAG, George (d. 1893). California train robber and outlaw. He and his brother John, one-time owners of a California quartz mine, waged war against the Southern Pacific Railroad, whose practice of taking land from ranchers and farmers for rights-of-way infuriated them. The Sontag brothers and Chris EVANS led a gang of train robbers, the "California Outlaws," looting the Southern Pacific Railroad's express cars but never stealing from its passengers or touching the U.S. mails. In August 1892 George was caught during a gun battle with Pinkerton detectives and California lawmen, one of whom was killed. George was sent to Folsom Prison for life. In 1893, when he heard of his brother John's death, George staged a wild, one-man prison riot and was shot to death while attempting to escape over the wall. See also MORRELL, Ed; SONTAG, John.

SONTAG, John (d. 1893). California train robber and outlaw. He, his brother George, and Chris EVANS led the "California Outlaws," two dozen or more train robbers who held up and looted express cars of the Southern Pacific Railroad in and around the San Joaquin Valley, California, in the 1880s and early 1890s. Their raids were in retaliation against the railroad's appropriation of ranch and farm lands. John and the others eluded huge posses of railroad agents, Pinkerton detectives, and local lawmen. In August 1892 John and Evans shot their way out of a trap in the wooded hill country; George was captured. The California Outlaws kept up their war with the railroad by stopping and searching stagecoaches, hoping to kill some railroad detectives. In June 1893 John and Evans fought the famous eight-hour gun battle of Simpson's Flat against a large posse. John was wounded many times and died later on July 3, 1893; Evans was seriously wounded but survived. See also SONTAG, George; MORRELL, Ed.

SORGE, Richard (1895-1944). Russian-born Communist spy. He served in the German army during World War I (1914-18), secured a doctorate of philosophy from the University of Hamburg, turned Marxist, and went to Moscow where he began an intelligence career as a Soviet Communist party member. From 1929 to 1932 he headed a successful Soviet espionage operation in Shanghai. In 1933 Sorge was assigned to Japan to establish a spy ring in Tokyo after having worked his way as a supposedly loyal German into the National Socialist (Nazi) Party. Operating undercover as a German newspaper correspondent, he was the leader of a successful spy ring which consisted mainly of Max Klausen, Branko de Voukelitch, Miyagi Yotoku, and Ozaki Hotsumi and which collected and transmitted to the Soviet Union secret Japanese political, economic, and military information. His efficient operation penetrated into confidential negotiations between the German and Japanese governments. On May 15, 1941, Sorge radioed Moscow that between 170 and 190 German divisions would invade the Soviet Union during the next month, on June 22 (his prediction was right). In late August 1941 he told the Soviets, who were expecting the Japanese to attack through Manchuria, that Japan would instead strike south into Indochina and the Dutch East Indies; again Sorge was correct, thus enabling Soviet forces in the Far East to be shifted to Europe to stem the German advance. In October 1941 Sorge and his ring were uncovered by the Japanese, who arrested and later tried them after months of interrogation, during which they all confessed. Both Sorge and Hotsumi were condemned to die (September 29, 1943), made unsuccessful appeals, and were executed in Tokyo (November 7, 1944). Klausen and Voukelitch received life imprisonment; Yotoku, who was never sentenced, died in prison in 1943.

SPANISH, Johnny [real name: John Weyler] (1891-1919). New York gangster. A Spanish Jew, he operated as a lone-wolf slugger and killer in New York City until he formed a gang in 1908. Always carrying two pistols, sometimes four, Spanish held up saloons and other establishments, pistol-whipped belligerent customers, and shot up the places. In 1909 he joined KID DROPPER and his gang but soon severed his tie when Kid Dropper stole the affections of his girlfriend. For seriously wounding the girl (he shot her in the abdomen when she was pregnant), Spanish was sent to prison for seven years in 1911. Surprisingly, he and Kid Dropper joined together after World War I, but their mutual jealousy and dislike soon reappeared, causing an intra-gang war between the supporters of Spanish and those of Kid Dropper. When Spanish was fatally gunned down outside a New York City restaurant on July 29, 1919, Kid Dropper took complete control of the gang and its labor slugging and bootlegging rackets.

SPANISH LOUIE (d. 1900). New York gangster and murderer. He was a trusted underling of New York gang leader Humpty JACKSON in the 1890s. Spanish Louie, whose real name was never known and who claimed a Spanish noble ancestry, always dressed in funereal black and carried two pistols and two eight-inch daggers hidden in his pants. Skilled in the use of weapons, he engaged in robbery, beatings, and killings as a gangster-for-hire. In 1900 he was found shot dead on New York City's 12th Street. A Brooklyn man claimed his body and gave him an orthodox Jewish burial.

SPARA, Hieronyma (d. 1659). Italian poisoner. A crone who sold fragrances in Rome, she was also a self-proclaimed sorceress who developed a secret, ritualistic cult (Diana worship) for women only. Her female followers bought strong poisonous potions from "La Spara," as she was commonly called, and held nightly meetings in her house in Rome. In 1659 Catholic priests, learning that several women had confessed to poisoning their unwanted husbands, secured a papal order to investigate and sent a female spy who infiltrated the cult and was herself sold poison to kill her husband. Arrested soon after, La Spara revealed her doings under torture and was publicly hanged as a murderous witch, along with her chief associate, "La Gratiosa," and three other women who had poisoned their spouses.

SPECK, Richard [Franklin] (b. 1941). Chicago mass murderer. At the age of 19, he had the words "Born to raise hell" tattooed on his left forearm. When Speck, who was a drifter often high on alcohol and drugs, arrived in Chicago in 1966, he had been arrested 37 times on such charges as disorderly conduct, trespassing, and burglary. On the night of July 13, 1966, Speck, with a knife and a gun, forced his way into a nurses' residence for the South Chicago Community Hospital and tied up nine female student nurses. He then leisurely and brutally stabbed

and strangled to death eight of them, one of which he raped
(the ninth nurse hid under a bed and was overlooked; she later
identified Speck as the murderer). On July 17, 1966, Speck
was discovered attempting to slash his wrists in a Chicago flop-
house and was arrested. In 1967 he was tried, found guilty of
first degree murder, and sentenced to die in the electric chair.
The 1972 Supreme Court decision abolishing capital punishment
nullified Speck's execution. He was re-sentenced to eight consecutive terms of 50 to 150 years each.

SPEER, Albert (1905-81). German Nazi architect, leader, and war
criminal. He joined the German National Socialist (Nazi) party
in 1931 and became the official architect of the Third Reich
(Nazi Germany) after Adolf HITLER assumed power in 1933.
One of Hitler's closest associates, Speer, a skillful organizer,
drafted the plans for the country's autobahns (superhighways),
for the stadium at Nuremberg, and for other grand construc-
tions. From 1942 to 1945 during World War II, he served as
minister of armaments and war production, implementing a war-
economy policy using slave labor. Millions of foreign workers
and prisoners of war were rounded up, transported to Germany,
and forced to work in factories and mines and on fields. Hitler's barbarous 1945 "scorched earth" decrees to destroy all
German power plants, factories, stores, railways, bridges, ships,
military and communication installations in order to prevent them
from falling into enemy hands were strenuously opposed by
Speer, who contended then that the war was already lost to the
Germans. Later the International Military Tribunal at Nuremberg
tried Speer, who did not shirk his guilt for war crimes, found
him guilty, and sentenced him to 20 years' imprisonment in 1946.
Released from West Berlin's Spandau Prison in 1966, he later
published his memoirs, Inside the Third Reich (1970), which
was a bestseller. He died in London on September 1, 1981.
See also SAUCKEL, Fritz.

SPENCER, Al (d. 1923). American bank and train robber. In the
early 1900s he worked with robber Henry STARR, who was reportedly the first to use a car in robbing banks. From 1920 to
1923 Spencer's gang, which included Ray TERRILL, Earl Thayer,
and Frank "Jelly" NASH, committed numerous bank robberies
mainly in Oklahoma. His gang went into hiding after robbing a
mail train in Osage County, Oklahoma, on August 20, 1923.
Spencer was hunted down and shot to death by lawmen in Coffeyville, Kansas.

SPENCER, Henry (1880-1914). Illinois murderer. In 1914 he arrived in Wheaton, Illinois, and soon began to court spinster
Allison Rexroat, who was ten years his senior and had a large
bank account. Spencer took Rexroat on a picnic, clubbed her
to death with a hammer, and then buried her. Suspicion focused
on Spencer after she was reported missing and after he withdrew

money from her account (she had trustingly put her bank account in his name). Spencer confessed to the crime when her
body was found, was convicted, and sentenced to be hanged.
When two evangelists visited him in jail, Spencer said he had
reformed and joined "God's holy crusade." On the gallows with
the rope about his neck, he abruptly changed from deep piety
to desperation, shouting out, "It's a lie! I never killed her!
You're all dirty bastards! You got no right!" His execution
was delayed momentarily.

SPIDERMAN OF MONCRIEFF PLACE [real name: Theodore Coneys]
(fl. 1941-42). Denver murderer. Philip Peters, a well-to-do
elderly man, was found murdered in his home in Denver on
October 17, 1941. The police were baffled by the crime; no
one had been found in the house and all of its doors and windows had been securely locked from inside. On July 30, 1942,
during a periodic police inspection of the house (weird noises
had been heard and a dim light and creepy figure had been
seen there), a 60-year-old spindly vagrant named Theodore
Coneys was discovered living in a cubbyhole in the house's attic. Unknown to Peters, Coneys had settled in his hideaway
and had used a tiny trapdoor (thought too small for someone to
pass through) to descend into the house from his lair. Peters
had accidentally encountered Coneys in the kitchen and had
been clubbed to death by him. The murderer, dubbed the
"Spiderman of Moncrieff Place," received life imprisonment.

SPIES, August (1855-87). German born American anarchist. After
moving to Chicago as a young man, he became involved in the
labor movement and was editor of a leading anarchist newspaper,
the Arbeitzer-Zeitung (Worker News), in which he attacked the
capitalists for misrepresenting the cause of labor. Spies, a
noted speaker at strike rallies, attended a demonstration at
Chicago's Haymarket Square on May 4, 1886, when union workers were protesting the shooting deaths of six fellow workers
the day before during a strike at the McCormick Harvesting
Machine Company. Suddenly a dynamite bomb was thrown and
exploded in the ranks of the police who were attempting to disperse the crowd. Seven police officers were killed, and 70
others injured. Afterward police raids resulted in the arrest
of some 200 supposed anarchists who might have thrown the
bomb; 31 of them were indicted. However, 23 were never
brought to trial. Spies and seven others--Albert Richard PAR-
SONS, George ENGEL, Louis Lingg, Samuel Fielden, Michael
Schwab, Adolph FISCHER, and Oscar Neebe--faced the prose-
cutors and were convicted of conspiring to commit violence and
murder. All the defendants pleaded innocent. Lingg, a 22-
year-old German-born revolutionary, committed suicide in his
prison cell on November 10, 1887; Spies, Parsons, Engel, and
Fischer were hanged on November 11, 1887; Fielden, English-
born, and Schwab, German-born, had their death sentences

commuted to life imprisonment; and 36-year-old Neebe was sentenced to 15 years at the Joliet, Illinois, state penitentiary. In 1893 Illinois Governor John Peter Altgeld pardoned Fielden, Schwab, and Neebe on grounds that the trial had been prejudicial with a packed jury.

SPINELLI, [Evelita Juanita] "Duchess" (1889-1941). California robber and murderer. In the mid-1930s she turned to a life of crime, organizing a robbery gang in the San Francisco area. The "Duchess," as her colleagues called her, was a small, iron-willed, myopic woman with incredible strength; she could wrestle her tough henchmen to the ground and throw a knife with amazing accuracy. Her gang, which included Mike Simeone (her husband), Gordon Hawkins, Albert Ives, and Robert Sherrard, successfully committed auto theft, burglary, and robbery until 1940. After the gang killed a man during a robbery, it began to fall apart; Sherrard, who showed signs of confessing to police, was killed by Spinelli's gang. Ives, arrested for a petty crime, broke down and told the police about the gang's activities, and Spinelli and the others were apprehended and found guilty and sentenced to die in California's gas chamber. Ives was judged insane and committed to Mendocino State Hospital, where he died in 1951. Though her execution was delayed by appeals for about a year and a half, Spinelli stoically died in San Quentin's gas chamber on November 21, 1941, becoming the first woman legally executed in California.

SPOONER, Bathsheba [Ruggles] (1746-78). Massachusetts murderer. At the start of the American Revolution in 1776, her Tory father, Timothy Ruggles, fled to Canada. Bathsheba stayed behind in Brookfield, Massachusetts and married 63-year-old Joshua Spooner. In the winter of 1778 Bathsheba nursed a wounded American soldier, Ezra Ross, back to health and had an affair with him. She then persuaded Ross, accompanied by two passing British soldiers, James Buchanan and William Brooks, whom she bribed with gold, to murder her elderly husband. Spooner's body was dumped in a well and later discovered. The murderous trio were arrested when they were found foolishly wearing clothing that had been on the old man. Suspicion fell on Bathsheba, who soon admitted her part in the crime. The jury found the four guilty in the first capital case tried in American jurisdiction in Massachusetts; all were sentenced to be hanged. Bathsheba begged for her life, saying she was pregnant. Groups of male midwives and lawful matrons examined her; the majority said she was not pregnant. The four murderers were hanged at Worcester, Massachusetts, on July 2, 1778. Doctors examined Bathsheba's body afterward and reported that her womb carried a five- or six-month-old male fetus. Many believe Bathsheba would not have died if she had not been suspected of being a Tory like her father.

SPRING, Robert (1813-76). English-born American forger. As a young man he came to the United States where he opened a bookstore in Philadelphia. While searching for and collecting rare books and manuscripts, Spring practiced imitating the handwritings of George Washington (his favorite forgery), Thomas Jefferson, Benjamin Franklin, John Paul Jones, Martin Luther, and other famous persons. In the 1850s and 1860s thousands of his forgeries--autographs, letters, checks, and other documents (notably Washington's Revolutionary passes)--were sold by him to many unsuspecting customers, including rare book and autograph collectors. Usually an item went for a fee of ten to fifteen dollars. Spring, who frequently used aliases, operated most of his life in Philadelphia except for brief, successive stays in Canada, Baltimore, and England in the 1860s; he was arrested and imprisoned several times on forgery charges in Philadelphia, admitted guilt, vowed to reform, but continued to manufacture fakes after his release. Spring died destitute in a Philadelphia hospital's charity ward on December 14, 1876.

STACHER, Joseph "Doc" (b. 1902). Polish-born American gangster and racketeer. In New Jersey in the 1920s, Stacher, who used a number of aliases, including Joseph or "Doc" Rosen, operated gambling rackets for Abner "Longy" ZWILLMAN. In the early 1930s Stacher was instrumental in bringing together New York's "Jewish Mafia" and "Italian Mafia," which later resulted in the formation of the national crime syndicate. He moved to the West Coast in the mid-1930s and to develop gambling rackets there for Meyer LANSKY. Stacher helped set up gambling casinos in Las Vegas in the 1950s. In 1964 he was convicted of income-tax evasion and given the option of a five-year prison term or deportation to a country of his choice. At that time U.S. laws forbid anyone being deported to an Iron Curtain country like Poland. Stacher moved to Israel in 1965.

STAFFORD, Annie. See GENTLE ANNIE.

STALIN, Joseph [real name: Iosif Vissarionovich Dzhugashvili] (1879-1953). Russian Communist leader and Soviet dictator. Expelled from theological school as a revolutionary, he later joined the Bolsheviks in 1903 and was arrested five times for terrorist activity but always escaped during the next ten years. From 1913 to 1917 Stalin (a name meaning "man of steel" adopted by him) was imprisoned in Siberia. Granted amnesty, he took part in the October Revolution of 1917, when the Bolsheviks under Vladimir I. Lenin seized power in Russia. Stalin soon emerged as a leader of the new Communist regime. After Lenin's death in 1924 he eliminated his political rivals, strongest of whom was Leon Trotsky, and by 1927 was virtual dictator. He then launched programs for industrialization and forced collectivization of agriculture. His tyrannical rule resulted in a reign of

terror in the 1930s, during which he purged the Communist
party of all opposition to him (1936-39), holding trials at which
many old Bolsheviks, such as Lev. B. Kamenev, Grigori E.
Zinoviev, and Nikolai I. Bukharin, were found guilty of plotting
to overthrow Stalin. They and millions of other Russians, including army officers, secret police, and common citizens, were
executed for treason and other "crimes." In 1939 Stalin, who
had maximized his personal power in the Union of Soviet Socialist Republics (Russia), signed a nonaggression pact with Adolf
HITLER, whose Nazi invasion of the Soviet Union in 1941 caused
Stalin to ally himself with Britain and later the United States
during World War II (1939-45). Afterward Stalin cunningly established Soviet hegemony in Eastern Europe. Increasingly paranoid in his last years, he arrested "conspirators," mostly Jews.
On March 5, 1953, he suddenly died in Moscow of a cerebral
hemorrhage.

STANFORD, Sally [born: Marcia Busby] (1903-82). San Francisco
madam. Stanford, who took her name from Stanford University
at Palo Alto, California, operated San Francisco's most renowned
bordello in the 1930s and 1940s. Her girls serviced distinguished
gentlemen, businessmen, and others, including the statesmen who
assembled in San Francisco in 1945 for the founding conference
of the United Nations. Stanford's place was shut down by the
police in 1949. She was married eight times during her life and
was mayor of Sausalito, California, from 1976 to 1978.

STARKWEATHER, Charles (1940-59). Nebraska mass murderer.
Called "Little Red" because of his red hair and short stature,
Starkweather, who felt subjected to ridicule as a teenager,
modeled himself after movie star James Dean. In and around
Lincoln, Nebraska, in 1957 and 1958, accompanied by his girl
friend, Caril Ann Fugate, he went on a senseless murder spree.
Before Starkweather was apprehended near Douglas, Wyoming, he
had shot, stabbed, or choked 11 persons to death, including
Caril's mother, stepfather, and two-year-old sister. Starkweather was condemned to death, going to the electric chair in the
Nebraska State Penitentiary on June 25, 1959. Caril, who
claimed she was innocent, received life imprisonment and was
later released on parole in 1977 fully rehabilitated.

STARR, Belle [born: Myra Belle Shirley] (1848-89). American
horse thief and fence. She was called the "Bandit Queen" by
the Eastern press, which portrayed her as an attractive female
Robin Hood, but she was actually a hatchet-faced woman with
slicked down hair who engaged in horse-stealing in Texas and
Oklahoma in 1870s and 1880s. Belle often wore long velvet
gowns and leather girdles in which she carried her six-guns.
During her life she had a succession of lovers, including outlaws Cole YOUNGER and Jim REED, by both of whom she bore
children. In 1876 Belle married a Cherokee Indian named Sam

Starr (apparently the son of outlaw Tom STARR) and together the pair raided ranches and small towns in Oklahoma's Indian Territory, stealing horses and cattle and later fencing the stolen livestock. She and her husband were convicted of horse-stealing in 1883 and sent to jail for six months. In 1886 the two were arrested as horse thieves again but were released because of lack of evidence (Sam died during a shootout with an Indian deputy after their trial before "Hanging Judge" Isaac Parker at Fort Smith). On February 3, 1889, Belle was fatally shot by an unknown gunman on a secluded road in Indian Territory (many believe that her son, Ed REED, lay in ambush and killed her because of their incestuous relationship).

STARR, Henry (1873-1921). American bank robber and murderer. He was the last of the notorious Starr clan, which included Tom STARR and Belle STARR. In late 1892 Henry formed a gang that proceeded to rob banks in Texas, Oklahoma, and Arkansas. While fleeing from the law, Henry shot and killed one of "Hanging Judge" Isaac Parker's deputies. Henry was caught and, in 1894, sentenced by Judge Parker to be hanged. Through many appeals and to Parker's chagrin, Henry was saved and sent to prison. Released after serving less than five years (he received a pardon from President Theodore Roosevelt), Henry resumed his bank robbery career (one report says he committed 48 robberies during his life). About 1914 Henry began to use an automobile instead of a horse during his holdups (some people credit him with being the first U.S. criminal to use a car in a robbery). In February 1921 Henry was fatally wounded by a shot gun blast fired by banker W. J. Myers of the People's Bank at Harrison, Arkansas.

STARR, Tom (1813-90). American Cherokee Indian murderer and outlaw. Starr, a tall, full-blooded Cherokee, led an outlaw gang of Indians, whites, and half-breeds in Texas and Oklahoma's Indian Territory. The Starr gang, which operated from the 1840s to the 1880s, raided settlements, killing inhabitants and rustling cattle and horses. When the Starr homestead was attacked in 1845 and Tom's father and brother were killed, Tom sought revenge, tracking down and killing nearly all of the 32 who took part in the attack and killings. Tom died of old age, a beloved member of his Indian clan. See also REED, Jim; STARR, Belle.

STASHYNSKY, Bogdan (b. 1930). Ukrainian-born Soviet spy, assassin, and defector. Many Ukrainians, including his parents, opposed the Soviet occupiers of the Ukraine after World War II; in 1950 Stashynsky, cooperating with the Soviet to prevent his family's deportation, became a secret KGB agent among his own people. In the following decade, he worked under several aliases while carrying out espionage activities against anti-Communist groups. He became guilt-ridden by his cold-blooded assassinations

of two prominent anti-Soviet Ukrainians--Lev Rebet in 1957 and
Stefan Bandera in 1959--both of whom he killed in Munich, West
Germany, with a special spray gun which injected poison. On
August 12, 1961, Stashynsky and his wife defected to the West
across the border between East and West Berlin; the next day
the Soviets closed the border and began building the Berlin Wall.
Stashynsky confessed to his crimes and was sentenced to eight
years in prison; in 1966 he was freed and, with his wife, received a new identity.

STAVISKY, Alexandre Serge (1886-1934). Russian-born French
swindler. He immigrated to Paris before World War I and became involved in many murky dealings, including allegedly drug-
trafficking and white slavery. Stavisky, nicknamed "Sacha,"
was imprisoned for about 18 months (1926-27) for swindling
seven million francs from two suckers in one of his fraudulent
stock deals. He never entered prison again, spending much
money bribing high French officials and other influential people
who could be useful to him in his operations and his evasion of
the law. Stavisky owned two Paris newspapers, several gambling
saloons, a fancy theater, and various companies (many of them
dummy). Through worthless stock issues, he robbed countless
French investors of millions of francs. The bubble burst in December 1933, when a trusted accomplice informed French authorities about selling a series of worthless bonds in the Crédit
Municipal at Bayonne. The public and insurance companies had
bought them as a sound investment. Stavisky, who had founded
the credit organization, fled from Paris, having been told he
could no longer rely on protection from high personages. In
January 1934 he was found dead in his villa near Chamonix; he
either shot himself in the head or was shot by the police to prevent the revelation of a scandal involving French cabinet ministers, judges, police, and others. Political chaos occurred afterward until public confidence was restored through trials of corrupt officials.

STEVENS, Walter (1867-1939). Chicago gangster. From about 1900
to 1920 he worked as a slugger and hit man for Maurice "Mossy"
Enright's union-busting gang in Chicago. Later, as a freelanc-
er, Stevens supposedly carried out dozens of murder contracts
for Johnny TORRIO and Al CAPONE (police credit him with committing at least 60 murders). Stevens, who was given the sobriquet "Dean of Chicago Gunmen," was paradoxically well-
educated (he read the works of Robert Burns, Jack London,
and others) and a caring family man (for 20 years he cared for
his invalid wife and provided a good education for his three
adopted children). He also didn't drink or smoke until he was
50. Stevens retired in the late 1920s after an attempt was made
on his life.

STIEBER, Wilhelm [Johann Carl Eduard] (1818-82). Prussian spy.

Credited with the establishment of the German espionage system, Stieber was Prime Minister Otto von Bismarck's honored "king of sleuthhounds" while the German people were being consolidated under Bismarck's Prussian leadership. In disguise, he entered Austria to obtain successfully much vital military information which aided Prussia in defeating Austria and its allies in the Seven Weeks' War (summer of 1866). Stieber's secret work (1868-69) in France, where he gathered useful data about machine guns, rifles, and other military equipment, later helped Bismarck win the Franco-German War (1870-71); Stieber boasted that there were nearly 40,000 agents working for him in France at the time. Top secrets were also blackmailed out of important personages who indulged themselves at Stieber's vice-ridden "Green House" in Berlin. He was a wealthy, dreaded police commandant and confidential advisor of Bismarck when he lay mortally stricken with arthritis in 1882.

STILES, Billie (d. 1908). American lawman, outlaw, and train robber. Stiles, who early in life became a fast draw with a gun, worked as a deputy sheriff for several lawmen in the Arizona territory. In about 1898 the citizens of Willcox, Arizona, made Burt ALVORD and Billie Stiles their marshal and deputy marshal respectively, but the two lawmen quickly turned to crime, organizing a gang and engaging in train robbery. Pursued by the law, Stiles and Alvord tried to cover their trail by faking their own deaths; they once sent coffins supposedly containing their corpses to Tombstone, Arizona, but the ruse was found out. In 1904 Arizona Rangers captured Alvord but Stiles escaped and later became a lawman in Nevada under the name of William Larkin. In early 1908 Larkin-Stiles was killed by a shotgun blast by a 12-year-old boy, whose fugitive father had been hunted down and killed by Larkin (ironically Stiles himself had killed his father at the age of 12).

STOKES, [Edward S.] "Ned" (d. 1901). New York businessman and murderer. In the 1860s Stokes hooked himself to multimillionaire financier James Fisk and profited enormously from Fisk's stock manipulations. The two quarreled over beautiful Broadway star Helen Josephine "Josie" Mansfield and business matters. Fisk accused Stokes of embezzlement and blackmail, and Stokes was found guilty of the latter on January 6, 1872. Immediately that same day Stokes sought out Fisk at the Broadway Central Hotel and shot and killed him. Later Stokes was convicted of murder and sentenced to death. His lawyers won him another trial, where the verdict was changed to manslaughter and the sentence to six years in Sing Sing Prison.

STONE, John (1806-40). Canadian-born American robber and murderer. After serving time in prison in Canada for robbery and murder in New York for horse rustling, Stone moved to Chicago in 1838 and quickly became known as a suspicious "loafer" and

drunkard. Later arrested for the rape and murder of Lucretia
Thompson, a farmer's wife, Stone pleaded innocent but was convicted and, before a large crowd of male and female spectators,
was hanged near Chicago's lake shore on July 10, 1840, becoming the first person ever to be legally executed in Chicago.

STOPA, Wanda (1899-1925). Illinois lawyer and murderer. From an
impecunious childhood in Chicago's Polish community, she worked
her way up to become a brilliant assistant district attorney in
Chicago. This beautiful, young sophisticate of the jazz age fell
in love with her mentor, Y. K. Smith, a Chicago advertising
executive who was married and rejected her amorous advances.
Emotionally distressed, Wanda took a taxi to the Smith estate in
Palos Park, Illinois, fired several shots at Smith's wife, failing
to hit her but accidentally killing the Smiths' 68-year-old care-
taker, Henry Manning, in the garden, and then fled (April 24,
1924). Detectives later found Wanda hiding in the Hotel Statler
in Detroit, but before they gained entry to her room, she committed suicide by drinking a bottle of poison. Her funeral was
one of Chicago's largest, a tribute to her life and tragic end.

STORMS, Charlie or Charles (d. 1881). American gunfighter. He
always admired the shooting ability of two lawmen, James Butler
"Wild Bill" Hickok and Bat Masterson, and wanted to be respected
for his gunslinging prowess, too. Storms saw Jack McCALL
fatally shoot Hickok in the back of the head in a saloon in Deadwood, South Dakota, in 1876. Immediately afterward Storms
took one of Hickok's famous pearl-handled .45-caliber Colt pistols and used it in gun duels in Deadwood and other places. On
February 21, 1881, in Tombstone, Arizona, he quarreled with
gambler-gunfighter Luke SHORT, who shot him dead before he
could raise his famous gun to squeeze the trigger.

STOUDENMIRE, Dallas (1845-82). Texas lawman and gunfighter.
On April 11, 1881, Stoudenmire, a former Texas Ranger, was
made marshal of El Paso, Texas. With his two six-guns, which
he wore tucked into his belt for easy access, Stoudenmire quickly became known as the toughest lawman in Texas, killing several
men in gunfights in the town. He developed a private feud with
the three Manning brothers, whom he claimed had killed his
deputy. When Stoudenmire, drunk and angry, began impulsively to shoot up the streets, the citizens forced him to resign after
he had served a year as marshal. On September 18, 1882, a
wild barroom fight occurred between Stoudenmire and George
"Doc" Manning, both of whom were wounded by gun shots.
Manning wrestled Stoudenmire into the street, where one of
Manning's brothers, James, fired a bullet into Stoudenmire's
head, killing him instantly. The Mannings pleaded self-defense
and were released.

STRANG, Jesse (d. 1827). New York murderer. In 1825 he began to work on John Whipple's estate in Albany, New York. Within a short time Strang and Whipple's promiscuous wife, Elsie, became lovers. Elsie suggested that Strang kill her husband and eventually bought a rifle for him to use. Strang practiced many months with the rifle to perfect his aim for a long shot through a glass window. On May 7, 1827, Strang shot Whipple dead as he prepared to go to bed. In time suspicion focused on Elsie and Strang, who were often seen together on the estate. They were arrested, and Strang soon admitted his guilt and said Elsie had instigated the murder. The judge refused to allow Strang to testify against Elsie, who was acquitted. Strang was convicted and sent to the gallows in Albany on August 24, 1827.

STRAUSS, Harry (1908-41). American gangster and murderer. Well known as "Pittsburgh Phil" (though apparently he was never in Pittsburgh in his life but took the name because he liked its sound), Strauss was the top and most vicious "hit" man (paid killer) in Murder, Inc., the enforcement arm of the national crime syndicate. He was hired to carry out "contracts" (assignments to murder) against rival mobsters throughout the United States, and at least 28 killings have been attributed to him. (Some law officials have estimated that Strauss killed over 100, maybe even 500, persons during his career from the 1920s to 1940.) Strauss, a tall, handsome brute who wore flashy, expensive clothes, enjoyed killing and often told his cohorts, such as Frank "Dasher" ABBANDANDO, Buggsy Goldstein, and Abe "Kid Twist" RELES, about his hits and how he disposed of the victims. In 1940 Reles turned informer and told the authorities all he knew about Murder, Inc., and Strauss's killings. Arrested, Strauss pretended he was crazy as a defense during his trial but was found guilty and went to the electric chair on June 12, 1941.

STRAWAN or STRAWHIM, Sam[uel] (1845-69). Kansas gunfighter. In the 1860s he became known as a boisterous, vicious gunfighter in the Kansas cowtown of Hays City. Strawan ignored a vigilante committee's order to get out of town and contemptuously pistol-whipped one of the chief vigilantes. When James Butler "Wild Bill" Hickok was hired to keep the peace, Strawan departed for about a month. On September 27, 1869, Strawan, along with 18 wild cowboys, rode into town, took over a beer saloon, and began to use the glasses for target practice. Hickok, after telling Strawan to stop, turned his back and faced the bar mirror. As Strawan stepped behind Hickok and went for his gun, Hickok whirled, drew his gun, and shot Strawan dead.

STREICHER, Julius (1885-1946). German Nazi leader, journalist, and war criminal. In 1919 Streicher, a one-time elementary schoolteacher, began a virulent anti-Semitic campaign in Nuremberg, Germany, vilifying the Jews and arousing hostility against them. He joined the Nazi movement under Adolf HITLER and participated in the abortive Munich "beer-hall putsch" (coup) of November 1923. From 1923 until 1945 Streicher, who was a noted pornographer, served as managing editor of the Nuremberg weekly, Der Stürmer (The Assaulter), in which he rabidly condemned the Jews, Hitler's scapegoats, and published obscene caricatures of them. After 1933 he was gauleiter (Nazi district leader) of Franconia in southwestern Germany. After World War II (1939–45) the International Military Tribunal convicted Streicher of war crimes, especially crimes against the Jews (he was known to have sadistically whipped and beaten them during the Nazi reign). He was hanged at Nuremberg on October 16, 1946.

STROLLO, Anthony C. (1899–1962). New York bootlegger, racketeer, and gangster. In the 1920s Strollo, also known as Tony Bender, was a Mafia bootlegger in New York City. From about 1931 on, he worked as underboss to a number of syndicate chiefs, including Charles "Lucky" LUCIANO, Frank COSTELLO, and Vito GENOVESE, and controlled many gambling and drug rackets in the city, especially in Greenwich Village. Strollo also arranged contract killings of rival mobsters. He was last seen on April 8, 1962, allegedly killed by enemies in the syndicate.

STROUD, Robert [Franklin] (1887–1963). American murderer, convict, and ornithologist. At the age of 19, Stroud killed a bartender in a dispute over a dance-hall girl in Juneau, Alaska. He was convicted of manslaughter and sentenced to 12 years at McNeil Island prison in Washington state. In 1912 Stroud was moved to Leavenworth. There, shortly before he was to be released in 1916, Stroud inexplicably stabbed a guard, who later died. Stroud was now sentenced to die on the gallows, but his mother persuaded President Woodrow Wilson to commute his sentence to life imprisonment with the stipulation that he remain in solitary confinement for the rest of his life. In his Leavenworth cell, Stroud kept canaries, did experiments in canary diseases, studied ornithology, and wrote two books on bird diseases. His work attracted attention to his plight, and many people, including veterinarians and bird-lovers, launched campaigns to gain his release. In 1942 Stroud was transferred to Alcatraz and ordered to leave his birds, books, and other personal property behind. Deprived of the things needed to carry on his bird studies, Stroud turned to writing a massive study on federal prison reform, which has never been published. Known as "The Birdman of Alcatraz," Stroud became the subject of many newspaper and magazine articles, a book, and a movie. In 1959 Stroud, in poor health but still seeking parole, was moved to the Federal Medical Center in Springfield, Missouri, where he died four years later, having spent 56 years in prison.

STRUCK, Lydia. See SHERMAN, Lydia.

SUNDANCE KID [real name: Harry Longbaugh] (1863-1911?). American train and bank robber and outlaw. At the age of 14 he was arrested for horse stealing, spent 18 months in jail in Sundance, Wyoming, and as a result was dubbed the "Sundance Kid." He then took part in numerous robberies, hiding from the law with other outlaws in the Hole in the Wall, a nearly impenetrable natural fortress located on the Wyoming-Utah border. In 1896 the Sundance Kid hooked up with Butch CASSIDY and his Wild Bunch, a vicious group that rode in and out of the Hole in the Wall and successfully engaged in train and bank robberies. The Sundance Kid was a charming, witty ladies' man when sober, but when drunk (and he liked to imbibe heavily) he was a hell-raiser, shooting up brothels and other joints. By 1901 the Wild Bunch was falling apart (members had been caught), so the Sundance Kid and his beautiful outlaw mistress Etta PLACE, along with Cassidy, fled to South America, where they reportedly attempted to reform but fell back into robbery. Bolivian soldiers supposedly shot and killed Cassidy and the Sundance Kid during a holdup in San Vincente, Bolivia, in 1911. However, there are reports that the Sundance Kid later turned up in Utah and that he eventually lived in Mexico City with Etta Place.

SURRATT, John H. (1844-1901?). American Confederate spy and conspirator. Son of Mary E. SURRATT, he was known for his intelligent espionage work for the Confederacy. With John Wilkes BOOTH, John Surratt led the plot to murder President Abraham Lincoln and recruited George Atzerodt and David E. Herold as fellow conspirators. After Lincoln's assassination in 1865, John fled from the country and became a fugitive abroad. A worldwide hunt for him ensued. Found serving in the Swiss Guards in Italy, John was arrested but escaped. He was hunted down in Egypt and brought back to the United States for trial in 1867. Through clever legal maneuvers, his lawyers got him acquitted. John lived the rest of his life inconspicuously in Baltimore.

SURRATT, Mary E. (1817-65). Alleged American conspirator. She owned and operated a rooming house in Washington, D.C., in which John Wilkes BOOTH and other conspirators met and stayed in 1864 and 1865. After Lincoln's assassination, Mary was arrested, along with several male plotters. The testimony at her trial was vague, and no evidence was ever shown that she was a part of the conspiracy. Nonetheless, because her house was used by the plotters, Mary was found guilty and hanged with Lewis PAINE, George Atzerodt, and David E. Herold on July 7, 1865. She was the first woman to be hanged by the U.S. government. See also SURRATT, John H.

SUTCLIFFE, Peter (b. 1945). English mass murderer. One of the

longest (five and a half years and five million man hours) and
costliest (₤3.4 million or $8 million) police searches in British
criminal history ended on January 5, 1981, with the arrest of
Sutcliffe, a truck driver from Bradford in Yorkshire-West Riding.
Proven to be the "Yorkshire Ripper" (dubbed that after the
notorious 1888 killer JACK THE RIPPER) who had terrorized the
county of Yorkshire in a murder spree since July 1975, Sutcliffe
was found guilty of killing 13 women, many of them prostitutes,
and was sentenced to life imprisonment on May 22, 1971. Sutcliffe, who also attempted to murder another seven women during
the period, believed he was on a "divine mission" to rid the
world of prostitutes. A British government report in early 1982
claimed that errors in judgment and inefficiency by police, who
had sighted Sutcliffe some 50 times and questioned him nine
times before arresting him, may have allegedly resulted in the
needless killings of the Yorkshire Ripper's last three victims.

SUTHERLAND, Mary Ann [Bruce] (c. 1860-?). Scottish adventuress
and swindler. A pretty fisher girl from Scotland's Peterhead
area, she transformed herself by false pretenses into a smart,
well-dressed lady living in comfort in Dundee. Not paying her
creditors soon led to her arrest, conviction, and brief imprisonment. Under various aliases, including that of Mrs. Gordon-
Baillie, she subsequently carried on her masquerade as a state-
ly beauty, traveling to London and the continent (Paris, Rome,
Florence, Vienna, and elsewhere) and leaving behind a trail of
unpaid bills and dishonored checks. As Mrs. Gordon-Baillie
she married and bankrupted a wealthy Englishman named Frost,
whose liabilities amounted to ₤130,000 after two years of marriage. In around 1886, using the name Gordon-Baillie she began collecting money to help the hard-pressed crofters on the
Scottish island of Skye and traveled to Australia where she
induced the colonial government of Victoria to grant a 70,000-
acre tract of land (worth ₤140,000) for the crofters to settle on.
Suspicion about the accounting of monies received by her on
the crofters' behalf resulted in her arrest in London (1888).
Tried and convicted of fraud, Sutherland-Gordon-Baillie received five years' imprisonment (October 24, 1888). She evidently resumed her old practices upon her release and died in
poverty in the end.

SUTTON, Arthur (b. 1950). Maine forger. While residing and
working in his hometown of Rumford, Maine, he developed ex-
traordinary skill at imitating the signatures of famous people
and during a three-year period (1973-76) sold his forgeries to
unwary autograph dealers, collectors, and others. Contemporary U.S. political figures and movie stars were frequently his
chirographic targets, though Sutton produced expert bogus
signatures of George A. Custer, Sitting Bull, and Adolf Hitler.
In Portland, Maine, in December 1976, Sutton was indicted on
12 counts of mail fraud, but received a suspended one-year

prison sentence; afterward he promised never to forge autographs again.

SUTTON, Willie "The Actor" [born: William Francis Sutton] (1901-1980). American bank robber and prison escapee. Sutton claimed to have robbed nearly 100 banks of more than $2 million because, in his words, "that's where the money was." Sutton, who worked single-handedly, was a master of disguise (hence his nickname "The Actor"), wearing facial putty, false beards and noses, and elevator shoes and affecting different mannerisms, such as lisps and odd limps. At times he posed as a postman, police officer, bank guard, window cleaner, moving man, and diplomat. Sutton was in and out of jail from 1926 to 1969 (he served a total of 33 years behind bars). Three times Sutton excaped, once from Sing Sing in 1932 and twice from Holmesburg Prison near Philadelphia in 1945 and 1947, only to be recaptured sooner or later. In 1969 he was paroled from the Attica State Correctional Facility in New York after serving 17 years for the $64,000 robbery of a Queens, New York, bank in 1950. He reformed himself and became a consultant to banks on security matters. On November 2, 1980, Sutton died in a retirement community in Spring Hill, Florida. See also TENUTO, Frederick J.

SVERDLOV, Jacob [Mikhaylovich] (1885-1919). Russian revolutionist and leader. A mastermind of the successful Bolshevik Revolution (1917), he virtually controlled the Bolshevik (Soviet Communist) party organization. Sverdlov's henchmen took Czar Nicholas II, his wife, Alexandra, and five children to the town of Ekaterinburg (now called Sverdlovsk in honor of Sverdlov) in the eastern Ural Mountains. On his orders, while the enemy White Army advanced on the town to liberate the royal Romanov family, the czar and his family, along with four faithful servants, were herded (on the night of July 29-30 [July 16-17, O.S.], 1918) into the basement of the house in which they had been held prisoner. Red guards, led by Jacob Yurovsky, unexpectedly and coldbloodedly shot to death Nicholas and the ten others, who thought exile was their eventual fate, having been led to believe this. Their bodies were cut into pieces and burned in gasoline in a mine shaft. The atrocity was discovered by the Whites, but Sverdlov blamed it on subversives, five of whom were found guilty and executed. Sverdlov died of pneumonia in 1919, but some claim he was murdered. Some also claim, without any proof, that the czar's youngest daughter, Anastasia, survived the massacre.

"SWAMI, THE." See SALOMEN, Edith.

SWEARINGEN, George (d. 1829). Maryland lawman and murderer. As the local sheriff in Washington County, Maryland, Swearingen, a married and rich landowner, was supposed to "do something about" the county's most beautiful harlot, Rachel Cunningham. The citizens were scandalized when he began having an affair with her. One day in early 1829 Swearingen went horseback riding with his wife and returned with her dead body, claiming she was killed during a fall. Shortly afterward Swearingen and his hussy vanished but were located in New Orleans, arrested, and returned to Maryland. Despite inconclusive evidence, Swearingen was tried, found guilty of murder, and hanged at Cumberland, Maryland, on October 2, 1829.

SWEENEY, Jim (fl. 1915-21). Chicago bomber. He organized and directed probably the first professional gang of terrorist bombers in the United States. During and after World War I, "Sweeney's Bombers," as they were dubbed, were frequently hired by union gangsters who wanted to enforce their authority over labor unions and the members. Sweeney, along with his gang's explosive expert "Soup" Bartlett and its chief labor agitator "Con" Shea, was said to be responsible for scores of bombing attacks in which dozens of persons were killed. In 1921 Andrew Kerr, a member of the Steam and Operating Engineers Union, testified that he had used Sweeney's Bombers to blow up laundries against which the engineers were conducting a strike. Sweeney was soon arrested and sent to Joliet prison for a long time, and his position as "king of the bombers" was then taken by Joseph SANGERMAN.

SWIFT, Delia. See BRIDGET FURY.

SYKOWSKI, Abram (1892-after 1975?). Polish-born swindler. For about 40 years he was an international swindler under such aliases as Carlos Nunn, Carlos Ladenis, and Count Alexander Novarro as he successfully fleeced wealthy persons in confidence games in Europe and Latin America. In 1921, while entering the United States with a fake passport under an alias, he was arrested and served two years' imprisonment. Deported from America as an undesirable alien in 1929, he carried on his scams (like bilking Russian refugees by selling them phony passports) and made much money through dope-smuggling and gunrunning. In 1946 he was arrested by the FBI in Miami, was sentenced to three years in prison for fraud, and was deported in 1949. A high-living, multilingual playboy, he succeeded in bilking about $200,000 from Egypt's King Farouk in 1952 on a promise of giving the king 10 percent of a fictitious multimillion-dollar bootleg fortune which he had often claimed to have hidden in U.S. banks. In 1953 French police took him into custody, but he soon escaped and disappeared forever in West Germany.

- T -

TABORSKY, Joseph (1923-60). Connecticut robber and murderer. in 1951 he and his brother Albert were convicted of killing a West Hartford, Connecticut, liquor store merchant named Louis

Wolfson. Because Albert had confessed to the crime, had implicated Joseph, and had testified against him, he was sentenced to life imprisonment, while Joseph, declaring he was innocent and his brother was crazy, was sentenced to die in the electric chair. Appeals were made by Joseph, who waited on death row in the Connecticut State Prison at Wethersfield. After Albert was moved to a state mental hospital, the state supreme court ordered a new trial, at the end of which Joseph was set free (1955). Later Connecticut experienced a series of robberies and killings (dubbed the "Chinese Executions" because the murder victims were all shot in the head). Joseph and an accomplice, Arthur Culombe, were eventually arrested and identified as the culprits. Joseph confessed to six murders and then a seventh, that of Louis Wolfson about nine years earlier. He was electrocuted in 1960.

TARNOWSKA, Maria [born: Maria Nicolaicvna O'Rourk] (1878 1923). Russian noblewoman, libertine, and murderer. A stunning beauty with many suitors by the age of 16, she eloped (1884) with the lascivious Count Vassili Tarnowska of Kiev; their marriage soon fell apart, with the count and countess each pursuing love affairs. Maria attracted rich lovers who lavished priceless jewels upon her, hoping to persuade her to run away with them; at least a half dozen of them killed themselves in frustration over her. A divorce freed the countess to indulge in sadistical and nymphomaniac urges. As numerous wealthy admirers came under her erotic spell, she came to be called "The Russian Vampire" and "The Sphinx of Crepe" while traveling around Russia and Europe. In 1907 she conspired with two lovers (Dr. Nicholas Naumoff and Donat Prilukoff) to murder Count Paul Kamarowsky, another lover, who had taken out a large life insurance policy in her favor. Kamarowsky was shot dead in Venice (1907), and the three conspirators were arrested, each blaming the others for the crime. They were tried and convicted in Venice (March 1910), receiving prison terms: Naumoff, two years; Maria, eight; and Prilukoff, ten. Released from Trani prison because of bad health in 1912, Maria became addicted to cocaine, roaming from Vienna to Russia to Paris, and died in obscurity in 1923. Naumoff and Prilukoff died shortly after.

TAYLOR, John (fl. 1715-25). English pirate. Based in New Providence in the Bahama Islands, he plundered ships in the West Indies until the Bahamian Governor Woodes Rogers succeeded in driving him to the shores of Africa and India. In August 1720 near Madagascar, the Victory captained by Taylor helped the Fancy captained by Edward ENGLAND seize the British East Indian ship Cassandra, which Taylor then converted to his flagship. Perhaps the single richest prize ever taken by pirates was the Portuguese East Indian ship Nossa Senhora do Cabo, seized by Taylor's pirate fleet off the island of Bourbon in the Mauritius island group on April 26, 1721. The loot belonging

to the Portuguese Count of Ericeira, which included silks, por-
celain, gold, and diamonds, was worth more than Ł1 million.
In 1723 Taylor received a Spanish pardon. He became a well-
to-do captain of a Spanish patrol ship in Panamanian waters.

TAYLOR, Louisa [Jane] (1846-83). British poisoner. An attractive
brunette widow at the age of 36, she went to live with an aged
friend of her husband's, William Tregillis, and his elderly, sick
wife, Mary Ann. Louisa, who agreed to pay for room and board
in the Tregillis home in Plumstead by nursing the ailing Mary
Ann, inexplicably fed poisonous sugar of lead (lead acetate) to
her patient until she died on October 23, 1882. Strangely,
though poisoning from sugar of lead requires large amounts to
be administered over a long while and symptoms from such
poisoning are easily evident, nobody (including the family doctor who gave Louisa sugar of lead because through "injections"
it smoothed her complexion) accused Louisa of foul play until
an autopsy revealed much sugar of lead in the victim. Tried,
convicted, and hanged (January 2, 1883) in Maidstone Prison,
Louisa Taylor never admitted guilt nor gave a motive for the
crime.

TEACH, Edward. See BLACKBEARD.

TENNES, Mont (1865-1941). Chicago gambler. In about 1900 he
formed a powerful gambling syndicate in Chicago. His men
busted up the saloons of rival gamblers, such as John O'Malley,
and made Tennes the "King of the Gamblers" by 1910. Tennes
established the General News Service, which virtually monopo-
lized horse racing news in Chicago until 1924. His gambling
saloons and dens were raided that year on orders from Chicago
Mayor William Dever, and many were shut down. Tennes then
retired, selling some of his businesses to friends. He died of
old age in 1941.

TENUTO, Frederick J. (1915-52?). American robber, prison escapee, and murderer. In the 1930s he was in and out of prison
several times on convictions of burglary and robbery. Convicted
of killing a Philadelphia man in 1940, Tenuto received a 10 to 20
year prison sentence, broke out two years later, was quickly
caught, broke out again in 1945, and was again recaptured a
month later. Incarcerated in Pennsylvania's Eastern State
Penitentiary (Holmesburg Prison) near Philadelphia, Tenuto and
four other convicts, including bank robber Willie "The Actor"
SUTTON, made the first successful escape from that institution
since its construction in 1894, using an extension ladder to
climb over the prison wall during a heavy snowstorm on February 9,1947. Tenuto, one of the FBI's ten most wanted
criminals, joined the mob of Mafia crime boss Albert ANASTASIA
and carried out numerous "contracts" (murder assignments), including the 1952 killing, on Anastasia's orders, of salesman

Arnold Schuster, who had turned Sutton in to the police (although Sutton had no connection with organized crime, Anastasia was enraged at Schuster for being a police informer). Afterward, in order never to be linked to the Schuster murder, Anastasia put out a contract on Tenuto, who soon disappeared forever.

TERESA, Vinnie or Vincent [Charles] (b. 1930). American gangster, racketeer, and informer. During a 25-year crime career, he rose to be the number three man in the Mafia in New England, working out of his home base in Massachusetts. In the late 1960s Teresa, an overweight man with a heart problem, turned "squealer" (the underworld's term for betrayer-informer) and gave much detailed information in court about organized crime and Mafia rackets, such as horse-race fixing at tracks in New England. His testimony helped either indict or convict about 50 mobsters, including Meyer LANSKY. The Mafia has reputedly issued a $500,000 contract for Teresa, who went into hiding under the U.S. Justice Department's Witness Relocation Program in the early 1970s.

TERRANOVA, Ciro (1891-1938). New York racketeer and gangster. In 1918 he became a Mafia leader in Harlem, where he made much money in the numbers racket as a partner of Dutch SCHULTZ. Terranova also bought, hoarded, and sold most of New York City's artichokes in the 1920s, earning the sobriquet, "The Artichoke King." In the mid-1930s he was stripped of his power by more ruthless gangsters, such as Charles "Lucky" LUCIANO and Vito GENOVESE, who called him weak and a coward. Terranova failed to take control of Schultz's numbers racket and retired to die later as a powerless Mafia boss.

TERRILL, Ray (d. 1931). American bank robber. At various times in the 1920s he joined with other robbers, including Al SPENCER, Frank "Jelly" NASH, Herman BARKER, and Matt and George Kimes, to go on bank-robbing sprees in Oklahoma, Texas, and Missouri. Terrill's biggest heist was with the Kimes brothers in 1927, when they stole $35,000 from the bank in Pampa, Texas. Lawmen pursued Terrill continuously until killing him in 1931.

TESSOV, Ludwig (d. 1901). German mass murderer. Between 1898 and 1901 he roamed from place to place in Germany as an itinerant woodworker, kidnapping and killing youngsters when the opportunity arose. Sometimes the bodies of his victims were cut up and the parts cast about, as was the case after he strangled to death two young girls in a forest near Osnabrück (1898). Finally he was taken into custody on Rügen, a German island in the Baltic Sea, when suspicion there about the murders of two boys (1901) focused on him (the victims, just before their deaths, had been seen with Tessov, whose clothing was apparently bloodstained). The noted scientist Paul Uhlenhuth verified that the stains were from human blood, not from wood as Tessov claimed. Promptly tried and convicted and executed, Tessov was said to have murdered at least 30 children before being caught.

TEW, Thomas (d. 1695). American privateer and pirate. In 1692 the English governor of Bermuda sold Tew a privateering commission to attack a French trading station on the West African coast. Instead, Tew on the 70-ton sloop Amity, armed with eight cannons, cruised along the coasts of India and Arabia and plundered shipping. On his return to his hometown of Newport, Rhode Island, in 1694, he was lionized by the people, who saw his piratical exploits as high adventure and a means to wealth. Obtaining another privateering commission, this one from New York's shrewd Governor Benjamin Fletcher, Tew aboard the Amity sailed again to the Eastern seas. In September 1695 he was shot to death while his crew attempted to loot a captured Indian Mogul galleon.

THATCH, Edward. See BLACKBEARD.

THAW, Harry K[endall] (1872-1947). American murderer. Thaw, the heir of a multimillionaire Pittsburgh, Pennsylvania, railroad tycoon, moved to New York City, where he met beautiful Evelyn Nesbit, a Floradora Chorus girl and mistress of world-renown architect Stanford White. In 1906 Nesbit left White to marry Thaw, who whipped her until she "confessed" her so-called sexual sins with White. Thaw became insane with jealousy and vowed revenge. On June 25, 1906, he and his wife attended a dinner-theater on the roof of Madison Square Garden. Also attending was White. Thaw went over to him and fired two bullets into White's head, killing him instantly. Promptly apprehended, Thaw was put in the Tombs, where he had all his meals catered from Delmonico's. He insisted he was innocent at his trial, during which his lawyer, Delphin Delmas, said that Thaw had temporarily suffered at the time of the killing "dementia Americana," a neurosis that makes an American male believe that his wife is sacred. Thaw was found "not guilty, on the grounds of his insanity at the time of the commission of the act." He was imprisoned, however, in the asylum at Matteawan, New York. In 1913 he escaped, fled to Canada, but was finally caught. A court declared Thaw sane in 1915, whereupon he left the asylum. The following year Thaw, who at that time divorced his wife, was returned to Matteawan after horsewhipping a teenage boy and was kept there until his second release in 1922. For the rest of his life, Thaw lived a wild, playboy existence, roaming the world and spending his money.

THIEL, Alexander D. L. (1890-1956). American forger. He first discovered his superior ability at forging signatures while working as a croupier in illegal gambling houses. Thiel, a John Barrymore look-alike, began breaking into businesses, stealing blank checks, and successfully passing bad checks throughout the United States. He once stole blank checks belonging to New York millionaire Messmore Kendall and swindled over $160,000 from Kendall's account (Thiel's biggest caper). To attract less attention, Thiel, who enjoyed the good life and was seen in New York nightclubs regularly, usually cashed forged checks of $5,000 to $15,000; he remained undetected for about 25 years. His forging operations were so expert and multifaceted that the authorities believed they were the work of a professional criminal gang led by a "Mr. X." In 1938 securities salesman Bertram Campbell, identified by bank tellers as Mr. X, was wrongfully convicted of forgery and spent over three years in Sing Sing Prison before being paroled. Meanwhile, Thiel, by then a drug addict, carried on his scams and was finally arrested by FBI agents in Lexington, Kentucky, in 1945. Brought back to New York and identified by witnesses in the Campbell case, Thiel confessed and was sentenced to nine years imprisonment. Upon his release he moved to Chicago, where he later was tracked down by police after forging a $100 check; Thiel, in wretched health, died several days later (1956).

THOMAS, Alvin Clarence. See THOMPSON, Titanic.

THOMPSON, Ben (1842-84). English-born American gunfighter, gambler, and lawman. Thompson, an expert shot with a six-shooter, was considered one of the fastest gunfighters of the Old West. He was credited with about 32 killings in Austin, Texas, Dodge City, Kansas, and elsewhere. In 1871, after serving a two-year prison term for a shooting, Thompson and his friend Phil COE established a gambling saloon in Abilene, Kansas, and made much money there in monte games. Thompson moved on to Ellsworth, Kansas, where he plied his gambling trade, again making large suns. In 1873 he helped his brother Billy, who had shot and killed the sheriff, escape from Ellsworth. In Austin where Thompson opened several gambling houses in late 1879, he was elected sheriff in 1880, did a good job keeping the peace, and was reelected the next year. However, the citizens forced him to resign in 1882 when he turned to drinking and shooting up the streets to create some excitement in town. At a vaudeville theater in San Antonio, Texas, on March 11, 1884, Thompson and his friend John King FISHER got into an argument with three gunslingers--Billy Simms, Joe Foster, and Jacob Coy--and were shot and killed. See also THOMPSON, Billy.

THOMPSON, Billy (1845?-88?). English-born American gambler and gunfighter. He tried to emulate his big brother, Ben, as an expert gunfighter and shrewd gambler. Billy, however, became known as an habitual drunk and a vicious, cold-blooded murderer.

In Ellsworth, Kansas, in August 1873, he blasted Sheriff
Chauncey B. Whitney with Ben's English-made, double-barreled
shotgun, killing him instantly. Afterward Billy told Ben he
would have shot "if it had been Jesus Christ." With Ben's
help, Billy managed to escape and later became head of an outlaw band in Buena Vista, Colorado. Billy was caught by Texas
Rangers and sent back to Kansas to stand trial. Reputedly,
Ben's bribery of officials helped gain his acquittal. Billy, a
roaming gunfighter until his death, was evidently shot and
killed in Laredo, Texas, in around 1888. See also THOMPSON,
Ben.

THOMPSON, Gerald (1910-35). Illinois rapist and murderer. Between November 1934 and June 1935, Thompson, a toolmaker,
raped 16 young women in Peoria, Illinois. He brutally beat to
death his last rape victim, Mildred Hallmark. An anonymous
tip, most likely from one of his victims, led to the arrest of
Thompson, who soon confessed to the murder and the rapes.
Thompson's modus operandi was as follows: he would pick up
the female with his car, imprison her there by a clever wiring
system (she would receive a powerful electrical charge when she
touched the car's door handle), drive to a secluded spot where
he would cut away the woman's clothing with sharp scissors,
and then rape her. Finally he would force the naked woman to
pose with him in weird sexual positions in front of his car's
headlights, while a self-timing camera took pictures of them.
He later used these photos to blackmail the women into silence.
These lewd pictures, along with a diary in which he recorded
his 16 victims and what had happened, were found in Thompson's home. Violent, angry mobs threatened to lynch Thompson before he was tried, convicted, and sent to the electric
chair in the Joliet State Penitentiary on October 15, 1935.

THOMPSON, Miran Edgar "Buddy" (1917-48). American robber,
prison escapee, and murderer. In the late 1930s and early
1940s, he was arrested eight times for robbery in the South
and Southwest and successfully broke out of prison eight times.
Caught for fatally shooting the police officer who killed his
brother, Thompson was given a 99-year prison sentence. At
Alcatraz on May 2, 1946, he participated in the famous rebellion-
breakout planned by Bernie COY. Along with Sam Richard
SHOCKLEY, Thompson goaded Joseph Paul "Buddy" CRETZER
into shooting the nine guards taken hostage during the break
(one guard died). After the rebellion was crushed, Thompson
and Shockley were tried and sentenced to die for murder. Both
died in San Quentin's new gas chamber on December 3, 1948.

THOMPSON, Titanic [real name: Alvin Clarence Thomas] (1892-c.
1970). American gambler and con man. His nickname derived
from his having been a surviving passenger of the Titanic, the
famous liner which sank in the North Atlantic in 1912, and his

claim afterward for phony insurance on lost valuables. A dandy who liked to gamble, Thompson specialized in deceiving moneyed golfers by pretending to be an unskilled player, losing at first on the golf course, doubling his bets to "get even," and then handily winning by playing either right or left-handed (he was an expert golfer and a southpaw, too). His golfing confidence games, which were usually played in Texas, supposedly netted him an average of about $200,000 a year until his death.

THORN, Martin George (1868-97). New York murderer. In June 1897 he and his lover Augusta Nack lured Willie Guldensuppe, Nack's ex-boyfriend, to Nack's house in Woodside, New York, where Thorn shot and stabbed him to death. They then cut up Guldensuppe's body, wrapped the pieces in oilcloth, and threw them into surrounding rivers. Police found parts of Guldensuppe's corpse in the rivers, and neighbors reported human blood in the drainage pool near Nack's house. Arrested for murder, the two lovers turned against each other, accusing the other of the crime. Nack was given a 20-year prison sentence (she was paroled after 10 years), and Thorn was sent to the electric chair (strapped in the chair, he said he had no fear and God would surely forgive him).

THREE-FINGER BROWN. See LUCCHESE, Tommy.

THURMOND, Thomas Harold (1909-33). California kidnapper and murderer. On November 9, 1933, he and his friend John Maurice Holmes kidnapped 22-year-old Brooke Hart, son of a wealthy department store owner in San Jose, California. They tied Hart up with wire, attached blocks of cement to his body, and dropped him into San Francisco Bay, thus drowning him. Thurmond's calls afterward to Hart's father, demanding $40,000 for the release of his son, were traced by police, who arrested Thurmond while he was arguing on the phone about the pickup spot for the ransom money. Thurmond confessed but blamed Holmes for the planning and execution of the crime; Holmes accused Thurmond. On November 26, 1933, when Hart's body washed ashore, more than 15,000 angry citizens stormed the Santa Clara County Jail in San Jose where Thurmond and Holmes were prisoners, beat the killers, dragged them out, and lynched them in the park across from the jail. No one was ever indicted for the hangings.

TILH, Arnaud du ["Martin Guerre"] (d. 1560). French impostor. One of the most infamous cases of impersonation occurred in Artigues in southwest France in the 1550s when Tilh was accepted there as the eight-year-long missing Martin Guerre, a runaway husband and heir to a large estate and fortune. Tilh, Martin's look-alike, was pronounced as genuine by Martin's pretty wife, Bertrande, and Martin's uncle, Peter Guerre, who however later quarreled violently with him over proprietorship

of the Guerre lands. After three years, a visiting soldier in
the town declared that the "Martin Guerre" living in the family
mansion with Bertrande was an impostor and that the real one
was a close friend of his who had lost a leg in a war in Flanders. The authorities investigated and held a public trial to
determine which was the real Martin Guerre. The soldier's
friend with a wooden leg arrived to testify, looking just like
Tilh-Guerre, and he was affirmed as real after Tilh openly admitted to the court his imposture. Condemned by the Toulouse
high court, Tilh was first publicly abused and then slowly hanged
to death in front of Martin Guerre's home. However, speculation
later arose that Bertrande was an accomplice to the fraud and
that the peg-leg man was an impostor, too.

TINKER, Edward (d. 1811). North Carolina swindler and murderer.
He was the first American sea captain to have attempted to defraud an insurance company by sinking his own ship. Tinker
scuttled his ship off Roanoke Island, North Carolina, and claimed
the loss of the cargo, which he had previously sold. Two of
Tinker's crew, Durand and Potts, joined his scheme, but a crew-
man named Edwards refused and was killed by Tinker, who
weighted Edwards' body down with rocks and threw it into the
sea. The corpse, however, washed ashore and was found.
Since Tinker was the last one to be seen with Edwards, he was
arrested. Durand, after receiving a letter from Tinker asking
him to testify that Potts was responsible for the murder and the
loss of the ship, grew afraid that Tinker might turn the tables
and induce Potts to blame him. Thus, Durand told the authorities about Tinker, who was then convicted of Edwards's murder
and hanged in Carteret, North Carolina, in September 1811.

TIRRELL, Albert J. (fl. 1845-46). Massachusetts accused murderer.
In 1845 Tirrell, the 25-year-old dissolute married son of a
wealthy Boston family, had a wild, passionate love affair with
23-year-old Maria Bickford of New Bedford, Massachusetts.
Tirrell's wife had him jailed on a criminal charge of adultery,
but Tirrell, contritely asking forgiveness, was soon released
and promptly renewed his affair with Maria. On October 27,
1845, Maria was found naked with her throat slit in a burning
rooming house in Boston's Beacon Hill district, the lovers'
trysting place. Tirrell, who had been seen leaving the house
just before the fire and whose bloody shirt had been found in
the murder room, shortly thereafter became a seaman and in
February 1846 was discovered aboard a schooner in New York
harbor and brought back to Boston to stand trial for Maria's
murder. Rufus B. Choate, a prominent lawyer hired by the
Tirrell family to defend Albert, claimed that indeed the defendant had killed Maria but he had done so while in a somnambu-
listic trance (witnesses testified to Albert's past history of
chronic sleepwalking, during which he had often acted reck-
lessly and violently). The jury found Albert not guilty, marking

the first time in the United States that sleepwalking had effectively been used as a legal defense. Later the Tirrell family, upset by the adverse public opinion concerning the verdict, committed Albert to an institution.

TOFFANIA, LA (1653-1723). Italian mass poisoner. For many years in Naples she concocted poisonous potions which she sold to wives who wanted to get rid of their husbands. La Toffania, as she was commonly called, operated undetected until 1719, when the viceroy of Naples found out that she was responsible for the poisoning deaths of numerous married men and issued an order for her arrest. Although she received refuge in a nearby convent, the viceroy sent troops to seize her there, causing a controversy when she was taken in violation of the convent's sanctity. Cast into a dungeon, La Toffania subsequently confessed under torture to having killed over 600 persons (mostly men), some of whom she poisoned herself, the rest dying at the hands of others who bought her "Aqua Toffania." She was strangled to death and her body thrown into the convent where she had gained sanctuary.

TOKYO ROSE [real name: Iva Ikuko Toguri D'Aquino] (b. 1916). Japanese-American propagandist and traitor. Born in the United States, she became well known as "Tokyo Rose" because of her seductive English-language radio broadcasts from Tokyo during World War II. American GIs and other Allied servicemen and women throughout the Pacific listened each evening (from about 8 to 9 p.m.) as she broadcast good dance music and other entertainment. She talked about both war and non-war news, hoping to undermine the morale of Allied forces by urging them to surrender and saying their fight was futile. But her pro-Japanese propaganda eventually ended with her arrest after the war and her conviction (1949) for treason. Sentenced to ten years' imprisonment, she was released after serving about six and a half years (she also paid a $10,000 fine). On January 19, 1977, U.S. President Gerald R. Ford pardoned her and reinstated her American citizenship.

TOPPAN, Jane [born: Nora Kelley] (1854-1938). American mass poisoner. Raised in an orphanage after her mother died and her father was sent to an insane asylum, she was adopted at the age of five by the Abner Toppans of Lowell, Massachusetts, who renamed her Jane Toppan. Later, jilted by her husband-to-be, Jane, at the age of 26, became a student nurse in a Cambridge, Massachusetts, hospital but before long was discharged when patients in her care began to die. Hired by another Cambridge hospital, she was soon fired when administrators learned she was not a graduate nurse and had forged her certificate. After 1880 Jane turned to private nursing, working in many homes in New England. One by one her patients, mostly elderly persons, died, until suspicions about their deaths focused on nurse Jane. Some of the bodies of her former patients were exhumed, examined, and found heavily loaded with poison. In 1901 Jane was charged with murder and confined in Massachusetts's Barnstable County Jail, where she confessed to murdering some 31 persons (later she claimed over 100 victims), using morphine and atropine (belladonna). She had covered up the telltale signs of morphine poisoning, which causes the pupils of the eyes to constrict, with atropine, which enlarges the pupils. Jane admitted to reveling in ecstasy watching the agonizing deaths of her trusting patients. In June 1902 she was tried, found insane, and sentenced to life imprisonment at the Taunton, Massachusetts, State Asylum for the Criminally Insane, where she remained until her death of old age on August 17, 1938.

TORRESOLA, Griselio. See COLLAZO, Oscar.

TORRIO, Johnny or John (1882-1957). Italian-born American gangster and racketeer. In New York City in the early 1900s Torrio, called "Terrible Johnny" at that time, led a cruel mob of pickpockets, burglars, fences, and sluggers--the James Street Gang. He also worked with gangster Frankie YALE, extorting money from rich businessmen in Brooklyn. In 1909 Torrio moved to Chicago to work for James "Big Jim" COLOSIMO, for whom he established a lucrative city-wide brothel system. Later, in 1920, Torrio, called "The Brain" now, hired Al CAPONE to "rub out" (execute) Colosimo and took over Colosimo's brothel empire. During Prohibition, Torrio and Capone operated breweries and gambling casinos throughout Chicago and made a fortune. At various times Torrio's gunmen engaged in gangland wars against other gangsters and bootleggers, such as Edward "Spike" O'DONNELL, Angelo GENNA, and Charles Dion O'BANNION. After he was severely wounded in a shootout with Earl "Hymie" WEISS, George "Bugs" MORAN, and Vincent DRUCCI on January 20, 1925, Torrio turned his rackets over to Capone and left Chicago, later retiring to Naples, Italy, for about three years. In 1928 he returned to the United States and became head of a multimillion-dollar bootlegging operation along the eastern seaboard. Torrio helped Charles "Lucky" LUCIANO, Meyer LANSKY, and others form the national crime syndicate in 1934 and sat for many years on the syndicate's board of directors. In 1939 he was convicted of income tax evasion and sent to Leavenworth. Paroled in 1941, Torrio gradually retired, becoming "crime's elder statesman." He died of a heart attack on April 16, 1957.

TOUCHY, Roger (1898-1959). Chicago bootlegger. In 1927 he set up a successful bootlegging operation in Chicago's suburban area of Des Plaines. He and his partner Matt Kolb brewed quality beer and trucked it to the saloons and speakeasies in the area. Touchy often bought off police and other officials with gifts of specially brewed bottled beer. For years Al

CAPONE tried to take over Touchy's operations, but he was uncertain of Touchy's impressive (but imaginary) gang of hoods. Finally in 1931 Capone's gunmen killed Kolb. Touchy was arrested for allegedly abducting brewer William A. Hamm, Jr. in 1933 but was found not guilty (members of the Barker-Karpis gang were later convicted). That same year, Touchy and others were arrested for allegedly kidnapping John Factor, an international swindler with ties to Capone. Touchy, nicknamed the "Terrible Touchy," was convicted of the crime and sentenced to 99 years in the state prison at Joliet, Illinois. Claiming he was framed and was innocent, Touchy broke out of prison with six other inmates on October 9, 1942. Caught in December of that year, Touchy was given an additional sentence of 199 years. His lawyers filed many appeals, finally succeeding in obtaining his release on November 25, 1959 (it was discovered that Touchy, in the Factor kidnapping case, had been framed on perjured testimony). On December 17, 1959, unknown gunmen shot and killed him outside his sister's home in Chicago.

TOURBILLON, Robert Arthur (1880-1950). American robber and con man. In the early 1900s in New York, Tourbillon formed a blackmail ring to extort money from rich society ladies. Tourbillon, who used several aliases, including Dapper Don Collins (his best known), was a smooth talker and a fine dresser. He used his charms to seduce women and bilk them of their money. Tourbillon accumulated a small fortune from his confidence games, as well as from robbery, bootlegging, drug smuggling, and alien smuggling. He served some time in jail but usually managed to evade conviction, helped by his crafty lawyer, Bill Fallon, and by the refusal of many of his victims to testify against him for fear of public scandal. In 1924 Tourbillon fled to Paris to avoid arrest for grand larceny. There and in Berlin he continued his swindling capers. New York police officers found him in a Paris jail; he had been arrested for not paying his hotel bill and for pushing a wealthy American woman off her Paris hotel balcony. Extradited to the United States, Tourbillon won the larceny case and then went into hiding for a while. In 1929 he was convicted of swindling a New Jersey apple farmer of $30,000 and was sentenced to three years in prison. Later he swindled a poor immigrant woman out of several hundred dollars, was apprehended, convicted, and sentenced to 15 to 30 years in prison. He died in Attica prison in June 1950.

TRACY, Ann Gibson (b. 1935). California murderer. In 1958 Tracy, a cocktail waitress in Laguna Beach, California, met and fell in love with Amos Stricker, a wealthy building contractor. During their two-year romance, Stricker dated other women and taunted Tracy with stories about his other love affairs. Tracy asked Stricker not to tell her about his other paramours, but he persisted. Finally, on November 14, 1960, Tracy shot and killed Stricker at his Laguna Beach home. Apprehended and

tried, she was convicted of first degree murder after first deny-
ing her guilt and then confessing. Before she was sent to the
Corona Women's Prison for life, Tracy was asked why she killed
Stricker and replied, "Because I loved him."

TRACY, Harry (1875?-1902). American robber, outlaw, escapee,
and murderer. In about 1895 he appeared at the Hole in the
Wall, a notorious outlaw hideout on the Wyoming-Utah border,
and soon pulled off several robberies before being caught and
sent to prison in Utah. In 1897 Tracy broke out and joined the
Wild Bunch led by outlaw Butch CASSIDY. Known as the "Mad
Dog of the Bunch" because of his brutal, murderous nature,
Tracy was arrested and charged with murder several times but
managed to break free. Sent to the Colorado State Prison for
life on a conviction of murder, Tracy and his friend Dave Merrill, another convict, stole a guard's rifle, killed two guards,
and escaped on June 9, 1902, fleeing to Oregon where they stole
guns and ammunition and robbed a bank. Tracy strangled Merrill to death when he came across a newspaper article saying his
companion had informed on him years earlier in order to get a
lighter sentence for a robbery they had committed together.
Written up as a "heroic" desperado, Tracy singlehandedly fought
off pursuing posses in July 1902. Finally cornered at a farm
near Davenport, Washington, on August 3, 1902, he held about
100 lawmen at bay in a furious day-long gun battle and then
committed suicide by firing a bullet into his head.

TRAFFICANTE, Santo, Jr. (b. 1915). American racketeer. As a
henchman for New York Mafia boss Vito GENOVESE, Trafficante
was allegedly involved in the slaying of rival boss Albert ANA-
STASIA in 1957. He managed mob-owned casinos in Cuba until
Castro closed them down in 1959 and rose to be a top kingpin
in the Mafia-oriented syndicate, a cartel controlling organized
crime in the United States. In 1975 Trafficante, who was a good
friend of Meyer LANSKY, told a congressional committee he had
helped recruit gangsters like John ROSELLI in the early 1960s
to assassinate Fidel Castro. Trafficante is today the reputed
syndicate boss of Tampa, Florida (some say he is underworld
boss of all Florida) and supposed to be involved in numerous
rackets, such as narcotics and gambling.

TRASH BAG MURDERER. See KEARNEY, Patrick.

TREBITSCH-LINCOLN, Ignatius Timothy (1875?-1943). Hungarian-
born adventurer and spy. Well educated with linguistic and
journalistic abilities, he was involved in various intrigues and
public disturbances in Europe, America, and Asia, having a
long checkered career run on bluff as a journalist, minister,
member of parliament, spy, political advisor, Buddhist monk,
and mandarin. This ex-Hungarian Jew, who changed his faith
to become a Lutheran missionary in Canada and then an Anglican

minister in England, ingratiated himself with British political
personages and in 1910 gained election to the House of Commons.
Later, distrusted and snubbed by many acquaintances, Trebitsch
(the name he was born with) betrayed the British by becoming
a double agent in World War I, pretending to procure information
for British intelligence while actually working as a German spy.
However, the discovery of his earlier forgery of the signature
of a distinguished Liberal Party member led to his arrest (1915)
in New York and extradition to England. Released from prison
in mid-1919, Trebitsch-Lincoln was deported to his native Hungary and subsequently became entangled in revolutionary movements both in Germany and Hungary. Much money was gleaned
by him for purposes of conspiracy and underhanded work, which
he later carried on in China as an anti-British propagandist, a
political advisor of Wu P'ei-fu, and a Buddhist abbot named
Chao-kung. He died in Shanghai on October 7, 1943.

TREGOFF, Carole. See FINCH, [Raymond] Bernard.

TRIFA, Valerian (b. 1914). Rumanian-American clergyman accused
of Nazi war crimes. When the German Nazis took over Rumania
in 1940 during World War II, Viorel Trifa (his name then) was
a member of the Rumanian Iron Guard, a fascist organization
which conducted pogroms against the Jews and others. He reportedly incited anti-Semitic violence as a speaker at rallies in
Bucharest in 1941. When the war ended he gained refuge in
Italy, where he taught history as a layman at a Catholic college
in Pesaro. In 1950 he entered the United States under the 1948
Displaced Persons Act, denying ever having been an Iron Guard-
ist. Consecrated as a bishop in the Rumanian Orthodox Church
in 1952, Trifa secured American citizenship in 1957 and became
an archbishop residing in the church's estate in Grass Lake,
Michigan. In 1975 the U.S. Justice Department began investigating Trifa as a war criminal, and in 1982 he was tried and
admitted to covering up his fascist activities when he came to
America. Portugal, which accepted Trifa as a U.S. deportee
in 1984, has since ordered him expelled.

TROPPMANN, Jean-Baptiste (1848-70). French mass murderer. In
1869, pretending to have found a gold mine in the Vosges Mountains in northeast France, he persuaded his newly acquired rich
friend Jean Kinck of Roubaix (French town near the Belgian
frontier) to loan him money to develop the fictitious mine. Soon
Kinck, who had also given Troppmann power of attorney, was
poisoned by Troppmann, who cut up his victim's corpse afterward and scattered the parts in a field outside Paris. Then
Troppmann induced Kinck's wife and six children to come to
Paris, where he knifed and strangled them all to death (September 1869). The authorities soon discovered the bodies buried in shallow graves and subsequently associated the crime
with Troppmann, whom local police in Le Havre had taken into

custody following his failure to produce a passport while seeking ship passage to America. Documents with the name Jean Kinck were found on him. After being brought to Paris, Troppmann gave his true name but denied the murders at first, feigning sorrow when he was shown his victims' bodies. However, while awaiting trial in prison, he finally admitted that he had killed the Kincks to gain their money and valuables. About two months later, on January 19, 1870, his death sentence was carried out as many French notables and others watched Troppmann, calm and collected, be guillotined. People were struck by his singularity, especially his height (only five feet tall) and his thumbs, which were as long as his index fingers.

TUFTS, Henry (1748-1831). American horse thief. At the age of 16 he stole his first horse and thereafter became proficient at breaking into locked barns and stables from which he stole scores of horses during his lifetime. Tufts used saws and corrosives to enter buildings, cork horseshoes to deaden the sound of horses being taken, and paints to disguise the animals afterward so they could be sold more easily to unsuspecting buyers. During the American Revolution (1776-83) he profitably sold stolen horses to both the Americans and the British in the New England area. Tufts eventually retired in 1807 and under a pseudonym published his autobiography, aptly titled The Autobiography of a Criminal, which was widely read, particularly by horse thieves. The book was the first autobiography by an American criminal. As a reformed and respectable citizen, he lived to a ripe old age, dying in 1831.

TURLEY, Preston S. (b. 1858). Virginia minister and murderer. His heavy drinking led to his dismissal as minister of the Baptist church in Charleston, Virginia (now West Virginia). On a summer night in 1858 Turley and his wife, Mary Susan, whom he had inveigled to participate in many of his carousals, arrived home drunk and got into a furious argument. Turley, reciting scripture, suddenly strangled Mary Susan to death in front of their three children and then disposed of her weighted-down corpse in a nearby river. The children, whom oddly he had not thought would tell the authorities, did so, and Turley was arrested, convicted, and sentenced to death. While standing on the gallows before a large crowd on September 17, 1858, he made his final remarks, a three and one half hour lecture on sin and demon rum. Turley was unhappy to see the hangman approach and not to see his children, who had stayed away despite Turley's letters from his death cell urging them to attend (one letter had said, "Don't you want to go and see Pa hung?").

TURNER, Joyce (b. 1928). South Carolina murderer. Owner of a nursery school in Columbia, South Carolina, she begrudgingly supported her indolent husband, Alonzo, until she fatally shot him in his sleep in June 1956. Two neighbors, Audrey Noakes and Clestell Gay, had urged her to do it; afterward the murder weapon, a .22-caliber pistol bought by Gay, was found and helped lead to the arrest of the three schemers, who admitted guilt and were sentenced to life imprisonment. At her trial's end, Joyce Turner scoffed about her husband's always wanting "to die in bed," as he used to say, a fate which she "simply arranged."

TURNER, Nat (1800-1831). Virginia murderer and insurrectionist. Turner, a black preacher and slave foreman, claimed he had been called by God to lead a revolt against the white plantation owners of Southampton County, Virginia. On the night of August 21, 1831, Turner and seven fellow black slaves invaded the manor house of Joseph Travis, Turner's master, and killed Travis and his family. Soon joined by about 75 other blacks, Turner went on a bloody two-day rampage of destruction and killing. His band murdered 51 whites before a massive counter-attack by white militiamen and federal troops--more than 3,000 men in all--crushed the insurrection. More than 100 black followers of Turner were rounded up and hanged, shot dead, or decapitated. Turner eluded capture for nearly two months but was finally caught in the woods and brought to trial. He confessed and was found guilty and was hanged in Jerusalem, Virginia, on November 11, 1831.

TURPIN, Dick or Richard (1706-39). English robber. At the age of 21, Turpin opened his own butcher shop which he stocked by stealing sheep, cattle, and horses. Later he turned to highway robbery with great success, operating out of a cave in Epping Forest northeast of London, generally working alone, and often preying on travelers on the road between London and Oxford. At one period Turpin committed robbery almost every night. After a Ł200 reward was offered for his capture, dead or alive, Turpin disappeared for about a year. Then a well-to-do gentleman, John Palmer, was caught illegally shooting gamecock in Yorkshire. Palmer turned out to be Turpin, who was later convicted of horse stealing and sentenced to death. He was hanged at York on April 7, 1739. Turpin's life was the basis of William H. Ainsworth's novel Rookwood, published in 1834.

TUTT, David or Davis (d. 1865). American gunfighter. By 1865 he had shot several men in head-on gun duels and gained some fame as a hardened gunfighter. Recently discharged from the Union Army, Tutt stopped in Springfield, Missouri, where he got into an argument with James Butler "Wild Bill" Hickok over Susannah Moore, a beautiful girl from the Ozarks. They challenged each other to a gunfight. In the classic Hollywood movie style, Tutt and Hickok walked toward each other in the middle of the town square on July 21, 1865. Tutt drew first, hastily fired several shots, and missed Hickok, who coolly drew, steadied his gun with both hands, and fired, hitting Tutt in the heart, killing him.

TWEED, [William Marcy] "Boss" (1823-78). New York politician and Tammany leader. Elected New York alderman in 1851, Tweed was one of the so-called "Forty Thieves." After serving as a U.S. Congressman (1853-55), he held important positions in New York City government and gained absolute control of Tammany Hall, the Democratic Party political machine that controlled the city's votes. Tweed and his cronies, the "Tweed Ring," dispensed special favors to businessmen, corporations, judges, police officers, gamblers, gangsters, and anyone who was of service to the machine at election time. Elected state senator in 1868, Tweed forced the state legislature to pass a city charter that allowed him and his cronies great leverage to manipulate expenditures. The Tweed Ring plundered the city treasury of some $45 million and robbed New York of almost three times that amount in uncollected taxes. Revelations of fixing contracts, falsifications of public accounts, and other fraudulent dealings were made in The New York Times, arousing public indignation. Tweed was charged with forgery and larceny, brought to trial, convicted, and sentenced to 12 years' imprisonment (the sentence was reduced by a higher court). Tweed was released in 1875 after spending one year in prison, but was arrested on a civil charge and imprisoned again. He escaped, fled to Cuba, and then to Spain. Again arrested, Tweed was extradited to the United States in 1876 and imprisoned in New York City's Ludlow Street Jail, where he died on April 12, 1878.

TYPHOID MARY. See MALLON, "Typhoid" Mary.

- U -

UNDERHILL, Wilbur (1897-1934). American bank robber. In 1933 Underhill, who was serving time for robbery, broke out of the Kansas State Penitentiary with several other inmates and went into hiding in the Cookson Hills of Oklahoma. He soon became head of Ford Bradshaw's gang and went on a wild bank robbery spree in Oklahoma, Arkansas, and Kansas. Underhill, nicknamed the "Tri-State Terror," and his recent bride were found by FBI agents in Shawnee, Oklahoma, on New Year's Day, 1934. A fierce gun battle ensued during which Underhill, bleeding from many wounds and wearing only his longjohns, dashed wildly firing a shotgun through police lines. He was found unconscious after driving through a store's plateglass window and died in the hospital at McAlester, Oklahoma, on January 6, 1934.

UNRUH, Howard (b. 1921). New Jersey mass murderer. Unruh, a Bible reader, became infatuated with weapons while serving as a U.S. soldier in Europe during World War II. After the war he acquired several guns and practiced his marksmanship in his basement. He grew to hate his neighbors, whom he believed ridiculed him behind his back. Using a 9-mm German Luger, Unruh went on a shooting rampage on the streets of his hometown, Camden, New Jersey, on September 6, 1949. He killed 13 persons in 12 minutes, then surrendered to police. Judged incurably insane by doctors, Unruh never faced trial and was incarcerated for life in a New Jersey mental hospital, where he still remains.

URSINUS, Sophie [born: Sophie Charlotte Elizabeth Weingarten] (1760-1836). German aristocrat and poisoner. Living in grand style in a villa outside Berlin, she was accused of fatally poisoning with arsenic a young Dutch officer with whom she had an extramarital affair and who threatened to leave her, her elderly husband, Ursinus, who died in 1800, and her rich maiden aunt Christina Regina Witte, who died in 1801 and whose estate she inherited. One of Sophie's servants, Benjamin Klein, became her confidant and told authorities about the poisonings; Klein himself was being poisoned by Sophie, who had decided that he knew too much. Convicted only of murdering her aunt, she was imprisoned in the huge castle of Glatz (Klodzko, Poland), where she was allowed to live in the luxury she had always known. There she had servants, some rooms in the castle's uppermost part, and gorgeous clothes; her fortune had not been taken away, owing to her upper-class position. Until her natural death on April 4, 1836, Sophie remained a genteel inmate, for 30 years hosting highborn guests and sumptuous dinners while prisoners in the dungeons below starved and labored to death in chains.

- V -

VACHER, Joseph (1869-98). French mass murderer and necrophile. A chronic loafer as a boy, he became a wandering derelict in France in the 1890s. As the so-called "French Ripper" he committed crimes and murders undetected until his apprehension in 1898. He assaulted and killed at least ten (maybe as many as 20) women and young girls and boys, whose corpses he mutilated and sexually abused. After he was caught Vacher claimed he was insane, having once been an inmate in an asylum, and was not responsible for the murders he had perpetrated. Closely examined as a "mental curiosity" before his trial, he seemed utterly without self-reproach and was judged a common criminal without redemption. The death sentence given him was carried out the last day of 1898.

VAILLANT, Auguste. See CASERIO, Sante Geronimo.

VALACHI, Joe or Joseph [Michael] (1904-71). American gangster and informer. In the early 1930s he worked as a "hit man" (hired killer) for Mafia boss Salvatore MARANZANO. Then he became involved in gambling, numbers rackets, and sale of narcotics in New York, working for Anthony C. STROLLO and other racketeers. Valachi was convicted of narcotics violations in 1959 and sent to prison in Atlanta for 15 to 20 years. There he supposedly was given the "kiss of death" by inmate Vito GENOVESE, who had been told Valachi was an informer. Valachi did decide to "sing" in order to get federal protection: In 1963 he publicly revealed the inner workings of the Cosa Nostra and the crime syndicate to the Senate Permanent Investigations Subcommittee chaired by Senator John L. McClellan. Valachi also identified more than 300 Mafia members. The Mafia reportedly issued a $100,000 contract to anyone who could kill Valachi, the "squealer," who was held in special custody while in prison. In 1968 he was transferred to the La Tuna Federal Prison in El Paso, Texas, where he died of a heart attack in 1971.

VAN DER LUBBE, Marinus (1909-34). Dutch arsonist. The Reichstag building, seat of the parliament in Berlin, went up in flames on the night of February 27, 1933. Van der Lubbe, caught at the scene of the fire, and four others--Ernest Torgler (a former German deputy), Georgi Dimitrov (a Bulgarian Communist writer), Blagoi Popoff (a Bulgarian student), and Wassil Taneff (a Bulgarian shoemaker)--were accused of responsibility for the fire and tried at Leipzig in 1933. Many believed the charges against Van der Lubbe and the others were contrived by the Nazi government to incite public hysteria against its political enemies and thus to gain emergency powers. The day after the fire, freedom of speech and freedom of the press was abolished in Germany and agitation against Communists and Jews increased. During the three-month-long trial, Van der Lubbe took little notice of the proceedings, laughing occasionally at the court and asserting his guilt (he had earlier stated to the police that he had set the fire himself for "personal reasons"). He was convicted and sentenced to death; the other defendants were acquitted. Despite a strong but vain appeal by the Dutch government, Van der Lubbe was beheaded in Leipzig prison on January 10, 1934.

VANE, Charles (d. 1719). English pirate. By 1715 he was one of the most feared pirates along the North Atlantic coast and in the West Indies. With BLACKBEARD, Vane engaged in wild merrymaking on North Carolina's Ocracoke Island. In 1718 Vane openly defied the arrival of Governor Woodes Rogers in Nassau harbor in the Bahamas, setting fire to a captured French ship loaded with explosives and sending it adrift toward two British warships, which were forced to retreat out to sea. Vane's pirate ship was wrecked on a desolate island in the Bay of Honduras; he nearly starved to death before his rescue by a passing ship. Vane was subsequently recognized and later hanged in Jamaica.

VAN MEEGEREN, Hans (1889-1947). Dutch painter and forger. When his own work lost favor with the critics, Van Meegeren decided to paint forgeries. Between 1936 and 1942 he created seven paintings attributed to the famous seventeenth-century Dutch artist Jan Vermeer, whose painting technique Van Meegeren researched and perfected. "Christ at Emmaus," probably Van Meegeren's most noted forgery, was pronounced a genuine masterpiece and the earliest known Vermeer and was bought by the Boymans Museum in Rotterdam. Van Meegeren, whose successful forgeries fetched about $3 million in all, was never detected as a forger. After World War II, when one of his paintings was discovered to have been sold to German Nazi leader Hermann GOERING, Van Meegeren was arrested and accused of collaborating with the enemy. In order to establish his innocence, Van Meegeren revealed himself as a forger and produced a painting in the Vermeer manner while in his jail cell. He died before he served out his one-year prison sentence.

VAN VALKENBURGH, Elizabeth (1799-1846). New York poisoner. As the temperance movement grew in America, she apparently over-reacted in her efforts to reform her two heavy-drinking husbands, both of whom she later confessed to killing by lacing their tea with arsenic poisoning. At her trial she calmly said that her second husband, John Van Valkenburgh, like her first spouse, had angered her because of excessive use of liquor, consequently she hoped to effect a cure through poison. About ten months after the death of her last husband, she was hanged in Fulton, New York, on January 24, 1846.

VANZETTI, Bartolomeo (1888-1927). Italian-born anarchist. He and Nicola SACCO, two Italian aliens and self-proclaimed anarchists in the United States, were charged with killing a shoe-factory paymaster and a guard during a robbery in South Braintree, Massachusetts, on April 15, 1920. Vanzetti, a fish peddler, and Sacco, a shoemaker, both of whom had evaded the army draft and feared deportation by the Justice Department, were found carrying guns and made false statements at their arrest. Brought to trial in Dedham, Massachusetts, the two defendants were found guilty by a jury on July 14, 1921. A storm of protest greeted the verdict, which was allegedly arrived at on flimsy evidence and influenced in part by anti-foreign, anti-Communist hysteria in the country. Prominent persons and others attacked the trial's testimony, saying it was false and biased in many parts. When the Massachusetts Supreme Court upheld the denial of another trial, appeals were made to Governor Alvan Tufts Fuller, who delayed the execution of Sacco and Vanzetti (they had been sentenced to death on April 9, 1927) and appointed an independent commission to review the case (June-August 1927). The commission ruled that their trial had been fair, Governor Fuller denied clemency, and

the two convicted immigrants, who had spent seven years in
prison, were sent to the electric chair on August 23, 1927.
Whether their executions were miscarriages of justice remains
debatable. There is some evidence that Vanzetti's only crime
was knowing the alleged guilt of Sacco.

VASQUEZ, Tiburcio (1835-75). Mexican-born California outlaw and
murderer. From 1870 to 1875 Vasquez and his band of outlaws,
mostly Mexicans, raided and robbed stores, ranches, hotels,
stagecoaches, and travelers in Southern California. He killed
three unarmed inhabitants of Tres Pinos during an attack on
the village on August 26, 1873. A large reward was posted
for his capture, dead or alive. One of Vasquez's band, Abdon
Leiva, caught Vasquez making love to his wife and betrayed
him, telling possemen about his hideout in Cahuenga Pass (now
the site of Hollywood). Vasquez was wounded in a shootout
there with a posse led by George Beers and was caught. He
was tried, convicted of murder, and hanged in San Jose,
California, on March 19, 1875.

VAVOUDIS, Nicholas (1903-51). Russian-born Communist Greek
spy. His parents brought him to Greece after the Bolshevik
Revolution, and there he became an active Communist Party
member closely connected to the Soviets. Arrested (1932) for
illegal Communist activities and sent to prison for four years,
Vavoudis escaped two years later by tunneling under the prison
walls and fled to the Soviet Union to become a highly trained
espionage agent. He later returned secretly to Greece to work
with Nicholas Kaloumenos and other Communist agents in the
underground before and during World War II (1939-45). After
the war, Vavoudis directed successful underground operations
as part of the Soviets' drive to control the Greek government.
For five years, he collected confidential military, political, and
economic information which he transmitted by radio in coded
messages to Communist confederates in Rumania, who relayed
them on to Moscow. By 1951 Greek security officials had uncovered and arrested many members of the Communist underground. They soon pinpointed where Vavoudis and Kaloumenos
had their hidden radio in Athens, arrested Kaloumenos (who
was later sentenced to death), but found that Vavoudis had
mortally shot himself (November 14, 1951) as he lay in a
secret underground room from which the messages had been
sent.

VELGO, Marie [Havlick] (b. 1916). Czechoslovakian murderer. In
1936 this gorgeous young wife of Jan Velgo, a well-to-do judge
whom she had recently married, learned that her husband had
only wedded her for convenience (as a married man he had a
better chance to gain a higher, vacant judgeship) and planned
to divorce her in the future. A thug named Wenzel Cerny,
whom Marie hired to kill Jan so that she would be assured of

inheriting his large estate, carried out the murder, but was surprised and shot by Marie at the scene in the Velgo apartment in Brno, Czechoslovakia (March 16, 1936). Cerny lived to show the authorities a letter signed by Marie in which she agreed to pay him 5,000 korunen (around $200) for some "services." Nonetheless, Marie was acquitted (reportedly her striking beauty swayed the all-male jury); Cerny was convicted and sentenced to life in prison. Later Marie was retried (October 1937), convicted, and received a 12-year prison sentence.

VELTHEIM, Franz von (fl. c. 1890-1908). German thief and blackmailer. Tall, handsome, and cunning, Veltheim used numerous disguises and aliases during a lucrative criminal career in London, Paris, Rome, Naples, Antwerp, Johannesburg, and other places. For years he baffled Scotland Yard, which considered him dead in 1896 when a corpse identified as his was found in the Thames. But he turned up again and again in the early 1900s: swindling £20,000 from some wealthy people in Rome on promises to recover for them the mythical lost Kruger treasure, whose whereabouts he professed to know; robbing money and jewels from young and old European and American ladies whom he betrayed after they fell in love with him; and blackmailing rich men and women on threats of murder. Scotland Yard finally caught Veltheim in London in 1908, and he received 20 years' imprisonment on a blackmail conviction. After World War I he was secretly deported to his native Germany, along with other undesirables, and he vanished completely.

VERZENI, Vincenz (1849-?). Italian mass murderer. Of ignoble ancestry, he prowled the streets of his native Rome and its environs, spasmodically seeking sexual pleasure through killing. At least a dozen murdered young women were credited to Verzeni, who was known to have disemboweled some victims and sucked their blood. In 1873, after several years of victimizations, he was arrested, convicted of murder, and imprisoned for life. Phrenologists and others, after examining him, deduced that the defectively bulky shape of his head and the aberrant history of his family (with arrested developments and mental problems) accounted for his extreme deviant character and behavior. But Verzeni, claiming he was not insane, said he felt ecstasy at the moment of killing.

VESCO, Robert [Lee] (b. 1935). American financier and fugitive. He fled from the United States to Costa Rica in 1972 when the Securities and Exchange Commission (SEC) was investigating his murky financial dealings. Vesco, who had invested heavily in Costa Rica's economy, "loaned" $3.5 million to Costa Rican President José Figuéres Ferrer, who sheltered Vesco from extradition to the United States where he faced charges of embezzlement. Rodrigo Carazo Odio, who pledged to rid Costa Rica of "corruption" and to expel Vesco, was elected the country's president in February 1978. Vesco then fled to the Bahamas. He faces charges in the United States of "misappropriating" about $224 million from Investors Overseas Services, his mutual funds company, and of giving illegal contributions to President Richard M. Nixon's 1972 reelection campaign. Vesco is also wanted on charges of swindling and bribery in Europe.

VESEY, Denmark (c. 1767-1822). West Indian-born Carolina slave insurrectionist. In 1800 Vesey, an intelligent and energetic black slave, purchased his freedom from his master for $600 he had won in a lottery. Working as a carpenter, he became dissatisfied with his second-class, freedman status and the wretched status of most blacks. Vesey, Peter Poyas, and some other blacks planned and organized an insurrection of all slaves in and around Charleston, South Carolina, to take place on July 2, 1822. The rebels hoped to seize arsenals, free the slaves, and take over the area. When the authorities were alerted to the scheduled July uprising, Vesey moved the date forward to June 16, on the eve of which Vesey, Poyas, and others were arrested (they were betrayed by informers). Shortly afterward 37 blacks including Vesey and Poyas were tried, convicted of actively inciting an insurrection, and hanged. Some 32 blacks were condemned to exile; four white men were fined and briefly jailed for encouraging the insurrection.

VICARS, Henry Edward (1888-1942). English burglar. Vicars, said to have committed more than 1,000 offenses, had a 20-year career of undetected burglary and housebreaking. He always worked alone, constantly varied his field of operation, never left any fingerprints or footprints, and never used or threatened violence while committing his crimes. Vicars was given the name "Flannelfoot" by the press because he wore socks or pieces of flannel over his shoes when entering the premises. Officers of Scotland Yard finally tracked him down, arresting him in the act of burglary in Eastcote, Middlesex, in October 1937. Vicars pleaded guilty to numerous offenses and was sentenced to five years' imprisonment. He died shortly after his release.

VIDAL, Ginette (b. 1931). French murderer. In Paris in 1972 she and her 29-year-old lover, Gerard Osselin, both of whom were married, signed an unusual contract in which each swore lifelong fidelity to the other, reserving the right to kill the other if that one became unfaithful. At the time both had left their families and were living together. Discovering that Osselin had begun secretly to see his wife again, Vidal fatally shot him as he slept, but she was found with the corpse and arrested while showing her supposedly lawful murder pact. It had no validity under French law, and Vidal, extremely piqued because of this, was found guilty and sentenced to ten years in prison.

VILLA, Francisco or "Pancho" [born: Doroteo Arango] (1878-1923).
Mexican cattle thief, outlaw, and revolutionary. Involved at an
early age in cattle rustling and other thievery in the Mexican
states of Chihuahua and Durango, he became a fugitive with a
reward for his capture offered by Mexican President Porfirio
Díaz. He joined Francisco Madero's revolutionary forces that
overthrew Díaz in 1911 and later in 1914 joined Venustiano Carranza in a revolution against President Victoriano Huerta, who
had ousted Madero in 1913. Bitter rivalry between Carranza
and Villa caused them to split apart, with Villa allying himself
with Emiliano Zapata in rebellion against Carranza, whose forces
were victorious in 1915. After the United States recognized
Carranza's Mexican government, Villa, who had fled to the
mountains in northern Mexico, ordered the execution of 16 U.S.
citizens at Santa Isabel, Chihuahua, in January 1916 and then
led a raid on Columbus, New Mexico, on March 9, 1916, killing
other Americans and partly burning the town. A U.S. military
expedition under Brigadier General John J. Pershing failed to
capture Villa and his outlaw band after a 300-mile chase through
Chihuahua and withdrew in 1917. Villa continued his depredations until 1920, when President Carranza was killed in a successful revolution led by Álvaro Obregón. Pardoned by the
new Mexican government with the stipulation that he would re-
tire from politics, Villa settled on a large ranch near Parral,
Chihuahua. There, on June 20, 1923, he was assassinated by
Melitón Losoya, a rich rival rancher, and his henchmen. The
killers supposedly were supported by Obregón, who now considered Villa a foe.

VILLIERS, Henry [Stuart] (fl. latter 1800s). British pickpocket,
forger, blackmailer, and burglar. A gentleman's servant who
had been the personal valet of a prominent nobleman for three
years, Villiers became a supposedly cosmopolitan man of wealth
in London, where he lived and hobnobbed with the upper class.
However, he lived a typical Jekyll and Hyde existence, indulging secretly in criminality with underworld associates who be-
stowed on him the sobriquet "Henry the Valet" because of his
past and gentlemanly life. Traveling in Britain and Europe,
this handsome rogue was especially deft at deceiving rich
women--his ladyloves--who sometimes loaned him much money,
with which he disappeared. Villiers was finally arrested in
London for stealing the Duchess of Sutherland's jewels in a
railway station in Paris. Found guilty, he received a seven-
year prison term and afterward vanished.

VLAD TEPES (1431?-77). Walachian prince and impaler. After
taking the throne of Walachia (southern Rumania) in 1456, he
continued the fight to hold back the Ottoman Turks who threatened to ruin the Walachian state. A fearless defender of law
and order and of Christianity, Vlad Tepes was nevertheless a
mercilessly cruel ruler. He was known as "Vlad the Impaler"

because of the way he often executed captive enemies (Turks, court rivals, and subjects who offended him): he impaled his victims alive upon wooden stakes in the ground. He also maimed, scalped, beheaded, and boiled alive some victims. But many of the peasants of Walachia and neighboring Transylvania considered him their savior, for he punished the landed nobility who rejected his efforts to create a "free market" that would help the peasants economically. In 1462 the Turks deposed Vlad Tepes, who went to Hungary and tried vainly to secure aid to regain the Walachian throne. In 1476 Transylvanians aided him in Walachia, which again came under his rule until a Turkish-supported rival ambushed and killed him about one year later. This bloodthirsty prince became the basis of the character of Count Dracula created by Bram Stoker in his 1897 novel, Dracula; during his lifetime Vlad Tepes had called himself at times "Dracula" (son of dragon or devil) in memory of his father, Prince Vlad Dracul.

VOIRBO, Pierre (d. 1869). French murderer. After suffering a miserable boyhood with a cruel father, he turned to crime for a livelihood and evidently was a killer-for-hire in and around Paris in the 1860s; at least ten murders are imputed to him. In his Paris lodgings in early 1869, Voirbo killed Désiré Bodasse, an elderly man who had loaned him 10,000 francs and now wanted repayment. Bodasse's body was cut into pieces which were chucked down a well, all except for the head, which Voirbo later claimed he filled with hot lead and sank in the Seine River. The body parts were found in the well, and an investigation began under Gustave Macé, who later became one of France's most skillful detectives. Although Voirbo had taken great pains to clean Bodasse's bloodstains off his floors and so had scoured his usually dirty lodgings thoroughly, suspicion centered on him after Macé traced the crime to him and reasoned that Voirbo's apparent effort to wash away the stains made him guilty. Voirbo made a dramatic confession when openly challenged by Macé. While in prison awaiting trial, he cut his throat with a knife (which had been sent to him hidden in a loaf of bread) and died.

VOUKELITCH, Branko de. See SORGE, Richard.

- W -

WADDELL, Reed (1859-95). American swindler. Waddell, born into a rich and respected Illinois family, became a successful gold-brick and "green-goods" swindler in New York City, Paris, London, and other places. Between 1880 and 1890 he reportedly made more than $250,000 from his con games. Scores of suckers bought his gold bricks, which were lead bricks covered by three coats of gold paint and containing slugs of pure gold to convince the suckers of their genuineness. Waddell sold his first gold brick for $4,000 in New York City in 1880. In his "green-goods" scheme, Waddell sold at so-called bargain prices what victims thought were perfect counterfeit bills after they had been lured by genuine bills. Suckers quickly discovered they had bought worthless green paper. In March 1895 in Paris, Waddell was shot and killed by Tom O'Brien, another swindler, during an argument over the spoils of a swindle.

WAGNER, Franz (1874-1938). German mass murderer. As a studious, intelligent youth, after the death of his father, he saw his mother, sister, and brother fall into a life of gross debauchery, which undoubtedly greatly troubled him. He became a teacher, married, and had five children (whose births were unwelcome by him, according to his diary) while growing increasingly melancholic and suicidal. About a year after moving to a town near Stuttgart, West Germany, Wagner went berserk without any apparent reason on the night of September 3, 1913. He knifed to death his wife and children, then wildly ran about the town firing guns at whomever he saw, killing nine persons; afterward he set fire to houses and barns and shot cows and horses fleeing from the flames. Finally police and numerous others clubbed him senseless to end his raving. The authorities pronounced Wagner an incorrigible paranoid and incarcerated him, despite his pleas to be executed, in a mental institution for the rest of his life.

WAGNER, Gustav Franz (1911-80). Austrian-born Nazi officer and war criminal. An important Nazi SS officer in World War II, Wagner was accused of being responsible for the gas-chamber deaths of about 250,000 Poles and Jews at the concentration camps of Sobibor and Treblinka, located in Poland. Known as "The Human Beast," Wagner used a forged passport issued in Damascus, Syria, to flee to Brazil in 1950. He was tried in absentia by a German court in 1965-66 and was found guilty of the deaths of 152,000 Jews at Sobibor, where he was allegedly assistant chief in 1942-43. Wagner, who lived under the name of Ganter Mende in Brazil, was identified by Treblinka survivors in 1978 and imprisoned. In 1979 Brazil's Supreme Court set him free, denying extradition requests from West Germany, Austria, Poland, and Israel on the grounds that the time for prosecution had lapsed. Wagner killed himself with a knife at his farm outside São Paulo on October 3, 1980. He had attempted suicide four times previously.

WAINEWRIGHT, Thomas Griffiths (1794-1852). English painter, art critic, and forger. His paintings were shown at the Royal Academy in London between 1821 and 1825. Wainewright wrote essays on the arts for the London Magazine under the pen names of Janus Weathercock and Egomot Bonmot. He acquired a sinister reputation for allegedly poisoning his uncle (whose

money he inherited), his mother-in-law, and his sister-in-law
(whose life he had insured for Ł16,000). The suspicious death
of his sister-in-law resulted in an investigation by the insurance
company, which concluded that murder possibly had been committed but produced no real evidence. Wainewright, who had
gone to France in 1831 when the insurance case was being argued, did not return to England until 1837. He then was arrested, tried, and convicted on an 1826 forgery charge (he had
forged powers of attorney to secure capital willed to him when
he was entitled only to the interest). Wainewright was transported to Tasmania, where he later died.

WAITE, Arthur Warren (1887-1917). New York dentist and murderer.
In 1916 Waite, a handsome, urbane dentist who gadded about in
New York society, killed his wife's millionaire parents, Mr. and
Mrs. John E. Peck, because she stood to inherit about $1 million
on their deaths. Waite purposely caused Mrs. Peck to catch
pneumonia by driving in a downpour with the windshield open.
Pretending he was giving her medicine, Waite sprayed her throat
with deadly bacteria and viruses, resulting in her death on January 30, 1916 (doctors ruled it death from kidney disease, and
Waite promptly had Mrs. Peck's body cremated). Waite now attempted unsuccessfuly to have Mr. Peck catch pneumonia; he
then put chlorine gas in his bedroom, fed him Veronal (a bar-
bital), and gave him a nasal spray with a tuberculosis bacteria
in it. When Mr. Peck failed to become ill, Waite gave him some
arsenic, which put him in bed but didn't kill him. The dentist
finally suffocated his father-in-law with a pillow. Afterward a
suspicious family friend anonymously accused Waite of murdering
the Pecks. An autopsy of Mr. Peck revealed arsenic poison,
which was traced to the dentist, who soon confessed to his
crimes. On May 24, 1917, Waite was electrocuted at Sing Sing
Prison (now the Ossining Correctional Facility), New York.

WALL, Tessie (1869-1932). San Francisco madam. Tessie, a buxom
blonde, operated a famous bordello on O'Farrell Street in San
Francisco in the early part of the twentieth century. Her establishment had only beautiful, lusty blondes, all somewhat
fleshy, like herself, who charged high prices. Tessie never
seemed to have a shortage of well-paying, satisfied clients and
indulged herself in wild living and gambling. In 1916 she shot
and seriously wounded her divorced husband, Frank Daroux,
who had refused her request for reconciliation (Tessie said she
shot him "because I love him--damn him!"). Daroux, also a
brothel keeper, didn't testify against Tessie, who went free.
She retired one year later and lived comfortably until her death
in April 1932.

WALLACE, William Herbert (1878-1933). English alleged murderer.
As an adventurous, educated young man, he traveled abroad
only to end up with routine clerical jobs in India and China.

In 1913, after returning to England, he married Julia Thorp
with whom he lived quietly and respectably in Liverpool while
working as an insurance businessman. The unexpected occurred with the discovery of the murder of Julia on January 20,
1931; she had been bludgeoned to death in their house's parlor
room upstairs. Despite Wallace's alibi that he had gone to meet
a Mr. Qualtrough (who remained a mystery) on the evening of
the crime, he was charged with the murder of his wife and
brought to trial on April 22, 1931. After hearing confusing
testimony and only circumstantial evidence against Wallace, the
jury reached a verdict of guilty; Wallace calmly and repeatedly
insisted he was innocent. Less than a month later the Court of
Criminal Appeal overturned the conviction, but afterward public opinion, which had favored Wallace during the trial, began
to turn against him until he was eventually forced to live an
almost friendless existence in Liverpool. On February 26, 1933,
he died in the hospital from a long-time kidney disease.

WALSH, Johnny "The Mick" (d. 1883). New York gangster. In the
1870s and early 1880s he was a ruthless gangster, heading a
gang of pickpockets, thieves, and muggers in the Bowery (lower
Manhattan). Walsh feuded with rival gang leader Johnny IRVING,
head of the "Dutch Mob." In Shang Drapper's Sixth Avenue
saloon in late 1883, Walsh encountered Irving and his friend
Billy Porter, drew his gun, and fatally shot Irving. Porter immediately drew his pistol and killed Walsh.

WALTERS, Annie. See SACH, Amelia.

WANDERER, Carl Otto (1887-1921). Chicago murderer. In 1920
Wanderer, a hero in World War I, claimed his wife had been shot
dead by an unknown robber whom Wanderer had then gunned
down with his service revolver. Discrepancies in the crime led
to the police and newsmen Ben Hecht and Charles MacArthur
learning the truth: Wanderer had actually hired a ragged
stranger to stage a robbery and then shot and killed both
the stranger and his wife, who was pregnant at the time.
Wanderer said he was homosexual, had married his wife for her
money and had become repulsed by the thought of her giving
birth, and had thus arranged his robbery-murder scheme.
Wanderer was found guilty and sentenced to be hanged. Hecht
and MacArthur arranged to have Wanderer as he stood on the
gallows read attacks on their editors, but Wanderer, tied hand
and foot as all hanged persons are, was unable and instead
broke into song. He died on schedule.

WANSLEY, Thomas G. See GIBBS, Charles.

WARD, Return J. M. (d. 1857). Ohio murderer. Ward, an enormous brute, was known to often beat his wife Olive, who finally
left him. In early 1857 she visited Ward and disappeared.

Suspicious neighbors accused Ward of killing her, but they failed to find her body (they had thoughtlessly not looked under the couple's bed, where Olive's corpse was hidden). Later Olive's jawbone was discovered in the fireplace ashes Ward had discarded. Ward was arrested and tried; he said he had killed Olive by accident and then panicked, cutting her body into pieces to be burned in the fireplace. The jury stopped his sickening testimony halfway through and promptly sentenced him to death on the gallows. Some say Ward was "legally lynched" but the jury reached an illegal verdict.

WARDER, Alfred (1820-66). British physician and poisoner. He was married three times during a successful career practicing medicine and lecturing in Great Britain, but each of his wives died under a cloud of suspicious poisoning. A thorough toxicological examination of the body of his third spouse, Ellen Vivian, confirmed that she had died from tincture of aconite, tiny amounts of which had been administered to her by Warder, an expert on forensic toxicology himself, in the form of an oral sedative taken over a long time. Although he knew aconite was strictly for external use, Warder had his wife take it internally for her bladder trouble. A guilty verdict seemed imminent by a jury at the inquest; before being taken into custody Warder ingested lethal prussic (hydrocyanic) acid at his home and died. He was held responsible for Ellen's murder.

WARDLAW, Caroline (d. 1913). American presumed murderer. In 1901 Caroline's husband, Colonel Martin, was poisoned to death in New York City. Caroline was awarded $10,000 on the life insurance policy she had recently taken out on him. She then took her daughter, Oscey, to live with Virginia WARDLAW, a sister who was the head of Soule College in Murfreesboro, Tennessee; they were soon joined by Mary, Caroline's other sister (Mary's son had strangely died when his clothes caught fire in 1900). The Wardlaw sisters drew much attention with their long black dresses, black shawls, and black veils. They lived in a large, dark mansion that had little furniture. In 1909 Oscey died and the Wardlaw sisters attempted to collect a $32,000 life insurance policy on her. Doctors seemed to think Oscey died of drugs and starvation, and the sisters were arrested. Virginia starved herself to death in prison. Caroline was tried and judged criminally insane; she was first sent to prison and later transferred to an asylum, where she died in 1913. Mary was acquitted.

WARDLAW, Virginia (d. 1910). American presumed murderer. She was the leader of the sinister Wardlaw sisters--Virginia, Caroline, and Mary--who always dressed in black and lived in dark, drab houses and mansions in Virginia, Tennessee, New Jersey, and New York in the early part of the twentieth century. In 1900 Mary's son, John, suddenly died and the Wardlaw sisters collected $12,000 from a life insurance policy recently taken out on him. Soon afterward, Caroline's husband, Colonel Martin, died of poisoning in New York City; Caroline collected $10,000 in insurance. Caroline and Mary often stayed with Virginia, who never married and who had stints as the head of two southern colleges during the early 1900s. In 1909 Caroline's daughter, Oscey, died; doctors said she was starved to death. Virginia and her sisters were then arrested. While in prison awaiting trial, Virginia refused to eat and gradually starved herself to death in 1910. See also WARDLAW, Caroline.

WARNER, Matt [born: Willard Erastus Christiansen] (1864-1938). American robber and lawman. In the late 1880s Warner, nicknamed the "Mormon Kid" (he was the son of a Mormon bishop), rode with robbers out of Robber's Roost, a mountain outlaw hideout in the Utah territory. There he met up with Butch CASSIDY, Tom McCARTY, and other outlaws, helping them steal horses and cattle and rob banks in Colorado in 1889. With robbery money, Warner set up a saloon in Star Valley on the Utah-Wyoming border in 1890; many stolen bills, including a $10,000 bank note, were tacked to the wall behind the saloon's bar. Warner, who had managed to beat a bank robbery charge in 1892, was arrested for a bank job in 1896, convicted, and sent to prison for five years. After his release he reformed and became a respected citizen in Carbon County, Utah, where he was elected deputy sheriff. Warner lived to a ripe age, dying in 1938.

WATERFORD JACK [real name: Frances Warren] (1840-after 1880). Chicago prostitute. Pug-nosed and homely, Waterford Jack, as she was curiously called, was a noted streetwalker (prostitute who solicits in the streets) in Chicago in the 1870s. She claimed she sought customers (some five to 25) every night, charging them from $1 to $10 for a "trick." In 1875 she formed a band of streetwalkers whom she took care of like a mother; she always put some of their earnings in bank accounts for them, taking a small amount for herself and banking it (she is credited with having never stolen a cent from her "girls'" savings). When Waterford Jack's savings account had reached $30,000 (her goal for retirement), she disappeared in 1880 from the Chicago streets.

WATSON, Ella. See CATTLE KATE.

WATSON, J. P. [born: Charles Gillam] (1870-1939). American mass murderer. In 1893 he poisoned to death a country girl who had eloped with him and announced she was pregnant; he then took off with her possessions. Afterward J. P. Watson (he had assumed that name after running away from home as a young teenager), pretending to be a respectable, well-to-do gentleman, sought young women or widows for marriage partners, passionately wooing them with poetry, flowers, and other things. Through newspaper advertisements about himself, he received hundreds of replies from forlorn females and chose likely candidates for marriage. By 1913 Watson had married ten women, four of whom he had killed and the rest he had deserted, later carrying off their money, jewelry, and other possessions. For the next half a dozen years he operated on the West Coast, soliciting in the press, marrying innocent victims, disposing of murdered wives in lakes and rivers (weighting their corpses so heavily that they would never resurface) and in deep, earthen graves, and absconding with the women's riches. One suspicious wife hired a detective to follow him, allowing police to discover much sought-after loot in his possession. However, only one of his murder victims was found, when Watson led authorities to her burial site in the southern California desert after making an agreement that he would receive no more than life imprisonment if he exposed the grave of one of his victims. He confessed to murdering eight women, was found guilty in 1920, and was given a life sentence; he died in San Quentin on October 15, 1939, having been given the epithet "Bluebeard." It is estimated Watson married at least 40 women, 25 of whom he evidently poisoned, clubbed, strangled, or in some other way killed.

WEBER, Jeanne (1875-1910). French mass murderer. A bourgeois Parisian housewife, she was first accused of killing her own two little girls, her young son, and three small nieces, all of whom had died mysteriously while in her care in 1905. But Weber's innocence was upheld by a leading French forensic scientist at her sensational trial in 1906, thus resulting in her acquittal. Afterward she disappeared for over a year until authorities found her under the alias of Madame Moulinet, working as a housekeeper near Villedieu in Indre province; again accused of killing a child, Weber was released when experts publicly denounced those who sought to try "this poor persecuted soul." In 1908 she was finally caught in the act of strangling a boy (all her victims showed black-and-blue marks around their throats, but their deaths had been attributed to fevers or disease). Declared insane (1908), she was locked up in a mental institution at Mareville, where she went steadily madder until strangling herself to death two years later. The eight murders she undoubtedly committed (there may have been 20 or more in all) gave her sexual ecstasy according to studies about her.

WEBSTER, John White (1791-1850). Boston professor and murderer. Dr. Webster, a professor at the Massachusetts Medical College, lived an extravagant life in Boston in the 1840s. In need of financial help, Webster borrowed money from a colleague, Dr. George Parkman, who many months later confronted Webster in his office and demanded payment of the loan. In anger, Webster

hit Parkman on the head with a piece of kindling wood, killing
him. To destroy the body, Webster cut it up and burned most
of the pieces. Later a suspicious college janitor, Ephraim Lit-
tlefield, uncovered some pieces and told authorities, who arrested Webster. At a sensational trial attended by more than
60,000 spectators, Webster pleaded not guilty but was convicted
of murder and sentenced to the gallows. Before hanging on
August 30, 1850, Webster confessed to the killing, which he
said he had not intended to do.

WEBSTER, Kate (1849-79). Irish-born British thief and murderer.
As a teenager she ran away from home, becoming first a pickpocket in Liverpool and then a thief in London, where she was
arrested many times and served short stints in jail in the 1870s.
Moving to Richmond in early 1879, Webster became the housemaid
for Julia Martha Thomas, a recluse, who soon tried to fire her
because of drunkenness. In mad revenge, Webster used an axe
to kill her well-to-do employer and to cut up her body. The
human parts were then boiled in a large pot, packed in a box,
and thrown into a river. Webster passed herself off as Mrs.
Thomas until the box was found (the remains were unrecognizable) and a suspicious neighbor obtained a police inquiry. She
fled to Ireland but was tracked down and returned to Richmond.
Throughout her trial she screamed her innocence and wildly
blamed others for the murder but was convicted and later hanged
(July 29, 1879), having admitted her guilt on the night before
her execution.

WEGER, Chester (b. 1939). Illinois murderer. When three married,
affluent Chicago ladies were found bound with cord and beaten
to death in Starved Rock State Park, Illinois, in March 1960,
the police began a lengthy interrogation of suspects. Their
attention eventually focused on Weger, a dishwasher employed
at the park's lodge. Claiming he was innocent (although a
bloodstained jacket was found in his possession), Weger readily
took two lie detector tests, both of which showed he was not
lying. An analysis of the bloodstains indicated they were from
animal blood. Investigators later studied the cord used to tie
up the victims, found it to be a unique kind used no where in
Illinois except in the park, and learned that the same kind of
cord had been used to bind a girl who had been raped not long
before the murders occurred. The bloodstained jacket was sent
to the FBI laboratory in Washington, D.C., which reported that
the stains were human blood. The raped girl identified Weger
as her attacker. After taking another polygraph test, which incriminated him, Weger confessed and was found guilty of murder
on March 4, 1961 (his twenty-second birthday). He later received life imprisonment. Asked how he had failed the third
lie detector test, Weger said he had not taken plenty of aspirin
with Coke to calm himself down as he had before the first two
tests.

WEHRING, Alfred (c. 1895-?). German spy. An intelligence officer
in the Kaiser's navy during World War I, he became part of
Germany's new espionage network in the 1920s. After training
in watchmaking in Switzerland and entering (1927) Britain posed
as a Swiss national named Albert Oertel, Wehring set up shop
in Kirkwall in the Orkneys, not far from Scapa Flow (an important British naval anchorage). He became a naturalized British
subject in 1932, but secretly gathered military plans which he
sent in code by shortwave radio to the German Nazi naval attaché in Holland. Wehring's information enabled a U-boat (submarine) to sneak into Scapa Flow at the start of World War II
and, undetected, sink the battleship H.M.S. Royal Oak (October 14, 1939). Wehring soon left Britain, and his subsequent
career is shrouded in mystery.

WEIDMANN, Eugene (d. 1939). French thief and murderer. While
vacationing with her aunt in Paris, Jean De Koven, a young,
beautiful, professional dancer from Brooklyn, New York, disappeared from her hotel on the Left Bank on the night of July 23,
1937. When her American Express traveler's checks were soon
after cashed under her forged signature, the police began an
intensive manhunt that eventually (through the efforts mainly
of a young criminal investigator, M. Primborgne, of the Sûreté
Nationale) led to Weidmann, an ex-convict who had served 16
years for theft. At his small abode outside Paris, Weidmann
resisted and had to be clubbed unconscious by the police; the
dead body of De Koven was found buried in clay beneath his
porch. Charming, handsome, and multilingual (he had learned
English while in Canada), Weidmann gained great notoriety during his trial (French women were enamored by him) and spoke
openly about himself and his criminal life. Finally convicted of
strangling De Koven and killing five others (just to steal their
money), he was condemned to die by the guillotine. In a
carnival-like atmosphere created by the many sadistic spectators
at the execution, Weidmann calmly became the last man to be
guillotined publicly in France (June 17, 1939), for much public
condemnation of the grisly show resulted in passage of a law
several days later banning further public executions.

WEIL, Joseph "Yellow Kid" (1875?-1976). American con man. Weil,
who always affected a dignified appearance, was probably the
most successful con artist of the twentieth century. He
swindled (by his own count) about two thousand suckers--
industrialists, manufacturers, bankers, and others--out of some
$3 to $8 million in his varied and complex confidence games,
such as selling fake pedigreed dogs, phony pills to turn water
into gasoline, valueless "free" land, and worthless stock certificates in copper mines and other ventures. Weil, nicknamed the
"Yellow Kid" because of his resemblance to a flimflam cartoon
character of the same name, usually worked alone but occasionally with friends, such as Fred BUCKMINSTER. Weil was

convicted several times and served time in local and federal
jails. After nearly being caught in an intended swindle in
Peoria, Illinois, in 1934, Weil announced that he was going
straight. He disappeared from public view until the late 1940s,
when he showed up in Chicago and reported that he was writing
his memoirs with the help of journalist W. T. Brannon. Weil
died penniless on February 26, 1976, and was buried in an un-
marked grave in Chicago's Archer Woods.

WEISBERG, Charles (d. 1945). American forger and swindler. He
was a talented, university-educated fabricator and peddler of
bogus handwritten documents in the Philadelphia and New York
areas, having much success in his forgeries of letters and signatures of George Washington, Abraham Lincoln, and Walt Whitman, of manuscripts by Stephen Foster, and of original surveys
of Mount Vernon. A stocky dandy who often sported a mustache
or goatee, "the Baron," as Weisberg was nicknamed (he used
many aliases during his career), sometimes sold his fakes through
the mail, collecting payment in advance; in Philadelphia he was
arrested several times for mail fraud and selling forgeries and,
after his trials and convictions in 1935 and 1941, was sent to
prison to serve 18-month and 30-month sentences respectively.
In 1944 Weisberg, arrested again, posted bond for $1,000 to
gain release, fled from Philadelphia to his New York hangout,
but was tracked down by postal authorities. Tried and convicted of defrauding a book buyer with a Katherine Mansfield
autograph, Weisberg received 30 months in the Lewisburg,
Pennsylvania, prison, where he died on May 4, 1945.

WEISS, Carl Austin. See LONG, Huey [Pierce].

WEISS, Earl "Hymie" [born: Earl Wajciechowski] (1898-1926).
Chicago bootlegger and gangster. In about 1916 he joined
Chicago's North Side Gang led by Charles Dion O'BANNION
and participated in a number of burglaries and killings. In
1921 Weiss instituted the "one-way ride," a way of permanently
getting rid of one's enemies. He helped O'Bannion build a
large and lucrative bootlegging operation and took part in gangland wars against Johnny TORRIO and Al CAPONE. After
O'Bannion's death in 1924, Weiss took over the North Side Gang
and made several attempts to kill Capone during the next two
years. On September 20, 1926, Weiss's gunmen drove past
Capone's stronghold, the Hawthorne Hotel in Cicero, Illinois,
and fired more than 1,000 machine-gun bullets into it; Capone
miraculously escaped. Unknown gunmen shot and killed Weiss
and his bodyguard, Paddy Murphy, in Chicago on October 11,
1926. See also MORAN, George "Bugs."

WEISS, Jeanne [Daniloff] (1868-91). French poisoner. An illegitimate child raised in Nice, she married a young French officer
named Weiss in 1886 and went to live with him in a town near

Oran, Algeria. There, in late 1889, she fell madly in love with a young engineer, Felix Roques, who dominated her sexually and insisted that she kill her husband so that they could marry. She fatally poisoned Weiss (October 1890) despite grave doubts about what would happen to the two young Weiss children, whom Roques seemed to disregard. Letters between the lovers were uncovered revealing the murder plot, and Roques shot himself to death after his arrest in Madrid. Jeanne Weiss was tried in 1891, convicted of attempted murder (she said her will had been ruled by Roques at the time of the crime), and given 20-years' imprisonment. In her prison cell on May 30, 1891, she committed suicide with some poison hidden on her person.

WELCH, Bernard [Charles, Jr.] (b. 1940). American burglar and murderer. A master burglar who worked alone, Welch specialized in stealing valuable furs, silverware, jewelry, coins, and objects d'art. Between 1965 and 1980 he was arrested 25 times and managed to evade incarceration several times by jumping bail; he also escaped from prison on occasions (he cleverly broke out of New York's Dannemora Prison in 1974). Passing himself off as a successful stockbroker, Welch lived in grand style with his family in the affluent suburb of Falls Church, Virginia. After burglarizing four houses in the Washington, D.C., area on December 5, 1980, he entered the house of Dr. Michael J. Halberstam, a prominent cardiologist and author who encountered Welch during the burglary. Welch shot and fatally wounded the doctor, who managed to get into his car to drive to the hospital and, while driving, to smash into Welch, fleeing. Police found over $4 million worth of loot in Welch's home in Virginia. Convicted of murder and burglary, he was sentenced to 143 years in prison before any eligibility for parole. In 1985 he escaped from a Chicago jail and reverted, evidently, to his former criminal livelihood until his recapture four months later.

WELCH, Ed (1865?-1912). American robber. Welch, who often used aliases, such as Howard Benson and Ole Hobeck, served time for robbery in the Atlanta penitentiary, where he met inmate Ben KILPATRICK, a former member of the Wild Bunch, an infamous outlaw gang. Upon the release of Welch and Kilpatrick in 1911, the two decided to rob together (the Wild Bunch had disbanded years before, to Welch's disappointment; he had always wanted to ride with the Bunch). On March 14, 1912, the pair attempted to rob a Southern Pacific express train at Dryden, Texas, but a guard, David A. Truesdale, clubbed Kilpatrick to death with an ice mallet, snatched Kilpatrick's rifle, and fatally shot Welch.

WEST, Dick (1870?-98). American stage, bank, and train robber. Orphaned or deserted as a youngster, "Little Dick," as he came to be called, was raised by cowboys in the Oklahoma Indian territory, where he also mingled with outlaws. By the summer of

1892 he had joined Bob, Bill, Grat, and Emmett DALTON and had taken part in a number of robberies. After most of the Dalton gang was destroyed at Coffeyville, Kansas (West was not there), he became a member of another robbery gang led by Bill DOOLIN and helped hold up stagecoaches, banks, and trains in the Oklahoma territory until the Doolin gang split apart in 1895. Later West committed several robberies alone until a posse shot him dead near Guthrie, Oklahoma, on April 7, 1898.

WESTERVELT, William (1831-?). American kidnapper. His plot to kidnap four-year-old Charley Ross, son of a Germantown, Pennsylvania, grocer, was carried out by Joseph Douglass and William Mosher on July 1, 1874. Ransom notes demanding $20,000 for the release of the boy were traced by police to Mosher. Douglass and Mosher were shot to death during an attempted burglary in Brooklyn, New York, on December 14, 1874. Before dying, Mosher admitted to kidnapping Ross. Suspicion focused on Westervelt when he showed up in Germantown asking personal questions about the Ross family. He was arrested and tried. Westervelt, who insisted he was innocent, was convicted of kidnapping and served seven years in solitary confinement in prison. After his release, Westervelt vanished. It is alleged he had drowned the Ross boy in New York's East River after failing to obtain the ransom money at the time of the abduction.

WEXLER, Irving. See GORDON, Waxey.

WEYLER, John. See SPANISH, Johnny.

WEYMAN, Stanley Clifford (fl. c. 1915-43). American con man. A clerk in New York, he turned impersonator for the sake of adventure, playing numerous roles during a checkered con career. He was arrested and imprisoned for posing as an American consul delegate to Morocco, a Serbian military attaché, an American naval officer, and a Rumanian military officer, among others. Between 1920 and 1921 Weyman, pretending to be an important doctor, was hired by a New York development company and sent to Peru to improve medical care in U.S.-controlled areas. Afterward, convincingly disguised as a U.S. State Department undersecretary, he showed Afghanistan's Princess Fatima around Washington, D.C., and New York City and conned her out of $10,000, saying the money was required for diplomatic gifts. Before finally landing in jail for a long stint, Weyman succeeded at times in duping doctors and others by posing as an authority on medicine or on penal reform.

WHALEN, William H. (b. 1915). American army officer and Soviet spy. He was commended for 21 years of distinguished service when a heart problem forced his early retirement from the U.S.

Army in 1961. At that time Whalen, who had worked in U.S.
Intelligence since 1947, was an intelligence officer connected to
the Joint Chiefs of Staff. The FBI, however, had been suspicious of him since 1959 when he had begun having recurrent
meetings with two Soviet embassy officials in public areas not
far from the Pentagon, Arlington, Virginia. Lieutenant Colonel
Whalen, arrested in 1966, became the first U.S. officer ever
accused of spying for the Soviet Union; he was found guilty of
revealing U.S. military secrets and received a 15-year prison
sentence in 1967.

WHITE, Dan[iel] (1946-85). San Francisco manslayer. Ex-Supervisor
White fatally shot San Francisco Mayor George Moscone and
Supervisor Harvey Milk in their city hall offices on November 27,
1978. He was promptly taken into custody and later brought to
trial, during which the defense showed that White had become
deeply agitated after quitting his supervisor's job (he had
claimed his $9,600 salary was too low for his family's needs)
and attempting unsuccessfully to get it back. On May 22, 1979,
a jury convicted White of manslaughter, immediately setting off
a storm of protest from many of San Francisco's citizens, including the large gay community (Milk was an avowed homosexual)
which believed White was guilty of premeditated murder. On
July 3, 1979, White was given the maximum prison sentence
permitted by the verdict--seven years and eight months. Paroled on January 6, 1984, he gained his complete freedom a
year later. But he had to live undercover, feared for his own
safety (many thought he had been treated much too leniently),
expressed remorse for what he had done, and unexpectedly
committed suicide (by carbon monoxide poisoning) in San Francisco in early November 1985.

WHITE, John Duncan (d. 1826). American thief, murderer, and
mutineer. Sought by Massachusetts authorities for robbery, he
and his friend Winslow Curtis (using the aliases Charles Marchant
and Sylvester Colson respectively) sailed as seamen aboard the
merchant ship Fairy bound for Sweden. The two, however, mu-
tinied, killing the captain and first mate, jettisoning their corpses
in the sea, taking control, and sailing the ship to Nova Scotia.
Shortly thereafter they were seized and brought to Boston,
where they were tried, convicted, and condemned to die. The
hangman killed Curtis but not White, who "robbed" him by hanging himself in his cell the night before.

WHITMAN, Alonzo James. See JIM THE PENMAN.

WHITMAN, Charles (1942-66). Texas mass murderer. On August 1,
1966 Whitman, a former U.S. Marine and an expert shot, went
on a murderous 96-minute shooting rampage from atop the 307-
foot-high observation tower on the University of Texas campus
at Austin. He had with him an arsenal of weapons (including

a 35-mm rifle with a telescopic lens), many boxes of ammunition, food, water, a transistor radio, a roll of toilet paper, and a bottle of spray deodorant. Whitman, who had stabbed and killed his mother and wife the day before, proceeded to shoot and kill students and townspeople with extraordinarily accurate shots. Finally, a police assault led by patrolman Ramiro Martinez overwhelmed Whitman, who was shot to death. The death toll from Whitman's 24-hour killing spree was 18 people dead and 30 others wounded. Ironically, Whitman had earlier told a psychiatrist that he had feelings of uncontrollable hostility and was "thinking about going up on the tower with a deer rifle and start shooting people."

WILBY, Ralph Marshall (1904-?). Canadian embezzler. Charged with embezzlement in Norfolk, Virginia, in 1935, he was deported to his native Canada but soon returned under the alias James W. Ralston to work in San Francisco as a bookkeeper. Arrested again for embezzlement in 1939, he received a suspended sentence and promised to never return to the United States. In 1940, however, Wilby returned from Canada and posed as Alexander Douglas Hume (a real certified public accountant whose credentials he usurped) to be hired by the William T. Knott Company, a department store corporation in New York City. In 1942 Wilby-Hume, working as a traveling auditor going from one store to another of the Knott Company, was made chief accountant and assistant treasurer; he then began, through fraudulent bookkeeping and masterly manipulation of money deposited in fictitious firms doing business with Knott, to steal funds which eventually amounted to a total of $387,000 by early 1944, when he mysteriously disappeared. An investigation uncovered his deft defalcations. Later that year he was tracked down in Victoria, British Columbia, arrested and extradited to New York to stand trial; he restored all of the stolen money except for some $80,000 paid to lawyers who fought his extradition. Wilby confessed and received five to seven years at Sing Sing prison; he dropped out of sight afterward.

WILCOXSON, Bobby Randell (b. 1929). American bank robber and murderer. Nicknamed "One Eye" (he had lost his right eye in an accident as a youngster), Wilcoxson ran into trouble with the law for wife beating and auto theft in the 1950s. After serving time in Ohio's Chillicothe Prison for car theft, he teamed up with Peter Curry and Albert Frederick Nussbaum and pulled off several robberies in the early 1960s, including the 1961 robbery of Brooklyn's Lafayette National Bank in which Wilcoxson shot and killed a guard while Curry seized $32,000 (Nussbaum drove the getaway car). Curry soon surrendered himself to authorities, saying he hadn't expected to kill anyone in his robbery career and identifying Wilcoxson and Nussbaum as associates. FBI agents captured Nussbaum after a high-speed chase through the streets of Buffalo, New York, in November 1962. About one week later Wilcoxson was arrested by the FBI in Baltimore and subsequently he and Curry were sentenced to life imprisonment. Nussbaum received a 20-year prison term.

WILD, Jonathan (1682-1725). English robber, fence, and thieftaker. While serving four years in debtors' prison, Wild became acquainted with thieves and their ways. After his release he established a highly organized gang of thieves and masterminded countless robberies throughout the city of London for about ten years. Known as the "Prince of Robbers," Wild had criminal branch offices, numerous warehouses for stolen property, and a fast-sailing sloop to smuggle goods in and out of England. Wild was also known to be a thieftaker, helping authorities capture criminals who were independent of or disobedient to his control. It is estimated he helped send about 100 criminals to the gallows before he himself followed them in 1725. A rebellious highwayman named Blueskin, whom Wild framed, slit Wild's throat in court; Wild recovered, but Blueskin was hanged. Soon afterward Wild was brought to trial as a receiver of stolen goods and was found guilty. The night before his execution, he tried unsuccessfully to commit suicide with laudanum. Wild was hanged at Tyburn on May 24, 1725.

WILLIAMS, Wayne [Bertram] (b. 1958). Georgia murderer. Twenty-eight black youngsters were found dead in and around Atlanta between 1979 and 1981, setting off a huge manhunt for the killer or killers. Large rewards were offered for information, and local and federal investigators questioned numerous suspects. In early June 1981 FBI agents picked up Williams, an aspiring talent promoter and former radio station manager, interrogated him, and released him because of insufficient evidence. Later that month, Williams was arrested, charged with murder, and indicted by an Atlanta grand jury for the slaying of two young black men whose bodies had been found in the Chattahoochee River. Williams pleaded not guilty to the charges. On February 27, 1982, he was convicted of the two murders and given life imprisonment.

WILLIAMS, [William S.] "Old Bill" (1787-1849). American mountaineer, scalp hunter, and horse thief. In about 1806 he became a fur trapper and trader in the Arizona territory, living and dealing with the Indians until about 1830. Williams then was known as a hunter of Indian scalps, some of which were "war trophies" he stole from the Indians themselves. With Jim BECKWOURTH and Thomas L. "Pegleg" SMITH, Williams formed a large horse-stealing ring that flourished in California in the 1840s. In 1848 Williams served as a guide for John C. Frémont on an expedition to locate passes for a transcontinental railroad. After members of the party froze to death in Colorado's La Garita Mountains, Williams was held responsible, accused of cannibalism (he had lived to return to base), and was fired by Frémont. Some Ute

Indians killed Williams in 1849 to avenge the murder of tribesmen by him the year before.

"WILLIAMSONS" (fl. 20th cent.). Itinerant con artists and swindlers. "The Terrible Williamsons," an infamous inbred gypsylike clan of crooks, established themselves in the New World around the turn of the century after Robert Logan Williamson, a Scottish-born immigrant swindler, settled with his wife in Brooklyn, New York, in the 1890s and subsequently encouraged others of his conniving clan to come to America, where the pickings were easy. Attractive, honest-looking, and smooth-talking, the Williamsons--who also bear old Scottish and Saxon names like McDonald, McMillan, Stewart, Reid, Keith, Johnston, and Gregg--roam throughout the country, cleverly inducing homeowners and others, especially older people, to buy their poor services and products; they pretend to be honest salesmen and women or skilled, inexpensive workers and repairmen (electricians, roofers, painters, driveway pavers, sellers of imported British woolens, Irish lace, lightning rods, etc.). This secretive clan, which has fleeced thousands of gullible Americans, is usually on the go in expensive cars, trucks, and trailers, living well and keeping one step ahead of the law; members often quarrel violently among themselves, especially when two "Williamson" families run into each other while canvassing the same area. Clan members, however, seldom fight in Cincinnati, Ohio, where they meet to bury their dead and to assign swindling territories for the following year. A law unto themselves, the Terrible Williamsons, some 2,000 strong today, have generally only been charged with misdemeanors, such as misrepresentation, selling without a license, or ignoring local sales-tax laws.

WILSON, Billy (1858-1911). American outlaw and sheriff. Born in Texas, he rode with outlaw Dave RUDABAUGH until together they joined BILLY THE KID and his gang in New Mexico territory in the late 1870s. Wilson took part in numerous depredations and shootings with the Kid, with whom he was finally taken captive by lawmen in late 1880. Imprisoned in Mesilla, New Mexico, Wilson later escaped by digging a tunnel to the outside and was not heard from again until 1886 when he began working as a cowboy under the name of Anderson. Wilson became a prosperous rancher in Terrell County, Texas, and was made county sheriff in 1900. Sheriff Patrick Floyd Garrett, who recognized Anderson as the fugitive Wilson, kept this secret and secured the aid of U.S. President Theodore Roosevelt in gaining a pardon for Wilson as a reformed citizen. Later a crook shot Wilson to death in 1911.

WILSON, Catherine (1842-62). British mass poisoner. For several years until found out in 1862, she worked as a nurse in the London area, caring for sick, wealthy persons whom she secretly poisoned to death after inducing them to leave most of their

money to her. She also evidently poisoned her husband, on
whom an autopsy was not done because she beseeched doctors
to respect his wish not to be "mutilated." The discovery of
sulfuric acid in a drink she tried to give a patient led to Wilson's arrest, trial, and conviction; various kinds of poison were
found in her victims, seven of whom were disinterred. Showing
no remorse, she was hanged (October 20, 1862) before a large
throng outside the Old Bailey (Central Criminal Court) in London.

WILSON, Edwin P. (b. 1929). American intelligence agent, gunrunner, and conspirator. From an improverished Idaho farm family,
he worked his way through college in Oregon, enlisted in the
U.S. Marines in 1951, and then joined the Central Intelligence
Agency (CIA) in 1955. Wilson was a CIA undercover agent until his retirement (actually firing) in 1971, and afterward he
amassed a fortune as an international entrepreneur, falsely
creating an illusion that his business dealings had the sanction
of the CIA. He penetrated the U.S. intelligence system through
the clandestine recruitment of CIA personnel and others, who
helped him steal secrets about weapons technology and other
technical information. After 1976 U.S. government authorities
became suspicious of Wilson, who lavishly entertained high U.S.
officials at his large farm-estate in Virginia and owned properties in North Carolina, Switzerland, England, Libya, Lebanon,
and Mexico. Accused of various illicit activities, Wilson went
into self-imposed exile in Libya for about two years until the
U.S. Marshalls Service tricked him into leaving and arrested
him in New York on June 15, 1982. In November that year he
was tried and convicted of smuggling guns to Libya, for which
he received a 15-year prison sentence and was fined $200,000.
At a second trial Wilson was convicted (February 5, 1983) of
smuggling plastic explosives to Libya in 1977, and he faced
other trials on illegal shipping and conspiracy charges while
serving time in the federal prison at Otisville, New York.

WILSON, Roger. See NELSON, Earle Leonard.

WILSON, Sarah (1750-?). British thief and impostor. In 1771 she
was exiled from England to America as an indentured servant,
having transgressed as a maid in the royal retinue of Britain's
Queen Charlotte Sophia by donning the royal jewels. After
Sarah Wilson landed aboard a convict ship in Maryland, she
slipped away from her master and traveled southward posing
for about 18 months as Princess Susanna Carolina Matilda, sister of Queen Charlotte Sophia. Several royal dresses and jewels with which she had absconded made her appear genuine in
the eyes of numerous Southern gentlemen, to whom she assured
royal appointments in return for gifts and lodgings. Apprehended in South Carolina in 1773, she later managed to break
free from her indenture during the American Revolution by
marrying a British officer and afterward disappeared.

WILSON, Tug (c. 1862-1934). New Orleans thug. For about 50 years he worked as a hired thug in New Orleans, especially in the city's French Quarter. Wilson, a powerful stocky brute, was arrested over 100 times during his heyday, the 1880s and 1890s, and became known for using his brawn to bust out of jail. Politicians employed Wilson to bully voters to vote for them on election day, and speakeasy (saloon) owners in New Orleans's red-light district hired him as a bouncer during Prohibition.

WISE, Martha [Hasel] (fl. 1925). Ohio burglar, arsonist, and poisoner. As a 40-year-old widow maintaining a meager farm in Medina, Ohio, she was ridiculed by her mother and relatives, the Geinkes, for her love affair with Walter Johns, a man much younger than herself. In retaliation she killed first the mother and, about one month later, the Geinke aunt and uncle. Wise, questioned after poison was found in the three corpses, admitted guilt, saying "the devil" had hounded her to commit the murders. Furthermore, she confessed to having committed burglary and arson many times in the area. At her trial, during which an insanity plea failed on her behalf, Walter Johns testified unabashedly that plain-looking Martha had "barked like a dog" when they had sex. She received life imprisonment.

WITTROCK, Fred[erick] (1858-1921). Missouri train robber. He was deeply impressed by the daring train robberies of Jesse JAMES and others he had read about in dime novels. Wittrock, wearing a black bandanna and brandishing two loaded six-guns, held up an express train in St. Louis in November 1886 and made off with $10,000 from the Adams Express safe. Detectives caught and arrested "Terrible Fred," as Wittrock wanted to be called, after he foolishly sent a letter to a newspaper saying where the robber's tools could be found. Wittrock was given a long prison sentence, and after his release he indulged in telling tales about his bold robbery. See also JENNINGS, Al.

WOLLWEBER, Ernst Friedrich (1900-?). German-born Soviet Communist saboteur and spy chief. Having espoused Communism in Germany in 1917, he participated in revolutionary activities there and abroad in the 1920s. A short, obese, self-educated Communist agent nicknamed "The Pancake," Wollweber headed the Western European division of Communist Internationale (Soviet spy organization) when Adolf HITLER came to power in 1933. His gang of saboteurs and spies, trained and equipped by the Soviets, inflicted severe destruction on Fascist countries --Germany, Italy, and Spain--and later on "imperialist" enemies of the Soviet Union. In the 1930s and during World War II they dynamited ships, docks, trains, railheads, airfields, bridges, and buildings; Wollweber himself, using many aliases as the "king of saboteurs," was credited with blowing up 21 Axis ships (1941) and served 18 months' imprisonment in Sweden on sabotage charges (1943-45). After the war he established (1945) the East German secret service, maintained Soviet Communist spy rings in European capitals, and instigated numerous kidnappings and assassinations. In the East German purge of 1958, Wollweber lost his political and military posts and went to Moscow, where he was welcomed, honored, and soon made chief of intelligence of all Soviet-satellite countries.

WOOD, Isaac L. (d. 1858). American mass poisoner. In May 1855 Isaac's brother David died suddenly on his estate in Dansville, New York. Later that year David's wife and three children died, and Isaac became administrator of the estate. Isaac moved to New Jersey with his wife and child, who thereafter died, and Isaac moved on to Illinois to start a new life. Before leaving Dansville he had rented the estate to a man named Welch, who discovered in the barn three packages of arsenic wrapped in legal papers giving Isaac authority over the estate after the death of David and his family. Isaac was hunted down and brought back to stand trial. He was convicted of murder and hanged in Geneseo, New York, on July 9, 1858.

WOODHOUSE, Henry [born: Mario Terenzio Enrico Casalegno] (1884-?). Italian-born American entrepreneur and forger. An audacious, amiable little gentleman who came to the United States in 1904 and was naturalized in 1917, Henry Woodhouse (the name in English into which he had translated his Italian name) lived and worked most of his career in New York City, founding and publishing three aviation magazines, writing some textbooks on aeronautics and publishing, and advising the U.S. government on aviation and other matters, such as Arctic and Antarctic exploration. Woodhouse was a big wheeler-dealer who promoted commerce and the arts, hobnobbed with illustrious friends (famous aviators, explorers, industrialists, inventors, presidents, and poets), and secretly indulged himself in producing and selling forgeries. Although he collected and displayed genuine autographs and rare books, he also turned out countless fakes by skillfully imitating the handwriting of distinguished persons and scribing their signatures on authentic documents, ancient or contemporary; he liked especially forging the signatures of American patriots and signers of the Declaration of Independence. In the 1930s the Henry Woodhouse Historic Exhibit in downtown New York City displayed both real and bogus autographs. Woodhouse's fakes were never publicly revealed until after his death.

WOODS, Frederick N. See SCHOENFELD, James L.

WORKMAN, Charles "the Bug" (fl. 1930s). American gangster and murderer. A cold-blooded killer-for-hire connected with the mob, he achieved notoriety primarily for single-handedly killing New York racketeer Dutch SCHULTZ. The newly established national crime syndicate, especially its board member Louis

"Lepke" BUCHALTER, wanted Schultz killed after Schultz threatened to "erase" Special Prosecutor Thomas E. Dewey, who was trying to break up the New York rackets (the syndicate thought that Dewey's death would bring legal retribution and destroy it). Thus the syndicate hired Workman, who along with gunman Mendy Weiss motored to the Palace Chop House and Tavern in Newark, New Jersey, on October 23, 1935. There Workman, carrying two .38 automatics, found and fatally shot Schultz and three of his bodyguards. Identified by witnesses as the killer, Workman was arrested, convicted, and sent to the New Jersey State Prison; he was released in 1958.

WORLEY, Richard (fl. 1718). American pirate. He probably committed more robbery on the high seas in less time than any pirate on record. For six weeks, first sailing in an open boat with eight other men and later in an armed English sloop which he had captured, Worley roamed the coastal waters of New York, New Jersey, and Delaware Bay, seizing and plundering fishing vessles and merchant ships and quickly earning a reputation as a desperate pirate, which he really was not. To escape a British man-of-war, he sailed southward to Charleston, South Carolina, where his pirate sloop was taken into custody offshore after a vain sea battle against a colonial fleet; Worley and his crew were jailed.

WORTH, Adam (d. 1907). British thief. Scotland Yard estimated that Worth, an astute and daring gentleman, stole more than one million pounds sterling during his long career of crime. His most sensational theft involved Thomas Gainsborough's famous portrait, "The Duchess of Devonshire," which he stole from Messrs. Agnew's art gallery in London on May 25, 1876, and then offered to return in exchange for an arrested gang member of his. The colleague, however, had already been released on a technicality, and Worth kept the picture and secretly shipped it to the United States where it remained hidden in storage for the next 25 years until Worth, in ill health and needing money, handed it over for a large, undisclosed amount in 1901. (Worth, who remained free, then lived in Chicago and had been tracked down by Alan Pinkerton, the famous American detective, with whom he made the deal to return the portrait to Messrs. Agnew.) Robberies of uncut diamonds in mail bags in transit in South Africa (1881) and England (1881), as well as of securities from mail trains in France (1880s), were committed by Worth and his associates with great skill. Worth devised various ingenious methods of passing off his stolen diamonds to merchants and others for handsome profits. Never jailed, Worth died in London's East End in 1907.

WORTMAN, [Frank] "Buster" (1903-70). St. Louis bootlegger, racketeer, and gangster. In the mid-1920s he became involved in the bootlegging operation run by Carl, Bernie, and Earl

Shelton in St. Louis and took part in gangland wars. In 1933 Wortman, nicknamed "Buster" because of his boyish antics, was convicted of helping kill a federal Prohibition agent and sent to Alcatraz Prison. Upon his release in 1941, Wortman organized a gang and warred against the Shelton brothers; his gang killed Carl Shelton in 1947 and Bernie Shelton in 1948. Wortman then controlled the gambling, vice, and drug rackets in St. Louis and southern Illinois. He reputedly had much influence with important Missouri and Illinois politicians. In 1962 Wortman was convicted of federal income tax evasion but was never sentenced. He died of cancer in 1970.

WYNEKOOP, Alice (1870-1952). Chicago doctor and murderer. A long-time prominent physician and respected charity worker in Chicago, she was charged with the murder of her beautiful, young daughter-in-law Rheta Gardner Wynekoop, whose practically naked body had been found (November 21, 1933) lying on a surgery table in the basement of her Monroe Street mansion. Allegedly, Dr. Wynekoop resented Rheta for recently marrying her darling son Earle, whom she had spoiled. Under intensive police interrogation, the elderly doctor said the killing had occurred accidentally but later recanted the confession, which said she had fatally overdosed Rheta with chloroform (none was found in the corpse) while examining her for a "mysterious" pain and then, to cover up her professional blunder, had tried to make it appear as if Rheta had been shot by unknown intruders. A jury convicted Dr. Wynekoop of first degree murder beyond a reasonable doubt. Sentenced to life imprisonment, she was later paroled in 1949.

- Y -

YAGER, [Erastus] "Red" (d. 1864). American outlaw and informer. Nicknamed "Red" because of his flaming red hair and whiskers, Yager was a member of the "Innocents," a large group of outlaws secretly led by sheriff-outlaw Henry PLUMMER, who robbed stagecoaches, bullion wagons, and miners in what is now southeastern Montana in the early 1860s. Apprehended in late 1863, Yager divulged how Plummer masterminded the depredations of the outlaws while pretending to weed them out; he also named some 26 important members of the Innocents. Despite his having turned informant, which led to the arrest and hanging of Plummer and others, Yager was shown no mercy by the Montana vigilantes and was hanged on January 4, 1864.

YALE, Frankie [born: Francesco Uale] (1885-1927). American racketeer and gangster. In Brooklyn, New York, in 1908, Yale and Johnny TORRIO ran an extortion racket, forcing Italian businessmen to pay protection money under threats of robbery, kidnapping, and murder. In 1918 Yale took control of the Unione Siciliane, a powerful national Sicilian crime cartel with branches in New York City, Chicago, and other cities. During Prohibition Yale was a major bootlegger and rum-runner and forced tobacco dealers to order his cheaply-made cigars, which were sold in boxes with Yale's face stamped on them. "A Frankie Yale" came to stand for anything cheap and lousy. Yale carried out a number of gangland slayings for Torrio and Al CAPONE, with whom he quarrelled over delivery of liquor shipments from New York. Mobsters driving a large sedan machine-gunned Yale in his car along a Brooklyn street on July 1, 1927; he died instantly.

"YELLOW KID." See WEIL, Joseph.

YORKSHIRE RIPPER. See SUTCLIFFE, Peter.

YORKSHIRE WITCH. See BATEMAN, Mary [Harker].

YOTOKU, Miyagi. See SORGE, Richard.

YOUNGBLOOD, Herbert (1899-1934). American murderer and prison escapee. Youngblood, a black prisoner awaiting trial for murder, joined fellow prisoner John DILLINGER to successfully break out of the Crown Point, Indiana, jail (the so-called "escape-proof jail") on March 3, 1934. They separated in the country, and 13 days later, on March 16, Youngblood was trapped by three lawmen in a store in Port Huron, Michigan. In a wild gun battle, he killed one of them, wounded the other two, but was mortally wounded himself. As he lay dying, Youngblood, loyal to Dillinger to the end, falsely reported that he had been with the much-wanted fugitive the day before, thus touching off a widespread but futile manhunt in the area.

YOUNGER, Bob or Robert (1853-89). American bank and train robber and outlaw. The youngest of the outlaw Younger brothers, Bob took part in several bank and express train robberies in Missouri and other midwestern states in the 1860s and 1870s. Severely wounded during the James-Younger gang's abortive and disastrous attempt to rob a bank in Northfield, Minnesota, on September 7, 1876, he was captured by pursuing lawmen and later, after pleading guilty to robbery and murder, was sentenced to life imprisonment at the Minnesota State Penitentiary, where he became a model prisoner. Bob developed tuberculosis in the prison and died there on September 16, 1899, at the age of 32. See also YOUNGER, Jim or James; YOUNGER, John; YOUNGER, [Thomas] Cole[man].

YOUNGER, Jim or James (1848-1902). American bank and train robber and outlaw. The handsomest of the outlaw Younger brothers, Jim helped the James-Younger gang rob banks and trains in several midwestern states between 1866 and 1876. Near

Osceola, Missouri, in 1874 he and his brother John killed two
lawmen during a shootout; John was also killed, but Jim,
wounded, managed to escape. In 1876 Jim was again wounded
(his jaw was nearly shot off) during an attempted robbery of a
Northfield, Minnesota, bank. Pursued by posses, he and surviving members of the James-Younger gang fled into the country,
where they split up into two parties, the James brothers going
one way, the Youngers another way. On September 21, 1876,
possemen trapped the latter outlaw party, shot dead Charlie
Pitts, who had taken part in the Northfield raid and had accompanied the Youngers, and then captured Jim, Bob, and Cole
Younger, who were all badly bleeding from bullet wounds. The
three brothers received life terms at the Stillwater, Minnesota,
state prison. Paroled with Cole in July 1901, Jim moved from
menial job to menial job, grew despondent, and, after being rejected by a young woman whom he had been courting, committed
suicide on October 19, 1902, putting a bullet in his temple.
See also YOUNGER, Bob or Robert; YOUNGER, John; YOUNGER,
[Thomas] Cole[man].

YOUNGER, John (1851-74). American bank robber and outlaw. A
member of the infamous James-Younger gang, John helped rob
several banks, including the $45,000 heist from the Ocobock
Bank in Corydon, Iowa, on June 3, 1871. He was also involved
in several killings during holdups and, along with his brothers
and Frank and Jesse JAMES, was sought by Pinkerton detectives
and sheriffs for many years. In a gun battle with three lawmen
near Osceola, Missouri, on March 16, 1874, John and his brother
Jim shot and killed Pinkerton Captain Louis J. Lull and Sheriff
Ed B. Daniels, but John died of multiple bullet wounds and was
left; Jim, wounded, fled to rejoin the gang. See also YOUNGER,
Bob or Robert; YOUNGER, Jim or James; YOUNGER, [Thomas]
Cole[man].

YOUNGER, [Thomas] Cole[man] (1844-1916). American bank and
train robber. He rode with Southern guerrilla leader William
Clarke QUANTRILL during the U.S. Civil War and participated
in the bloody raid on Lawrence, Kansas, in 1863. In 1866 Cole
and his brothers Bob, Jim, and John formed a robbery gang
with Frank and Jesse JAMES, and for the next ten years the
James-Younger gang held up banks and express trains in Missouri, Iowa, Kansas, and other midwestern states, killing at
least ten persons and stealing some $250,000 in cash, securities,
gold, and jewelry. A happy-go-lucky ladies' man, Cole had a
brief affair with Belle STARR, a notorious horse thief; he considered settling down in Dallas, but was persuaded by Jesse
James to return to the outlaw trail. During an attempted robbery of a Northfield, Minnestoa, bank on September 7, 1876,
enraged citizens opened fire on the James-Younger gang, killing
two gang members, Clell Miller and Bill Chadwell, and seriously
wounding Cole, Bob, and Jim Younger (brother John had been

killed by lawmen in 1874), all of whom were captured two weeks later. The lesser-wounded James brothers managed to escape. The Youngers all pleaded guilty in order not to be hung and received life sentences at the Minnesota State Penitentiary at Stillwater. In 1901 Cole was paroled, earned a living selling tombstones for awhile, received a pardon in 1903, and then returned to the Youngers' homestead, Lee's Summit, Missouri, where he lived as a peaceful citizen, working at various jobs. For a few years he appeared at local carnivals and in a touring wild West show. Cole died of a heart attack on March 21, 1916. See also YOUNGER, Bob or Robert; YOUNGER, Jim or James; YOUNGER, John.

- Z -

ZANGARA, Joseph or Giuseppe (1900-1933). Sicilian-born American assassin. Zangara, an unemployed mill worker who railed against "capitalists," moved from New Jersey to Florida to find work in early 1933. On the morning of February 15, 1933, he attempted to kill President-elect Franklin D. Roosevelt, firing several shots at him as he and Chicago Mayor Anton J. Cermak drove in an open car through the streets of Miami. Zangara's bullets missed Roosevelt but hit some bystanders and Cermak, who was fatally wounded (he died on March 6, 1933). Seized immediately after the shooting, Zangara was tried, convicted, and sentenced to death. On March 21, 1933, he died in the electric chair, showing no remorse.

ZELIG, Jack [born: William Alberts] (1882-1912). New York gangster and murderer. In New York City in the early 1900s Zelig worked for Monk EASTMAN and KID TWIST, Eastman's successor. About 1908 he formed his own gang of muggers, robbers, and murderers. His gang members rendered their services for set fees (murder cost $10 to $100). Zelig's two top lieutenants, Jack Sirocco and Chick Tricker, turned against him and tried to take over his gang, causing a gangland war to break out between Zelig and them in 1911. On December 2, 1911, Zelig, called "Big Jack" because of his huge size and his ambition to become New York's top crime boss, shot and killed gunman Julie Morrell, who had been sent to kill him. Zelig and his men were hired by Charles BECKER to "rub out" Herman Rosenthal, a gambling casino owner who had blown the whistle on payoffs to Becker and other policemen. On October 5, 1912, Zelig was shot to death on a Manhattan trolley car by Red Phil Davidson. See also GYP THE BLOOD.

ZERILLI, Joseph (1897-1977). Sicilian-born Detroit gangster. In the 1920s Zerilli became an important member of the Purple Mob in Detroit. The mob was involved in bootlegging, hijacking, extortion, prostitution, loansharking, drugs, murder, and other criminal activities. Although Zerilli was known to have been mixed up in illegal pursuits, he was convicted of breaking the law only twice. In 1919 he was fined for carrying a concealed weapon and for speeding. By the mid-1950s Zerilli was reputedly the highest-ranking Mafia-syndicate leader in Detroit. He was implicated in the 1975 disappearance of former Teamster President James R. Hoffa. When Zerilli died on October 30, 1977, he had revealed nothing about the Hoffa case to local or federal authorities.

ZHELYABOV, Andrei. See PEROVSKAYA, Sophia.

ZIEGLER, "Shotgun" [George] [real name: Fred Goetz] (1897-1934). American gangster, robber, and kidnapper. A university graduate, he inexplicably abandoned the straight life for a crime career, working as a gunman for Al CAPONE in Chicago and robbing banks with other gangsters in the Midwest in the 1920s. His use of the shotgun in crime earned him his nickname for that weapon. Ziegler, who apparently was involved in at least one dozen mob killings, was reputed to have been one of the machine gunners in the 1929 St. Valentine's Day Massacre of henchmen of mob-boss George "Bugs" MORAN. In St. Paul, Minnesota, in 1933 he helped "Doc" and Fred BARKER, Alvin KARPIS, and others kidnap millionaire brewer William A. Hamm, Jr., whom they released for $100,000 ransom. Ziegler supposedly masterminded the 1934 kidnapping of millionarie banker Edward G. Bremer in Minneapolis, Minnesota; Bremer was released for a $200,000 ransom. The Barker-Karpis gang became annoyed when Ziegler bragged openly about the Bremer job. On March 22, 1934, unknown mobsters killed Ziegler outside his favorite cafe in Chicago; a shotgun blast at close range tore away his face.

ZINGARA, Madam [born: Elizabeth McMullin] (fl. 1890s). American con seeress and swindler. Born in New York, she left home to travel about the United States and abroad, using numerous aliases while practicing a spiritual confidence game. Taken in by her supposed mystic or psychic powers, many persons paid her large fees in the belief that she foretold the future. (She was skilled at wheedling information from dupes and then giving it back as if it were sheer prophecy.) Although having the name of Fitzgerald (from a short marriage to a Worcester, Massachusetts, man whom she had divorced), she was best known as Madam Zingara in New York City, where she was finally apprehended in 1899. Convicted of fraud in early 1900, she went to prison at the age of 37 and served a long term.

ZODIAC KILLER (fl. 1968-75). California mass murderer. An unknown person, dubbed the "Zodiac" because of cryptic, astrological notes sent by him to the police and the newspapers in California, claimed to have killed some 37 people, mostly young females, but the police failed to find the bodies of many of his

claimed victims and attribute no more than half a dozen killings
to him. A young couple shot to death near Vallejo, California
(1968) and a young woman similarly killed outside Vallejo (1969)
were the Zodiac's first admitted victims. Witnesses to his murder of a young San Francisco cab driver described him to police:
a male about 40 years old, of average height, with reddish-brown
hair, and wearing thick eyeglasses. Correpondences from the
Zodiac ended in 1975, and today his identity remains a mystery.

ZOTOW, Eugene [real name: Ivan Miassojedoff] (d. 1953). Russian-
born artist and counterfeiter. A talented art professor in
Petrograd (Leningrad), he and his pupil-friend Solomon
SMOLIANOFF left Russia when Joseph STALIN began his actions
against Jews in the early 1920s. Calling himself Professor Eugene Zotow, he sold his paintings and etchings while also producing and selling counterfeit British and American paper money;
the latter activity got him in trouble with the law several times
in Germany and other European countries. He went into hiding
in Liechtenstein as World War II began in 1939. There, in the
capital town of Vaduz, Zotow became known for his wonderful
oil paintings and etchings and, on commission, produced five
exceptionally beautiful stamps for Liechtenstein. In 1947, claiming that U.S. currency was the easiest to counterfeit because
each bank note was the same size regardless of its worth, Zotow
turned out bogus $100 bills, but Swiss authorities soon learned
of the counterfeiting, notified the Liechtenstein police, and obtained the professor's arrest. He received two years' imprisonment and eventually was deported to Argentina, where he died
of cancer three days after his arrival in 1953.

ZWANZIGER, Anna Maria (1760-1811). German mass poisoner.
Thickset and plain-looking, she worked as a housekeeper and
cook in a succession of households in towns in northern Bavaria;
earlier, as a young married woman who had been born in Nuremberg, she had run away from her husband because of his dip-
somania. For about ten years, until she was arrested in 1809,
Zwanziger secretly poisoned with arsenic as many as one dozen
persons in Bavarian households in which she was employed; in
Pegnitz, the wife of a judge whom Zwanziger wanted to marry
died from poisoned coffee and wine. When the judge showed no
interest in her, she went to work for another judge whom she
killed with arsenic-spiked tea after he too showed indifference
to matrimony with her. Moving to another family, she poisoned
the wife in the hope of marrying the husband, a magistrate,
but she was crazily mistaken once again. Now vengeful, Zwanziger fed poisoned food to everyone in the household--servants,
guests, and the baby--whenever she could. Suspicion about her
cooking led to her dismissal, and afterward arsenic poison was
found in the sugar, salt, and coffee in the kitchen. Later, when
some bodies of her former victims were exhumed, the authorities
apprehended Zwanziger in Nuremberg and brought her to trial,

during which she craftily evaded the prosecutor's questions, all the while proclaiming her innocence. The trial dragged on for two years until one day she suddenly broke down in court and shrieked that she was the killer, with a thirst for more. She was convicted and beheaded in July 1811.

ZWEIBACH or ZWERBACH, Max. See KID TWIST.

ZWILLMAN, Abner "Longy" (1899-1959). New York and New Jersey gangster and racketeer. Zwillman, an early associate of Meyer LANSKY and Benjamin "Bugsy" SIEGEL, became involved in the bootlegging and gambling rackets in New York during Prohibition. He helped form the national crime syndicate in 1934 and was made head of most rackets in New Jersey the following year. Zwillman, nicknamed "Longy" because of being long on talk, grew enormously rich from his operations and held influential power in New Jersey politics for many years. In the 1950s he attempted to change his image, donating large sums of money to civic organizations and charities, but his public appearance before Senator John L. McClellan's Senate subcommittee investigating rackets in the late 1950s harmed him and allegedly made members of the syndicate think Zwillman might turn informer. Zwillman was found strangled to death by a plastic cord in the cellar of his mansion in West Orange, New Jersey, on February 27, 1959; his death was ruled a suicide.

APPENDIX: LIST OF CRIMINALS BY
TYPE OF CULPRIT

The names of the dictionary's biographical subjects have
been alphabetically grouped here under various broad law-
breaking occupational categories, such as assassin, con
artist, gunfighter, impostor, kidnapper, murderer, thief,
swindler, and war criminal. If the reader can not find a
particular person under a category, he or she should look
under another heading, for a name may be listed under a
related and comparable category; for instance, check both
agitator and terrorist, murderer and poisoner, and burglar, robber, and thief. There is also a miscellaneous
category.

AGITATOR--See also Conspira-
    tor; Terrorist.

Armstrong, Karleton
Berkman, Alexander
Blood, Thomas
Buntline, Ned
Caserio, Sante Geronimo
Czolgosz, Leon F.
Davis, Angela
DeFreeze, Donald
Dunne, Reginald
Engel, George
Fischer, Adolph
Gabriel
Goldman, Emma
Lebron, Lolita
Meinhof, Ulrike
Nation, Carry
North, John
Parsons, Albert Richard
Pavelić, Ante
Sacco, Nicola
Saxe, Susan
Spies, August
Turner, Nat

Vanzetti, Bartolomeo
Vesey, Denmark
Villa, "Pancho"

ARSONIST

Cream, Thomas Neill
Harris, Leopold
Holmes, H. H.
Kürten, Peter
Panzram, Carl
Van der Lubbe, Marinus
Wise, Martha

ASSASSIN and WOULD-BE
ASSASSIN

Abdul Aziz, Faisal ibn Musad
Agca, Mehmet Ali
Booth, John Wilkes
Bremer, Arthur
Caserio, Sante Geronimo
Chernozamsky, Vlada
Clément, Jacques

ASSASSIN (cont.)

Collazo, Oscar
Corday, Charlotte
Czolgosz, Leon F.
Ford, Bob
Fromme, "Squeaky"
Gérard, Balthazar
Godse, Nathuram
Grinevitsky, Ignaty
Guajardo, Jesús
Guiteau, Charles Julius
Hayer, Talmadge
Hinckley, John W.
Lacenaire
McCall, "Black Jack"
Mercader, Ramón
Moore, Sara Jane
Nicholson, Margaret
Orchard, Harry
Oswald, Lee Harvey
Perovskaya, Sophia
Planetta, Otto
Princip, Gavrilo
Ravaillac, François
Ray, James Earl
Schrank, John N.
Sirhan, Sirhan
Stashynsky, Bogdan
White, Dan
Zangara, Joseph

BOOTLEGGER--See also
    Gangster; Racketeer.

Aiello, Joey
Alterie, Louis "Two-Gun"
Capone, Al
Colbeck, Dinty
Drucci, Vincent
Esposito, Joseph "Diamond Joe"
Fay, Larry
Genna, Angelo
Genna, Mike
Genna, Tony
Gordon, Waxey
Kelly, "Machine Gun"
LeMarca, Angelo John
McErlane, Frankie
Madden, Owen
Maranzano, Salvatore

Masseria, Joe
Moran, George "Bugs"
O'Bannion, Dion
O'Donnell, "Spike"
O'Donnell, "Klondike"
Remus, George R.
Saltis, "Polock Joe"
Schultz, Dutch
Sheldon, Ralph
Strollo, Anthony C.
Touchy, Roger
Weiss, Earl "Hymie"
Wortman, "Buster"

BURGLAR--See also Gangster;
    Robber; Thief.

Bliss, George M.
Cochrane, Henry S.
Coppola, Frank
Dinsio, Amil
Doty, Sile
Haarmann, Fritz
Hope, Jimmy
Ingenito, Ernest
Karpis, Alvin
Lemay, Georges
Lutz, Rudolf
Lyons, Sophie
Mahaney, Jack
Merrick, Suds
Murphy, Jack
Panzram, Carl
Peace, Charles
Reiser, Charles
Shinburn, Mark
Singer, Joel
Vicars, Henry Edward
Welch, Bernard
Wise, Martha

BROTHEL KEEPER--See Madam.

CANNIBAL--See also Murderer.

Bean, Sawney
Denke, Karl
Fish, Albert

CANNIBAL (cont.)

Layfayette, Justine
Packer, Alfred

CON ARTIST--See also Swindler.

Arnold, Philip
Beck, Sophie
Blonger, Lou
Buckminster, Fred
Cagliostro, Count Alessandro
DeAngelis, Anthony "Tino"
Deeming, Alfred
Engel, Sigmund Z.
Enricht, Louis
Estes, Billie Sol
Gondorf, Charley
Gray, George
Guimares, Alberto Santos
Hill, Mildred
Humbert, Theresa
Jim the Penman
Jones, Edward
Jones, William
Kid Duffy
Law, John
Lustig, "Count"
McDonald, Mike
Means, Gaston Bullock
Novena, Colonel M.
Osman, Sülün
Patten, C. Thomas
Peters, Frederick Emerson
Reis, Arturo Alves
Salomen, Edith
Serafina, Countess
Skaggs, Elijah
Smith, "Soapy"
Smith, "Pegleg"
Sykowski, Abram
Thompson, Titanic
Tourbillon, Robert Arthur
Weil, Joseph "Yellow Kid"
Weyman, Stanley Clifford
"Williamsons"
Zingara, Madam

CONSPIRATOR--See also Agitator; Spy; Terrorist;
Traitor.

Babington, Anthony
Catesby, Robert
Dimitrijević, Dragutin
Fawkes, Guy
Fieschi, Giuseppe Maria
Murrel, John A.
Oates, Titus
Paine, Lewis
Perovskaya, Sophia
Princip, Gavrilo
Surratt, John H.
Surratt, Mary E.
Wilson, Edwin P.

COUNTERFEITER--See also
Con Artist; Forger;
Swindler.

Bristol Bill
Butterworth, Mary
Carson, Ann
Harris, Phoebe
Kent, Frank
Loomis, Grove
Lupo, Ignazio
Peglow, Karl
Smolianoff, Solomon
Zotow, Eugene

EMBEZZLER--See Con Artist;
Racketeer; Swindler.

EXTORTIONIST--See also
Gangster; Kidnapper, Racketeer; Swindler.

Becker, Charles
Belcastro, James
Bioff, Willie
"Cooper, D. B."
Luciano, Charles "Lucky"
Lupo, Ignazio
Masseria, Joe
Roselli, John

EXTORTIONIST (cont.)

Tourbillon, Robert Arthur
Zingara, Madam

FENCE--See also Gangster;
Racketeer; Thief.

Cutpurse, Moll
Dobbs, Johnny
Grady, "Travelling Mike"
Mandelbaum, Fredericka "Marm"
Starr, Belle
Wild, Jonathan

FORGER--See also Counter-
feiter; Swindler.

Byron, Major George
Cline, Alfred L.
Cosey, Joseph
Cox, Seymour Ernest J.
Dawson, Charles
de Hory, Elmyr
Field, "Pinny"
Ireland, William Henry
Irving, Clifford
Lacenaire
Laffite, John
Patrick, Albert
Reavis, James Addison
Reis, Arturo Alves
Saward, James
Simonides, Alcibiades
Smolianoff, Solomon
Spring, Robert
Sutton, Arthur
Thiel, Alexander D. L.
Trebitsch-Lincoln, Ignatius
Timothy
Van Meegeren, Hans
Villiers, Henry
Wainewright, Thomas Griffiths
Weisberg, Charles
Woodhouse, Henry

GAMBLER--See also Con Artist;
Gangster; Racketeer;
Swindler.

Adams, Al
Ashby, James
Coe, Phil
Cohen, "Mickey"
Devol, George H.
Grannan, Riley
Hargraves, Dick
Holliday, "Doc"
Johnny Behind the Deuce
Johnson, "Mushmouth"
Jones, William
Law, John
Le Roy, Kitty
Loving, "Cockeyed" Frank
Lowe, Joseph "Rowdy Joe"
McDonald, Mike
North, John
O'Leary, "Big Jim"
Poker Alice
Rothstein, Arnold
Short, Luke
Skaggs, Elijah
Smith, "Soapy"
Tennes, Mont
Thompson, Ben
Thompson, Billy
Tompson, Titanic

GANGSTER--See also Bootlegger; Racketeer.

Abbandando, Frank "Dasher"
Accardo, Tony
Aiuppa, Joseph John
Alderisio, Felix Anthony
Amatuna, Samuzzo "Samoots"
Amberg, "Pretty"
Anastasia, Albert
Anselmi, Albert
Battaglia, Sam "Teets"
Belcastro, James
Bonanno, Joseph C., Sr.
Brady, Al
Brothers, Leo Vincent
Buccieri, Fiore "Fifi"
Buffalino, Russell A.

GANGSTER (cont.)

Burke, Elmer "Trigger"
"Buster from Chicago"
Calamia, Leonard
Campagna, Louis
Capone, Al
Capone, Frank
Cohen, "Mickey"
Colbeck, Dinty
Coll, Vincent "Mad Dog"
Colombo, Joe
Colosimo, James "Big Jim"
Coppola, Michael "Trigger Mike"
Costello, Frank
Cyclone Louie
Dillinger, John
Dio, Johnny
Dolan, "Dandy Johnny"
Driscoll, Danny
Drucci, Vincent
Eastman, Monk
Egan, "Jellyroll"
Fitzpatrick, Richie
Floyd, "Pretty Boy"
Galante, Carmine
Gallo, Joey
Gambino, Carlo
Genovese, Vito
Giancana, Sam "Momo"
Gigante, Vincent
Guzik, Jake
Gyp the Blood
Humphreys, Murray
Hunt, Sam "Golf Bag"
Jackson, Humpty
Kelly, "Machine Gun"
Kid Dropper
Kid Twist
Lansky, Meyer
Lingley, William "Big Bill"
Lombardo, Antonio
Lucchese, Tommy
Luciano, Charles "Lucky"
Lyons, Danny
McErlane, Frankie
McGurn, "Machine Gun" Jack
Madden, Owen
Maranzano, Salvatore
Marcello, Carlos
Masseria, Joe

Moran, George "Bugs"
Moretti, Willie
Morton, Samuel J. "Nails"
Nelson, George "Baby Face"
Nitti, Frank
O'Bannion, Dion
O'Donnell, "Klondike"
Orgen, Jacob "Little Augie"
Patriarca, Raymond L.S.
Poole, William
Prio, Ross
Profaci, Joe
Reles, Abe
Ricca, Paul
Roselli, John
Saltis, "Polock Joe"
Scalise, Frank
Scalise, John
Schultz, Dutch
Shapiro, Jacob "Gurrah"
Siegel, Benjamin "Bugsy"
Socco the Bracer
Spanish, Johnny
Spanish Louie
Stacher, Joseph "Doc"
Stevens, Walter
Strauss, Harry
Strollo, Anthony C.
Teresa, Vinnie
Terranova, Ciro
Torrio, Johnny
Valachi, Joe
Walsh, Johnny "The Mick"
Weiss, Earl "Hymie"
Wilson, Tug
Workman, Charles "The Bug"
Wortman, "Buster"
Yale, Frankie
Zelig, Jack
Zerilli, Joseph
Ziegler, "Shotgun"
Zwillman, Abner "Longy"

GUNFIGHTER--See also Western
    Outlaw.

Allison, Clay
Billy the Kid
Brocius, William "Curly Bill"
Claiborne, Billy

GUNFIGHTER (cont.)

Clanton, Billy
Coe, George
Colbert, Chunk
Cooley, Scott
Courtright, "Longhair Jim"
Daly, John
Earp, Wyatt
Fisher, John King
Grannan, Riley
Hardin, Wes
Hedgepeth, Marion
Higgins, "Pink"
Holliday, "Doc"
Johnny Behind the Deuce
Kid Curry
Leslie, Frank "Buckskin"
Longley, William P. "Wild Bill"
Loving, "Cockeyed" Frank
Lowe, Joseph "Rowdy Joe"
McKinney, James
Meldrum, Robert
Miller, Jim
Musgrove, Lee H.
O'Folliard, Tom
Poker, Alice
Raynor, William P.
Richardson, Levi
Ringo, Johnny
Selman, John
Short, Luke
Slade, "Jack"
Slater, Oscar
Storms, Charlie
Stoudenmire, Dallas
Strawan, Sam
Thompson, Ben
Thompson, Billy
Tutt, David

GUNRUNNER--See Smuggler.

HIGHWAYMAN--See also Robber;
    Thief; Western Outlaw.

Abershaw, Jerry
Cutpurse, Moll
Duval, Claude

Garcia, Manuel Philip
Hare, Joseph T.
Harpe, "Big"
Harpe, "Little"
Lightfoot, Captain
Mason, Sam
Nevison, William
Rann, Jack
Turpin, Dick

IMPOSTOR--See also Con Artist;
    Swindler.

Baker, Mary
Demara, Ferdinand Waldo, Jr.
Hamilton, Mary
Mina, Lino Amalia Espos y
Orton, Arthur
Peters, Frederick Emerson
Psalmanazar, George
Salomen, Edith
Sutherland, Mary Ann
Tilh, Arnaud du
Trebitsch-Lincoln, Ignatius
    Timothy
Weyman, Stanley Clifford
Wilson, Sarah

INFORMER--See also Gangster;
    Racketeer; Robber; Thief.

Bioff, Willie
Murphy, Jim
O'Keefe, "Specs"
Reles, Abe
Teresa, Vinnie
Valachi, Joe
Yager, "Red"

KIDNAPPER--See also Murderer;
    Pirate; Robber.

Abbott, "Bud"
Anderson, Bella
Ba Cut
Barker, "Doc"
Bogle, James H.
Calico Jim

KIDNAPPER (cont.)

Chang Hsüeh-liang
Chessman, Caryl
DeFreeze, Donald
Eiseman-Schier, Ruth
Fish, Albert
Gooch, Arthur
Hall, Carl Austin
Harris, William
Hauptmann, Bruno Richard
Heady, Bonnie Brown
Hickman, Edward
Karpis, Alvin
Kelly, "Bunco"
Kelly, "Machine Gun"
Krist, Gary Steven
LeMarca, Angelo John
Leopold, Nathan F., Jr.
Loeb, Richard A.
Rais, Gilles de
Schoenfeld, James L.
Seadlund, John Henry
Shanghai Kelly
Shockley, Sam Richard
Smith, "Pegleg"
Thurmond, Thomas Harold
Westervelt, William
Ziegler, "Shotgun"

MADAM--See also Procurer;
   Prostitute.

Adler, Polly
Allen, Lizzie
Arlington, Josie
Briggs, Hattie
Bulette, Julia
Connors, Babe
Coo, Eva
Cornelys, Madame
Everleigh, Ada
Everleigh, Minna
Gentle Annie
Gourdan, Madame
King, Kate
Poker Alice
Silks, Mattie
Stanford, Sally
Wall, Tessie

MISCELLANEOUS

Alexander VI
Beck, Dave
Bergdoll, Grover Cleveland
Binaggio, Charley
Burroughs, George
Cagliostro, Count Alessandro
Calley, William L., Jr.
Christian, Fletcher
Cinqué
Coplon, Judith
Fall, Albert B.
Gallus Mag
Green, Eddie
Harrison, Carter
Haywood, William Dudley
Hearst, Patty
Hill, Virginia
Hiss, Alger
Hitler, Adolf
Jones, Jim
Lalaurie, Delphine
Little Pete
Long, Huey
Maledon, George
Mallon, "Typhoid" Mary
Metesky, George
Mock Duck
Monk, Maria
Moore, Flossie
Morrell, Ed
Mussolini, Benito
Pendergast, Tom
Place, Etta
Porteus, John
Rasputin, Grigory Yefimovich
Restell, Madame
Ribbentrop, Joachim von
Rose, Della
Ruef, Abraham
Sade, Marquis de
Sangerman, Joseph
Shannon, Robert K. G.
Slovik, Eddie
Stalin, Joseph
Sweeney, Jim
Tweed, "Boss"

MURDERER and ALLEGED
  MURDERER (before 1900)--
  See also Assassin; Gangster;
  Pirate; Poisoner; War Crimi-
  nal; Western Outlaw.

Abrams, "Big Mike"
Aikney, Thomas
Allen, Bill
Allman, "Bad John"
Anderson, Bill
Antonini, Theresa
Apache Kid
Aram, Eugene
Arden, Alice
Arnold, Stephen
Avinain, Charles
Baker, Cullen M.
Baker, Joseph
Báthory, Elizabeth
Beadle, William
Bean, Sawney
Beauchamp, Jereboam O.
Bender, Kate
Bender, William John "Old Man"
Bevan, Catherine
Bichel, Andreas
Billee, John
Billington, John
Bompard, Gabrielle
Borden, Lizzie
Boston, Patience
Boyd, Jabez
Branch, Elizabeth
Bras-Coupé
Braun, Tom
Bridget Fury
Briggen, Joseph
Brown, Sam
Brownrigg, Elizabeth
Buchanan, Robert
Buck, Rufus
Buhram
Burke, William
Burrow, Rube
Captain Jack
Carlton, Harry
Casey, James P.
Chappleau, Joseph Ernst
Christie, Ned
Coleman, Edward

Colt, John C.
Cooley, Scott
Coolidge, Valorus P.
Copeland, James
Corder, William
Cunningham, Charles
Deeming, Alfred
Deshayes, Catherine "La Voisin"
Dixon, Margaret
Dolan, "Dandy Johnny"
Donnelly, Edward
Driscoll, Danny
Druitt, Montague John
Duell, William
Dumolard, Martin
Durrant, Theo
Dyer, Amelia Elizabeth
Espinosa, Felipe
Fenayrou, Marin
Fieschi, Giuseppe Maria
Flores, Juan
Gibbs, Charles
Glanton, John J.
Goldsby, Crawford
Graves, Thomas Thatcher
Green, Edward W.
Hayes, Catherine
Hellier, Thomas
Helm, Jack
Helm, Boone
Hendrickson, John, Jr.
Hicks, Albert E.
Holmes, Alexander William
Holmes, H. H.
Jackson, "Bricktop"
Jack the Ripper
Johnson, John
Johnson, Richard
Keene, John
Kelly, Ned
Kemmler, William
Kennedy, "Spike"
Kent, Constance
Ketchum, Tom
Ketchum, Sam
Kid Curry
Knapp, Joseph
Latimer, Irving
Layfayette, Justine
LeBlanc, Antoine
Lechler, John

MURDERER (before 1900) (cont.)

Lee, John D.
Longley, William P. "Wild Bill"
Loomis, Cornelia
Loomis, Wash
Loomis, Grove
Luetgert, Adolph Louis
Lyons, Danny
McConaghy, Robert
Malcolm, Sarah
Manning, Maria
Miller, John
Muller, Franz
Murrel, John A.
Ocuish, Hannah
Ogilvie, Patrick
O'Kelly, Edward
Olive, "Print"
Packer, Alfred
Palmer, Annie
Peach, Arthur
Peltzer, Armand
Peltzer, Leon
Phillipe, Joseph
Piper, Thomas W.
Place, Martha M.
Plummer, Henry
Pomeroy, Jesse H.
Poole, William
Prescott, Abraham
Probst, Antoine
Quantrill, William Clarke
Rais, Gilles de
Reed, Ed
Ruloff, Edward H.
Russell, Baldy
Skull, Sally
Slade, "Jack"
Smith, Madeleine
Smith, Richard
Spanish Louie
Spooner, Bathsheba
Starr, Henry
Starr, Tom
Stokes, "Ned"
Stone, John
Strang, Jesse
Tessov, Ludwig
Thorn, Martin George
Tinker, Edward

Tirrell, Albert J.
Tracy, Harry
Troppman, Jean-Baptiste
Turley, Preston S.
Turner, Nat
Vacher, Joseph
Vasquez, Tiburcio
Verzeni, Vincenz
Vlad Tepes
Voirbo, Pierre
Ward, Return J. M.
Watson, J. P.
Webster, John White
Webster, Kate
White, John Duncan

MURDERER and ALLEGED
MURDERER (after 1900)

Abbandando, Frank "Dasher"
Abbott, "Bud"
Abbott, Jack Henry
Abdullah, Mohammed
Adams, Millicent
Adorno, George
Agca, Mehmet Ali
Allen, Floyd
Allen, Margaret
Anselmi, Albert
Arbuckle, "Fatty"
Ba Cut
Ball, Joe
Baniszewski, Gertrude Wright
Barker, Fred
Barker, Herman
Barrow, Clyde
Beck, Martha
Becker, Charles
Bianchi, Kenneth
Biddle, Ed
Bjorkland, "Penny"
Bolber, Morris
Bolton, Mildred Mary
Bonnot, Jules
Boyle, W. A. "Tony"
Bradford, Priscilla
Brady, Al
Brady, Ian
Braun, Tom
Briley, Linwood

MURDERER (after 1900) (cont.)

Brooks, Charles, Jr.
Brothers, Leo Vincent
Browne, Frederick Guy
Brühne, Vera
Buchalter, Louis "Lepke"
Buisson, Émile
Bundy, Ted
Buono, Angelo
Caillaux, Henriette
Capone, Al
Caritativo, Bart
Carpenter, Richard
Chapin, Charles E.
Chapman, Gerald
Chapman, Mark David
Christie, John Reginald Halliday
Christofi, Mrs. Styllou
Ciucci, Vincent
Clark, Lorraine
Clements, Robert George
Cline, Alfred L.
Coll, Vincent "Mad Dog"
Collins, John Norman
Columbo, Patty
Coo, Eva
Cook, William
Coppola, Frank
Coppolino, Carl
Corll, Dean
Corona, Juan
Cretzer, Joseph Paul "Dutch"
Crimmins, Alice
Crimmins, Craig
Crowley, Francis "Two-Gun"
Daniels, Murl
D'Autremont, Hugh
De Feo, Ronald, Jr.
De Kaplany, Geza
Denke, Karl
DeSalvo, Albert
Diamond, Jack "Legs"
Dillinger, John
Dobbert, Ernest John, Jr.
Dominici, Gaston
Dreher, Tom
Dubuisson, Pauline
Ellis, Ruth
Fernandez, Raymond
Finch, Bernard

Fish, Albert
Floyd, "Pretty Boy"
Francis, Willy
Franklin, "Whitey"
Fugmann, Michael
Gacy, John Wayne, Jr.
Galante, Carmine
Gein, Ed
Genna, Angelo
Genna, Mike
Genovese, Vito
Gillette, Chester
Gilmore, Gary Mark
Glatman, Harvey Murray
Gohl, Billy
Goldsborough, Fitzhugh Coyle
Goolde, Marie
Goolde, Vere
Gossmann, Klaus
Graham, Barbara
Graham, John
Gray, Judd
Guay, Albert
Gunness, Belle
Gyp the Blood
Haarmann, Fritz
Haigh, John George
Hall, Carl Austin
Hamilton, Ray
Harris, Jean
Harvey, Julian
Hauptmann, Bruno Richard
Heath, Neville
Heirens, William
Held, Leo
Henley, Elmer
Herrin, Richard
Hickman, Edward
Hirasawa, Sadimacha
Horn, Tom
Housden, Nina
Huberty, James
Hunt, Sam "Golf Bag"
Ingenito, Ernest
Irwin, Robert
Jackson, Humpty
Judd, Winnie Ruth
Kearney, Patrick
Kemper, Ed
Kid Curry
Kiss, Béla

MURDERER (after 1900) (cont.)

Kürten, Peter
Labbé, Denise
Landru, Henri Désiré
Leopold, Nathan F., Jr.
Lincoln, Warren
Lingley, William "Big Bill"
Loeb, Richard A.
Lonergan, Wayne
Lucas, Henry Lee
Luccas, Jimmy
Lüdke, Bruno
Lupo, Ignazio
Lutz, Rudolf
McCollum, Ruby
MacDonald, Jeffrey
McGurn, "Machine Gun" Jack
McKinney, James
Madden, Owen
Manson, Charles
Massie, Thomas H.
Miller, Bill "the Killer"
Miller, Lucille
Monge, Luis José
Mullin, Herbert
Murphy, Jack
Myrtel, Herá
Nash, Frank "Jelly"
Nelson, Earle Leonard
Nelson, George "Baby Face"
Newell, Susan
New Orleans Axeman
O'Bannion, Dion
O'Connor, "Terrible Tommy"
Panzram, Carl
Pardue, John
Parker, Bonnie
Patterson, Nan
Peete, Louise
Petiot, Marcel
Phillips, Clara
Podola, Guenther
Queripel, Michael
Rees, Melvin David
Reles, Abe
Ricca, Paul
Rogers, George
Ruby, Jack
Sach, Amelia
Scalise, John

Schmid, Charles Howard, Jr.
Schreuder, Frances
Schroeder, Irene
Schwartz, Charles Henry
Seadlund, John Henry
Selz, Ralph Jerome von Braun
Sheppard, Sam
Shockley, Sam Richard
Smith, Edgar
Smith, George Joseph
Smith, Mary
Smith, Perry E.
Smith, Robert
Snyder, Ruth
Son of Sam
Speck, Richard
Spencer, Henry
Spiderman of Moncrieff Place
Spinelli, "Duchess"
Starkweather, Charles
Starr, Henry
Stopa, Wanda
Strauss, Harry
Stroud, Robert
Sutcliffe, Peter
Swearingen, George
Taborsky, Joseph
Tarnowska, Maria
Tenuto, Frederick J.
Thaw, Harry K.
Thompson, Gerald
Thompson, Miran Edgar "Buddy"
Thurmond, Thomas Harold
Tracy, Ann Gibson
Tracy, Harry
Turner, Joyce
Unruh, Howard
Velgo, Marie
Vidal, Ginette
Wagner, Franz
Waite, Arthur Warren
Wallace, William Herbert
Wanderer, Carl Otto
Wardlaw, Caroline
Wardlaw, Virginia
Watson, J. P.
Weber, Jeanne
Weger, Chester
Weidmann, Eugene
Welch, Bernard
White, Dan

MURDERER (after 1900) (cont.)

Whitman, Charles
Wilcoxson, Bobby Randell
Williams, Wayne
Workman, Charles "the Bug"
Wynekoop, Alice
Youngblood, Herbert
Zelig, Jack
Zodiac Killer

PICKPOCKET--See also Robber;
Thief.

Cutpurse, Moll
Diver, Jenny
Gordon, Waxey
Irving, Johnny
Jackson, Eddie
Mahaney, Jack
Moran, Thomas B. "Butter-
fingers"
Sheppard, Jack
Villiers, Henry

PIRATE

Angria, Kanhoji
Angria, Tulaji
Baker, Joseph
Baldridge, Adam
Barbarossa I
Barbarossa II
Bellamy, "Black"
Blackbeard
Bonnet, Stede
Bonny, Anne
Colonel Plug
Condent, Christopher
Copeland, James
Dampier, William
Davis, Howell
de Lussan, Raveneau
de Soto, Benito
Diabolito
England, Edward
Esquemeling, Alexander Olivier
Eustace the Monk
Every, Henry

Gambi, Vincent
Gibbs, Charles
Gilbert, Pedro
Gordon, Nathaniel
Henszlein, Klein
Kidd, Captain
Laffite, Jean
L'Olonnois, Francis
Low, Edward
Mainwaring, Sir Henry
Mansvelt, Edward
Merrick, Suds
Morgan, Henry
Philipse, Frederick
Plantain, John
Portuguez, Bartholemy
Rackham, Jack
Read, Mary
Roberts, Bartholomew
Roc the Brazilian
Socco the Bracer
Taylor, John
Tew, Thomas
Vane, Charles
Worley, Richard

POISONER--See also Murderer.

Ansell, Mary
Archer-Gilligan, "Sister Amy"
Bateman, Mary
Becker, Marie
Blandy, Mary
Botkin, Cordelia
Brinvilliers, Marie de
Bryant, Charlotte
Carew, Edith Mary
Carr, Robert
Castaing, Edmé
Chapman, George
Cotton, Mary Ann
Cream, Thomas Neill
Crippen, Hawley Harvey
Cross, Phillip
de Melker, Daisy Louisa
Doss, Nannie
Eustachy, Lauren
Fazekas, Mrs. Julius
Fullam, Augusta
Gottfried, Gesina

POISONER (cont.)

Grinder, Martha
Hahn, Anna Marie
Hoch, Johann
Howard, Frances
Hyde, Bennett Clarke
Jeanneret, Marie
Jegado, Hélène
Klimek, Tillie
Lafarge, Marie
Lehmann, Christa
Lyles, Anjette
Major, Ethel Lillie
Marek, Martha
Mercier, Euphrasie
Merrifield, Louisa
Mina, Lino Amalia Espos y
Molineux, Roland B.
Nozière, Violette
Olah, Susanna
Palmer, William
Panchenko, Dimitri
Pritchard, Edward William
Rendall, Martha
Robinson, Henrietta
Robinson, Sarah Jane
Scieri, Antoinette
Sherman, Lydia
Spara, Hieronyma
Struck, Lydia
Taylor, Louisa
Toffania, La
Toppan, Jane
Ursinus, Sophie
Van Valkenburgh, Elizabeth
Warder, Alfred
Weiss, Jeanne
Wilson, Catherine
Wise, Martha
Wood, Isaac L.
Zwanziger, Anna Marie

PRISON ESCAPEE--See also
    Gangster; Murderer; Robber;
    Thief; Western Outlaw.

Biddle, Ed
Briley, Linwood
Burns, Robert Elliott

Evans, Chris
Gardner, Roy
Guerin, Eddie
Judd, Winnie Ruth
Kid Curry
Lemay, Georges
Lustig, "Count"
Mahaney, Jack
Miller, Bill "the Killer"
Nash, Frank "Jelly"
O'Connor, "Terrible Tommy"
Sheppard, Jack
Tenuto, Frederick J.
Thompson, Miran Edgar "Buddy"
Tracy, Harry
Vavoudis, Nicholas
Welch, Bernard
Wilson, Billy
Wilson, Tug
Youngblood, Herbert

PROCURER--See also Madam;
    Prostitute; Racketeer.

Allen, John
Bassity, Jerome
Bioff, Willie
Colosimo, James "Big Jim"
Earp, Wyatt
Messina, Attilo
Messina, Carmelo
Messina, Eugenio
Purdy, Sam

PROSTITUTE--See also Madam.

Adams, Mary
Allen, Lizzie
Arlington, Josie
Brécourt, Jeanne
Bridget Fury
Bulette, Julia
Cattle Kate
Churchill, "Chicago May"
Clark, Mary Anne
Coo, Eva
Frisco Sue
Gentle Annie
Hayes, Catherine

PROSTITUTE (cont.)

Jackson, "Bricktop"
Juanita
Mata Hari
Moders, Mary
Pearl, Cora
Peel, Fanny
Serafina, Countess
Waterford Jack

RACKETEER--See also Boot-
legger; Gangster; Swindler.

Adams, Al
Adonis, Joe
Aiello, Joey
Amberg, "Pretty"
Anastasia, Albert
Barnes, "Nicky"
Battaglia, Sam "Teets"
Beland, "Ma"
Berman, Otto "Abbadabba"
Bioff, Willie
Bonanno, Joseph C., Sr.
Buchalter, Louis "Lepke"
Buffalino, Russell A.
Campagna, Louis
Capone, Al
Capone, Ralph J. "Bottles"
Cardinella, "Sam"
Costello, Frank
Diamond, Jack "Legs"
Dio, Johnny
Esposito, Joseph "Diamond Joe"
Fay, Larry
Galante, Carmine
Gallo, Joey
Gambino, Carlo
Genovese, Vito
Giancana, Sam "Momo"
Gordon, Waxey
Johnson, "Mushmouth"
Kid Dropper
Lansky, Meyer
Lucchese, Tommy
Luciano, Charles "Lucky"
Moretti, Willie
Orgen, Jacob "Little Augie"
Patriarca, Raymond L. S.

Prio, Ross
Profaci, Joe
Roselli, John
Rothstein, Arnold
Schultz, Dutch
Shapiro, Jacob "Gurrah"
Siegel, Benjamin "Bugsy"
Stacher, Joseph "Doc"
Strollo, Anthony C.
Teresa, Vinnie
Terranova, Ciro
Torrio, Johnny
Trafficante, Santo, Jr.
Wortman, "Buster"
Yale, Frankie
Zwillman, Abner "Longy"

RAPIST--See also Kidnapper;
Murderer.

Apache Kid
Buck, Rufus
DeSalvo, Albert
Glatman, Harvey Murray
Miranda, Ernesto
Nelson, Earle Leonard
Piper, Thomas W.
Rees, Melvin David
Thompson, Gerald

ROBBER (before 1900)--See
also Burglar; Highwayman;
Pirate; Thief; Western Outlaw.

Apache Kid
Barter, "Rattlesnake Dick"
Bass, Sam
Bell, Tom
Beni, Jules
Black Bart
Brady, Al
Bras-Coupé
Bunch, Eugene
Burrow, Rube
Cassidy, Butch
Chapman, John T.
Churchill, "Chicago May"
Clifton, Dan

ROBBER (before 1900) (cont.)

Cornett, Brack
Curry, George "Flat Nose"
Dalton, Bill
Dalton, Bob
Dalton, Emmett
Dalton, Grat
Daughtery, Roy
Davis, Jack
Diver, Jenny
Doane, Moses
Dobbs, Johnny
Doolin, Bill
Evans, Chris
Fitzpatrick, James
Flores, Juan
Ford, Bob
Ford, Emma
Frisco Sue
Garcia, Manuel Philip
Green, Edward W.
Guerin, Eddie
Hanks, O.C. "Camilla"
Hart, Pearl
Hedgepeth, Marion
Herring, Bob
Hite, Wood
Jackson, Frank
James, Frank
James, Jesse
Jennings, Al
Kelly, Ned
Ketchum, Tom
Ketchum, Sam
Kid Curry
Kilpatrick, Ben
Lay, Elzy
Leslie, George Leonidas
Little, Dick
Loomis, Cornelia
Loomis, Wash
McCarty, Tom
Miner, "Old Bill"
Mullinen, Joe
Murrel, John A.
Newcomb, George "Bitter Creek"
Parish, Frank
Perry, Oliver Curtis
Plummer, Henry
Reed, Jim

Reed, "Texas Jack"
Reno, Frank
Reno, John
Reno, Simeon
Reno, William
Robin Hood
Rob Roy
Romaine, Henry G.
Rudabaugh, Dave
Ruloff, Edward H.
Russell, Baldy
Sheppard, Jack
Skinner, Cy
Sontag, George
Sontag, John
Starr, Henry
Stone, John
Sundance Kid
Tracy, Harry
Turpin, Dick
Warner, Matt
West, Dick
White, John Duncan
Wild, Jonathan
Wittrock, Fred
Worth, Adam
Younger, Bob
Younger, Cole
Younger, Jim
Younger, John

ROBBER (after 1900)

Abbott, Jack Henry
Adorno, George
Alvord, Burt
Ashley, John
Bailey, Harvey
Barker, "Doc"
Barker, Fred
Barker, Herman
Barker, Lloyd
Barrow, Clyde
Bonnot, Jules
Buisson, Emile
Carpenter, Richard
Cesaroni, Enrico
Chapman, Gerald
Chessman, Caryl
Colbeck, Dinty

ROBBER (after 1900) (cont.)

Cook, William
Cooney, Celia
Coy, Bernie
Cretzer, Joseph Paul "Dutch"
Crowley, Francis "Two Gun"
Daugherty, Roy
D'Autremont, Hugh
Dean, Margie
Dillinger, John
Fahy, Bill
Floyd, "Pretty Boy"
Ford, Emma
Franklin, "Whitey"
Gardner, Roy
Guerin, Eddie
Hamilton, Ray
Hirasawa, Sadimacha
Irwin, Stella Mae
Karpis, Alvin
Keene, John
Kid Curry
Kilpatrick, Ben
Kiss, Béla
Lamm, "Baron"
Liebscher, William Jr.
Lucas, Jimmy
McGinnis, "Big Joe"
Miller, Bill "the Killer"
Miner, "Old Bill"
Moran, George "Bugs"
Morris, Earl
Nash, Frank "Jelly"
Nelson, George "Baby Face"
O'Keefe, "Specs"
Panzram, Carl
Pardue, John
Parker, Bonnie
Rudensky, Morris "Red"
Russell, Baldy
Schroeder, Irene
Seadlund, John Henry
Shockley, Sam Richard
Singleton, Ed
Spencer, Al
Spinelli, "Duchess"
Starr, Henry
Stiles, Billie
Sutton, Willie "The Actor"
Taborsky, Joseph

Tenuto, Frederick J.
Terrill, Ray
Thompson, Miran Edgar "Buddy"
Tourbillon, Robert Arthur
Tracy, Harry
Underhill, Wilbur
Welch, Ed
Wilcoxson, Bobby Randell
Ziegler, "Shotgun"

SCALP HUNTER--See also
  Western Outlaw.

Hobbs, James
Glanton, John J.
Kirker, James
Williams, "Old Bill"

SPY--See also Conspirator;
  Traitor.

Abel, Rudolf
André, John
Beria, Lavrenti
Blake, George
Boyce, Christopher
Boyd, Belle
Carr, Sam
Chambers, Whittaker
Eastern Jewel
Éon, Chevalier d'
Fuchs, Klaus
Gold, Harry
Greenhow, Rose
Ivanov, Igor A.
Kuehn, Bernard
MacLeod, Banda
Mata Hari
May, Alan Nunn
Philby, "Kim"
Poyntz, Juliet
Prime, Geoffrey A.
Rintelen, Franz von
Rose, Fred
Rosenberg, Ethel
Rosenberg, Julius
Schulmeister, Carl
Sobell, Morton
Sorge, Richard

SPY (cont.)

Stashynsky, Bogdan
Stieber, Wilhelm
Surratt, John H.
Trebitsch-Lincoln, Ignatius
 Timothy
Vavoudis, Nicholas
Wehring, Alfred
Whalen, William H.
Wilson, Edwin P.
Wollweber, Ernst Friedrich

SMUGGLER--See also Racketeer.

Carter, John
Coppinger, Daniel
Kirker, James
Laffite, Jean
Luciano, Charles "Lucky"
McCall, "Black Jack"
Murray, George C.
Sykowski, Abram
Wilson, Edwin P.

SWINDLER--See also Con Artist;
 Counterfeiter; Forger;
 Gambler; Racketeer.

Balfour, Jabez Spencer
Beck, Martha
Beck, Sophie
Belle, Earl
Birrell, Lowell McAfee
Bottomley, Horatio William
Brécourt, Jeanne
Byron, Major George
Chadwick, Cassie L.
Churchill, "Chicago May"
Clarke, Mary Anne
Cox, Seymour Ernest J.
DeAngelis, Anthony "Tino"
Deeming, Alfred
Fernandez, Raymond
Gee, Dorothy
Gondorf, Charley
Gordon-Gordon, Lord
Graiver, David
Guimares, Alberto Santos

Harris, Leopold
Hartzell, Oscar Merrill
Hoffman, Harold
Hohenau, Walter
Holmes, H. H.
Hooley, Ernest Terah
Humbert, Theresa
Insull, Sam
Jones, Edward
Keely, John E. W.
Koretz, Leo
Kreuger, Ivar
Laffite, John
Landru, Henri Désiré
Lemoine
Lennon, "Packy"
Lustig, "Count"
Lyons, Sophie
Marek, Martha
Mead, Elmer
Miller, Bill
Moders, Mary
Musica, Philip
Newman, Julia St. Clair
Novena, Colonel M.
Osman, Sülün
Peck, Ellen
Poillon, Charlotte
Poillon, Katherine
Ponzi, Charles
Reavis, James Addison
Salomen, Edith
Schwartz, Charles Henry
Smith, Mary
Spring, Robert
Stavisky, Alexandre Serge
Sutherland, Mary Ann
Sykowski, Abram
Tinker, Edward
Veltheim, Franz von
Vesco, Robert
Villiers, Henry
Waddell, Reed
Weisberg, Charles
Wilby, Ralph Marshall
"Williamsons"
Zingara, Madam

TERRORIST--See also Agitator;
Assassin; Conspirator.

Agca, Mehmet Ali
Ba Cut
Chernozamsky, Valda
Chesimard, Joanne
Dunne, Reginald
Lebron, Lolita
Meinhof, Ulrike
Pavelić, Ante
Perovskaya, Sophia
Saxe, Susan
Sverdlov, Jacob
Wollweber, Ernst Friedrich

THIEF--See also Burglar; Con
Artist; Highwayman; Pick-
pocket; Robber; Swindler.

Adams, Mary
Antonini, Theresa
Bateman, Mary
Beckwourth, Jim
Bonner, Antoinette
Bonnet, Jeanne
Brooks, Bill
Cattle Kate
Clanton, "Ike"
Clanton, "Old Man"
Cosey, Joseph
Curry, George "Flat Nose"
Cutpurse, Moll
Dagoe, Hannah
Dutch Henry
Engel, Sigmund Z.
Enricht, Louis
Fieschi, Giuseppe Maria
Grady, "Travelling Mike"
Hellier, Thomas
Lacenaire
Larn, John M.
Lyons, Sophie
Mina, Lino Amalia Espos y
Moders, Mary
Newman, Julia St. Clair
Osman, Sülün
Packer, Alfred
Parish, Frank
Perkins, Josephine Amelia

Peruggia, Vincenzo
Reed, Ed
Reed, Jim
Robin Hood
Rob Roy
Scieri, Antoinette
Selman, John
Shanghai Chicken
Smith, Mary
Smith, "Pegleg"
Starr, Belle
Tufts, Henry
Veltheim, Franz von
Weidmann, Eugene
Wild, Jonathan
Williams, "Old Bill"
Wilson, Sarah
Worth, Adam

TRAITOR--See also Conspirator;
Spy.

Arnold, Benedict
Axis Sally
Ba Cut
Casement, Sir Roger
Eastern Jewel
Joyce, William
Quisling, Vidkun
Tokyo Rose

WAR CRIMINAL--See also Spy;
Traitor.

Barbie, Klaus
Bormann, Martin
Doenitz, Karl
Eichmann, Adolf
Fedorenko, Fyodor
Frank, Hans
Frick, Wilhelm
Funk, Walter
Goebbels, Joseph
Goering, Hermann Wilhelm
Grese, Irma
Hess, Rudolf
Heydrich, Reinhard
Himmler, Heinrich
Hitler, Adolf

WAR CRIMINAL (cont.)

Hoess, Rudolf
Jodl, Alfred
Kaltenbrunner, Ernst
Keitel, Wilhelm
Koch, Ilse
Krupp, Alfried
Ley, Robert
Mengele, Josef
Menten, Pieter
Neurath, Konstantin von
Pavelić, Ante
Quisling, Vidkun
Raeder, Erich
Rosenberg, Alfred
Sauckel, Fritz
Schirach, Baldur von
Seyss-Inquart, Arthur
Speer, Albert
Streicher, Julius
Trifa, Valerian
Wagner, Gustav Franz

WESTERN OUTLAW--See also
    Gambler; Gunfighter; Scalp
    Hunter.

Alvord, Burt
Baker, Cullen M.
Barker, "Ma"
Bass, Sam
Beni, Jules
Billee, John
Billy the Kid
Black Bart
Bowdre, Charlie
Brocius, William "Curly Bill"
Brown, Hendry
Calamity Jane
Canton, Frank M.
Cassidy, Butch
Christie, Ned
Clanton, Billy
Clanton, "Ike"
Clanton, "Old Man"
Clifton, Dan
Cortina, Juan
Dalton, Bill
Dalton, Bob

Dalton, Emmett
Dalton, Grat
Daly, John
Daugherty, Roy
Davis, Jack
Donahue, "Lame Johnny"
Doolin, Bill
Espinosa, Felipe
Evans, Chris
Farrington, Hilary
Farrington, Levi
Flores, Juan
Ford, Bob
Goldsby, Crawford
Hanks, O.C. "Camilla"
Heath, John
Helm, Boone
Herring, Bob
Hite, Wood
Jackson, Frank
James, Frank
James, Jesse
Kelley, Daniel
Kelly, Ned
Kilpatrick, Ben
Lay, Elzy
Little, Dick
Mather, David
Murieta, Joaquin
Murphy, Jim
Musgrove, Lee H.
Newcomb, George "Bitter Creek"
O'Folliard, Tom
Place, Etta
Reed, Jim
Reno, Frank
Reno, John
Reno, Simeon
Reno, William
Ringo, Johnny
Rose, Della
Rudabaugh, Dave
Russell, Baldy
Russian Bill
Skinner, Cy
Sontag, George
Sontag, John
Starr, Tom
Stiles, Billie
Sundance Kid
Tracy, Harry

INDEX